AMERICAN JEWISH ARCHIVES, NO. V

HISTORY OF THE JEWS
OF THE
NETHERLANDS ANTILLES

By Isaac Samuel Emmanuel

HISTOIRE DE L'INDUSTRIE DES TISSUS
DES ISRAÉLITES DE SALONIQUE, 1935

HISTOIRE DES ISRAÉLITES DE SALONIQUE, 1936

GUEDOLÉ SALONIKI LEDOROTÁM, 1936

PRECIOUS STONES OF THE JEWS OF CURAÇAO:
CURAÇAON JEWRY, 1656-1957, 1957

MAZAVOTH SALONIKI, 2 VOLUMES, 1963-1968

TOLEDOTH YEHUDÉ SALONIKI, IN PRINT

With Suzanne A. Emmanuel:

HISTORY OF THE JEWS OF THE NETHERLANDS ANTILLES, 1970

Isaac S. and Suzanne A. Emmanuel

HISTORY
OF THE JEWS
OF THE
NETHERLANDS
ANTILLES

SECOND VOLUME - APPENDICES

AMERICAN JEWISH ARCHIVES

CINCINNATI – 1970

ABREVIATIONS OF NAMES

Ab ⎫
Abm ⎭ — Abraham

A. Correa — Alvares Correa

A'dam — Amsterdam

A. de Neyra — Athias De Neyra

Alvs. — Alvares

Benj ⎫
Benjn ⎪
Bij ⎬ — Benjamin
Binj ⎪
Bn ⎭

C. — Cohen

C. d'Azevedo — Cohen d'Azevedo

C. Gomes — [Da] Costa Gomes
 (Gomez) — (Gomez)

C. Henriquez — Cohen Henriquez

C. Peixotto — Cohen Peixotto

D ⎫
D' ⎭ — Da or De

Danl ⎫
Dl ⎭ — Daniel

D. C. Gomes or — Da Costa Gomes
 Gomez — (Gomez)

Dd — David

Delv. — Delvalle

G. Casseres — Gomes or Gomez
 Casseres

Gab ⎫
Gabl ⎪
Gl ⎬ — Gabriel

Gs — Gomes

Gz — Gomez

Henriqz — Henriquez

Hisq ⎫
Ho ⎬ — Hisquiao, Hisquiau
Hu ⎭

Hm — Haim

Hs — Henriques

Hz — Henriquez

Ib — Iacob

Ic ⎫
Is ⎭ — Isaac

Id. — Idanha

Iml — Imanuel

Isl ⎫
Ysl ⎭ — Israel

Jb — Jacob

Jeos — Jeoshua, Jeosua,

Jh — Jeudah   [Jeosuah

Jn — Jesurun

Jos — Joseph

L. Henriques or — Lopes or Lopez
 Henriquez   Henriques or
                  Henriquez

L. Maduro — Levy Maduro

L. Penha — Lopes or Lopez
            Penha

Ls ⎫
Lz ⎭ — Lopes, Lopez

L. Raphael — Lopes Raphael

M. Chumaceiro — Mendes Chumaceiro

M. Gama — Mendes [da] Gama

M. Monsanto — Mendes Monsanto

Ml — Manuel

539

Mord		Sal	– Salomon
Mordhy	– Mordechay	Sam	
Mordy		Saml	
My		Sem	– Samuel
Ms	– Mendes, Mendez	Seml	
Mz		Sl	
		S. D.	– Salom or Shalom Delvalle
N. de Crasto	– Namias de Crasto		
Ns. de Crasto		S. Delvalle	– Salom or Shalom Delvalle
Ns	– Nunes		
Nz	– Nunez	Sh. Ferro	– Semah or Semach Ferro
		So	– Salomo, Selomo
P. Brandao	– Pereira Brandao		
Pa. Brandao			
Po.	– Pinedo		
Rl	– Raphael		
Rois			
Roiz			
Roz	– Rodrigues or Rodriguez		
Rs			
Rz			

THE OLDEST HASCAMOTH OF CONGREGATION MIKVE ISRAEL
1671-1750

INTRODUCTION

J AN DE YLLAN and his companions must have drawn up a constitution for the government of their small community. That constitution naturally had to be amplified and modified in 1659 and again in 1671 to meet the needs of the growing colony. That there was a constitution in 1671 is definitely known; it is referred to in the *Hascamoth* "A" of this appendix* and in a letter written by the Curaçao parnassim to the Amsterdam parnassim in 1674 (page 55 above).

In Tishri, 5449 (1688), the *Hascamoth* of 1671 were revised to include the regulations adopted over the years. In 1739 the Mahamad charged Samuel Idanha de Casseres (*Precious Stones*, pp. 325-27) and Mordechay Haim Senior (*ibid.*, pp. 313-14) to "review all the *Hascamoth* and make a compilation of all of them" ("Memorias Senior," 3 Sivan, 5499).

The *Hascamoth* "A" here presented were submitted by the Mahamad of 1751 to the Amsterdam parnassim as a basis for formulating new ones, or the *Hascamoth* "B" of this appendix (PJCAA, bundle). Unfortunately they do not constitute all the resolutions to that date, but only those considered indispensable for drawing up new regulations. The "Memorias Senior" and "Memorias Curiel" refer to many missing resolutions of importance, notably those about the building of the Synagogues of 1674, 1690, 1703 and 1732, respectively.

The transliteration of the Hebrew words appears as in the original i.e., soguet, Sefre, Talmut, etc.

As the oldest documents of the community, the *Hascamoth* "A" are worthy of being preserved for posterity.

* See below, p. 577.

HASCAMOTH "A"

Translated from the original Portuguese by the co-authoress

IN THE NAME OF BLESSED GOD, AMEN

ON 12 TISRY, 5449 [1688], the Mahamad and Council met and, for the purpose of our conservation, examined and revised the Regulations of this Holy Congregation Mikve Israel and had them signed by all the members of the Congregation who promised, under penalty of excommunication, not to violate them. And these having been found in good form were applauded and reinstated with all their former requirements and penalties for the service of Blessed God, Amen.

1. That on rosassana (Rosh Hashanah) Eve the gentlemen of the Mahamad shall meet for the purpose of electing two pernassim [parnassim] and Gabay to serve for one year, as well as two Bridegrooms of the Law, of whom the Hathan Thora shall be a married man. Announcement of those elected shall be made from the pulpit on the first day of rosassana. They shall be given until Kipur Eve to accept or withdraw and in the latter event another of those originally approached, in his turn, shall be elected in his place the same night. If he [too] does not accept, he shall incur the same fine as the first of 24 florins which he shall pay at once to the Sedaca, and until he does so shall be denied admission to the Synagogue. The Mahamad shall be unable to make the slightest allowance to anyone, as that would be construed as robbing the Sedaca. Persons in these degrees of relationship prohibited by our Law shall not serve together: Father with son, father-in-law with son-in-law, brothers with brothers, and brothers-in-law...

2. On Sebuoth (Shabu'oth) Eve the Parnas of Talmut Thora in service shall convoke the gentlemen of the Mahamad for the election of another well-deserving person for that post, such election to be announced on the first day [of Shabu'oth]. On his refusal to serve, he shall pay twelve florins, and another shall be nominated on the second day under the same penalty.

3. The gentlemen of the Mahamad shall be obliged, without taking refuge in the fact that they are going out, to instruct the new Mahamad in running things carefully. They shall order the Parnas of Talmut Thora to try to help the Ruby in his schools, two hours in the morning and two in the afternoon; also, to assist the said hazan with the Sefre thora when the congregation is not in prayer, and to attend [services] daily at the usual hours. He must also go

to slaughter and inspect [the animals], if called, excepting on the eves of the Sabbath and of festivals. And he shall take care of this himself. For neglecting any of these duties — and it not being an exceptional case — he shall be fined one soldo by the Gabay on each occasion, such being Holy money, etc.

4. The gentlemen of the Mahamad functioning shall take care that no disputes among the congregants arise within the Synagogue and, to discourage such occurrences, witnesses thereto shall give an account of same to the said gentlemen of the Mahamad. Anyone raising his voice against another shall, in addition to the fine of twenty-four florins, not only pay a fine of three florins — and six florins if he uses injurious words — but shall also ascend the pulpit to ask the forgiveness of God and of the Congregation for such disrespect. No one may free himself from ascending [the pulpit] without paying forty-eight florins and no one unable to pay shall be exempted, but shall be punished by the gentlemen of the Mahamad according to the offense committed. No exceptions shall be made for anyone, as that would be tantamount to robbing Holy money, and such person shall not be admitted to the Synagogue before paying such debt.

5. On leaving the Synagogue every person shall continue walking and wishing to converse shall do so without raising his voice, as otherwise it might be construed as quarreling. If this occurs in the presence of a member of the Mahamad, he shall separate them and if they refuse to obey, they shall incur the penalty of *Beraha* which shall not be removed before payment of the twelve florins' fine. In the absence of one of said gentlemen [of the Mahamad], one of the oldest [members present] shall do what he deems best to pacify them in order to avoid a scandal, it being understood within a radius of three houses on either side of the Synagogue.

6. Should any question arise between the Congregants, [then] through the Semas to whom five placas shall be given for citation, they shall be obliged to present the matter to the gentlemen of the Mahamad for adjustment. If the latter cannot settle it, they will grant permission to refer the matter to the Governor if they deem it a proper one and will prevent anyone acting otherwise by imposing a fine of twelve florins payable in cash and by denying him admittance to the Synagogue until such payment. Should he absent himself from the Synagogue for three months thereby demonstrating his meager interest in Judaism, he as well as his entire household shall be denied meat and burial. Guarding against that hour to which we are all subject, he shall be fined double, etc. [See *Hascama* of the 14th of Hesvan, 5482, pages 561-62 below.]

7. The community tax of 1/4% levied in the year 5431 [1670-71] on goods coming from Holland shall remain in force. It is again ordered that the same tax shall apply to all those doing business with the Islands, and that careful accounts be kept by all to avoid incurring the pain of *Baraja*. Such account and other offerings shall henceforth be adjusted from Rossassana to Rosassana (sic). Anyone neglecting to make timely payment of donations owing

543

for six months past shall be excluded from the Synagogue unless there be sufficient pledge against his debt.[1]

8. In the event of an ordinary or extraordinary expense, the gentlemen of the Mahamad are given discretionary power to employ the Sedaca and tax moneys considered as one fund, it being understood up to twenty-five patacas and in excess of that amount a meeting shall be convoked of seven of those who framed these Regulations, etc.

9. The distribution of seats shall be at the election of the gentlemen of the Mahamad, who are empowered to make room on a bench for a stranger or for a bachelor since married, without any objection on the part of the congregants. In signal of respect, a member may move down the bench to offer the first place to an elderly person, etc.

10. The assignment of the Misvot and calling one to the Torah shall remain within the discretion of the presiding parnas, who shall seek to give everyone his place, as is proper. No parnas may deprive anyone of his due for personal reasons and any member refusing to perform the Misvot shall be excluded from such privilege for a period of three years. For the Song of Moses and [Ten] Commandments two elderly men shall be called until God grant there be a H: H: (Haham or Rabbi) of the Congregation, in which event he shall be granted this privilege which devolves upon him by right, etc.

11. There shall at no time be erected or procured in this fortress another house as a Synagogue outside of what we now have. In the event that an arrogant, bold or headstrong person attempts to do so, whoever he may be, he shall incur the penalty of *Beraha*, he and his followers. He shall be given an opportunity to desist from that plan within eight days. But if he continues with his intention of disrupting the general union, a report shall be given to the gentlemen of the Mahamad immediately to remedy the situation. They, in the company of the other signatories, shall seek to prevent that design through the intermediation of the Honorable Governor should all other means fail. The penalty shall not be removed until the payment of forty-eight florins to the Sedaca. However, if in time some [i.e., planters distant from the city] for their convenience find it best and have enough people for a congregation, they shall be given a Sefre and the necessary assistance so that everywhere we may serve God as we should, etc.

12. No person may take the letter of his fellowman except for immediate delivery and, when opening his mail, shall take great care not to open that of a stranger's. Acting otherwise, he shall incur the penalty of *Beraja* and also a fine of 24 florins if the Mahamad learns that it was done maliciously, the penalty not to be removed before payment of the fine, etc.

13. The gentlemen of the Mahamad shall take care that no one among our nation leads an indecent life. On receiving such notice, they shall warn him once, then once again. If he be stubborn and not mend his ways, they shall give a report, in all secrecy, to the Governor, requesting the man's banishment

---

[1] See below, pp. 556, 561, 600.

from the island. For if we do not do so, it will be said that we approve of improper conduct and on that account we may suffer some prejudice, etc.

14. The gentlemen of the Mahamad give warning that no one among us, under penalty of *Beraha*, may in jest or otherwise compose a verse, sonnet or pasquin injuring his fellowman. He shall not be admitted to the Synagogue nor enjoy his prerogatives before paying twenty-four florins the first time; the second [time] he shall be set apart as a disturber [of the peace]. Anyone having knowledge [of such a troublemaker] shall immediately denounce him to the gentlemen of the Mahamad, and in failing to do so shall incur the penalty of *Beraha*, etc.

15. Any member feeling that his honor is being prejudiced by a fellowman in his looks and actions shall so manifest that to a gentleman of the Mahamad who, being of the same opinion, shall communicate it to his colleagues. They shall try to avoid all scandal. If they do not deliberate upon it among themselves, they shall call two or four of the signatories to decide on the best procedure to follow, in all secrecy and under oath not to divulge the proceedings. If, instead of cooperating with the Mahamad, the slanderer tries to ruin his fellowman, he as well as his listeners who do not denounce him shall incur the penalty of Beraha which shall not be removed until the payment of twenty-four florins to the Sedaka, etc.

16. The Treasurer [shall] read the foregoing Regulations every six months, on the first day of Pesah and Sucot, respectively. These shall be observed and shall be made to be observed by everyone without exception. No Mahamad may add to or diminish these Regulations without the opinion of the Seven who shall be the three who serve with four others of the signatories not in the degree of kinship as defined in the Book of which he shall be in charge. The Treasurer shall deliver it to whoever is elected. Failing to do so, he shall be set apart from the Nation as a disturber of it[s peace] and shall pay twenty-four florins to the Sedaka before the penalty is removed. All the foregoing Regulations shall be binding upon this congregation forever.

17. The gentlemen of the Mahamad, in behalf of the general welfare and in consideration of the great difficulties and damages that may result in disputes with Gentiles over matter[s] of Religion, and the due care that must be exercised for their avoidance, and in attempting by all lawful means to maintain ourselves in peace and quiet with our natural neighbors among whom the Lord God has conceded us freedom of religion in their lands,

ORDER, under penalty of *Beraha*, that no one of this Holy Congregation, whether man or woman, shall in any way dare discuss the subject of another religion or scandalize it by curse words or disparagement of their gods. For violating this Regulation he shall pay six florins [the first time] and twelve florins the second [time], and shall be denied admittance to the Synagogue until the payment of such fine.

18. Said gentlemen, having noticed the delays caused in the Synagogue on the first Saturday after a marriage, order that henceforth no more than nine persons may be called to the Torah in the special privileges offered, as is the

style of the H[oly]. C[ongregation]. of Talmud Thora of Amsterdam, which may God increase and which we ought to follow. The Hatan Thora and [Hatan] Beresit shall be permitted to call two more people besides those who may wish to ascend the Torah in Honor of the Law, etc.

19. If a member gives sufficient cause to be ordered out of the Synagogue, no one shall arise from his seat to offend or defend him so that the gentlemen of the Mahamad may handle the matter without the clamor attendant in similar occurrences and because no one outside of the gentlemen of the Mahamad may act by word or deed. If a person obstinately refuses to leave at once in obedience to the orders of the gentlemen of the Mahamad, he shall be fined twenty-five florins and, until giving due satisfaction, shall not be admitted to the Synagogue or [perform] the other duties that devolve upon us. If he wishes to exclude himself [from the community], he shall not be exempted from his due contribution toward the expenses of the Holy Synagogue, etc.

20. If a member has not fulfilled his obligation of contributing toward the [Synagogue] expenses during the course of the year, the gentlemen of the Mahamad and their councillors shall meet for the purpose of taxing him, as is most just, to prevent the Holy Synagogue from running into debt. May everything be for the honor of blessed God, Amen.

21. From Rosassanah to Rosassana the Treasurer shall be obliged to deliver these Regulations in proper form to the incoming Treasurer. If some ill-natured person does not hand them over, he shall be fined fifty patacas, half to go to the poor of this Island and the remainder to be used in the discretion of the gentlemen of the Mahamad then serving. And may all be for the good of Israel, Amen.

22. On (15) [5] Tisry of the year 5452 [1691], the gentlemen of the Mahamad and their councillors met to consider the great annoyance and delay that the reading of the numerous *hashcaboth* causes the Holy Congregation on Saturdays and holidays. That being contrary to the practice followed in other congregations, they ordered that this Regulation be revised to provide that no memorial prayers may be offered except when a member has been called to the Torah from where he shall be permitted to make it and also on the holy day of Kipur. Outside of that time and place only to those in mourning during the entire first year and no more. If some devout person wishes memorial prayers said for him yearly on a fixed day, that shall be permitted on his making a bequest for the expenses of this Holy Synagogue; [memorial prayers] shall also be offered for the exalted Chief Rabbi Josiau Pardo[2] for having been of this Holy Congregation, on the festive days of every holiday, once by the Congregation in general and no more. And may God bless His people with Life and Peace, Amen!

[2] See pp. 60-61 above re his death anniversary; also, p. 554 below.

IN THE NAME OF BLESSED GOD, AMEN

On the 19th of Tisry of 5456 [1695], the gentlemen of the Mahamad met with their councillors to cogitate over the poor observance of these Regulations and, motivated by their love and reverence for God who helps us, they resolved to make the following additions:

1. Henceforth no member of this Holy Congregation may flaunt his lax observance of the Regulations. The parnazes and the entire Holy Congregation, as well as their successors, take it upon themselves to enforce observance [upon all] without exceptions and to execute the penalties therein contained on all violators. To have the necessary force so that no one may exempt himself by alleging that he is not a member of this Holy Congregation, said gentlemen and their councillors order that anyone not wishing to be subject to these regulations and wanting to exclude himself from the members of this Holy Congregation must so declare himself before the Treasurer within three days. Failing to do so, he shall be considered on the same plane as the other members, subject to [all] the penalties and [duty of] contributing according to his means toward the upkeep of this Holy Congregation [on pain of] being taxed for each year of non-payment as seems best to the gentlemen of the Mahamad.

2. And it coming to the attention of said gentlemen that games of chance are being played freely on the pretext that the ban against such, with the attendant penalty of Beraha, has been removed from these statutes, the gentlemen of the Mahamad and their councillors serve notice that the ban is restored with the same penalty and extends as well to any individual who, knowing or hearing of such offense, neglects to report the offender to the gentlemen of the Mahamad in whose discretion shall rest the fixing of the fine and the punishment upon non-payment thereof, etc.

3. Also, in the allotment of the Misvot and calling to the Torah, the presiding parnas shall act impartially, giving each one his due and showing respect for age and seniority. Anyone refusing such Misva shall be subject to the fines specified in these Regulations, but through the Samas shall be given a chance to retract, thereby showing his staunch faith and reverence for God, in which event such fine shall be commuted to four patacas for the Sedaca. But if he remains obstinate in his stand by telling the gentlemen of the Mahamad in person or otherwise that he will not perform any Misva assigned to him during their tenure, he shall be subject to the penalties of this statute and for three years shall be denied any [Misva]. And so that all incoming parnazes during that period may know of such punishment, the Treasurer is instructed to enter a resolution [to that effect] in this book.[3]

4. The Treasurer is also obliged to keep a separate book containing all these Regulations with [a list of] the fines incurred by the offenders. At the end of his year of office he shall deliver it to the newly-elected [Treasurer] with a resolution to be signed by both as to its delivery and receipt in perfect con-

[3] See below, pp. 559-60, 575, 610-11.

dition so that at no time can it be said that the Regulations were revoked; and in like manner shall the book be given to the latter's successor. Any treasurer defaulting in these provisions shall pay twenty patacas to the Sedaca and in neglecting to make payment shall be punished with all the means available to us in having him set apart from the Nation. May God give us the faculty to observe His precepts, Amen!

On 13 Nisan, 5456 [1696], the gentlemen of the Mahamad and their councillors met to consider means to assure the absolute *Kashruth* of meat killed for public sale.

Said gentlemen order that from today on any meat sold without two lead tags with the Casser seal shall be considered trefa, excepting meat slaughtered by an individual having a permit to kill and inspect for his own household or business, provided that he shall affix two wafers of sealing wax with his own mark in identification thereof.

Said gentlemen also order that the examiner shall place a lead tag on the ear of a lamb or goat to identify him as the slaughterer. That tag may not be removed by the owner of said animal so that purchasers may be able to recognize it as Casser. Another lead tag or a seal with sealing wax must be placed on the vital organs when the slaughterer is a private individual. By exercising such care we shall avoid eating treffa meat (as has occurred).

This same procedure applies to the hind quarters as well. In the absence of leaden tags or seal thereon, such meat shall be considered treffa.

It is also ordered that a cow slaughtered for casser [use] cannot be put for sale unless the Samas or another Jew is present to assure the purchaser that it was slaughtered and examined for casser.

Observing also that fowl are taken by a slave to slaughter, the said gentlemen [remind that] such cannot be eaten unless a Jew accompanies the slave to the examiner's house and delivers the fowl to the house of her masters. All members are urged not to be negligent in observing this important rule so easy to follow.

Notice is also given that anyone wishing to buy casser fat should not send his slaves for it unless they are accompanied by a Jew.[4]

IT IS VERY WELL KNOWN to you that when Chief Rabbi Jossiao Pardo (May he rest in peace!) came here, the Erub of the city was established since it was walled. One street was designated as out of limits for us to walk through on [the] Sabbath. Since subsequent governors closed down that street for the convenience of said city, it is warned that said Erub continues with the same force as when it was initiated, with the proviso that the prohibited street be included within the fortress, [that is, the street] in back of the church, beginning from the "kat" up to the battery where the flagpole stands. And may the blessed Lord inspire us to serve and revere Him, Amen!

4 See below, p. 550.

On 4 Tisry [of the] year 5460 [1699] the membership having been made aware how tremendously important it is for our conservation and the prosperity of this Holy Congregation to observe the Regulations, it was unanimously agreed that those previously made and signed by all continue in effect. The gentlemen of the Mahamad, each one in his time, shall try by all means to enforce their observance with the cooperation and assistance of all so that no one may excuse himself on the ground that they were or have been revoked since they remain in the same vigor as when first established. In further support thereof, the members were pleased that the Haham [Lopez] (following the opinion of the Elders of the Nation and of the heads of families), in the company of the gentlemen of the outgoing Mahamad, was disposed to explain and discuss some of the Regulations and especially to establish (divine) [due] obedience to the gentlemen of the Mahamad, all of which briefly follows in this form, etc.

1. As to relatives permitted to serve together as members of the Mahamad, it must be explained that although there are different degrees of affinity prohibited under our laws, nevertheless, if these very ones were classed and legally accepted by the Holy Congregation with the consent of the entire membership, then under the Din (law) they could lawfully serve together. For the convenience of the Holy Congregation, this Regulation allows one to serve together with the husband of a niece or of a cousin and with strangers whose wives are in the relationship of aunt and niece, or of cousins. Such relatives shall be allowed whenever the gentlemen of the Mahamad find it necessary and convenient to elect them. All others of closer affinity or consanguinity shall be prohibited, etc.

2. The penalty of Beraha shall be imposed on any person or persons who may insult the gentlemen of the Mahamad [as a whole] or any of them in their official but not private capacity, either by word or deed, or by raising his voice insolently against them to contradict their orders or to criticize the distribution of the Misvoth in the Synagogue and outside of it, or to disparage their work of an official nature.

   The gentlemen of the Mahamad shall be unable to pardon such effrontery, but shall be forced to proceed against such a person or persons, without exception, by denying [admittance to] the Synagogue. For the enlightenment of all, that [punishment] shall be announced from the pulpit. Former members of the Mahamad, as well as other disinterested individuals, shall use all their efforts in carrying out this Regulation. Such person or persons incurring this penalty shall not be excused until giving full satisfaction to the gentlemen of the Mahamad and paying the fine of twenty-five pesos. The penalty of Beraha shall thereupon be removed with the ceremonies necessarily held in such cases, at the disposition of the Haham.

3. In consideration of the fact that some gentlemen take advantage of paying the slight fine rather than accept some worthy office of this Holy Congregation, it has been deemed fitting to increase the fines as follows:

549

For refusing the office of Mahamad, fifty pezos;

For refusing the office of Parnas of Hebra or of Talmud Torah, twenty-five pezos;

For refusing the honor of Bridegrooms of the Law, twenty-five pezos;

For raising one's voice insolently in the Synagogue against a neighbor, whether man or woman, twenty-five pezos; and

For offending, by deeds (i.e., striking), a neighbor, whether man or woman, in the Synagogue, fifty pezos, etc.

4. If any of these fines, as well as others imposed in the discretion of the Mahamad, are not paid within the time ordered, the gentlemen of the Mahamad shall proceed against such [delinquent] by denying him admittance to the Synagogue. If he remains obstinate and the case is one requiring the protection of our Holy Law, they are empowered to deny him circumcision, burial and the like. Those gentlemen of the Mahamad succeeding in office shall be obliged to proceed with the same rigor and without any mitigation in order to obtain full satisfaction. It is hoped that the zeal of all the members of this Holy Congregation will not give occasion for the execution of such punishment. May God implant in us love and reverence for Him to serve Him as we should. And may peace reign over Israel, etc.

Done in the H[oly] C[ongregation] of Mikve Israel the 8th of Tisry, 5460 [1699].

Signatures of the immediately past Mahamad:	With the approval of the worthy Elders and Heads of Families, we sign as mediators, in the name of all, in Curaçao, in the H[oly] C[ongregation] of Mikve Israel the 8th of Tisry, 5460.
The Messrs. Issaque de Marchena Isaq Prareira (sic) Gabriel Levy, Treasurer	(*Signed*) Eliau Lopez Joseph da Costa de Andrade Mordehay Namias de Crasto

On the 25th of Adar Seny, 5461 [1701], the gentlemen of the Mahamad met to consider the many disorders arising out of the marking of casser meat with papers. Since notice has come that trefa meat has been cooked for casser, it is again ordered that every Treasurer shall see to it that lead tags are handed down from Treasurer to Treasurer to avoid such irregularities.

Therefore, we order the slaughterer and examiner of the community to leave his house at the strike of the [town] bell to kill and examine for the entire Nation, and the Samas to mark with lead tags all meat [destined] for all of our people.

Since we have notice that many are slaughtering for Gentiles — a thing that should not be done since it deprives the soguet and bodek of the Nation from their rightful profits and the Synagogue assumes the cost of the lead tags and the labor of marking — we again order that no member may, directly or indirectly, kill or send to kill for any Gentile without the Soget's benefiting therefrom, unless he purchases [the animal] alive with his money; but, if otherwise, he shall be found guilty and sentenced to pay a fine of ten pezos [N.B. - The text seems contradictory.]. For these reasons all meat marked with papers shall be considered null and void, as treffa and Nebala [i.e., unclean and carrion]. May God establish peace among His people, Amen.[5]

IN THE NAME OF BLESSED GOD, AMEN

On the 1st of Sivan of the year 5462 [1702], the gentlemen of the Mahamad and their councillors met to assign seats in this Holy Synagogue of Mikve Israel, which may God increase and help us inaugurate and enjoy for the furtherance of His Holy Law, and for the good, peace and union of all the members of the congregation. Inasmuch as the said gentlemen acted with their customary fairness, there is no doubt that the assignments will prove satisfactory. They also resolved that:

1. No one may occupy the seat of his neighbor; neither men nor women may bring chairs to the Synagogue as they will not be admitted.
2. No one may raise his voice in the Synagogue because of the seats [assigned] or for any other reason, under pain of *Beraha* as well as the fine specified in our statutes.
3. If a seat in this Holy Synagogue becomes vacant through absence or for any other reason, neither the neighboring person nor any other may occupy it, as such vacancy shall be filled at the election of the gentlemen of the Mahamad.[6]
4. No women other than the Brides of the Law or of a Marriage, together with their bridesmaids, may sit in the front part of the ladies' gallery.

May God give us the grace to serve Him and may He bless us with peace, Amen!

Signed: Abraham Jesurun

On the 12th of Kisleu of the yr. 5465 [1704] the gentlemen of the Mahamad and their councillors met to reduce the great annoyance and delay caused by certain customs followed in this Holy Congregation and nowhere else.

First among these are the numerous ascavot [memorial prayers] made daily and on holidays by certain gentlemen contrary to Chapter [Article] 22 of the Regulations adopted on the 5th of Tisry of the yr. 5452 [1691]. It has been

[5] See above, p. 91.
[6] See below, pp. 556, 564, 569.

deemed fitting to reinstate this Article with all rigor. All persons are forbidden to offer such prayers with the exception of a member called to the Torah if he or his wife is in mourning. No one else may say the memorial prayers already offered by the said member called to the Torah or make a donation during the reading of the Sepher on pain of forfeiting four patacas to the Sedaka.

The first memorial prayer of the seven days [of mourning] shall be offered by the mourner in behalf of whoever died in this city or elsewhere, on Saturday evening and on the days the Torah is read, as is customary in other congregations. Services shall begin for the one who died here and if there are two deaths, then for the first decedent though the younger. Offerings shall be restricted to the mourners and relatives of the first decedent in order not to delay [services] for the second [decedent], after which those so desiring may make donations. The private memorial prayer is permitted to those in mourning until the end of the year at their request, and only one to whatever member requesting it (after the public memorial prayers have been offered) for a relative or friend not having died away from here.

It was also decided that our Chief Rabbi may on no account preach more than once every 15 days, excepting sermons for Bridegrooms of the Law and on the installation of officers. And may the Lord God instill us with reverence for Him for the preservation of this Holy Congregation, which may He increase.

On the 29th of Elul, the members of the Mahamad met and resolved that henceforth, in view of the large increase of this Holy Congregation, which may God prosper, and in order to lend dignity to the post, no bachelor may hereafter be elected Hatan Beresit or the Second Bridegroom of the Law.[7]

Signed: J. Pereyra

On the 21st of Kisleu, yr. 5466 [1705], the gentlemen of the Mahamad and their councillors having met to remedy the little or no zeal manifested by the members when called to the general meetings, it was resolved to elect councillors who shall attend whenever summoned by the present gentlemen of the Mahamad, or their successors, jointly to conduct elections, [impose] fines or act on any matter whatsoever before the said gentlemen of the Mahamad. Those councillors shall not be excused from attending unless they are away [from the island] or confined to bed. The gentlemen elected as councillors promise faithfully to observe the foregoing under penalty of Beraha and obligate themselves to pay the fine of fifty pezos for any absence other than the occasions specified, it being understood that the penalty of Beraha shall not be removed until such payment.

So that all is done properly, with love and fear of God, said gentlemen of the Mahamad and the new councillors, in the presence of the Chief Rabbi, promise under solemn oath henceforth to make no exceptions for anyone on any occa-

---

[7] See below, pp. 559, 563, 564, regarding bachelors.

sion; to show equality for all without partiality or passion, and to use all efforts scrupulously to observe all our regulations — those already established as well as those to be enacted — for the conservation of this Holy Congregation, which may God increase.

Under the same oath the said gentlemen of the Mahamad and councillors promise not to relate or divulge to any person, directly or indirectly, the proceedings of any meeting in order to avoid any possible unpleasantness.

In confirmation whereof, said gentlemen of the Mahamad and councillors signed this Regulation in the Book of Regulations. May the Lord God inspire us with His divine love and reverence, for the preservation of our peace.

Signed:

Isaque de Marchena	Manuel Alvares Correa
Jeudah Touro	Abraham Penso
Moseh Lopez Henriques	Gabriel Levy
Ab^m. Orobio de Mattos	David Senior
Mord^y Henriques	Ab: Henriq^z Morao
Abraham de Chaves	Jacob de Crasto
M D Crasto	Moseh Levy Mad$^{ro}_.$

At the request of several members, the gentlemen of the Mahamad and their councillors resolved to allow the offering of memorial prayers from the Torah for a grandfather, blood uncle, son-in-law, brother-in-law or cousin, provided that a member ascending the Torah, or his wife, bears the relationship set forth. Memorial prayers forbidden for all others remain as specified in the Regulations.

May God give Life to His people and may there be Peace over Israel.

Done in the H[oly]: C[ongregation]: of Mikve Israel on the 21st of Menahem, 5467 [1707].

Signed: Isaq Levy Maduro

On the 28th of Tisry, yr. 5468 [1707], the gentlemen of the Mahamad and their councillors met to correct the disorders caused in this Holy House by the big boys and lads who do not attend the Medras. The boys believe that they are accountable to no one, that they are free from punishment by the schools for non-attendance, and that since they are under age the punishment specified in the Regulations cannot apply to them. Since this insolence has reached the extreme where the boys have lost respect even for the parnassim of the T[almud]: T[orah]: and the Rubisim, the said gentlemen of the Mahamad and their councillors have found it expedient to fix the proper correction for the decorum of this Holy House.

With the approval of G[Hazan]. Samuel Levy Maduro who is busy with his cantorial duties and on the zealous offer of Mr. Gabriel Levy [to serve], said gentlemen elected him as Parnas of T[almud]: T[orah]: in Mr. Sam[ue]l Levy

Maduro's stead, with full [faculty and power to punish all boys who are boisterous in the Synagogue. The same power is given to his colleague, Mr. Joseph Fidanque, and to all the gentlemen who may succeed him in this charge and, in his absence, to the teachers or any of them (proposed but not accepted).

When a boy gives the parnas cause to send him to the school for punishment which shall be meted out at the election of the parnassim of T[almud]: T[orah]:, his father shall be unable to prevent this unless he pays the fine specified in our Regulations.

All the gentlemen who do not wish their sons to be under the vigilance of the parnassim of T: T: should declare that before the gentlemen of the Mahamad so that the boys may be noted down as being subject to the *Escamoth*.

The fathers are also forbidden to take their sons to their seat[s] or to put them in through the window or to take them to the women's Synagogue [gallery], unless they are four years of age or under. All lads over that age shall remain under the [vigilance of the] parnassim of T: T: who will be vigorously supported by the gentlemen of the Mahamad and councillors. By this means do we hope to attain tranquility and divine decorum in this Holy House. There is no doubt of the interest of all the members in schooling their children to be respectful and obedient to the parnassim of T: T: and the teachers, for by these means can we hope the Lord God to prosper the entire membership of this H[oly]: C[ongregation]: And may there be peace over Israel.[8]

Signed: Abraham Naar, Treasurer

On the 27th of Nisan, 5468 [1708], the gentlemen of the Mahamad and councillors convened and resolved to permit all gentlemen so desiring to make a bequest to this Holy Congregation for the saying of annual memorial prayers for one of their departed on whatever day they may designate, provided that the legacy for each decedent is for p[ezo]s: 40: and no less, as otherwise it will not be considered. Those gentlemen making a bequest shall, in addition to the public memorial prayer on the day fixed, be entitled to another on the Holy day of Kipur every year.

A resolution to this effect shall be entered in the Congregational Book which shall include Haham Jossiao Pardo (May he rest in peace!) and those gentlemen who have left their wealth to this H: C: May it all be for the increase of the divine service and may God grant long life to the entire H: C: And may there be peace.

Signed: Abraham Naar, Treasurer

On the 5th of Sivan, 5468 [1708], the gentlemen of the Mahamad and their councillors met to elect two well-deserving gentlemen to occupy the post of

---

[8] See below, pp. 555, 557, 569.

parnassim of T[almud]: T[orah]: May those elected be under very good augury (Besimantob)!

In view of the little obedience shown by the students in the Synagogue and at school, it is again admonished that the gentlemen elected shall be given full authority over all the boys who are not subject to the Regulations. They shall be permitted to mete out punishment as they deem necessary and shall have the full support of the gentlemen of the Mahamad and councillors. Those members who do not wish their sons to come under this [ruling] shall be subject to the letter of our Regulations. And may there be peace over Israel.[9]

1st parnas of T: T: -   Gabriel Levy
2: d[itt]o   -   Ishac Levy Maduro

On the 29th of Elul, 5468 [1708], the gentlemen of the Mahamad and their councillors convened and, for the greater increase of our Holy Law and those who honor it, found it fitting to provide that the gentlemen who are elected Bridegrooms of the Law and decline (which, it is hoped, will not occur because of the devotion of all the members) shall pay a fine of fifty patacas. And may God bless His nation with peace, Amen!

Signed: Abraham Naar, Treasurer

On the 11th of Nisan, 5469 [1709], the gentlemen of the Mahamad and their councillors convened to consider the great disorder caused when some members leave their seats to occupy others. In keeping with our Regulations, all gentlemen having a seat are requested to sit there. No one, excepting certain elderly gentlemen of sixty years and upwards who may find it more comfortable to sit elsewhere, shall hereafter be allowed to occupy any seat other than his in this Holy Synagogue.

Anyone disobeying this order for the first time shall be fined five pezos; on the second time, ten pezos. The third time he shall incur the penalty of Beraha which shall not be removed until payment of the fine imposed by the gentlemen of the Mahamad and their councillors, at a minimum of twenty-five pezos.

All members are expected to cooperate and realize the importance for each one to occupy his own seat for the better preservation of the peace and union of this Holy House. And may God endow us with Peace and Blessing. Vesalom (And may there be peace over Israel).

Signed: Salamao Senior

Although on the 11th of this [month] it was forbidden for anyone to occupy the seat of another and since some gentlemen having done so pleaded ignorance as an excuse, it is warned that no one shall hereafter be excused. Anyone in doubt

---

[9] See above, pp. 117, 175, 553; below, pp. 557, 560-61.

about his seat may ask the Treasurer to enlighten him. Notice is given that the fine specified in the Regulation does not apply to those who sit a little farther up or down their bench unless this disturbs the owner of the [adjoining] seat. In that event they shall be subject to the fine under the Regulation.

As some gentlemen, in order to avoid occupying the seat of another when leaving theirs, remain standing and thus block the space and aisle of this Holy Synagogue, it is admonished that all members who are not seated at their places and remain standing shall on no account be allowed to pass through the back of the pulpit in order to go inside unless they wish to perform a Misva or [H]agomel or make an offering before the doors of the Holy Ark. If for any other reason he enters beyond the limit specified, he shall incur the same fines as those occupying the seat of another.

And may God put his Blessing upon us and grant us peace and union.[10]

Done in the H: C: of Mikve Israel the 17th of Nisan, 5469 [1709].

The gentlemen of the Mahamad and councillors give notice that the foregoing Regulation is in full force and effect and that no one is permitted to occupy another's seat during prayer except on the Holy day of Kipur and [the] 9th of Abb (sic).

Signed: Salamao Senior, Treasurer

The Tax of the Nation instituted in the Yr: 5431: and renewed on the 12th of Tisry, 5449, for the payment of the 1/4% duty on all imports for the account of another, whether or not on commission, remains in force.[11]

All members are warned to keep a good record of it since they are subject to the penalty of *Beraha* which also extends to those who erroneously imagine that they do not have to pay it if they apply it (the tax money) toward a charity here or abroad or deduct their fines from same.

Everyone is admonished to appear before the Treasurer between now and Rosasana Eve to pay all arrears due and make adjustments on estimated income if one is behind in his cargoes. Henceforth the tax and adjustment on estimated income shall be paid from Rosasana to Rosasana under pain of *Beraha*. It therefore behooves us to get together with them [the Gabay] to avoid such penalty. The gentlemen of the Mahamad and their councillors shall take strict measures against those who are delinquent.

The zeal of the members is counted upon in making payments punctually, for in so doing they will be assisting those in charge of it, and by paying every year they will make it easier for themselves and more advantageous for the Sedaca.

10 See above, p. 551; below, pp. 564, 569.
11 See above, p. 543; below, pp. 561, 600.

[Done] In Curaçao, Sivan, Yr. 5469 [1709].
The gentlemen of the Mahamad, to help
members from incurring the penalty of
Beraha of this Regulation, permit one
not in funds to give his handwritten
obligation or to make payment with
Letters of Bottomry.

Signed: Salomon Senior
Treasurer

On the 18th of Sivan, Yr. 5471 [1711], the gentlemen of the Mahamad and their councillors convened to elect two more Parnasims to carry out the meritorious Misva of T: T: May those who were elected be under good augury (Besimantob)!

As is known, the dissensions due to the little obedience the boys pay the Messrs. Parnassim make necessary the reinstatement of the Regulation enforcing their obedience, with the specification that all boys up to sixteen years of age, without any exception, shall be subject to the Messrs. Parnassim of T: T: and thereafter to the Regulations of this H: C:, which may God increase for His Holy Service.[12]

Signed: Benjamin Motta
Treasurer

The gentlemen of the Mahamad make known to all the gentlemen of this H: C: that henceforth all members wishing to open a Jesiba may do so on obtaining permission from the gentlemen of the Mahamad with the understanding that when the Haham[13] happily arrives, he shall head all of them and all those already established, all the *Jesiboth* to be subject to the gentlemen of the Mahamad.

Done in the H: C: of Mikve Israel in Curaçao [on] the 13th of Tisry, Yr: 5474 [1713], by order of the gentlemen of the Mahamad and councillors.

[Signed]: David Aboab Cardozo
Treasurer

IN THE NAME OF BLESSED GOD

The gentlemen of the Mahamad and their councillors, observing the arrears of this H: C:, which may God increase, and the expenses which keep growing daily, resolved to collect all moneys from the Sedaca and Hebra [funds] remaining in the hands of some members of this H: C: so that they can handle any emergency that may arise.

It is therefore ordered that all gentlemen having any money of said Misvot appear before the Treasurer and administrator and deliver it, without fail, before Pesah. This applies to capital as well as gifts [interest].

---

[12] See above, pp. 553, 555; below, pp. 560-61.
[13] Haham David Nunes Torres remained at The Hague at his congregation's behest (p. 116).

557

Those gentlemen having pledges deposited with the Treasurer are instructed to go and claim them within three months, as otherwise such will be sold without further notice.

For the greater prosperity of this H: C:, which may God increase, said gentlemen of the Mahamad and their councillors resolved that henceforth no moneys belonging to the Sedaca or Hebra shall or may on any account be given to any member of this H: C: on interest, collateral or otherwise. But the Treasurers of Sedaca and Hebra, respectively, may lend moneys which these Misvot may have left, on good and sufficient mortgages to residents of this Island of the nation of the land [i.e., non-Jewish Hollanders], and to no others, because so they deem fitting for the increase of both Misvot.

May God make all prosper and may there be peace.

Done in the H: C: of Mikve Israel, the 18th of Tisry, Yr. 5474 [1713].

Signed: President Mordy Henriquez & Ishac Touro, and the
Messrs. Councillors Manuel Alvares Correa, Abraham Penso,
Gabriel Levy & Abraham Henriquez Morao.

David Aboab Cardozo
Treasurer

IN THE NAME OF BLESSED GOD

Since several questions have arisen concerning the money offered for the meritorious deed of marrying orphan girls, explanations were made by the gentlemen of the Mahamad and their councillors in order to avoid any doubts in the future. Henceforth deposits are to be made in care of the Treasurer for investment at the best possible income. The application of that money shall remain at the disposition of the said gentlemen of the Mahamad who will carry out the donor's wishes of paying it to the first, second or third [drawing] and keep a record of such designation.

May the Lord God give us greater desire for the accomplishment of all good deeds.

Curaçao, 13 Elul of the year 5474 [1714].

On the 29th of Elul of 5474 [1714] the gentlemen of the Mahamad and their councillors convened and, after deliberating on reaffirming the deliberations and dispositions made by the gentlemen of former Mahamads and councillors, resolved that the outgoing parnazes de banca, who automatically become councillors, shall assist the newly-elected Mahamad in the company of two other councillors whose turn it is to serve by rotation, excepting those in the degrees of relationship forbidden in the Regulation covering this particular.

And may the Lord God grant us Peace and Union, etc.

214. HASCAMOTH AMENDED IN 1786 AND 1809,
FIRST PAGE

213. HASCAMOTH OF 1753 IMPLEMENTED IN 1756,
FIRST PAGE

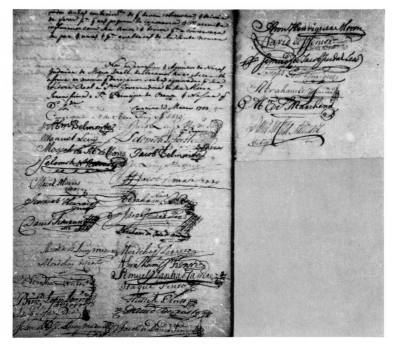

215. SIGNATURES, PARNASSIM AND ADJUNTOS APPROVING
HASCAMOTH OF 1753, PAGE 232

216. OLDEST PRINTED MIKVE ISRAEL
BYLAWS EXTANT

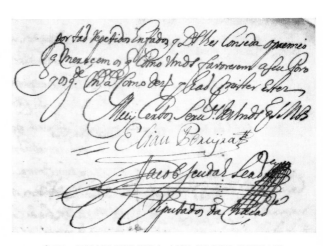

217. ELIAU PEREIRA AND JACOB JEUDAH
LEAO, JEWISH REPRESENTATIVES,
1719-1738, APPENDIX 13

In view of the disorder occurring on the evening of Simha tora (sic) during the circuits with the Holy Scrolls of the Law, it was resolved that henceforth on Simha Torra (sic) as well as on the occasion of donating a Sepher to the Synagogue, [the privilege of] carrying the Sepher or candle shall be granted to no one but a married man, excepting when a Sepher is donated to the Synagogue by a bachelor who at that time and only then will be permitted to carry and place it [in the Holy Ark].[14]

IN THE NAME OF BLESSED GOD

Because of our sins we witness the little zeal displayed in the divine worship and the disorders committed in this H: C: against the Blessed Lord and His Holy Law, in that His Holy House is used as a means of avenging wrongs for the least [grievance] some have (or think they have) against one of the gentlemen of the Mahamad. While they believe they are retaliating in refusing the Misvoth assigned them by said gentlemen who certainly take no offense in this, they are indeed committing a grave sin against the Lord God whose worship is profaned, whose divine Law is disparaged and whose Holy House is outraged.

The slight fine may be responsible for the commission of such a grievous sin, for our Regulations provide that a transgressor may elect to pay four pezos' fine or be excluded from a Misva for three years, [a deprivation] which some of meager devotion regard as of minor importance. This practice must be stopped and a remedy found.

The gentlemen of the Mahamad and their councillors, in honor of the Lord God, His Holy Law and for its protection, and in order to end these disorders, have found it desirable to forgive and pardon all those members who incurred the sin of refusing Misva (which they were denied for three years) by allowing them immediately to pay the Treasurer the fine of 4 P[ezo]s. stipulated in our Regulations, whereupon they shall all be able to enjoy the Misvoth.

It is hoped that the Lord God will imbue our hearts with divine love and reverence for Him in order that we may cherish, esteem and put His commandments into practice. So that none among us may foil such a devout intention, it is ordered that henceforth any member, without any exception, who is accorded a Misva by the gentlemen of the Mahamad or, in their absence, by one of the worthy Elders or by a *Bahal Asura*, while in this Holy House or in the courtyard or in its district, shall not be excused therefrom unless on refusing he goes to the gentlemen of the Mahamad and proves to their satisfaction that an indisposition totally impedes his performing it. Anyone else refusing shall be immediately ordered out of the Synagogue and its vicinity by the Mahamad and not allowed to re-enter it or the courtyard until paying a fine of thirty pezos, which the gentlemen of the Mahamad may on no pretext whatsoever condone or pardon, for that would be tantamount to stealing sacred money.

The same fine shall apply to one entering the Synagogue after the assignment

---

[14] Regarding bachelors, see above, p. 552, and below, pp. 563, 564.

of the Misvoth and failing to perform his Misva before the Sepher is returned. All successors to the gentlemen of the Mahamad shall be required to proceed against one refusing a Misva as though he had actually done so during their year [of office].

Although it is hoped that none among us contemplates this sin, if anyone committing it seeks to convince the gentlemen of the Mahamad that he cannot pay the fine, it is warned that they will take no stock of this but will proceed summarily and impartially to deny him the Synagogue immediately.

To be readmitted [to the Synagogue], a person unable to pay the thirty pezos' fine must ascend the pulpit on the Holy Day of Sabath[15] after the Amida [of the morning service] and before the removal of the Torah, to ask forgiveness of the Lord for the wrong committed against [His] Divine Majesty, His Holy Law and the proper decorum of this Holy House. And unless satisfaction is given, either by money for one who can pay or by ascending the pulpit for one who cannot, he shall under no circumstances be admitted to this Holy Synagogue or its courtyard.[16]

May the Lord incline our hearts to His Holy Service so that in unison we may praise His Holy Name, observe His Divine Law and Conserve the worship of this Holy House, as we should, in order that He may thus put His blessing upon us and bring prosperity to this entire H: C:, amen!

IN THE NAME OF BLESSED GOD

By virtue of the Regulation made and published on the 18th of Sivan, Yr: 5471 [1711], holding those [boys] of the age of 16 years subject to the orders of the parnasims of T: T:, and in view of the scant respect paid to it, and the Messrs. Parnasims [of T: T:] giving as an excuse that they do not execute its terms since the youths are over the age referred to,

We hereby order and fully empower the said Messrs. Parnasim of T: T: to eject from the Synagogue, for the slightest provocation, whatever person or persons may be sitting on the sides of the pulpit who are still under the care of their parents or guardians, no matter of what age. The Parnassim of T: T: can eject them from the Synagogue for the least cause and for that purpose shall call the Samas Ab[raha]m: Lopez Silva.[17] The gentlemen of the Mahamad will give their assistance for this and consider the case on the following day. If [the offense is] one of word or deed, he [the culprit] shall pay the fine[s] set forth in the Regulation, which are 50 and 25 Ps., respectively. If he does not have the means to pay, he shall be punished in the schools (sic) like any other pupil, for experience shows us that they imagine that they can keep on causing these disorders because they are not subject to the teachers.

The zeal of all the gentlemen is counted upon in not giving occasion for the

---

[15] The absence of a Haham at the time may account for such unusual procedure on the Sabbath.
[16] See above, p. 547; below, pp. 570, 575, 610-11.
[17] Samas since 1696.

execution of the foregoing. And may the Lord inspire us with love and reverence to serve Him, amen.

Done in the H: C: of Mikve Israel, the 22nd of Kisleu, Yr. 5478 [1717], and signed in the presence of the gentlemen of the Mahamad and councillors.

Signed: David Vas Farro
Treasurer

IN THE NAME OF BLESSED GOD

On the 14th of Hesvan, y. 5482 [1721], the gentlemen of the Mahamad and their councillors met to confirm the Regulation dealing with the payment of the 1/4% Imposta [sales tax] of the [Jewish] Nation, on all businesses [operated] on commission or not being of others.[18] This is also understood to include strangers visiting and congregating with us in this Holy House during their stay on this Island. Thus, all are warned that the same penalty of Beraha fixed for the members also extends to strangers and will be strictly executed against any violator. It is hoped that the zeal of the gentlemen will impel them to contribute heartily toward the foregoing which, they should realize, is directed for the furtherance of Charity. In this manner they will discharge the obligation they assume, for Blessed God urges it upon us and for our almsgiving promises to deliver us from our enemies.

So, also, are the members and this entire H: C: admonished that the Regulation[19] made on the 9th of Tisry of the Year 5476 [1715], forbidding cases, and particularly [those] involving questions of honor, to be brought before the Council of this Island without the permission of the gentlemen of the Mahamad, is still in force. It is poorly kept because people let themselves be moved constantly by passion and private hatreds, not realizing the pain of Beraha they incur, plus [the fine of] 25 Pezos for the Sedaca (since the one speaking of four pezos has been revoked), in addition to the scandal.

Since the Blessed Lord calls us his sons and as such we are [therefore] brothers, we must be guarantors for one another in seeking to prevent lawsuits from being instituted against any member. For we well know that those who do not care much for us will take note and with this pretext will withhold the little affection they have for us by saying that we are as hateful as pagans. We therefore count on the devotion of all members in not permitting themselves to be swayed by passion. When approached with their (members') grievances, the gentlemen of the Mahamad will seek to mete justice fairly in order to give no one cause for complaint, and will punish the guilty with all rigor.

May the Lord God imbue us with love and fear of Him, etc.

---

[18] See above, pp. 543, 550, 556.
[19] This *Hascamah* is missing. See Article 6 of the *Hascamah* of 12 Tisry, 5449, at p. 543 above.

Done in the H: C: of Mikve Israel in Curaçao in the presence of the gentlemen of the Mahamad and councillors, etc.

Signed: Abraham da Costa de Andrade
Treasurer

IN THE NAME OF BLESSED GOD

Notice is given to all of you in general, and everyone in particular, by the Chief Rabbi and the Mahamad, that no one of this H: C: may purchase from Gentiles cheeses arriving from Amsterdam without the certification of the Chief Rabbi of the Holy Congregation of Amsterdam, or of any other well-known person, that they are *Caserim* [casher], which [certification] must be shown to our Chief Rabbi.

May God keep us from falling into sin, and peace be among you.

Done in the H: C: of Mikve Israel on the 21st day of the Homer, y. 5483 [1723].

Signed: Is[aac]: de Marchena
Treasurer

Notice having come (from) [to] the gentlemen of the Mahamad about the disorders of yesterday morning and today over ordering the commencement of prayers, the said gentlemen of the Mahamad and their councillors, in seeking the peace and union of this Holy Synagogue and the avoidance of greater disturbances, resolved to order, as they now order, that if a member of the Mahamad is not in the Synagogue before prayers are started, the Chief Rabbi shall conduct them in his stead, and if he, too, is absent, [then] one of the Messrs. Parnassim of Talmut Tora (sic) who may be present.

And may God grant us Peace and Union.

Done in the H: C: of Mikve Israel, the 12th of Elul, y. 5483 [1723].
Present, the gentlemen: Ishac Levy Mad[u]ro, President; Ishac de Marchena, Treasurer; Councillors, Jacob de Ephraim Jesurun Henriquez, Jacob Abenatar & Jacob Jeudah Leao.

Signed: Is. de Marchena
Treasurer

In the meeting held on the 13th of Elul, y. 5483 [1723], the above-mentioned resolution was shown to Messrs. Gabriel Levy, Ishac Touro and Abm. Naar, councillors of this H: C:, which may God increase, and they ratified it: Resolved [as] above.

Done in the H: C: of Mikve Israel.
Present: The gentlemen of the Mahamad and their councillors, etc.

Signed: Is. de Marchena
Treasurer

IN THE NAME OF BLESSED GOD

At a meeting of the gentlemen of the Mahamad and their councillors, it was resolved that the bachelor Mord[echa]y Levy Mad[u]ro, assistant-teacher of this H: C:, has the permission of the gentlemen of the Mahamad to pray on any day [in the Synagogue] when one of the hazanim is ill, excepting the ten days of Tesuba (Penitence).[20]

Done in the H: C: of Mikve Israel, the 16th of Sebath, Yr. 5484 [1724].
Present: The Chief Rabbi, the gentlemen of the Mahamad and their councillors.
Absent: Mr. Abraham de Chaves.

Signed: Eliau Jeudah Leao
Treasurer

IN THE NAME OF BLESSED GOD, AMEN

The Messrs. Parnassim of T: T: having complained at a meeting of the gentlemen of the Mahamad and their councillors about the poor attendance of the teachers in the schools and Synagogue of this H: C:, which may God increase, the lack of instruction among the students and the little respect and decorum said teachers manifest toward the Messrs. Parnassim of T: T:, to the extent of contradicting their orders and staying away from school without permission, all of which is contrary to how it should be, the gentlemen of the Mahamad and their councillors therefore announce:

That they have given the Messrs. Parnassim of T: T: full power and faculty to dismiss, if need be, without further notice to the gentlemen of the Mahamad (who will fully uphold their actions in this regard), any teacher who shirks his duty by absenting himself from the school and Synagogue without permission and by neglecting to show proper respect toward any of the Messrs. Parnassim in their official capacity.

The devotion of all the teachers is counted upon in seeking not to give cause for this [action] and in performing their bounden duty to further the instruction of the Divine Law among the students, for it is through them that we can expect divine blessing and aid which God inspires within our hearts.

Done in the H: C: of Mikve Israel, the 16th of Sebath, Yr. 5484 [1724].
Present: The gentlemen of the Mahamad and their councillors.
Absent: Mr. Ab[raha]m. de Chaves

Signed: Eliau Jeudah Leao
Treasurer

[20] Regarding bachelors, see above, pp. 552, 559, and below, p. 564.

IN THE NAME OF BLESSED GOD, AMEN

The gentlemen of the Mahamad and councillors, observing the present need for distributing the seats of this Holy Synagogue and seeking to accommodate all the members as far as possible, urge everyone henceforth not to occupy another's seat, or to remain standing or seated behind the pulpit, or by any means to gather in the courtyard of the Synagogue, because the Regulations prohibiting the foregoing with pain of Beraha, [namely,] that of the 21st of Sebath of the yr. 5476[21] as well as those ratified thereafter, remain in all their vigor.[22]

The zeal of all the members of this H: C:, which may God prosper, is counted upon [in observing this], as it is most necessary for the Union and Tranquility of this Holy House. And may God bless us all with peace, Amen!

Done in the H: C: of Mikve Israel on the 12th of Tisry, 5485 [1724].
Present: The gentlemen of the Mahamad and councillors.

Signed: Eliau Jesurun Henriquez
Treasurer

The gentlemen of the Mahamad and councillors admonish the membership that no Sohet-Bodec without a license of Sohet-Bodec of the community may under any pretext whatsoever kill any cattle for any member or individual of this H: C: Those having [a] license of Sehitta (sic) and bedeha (sic) shall not be able to slaughter at their home or outside of it without the permission of the gentlemen of the Mahamad, who will grant it for their (applicants') private use.

Done in the H: C: of Mikve Israel, the 26th of Hesvan, Yr. 5485 [1724].
Present: The gentlemen of the Mahamad and councillors.

Signed: Eliau Jesurun Henriquez
Treasurer

IN THE NAME OF BLESSED GOD

On the 12th of Sebath, Yr. 5486 [1726], the gentlemen of the Mahamad and councillors convened and, because of the great veneration which we owe the Sepher Thora, resolved that, henceforth the Raising of the Sepher Thora shall be accorded neither to married men nor to bachelors, but only to the Levantadores by turn. Those wishing to enroll for it, if married, must first submit to an examination by the Messrs. Levantadores who will admit no bachelor to the test,[23] for so have the gentlemen of the Mahamad and councillors found proper for the divine respect toward the Sepher Thora.

Hereafter [neither] the gentlemen of the Mahamad, nor any Bahal Asurah, nor any other entitled to distribute the Misvot, nor the person having the duty

---

[21] This *Hascamah* is missing, but is mentioned in the "Memorias Senior" and "Memorias Curiel."
[22] See above, pp. 551, 556 and below, p. 569.
[23] Regarding bachelors, see above, pp. 552, 559, 563.

of performing a Misva for an absentee, may on any account assign the said Misva to a young bachelor or to a married [Levantador] before his turn, but only to the gentlemen currently so functioning [as Levantadores] and those married men who, having been examined and found capable of performing that Misva properly, have been admitted by the gentlemen of the Mahamad. As this is for the honor of our Holy Law, we trust that it will protect us and that the Lord God will imbue us with His divine Love and Fear and bless all His people of Israel and this H: C: with Peace, Amen!

The said gentlemen of the Mahamad and councillors further order that no one may leave his seat to accompany the Sepher Thora and [thereby] annoy others, under pain of incurring the same penalty expressed in the Regulation about occupying the seat of another, because they find this proper for the Tranquility, Peace and Quiet of this Holy House, and they count on the zeal of all the members in observing it. May God bless His Nation with peace, amen!

Done in the H: C: of Mikve Israel.
Present: The gentlemen of the Mahamad and councillors.

Signed: Mordehay Senior
Treasurer

IN THE NAME OF BLESSED GOD

The gentlemen of the Mahamad and councillors, observing that marriages celebrated among our Nation in the presence of two witnesses, though valid, give rise to many difficulties, have consulted with our H: H: M: V: R: (the omniscient sage, our teacher and lord) Reph[ae]l Jesurun to remedy the situation. Said G[Haham]. found it expedient, with the approval of the gentlemen of the Mahamad and councillors, to enact a Regulation henceforth prohibiting anyone, under pain of *Beraha*, from performing marriages without the attendance or approval of the Haham and prohibiting under the same penalty any member or stranger from acting as witness for those marriages celebrated without the attendance or approval of our Haham. In addition to the marriage performer and the witnesses' incurring the penalty of *Beraha*, such marriages shall be considered null and void.[24]

It is hoped that out of zeal and reverence for God all the members and all those who congregate with us will flee from these searing flames, that God will deliver us therefrom and establish Peace upon us and His Nation Israel, Amen!

Done in the H: C: of Mikve Israel, the 24th of Tamus, Yr. 5486 [1726].
Present: The gentlemen of the Mahamad and councillors and
    H: H: M: V: R: Reph[ae]l Jesurun.

Signed: Mord[eha]y Senior
Treasurer

[24] This is a startling decision since it is against accepted law. See below, p. 579, for the Beth Din's reservation to this *Hascamah*, which was slightly amended in 1749.

N.B. The foregoing Regulation was announced from the pulpit that day at Minha (afternoon services) and on Thursday morning, [the] 26th d[itt]o before taking out the Sepher Tora.

N.B. On the 17th of Hyar, 5509 [1749], the gentlemen of the Mahamad and councillors republished and reread this Regulation in the Synagogue and, with the approval of the Bethdin, strengthened and amplified it, as appears in f[oli]o[s]: 47 & 48 [of the Book of Regulations].

IN THE NAME OF BLESSED GOD

The gentlemen of the Mahamad and councillors have observed that the greatest disorders are experienced on those occasions when the utmost attention should be given in this Holy House, such as on the nights of Tucum [Ticun] when [with] contrite [heart] we should appeal to God, on the evenings of Sebuoth when with love and divine reverence we should give God thanks for having chosen us for His people and, while reciting His divine precepts, remind ourselves of the giving of the Law, and also on the night and day of Tishabeab when we should bring to mind the trials suffered by our ancestors and sense them as present ones because on account of our sins we are still deprived of the wealth that they had, for which reason our sages instituted the Kinoth to assuage the spirit and, while shedding tears, to beg God for charity's sake to make this day again a happy one for us. On these days there is the greatest disorder. There is so much noise and commotion that very often some interrupt others and thus disrupt the devout attention which should be lent.

For this reason it has already been announced in this Holy Place, by order of former gentlemen of the Mahamad, that all members wishing to say Kinoth should so inform the eminent Haham four days before so that he may assign them and in this manner avoid the confusion of voices in this Holy House.

The gentlemen of the Mahamad and councillors, having noticed that when these disorders occur some allege ignorance of the foregoing announcement because it is not recorded in the Book of Resolutions of this H: C:, again hereby ratify it and order that on the nights of Ticun of Osahana Raba and Sebuoth for the verses of Ruth, as well as on the night and day of Tishabeab, no one shall be permitted to say Chapter, Verse or Dirge before having consulted with our Haham four days earlier so that he may place it in the order he finds most proper for the quiet and tranquility of this H: C:

It is also admonished that whoever violates this order and raises his voice without previously having consulted with our Haham shall incur a fine of four patacas for the Sedaca. If he does not obey immediately when ordered to be still, he shall incur a fine of twenty-five pezos for disturbing the quiet of this H: C:

So that no one may plead ignorance, this shall be entered as a resolution in the Book of Resolutions of this H: C: and each of the Treasurers succeeding in office must, during his year [of service], read this Regulation on the first day of Sucoth or [on the] Sabbath before Sebuoth and Sabbath Semhu (Shimhu = the second Sabbath before Tish'ah be-Ab).

May God implant in us His divine love and reverence, and bless His Nation with Peace, Amen!

Done in the H: C: of Mikve Israel on the 11th of Menahem, Yr. 5486 [1726]. Present: The gentlemen of the Mahamad and councillors.

Signed: Mordehay Senior
Treasurer

IN THE NAME OF BLESSED GOD

The gentlemen of the Mahamad and councillors, having observed the disorders occurring in the burial of our dead in the old cemetery because of the absence of regular rows, have resolved to take the necessary measures to divide the new extension to said cemetery into regular rows eight feet in length. Each of these rows shall provide for [two] graves four feet in width. The first of these rows shall start immediately from the wall where lies the tomb of the youngster Jacob da Motta [C 850] — May he rest in peace — [and shall run] up to the House [of Circuits]. In that order and not beyond the rows.

Notice is hereby given that the first one to pass on — and may it be at a ripe old age — shall be buried in said first row in a cost-free grave, whether he be rich or poor. A married person desiring to reserve another grave immediately next to his, for husband or wife, may do so without any charge. The Parnas de Hebra shall note such [reservation] in the Register.

Additional graves may be reserved in the general row on giving immediate notice to the Parnas de Hebra. These shall be listed in the Book of Rows, in charge of the Parnas de Hebra, as reserved for the burial of the person or persons designated by the one making the reservation or his heirs, and no other. For each grave reserved in said row for other than a spouse, there shall be paid at once to the Parnas de Hebra four pesos to be applied toward the meritorious services of the Gemilut Hasadim.

Any member desiring to reserve a grave in any row other than the general row of the new extension to the cemetery may do so on paying six pesos cash, to be applied as above, which shall be noted in the Register to avoid errors.

Since many members have several graves reserved in the old cemetery also, they are instructed to report same within fifteen days to the Parnas de Hebra so that he can notify the gentlemen of the Mahamad and councillors, who shall thereupon assign a cost-free grave beside a deceased husband or wife, if there is an open space. The Parnas de Hebra shall list it at once in the Cemetery Register to be made.

Any member desiring additional graves in the old cemetery shall be granted same on paying three pesos for each grave, to be applied as above. Such reservation shall be noted down in the Cemetery Register in the name of the person making the reservation or of his heirs.

567

So that everything is conducted properly, the Parnas de Hebra shall furnish Mr. Isaac Aboab, caretaker of the cemetery, a copy of the Cemetery Register to be made, in which he shall record [the names of] those [deceased] as they are buried in the general row or in the graves reserved by members in other rows of the new cemetery, and in the old cemetery as well.

The gentlemen of the Mahamad and councillors further order that henceforth no burial shall be made in the cemetery without the Parnas de Hebra's ticket which must be delivered to the Head of the Company of Gravediggers (whose turn it may be to serve) with instructions where to bury the deceased. That shall be in the general row and in the grave immediately after the last interment.

It is well understood that if the deceased was married, as has been provided there shall be allowed him an open grave for the surviving spouse, or more [graves] if previously reserved.

If a deceased person has a grave reserved in any other row [outside of the general row] of the new extension or in the old cemetery, or if a relative or friend of his wishes to have him interred in one of their [reserved] spaces, the Parnas de Hebra shall, on receiving a written request, indicate at the foot thereof to the Head of the Gravediggers' Company then serving in which row and grave of the new extension or of the old cemetery he should bury said deceased. The Heads of the Gravediggers' Companies, or their substitutes, are enjoined from consenting, nor may they consent, to bury any decedent outside of the place designated on the Parnas de Hebra's ticket, which must be delivered in the cemetery to Mr. Isaac Aboab. At the end of the year, he shall surrender those [tickets] to the Parnas de Hebra for comparison with his Register in order to avoid discrepancies.

A copy of this resolution, which is to be entered in the Book of Resolutions of this H[oly]. C[ongregation]., shall be delivered by the Gabay to the Parnas of Gemilut Hasadim so that he may have it head the Cemetery Register to be drawn up, for the guidance of all future Parnassim serving such worthy cause.

May the Lord God implant in us His love and reverence and may He grant us life to serve Him until we reach that happy day which he has promised us [25] בלע המות לנצח וכו'/

Done in the H[oly]. C[ongregation]. of Mikve Israel on 7: Tisry, Yr. 5489 [September 10, 1728].
Present: The gentlemen of the Mahamad and councillors in the company of the Parnassim of Guemilut Hasadim.

Signed: Abraham Naar
President[26]

---

[25] "He will swallow up death in eternity" (Isaiah 25:8).
[26] Compare *Precious Stones*, pp. 48-50.

IN THE NAME OF BLESSED GOD

The gentlemen of the Mahamad and councillors having, by virtue of resolution made on Sebath 21, yr. 5476,[27] and revised the 14th of Tisry, yr. 5477,[27] distributed the seats of this Holy Synagogue and tried wherever possible to accommodate all the members, urge all the gentlemen neither to occupy the seat of another, nor to remain standing, nor seated behind the pulpit, nor by any means to gather in the Synagogue courtyard since the Regulations prohibiting the foregoing remain in all their vigor.

The devotion of the members is counted upon in observing [this] as necessary for the union of this Holy House. May God establish Peace over Israel, Amen!

Done in the H: C: of Mikve Israel on the 7th of Tisry, yr. 5489 [1728]. Present: The gentlemen of the Mahamad and councillors.

Signed: Abraham Naar
President

IN THE NAME OF BLESSED GOD

The Messrs. Parnassim of T: T: having disclosed to the gentlemen of the Mahamad and councillors the liberty which the students take on becoming Bar Misva, [in that,] contrary to the divine commandments, like libertines they discard and abandon all the[ir] previous education whose only purpose was to prepare them for the study and cultivation of the divine law on reaching this age; [and whereas] this should not be expected [tolerated] if we do not want it to seem as though we approved of our sons' wandering from the meditation of God's Law [and] with some following [the example of] the others, the Lord God withdraw His protection, heaven forbid, because this [the study of the Torah] is our only means of attaining divine mercy, of expecting Him to take us under His wing and making us prosper in our careers out of the zeal and love for our divine Law that plead for us;

The gentlemen of the Mahamad and councillors resolved that all boys up to the age of sixteen years must attend school and under no pretext may refuse to attend. The Messrs. Parnassim of T: T: are hereby given the faculty and absolute power of enforcing this in the manner they deem necessary in order to teach said [boys] with their life and by force if need be — all for the service of God.[28]

The devotion and love of all the members is counted upon in making their sons fulfil this sacred duty, for the achievement of which we can hope God will bestow the blessing He promises, that He will open the windows of heaven and pour His blessing upon us until we cry out, Enough!

May God make us worthy of this grace and prosper this entire H: C: And may there be peace unto all.

Done the 26th day of Hesvan, Yr. 5489 [1728].

Signed: Mosseh de Chaves
Treasurer

[27] Both resolutions are missing; the first is cited in the "Memorias Senior." See the *Hascamoth* of 11 and 17 Nisan, 5469; also, pp. 555-56 and 564 above.

[28] See above, pp. 117, 175, 557.

IN THE NAME OF BLESSED GOD

The gentlemen of the Mahamad and councillors, having observed the disorders arising over the Misvot, give notice that every member assigned a Misva must fulfil it under the penalty expressed in the Regulation,[29] except and when on such assignment he is ill or unable to perform it and so notifies the gentlemen of the Mahamad who, being satisfied that he has sufficient cause, shall permit another to do it in his place. In that event, if he is in the Synagogue, he may have it done by another without the intervention of the person charged with performing a Misva for one not in the Synagogue.

Notice is also given that whoever has the charge of substituting for an absentee must, in the absence of a person from the Synagogue, perform the Misva for the absentee; in the absence of more than one person, he shall perform one Misva and allot the others to whomever he wishes. [A designee of his] for refusing to carry out a Misva for an absentee shall incur the same fine as one turning down a Misva other than the Misvot of removing the band [of the Sepher Torah] and of eshaim [to put on or remove the ornaments, e.g., the *rimmonim*, etc., of the Sepher Torah], which he can always do or have done.

The zeal of all the members is counted upon in regarding an assignment of the Misvot as a prize to be exercised by everyone with devotion.

May God make our hearts as one and implant in us His divine Love and Fear. Peace unto Israel.

Done in the H: C: of Mikve Israel on the 14th of Adar of 5496 [1736].[30]

Signed: Jacob Lopez Dias
Treasurer

IN THE NAME OF BLESSED GOD

The gentlemen of the Mahamad and councillors, observing that on the occasions when the Kadis of Rabanan [Rabbis' Kaddish] is distributed the person given the Misva is prevented from saying it alone, admonish all members that henceforth, to avoid disorders, only the person to whom the Misva is assigned shall say it without being joined, in a loud voice, by any of the others saying Kadis.[31]

May God grant life to His entire Nation and peace unto Israel.

Done in the H: C: of Mikve Israel on the 8th of Nisan, Yr. 5496 [1736].
Present: The gentlemen of the Mahamad and councillors.

Signed: Jacob Lopes Dias
Treasurer

---

29 See above, pp. 547, 559-60; below, pp. 575, 610-11.

30 Especially amazing is the absence of a resolution relating to the construction of the Synagogue of 1730 and another for its dedication in 1732!

31 See *Precious Stones*, pp. 91-92.

IN THE NAME OF BLESSED GOD

It having come to the attention of the gentlemen of the Mahamad and councillors that some of our Nation are inclined to discuss matters which concern only the Government and Courts of this Island, which discussions may cause trouble and annoyance to the [Jewish] Nation, God forbid, notice is hereby given for everyone to refrain from and to have their children refrain from interfering in any matter concerning the Government or Courts of the Island, either by word or deed. For so it behooves us for our Conservation; the Lord God commands us to obey and respect our Superiors, and our ancestors did so ordain in this H: C: for having recognized this [policy] as the best means for [assuring] our peace and tranquility.

For these reasons the gentlemen of the Mahamad and councillors have found it advisable to issue this warning. They expect everyone to cooperate in order to prevent any possible difficulties to the offender and the Nation as well.

Lest anyone violating this warning thinks that the congregation will pledge itself for him, be it known that not only will they refuse to help him, but, in order to satisfy the Governor and Council, they will also proceed against the transgressor with all the powers under our Regulations and other measures which the gentlemen of the Mahamad and councillors may deem necessary according to the requirements of the case.

May God move our hearts to work for peace and union so that we may remain in the grace[s] of our Superiors, and may He bless His people with peace, Amen.

Done in the H. C. of Mikve Israel, 20 Sivan, 5499 [1739].[32]
Present: The gentlemen of the Mahamad and councillors.

Signed: Jacob de Eliau Pereira
Treasurer

IN THE NAME OF BLESSED GOD

The gentlemen of the Mahamad have received a letter from the very illustrious gentlemen of the Mahamad of the Holy Congregation of T: T: of Amsterdam, disclosing that a member [of ours] had written to various merchants of that city against the interests of a fellowman. In telling strangers that there is among us an evil person capable of such a deed, he not only trespassed against the commandments of God's Holy Law, but also profaned His Holy Name. [Their letter] firmly recommends a careful investigation of the person guilty of this act so that he may be punished in accordance with his crime and in accordance with the rigor of our Holy Law so that there is no repetition of it in the future.

The gentlemen of the Mahamad and their councillors, in the company of our eminent Haham R[ephae]l. Jesurun, after investigating the matter as far as possible, decided with the approval of our worthy Haham upon the proper punishment to be meted out under our Holy Law.

[32] See p. 149 above.

Since in the Yr. 5449 it was resolved to forbid, under penalty of the small ban, the composition of verses, sonnets or pasquins injurious to one's fellow-men, which [offense] is less grievous than the foregoing case, said gentlemen resolved to enact a Regulation, as they now enact, whereby any member or resident of this Island, or even visitors, committing an offense similar to this, either directly or indirectly, by inciting or causing to incite, by writing or causing to be written anything frivolous against his fellowman or against his interests, shall be under penalty of the small ban and shall be punished with all the rigor of our Holy Law, as a disturber of the peace and general welfare. His crime shall be announced in the Holy Synagogue so that everyone may avoid him and especially his mischief. He shall not be relieved or released from such penalty until paying a fine of fifty pezos for the Sedaca and giving public satisfaction from the pulpit, [namely,] by asking God, the Holy Congregation and the person he has injured for forgiveness of his sin.[33]

So that no one may plead ignorance as an excuse, said gentlemen order that this Regulation be announced from the pulpit.

May Blessed God help us with His divine aid so that we may incline our hearts to keep His divine laws with love and reverence by loving our fellowmen as His Holy Law commands and by driving away all evil from us. May He bless His people with peace and union, Amen!

Done in the H. C. of Mikve Israel, the 3rd of Nisan, Yr. 5500 [1740].[34]
Present: The gentlemen of the Mahamad and councillors in the Company of the eminent Haham.

Signed: Josseph Jess[uru]n. Henriquez
Treasurer

The gentlemen of the Mahamad and all the councillors having convened to discuss various matters before them, several of them proposed that, whereas all the worthy councillors are now called to elect parnassim and to distribute the [Synagogue] seats; and [whereas] it is inevitable for the said councillors to have brothers, brothers-in-law and cousins sitting in the junta who, in all justice, should not vote together for those purposes or for the distribution of the Misvot of Rosasana and Kipur (about which more will be said by the said gentlemen of the Mahamad and councillors); and [whereas] it would be more desirable for the tranquility, peace and union of the junta and of this Holy Congregation, which may God increase; and [whereas] several of the gentlemen have proposed that these sections should be annulled or amended to provide that henceforth those functions should be vested in the ordinary junta of seven persons in the degrees of relationship not forbidden to sit together in judgment;

Now, therefore, it is resolved that these sections be annulled and abolished

---

[33] See above, p. 545, art. 14.
[34] See p. 147 above.

and that henceforth elections for the Mahamad and the distribution of the Misvot of Rosasana and Kipur, as well as the distribution of [Synagogue] seats when necessary, shall be vested in the said seven members (in the degrees of relationship not forbidden) of the ordinary junta of this year.

Considering that some gentlemen may see in this delegation of power also some injury to honor, the said seven [members] of the ordinary junta shall not nor may not have the power or faculty to elect as parnas anyone not actually a councillor or to nominate any member [of the congregation] as a new councillor without the consent and approval of all the worthy councillors. Insofar as these two points are concerned and in other urgent matters that may arise, the gentlemen of the Mahamad presiding [that is, the ordinary junta] shall be obliged to hold a general junta of all the worthy councillors so that these matters can be decided by a majority vote.

May God assist us with His divine aid so that with love and reverence we may serve Him and keep ourselves in peace and union, Amen.

Done in the H. C. of Mikve Israel, the 4th of Tisry, 5504 [1743].
Present: The gentlemen of the Mahamad and all the councillors.

Signed: Selomoh Lopez Henriquez
Treasurer

[The following five Hascamoth relate to the conflicts of 1744-1750, discussed in Chapter IX.]

REGULATION, that all persons called to the Torah must offer as their final donation at least a half soldo for the health of the Parnas President and the Holy Congregation

IN THE NAME OF BLESSED GOD

Whereas, it is the custom in this Holy Congregation and in all the congregations of Israel governed by the law of good manners and courtesy for all those called to the Torah to make as the last of their offerings, a donation for the health of the Parnas President and of the H. C., in signal of respect and reverence toward the Congregation and those governing it; and

The gentlemen of the Mahamad and their councillors, having observed for some time past and even as recently as last Saturday that several members of this H. C., because of some actual or imagined grievance or complaint against the Parnas President or one of the gentlemen of the Mahamad, disregard this so courteous and well-founded institution and custom, by refusing to make a donation for the health of the Parnas and the H. C.; and

Deeming it necessary eventually to put a stop to this shameful neglect, as it may be the cause of fomenting disorders and the dissolution of this H. C., and as this flagrant practice though meant to offend does not offend the gentlemen of the Mahamad but above all demonstrates and evinces the little reverence held for this Holy House which they use as a battleground to take revenge and meanwhile dishonor the Sepher Torah and the Holy Law therein inscribed which forbids such behavior;

Now, therefore, the said gentlemen of the Mahamad and their councillors have unanimously resolved to institute by Regulation, as they institute by this, that henceforth anyone called to the Torah must offer at least one-half soldo for the health of the Parnas President and the H. C., and if he refuses to do so, the Hazan who reads the Parasah is hereby ordered to offer the said half soldo for the Parnas President and H. C. However, as it is the intention of the gentlemen of the Mahamad and their councillors only to prevent disunity and disorders and to see that the divine decorum of this Holy House and its Holy Law is preserved and not to force anyone to offer more than he wishes since donations must be voluntary, whoever does not wish to pay this half soldo offered against his will may so manifest that to the Treasurer after all have left the Synagogue and not before. In that event, he (the Treasurer) shall have to deduct this half soldo from the [member's] pledges. If anyone objects to the terms of this Regulation — an objection not to be expected — the Parnas shall order him to become quiet and on not obeying but stubbornly raising his voice in disagreement, he shall incur the penalty of the small ban. The gentlemen of the Mahamad shall make him leave the Synagogue and shall not remove said penalty until he pays a fine of 25 pezos for the Sedaca and gives satisfaction to the gentlemen of the Mahamad as provided in the Regulation with regard to raising one's voice in the Synagogue. Successors to the Mahamad in office, as well as the worthy councillors, shall be obliged to give their full assistance in carrying out this Regulation fully.

As it is the object of the gentlemen of the Mahamad and their councillors to prevent disorders, to avoid unpleasant developments and to strive to maintain peace and union in this H. C., which may God increase, they count on the zeal of all the members and congregants of this Holy Congregation in performing their obligation and contributing as much as possible for our conservation in this prolonged exile, so that the Blessed Lord may redeem us and move us nearer to this much desired goal, so that united we may serve Him with a perfect heart.

May He bless us with peace and union, Amen!

Done in the H. C. Mikve Israel, the   Elul, Yr. 5505 [1745].
Present: The gentlemen of the Mahamad & their councillors.

Signed: Abm: d[e] Jacob Jeudah Leao
Treasurer

219. SILVER RIMMONIM DONATED TO SYNAGOGUE
MIKVE ISRAEL, CURAÇAO

218. SILVER RIMMONIM DONATED TO SYNAGOGUE
MIKVE ISRAEL, CURAÇAO

220. SILVER TORAH CROWN BEQUEATHED BY MORDECHAY NAMIAS DE
CRASTO TO SYNAGOGUE MIKVE ISRAEL, 1716, PAGE 95

221. SILVER PURIM BOWLS DONATED TO SYNAGOGUE MIKVE ISRAEL BY DAVID
MORDECHAY DE CRASTO AND HAIM GABRIEL DA COSTA GOMEZ, PAGE 260

REGULATION with regard to what the gentlemen of the
Mahamad and the councillors of the H. C. Mikve Israel
resolved on the obedience and respect required of the
members of this H. C. as well as those of the H. C.
Neve Salom toward the Parnasim and in the Synagogue
of said H. C. Neve Salom

IN THE NAME OF BLESSED GOD

The gentlemen of the Mahamad and councillors of the H. C. Mikve Israel make
known and hereby admonish all members of the H. C. Neve Salom that they
have given, and hereby give, full power and faculty to the Mahamad of the
said H. C. Neve Salom, if it should be necessary (God forbid), to eject from
the Synagogue any members of the said H. C. Neve Salom who may create a
disturbance in the Synagogue by word or deed and refuse to quiet down when
so ordered by the Parnasim, and to fine them in accordance with the Regulations
(and the same applies to any person or persons going to Outrabanda for a walk
[and visiting the said Synagogue]). The Mahamad and councillors or the H. C.
Mikve Israel shall extend all the necessary assistance as provided in the Regulation effected on the 7th of Tebeth, Yr. 5493,[35] which remains in full force
and is hereby reaffirmed.

Notice is given that the fines shall hereafter be as follows:

For refusing the office of Parnas, Treasurer, Hatan Torah or [Hatan] Beresith,
respectively, twenty pezos
For refusing the office of Parnas of Talmud Torah, ten pezos
For refusing any of the following Misvot, such as opening the doors of the
Ark, carrying the Sepher Tora, unwinding the band [on the Sepher Torah],
Eshaim, raising the Sepher, accompanying [the Torah], substituting for an
absentee having a Misva, and for calling to the Torah, respectively, five
pezos[36]
For creating a disturbance in the Synagogue and refusing to become quiet
when so ordered by the gentlemen of the Mahamad, five pezos; and if one
comes to blows, ten pezos.

It is hoped that out of their deep devotion and reverence for God no one will
disregard the usages of the Holy House of God. If any members of [the] H. C.
Neve Salom or any visitors attending the Synagogue of the said H. C. give cause
for being fined and refuse to pay, then they shall be vigorously prosecuted.

May God imbue us with love and reverence for Him so that His Holy Law may
be observed in Peace and Union.

35 Missing.
36 See above, pp. 547, 559-60, 570; below, pp. 610-11.

Done in the H. C. Mikve Israel, the 19th of Elul, Yr. 5505 [1745], by order of the gentlemen of the Mahamad & councillors.

Signed: Abm. de Jacob Jeudah Leao
Treasurer

IN THE NAME OF BLESSED GOD

The members of the H. C. of Neve Salom living on the other side of this harbor (Otrabanda) having resolved, with the approval of the gentlemen of the Mahamad and councillors and with the assistance of the entire illustrious H. C., to build a prayer house for divine worship; and the gentlemen of the Mahamad and councillors, on perceiving some dissension among them and in an effort to stop it from worsening, found it prudent, with the approval of our eminent Hahamim to forbid, as they do hereby forbid, any member of said H. C. Neve Salom, or anyone of this H. C. of Mikve Israel, or even a stranger, to gather together to pray with a quorum in Otrabanda in any house outside of Synagogue Neve Salom, whether or not such house is located within the Saturday limits comprising a district of two thousand paces from the Synagogue in either direction. Excepted are the houses of a bride and groom and of mourners where it shall be permitted to them to pray during the seven days of marriage or of mourning. It is well understood to mean on weekdays [only], because on Saturdays and holidays a newly married couple as well as mourners can attend the Synagogue. They shall not be permitted to pray with a quorum in their homes without the express order [consent] of the parnasim and treasurer of Otrabanda and the approval of the gentlemen of the Mahamad of this H. C.

All those wishing to pray with a quorum shall be obliged to congregate with the rest of the members in the Synagogue Neve Salom, in the building currently used or which, with the grace of God, they shall occupy when built.

Notice is given that all those violating or overstepping the bounds of this resolution shall incur the penalty of Beraha. They shall be prosecuted with all the rigor of our Regulations which prohibit worshiping with a quorum outside of the Synagogue. That penalty shall not be removed until there is proof of repentance and payment of the fine of twenty-five pezos for [the] Sedaca of the H. C. Neve Salom. This resolution carries the same force and prohibition as the one applying to those of us who live in the City.

So that everyone may know of this [ruling] and none may plead ignorance, the said gentlemen have ordered it to be announced in this H. C. and in the Neve Salom in Otrabanda, and in this manner seek to maintain peace and union among us.

All members and congregants of both congregations, out of their devotion and reverence for God, are expected to make every effort to follow through, by worshiping in the official Synagogue as our Holy Law commands.

May Blessed God make us prosper and bless us with the blessings and happiness He promises to those who keep it (His Holy Law), Amen!

Done in the H. C. of Mikve Israel, the 21st of Sivan, Yr. 5506 [1746].
Present: The gentlemen of the Mahamad with their ordinary & extraordinary councillors and the Elders of the Nation with the approval of the eminent Hahamim.
May there be peace all over Israel!

Signed: Semuel de Is[aac]. Levy Maduro
Treasurer

IN THE NAME OF BLESSED GOD

In view of the disturbances which have been prevailing for some time now in this H. C. through the perpetration of some individuals and which, because of our sins, keep growing daily, and since most of them refrain from congregating in this Holy House and, according to what they themselves say, intend to find a way to have a separate Synagogue or to congregate with a quorum in some private home,

The gentlemen of the Mahamad met on the 15th of this [month] with all their ordinary and extraordinary councillors to perform their duty and what our Regulations order to find how to check this very harmful design and save those [people] from incurring the penalties imposed by our said Regulations which were first promulgated with so much devotion and reverence for God by our ancestors in the Yr. 5431 for the maintenance of the good government of this Holy Congregation and our own preservation, and which they confirmed on 12 Tisry, yr. 5449, and reinstated with all vigor on the 8th of Tisry, yr. 5460.[37] At that time, with the approval of the Elders of the Nation & of the entire Holy Congregation, they delegated the eminent Haham Eliau Lopez of glorious memory, in the company of Messrs. Ishac de Marchena, Ishac Pereira & Gabriel Levy who had served the year before as Mahamad, and the Messrs. Joseph da Costa de Andrade and Mordechay Namias de Crasto (who God has), to amplify [them] and prepare an explanation and necessary additions to some Regulations, as they did. Finally, on the 21st of Sivan, yr. 5506, while Mr. Samuel de Is. Levy Maduro was Treasurer, with the approval of the gentlemen of the Mahamad and all their councillors, as well as of the venerable Elders of the Nation and the eminent Hahamin — at the time when the Synagogue of the H. C. Neve Salom on the other side of the harbor was being built with the aid of this entire H. C. — in order to stop the conflicts which existed among those living there, they again amplified and explained some points concerning the said Regulations and government of this Holy Congregation and of the Neve Salom in Otrabanda.

Since all the Regulations and resolutions mentioned prohibit, under penalty of the small ban and pecuniary fine, the attempt or intent to build another Synagogue outside of the official one which we have in the city and [also] on the other side of the harbor, or to congregate with a quorum in any private house in the district of Saturday limits consisting of two thousand paces on all sides,

---

[37] See above, pp. 542, 549.

in the city as well as in Otrabanda, excepting the home of a bride and groom and/or of mourners where it is permitted to pray with a quorum during the seven days of marriage or mourning, that is, on weekdays but not on Saturdays and holidays when the newlyweds as well as the mourners can attend the Synagogue, the said gentlemen of the Mahamad and all their councillors resolved, with the approval of the eminent Hahamim, again to ratify and reinstate all the Regulations and resolutions referred to, in all their points and requirements, as they do by these presents, with the same penalties specified in those Regulations.

So that no one may at any time allege ignorance, they ordered that this resolution or Regulation should be announced in this H. C. Mikve Israel as well as in the Neve Salom, with the warning to all members and individuals of this H. C., under which are included those of the Neve Salom, and all strangers, that all the Regulations referred to are and remain in their [full] force and effect over all the [Jewish] inhabitants of this Island, and that all violators will be prosecuted with all the rigor permitted to us by the said Regulations, our Holy Law and its professors.

All of us, out of our devotion and reverence for God, should heed this important as well as kindly warning in order to avoid the difficulties which may arise. We implore God to fill our hearts with His divine love and fear and to keep us in peace & union, Amen.

Done in the H. C. Mikve Israel on the 15th of Jiar, Yr. 5508 [1748].

Present: The gentlemen of the Mahamad and all their ordinary and extraordinary councillors; communicated to the eminent Hahamim and announced on the 19th of said month and year.

Signed: Mosseh Henriq[ue]z Cotino
Treasurer

17. HYAR YR: 5509 [1749]

For just reasons entertained, the gentlemen of the Mahamad and their councillors today ordered that there be reread and reannounced in the Synagogue the Regulation effected on the 24th of Tamus, Yr. 5486,[38] and entered in f[oli]o: 30, under which it is forbidden to perform marriages and to serve as witness thereto unless done in the presence of or with the approval of our eminent Haham. They, together with the gentlemen of the Beth Din, strengthened it with the following Regulation thereafter published and read:

IN THE NAME OF BLESSED GOD

The gentlemen of the Mahamad and their councillors, together with our eminent Haham Semuel Mendes de Solla and the gentlemen of his Beth Din, for just reasons found it imperative again to repeat, reread and republish the foregoing

[38] See above, p. 565; below, p. 602.

Regulation so that no one may allege ignorance. They declared that this Regulation remains in full force and effect and also prohibits anew, under the same penalty, anyone, whether resident or stranger, from performing marriages on this Island or serving as a witness thereto unless in the presence and with the consent of our worthy Haham.

They also declared that by virtue of the authority and power vested in them by Din, henceforth if anyone acts to the contrary, such marriage as well as the witnesses to it will be held totally invalid, null and void, and the woman receiving such ceremony considered single under our Holy Law.

All members and strangers, out of their devotion and reverence for God, are expected to pay close attention to this well-meant notice so that it may not be necessary to prosecute the transgressors with the rigor of our Holy Law.

May God save us from running into similar difficulties and may He bless everyone of this H. C. with peace and union, Amen!

Done and published in the H. C. of Mikve Israel, the 17th of Iyar, Yr. 5509 [1749]. Present: The gentlemen of the Mahamad, their councillors & the eminent Haham with the gentlemen of his Beth Din.

Signed: Semuel de David Hoheb
Treasurer

N.B. The above Regulation was announced from the pulpit on that day before Harbit & on Thursday morning, the 20th of said [month] before taking out the Sepher Thora.

N.B. The gentlemen of the Beth Din, for reasons reserved to themselves, have requested the gentlemen of the Mahamad to make this notation below the foregoing Regulation:

> Because Kedusim [marriage] is such a delicate and important matter, and since all cases are not alike and there may be certain helpful circumstances not present in others that may come to change the view of the Law, when such a case arises (God forbid), before doing anything one should communicate with the said gentlemen of the Beth Din so that, after due and meticulous examination of the matter, they may give a report to the gentlemen of the Mahamad as to what should be done in order to avoid all sorts of doubts.

We, the undersigned Parnassim, Treasurer & councillors of the H. C. Mikve Israel, declare that the above Regulations are faithfully copied from the Book of Our Regulations & compared by us.

In witness whereof, we sign it in our hand in Curaçao, [the] 22 January, 1751:

David Jesurun	Selomoh N[une]s Redondo
1751	
Binj[ami]n Lopez Henriq[ue]z	Abraham de Is[aac]: Senior
Jacob Levij Madúro	Jacob Fidanque
Josseph Jess[uru]n Henriques	

B. THE HASCAMOTH OF 1750-1810

INTRODUCTORY NOTE

BㅂㅌWEEN 1750 AND 1756 the Amsterdam parnassim promulgated new Hascamoth for Curaçao based on amendments and modifications submitted by their colleagues of Curaçao. Signed and approved by Prince William IV of Holland in 1750, these were further amplified between 1751 and 1755 and ratified by Princess Anna and the directors of the Dutch West India Company in 1755 (pages 231-33 above). There are at least four copies extant: one among the loose papers of the Mikvé Israel Archives, another in a bundle of the Archives of the Portuguese Jewish Community of Amsterdam, the third in the Royal Dutch Archives at The Hague and the fourth at the American Jewish Historical Society Library at Waltham, Mass. The Curaçao parnassim made certain changes in these Regulations in 1786 and in 1810 (pages 275, 290 above). These were translated from Portuguese into English in 1810 by Abraham Salom Delvalle, a sworn translator, during the English occupation of Curaçao (Ministerie van Koloniën no. 3740, 2nd half 1816; re Delvalle, *Precious Stones*, pp. 417-19). Referred to as reforms, these modifications of 1810 were signed by 24 representatives of the community: the Mahamad, their councillors, and Delvalle as councillor and translator. They were further signed and approved by William Prince, Government Secretary and Court Clerk, on January 10, 1810, and on May 21, 1811.

Although Delvalle's translation contains many errors in grammar, punctuation, spelling and sometimes of text, it has nevertheless been retained almost entirely. He did not translate one thing or another and took the liberty of making certain changes and additions. Sometimes we have set off his expression in parentheses and followed it directly with the correct term in brackets. In some instances it was necessary to include important omissions; these additions we have set off in brackets. For example, in Article 10 of the First Section relating to "ceremonies with the Books of Moses" or ceremonies requiring one to go before the Torah, he forgot to include the Bar Misva ceremony which, as late as 1750 and 1756, ranked in the same plane of importance as the Synagogue ceremonies conducted on Saturday for a bridegroom or for the father of a newborn son. In still other instances it was necessary to retranslate the confusing or incorrect portions, or the whole, of these Regulations, as in Articles 5th, 9th and 10th of the Fifth Section, and so on. Such inclusions or corrections are enclosed in brackets.

The "Domestical Regulations" of 1810 show the inevitable influence of the

English occupation on the parliamentary procedure, the decorum, dress, etc., prescribed for the parnassim and councillors in their meetings.

TRANSLATION
[by Abraham S. Delvalle]

Extract from the Records of Resolutions, of the Portuguese Hebrew Consistory, of this Island of Curaçao.

Thursday the 8th of the month "Yar" A.M. 5571, or the 2nd of May 1811 Present all the Members.

Nº 1. The president, considering the mode of voting in our Assemblies, as ordered, by our "Ascama" (or Church-ordinancies) to be very irregular, and that it would be more proper, to follow in that respect, the Example, as well of the respective Tribunals, of this Island, as in General, of all Colleges, and Assemblies, properly constituted, he, said President, proposed, that henceforth, the President of this Consistory at our different meetings, will be the last, to give his vote, or opinion, and that in General, all matters before this Consistory, will be decided, by a Majority of votes, observing, that when with the Concluding opinion, of said President, the votes are Equal, the matter shall be resolved, or decided on, in favor of the vote, of said President.

And the opinion, of all the Members, having been asked, it unanimously was resolved and agreed, and it is hereby resolved and agreed accordingly.

1st. To accept of said proposal, and the same is hereby accepted accordingly, and that in consequence thereof, the votes shall in future be taken, in manner as aforesaid.

2nd. That in general, all matters, before this Consistory, shall be decided by the Majority.

3rd. and finally, that when the votes are equal, the concluding vote, of the President, will have the preference, and the matter be decided accordingly.

Nº 2. The President having experienced, that the Members of this Consistory do not properly attend, at our Assemblies when Convoked, and that some by paying the fine, stipulated by our ordinancies, and others, in consequence of indispensable business remain absent, and also that the Planters among us, as well from their distance from Town, as in consequence of the Season, are often entirely unable to attend, which inconveniencies from 22 Effective Members (in appearance) of which this Consistory, is composed, we finally will be reduced, to an incompetent number to meet — said President, together with his Colleagues (the vice President and the Treasurer) after having meditated on the Subject, in order to find a Medium, which preventing the above-mentioned inconveniency, would at the same time accomodate all parties, promote the Harmony of this Consistory, and leave each Member remain with their prerogatives, without depriving them, of their right, to be participated, of all the Occurrencies, found proper, to submit to this Assembly, a certain plan containing 17 Articles, and framed by them to that effect which, having been seen, read and examined, after a mature deliberation it unanimously was found proper and resolved, and it is hereby resolved accordingly to approve, of said plan, and the same is hereby approved accordingly, in order to be adopted, and Strictly to be followed, in the manner as is hereafter described, and to be annexed, to our "Ascamot" or Church Ordinancies, to form an integral part, of the same, together with the foregoing Resolution, respecting the manner of voting in our Assemblies, under this positive restriction however, that the same, shall not be acted upon, or have any authenticity whatever, previous, it shall have been submitted to the Honorable Council of this Island, to be approved by the same, agreeably to the 19th Article of the first Section, of the Reform of our said "Ascamot" or Church Ordinancies.

(*signed*)   Salomon Senior
Treasurer

(*signed*)   Moize Cardoze
President

Agrees with the Original

By me [*signed*]
delvalle
Sw[orn]. Int[erpreter].
A true Copy
W. Prince
Sec.

TRANSLATION

No. 9
Approved and signed the 21st of May, 1811, by Wm Prince, Government Secretary and Court Clerk

Scheme of a new Institution proposed by the President and his Colleagues (the vice President and the Treasurer) at the Assembly of our Consistory, held on the 2nd of May instant, as appears by the annexed Resolution, to form an integral part of our Ascamot or Church Ordinancies.

Art 1st

An Election will be made of Six Members from the Consistory, to form nine with the three Members of the Regency, for the Establishment of a Congress.

2nd

This Congress will be authorized, and be stiled The General Assembly, with ample Power to resolve and to dispose in all cases whatever respecting the Political Government of the Sinagogue — observing that if in matters of great consequence they find any difficulty to conclude, they will request the Elders to Join and to assist them in their deliberations.

3rd

In same manner if any Circumstances should urge them to make some alterations in our Ascamot or Church Ordinancies they will have to convoke the Elders to proceed in the manner as prescribed by said Ordinancies.

4th

Those Members of our Consistory who are not Elected for the Congress will remain in the same degree of respectability and rank with those of our said Consistory heretofore stiled "Members of 70 Years" and in General enjoy every prerogative and be called Elders of the Nation.

5th

Respecting the distribution of any particular performance of our Ceremonies and that of the Selected Seats in the Sinagogue and also the periodical Election of the administrators of the Public Schools they shall continue to act as heretofore without any distinction or taking any new prerogative to themselves.

6th

The Elders of the Nation will be obliged to attend unless prevented by any plausible cause at the last General Joint meeting of our Consistory to take Cognizance of all the Occurrencies of the last year and Especially to examine the Books and to resolve on the different branches of our finance on pain of forfeiting a fine of Ten Pieces of eight each.

7th

This Congress will continue for Seven Years and the Members thereof be obliged to attend without exception at all the meetings on pain of forfeiting a fine of Ps 100 each time unless they produce an Excuse for their nonattendance to the satisfaction of the Congress.

8th

If a Member of said Congress would wish to resign his place during the above-mentioned period of Seven Years he shall have to pay a fine of Ps 300 to the benefit of the Poor after which he shall again be considered as an Elder of the Nation with the rest of the Members of our Consistory.

9th

No misunderstanding or Enmity between the Members will be admitted as an Excuse for the nonattendance of any Member at the General meeting of the Consistory as all matters discussed in that Assembly only relate to the Political Government of the Sinagogue.

10th

In case any of the Six Members who compose the Congress should depart this life during the aforesaid period of 7 years another Member from the Consistory or Assembly of elders will be elected in his place who immediately will be considered as an Effective Member of said Congress.

11th

The Congress will meet as many times as it shall be convoked by the President, and Seven Members be Sufficient and Competent to deliberate in all matters.

12th

If unexpectedly the aforesaid number of Seven Members to form a Legal meeting cannot be obtained either because the Members of the Regency of the Sinagogue happen to be also of the Six elected for the Congress or in consequence of any other reason, one or more of the Elders (if necessary) shall be convoked to complete said number of Seven which latters will be obliged to attend if not prevented by impossibility on pain of forfeiting a fine of Ps 10.

13th

The first Election for this Congress will be made by the Mahamad or Court of Justitie which will be properly authorized to that effect.

14th

A proper Instrument or authority will also be granted by the General Assembly of the Elders of the Nation to the Congress with full power to act in all cases under the aforesaid restrictions and Regulations as they shall find proper — observing that the Resolutions and all other proceedings of said Congress will have the same force and Legality as those of the former Joint General Assembly of the Elders without any person being allowed to oppose or to contradict the same in any manner whatever and much less to Speak against the same Especially with Strangers who have nothing to do with their deliberations on pain of forfeiting a fine of Ps 100 to the benefit of the Poor for the first time and if repeating the same Offence such persons will be excluded for their imprudence from all the Honors as Members of the Consistory.

15th

After the expiration of the abovementioned Seven Years a new Election shall be made by said Congress of which only three Members will be allowed to be re-Elected (if they agree to it) for the new Congress and so Successively.

16th

The three Members of the Regency of the Sinagogue — to wit — The President, the vice President and the Treasurer, the late Regent and three of the Members of the New Congress will form the Mahamad or Court of Justice by which

E[l]ection the restriction made by our Ascamot or Church Ordinancies that persons related together shall not meet together in said Court will be observed. If therefore it is impossible to Complete said Court of seven Members out of the nine Members of the Congress, five will be Sufficient to deliberate with the Majority of votes, and if finally, it should be the case, that even those five cannot be obtained, one or more of the Assembly of the Elders, will be convoked to attend.

17th

The Reform or amplification of our Ascamot or Church Ordinancies Sanctioned by the Honorable Council of this Island on the 10th of January 1810, will remain in full force except in such Articles which are contrary to this Institution, and especially that respecting the manner of voting in our Assemblies, which has entirely been altered, as mentioned in our Resolution of this day.

By Command of the Consistory.

(*signed*)   Moize Cardoze

Presid[t]

[*Signed*] By me

delvalle

Sw[orn.] Int[erpreter].

A true copy.

W. Prince

[Secretary & Court Clerk]

TRANSLATED FROM THE ORIGINAL PORTUGUESE
BY A. S. DELVALLE AND AMENDED BY THE CO-AUTHORESS

Escamoth or Church Ordinances of the Portuguese Jewish Congregation of the Island of Curaçao of the year 1756 & the Alterations made in the same, in 1786, together with the Reforms of the present year 1809

SECTION FIRST
RESPECTING THE POLITICAL GOVERNMENT

Escamoth of the Years 1756 & 1786

Art: 1st

There shall be only one Chief Congregation to wit – That called *Mikvé Israel*, in Willemstadt of the said Island, to which that called Neve Salom, at the Otra Banda, shall be Subordinate, without it being allowed, to form any other Congregation whatsoever, in the said Island, nor shall any private Company, meet with ten persons, & Separate themselves from the said Congregation, to read prayers with *Minjan*, (that is with ten persons) except, in the mourning Houses, and at the Celebration of any Marriage (during the Nuptial days) and this only, on common [i.e., weekdays], and not on Saturday nor Holydays, or well, in case some private persons, without intention, to separate themselves from the Congregation, shall have assembled for some particular reasons, after having obtained permission for the same, from the President, for one or more times, without which permission, it shall by no means be permitted, to read the said prayers in the abovementioned manner, and those who shall separate themselves from the Congregation, either in Williamstadt, or Otra Banda aforesaid, and join in the

Reforms of the Year 1809

Art: 1st

This article has remained in its full force, with this distinction however, that instead of incurring in the Penalty of Excommunication, The Transgressors shall be considered, as disturbers of the Public peace, & traduced before the Judge of the Colony, to be corrected with the utmost rigor.

abovementioned manner, shall incur the Penalty of Excommunication, and be expelled from the Congregation and besides, the Mahamad (That is the Court of Justice) [the executives of the Congregation] at the time being, shall proceed against such Transgressors with every Rigor, and inflict such further Penalties, as they will deem proper to decree.

Art: 2nd

That the Mahamad, shall henceforth be composed of five persons – to wit – Four Wardens and a Treasurer, and two Members of the General Assembly of the last Election, each [in] their turn. The Mahamad shall nominate their successors in the following manner – to wit – On Ros-Ashana (or the Jewish New year's feast) Two Parnassim or Wardens, and a Treasurer – and on the Eve of the Passover's feast, Two Wardens, who shall serve each one year, In which manner there shall always be in service, persons who are acquainted with the former proceedings.

[Art:] 3rd

That henceforth, all Wardens Elected, accepting or not accepting, shall enter in the Rank of Members of the General Assembly, without any distinction whatsoever, and in case one or more of the five aforesaid persons, composing the Mahamad, from any Circumstances, may not be able to attend at the Assembly, the last Elected Warden or Wardens shall be convoked, in their place, and if the Treasurer cannot attend, his predecessor shall be convoked, provided he is not related to one of the Wardens in such degree as will be mentioned in the 11th Article.

Art: 2nd

The Mahamad shall henceforth consist of seven persons, to wit – Two active Church Wardens and Treasurer, Two Church Wardens who served the last year, and two Members of the General Assembly, to be elected agreeably to their age.

The Election of one Church Warden, and of a Treasurer, will be made on Ros-ashana or New Year's feast, and one Church Warden on Passover feast who shall serve each one Year – In which manner the Board shall always be attended by persons informed of the last Ocurrencies.

[Art:] 3rd

This article has remained in its full vigor, Except that instead of five persons, the Board shall consist of seven persons, as it is at present.

587

[Art:] 4th

Each Warden shall preside during three months.

[Art:] 4th

Each Warden shall preside Six months.

[Art:] 5th

In case any of the Wardens or the Treasurer of the 1st Election refuse to accept their places or shall leave the same previous the expiration of one year they shall have to pay a fine of Pˢ 100 each and those of the 2nd Election Pˢ 150 and after the said two Elections shall have been made and those elected having refused, all the Members of the General Assembly shall be lotted out (except those who have served the last Year and those who having been elected & have refused the situation) and he or they whose names shall be lotted out shall be obliged to accept the situation.

[Art:] 5th

Those who shall refuse to act either as Church Wardens or as Treasurer or taking their dismission before time is expired, shall pay a fine of Pˢ 150, as well for the 1st as for the 2nd Election and in case both elections refuse to accept, the order expressed by the said Article shall be observed.

Art: 6th

A Member of the General assembly who shall refuse to be one of the Mahamad shall pay a fine of Pˢ 25 and another be Chosen in his place who also refusing shall have to pay the same fine and so on.

Art: 6th

In force.

[Art:] 7th

It shall not be allowed to any person whatsoever to exempt himself from being Warden or Member of the General Assembly, unless he declares to the President that his situation in life does not admit to indulge himself to accept such place or that he has attained Seventy years of age.

[Art:] 7th

No person shall excuse himself, from being Warden, nor shall it be allowed to any Member of the General Assembly, to decline acting in that Capacity if required Unless he shall declare and prove to the President his Impossibility or that he has attained Seventy Years of age, observing that it never shall be permitted in any manner whatsoever to elect a person Member of the General Assembly, previous he shall have been Selected Warden, Unless in the Event that it shall be found convenient to elect a General Attorney who always is immediately considered a Member of the General Assembly.

[Art:] *8th*

Those who have served their time as Warden shall not be elected again for two Years Unless in a case of Urgency, that the election cannot be compleated in any other manner.

[Art:] *8th*

Those who have served during one year shall not [nor] may be elected for two Years after, unless they consent in the same, in which regulation the Treasurer, who shall be elected by Lot is also Comprehended – and in case of Urgency that the Election of the Passover cannot be properly completed (in order not to come and to remount to the ancient Members who already have been Church Wardens of that Election) it is hereby established that in such event the abovementioned dispensation and suspension of two Years shall not take place and in like manner it will be allowed to a Church Warden or Treasurer to continue two Years in Service (if the Board agree with them) provided they are immediately elected without making any other Election before them.

Art: *9th*

All cases shall be decided, by the Mahamad, with 5 Votes & if these cannot be completed all the Members of the General Assembly, except those related with the seven Members composing the Mahamad shall be convoked, (when) to render the assembly Lawful, there ought to appear at least Seven Members of the General Assembly when the matter in question shall be decided with the Majority of two votes but if among the said Members of the General Assembly there cannot be found 7, who are not related as aforesaid the matter will be decided with such Members as can be found, but always with a Majority of two votes and those who shall refuse to attend shall incur the little Ban & besides pay a fine of P^s 4 unless they are prevented by some pressing motives.

Art: *9th*

Only the little Ban is abrogated in this article.

589

[Art:] 10th

The Mahamad shall have full authority and Superiority in the Government of the Congregation and its Dependencies and no person shall be allowed to contravene their Resolutions nor to sign any Instrument to contradict the same on pain of Excommunication.

Confiding that those intrusted with the reins of Government will dispose every thing with particular Zeal and consideration, without partiality and in the fear of God – and therefore each Member of the said Mahamad at their avenement [installation] shall take a proper Oath before the Books of Moses [open doors of the Holy Ark] and in the presence of the late Mahamad that they shall conduct themselves in their Office with rectitude and Justice and for the love of God without any partiality [or prejudice], which point, ought strictly to be observed.

[Art:] 10th

In force, except the Excommunication, which is abolished and instead thereof a fine of Ps 100, established, and besides the Mahamad authorized to cause the Transgressors to be corrected as disturbers of the public peace.

Art: 11th

In the Mahamad, Father and Son, Brother [with Brother],[39] Grand Father & Grand Son, Father[-in-law][39] and Son in law, Uncle and Nephew (and) [,] full cousins [, Brother-in-law with Brother-in-law nor relatives in these degrees][39] shall not [nor] may be elected together, nor shall they vote in any matter relating to each other.

Art: 11th

In force.

[Art:] 12th

The Mahamad shall assemble as usual or as many times as the President shall deem proper and send a message by the Samas or Sexton, when all matters will be decided with the majority as aforesaid.

[Art:] 12th

In force, observing that the majority of Votes expressed, in the Ordinances of 1756 ought to be understood for a majority of two votes.

---

[39] This, and matter hereinafter in brackets, omitted by Delvalle.

[Art:] 13th

If a Member wishes to give in his vote in a secret manner he shall be allowed to do the same.

[Art:] 14th

The Members of the Mahamad upon their entering in Office shall also have to Swear to Keep [inviolably] Secret all the Elections and other circumstances depending on the same, and also all such matters which shall be (discuted) [discussed] in the Assembly and which the President or any other of the Members shall require to be kept Secret.

[Art:] 15th

The Treasurer after his year is finished shall publicly give a proper and distinct account of the revenue and expenditure of the Sinagogue, in order that the whole Congregation may be informed of the state of its finances after which he shall have to deliver all the Properties and Documents which are under his care to the new Elected treasurer in the presence of the (two) late Church Wardens.

Art: 16th

The Church Wardens and Treasurer, shall by themselves and whenever they shall find proper may dispose of Ps 25 and the Mahamad may annually spend the whole Revenue of the Sinagogue, but in case of any deficiency they shall have to convoke a General assembly to resolve accordingly.

[Art:] 17th

The Mahamad has no authority to dispose of the Capital of the Sinagogue nor to

[Art:] 13th

In force.

[Art:] 14th

In force, except if any of the Members should be so (indiscrate) [indiscreet] as to communicate any of the Debates of the Assembly or any other circumstances, which demand to be Kept Secret they shall for the first time forfeit a fine of Ps 100 for the Poor and if repeated and it being fully proved then they shall be excluded from the Assembly & forfeit their rights as Members of the same.

[Art:] 15th

In force, adding that in case the Treasurer does not comply with his duty and does not appear in the Sinagogue, to read his account Current and to proclaim the new Election as usual (unless it is absolutely impossible to him) he shall be dismissed and be fined in the same fine as if he had refused to accept the Office.

Art: 16th

The Church Wardens and the Treasurer agreeing together shall by themselves and whenever they shall find proper may dispose of Ps 25 that is to say, in all cases when some honest or distressed person shall claim their assistance and the Mahamad shall likewise yearly may dispose of what they shall find regular and necessary, but in case of Extra Expences they shall have to convoke a General Assembly to resolve.

[Art:] 17th

In force, adding only that the Mahamad shall neither may dispose of any property give any money on Mortgage without the concurrency and approbation of the Members of the General Assembly legally assembled.

of the Sinagogue without the Sanction of the General Assembly.

[Art:] 18th

The Mahamad is authorized to prohibit all kind of Hazard Games, and to inflict the pain of the little Ban on the perpetrators who shall be considered as disturbers of the Public peace.

[Art:] 18th

In force, but instead of inflicting the little Ban, they shall fine in Ps 50 and bring the Perpetrators before the Judge of the Island (if the Mahamad finds it proper) in order to prevent inconveniencies.

[Art:] 19th

The Mahamad shall not [nor] may increase nor diminish the number of Church Wardens or make any alteration in these *Escamoth* or Ordinances. But in case they find it very necessary for the benefit and welfare of the Congregation they shall have to demand the approbation of the Directors of West India Company.

[Art:] 19th

The assembly together with the Elders shall [or] may increase or diminish the number of the Wardens, and also make any alteration in these ordinances, when it will be necessary, observing that when agreeing in the same, they shall have to make a Representation to the Government of this Island, to demand their approbation in order that the said Government if necessary may intercede in their behalf to obtain the Ratification and Sanction of the Sovereign.

SECOND SECTION
RESPECTING THE ELECTIONS

Art: 1st

The Mahamad shall on every Eve of Ros Ashaná (or Jewish Year's feast) elect two Bridegrooms for the Law, (that is to say) one to finish and the other to Commence the Books of Moses and grant them time till two days before *Kipur*, or the Grand day of Atonement to accept or to refuse the situation and if refusing, they shall have to pay Ps 100 to the Poor and others be elected in their (room) [place] who likewise refusing shall have to pay the same fine of Ps 100 to the Poor, when if there are no Zealous and meritorious persons who offer them-

Art: 1st

The Mahamad shall on the eve of Ros-Ashaná elect two Bridegrooms for the Law, that is to say, two persons, one to finish and the other to Commence the Books of Moses, who shall have time to accept or to refuse till two days previous Kipur, or the grand day of Atonement and if not accepting they shall have to pay a fine of Ps 150 and others be elected in their place who also refusing shall have to pay the same fine of Ps 150 and then if there are no Zealous & meritorious persons who offer themselves to act in that Capacity all the Members of the

selves for the said situation all the Members [of the General Assembly] shall be lotted out and those whose Names are drawn shall be obliged to accept, However not be allowed to offer more than Ps 50 to the Poor [& officiants] in both days of their function, whereof the Banquet shall be held in the Mahamad's Hall.

General Assembly shall lot for the same and those whose names are drawn shall be obliged to accept the situation recommending as well to the Latters as to the Bridegrooms of the 1st & 2nd Election to remember their duty towards the poor, – to wit – to offer in a generous manner according to their means, observing however that as well the Bridegrooms of the 1st, as of the 2nd Election shall have to Offer Ps 100 in both days of their function, for the Poor and those elected by Lot, shall have to offer Ps 50 to the Poor and it is further hereby established that the said Bridegrooms shall form the lists as well of those to whom they shall wish to give *Mitsva* (that is to say, to perform any of the Ceremonies with the books of Moses) as that of the persons whom they shall wish to call to assist at the reading of the said Books of Moses in due order, and agreeably to our Customs, in order that the Presiding Warden may guide himself accordingly.

Art: 2nd

The Mahamad together with the Wardens to Superintend the Instruction of the Holy law to the Children, shall annually elect four Wardens, for the said Superintendance to serve one Year – to wit – two at Pentecost and two on Saturday, before the Hester feast and if refusing they shall have to pay Ps 25 and others elected under the same penalty (if refusing) in which case one of the Members of the General Assembly, shall be Elected by Lot unless there would be some Zealous and meritorious persons offering to serve in that Capacity.

Art: 2nd

In force.

[Art:] 3rd

Every year on the eve of *Ros ashaná*, the Mahamad shall elect a person to super-

[Art:] 3rd

In force.

593

intend the Burials and matter respecting the Burying Ground with the Title of Warden of Hebrá and on Sabath Agadol (that is) the Saturday before the Passover the Election made of an Inspector of the Buildings (to wit) the Sinagogue and other Buildings appertaining to the Congregation shall be proclaimed who shall cause the necessary repairs to be made on the Sinagogue and its Houses, however he shall make no new Buildings without having obtained an Express order from the said Mahamad. The fine for refusing both situations is regulated on that of the Inspectors on the Instruction in Holy Law to the Children.

[Art:] 4th

All fines for the Poor shall immediately be paid after the ensuing Holy Days being over, previous to be admitted in the Sinagogue.

[Art:] 4th

The fines mentioned by this article as well as all others decreed by the Mahamad, shall be paid in one year without further delay and the acting Wardens shall be obliged on their responsibility to proceed in prosecuting by law those who shall not pay (except) in case of impossibility which regulation shall be put in force from the date hereof.

Art: 5th

The Members of the General Assembly who from the refusal of any other person shall have been elected by Lot to serve in any Capacity, shall be free from being lotted out again, till all the rest of the Members shall have served in the same manner.

Art: 5th

In force.

THIRD SECTION
RESPECTING THE CHANTERS, SEXTONS & SLAUGHTER[ER]S

Art: 1st

The Chanters shall be Elected by the General Assembly, though some or any of the Members may be related to the Person in nomination, which said Chanters

Art: 1st

In force.

shall be bound to follow in every respect the order given them by the Mahamad.

[Art:] 2nd

The Sexton shall be Elected by the Mahamad and shall distribute the monthly allowances to the poor and also the pious Gifts & promises from time to time sent to them and further to obey the orders of the said Mahamad.

[Art:] 2nd

In force.

[Art:] 3rd

No person shall presume to kill animals, except the Slaughters engaged and authorized by the Congregation.

[Art:] 3rd

No person shall presume to kill for the public in Town, but the Slaughters authorized by the Mahamad, allowing however those Slaughters who have Certificates to kill for their Families.

[Art:] 4th

In case the [Mahamad and] General Assembly would at any time find proper to erect a Butchery [or establish a meat market] they may do the same and make such regulations as they shall find proper.

[Art:] 4th

In force.

FOURTH SECTION
RESPECTING THE SINAGOGUE AND THE CEREMONIES WITH THE BOOKS OF MOSES

Art: 1st

The Mahamad shall have at their free disposal the places in the Sinagogue and no person shall be allowed to occupy an other's place, [on pain of forfeiting a fine of Ps 10 and in case anyone has no seat], he shall have to apply for one to the President.

Art: 1st

In force – However the Wardens shall not be obliged to vigilate respecting the prohibition mentioned in this article – but in case any complaints are made on the subject, and when they know that any individual occupies the place of any other person in the Sinagogue, they shall order them to retire to their own, on pain of Ps 10 and at all times they shall have to impede any persons from retiring from one place to another and also to sit in the department of the Inspectors on the Children (except those who have already their places established at the same) and those who by leave of the President occupy the same. It shall be allowed to every stranger to sit in the Sinagogue wherever he pleases except on the places of Distinction but after a week residence in this Island the President shall allot a proper place to the same, as Usual.

[Art:] 2nd

It shall not be allowed to (speak) [raise one's voice] nor to insult any person in the Sinagogue or within its Districts on pain of forfeiting Ps 25 [for the Poor] previous to be[ing] admitted again in the said Sinagogue – [and whoever raises his hand against his fellowman or threatens him with a club or offensive weapon, in the Sinagogue or within its District, shall incur the penalty of Excommunication and shall not be admitted in the Sinagogue without asking pardon, and paying a fine of Ps 50 for the Poor, & to obviate all nature of disorder, no one may enter the Sinagogue with a club, sword or dagger – excepting a cane when needed for one's support – on pain of paying Ps 5 for the Poor.]40

[Art:] 2nd

The penalty of Excommunication and that of being Banished from the Sinagogue are hereby entirely abolished, but the fines continued, which latters ought to be paid without delay (in one Year) whereof the responsibility shall remain on the Wardens.

Art: 3rd

The District of the Sinagogue, while prayers are read ought not only to be understood to be its yard and schools but also the street of the said Sinagogue from the Ramparts to the first Corner of the said Street. But after prayers time the Penalties mentioned by the above article are only to be understood for such Trespasses committed in the Yard of the Sinagogue and in the Schools & in order to prevent all sorts of disorders and ir-regularities it is hereby prohibited, that during prayers' time, no (person) [member] shall presume to form any

Art: 3rd

In force – adding the most serious ad-monition to maintain a proper decorum in this Holy House and not to assemble behind the Thebá (that is the Pulpit) at any time, which causes so much Scandal and those who shall (prevaricate) [persist] therein shall have to pay Ps 25 for the poor.

---

40 Delvalle's translation is inaccurate; this is ours.

(Circles) [Circuits] in the Yard of the Sinagogue nor at the Door. – Except on Saturdays and Holydays in the afternoon, while the Children are exercised in singing Psalms and also between Passover and Pentecost.

[Art:] 4th

No person shall be allowed to [rise] in the Sinagogue to approve or disapprove, nor to give any advice in a loud manner, against any order given by the Mahamad, unless it shall be a person sent by the said Mahamad to cause such orders to be observed but no others shall be allowed to do the same and in case any person will deem it necessary to represent any thing he shall address himself in a private manner to the Presiding Warden [or his substitute] to avoid disorders and irregularities.

[Art:] 4th

In force, and those who shall be sent by the Mahamad, shall have to behave with decency and good manners.

Art: 5th

No person shall be allowed to read the Morning, Midday or Evening prayers with Minjan (or Ten persons) in the Sinagogue but on the stipulated hours, unless having obtained permission from the Mahamad or its representatives present.

Art: 5th

In force.

[Art:] 6th

When the President is not in the Sinagogue the Second Warden shall have the Command, and in his absence the Treasurer, but he not being in the Sinagogue, the Rabino shall command, and after him [the Superintendent of the Instruction of] the Children and if all these are absent the Eldest Member of the General Assembly present, shall preside.

[Art:] 6th

In force.

[Art:] 7th

The distributions of the different Ceremonies to be performed, with the Books of Moses and those to call to assist at

[Art:] 7th

In force, advertising that the Bridegrooms & the fathers of new born Children shall be obliged previous to the Saturday of

the reading of the same shall be at the disposal of the Presiding Warden except on *Ros-ashana* and *Kipur* when the same shall be distributed by the Mahamad. Except on the day when it is usual to call the Rabino or some Bridegrooms or when a person having newly got a Child, are called to assist at the said Reading.

[Art:] 8th

All persons who are called to assist at the reading of the Books of Moses shall have to offer at least 3 stivers for the health of the President and the Congregation.

[Art:] 9th

[A member celebrating a particularly happy ceremony in the Synagogue may call to the Sepher not more than nine persons; Bridegrooms of the Law shall be permitted to call only two more in honor of the Law].[41]

[Art:] 10th

On Holydays and on such Saturdays when there are any Public Ceremonies of the Congregation, no person shall be allowed any private Ceremony nor (pretend) [presume] to partake [of] any of those with the Books of Moses – [not even if he is a bridegroom, the father of a newborn son or of a Bar Misva].[42]

[Art:] 11th

Those who find themselves in the Sinagogue and do not perform the Ceremonies of the Books of Moses, whereto they shall be called and also at the reading of the same shall immediately be ordered to withdraw from the Sinagogue and not be admitted again previous they shall

their Ceremony, to participate their Situation to the three persons in Regency and if failing in this Civility it shall be optional to the presiding Warden to exclude them from giving them any participation in the Ceremonies with the Books of Moses.

[Art:] 8th

In force.

[Art:] 9th

For the first only *nine* shall be called, but the Bridegrooms of the Law shall be allowed to call fifteen persons.

[Art:] 10th

In force.

[Art:] 11th

All those present in the Sinagogue who shall not perform the Ceremony whereof they are Chosen shall be fined in Ps 30, but those, who having been called to assist at the reading of the Books of Moses and do not immediately attend, shall be sent out from the Sinagogue for

---

[41] Our translation.
[42] Omitted by Delvalle.

[have] paid Ps 30 and take off the penalty of the little Ban.

the disrespect shown to the law and be condemned in the fine of Ps 100 besides the penitence which shall be inflicted by the Rabino, advertising that such Transgressor shall be obliged to make proper atonement and [be] absolved from such penalty as the case shall require, previous to be admitted in the Sinagogue.

FIFTH SECTION
RESPECTING THE JEHIDIM OR (INDIVIDUALS) [MEMBERS] AND THE COMMERCIAL TAX

Art: 1st

In case a (person) [member] for any private reason or for (debt) [indebtedness to the Poor Fund] does not attend (at) the Sinagogue (if he has not transgressed any of the precepts of the Holy Law to be punishable for the same) the Mahamad shall endeavour to bring him back to the Congregation with docility & friendly manners. [Failing in this, the Mahamad shall take appropriate steps only to enforce payment of the tax due and donations outstanding for that and past years.]43

Art: 1st

Annulled [for] being (inconsequent) [inconsistent].

[Art:] 2nd

Every Six months an account shall be delivered to every (individual) [member] of (their) [his] Tax and promises due to the poor, which ought finally to be paid before the Day of Atonement and those who shall not comply herewith shall be prohibited to enter in the Sinagogue Unless their situation is such to render it impossible for them to pay their said account.

[Art:] 2nd

The accounts of the Offers made for the Poor, as well as of the Taxes (if any should be established hereafter) shall be given to the (Individuals) [Members] every Six months, (who) [which] ought to be paid before the day of Atonement leaving to the Zeal of each Individual without establishing any fine to pay such a Sacred Debt, (that is to say after three years time) and if then not paid, they shall be prosecuted in law except if they declare themselves unable to pay, and it is particularly recommended to the residing Wardens to vigilate at their reospnsibility in case of decease of any

43 Our translation; Delvalle's incomplete.

599

individuals to deliver to their Estate an account of what they are indebted to the Sinagogue and to endeavour to collect the same and if refusing they shall have to enforce payment in a Judicial manner.

Art: 3rd

No Fraternity or Particular Society shall be allowed to issue any Proclamation in the Sinagogue without the [express] Consent of the Mahamad.

Art: 3rd

In force.

[Art:] 4th

The Offers and other contributions for the poor shall continue as usual at the limited times which also shall take place after the Sermons Preached on Holy days and on all ordinary and Extraordinary occasions and the $\frac{1}{4}$ pC^t Charged by the Merchants on goods on Commission shall be paid to the Treasurer.

[Art:] 4th

In force.

Art: 5th

[All Members and Congregants, residents or transients, must pay, under penalty of the small Ban, the $\frac{1}{4}$% Community Tax on all business done on Commission or otherwise, which tax shall have to be delivered personally to the Treasurer every year before he steps down from office, and anyone not paying shall be prosecuted by all means at law. It shall be the duty of the Treasurer, on the arrival of a stranger, to acquaint him with this Regulation so that he does not violate it because of ignorance.][44]

Art: 5th

In force, altering the little Ban and establishing that the Wardens shall after six months have to enforce payment of the said Tax and in case of any contumacy in not giving proper notice of the amount of the said Tax the Mahamad shall prosecute such persons by Law.

Art: 6th

It shall not be allowed to any individual of the Congregation to (argument) [argue] or dispute in matters of Religion with any of the Dominating Religion, nor to offend in any manner whatsoever those

Art: 6th

In force.

---

[44] Delvalle's translation is inaccurate; this is ours.

who profess the same; and those who shall contravene this order [and thus make us disliked] shall be considered as disturbers of the liberty we enjoy, for which reasons a strict observation of this article is seriously recommended.

[Art:] 7th

No person shall be allowed to solicit any thing from the Government of this Island in behalf of the Congregation at large, except the Mahamad and those ordered by them, on pain of incurring the penalty of Excommunication, [the observance of this being deemed most necessary for the preservation of our union.]45

[Art:] 7th

The Excommunication excluded and a fine of Ps 50 established, besides to be corrected for the first time by the Mahamad and for the Second time by the Judge of the Island, whom the Mahamad shall acquaint of the Event.

[Art:] 8th

No person shall presume to write [or have written for him] any Pasquil or (Manderous) [Slanderous] papers, signed or not against the Mahamad, (Doctors) [professors] of the Holy Law, or any other persons, without exception, and those who shall do the same shall be considered as Excommunicated persons and as Disturbers of the public peace, because they have committed a Crime against the Holy Law & against their fellow Creature[s] and shall besides be fined by the Mahamad as they shall find proper.

[Art:] 8th

In force altering the penalty of Excommunication and establishing that the (prevaricators) [offenders] shall be traduced before the Judge of this Island to be punished according to their Crime.

Art: 9th

[Any Jew arrested by order of the Judge of the Island for robbery, fraud or other premeditated crimes or acts creating discord, is warned to dispel the notion that the Community will come to his assistance, for by this Regulation it is established that neither time nor money from the Poor Chest will be expended to free him, and that the Mahamad, instead of aiding him, will assent to his punish-

Art: 9th

In force.

---

45 Omitted by Delvalle.

ment by the Court in accordance with the crime, to set an example for others so that this evil is removed from our midst.][46]

[Art:] 10th

[No person whatsoever shall presume to give Kedusim (i.e., to marry a girl) clandestinely without the consent and presence of her elders or, in their absence, of her nearest relatives. In violating this article, he and the witnesses to the ceremony shall incur the penalty of Excommunication and shall not be absolved therefrom before he gives the maiden a divorce if she wishes it, and they also pay a money fine for the Poor in accordance with the circumstances. Since the object of this Regulation is to prevent all manner of deception and seduction, it is hereby announced that all those presuming to marry a maiden shall have to comply with all the preliminary public ceremonies customary unless an extraordinary occurrence such as illness, etc,. makes it necessary to perform the marriage sooner, and even then with the greatest publicity possible.][47]

Art: 11th

The (Individuals) [Members] of our Congregation shall not [nor] may summon each other in law previous [to referring the matter to] the Mahamad, who shall endeavour to settle [it amicably], and not succeeding they will grant [the petitioner such] permission [and the one prosecuting without permission shall forfeit P[s] 4 to the Poor and have the summons nullified];[48] for which reason the Mahamad shall have to meet every fortnight on Thursday unless any Urgency may call them together more often.

[Art:] 10th

No person whatsoever shall presume to give Kedussim (that is to Marry a girl) in a Clandestine manner without the Consent of their Parents & those who shall contravene, this article together with the witnesses to such Marriage shall have to pay P[s] 25, for the poor and the Marriage immediately be annulled agreeably to our Rites, and in case of opposition the Mahamad shall proceed in Law against the same, following therein the orders of our Superiors,[49] whereby it is positively mentioned that those who wish to marry agreeably to our Law shall have to pass thro' all public and usual ceremonies.

Art: 11th

The (Individuals) [Members] of our Congregation shall not summon each other in Law, previous [to] having manifested this intention and communicated the case to the President (in order to reconcile the Parties) and (if) failing therein they shall have to pay P[s] 4 and annul the Citation sent without permission.

---

[46] Delvalle's translation is inaccurate; this is ours.
[47] Delvalle's translation is inaccurate; this is ours.
[48] Bracketed portions omitted by Delvalle.

Art: 12th

The (Individuals) [Members] of our Congregation shall not take any letters, addressed to another person, unless (he) [they] deliver(s) them immediately to their owners, without opening the same, & in case from any malice, they transgress this article, they shall incur in the pain of the Little Ban, besides a pecuniary fine of Ps 10 for the poor, to be paid previous to be absolved, of the said Ban.

Art: 12th

In force — establishing instead of the Little Ban, to acquaint the Judge of the Island with the event being a Civil matter, in order that the Transgressor may be Corrected.

[Art:] 13th

In case any (individual) [member] does not obey the orders of the Mahamad, and refuses either to come to the Sinagogue, or to pay the fines forfeited by them, every exertion shall be employed, to reduce such persons with docility, but if still refusing, the Excommunication shall be proclaimed, against his person, and if persevering, the [Ritual][49] Bath, Circumcision, [Burial][50] and other Ceremonies, of our Holy Law, shall be prohibited (them) [him].

[Art:] 13th

Every individual who from contumacy does not obey the orders of the Mahamad will be reduced with Soft and docile manners to his duty; however, if persevering in their Error they shall be traduced before the Judge of the Island to be brought to order and to cause our Rights to be maintained, and if not appearing when the Wardens or Mahamad shall have ordered them for the third time (Unless giving a proper excuse in good and decent terms), they shall be treated as disobedients, with the utmost rigor.

[Art:] 14th

In case the Mahamad finds it proper at any time, to tax the (Individuals) [Members], of our Congregation, they shall [or] may do it with the concurrence of the General Assembly.

[Art:] 14th

In force.

SIXTH SECTION
RESPECTING THE RABINO

Art: 1st

The Rabino shall be obliged to hold [to] his Contract, unless the Mahamad [&

Art: 1st

In force.

---

[49] See above, p. 233.
[50] Omitted by Delvalle.

councillors]51 find it proper [under the circumstances] to exonerate him.

[Art:] 2nd

[No Rabino may attend any of the Assemblies of our Consistory unless called in cases concerning our Religion, nor may he impose the Excommunication upon any person except in such cases that are indisputably notorious and cannot be put off, and then only with the special order of the Mahamad and Elders.]52

[Art:] 2nd

In force, except that no Excommunication whatever shall henceforth take place.

[Art:] 3rd

[No person shall be excommunicated or put under the small ban for any difference of a commercial nature or otherwise, except]53 in questions respecting our Religion or the Government of the Sinagogue.

[Art:] 3rd

It is hereby reiterated that no Excommunication in any case whatsoever shall take place, except where our Holy Law inflicts the same for which the person incurring the same shall be obliged to atone and to make such Penitence as the Rabino in Equity shall find proper.

Art: 4th

Respecting marriages, divorces and Hallissoth (that is a renouncing act to marry the wife of a deceased brother) and other rites & Ceremonies of the (Holy) Law [and ordinances of our sages],54 the decision of the Rabino shall be followed.

Art: 4th

In force.

[Art:] 5th

[Any Member wishing a ruling by the Beth Din shall ask permission of the Mahamad who, allowing the same, shall order the Rabino to convoke his Beth Din which shall be obliged to execute its decision.]55

[Art:] 5th

In force.

---

51 Omitted by Delvalle.
52 This translation is ours; Delvalle's is confusing.
53 Our translation; Delvalle's is inaccurate.
54 Omitted by Delvalle.
55 Our translation; Delvalle's confusing.

[Art:] 6th

[The Rabino cannot grant a divorce or Halisa, nor can he marry any person without the permission of the Mahamad.][56]

[Art:] 6th

In force.

[Art:] 7th

No (Individual) [Member] shall read [in the Sinagogue][57] any (private prayers) [litany, verse or chapter][57] said on the [nights of][57] Pentecost and on the (Seventh day of the Tabernacle feast) [Hosana Raba],[57] without having acquainted the Rabino of such Intention four days before the execution thereof, to avoid Confusion.

[Art:] 7th

In force.

[Art:] 8th

The certificates to kill [and examine][58] animals agreeable to our rites shall be given by the Rabino, and the Emoluments of the Contracts of Marriage will also come to him. The said Rabino shall be considered as Chief of all the Fraternities whereof none shall be established without the permission of the Mahamad.

[Art:] 8th

In force.

Art: 9th

No Judge whatsoever [– even if a member of the Mahamad –],[59] being [an interested][59] party, shall decide in his own case; another [shall] be appointed in his place.

Art: 9th

In force.

SEVENTH SECTION
RESPECTING THE ESCAMOTH OR ORDINANCES

Art: 1st

There shall be kept a particular book for the Escamot, which together with the others of the Congregation shall be intrusted to the Custody of the Wardens & Treasurer.

Art: 1st

In force.

---

[56] Our rewording of Delvalle's translation.
[57] Omitted by Delvalle.
[58] Omitted by Delvalle.
[59] Omitted by Delvalle.

[Art:] 2nd

All [decisions or] resolutions shall be signed immediately by the gentlemen present and though they may not concur in their votes, they shall be obliged to follow the majority.[60]

[Art:] 2nd

In force – But if the resolutions cannot immediately be extended they shall be compleated on the following day, and in the meanwhile the principal facts and particulars shall immediately be signed in a compendious manner.

[Art:] 3rd

That no alteration whatsoever shall be made in these Escamot without the Communication and approbation of the Mahamad and all the Members of the General Assembly, & no Conclusion shall be taken without a majority of two thirds of the Votes, and to render said assembly lawful, the number of the Members of the General Assembly ought always to be superior to that of the Mahamad.

[Art:] 3rd

In force.

[Art:] 4th

All the Escamot shall be read every year by the Treasurer at the first meeting of the Mahamad at the (avenement) [installation] of the newly elected Members for their instruction [and of those again serving];[61] they also shall be read twice a year by the Chanter, in order that every one may be acquainted with the same & know (how to proceed) [what and what not to do to avoid sinning through ignorance];[61] praying the Almighty God to illuminate us with wisdom and respect for the Conservation of the peace and tranquility in the fear of His Holy name.

[Art:] 4th

In force.

ALTERATIONS OF THE YEAR 1786[62]

Art: 1st

The Wardens, Treasurer and Bridegrooms of the Law of the 1st Election shall pay

Art: 1st

This article is annulled by the 5th Article of the 1st Section, of the above reforms,

---

[60] Rewording of Delvalle's translation.
[61] Omitted by Delvalle.
[62] Made during the pendency of the Andrade case, pp. 271-75 above.

P 100 to the poor if refusing, and those of the 2nd Election P 200.

and also by the 1st Article of the 2nd Section.

Art: 2nd

The Members who shall not appear, when a General Assembly is convoked, shall pay a fine of P 10 and in the Mahamad P 4.

Art: 2nd

In force – and the payment of the said fines shall be enforced, from the New year's feast to the Passover, and from the Passover's feast to New year again – advertising that such Members, shall not be exempted from being convoked in future and if not appearing, without producing a laudable excuse they shall pay the same fine of P 10 and P 4.

[Art:] 3rd

All the attendants of the Sinagogue and all persons in General shall positively have to obey the orders of the residing Wardens and in case of disobedience or if failing in their duty, the said Wardens may dismiss them.

[Art:] 3rd

In force.

[Art:] 4th

The whole Congregation shall bear due obedience to the Rabino and the residing Wardens as well in the Sinagogue as out of the same and if any Individual has to form any complaints (they) [he] shall have to address the same to the Wardens in a decent and respectable manner to be deliberated on in Justice & equity & in case any Individual behaves in an improper manner against the said Wardens, (they) [he] shall forfeit a fine of P 100 besides being corrected, by the Judge of the Island, whom the said Wardens shall have to acquaint with the event.

[Art:] 4th

In force – also including the Rabino and the Treasurer, and that out of the Sinagogue, the Individuals shall have to bear due obedience to every one in their respective Capacity.

CONCLUSION

1st

The Wardens, Mahamad, and General Assembly, shall be obliged to maintain these Escamot, in all their points and in an inviolable manner, for which reasons it is particularly recommended to the President immediately after the grand day of atonement to cause the new Elected Members to sign under the Escamot that they oblige themselves to maintain the same and to cause them to be maintained as well as those of 1756, 1786 or any other, which may hereafter be enacted and also such resolutions as explained in the following article.

2nd

All resolutions and Proclamation[s], to be issued hereafter by the Mahamad and the General Assembly shall have the same force as if they were inserted by these presents and which shall only (may) be altered by a majority of one third of the Members of a General Assembly Legally assembled.

DOMESTICAL REGULATIONS TO BE OBSERVED IN THE ASSEMBLIES OF THE MAHAMAD AND AT THE GENERAL MEETING

Art: 1st

The Church Wardens shall all be dressed in black as well in the Sinagogue as in the Assemblies and further in all occasions where [they] shall have to appear in their Capacity.

Art: 2nd

Mahamad or Board of Justice means the assembly of Seven, mentioned in the 2nd article of the 1st section of the Reforms. There all the Elections shall be made, without it being allowed to the Members of the General Assembly to interfere with their resolutions & they also are constituted competent Judges to decide in all cases pending among the Congregation and to issue sentences.

[Art:] 3rd

General assembly is the concurrence of all the Members, there all matters respecting the Political Government of the Sinagogue are (discuted) [discussed] and also its finances in which assembly, father & son and other[s] related together shall [or] may assemble.

[Art:] 4th

The Treasurer is also in future, included when by any Resolutions, papers or documents the words Church Wardens are made use of, without any distinction, therefore on all points & particulars where we say Church Wardens the meaning is the three persons in regency.

[Art:] 5th

The Members of the Mahamad shall all be dressed in black when meeting, and those of the General Assembly shall also be dressed in a decent manner.

[Art:] 6th

The President shall sit at the Head of the Table, the Vice [President] at his right, and the Treasurer in middle of them — and the other Members, according to their age.

[Art:] 7th

It shall not be allowed to any Member to give his opinion before his turn, unless asking permission to the President.

[Art:] 8th

When a Member exposes his opinion, every attention shall be paid and he who shall interrupt him, shall for the 1st & 2nd time be admonished by the President and for the 3rd time, he shall have to withdraw.

Art: 9th

When the President calls for attention he shall be obeyed and he who does not perform the same, shall twice be admonished and for the 3rd time have to withdraw.

[Art:] 10th

No Member shall be allowed to quit the assembly, unless in case of Urgency when he shall have to expose the same to the President and by his leave he shall [or] may retire and those who shall act to the Contrary shall pay a fine of P 20 to the Poor.

[Art:] 11th

The above articles shall be posted up, in the Mahamad's Hall in order that every one may guide and regulate (themselves) [himself] accordingly.

(Signed) Mordy Hm Senior, President	Abm de Jb Iessurun
Moise Cardoze	Dd Cohen Henriquez Jr
Abraham de Mordy Senior	Manl Alvs Correa (Treasurer)
Ishac de Abm de Marchena	Rephael Penso
M[oses]: Cohen Henriquez	Dl de Dd Gomes Casseres
Ieosuah de Ib Naar	Benjn Iessurun
Ieosuah Rl Henriquez	Abm Haim Fidanque
Dd Hm Dovale	Dd de Ishac Henriquez
Dd Cohen Henriquez	Aron Pinedo
Ephraim Curiel	Abm Pinedo
Gabl de Dd dC Gomes	Samuel dCasseres
Rl Pinedo	Abraham Salom Delvalle

The above agrees with the Original lodged in our Archive.

Quod Attestor

(Signed)   Mordy Hm Senior

President

Translated by me
(Signed)   Delvalle Governmt Interpreter and Translator
Approved the 10th of January 1810   No 7.

(Signed)   Wm Prince

Secretary & Court Clerk

A true copy.
    Wm Prince

C. SUPPLEMENTARY HASCAMOTH OF 1756 AND 1768

Translated from the original Portuguese by the co-authoress

AMONG THE RECORDS of Congregation Mikvé Israel in Curaçao are three Regulations written in very poor Portuguese. One is of Tishri, 5517 (1756); the others are of the year 1768. The first was directed against members refusing to perform the honorary functions (Misvot) assigned in the Synagogue. The second, promulgated to protect maidens from abuse on the part of young men promising marriage, punished the girl's family more severely than the youth's (above, pages 269-70). The third fined the councillors and Elders of the Nation who did not attend meetings and members who declined the office of Parnas. It was effected during the conflict over the proposed introduction of the Finta or communal tax (above, pages 255-56). The translations of these Regulations follow.

1.

The gentlemen of the Mahamad and their councillors, having noticed and experienced the great impudence, insolence and dissoluteness with which many individuals [not only] refuse the Misvot assigned to them [by] sending others to perform them, but also voice their disapproval of the Misvot assigned to others, and by such behavior openly profane God's name, disturb their fellowmen and demonstrate their meager respect for this Holy House,

Said gentlemen [of the Mahamad, etc.], seeking to prevent and check such unspeakable insolence, called together the worthy Elders of the Nation in whose company they unanimously resolved, without any opposing vote, that henceforth anyone assigned a Misva while attending the Synagogue and not carrying it out, shall in addition to incurring the penalty of the small ban and [fine of] thirty pezos directed by the Regulation, be unable to give the Misva to another.[63] He must apply to the Parnas President with a legitimate, valid reason for his indisposition whereupon the said President shall order it performed by whomever he considers worthy. But if the excuse proves fancied and untrue, he then incurs the same penalty of the small ban. Also, whoever has the duty of substituting for an absentee assigned a Misva is admonished that he must select one of the Misvot if there are many, for he has no authority to bestow the remaining Misvot upon whomever he chooses, but must notify the President who shall have them executed by whomever he deems worthy.

[63] See above, pp. 547, 559-60. 570, 575.

By virtue of the authority our Regulation [i.e., concerning the Mahamad, etc.] vests in the Mahamad, the councillors and Elders to alter any Regulation if they so find it desirable, they resolved to give notice with respect to Article 7 of the Ordinances relating to the Misvot of Bahale Berit, Bridegrooms and those carrying out other religious functions, that any member who has given the Mahamad in general or anyone of them in particular cause to deny him a Misva, shall not be granted the said Misvot although he is entitled to one of them [i.e., as Bridegroom or as father of a son to be circumcised], unless he gives full satisfaction to the presiding Mahamad as well as the Mahamad he had given cause [to suspend this privilege].

Out of their devotion and reverence for God, all members are expected not to give cause for creating a disturbance or tumult. May God bless everyone of this H. C. with Peace and Union, Amen.

Done and Published in the H. C. of Mikve Israel, the 19th of Tisry, Yr. 5517 [1756].

Signed: Ishac de Marchena
Treasurer

2.

As honor and chastity of the daughters of Israel is one of the virtues so highly esteemed in our Holy Law and regarded as the true essence of their beauty the gentlemen of the Mahamad, their councillors and the Elders of the Nation, together with the eminent Haham, having remarked the wanton dissipation and unspeakable excesses between the young men and maidens of our Nation, their unbridled levity and frivolity which, because of their close association with each other, very often results in the girls yielding their honor on the young man's promise of marriage, and without [thought of] preserving the glory of their forebears they degrade it by their ugly, filthy, ignominious deeds and trample upon and disgrace their family honor; without caring about the betrayal of a negative precept of having carnal intercourse prohibited and forbidden by our Holy Law to a *Nidah* (menstruating woman) in which they become accomplices to a crime, the penalty for which is divine extirpation, all the while not foreseeing possible death for the young man after the commission of that vile deed, and perdition and dishonor for her;

The said gentlemen of the Mahamad, their councillors and Elders of the Nation, in the company of the eminent Haham,* unanimously and in general agreement resolved to take measures toward checking this indecency and preventing immodesty and levity among the daughters of Israel. Henceforth, (anyone) [those] committing such a base act shall not, without any exception, be protected by the gentlemen of the Mahamad or councillors and Elders of the Nation or by the eminent Haham, who, on the contrary, will abandon them and leave them for what they are, and when they, without... come to marry each

* Da Fonseca.

other, or if they are obliged to marry, neither the Haham nor the Hazanim [nor] the gentlemen of the Mahamad will sign their marriage contract, but shall have it executed by someone of their [i.e., Mahamad's] choice, nor will they (the transgressors) be assigned any Misva or honor customarily bestowed upon and performed by bridegrooms in this Holy House.

Should this happen to the daughter of one receiving a salary, stipend or monthly allowance from this Holy Congregation, except where it is patently clear that she was forced, God forbid, the father(s) of such [a] girl(s) shall be dismissed from service and [cut off] from any stipend or assistance they [he] had been enjoying from this Holy House.[64]

This notice shall serve as a warning to all fathers, brothers, custodians or guardians over these boys and girls, diligently to watch over their sons and daughters in order to avoid with vigor (?) all cause for scandal, ignominy and immorality in Israel.

Done and Published in the H. C. Mikve Israel, the 20th of Elul, Yr. 5528 [1768].

Signed: Jeosuah D Crasto
Treasurer

3.

N.B. *The twelve opening lines obliterated by water*

...and penalty of the small ban, [upon] whoever does not attend a meeting of the Mahamad when called, unless he is related [to one of the councillors or parnassim]. Since no mention is made of general meetings and [meetings] of the Elders [i.e., Article 5 of the Regulations of 1756, while fining a parnas for refusing to accept or complete his term of office, is silent about fining a councillor for not attending a meeting], we resolved that, besides having said article remain in full force and effect, it shall also provide that councillors to the general meetings and meetings of Elders [of the Nation] who have been notified and do not attend shall be fined 6 P[ez]os for the Sedaca unless [there is proof] of absolute [indisposition] (words erased), and on not paying the ...[fine] shall have it charged against their respective accounts at once...

If someone is elected for an office which he agrees to accept and does not call within a certain period [of days] to take office, he shall be obliged to pay the fine specified in the Regulations and another shall be elected at once in his place, under the same obligation. This [,however,] shall not apply to elections made by lot or to... [those for] Parnas of T[almud]. T[orah]. on the second ballot, or to a person elected Parnas on the refusal of another, which... (three lines obliterated by water).

Signed: Jeosuah de Crasto
Treasurer

[64] See above, pp. 269-70.

D. EXTRACTS FROM THE REGULATIONS ADOPTED
BETWEEN 1825 AND 1963

REGULATIONS OF 1825

The conflict over Hazzan Piza (Chap. XV) led to the enactment of new regulations at the end of 1825. These are the most important provisions:

Art. 22.   All members of the community 25 years of age and over, excepting religious employees and officiants, were eligible for the office of parnas.

Art. 29h.   Government proclamations and announcements by the parnassim and/or Great Council of the Synagogue had to be written in Dutch and placed on the synagogue wall with a translation in a language better understood by the members.

Art. 124.   The minutes of the Great Council of the Synagogue and of the Mahamad or parnassim had to be written in Dutch.
(N.B.   But they were also written in Portuguese!)

Art. 29m.   In his sermons the rabbi was not to speak against the government nor against the administration of the community by the parnassim nor against the members for their conduct whether in religious or civil matters.

Art. 32g.   The treasurer was to take care of distributing flour for *matza* for Passover to the ecclesiastical employees and the poor of the community, and "Harosset" for all members.

Art. 49a.   The two parnassim and treasurer, i.e., the Mahamad, were to be chosen by the Great Council of the Synagogue, defined in art. 47 as being the incumbent Mahamad and the Elders, i.e., all past parnassim.

Art. 56.   The rabbi had to know Hebrew, Dutch and Portuguese.

Art. 70.   All moneys, securities and certificates of indebtedness of the community were to be kept in the Consistorial Chamber in an iron chest provided with three different locks and three keys, one for each parnas and one for the treasurer. All three officers had to be present when it was opened.[65]

REGULATIONS OF 1833

These were called *Reglement voor de Nederlandsche Portugeesche Israelitische Hoffd Sijnagoge te Curaçao* (Curaçao: A. L. S. Muller & J. F. Neuman Wz., 1833, 39 pp.). They are the oldest *printed* Community Regulations extant.

Art. 15, p. 4.   The Parnas-elect refusing to serve shall be excused on paying 400 florins.

---

[65] RA, Koloniën na 1813, 3766, no. 205.

Art. 29c, p. 7. The Parnassim have the task of seeing that the religious services, ceremonies and usages are observed and carried out in the synagogue.

Art. 29r, p. 9. The Parnassim shall take care that the Rabbi or Assessors do not perform a marriage or divorce before obtaining their (the Parnassim's) consent and before the civil marriage or divorce has taken place.

Art. 47, p. 16. The Great Synagogue Council shall consist of (a) the Corresponding Member to the High Commission, (b) the Parnassim, Treasurer and two Assessors in office, and (c) the Elders, namely, those who formerly served as Parnas or Treasurer as well as those who were elected Parnas or Treasurer but were excused from serving on the payment of the ransom.

Art. 58, pp. 19-20. The Chief Rabbi or Rabbi shall be appointed by the Great Synagogue Council and seventeen Notables of the Community named by the Governor of the Island for the purpose. Such appointment shall not be legally binding until approved by His Majesty [the King of Holland].

Art. 59g, p. 20. The Rabbi shall take care that no other Rite or Liturgy is introduced.

Art. 60, p. 21. The Chief Rabbi or Rabbi, as an officiant of the Community, shall be entirely under the orders of the Parnassim. He shall always follow their orders so long as they are in keeping with religious principles.

Art. 87d, p. 27. Those receiving assistance from the Community Chest shall see to it that their children attend the Community schools on pain of losing such aid.

Art. 124, p. 34. Within the Community no Rite or Liturgy other than that of the Netherlands Portuguese Synagogue [of Amsterdam] shall be allowed.

Directly after these regulations is a reproduction of the agreement entered into by the Portuguese Jewish and German (Ashkenazic) Communities [of Amsterdam] during the French occupation in Napoleon's day, and approved by the Government. Just five of its seven articles are cited below.

1. No Jew belonging to one of these communities may be accepted by the other, excepting women in the event of marriage.
2. Where only one community exists all Jews are considered on an equal footing. A Jew returning to a city having different communities shall belong to his former community.
3. A woman married to a member of another community, as well as the children of such a marriage, shall belong to the husband's community.
4. The widow and her children shall remain members of the deceased husband and father's community. A widow who remarries shall have the privilege of belonging to the community of her choice if her husband died childless.
5. The children of the first marriage shall remain members of the community to which they belonged.

The Regulations of 1833 refer to this agreement at art. 115, pp. 32-33. The object ostensibly was to put Ashkenazic sojourners on an equal basis with the other members and to permit their return to their original community if they went back to Holland. This agreement was executed in Amsterdam on January 15, 1810, and signed by [Dr.] Im[anuel]. Capadose, Jacob de Isaac Teixeira de Mattos and Isaac Teixeira Jr. for the Portuguese Jewish Community, and by H[erz]. H. de Lemon, Benjamin Leemans and J[onas]. D[aniel]. Meyer for the Ashkenazic Community.

REGULATIONS OF 1849

These regulations, preserved in the archives of the High Commission, show that

1. The parnassim were still elected by the Great Council of the Synagogue and not by the members;
2. The rabbi had to be named by the High Commission and approved by the king.

REGULATIONS OF 1860

No record could be found of these regulations. Haham Chumaceiro, then visiting Holland, defended them against certain objections raised by some members on the High Commission.[66]

REGULATIONS OF 1875

After the schism of 1864, new regulations were drawn up by the attorney Abraham M. Chumaceiro[67] and printed in Curaçao in 1875. Amended in 1886 and printed in Curaçao in 1896, they remained in force until 1964.

The Reform Community Emanu-El drew up its bylaws in 1865. These were modified and printed in 1880, further amended in 1883, and again modified and printed in 1897.

CONCERNING THE INSISTENCE IN THE HASCAMOTH AND RESOLUTIONS ON MAINTAINING THE CUSTOMS AND RITE OF THE SYNAGOGUE

The Hascamoth and resolutions show how strongly the Jews of Curaçao insisted, generation after generation, on preserving the customs and synagogue rite, which was Sephardic.

In 1752 the cantors were forbidden to change words or make innovations in the prayers. They were obliged to follow the "old style."[68] The conflict over Hazzan Piza (Chap. XV) was partly due to trivial changes that he had introduced.

---

[66] See above, p. 358.
[67] According to a letter from his son, Isaac Haim M. Chumaceiro, to the author.
[68] MS, 8 Sivan, 5512. See above, p. 183, regarding the movements of the *lulab*.

According to Sephardic usage, an unmarried cantor could not officiate during the ten days of awe (Rosh Hashanah through Yom Kippur). In Curaçao they went so far as to forbid a bachelor to raise the Torah or to carry it during the Simḥath Torah procession.[69]

Art. 5 of the Royal Edict of April 2, 1825, made it mandatory for synagogues in the Netherlands West Indies to draw up their bylaws "in the spirit of the bylaws in use in the Mother Country," that is, the Portuguese Jewish Community of Amsterdam.

Art. 29c of the Regulations of 1825 charged the parnassim with the "responsibility of seeing that all the religious ceremonies, uses and customs were observed and carried out."

Art. 112 of the same Regulations obliged the parnassim to have all the religious ceremonies, uses and customs in burials executed according to ritual procedure.

As observed above, art. 124 of the Regulations of 1833 did not allow the existence in the community of any Rite or Liturgy other than that of the Netherlands Portuguese Synagogue. The original text reads as follows: "Binnen de gemeente zal geen ander Ritus of Liturgie toegelaten worden dan die der Nederlandsche Portugeesche Israelieten."

The government cooperated fully with the parnassim in upholding the traditions of the synagogue. By its Ministerial Decree of August 12, 1845, no innovations could be made in the synagogue services.[70]

Art. 138 of the Regulations of 1849 specified that "the language of the prayers shall be in Hebrew only. No prayer book other than that recognized by the Portuguese Jewish Community of Amsterdam shall be used."

REGULATIONS OF 1875

Art. 7.　"Membership is forfeited on the adoption of another religious creed or rite different from that of the Community."

Art. 83.　"Nothing conflicting with the principles of Jewish doctrine shall be taught in the religious schools."

Art. 85.　"No marriage shall be recognized religiously until it has been blessed according to religious prescriptions. By nuptial blessing is meant the consecration of a marriage according to Jewish prescriptions and in accordance with synagogue rite..." which is the Sephardic rite.

Art. 91.　"No reform whatsoever can be made of the established uses and customs of the community relating to the synagogal and religious ceremonies until the consent of the Council of Elders and the approval of the Chief Rabbi or Minister have been obtained. In the absence of a religious authority in the community, the Synagogue Council shall submit the [proposed] reforms to the Council of Elders for them to decide whether or not it is desirable to introduce them to the community and [also] to name three

---

[69] See above, pp. 552, 559, 563, 564.
[70] MIA, Minutas de Parnassim, Dec. 28, 1847.

orthodox rabbis of Holland or elsewhere to determine whether or not they (these reforms) are in conflict with religious laws."

These four articles were kept intact in the Regulations of 1886. They were still in vigor in 1963 when the two communities — Mikvé Israel and Temple Emanu-El — merged, became affiliated with the Jewish Reconstructionist Foundation and the World Union for Progressive Judaism, and thus abandoned their ancestral Sephardic rite.[71]

[71] See above, Chapter XXV.

PLANTATIONS, GARDENS AND "CUNUCUS"

THE AGRICULTURAL ACTIVITY of the Jews has been touched upon during the course of this work.[1] As agriculture played an essential role in the history of the community and of the island, a list of the Jewish plantations, gardens and "cunucus" (a patch of ground normally used for growing corn) is given below. The aim is not to furnish *the* list from generation to generation, but to demonstrate that since 1660, and possibly earlier, the Jews owned plantations and that 80% of the Curaçao plantations and 20% of the gardens at one time or another were in the possession of Jewish owners. The plantations that belonged to Protestant and Catholic clergymen are also included.

PLANTATIONS HELD BY THE JEWS FOR A HUNDRED YEARS OR MORE

Some plantations remained in Jewish hands for over a century — one for as long as 140 years. Notably among them were the Bloempot, Brakkeput, Girouette, Groot St. Michiel, Klein Piscadera, De Hoop (alias Judio), Mahaai, Poos Kabaai, Princenhoff, Rafael, St. Jago, Suikertuintje, Van Engelen, Wacauw. Several were owned by Jews for a hundred years with slight interruptions: Bloemhoff, Bottelier, Klein St. Michiel, Piscadera, Rooi Catochi, Zuurzak, and others.

Some families — the Alvares Correas, Da Costa Gomezes, Henriquezes, Maduros, Pinedos, among others — kept their plantations for three or four consecutive generations. It is not surprising that various parts of the island, now residential areas, are still known by the names of their old Jewish owners, e.g., Boca Juliao, Bonam, Daniel, Habaai (alteration of the name Gabay), Lena Belmonte, Maduro, Marchena, Moron, Parera, Penso's Park, Sasso, and so on.

NAMES OF THE JEWISH PLANTATIONS

As a rule the Protestant planters, and later the Jews, retained the names given by the first inhabitants, the Indians, before the Dutch occupation in 1634. Hence only a relatively few plantations and gardens — about twenty-three — bear saints' names. New owners who tried changing the old names found that these did not always "stick." The Jews did not name their plantations for relatives, biblical heroes or cities or with Hebrew expressions as in the case of their sailing

---

[1] See pp. 62-67.

vessels (appendix 3). Of course there were some rare exceptions in the 18th century. Jacob de Leon called his plantation *Beraha ve Salom* (Blessing and Peace). One Levy Maduro named his farm *Nayoth Barama* — an attempt to associate a relative Samuel with the city of the prophets led by the Prophet Samuel. Eliau Pereira likened himself to the Prophet Elias at Mt. Carmel and called his plantation *Berg Carmel*. One Isaac Calvo Andrade styled his plantation *Berg Sinai* (Mt. Sinai). The garden *Bethlehem*, for many years held by the Henriquez Juliao family, had been so named by its former Protestant owners. The plantation *Mikvé Israel* or *Esperanza de Israel* was known by its shortened form *De Hoop*, later as *Esperanza* and still later as *Judio*.

In the late 18th and early 19th centuries some Jews gave their plantations English names. For example, De Sola changed the *Welgelegen* (or *Habaai*) to *Pleasant Valley*; the Cohen Henriquez family changed its *Van Engelen* to *Mt. Vernon*. Neither name took root among the population. Although the Jews spoke Portuguese and later Spanish, there were relatively few plantations with Iberian names.

AREA

The Jewish-owned plantations varied between 4,000 hectares, more or less (e.g., Moses Penso's *Fuik* and *Santa Barbara* plantations held in 1751), and 35 hectares (e.g., the Pinedo family's *Koningsplein*). The gardens or *cunucus* ranged from 1.5 hectares to several tens of hectares.

FACTORS DETERMINING A PLANTATION'S VALUE

The value of a plantation depended on a number of factors: the area and fertility of the land, the existence of water wells and salt licks, the number of fruit trees, the presence of limekilns and fishing boats, and the condition of the planter's dwelling and of the slave quarters. Naturally the number of slaves, the livestock, fodder, etc., also entered into the picture. Ever since 1714 the Company collected a 2% transfer tax on the land[2] without its slaves, livestock and other chattels, and from 1765 1%, as did the Curaçao Government later on. In order to avoid disputes between the planters and the employees of the Fiscal (public prosecutor), the Company issued a proclamation in 1765 fixing the value of a plantation's inventory as follows: slaves, 150 pesos each; mules, 50; cows and horses, 20; calves, 10; donkeys, 6; sheep, 3; goats, 2; turkeys, 1; chickens, 1/2 peso; ducks, 6 reales; a bushel of lime, 2 pesos; a bushel of corn, 1 peso (OAC 194, no. 19).

This study gives us, as far as possible, the value of the plantations as found in different records. In the 18th century this varied between 1,000 and 67,500

[2] The transfer tax was 500 pesos on properties worth between 21,000 and 30,000 pesos; and 1,000 pesos on those 30,000 pesos and above (OAC 194, no. 19). In 18th century Curaçao there was no real estate or plantation (less its inventory) assessed at more than 28,000 pesos.

pesos.[3] The average plantation was worth 4,000 pesos and had three male slaves to one female slave. (Female slaves were usually sold in the city for domestic use.) Among the Jews, Moses Penso had the record number of 403 slaves on his plantations in 1754.

SALE OF PLANTATIONS

The Jews were compelled to sell their plantations more often than the Protestant and Catholic planters. The merchant-planter who needed ready cash to pay debts, or to replace his ships that had been sunk by pirates or the enemy, would dispose of his plantations as a last resort. A prolonged drought often spelled hopeless insolvency for a planter. Sometimes plantations were bought at auction solely for speculative purposes. Dominie Bosch, a plantation owner in 1827, wrote that several wealthy Jews had ruined themselves in that manner. This speculation virus also attacked a number of Gentiles who either lost vast sums in such ventures (*Piscadera*, 1874; *Parera*, 1874-75) or realized substantial gains (*Koningsplein*, 1782; *Welgelegen*, M.D., 1799-1802; *Santa Barbara*, 1875). As a result of these manipulations, a plantation would change hands as often as twice a year and, on one occasion, thrice in one day (*Blij en Heim*, 1779 — all three purchasers Gentiles). With the emancipation of the slaves in 1863, the plantations were gradually left untilled and used as country estates.

INCONSISTENCIES IN THE RECORDS

To prepare the list of Jewish-owned plantations it was necessary, as always, to pore over various records and even the old Mikvé Israel archives. These records include: (1) the mortgage registers, since almost every purchase carried a mortgage; (2) government reports of cash receipts, including transfer taxes on property, periodically submitted by the governor to the Company since 1714; (3) notarial documents and court records dealing with disputes between neighboring planters or lawsuits between creditors and debtors, including planters.

The year is given as it appears in the records and does not necessarily indicate the year of acquisition. Often a Jewish planter who had held a plantation for many years would take out a second mortgage or increase the first mortgage on his property. Although the transfer tax records state the year of sale, they do not always specify the date of purchase. Jewish and gentile planters of the 17th century often annexed, by purchase, various Company lands to their holdings. The archives have preserved the names of those purchasers for the years 1682, 1683 and 1709, and it is quite possible that they had acquired their farms many years earlier.

Until 1820 the notary invariably included in the sales contract or deed the names of neighboring planters. Unwittingly he brought to light, for us, various

---

[3] Plantation values from 1694 to 1827 are given in pesos; after January, 1827, in florins at the rate of 1.33⅓ florins to the peso, unless otherwise specified.

plantation owners heretofore not encountered. The year tagged to these "discovered" plantations is the year appearing in such a document and not necessarily the year of its acquisition which may have been much, much earlier. As the notary made use of earlier bills of sale to prepare the new papers, he would record the same neighbors although they had long since died and their plantations had already been sold or passed on to their heirs.

The documents often contradict themselves. The notary would sometimes have the deed to the plantation in one name and the inventory of the same property in another's. To illustrate, in 1886 when Isaac Pinedo Jr. sold his *Koningsplein* plantation, the records cited P. H. Maal just as often as H. Pietersz as the buyer. All efforts have been made to reach what in our opinion are the most exact facts.

As for area, two registers were consulted and not always did they coincide with each other.

PLANTATIONS AND GARDENS IN 1817

Shortly after the Dutch repossessed Curaçao in 1816, Governor Kikkert partitioned the island into three divisions: Eastern, Western and Central, and these in turn into districts. He then sent the Colonial Minister a list of all the plantations and gardens on the island (RA, Ministerie van Koloniën, no. 3741, 1st half 1817). Some still belong to Jews.

Since there are many plantations having the same name, since many are known under two or three names, and since the records do not always list the variations at one time, it follows that from time to time a plantation is listed without its second or third name and owner although it may be identical with the plantation and owner figuring under another name. Because of the repeated inconsistencies in the records, it was difficult for me to establish a definitive spelling of the plantations.

This is the key to the abbreviations and symbols employed in the following list of plantations and gardens compiled from various records:

a.	=	also known as	Kl.	=	Klein
b	=	before the year of	MD	=	Middle Division
BENQ	=	Beneden Quartier	OD	=	Eastern Division
BOA	=	Boven Altena	ps	=	pesos
BOQ	=	Boven Quartier	RQ	=	Ruiters Quartier
bt	=	bought	sl.	=	slaves
d.	=	daughter of	w.	=	wife of
fls.	=	florins	WD	=	Western Division
form.	=	formerly	wi	=	without inventory
h	=	hectares	wid.	=	widow or widower of
JQ	=	Joden Quartier	†	=	Gentile

Plantation or Garden	Year of ownership	Owner	Value	Slaves	Remarks
A					
ALIDA					
ALTENA, see also Family Graves	1802	Abraham Samuel L. Maduro	1,800		14 h
	1841	Jeosuah Naar			Sold to †M. Lingstuijl in 1802 (OAC 1104, no. 134)
ARARAT, a. Rosendaal; see also Family Graves	1825-27	M. H. A. Correa			CGAR VI, Feb. 26, 1841
"	1827	A. J. Jesurun			CGAR II, Feb. 25, 1825
"	1828	Abraham Is. Henriquez		20	
"	1847	Dr. Salomon Jos. de Jongh	650		CGAR IX, Feb. 12, 1847
ASENCION	1757	Dominie Wigboldus Rasvelt and †Wid. Wm. van Uytrecht		110	(OAC 873, no. 19); see San Pedro and Welgelegen; 490 h
ASENCION, a. St. Patrick					390 h
ASIENTO, see Family Graves					
B					
BACKER, BOA, a. Onverwagt	1718	Abraham Henriquez Moron	660wi		
"	1733-38	Aron & Joseph da C. Gomez	1,000	5	OAC 801, Aug. 20, 1733
"	1750-56	Benjamin Vaz Faro	3,250		OAC 833, Aug. 27, 1756
BAJADA VAN DANIEL	1825	Moizes Pinedo Jr.	19,500		63 h
BARBER, a. Cabrietenberg, WD	1832-38	De Marchena Family			283 h
BARON, see Family Graves					
BARTHOOLSCHE KUST, BENQ	1792	Gabriel Pinedo			See Wacauw.
	1802	Aron Gabriel Pinedo			"
					"

Name	Years	Owner		No.	Notes
BELLEVUE TUIN, see Charo					
BERAHA VESALOM,[4] JQ	1694?-1760	De Leon and G. Casseres		25*	*In 1760 (OAC 880, March 25, 1761)
BERG CARMEL, see Parera					
BERG SINAI, BOQ	1798	Isaac Calvo Andrade	450		OAC 1100, no. 95
"	1798-1806	Ester Alva Rodriguez Nunes	350		
BERG VAN SUZANNA (lot)	1754-68	Widow of Jeosuah Rephael Henriquez			See Groot St. Michiel.
"	1768	Mordechay Jeosuah Henriquez			
BETHLEHEM (garden)	1826-45	Abraham Henriquez Juliao		37ᵃ	ᵃ With those of Zegening in 1838 (CEOE 172)
BEURS, see Family Graves					
BEVER, a. Bona Vista; see also Family Graves	1890	Mordechay Fidanque Curiel			
"	1920 (?)	Benjamin L. Maduro			1.5 h
BIJGELEGEN, see also Welgelegen	1856	Benjamin A. Correa			
BLAUW, see also Oud St. Michiel	1768	Mordechay Jacob Henriquez			See Klein Blauw.
"	1777	David Jacob Henriquez			See Blijrust.
"	1795	Moses Frois			
"	1842	Eliau Penso		29ᵇ	ᵇ With those of St. Elizabeth (CEOE 172)
BLIJ EN HEIJM (Bleinheim), JQ; see also Nooit Gedagt, Family Graves	1763-66	Mordechay Jb. Henriquez	5,250	3	OAC 890, nos. 203, 219
"	1766-67	Jacob Elias Parera	6,000	9	OAC 900, no. 36
"	1767-69	†A. Bakker	6,400	8	OAC 901, no. 15
"	1769-79	Jacob Ho. Suares	6,100	6	

⁴ This plantation must be the same one owned by Balthazar (Abraham) de Leon before 1694 and inherited by his son Jacob (*Precious Stones*, p. 191). Jacob, in turn, left it to his niece Sarah, daughter of Dr. Isaac Gomes Casseres, in 1760 (*ibid.*, pp. 185-86). She died shortly afterwards, bequeathing it to Jacob Gomes Casseres.

623

Plantation or Garden	Year of ownership	Owner	Value	Slaves	Remarks
Blij en Heijm (Bleinheim), JQ	1779	†C. A. Roelans⁵	3,000	5	OAC 922, nos. 536, 537, 540, 543
"	1779	†Jan Schoon⁵	3,000	5	
"	1779	†Jan N. van Starckenborgh	4,500	3	OAC 922, no. 541
"	?	†Lodwijk van Schagen			
"	1800-79	Governor J. R. Lauffer and his descendants	2,740	2	Bt from the Van Schagen estate (OAC 1102, no. 5)
Blij Rusr, a. Grote Blauw, BENQ	1815-20	Gabriel Pinedo	13,150ᶜ	18	ᶜ In 1820wi; 226 h with St. Elizabeth (OAC 1058, no. 82)
"	b1841-43	Elias Penso	10,000	16ᵈ	ᵈ With those of St. Elizabeth (CEOE 792, no. 88)
"	1879	Manuel Penso Curiel	10,145		CC, March 31, 1882
Bloem en Hoof, see Ravenslot					
Bloemfontein	1900(?)	C. J. Henriquezᵉ			ᵉ Jewishness uncertain; 2.5 h
Bloemhoff, a. Nooit Gedacht, RQ; see also Kl. Bloemhoff	1760-62	Moses David Hz. Juliao	7,200	10	(OAC 879, Oct. 24, 1760); 7 h
"	1762	†J. Th. Vos	5,500	9	OAC 885, no. 75
"	1762-66	Rachel, wife of David Hz. Juliao	6,200	8	OAC 894, nos. 144-47
"	1766-67	Salomon Haim Calvo	6,600	8	OAC 899, no. 143
"	1767-81	†Jan Evertsz⁶	6,600	9	OAC 901, no. 6
"	1781	Manuel da C. Gomez & Bros.	5,300	6	OAC 993, no. 719
"	1797	Samuel Joseph da C. Gomez			
"	1806	David Lopez Raphael	2,800	2	OAC 1108, no. 72; sold to †J. de Langen
"	1808	Isaac da C. Gomez	4,500		
Bloemhoff, OD	1820-24	Manuel Hm. A. Correa	4,300 wiᶠ		ᶠ In 1820 (OAC 554, no. 508)
"	1825-47	Raphael Salzedo		7ᵍ	ᵍ In 1828 (CGAR II, Feb. 28, 1825)

624

			Price	No.	Notes
"	1847-51	Samuel C. Henriquez and	2,500	2	CGAT, 1851, nos. 10-11
		Aron da C. Gomez	5,200	2	CGAT, 1853, nos. 44-45
"	1851	†Jannetje S. Schotborgh	5,800	1	7 h
" a. Nooit Gedacht	1853	Moses Curiel	5,000 wi		h Sold to †M. B. Gorsira
" " "	1862	David Abm. Jesurun	1,000h		i Bt from Gorsira
"	1880	Abraham David Jesurun	1,000i		
"	1880-96	Moses David de Castro	9,000		
"	1896	Josias Lopez Henriquez			
"	1925(?)	S. Abinun de Lima Jr.			
BLOEMHOFF, BOA	1804	Wid. Moses Jesurun Lindo			Bt from Henriquez (CGAK, Jan. 8, 1879)
BLOEMPERK (Rust), BOQ	1828	Judith, wid. Aron Motta	860		
" (see Mahaai)	1879	Jacob Cohen Henriquez			
"	1879	Manuel A. Correa Jr.	3,000		
BLOEMPOT, a. Moron, RQ	1690-1745	David Senior	5,250	2	OAC 816, no. 102; WICA 592, p. 921b
"	1745-48	David Baruh Louzada7		44j	j In 1770
"	1754-84	Aron Henriquez Moron	5,230	1	OAC 1086, nos. 126-28; 22 slaves in 1791
"	1784-97	Manuel Moseh A. Correa	5,300		OAC 139, no. 39
"	1797	†Wilhelm Muller	4,000k		k In 1820wi (OAC 554, no. 18)
"	1816-20	Ephraim Curiel	5,700l	12*	l In 1833; * in 1827
"	1827-33	Haim aCohen	6,500m	12**	m In 1855; ** in 1842 (CEOE 172)
"	1833-67	Moses C. Henriquez and his estate			
"	1867-80	Alvares Correa Family			

5 Unable to pay the mortgage, Suares sold it to the mortgagee C. A. Roelans who sold it the same day to Jan Schoon for the same price. Schoon sold it later that day to Starckenborgh at a gain of 1,500 pesos and two slaves.

6 "Cornet over de cavallery en opperfactoor deeses Eylands."

7 The widow Louzada sold it in 1748 with three slaves for 7,450 pesos (OAC 819, Sept. 4, 1748).

Plantation or Garden	Year of ownership	Owner	Value	Slaves	Remarks
BLOEMPOT, a. Moron, RQ	1900(?)	Ida Penso			1.5 h
BOCA CHICA (lot)	1715-47	Elias Levy			See Union.
"	1802	Mordechay A. Correa	400		
BOCA JULIAO, a. Cornetsbaai	b1713	Henriquez Juliao Family			
BOCA DE PISCADERIS (cunucu)	1732	Daniel Aboab Cardozo			See Buena Esperansa (OAC 1138, Mar. 12, 1732).
BON PAIS, BENQ, a. de Chovaz	b1739-67	Jeosuah Naar			OAC 1548, Feb. 19, 1739
"	1767-71	David Jeosuah Naar	16,000	228	OAC 901, Oct. 6, 1767
"	1771	Sarah, D. J. Naar's wife	4,201	8	OAC 908, no. 19
"	1819	Jacob & Abraham Naar	14,000wi		OAC 554, no. 540
"	1819	†C. Schotborgh	18,500	6[9]	OAC 112, no. 70
"	1828	Jacob Naar and Wid. J. Naar		26	
"	1834-66	J. M. Pinedo	5,000		
"	1884	Manuel Penso Curiel	6,000		
BONAM, see Fortuin					
BONA VISTA, see Buena Vista					
BOTTELIER, I⁰ OD, see also Lange Tuin	1814-15	Mordechay Raphael A. Correa			75 h
"	1815	†H. Evertsz			CGAR I, Feb. 6, 1815
"	1816-43	David Capriles	3,700wi[n]		[n] In 1819 (OAC 554, no. 198)
"	1847	Estate Esther Abm. Jb. Jesurun	1,000		Sold to †Dr. C. J. Jonckheer
"	1855	Daniel Cohen Henriquez	5,500		CGAT, 1855, nos. 119-20
"	1862	Jacob J. Naar			
"	b1876	Benjamin G. Casseres			
"	1876	Moses Delvalle Henriquez	10,000		Bt from Casseres (CGAK, June 29, 1876)
"	1924	Moses E. Curiel	11,850		

BRAGASMIT, see Valantijn, Zorgvliet

Plantation	Years	Owner	Quantity	No.	Notes
BRAKKEPUT	b1726-30	Abraham Penso		2[o]	[o] In 1730 (OAC 1137, Apr. 28, 1730)
BRAKKEPUT ABAO, see Rust en Vrede					
BRAKKEPUT ARIBA, a. Nooit Gedacht, a. Groot Brakkeput	1826-42	Manuel Penso	2,000	31[p]	[p] In 1828 (CEOE 172); 76 h
"	1843-56	Benjamin Suares	16,000[q]	7	[q] In 1856 (CGAT, 1856, nos. 25-6)
"	1868	Moses Curiel			
"	1885	Penso Family	14,000		
"	1900	M. D. J. Cardoze	17,000		
BRAKKEPUT MEIMEI, a. Bragapoti	1920	Joseph A. Correa			80 h
BRIEVENGAT,[11] RQ	1747-60	Samuel Bn. de Casseres	24,000	87	478 h; OAC 818, March 23, 1747; OAC 877, May 7, 1760
"	1760	Dominie Johannes Ellis		68[12]	OAC 878, Sept. 3, 1760
BUENA ESPERANSA,[13] JQ, a. Marchena	b1729-32	Daniel Aboab Cardozo		20	OAC 1136, Sept. 5, 1729
"	1732	†Wid. P. de Velder	1,400 wi		Bt from Cardozo (WICA 580, p. 683v)
"	1775-82	Abigail, wid. Moses Penso	3,500		Bt from †Brugman (OAC 914, no. 26)

[8] The inventory also listed 58 bulls, 10 horses, 11 donkeys, 2 homing pigeons, and so forth.

[9] The inventory also listed 28 cows, 12 horses, 275 sheep, 225 goats and two corn mills.

[10] Apparently there were two plantations called Bottelier: that of 54 hectares also known as De Goede Tuin; the other of 140 hectares also known as Lange Tuin, or Grote Tuin, owned by Elias M. Curiel in 1870 (CGANA, 1870, no. 68).

[11] This plantation was known as "brievegat aan de noordkant" before 1708 and is mentioned in Governor Jacob Beck's will made in Curaçao on Aug. 31, 1708 (GAA, Notary Livinus Meyer, no. 5422, pp. 217-26).

[12] The inventory also listed 73 cows, 411 sheep, 322 goats and 8 horses. The Casseres heirs sold the Brievengat to Ellis along with the parcels Rantjes, Francisco, Catje and Juantje Christoffel.

[13] Also known by its Dutch equivalent Goed Hoop; later called Buena Vista (OAC 1084, no. 62).

Plantation or Garden	Year of ownership	Owner	Value	Slaves	Remarks
BUENA ESPERANSA, JQ	1782	†P. N. Christiaan	4,000		35 h with the Goed Gezicht, Vrijheid and Rust en Vrede
BONNA VISTA, RQ (lot)	1795	Jacob Jesurun Sasportas			
BUENA VISTA, BOQ, also Bona Vista	1788	Ester, wid. Manuel Abenatar	1,100	1	Sold in 1788 (OAC 1090, no. 116)
"	1818	Isaac and Moise Pinedo			
"	1824	Widow of Aron Pinedo			She sold it to Manuel Pinedo.
"	1824-25	Manuel Pinedo			CGAR II, Aug. 30, 1824
"	1825	†G. M. Ellis			CGAR II, June 13, 1825
"	1849-54	Leah Abraham Jesurun			She sold it to Elias Jn. Henriquez.
"	1854	Elias Jesurun Henriquez	1,000		
" (see Bever)	1856-62	Isaac Rz. Miranda Jr.	1,200		
BUENA VISTA	1925(?)	J. A. Henriquez			3.2 h
BUITENRUST, see Zapater					
BULLENBAAY	1660-1796	Dutch West India Company			
BURGH, see Rust en Burgh					
C					
CABAJE					87 h
CABO VERDE (lot)	1846	Abraham Henriquez Juliao			Adjacent to "Steenen Koraal"
CABRITENBERG, see Barber					
CARACAS BAAI (lots at)	1855	Rachel M. da Costa Senior	14,000		See Family Graves.
CAS ABAU					451 h
CAS ABAU, a. De Zegening	1828	Abraham Henriquez Juliao		37r	r With those of Bethlehem; 31 h
CAS CORA, a. Vredenberg, Penso's Park	1821	Mordechay Raphael A. Correa			75 h
"	1892	Jacob Elias Penso	14,000		Bt from †G. Ferguson

628

CAS GRANDI, a. Neidrust	1825-62	Manuel Penso	13,000s		s Value in 1862 wi; 61 h with Hoffi Bieuw
"	1910(?)	M. and J. Cardoze			
CASJOE TUIN, a. Cunucu Abao	1812	Moses Henriquez Juliao			See St. Nicolaas.
CATTENBERG, JQ	[1700?]-1737	Gabriel Levy and his widow		10t	t In 1737 (OAC 1140, Apr. 9, 1737)
"	1737-45	Benjamin Naar	3,101	15u	u In 1741 (OAC 807, Aug. 28, 1737)
"	1745	†G. A. de Quirigazoe	6,000	7	OAC 816, no. 157
"	1768-74	Leah, wid. Moses de Chavez	6,250v	11	v Purchase price (OAC 904, June 21, 1768)
"	1774	†David Muchart	4,600	9	OAC 913, no. 99
"	1787-1801	Abraham Calvo and his estate	4,500	5	OAC 1089, no. 58
"	1801	†W. Forbes	4,100	3	OAC 1103, no. 84
CATTENBERG, RQ	1745	Elias Parera	2,700wi		Sold to †C. Schotborgh (WICA 592, p. 924b)
CERITO, a. Vrede	1827-54	Esther Abm. Jesurun	2,000	12w	Value in 1854; w in 1828
"	1854-59	Jacob Abm. Jesurun			
"	1877	D. A. Jesurun			
"	1889-95	Abraham David Jesurun			
CHANGO, a. Mantancia	1895	Mordechay da Costa Gomez	6,900		Bt from A. D. Jesurun 31 h
CHARO, a. Bellevue	1819	Pastor Johan Joseph Perovani			OAC 1121, no. 81
CHER ASILE, see also Family Graves	1848-50	Esther Delvalle, wid. Abm. Is. Henriquez[14]	2,500x	1	x With Steenen Rijk
CHIROUETTE, see Girouette					
CHIROEMET (Girouette?), OD	1832	David S. Valencia			CGAR IV, Apr. 9, 1832 3.5 h
CHRISTOFFEL					

[14] She sold it to Dr. C. H. Jonckheer in 1850 for 2,000 florins (CGAT, 1850, no. 80) Today Cher Asile and Steenen Rijk — without the houses, churches and schools — are worth 2,000,000 florins.

Plantation or Garden	Year of ownership	Owner	Value	Slaves	Remarks
CORAAL PATIN, a. Eendragt	1876-98	Jacob J. Naar	5,000y		y In 1876
CORAAL SPECHT					145 h
CORAAL TABAK, BOQ, OD	1670-1796	Dutch West India Company			492 h according to Cadaster
"	1796-99	Abraham, a. Antoine, Delvaille	5,010		Bt from the Government (OAC 1098, no. 156); sold for 14,200 pesos
"	1798	†J. Brands	14,200	4	OAC 141, no. 30; OAC 1100, no. 183
"	1851-73	Aron da Costa Gomez	10,600	2¹⁵	Bt from the †Gorter Family
"	1873-90	Samuel C. Henriquez	9,075z		z In 1873
"	1890-1925	Julius L. Penha	8,500		Sold in 1925 for 20,000 florins
CORNETSBAAI, see Boca Juliao					
CORPORAAL, a. Zorgvliet	1766-99	Is. Hm. Rodriguez da Costa and his widow			87.75 h
"	1808	Widow of Aron Aeliona			a With Suikertuintje lots (OAC 1027, no. 57)
"	1845	Esther de Jb. Senior			CGAR VI, Sept. 29, 1845
"	1847	Abm. Is. Henriquez and wid.			With Zevenbergen
"	1889-1902	Abraham Henriquez			Sold to †J. C. Forbes with Zeven-huizen for 36,000 florins
CORRIE, a. Vreugdendaal					
CUNUCU ABAO, see Casjoe Tuin, Vredenberg, Family Graves	1910	S.A.L. Maduro			17 h
CUNUCU Poos	1828	Isaac Capriles			

D

DAMACÓR, see also Vreugdendaal   18 h

DAMASCO, OD, see also Jan Tiel; Family Graves	1737-42	Moses Penso	5,700	6	Bt from the †Jan Tiel estate (OAC 806, Jan. 6, 1737)
"	1742	†Claas Visser	16,000	40	OAC 813, no. 334
"	1767-84	Is. Hm. Rodriguez da Costa and his widow	17,000[16]	40	OAC 901, no. 92
"	1784	†C. Visser	15,800	5	OAC 1086, no. 120
"	1803	Wid. Judith Rz. Pimentel[17]	8,000	30b	b On her death in 1809 (OAC 482, no. 5)
"	1819-28	Moses Henriquez Juliao	40,000 wi		With Jan Tiel (OAC 554, no. 665)
"	1828	†Lauffer Brothers (?)[18]		14	MIA[18]
"	1829	Isaac Capriles			
"	1863	S.E.L. Maduro			CGAR IX, May 5, 1863
DANIEL,[19] WD, a. Malpais; see also Malpais, Family Graves	1713	Benjamin da Costa			WICA 205, p. 535v; 55h with Casjoe Tuin
"	1825-27	Moises Pinedo Jr.	19,500e		e With Casjoe Tuin and Bajada (OAC 497, no. 24)
DAVELAAR	1898	B. de Marchena			
DEYN, a. Stadszicht	1769	Josias de Casseres	2,200	3	OAC 906, Aug. 11, 1769
"	1900 ?	J. R. da Costa Gomez			37 h
DOKTERSTUIN, a. Klein Asencion					Known in 1742 as Doctor; 526h
DOMINEE ROOY					So known in 1716 (WICA 572, p. 391v); 88 h
DOMINGUITO, see Fortuin					
DONA PALIA, RQ (lot), see Union					80 h
DONKERBERG, see Ravenslot					

[15] Also listed in the inventory were 645 goats, 367 sheep, 12 cows, 4 bulls, 25 donkeys, 2 riding donkeys, a horse, a homing pigeon, two corn mills, and so forth (CGAT, 1851, nos. 73-74).
[16] This price included the slaves, a large limekiln, 38 cows, 20 calves, 254 sheep, 128 goats, 3 horses, 12 donkeys, and so forth.
[17] She had bought it from † N. Evertsz.
[18] According to MIA, Capriles bought it with 14 slaves from Lauffer Brothers on Feb. 24, 1829, for 13,307.16 florins.
[19] This plantation probably belonged to the first Daniel Aboab Cardozo since 1674 and thus bears his name.

Plantation or Garden	Year of ownership	Owner	Value	Slaves	Remarks
DRIE GEBROEDERS, see Union Veeris, Westerveld	1774	Jacob David Jesurun	13,000		OAC 913, no. 108
DUIVELSKLIP, see Fuik	1668-1796	Dutch West India Company			
"	1866-74	Hana de Abm. D. Henriquez	8,000		Sold to †W. P. Maal
DWARS IN DE WEG, BOQ	1786-87	Moses Frois[20]	7,200[d]	7	d With Grote and Klein Minguilito (OAC 1088, no. 121)
E					
EENDRAGT, see also Coraal Patin	1767	Rachel Bueno Vivas	3,550	4	OAC 901, no. 108
"	1785	Mordechay A. Correa			OAC 1087, no. 33
"	b1771	Rachel, wid. Dd Hz. Juliao			
"	1771-74	Jb. Hz. Moron de Losena and Ester, wid. Abm. Is. Hz. Moron	2,300	3[21]	OAC 908, no. 315
"	1819	The Widow Raphael Pinedo			OAC 1062, no. 24
EENSAMHIJD,[22] JQ, a. Nieuwe Wereld	1750	Isaac Samuel L. Maduro	2,000		OAC 824, Nov. 19, 1750
"	1764-66	Esther L. Raphael	3,000	2	OAC 892, no. 151
"	1766-93	Mordechay Motta	1,573	1	Worth only 575 pesos in 1793
"	1806	Abm. Samuel L. Maduro	420		Bt at public auction (OAC 1108, no. 153)
EIGEN VERDRIET, BOA (lot)	1764	Rachel Bueno Vivas	2,500	2	OAC 892, no. 144
ENGELENBERG, see Van Engelen					
F					
FAMILY GRAVES, see below, pp. 678-80					
FLIP, a. Klein Paradera, WD	b1802	Dominie Pieter Jan van Esch[23]			Sold to Manuel Pinedo
"	1802-20	Manuel Pinedo	6,020	1	OAC 1104, no. 81

FONTEIN, WD	1843	Jacob Jesurun and sisters		14[e]	e With those of Siberie (CEOE 172); 717 h
"	1846-52	Isaac de Castro and widow		10[24]	Sold in 1852 with 8 slaves for 6,267 fls. (CGAT, 1846, no. 41)
"	1861	Jacob Abm. Jesurun	4,000		Bt from †Emelie de Brot-Gorsira; sold for 8,400 in 1870 (CGANA, 1870, no. 206)
FORTUIN, a. Bonam	1900 ?	E. M. Curiel			47 h
FORTUIN, BOQ, a. Dominguito	1747-51	Joseph Bonan	3,200	15[f]	f In 1749 (OAC 819, no. 79)
"	b1777-99	Samuel and Jos. da C. Gomez	1,300		OAC 917, no. 115
"	1799	Jacob Jesurun Pinto	1,300		OAC 1101, no. 51
"	1826	Haim aCohen		1	CGAR III, Sept. 18, 1826
LA FORTUNA (lot)	1862-70	Jacob A. Jesurun	8,400		Value in 1870; 34 h
FRANCIA	1785	Moses Vas Nunes	225		OAC 972, no. 95
"	1803	Abraham Pinedo			
"	1905	Manuel S. L. Maduro			Bt from J. and A. A. M. Monsanto[25]; 5 h
FUBURG	1874-88	Hana Abm. Delv. Henriquez	5,000		Value in 1888
FUIK, BOQ	1751-58	Moses Penso and his estate	73,500[26]	300[g]	g With those of Sta. Barbara
"	1758	†Widow Willem Meyer	67,500	300	

20 Frois sold it for 8,000 pesos in 1787 with the parcel Vrede and seven slaves.

21 The inventory also included eleven paintings. Sold to †J. A. Kool in 1774 for 1,400 pesos with three slaves and five paintings (OAC 913, no. 158).

22 Originally called Nieuwe Wereld, it was named Eensamheid by †Jacobus van Veyder in 1752.

23 He married Catharina Struddels, widow of Willem van Uytrecht.

24 The inventory also included 30 cows, 206 sheep, 40 goats, 9 donkeys, and so forth (CGAR IX, Aug, 10, 1846).

25 Communication of the late Jossy M. L. Maduro.

26 Bought from †Willem Meyer together with the Sta. Barbara and a house on Breedestraat (OAC 1566, June 1, 1751). Penso also rented the Duivelsklip plantation from the WIC. Fuik, with Klein St. Joris and Duivelsklip, had a combined area of 4,326 h. Fuik and the Sta. Barbara of 1,202 h were the two largest plantations in Curaçao. At his death in 1754, Penso owned 403 slaves on these two plantations, 2,898 head of cattle on the Fuik, and 1,301 head on the Sta. Barbara (OAC 837, Aug, 8, 1758; OAC 871, no. 149). His heirs sold the two plantations to the widow of Willem Meyer, without the house on Breedestraat, for 67,500 pesos.

633

Plantation or Garden	Year of ownership	Owner	Value	Slaves	Remarks
G					
Gaito, a. Vergenoeging, see Vreeland					
Gasparito, a. Ma Retraite					28 h with Kl. St. Kruis, a. Koeimans
Gato, see Family Graves					
Gedachtenis, see Watervliet					
Genoegen is 't al, see Goed Heen Komen					
Gerustheid	1839-51	Obadia Ms. da Costa and daughter	2,100	1[27]	Value in 1851 (CGAT, 1851, nos. 78-79)
Gibraltar (lot)	1858	Mordechay Pinedo			CGAR IX, Feb. 10, 1858
Giftenberg	1873	Isaac Salas	1,000		Bt from †P. Evertsz
Girouette, a. Rijkenberg, BOQ	1715-21	Samuel L. Maduro	1,600 wi		(WICA 572, p. 91v); 34 h
" (see Chiroemet)	1801-04	Haim Gabriel da C. Gomez and his widow	3,500	3	Bt from †N. Evertsz (OAC 1103, no. 66)
"	1804	†M. L. Ellis	8,000	9	OAC 1106, no. 66
"	1809-51(?)	Jacob Senior	8,400 wi		Value in 1819 (OAC 554, no. 27)
"	1852-53	Henry Nathan	5,000		Value with the land Terra Sekoe
"	1853-56	Jacob A. Jesurun	5,200	5	
"	1856-57	Jeudith Jesurun Pinto	6,400	2	
"	1857-69	Moses Curiel	8,000	2	
"	1869	Ephraim Curiel	6,000		Bt from Rebecca, wife of Manuel Penso Curiel
"	1884-1910	Ephraim Curiel Jr.	6,000		
"	1910	Rebecca, wife of David M. Cardoze	7,500		Bt from My. Fidanque Curiel
Goed Begin, a. Jan We	1741-45	Joseph da Costa Gomez	650		WICA 589, p. 86v; OAC 811, no. 368

	Years	Name	Value	No.	Reference
"	1745-77	David Lopez Laguna	850		Laguna heirs (OAC 918, no. 355)
"	1777	Jacob and Samuel da C. Gomez	800		
"	1777-99	Samuel da Costa Gomez			
"	1799-1820	Jacob Jesurun Pinto	2,400	5	OAC 1101, no. 55; OAC 554, no. 37
"	1820	Jacob Lopez Penha			
"	1828	Benjamin de J. Henriquez		6	
GOED BEGIN, a. Kl. Zuurzak; see also Klein Zuurzak	1847	Mordechay Rl. A. Correa			
"	1855	Moses de Marchena	6,000	5	Bt from My. Correa's widow (CGAT, 1855, nos. 121-22)
"	1856-62	Jeosuah Naar	4,000	3	
"	1869-72	Sarah Penso, wife of David Pardo Jr.	6,000		CGANA, 1869, II, no. 140
GOED GEZICHT, see Buena Esperanza					
GOED HEEN KOMEN RQ, a. Zoutpan, Genoegen is 't al, Salina Abao	1738-42	Joseph da Costa Gomez	1,000		WICA 586, p. 396v
"	1742-45	†Willem Kock	9,000	14	Value with other lots (OAC 813, no. 33)
"	1745-47	Samuel de Casseres	8,000	14	OAC 816, no. 163
"	1747	†Jacob Berry	4,700		OAC 1549, Sept. 28, 1747
"	1768	Jacob Hisquiao Suares	3,000		Sold to †N. Evertsz (OAC 904, May 6, 1768)
"	1859-79	Jacob Abraham Jesurun	6,500		Value in 1862 without inventory
"	1879-1913	Esther, Ricot and Leah De Marchena	10,000		Sold in 1913 for 6,625 florins

[27] There also were 42 pitchers of aloe.

635

Plantation or Garden	Year of ownership	Owner	Value	Slaves	Remarks
GOED HOOP, a. Esperanza					
(DE) GOEDE HOOP, see Popo					
GOEDE TIELEN, see Lange Tuin					
GOESJE (cunucu)	b1715-42	Daniel Aboab Cardozo and his estate			19 h. With Boca Chica (OAC 1138, March 12, 1732; OAC 805, Oct. 11, 1736)
"	1742-44	Haim Abinun de Lima and his estate		2	
"	1744	†W. Lixraaven			OAC 815, no. 104; WICA 591, p. 740v
GRANATENBERG	1723-33	Elias Levy			Sold in 1733 (OAC 801, June 26, 1733)
"	1753	Jacob Elias Pereira	16,250	16	With Oud St. Michiel (OAC 828, June 5, 1753)
"	1765	Jacob Hz. Pereira, Elias Hm. Pereira and Jb. Pereira	15,000	19	OAC 1558, no. 35
GRAVES IN THE PLANTATIONS, see below, pp. 678-80					
GROOT BRAKKEPUT, see Brakkeput Ariba					
GROOT KWARTIER, see Vreeland, Vergenoeging, Rust en Burgh, Family Graves					
GROOT EN KLEIN MALPAIS, a. Mount Pleasant, see also Malpais	1874-86	Abraham Delvalle Henriquez	5,000		930 h.
GROOT MINGUILITO, see Dwars in de Weg.					

Plantation	Period	Owner	Value		Reference
GROOT PISCADERA,[28] also Piscadera, BENQ; see also Kl. Piscadera	1796-1807	Raphael A. Correa	7,840		Bt from the Government (OAC 1098, no. 89); 308 h
"	1807	Manuel Penso			OAC 1022, no. 3
"	1812-19	Samuel da Costa Gomez	47,000		OAC 1059, no. 36; OAC 497, no. 33
"	1820	Jeosuah de Sola	45,000 wi		OAC 554, no. 463
"	1834-70	David Delvalle Henriquez		54 h	h In 1843 (CEOE 172)
"	1870-74	†J. Southerland	29,900		CGAK, Sept. 19, 1870; bt from D. Henriquez
"	1874-99	Salomon Elias Curiel	20,000		Bt from the Widow Southerland
"	1899	†Jones	37,500		
GROOT SANDROH	1851	Benjamin A. Correa			
GROOT SANTA MARTHA	b1709-16	Manuel Gomes and his widow			554 h with Klein St. Jan
"	1716	†J. Schuurman	12,000 wi		WICA 203, p. 97; WICA 572, p. 391 v
"	1829-50	David Dovale[29]			
"	1850	†C. G. de Haseth	38,000	60[30]	CGAR VII, Apr. 15, 1851
"	1851	Jeosuah Naar & Co.			Bt from †J. Stuyling
GROOT SINT JORIS,[31] BOQ; see also Sint Joris	1753-98	Abraham and Isaac de Marchena			(OAC 900, no. 37); 454 h
"	1798	†C. Ringeling	40,000	28[32]	(OAC 1100, no. 10)

[28] Owned by the WIC until 1796, it was rented to Benjamin Lopez Henriquez from 1735 to 1777, first at 600 pesos yearly and later at 945 pesos. The inventory of slaves and other assets of Lopez Henriquez and his sons was worth 7,500 pesos in 1749 (OAC 821, Nov. 17, 1749). In 1738 he had 53 slaves on the plantation (OAC 1141, July 31, 1738). From 1777-1791 the land was rented to David Morales and afterwards to Raphael A. Correa, son-in-law of Lopez Henriquez (WICA 616, no. 1, Feb. 12, 1791). In 1795 Correa paid 450 pesos' rent, the highest rental paid that year for a WIC plantation (W. I. Comité 139, June 24, 1795).

[29] In 1842 the plantation had 8 horses, 52 cows, 6 donkeys, 320 sheep, 650 goats, and so forth (CEOE 172).

[30] The inventory lists, among other things, a sugar mill, 670 sheep and 700 goats (CGAT, 1850, nos. 73-74).

[31] In 1715 there were sugar mills on the plantation.

[32] The inventory also lists 130 cows, 1,500 sheep, 80 goats, 31 horses, 30 donkeys, fowl, 3 homing pigeons, and so forth (OAC 1100, no. 10).

Plantation or Garden	Year of ownership	Owner	Value	Slaves	Remarks
GROOT SINT JORIS, BOQ	1818-31?	David Haim Dovale and his widow	45,000	40[l]	[l] In 1820 (OAC 1059, no. 55); 44 slaves in 1828
"	1831-46	Jacob Haim Penso	60,000[33]	37[j]	[j] In 1837 (CGAN, 1846, July 14, 1746)
"	1847-69	†P. L. de Haseth	11,915	8	Bt from †Clasina de Haseth
"	1869-84	Dr. Isaac Jacob Senior	35,000		
"	1884	†A. Perret-Gentil	38,000		
GROOT SINT MICHIEL	1721-39	Jeosuah Henriquez			(OAC 1548, Feb. 19, 1739); 257 h See footnote 34.
"	1739-1855	Jeosuah Henriquez' descendants			
"	1855-74	Mordechay Jeos. Henriquez			
"	1874-75	Samuel L. Maduro Jr.	36,960		CGAK, Nov. 20, 1874
"	1875	†Genereux de Lima[k]	36,960		[k] Of Jewish descent (CGAK, Dec. 20, 1875)
"	1910?	J. A. Correa			
GROTE BERG (Grotenberg), see also Harmonie	1834	Jacob de Castro	5,500		
GROTE BLAUW, see Blauw, Blijrust					
GROTE ROZENDAAL, JQ (cunucu)	1733-36	Isaac Nunes Redondo		2	OAC 1139, Jan. 5, 1733
GROTE TUIN, see Bottelier					
GROTE ZOUT, see Zoutpan					
GROTE ZUURZAK, see Zuurzak					

H

HAAN EN WOENDERBERG	1844	Ribca Bueno Vivas			
HABAAI, see Welgelegen					
HANNEBERG, OD	1767-84	Isaac Hm. Rodriguez da Costa	1,200		OAC 900, no. 96

222. ESTHER, WIDOW OF ABRAHAM
JACOB JESURUN, 1770-1846,
PLANTATION OWNER

223. HERMAN C. HENRIQUEZ, 1831-
1906, PLANTATION OWNER; CONSUL OF
ITALY FOR MANY YEARS

224. JACOB ELIAS PENSO, 1839-1912,
NOTED MERCHANT

225. MOZES E. CURIEL, 1853-1933,
NOTED MERCHANT

226. JULIUS DAVID LOPEZ PENHA,
1855-1934, PLANTER, PAGE 465

227. MANUEL SALOMON L. MADURO,
1861-1932, PLANTER

228. BENJAMIN ABRAHAM B. JESURUN,
1867-1936, PLANTER, PAGES 465-66

229. EDWARD ABRAHAM B. JESURUN,
1870-1934, PLANTER, PAGES 465-66

	Year	Owner	Value (fls.)	Slaves	Notes
"	1784	†Claas Visser	1,200		CGAT, 1846, no. 10
"	1846	Ribca Bueno Vivas	400		Sold to †Igaris for 1,600 (CGAT, 1854, nos. 105-106)
"	1847-54	Hanah and Ribca de Manuel A. Correa	600		Bt from †Igaris (CGAT, 1860, no. 57)
"	1860	S.E.L. Maduro	200		2.40 h
HARMONIE, BENQ, a. Rameljosa, a. Grotenberg	1730	David Namias de Crasto and Isaac de Marchena			
"	1834-54	Jacob Rephael Pinedo	6,650	4l	Value in 1854 with the Grotenberg (CGAT, 1854, nos. 59-60); l in 1843 (CEOE 172)
"	1857-62	Lea Sasportas de Castro	8,800	4	CGAT, 1857, nos. 40-41
"	1910(?)	G. Marchena			
HATO, see also Family Graves	1660-1796	Dutch West India Co.	8,010		1,080 h
"	1796-1800	Raphael Pinedo			Bt from the Government (W. I. Comité 143a)
"	1800	†Nicolaas Evertsz	18,000	19	OAC 1102, no. 143
"	1807	Mordechay Rl. A. Correa (?)			
HERMANUS, a. Oud St. Marie	1715-16	Jacob Andrade	3,330		Sold for 5,200 ps. (WICA 572, p. 635); 250 h
"	1841	Manuel and My. A. Correa		37m	m In 1842 with those of Meiberg Tuin (CEOE 172)
HERONIMO, see Ligtenbergh					
HOEDIO, see (De) Hoop					
HOF EN BERG (Hoffenberg), BOQ	b1782	Isaac Pardo			
"	March 1782	Benj. and Moses C. Henriquez	2,000	3	OAC 938, no. 78

33 According to MIA, loose papers, Feb. 19, 1834, the plantation costs 60,000 fls.

34 The number of slaves for the years 1749, 1768, 1805, 1827 and 1843 was 50, 100, 43, 74 and 108, respectively. The value of the plantation for the years 1768, 1805, 1819, 1834, 1857, 1861 and 1874 was 36,000 ps., 27,000 ps., 27,000 ps. wi, 25,000 fls., 40,481 fls., 26,400 fls, and 36,960 fls., respectively. In 1874 the plantation also included the Ligtenberg, a. Heronimo, and the parcels Berg van Suzanna, Manuel Kuiper and Jan Boelhouder (CC, Oct. 24, 1874).

Plantation or Garden	Year of ownership	Owner	Value	Slaves	Remarks
HOF EN BERG (Hoffenberg), BOQ	June 1782	†Susanne Evertsz-Hansz	4,000	4	OAC 938, no. 221
"	1815	Abraham Salom Delvalle			
HOFFI BIEUW	1862	J. A. Jesurun	600		61 h with Cas Grandi
HOFFJE	1796	Raphael A. Correa			
(DE) HOOP, a. Jode Quartier, a. Judio, a. Hoedio	1660-1704	Jeosuah Henriquez			OAC 1534, no. 57
"	1704-15	His son Mordechay Henriquez[35]			OAC 1534, no. 57
"	1716-58	Rachel Naar (wid. My. Henriquez) and children		15[n]	[n] In 1758 (OAC 837, Feb. 25, 1758)
"	1759-1800	Jacob Mordechay Henriquez			
"	1800	†Joh. Martijn	11,500	11	OAC 1102, no. 125
(DE) HOOP [Esperanza?]	1762	Abraham A. Correa			OAC 885, no. 148

I - J

Plantation or Garden	Year of ownership	Owner	Value	Slaves	Remarks
INSIGHT	1742	Isaac da Costa Gomez	1,350	2	OAC 812, June 29, 1742
JACK EVERTSZ, see Ravenslot					
JALOUSIE, see Family Graves					
JAN DORET					4.90 h
JAN JONGBLOED, a. Vergenoeging, BOQ	1804	Isaac Cardozo	8,000	12	OAC 1106, no. 76; sold to R. Mz. Henriquez
"	1807	Rachel Ricardo Mz. Henriquez			Sold to Tavarez
"	b1811	David Tavarez			OAC 1039, March 8, 1813
"	1814-17	Gabriel Aron Pinedo		23[o]	[o] In 1816
JAN KOK, a. Zevenhuizen	1895-1902	Abraham Henriquez	32,000	34	Value in 1902 with Zorgvliet; 345 h (MIA, meeting of May 6, 1816); 360 h with Damasco
JAN TIEL, see also Damasco	1816	Moses Henriquez Julio			

640

JAN WE, see Goed Begin

JAN ZOUTVAT, a. Uijlenburg, Vredenberg; see also Family Graves

	David de Castro	1813-17		
"	Salomon S. Delvalle	1818	10,500 wi	OAC 554, no. 506
"	Abm. de Is. Henriquez	1820	4,500	OAC 1122, no. 80
"	Jb. Jeosuah Naar and children	1875-98	10,000	Bt in 1875 from †P. H. Maal

JODE (JOODE) QUARTIER PLANTATIONS unnamed by their owners

	Abraham de Leon and children	1694-1760		
"	Abraham de Campos Pereira	1716	1,300	
"	Salomoh Samuel L. Maduro	1719		OAC 794, Jan. 1, 1719
"	Daniel Aboab Cardozo	1719		OAC 794, Jan. 1, 1719
"	Abraham Orobio de Mattos	1719		OAC 794, y. 1719
"	Isaac de Marchena	1721		
"	Isaac de David Senior	1723		
"	Elishah Aboab [Cardozo]	1731		OAC 1138, Sept. 6, 1731
"	Isaac Henriquez Juliao	1731	3	
"	Mordechay A. Correa	1735		OAC 804, March 18, 1735
"	Moses Penso	1742		OAC 813, Dec. 13, 1742
"	Selomoh Nunes Redondo	1743		OAC 814, no. 297

JOONTJE, a. Mon Repos, OD	Moses de Castro Jr.	1832	2.25 h	
"	Edward and Benj. Jesurun	1888		CEOE 172

JORENKWEST TUIN

JUANA MATEO, see Family Graves

	Clara A. Correa	1843	

K

KANGA, see Savaan

KARPATA, see Rust en Vrede		8 h

KATTENBERGH, see Cattenberg

641

35 In 1746 it was worth Ps. 10,000 with its ten slaves; Ps. 17,000 in 1784 with Klein Tuin (OAC 1086, nos. 139-40).

Plantation or Garden	Year of ownership	Owner	Value	Slaves	Remarks
KERENBERGH	b1732	Joseph Abendana Pereira			By Piscadera
"	1732	Elias Levy	2,000		WICA 580, p. 584v
KIJKENBERG	1828	I. de Sola		12	
KLEIN ASENCION, see Dokterstuin					
KLEIN ARARAT (lot)	1810	Abraham Salom Delvalle			
KLEIN BLAUW, a. St. Elizabeth; see also Oud St. Michiel	1819	Gabriel Pinedo	6,000 wi		OAC 554, no. 640
"	b1823	Ester Peixotto, wid. David Henriquez Juliao	7,000		
"	1823	Lea, wid. Moses Penso		19p	OAC 596, Aug. 13, 1823; p in 1828
KLEIN BLOEMHOFF, see also Family Graves	b1762	David Lopez Laguna			
"	1762-68	Gabriel Pinedo	2,000	3	OAC 885, no. 101
"	1803	David Lopez Raphael	2,500	1	OAC 1105, no. 93
"	1812	Isaac Cardozo			Sold to †H. Evertsz (CGAR I, Oct. 5, 1812)
"	1815	Mord. de Rephael A. Correa			
KLEIN KLOOF, a. Pannekoek	1856(?)	S. da Costa Gomez	4,820		175 h
KLEIN KWARTIER, OD, see also Vrede	b1815-47	My. Jeosuah Henriquez and widow	18,000 wi	12q	Value in 1818; q in 1828; sold in 1847 with 8 sls. for 6,600 fls.
"	1867	Benjamin Jesurun Jr.			
"	1889	A. B. Jesurun			
"	1889-1915	Aron A. Correa[36]			115 h
KLEIN MALPAIS, a. Souax, Weitje	1847-88	Hana Abm. Delv. Henriquez	45,000		Value in 1874; 133 h
KLEIN MARCHENA					10 h
KLEIN MINGUILITO, see Dwars in de Weg					

KLEIN PARADERA, see Flip					
KLEIN PISCADERA-RAFAEL, a. Weltevrede, BENQ	1717?-1807	Raphael Manuel A. Correa and his descendants[38]			170 h with the Rafael[37]
"	1807	Joseph and My. A. Correa			OAC 1022, no. 3
"	1807-12	Haim Abinun de Lima			
"	1812-25	Isaac Capriles	25,900wi		Value in 1819 (OAC 590, no. 477; OAC 315, April 29, 1825)
	1826	Jeosuah de Sola			Bt from †F. G. Beutner (CGAR III, July 25, 1826)
"	1827-28	Isaac Capriles			Bt from Capriles[39]
"	1828	M. H. A. Correa			
"	1842-48	Moses Jesurun		40[r]	[r] In 1843 (CEOE 172)
"	1848-52	Sylvania Joseph Capriles[39]	10,000[s]	12[s]	[s] In 1848
KLEIN Sr. JAN, see also St. Jan	1829-50	David Dovale	2,000		Sold to †C. G. de Haseth in 1850 for 2,000 fls.; 554 h with Groot Sta. Martha
KLEIN Sr. JORIS, BOQ; see also Groot St. Joris and St. Joris	1805	Abm. Lopez Raphael	20,000	20	OAC 1107, no. 182
"	1807	Isaac Henriquez			4,326 h with Fuik and Duivelsklip
"	1833	Jeosuah Jacob Naar			
"	1842	Abraham Capriles		40	CEOE 172
KLEIN Sr. KRUIS, a. Koeimans, JQ (near the Beth Hahaim)					28 h with Gasparito

[36] Correa had bought it from Jesurun for 12,500 fls. and sold it to †Carlos Cadieres for 16,000.

[37] There was another Klein Piscadera plantation which, with the Ravenslot, measured 122 h.

[38] The plantation had 22 slaves in 1752, 20 in 1760, and 30 in 1783. In 1752 it was worth 13,000 pesos; in 1783, 22,000 ps. with the Vergenoeging and four other parcels (OAC 1143, Jan. 1, 1740; OAC 862, no. 213; OAC 855, no. 148; OAC 16, Oct. 26, 1752; OAC 877, April 17, 1760, and OAC 1084, no. 62).

[39] Together with the lots Preto (a. Nana), Savaan, Vergenoeging, Moontje and two other parcels (CGAR IV, July 15, 1828; CGAT, 1852, nos. 66-67).

Plantation or Garden	Year of ownership	Owner	Value	Slaves	Remarks
KLEIN STE. MARIE	1698	Abm Hz. de Mesquita and Aron L. Maduro			Comm. of the late J. M. L. Maduro
KLEIN STA. MARTHA (orig. St. Maarten)	b1709	Abraham Henriquez [Moron]			WICA 203, p. 97b
"	1709-19	Aron Levy Maduro	10,000		Sold to †Jan Henrix (WICA 573, p. 267v)
"	1819-56	Jacob Jeosuah Naar and his descendants	35,000	64t	Worth 50,000 pesos in 1824 (OAC 297, June 16, 1824); t in 1827.
"	1856-62	Joseph Jacob Henriquez	55,000[40]	41u	u In 1856; 480 h with Rustenpad and San Mango
KLEIN ST. MICHIEL, BENQ; see also Groot St. Michiel, Oud St. Michiel, Family Graves	b1709-22	Moseh L. Maduro and widow		5v	v With those of Montagnie (OAC 797, no. 306); 185 h with Slangenbaai
"	1722-36	Jeremiao and Is. Mh. L. Maduro			OAC 805, Feb. 27, 1736
"	1736	Is. L. Maduro and Jb. Henriquez[41]			
"	1746-60	Jacob Henriquez	12,400	48	Bt Maduro's half share (OAC 817, July 28, 1746)
"	1760-66	Ester L. Henriquez, wid. of Jeosuah Henriquez	18,001	4	Bt from the Jb. Henriquez estate (OAC 879, Oct. 10, 1760)
"	1766-68	†C. S. Hansz	18,500	12[42]	Sold by Henriquez (OAC 895, no. 47)
"	1768-73	Mosseh Henriquez	15,000	18	Bt from Hansz (OAC 904, June 10, 1768)
"	1773-81	Samuel and Michel Eliao Jeudah Leao	14,001	20	OAC 912, nos. 170-71
"	1781	†Domingo Schilepele	14,000	13	OAC 934, no. 1011
"	1805-06	Abm. Salomon L. Maduro	7,000	4	Bt from †Louis Brunnet (OAC 1107, no. 50)

"	1806-13	Salomon Samuel L. Maduro	7,000[43]	4	With the land Slangenbaai (OAC 1108, no. 79)
"	1813	Johebed, wid. of above		25[w]	[w] On her death in 1813 (OAC 1039, no. 25)
"	1813-19	Mord. Rephael A. Correa			
"	1819-36	Hanah, d. My. A. Correa	18,700[wi]	35[x]	Value in 1819 (OAC 554, no. 482); [x] in 1828
"	1836-51	Raphael Pinedo	16,000[44]	18[y]	[y] In 1843 (CEOE 172)
KLEIN TUIN, JQ, see also Lelienberg, (De) Hoop	1744-58	Rachel Naar, wid. Mord. Henriquez	3,660		OAC 176, no. 90; WICA 591, p. 744v
"	1758-1800	Descendants of R. Henriquez			
KLEIN ZUURZAK, see also Zuurzak, Goed Begin	1766-1803	Isaac Haim Rodriguez da Costa[45] and his widow			OAC 895, no. 224
"	1803	†Maria Frederick Hermes	13,020	13	With Groot Zuurzak
"	1805-38	Abm. Is. Henriquez	12,350	5946	Bt from Hermes with Groot Zuurzak and only five slaves
"	1838	Benjamin Is. Henriquez		4	
"	1850-60	Jb. Henriquez and Jb. J. Naar	29,000		With the Zuurzak
"	1860	Benjamin A. Correa	25,000		With the Zuurzak (CGAT, 1860, no. 61)
KLIP[47]					
KNITENPAD, WD	1723	Samuel Gomes	400[wi]		WICA 208, p. 108b
KOEDISJE, a. Soledad	1857	Jb. J. and Abm. Naar			
	1900(?)	E. and Ph. S. Cohen Henriquez		4[h]	

[40] The inventory also lists 62 bulls, 800 sheep, two horses, two canoes, and so forth (CGAT, 1856, nos. 115-16).

[41] Henriquez, son-in-law of Isaac Maduro, received half of the plantation as dowry.

[42] The inventory listed among other livestock 24 fowl.

[43] The bill of sale specified that the well on the "Hofje" was public domain for the use of all the neighboring plantations.

[44] Pinedo sold it to †Emilie Debrot-Gorsira in 1851 for 16,000 fls. (CGAT, 1851, nos. 8-9).

[45] Da Costa had to pay the WIC yearly rent of 4.5 pesos for a piece of land adjacent to the Klein Zuurzak.

[46] With those of the Zuurzak at his death in 1838 (CEOE, 776, no. 56).

[47] At the end of the 18th century the plantation belonged to †Pierre Brion, father of the admiral. In 1809 Admiral Brion owned a third part (CGAR I, July 14, 1809).

Plantation or Garden	Year of ownership	Owner	Value	Slaves	Remarks
KOEIMANS, see Kl. St. Kruis					
KOKOTE, see Rust en Dorp					
KONINGSPLEIN, RQ, see also Family Graves	1712-20	Governor Jeremias van Collen and his widow			
"	1720	Gov. Jonathan van Beuningen			35 h
"	1763-64	Rachel Bueno Vivas	11,000	8[48]	WICA 573, p. 144v; Bt. from †Jan Evertsz (OAC 889, no. 345)
"	1764-67	Is. Hm. Rodr. da Costa	11,000	8	OAC 891, no. 373
"	1767	†Juriaen Brugman	4,000		OAC 901, no. 91
"	1767-68	†Willem de Windt	4,000		
"	1768-72	†Mathias Pabst	4,000		OAC 904, Jan. 29, 1768
"	1772-80	Gabriel Pinedo	4,013[49]		OAC 912, no. 119
"	1780-82	†P. N. Christiaanz	10,500	11	OAC 926, no. 642
"	1782-1803	†Nicolaas Henricus and his estate	16,000	12	OAC 938, no. 240
"	1803-85	Abm. Pinedo and his descendants[50]	4,230	6	OAC 1105, no. 48
"	1885	†Pieter H. Maal	16,000		
KORAAL PATIN, see Coraal Patin					
KORAAL TABAK, see Coraal Tabak					
KORPORAAL, see Corporaal					
KORTIJN (lots)	1851	J. A. Jesurun			
L					
LABADERA					
LAND-ZEE-ZIGT, see Waterlo					7 h
LANGE TUIN, a. Goede Tielen; see also Bottelier, Union, Watervliet	1827-42	David Capriles		16[z]	[z] In 1827 (CEOE 172); 140 h

					CEOE 172
"	1842-45	Widow Abm. Jesurun			
"	1856	Jacob Henriquez			
"	1862	Jacob J. Naar			
LANGEWENST, RQ (lots)	1764	Manuel Moseh A. Correa	3,800[51]	3	OAC 891, no. 391
LELIENBERGH, a. Kl. Tuin, BENQ	1670-1796	Dutch West India Co.			395 h
"	1796-99	Gabriel Pinedo	4,800		Bt from the Government with Lange Tuin (OAC 1098, no. 154)
"	1799-1802	Abraham Pinedo	6,500	7	With Klein Tuin (OAC 1101, no. 58)
"	1802-20	Manuel Pinedo	10,000	13	Value in 1802 (OAC 1104, no. 142)
LESCH DEN DORST (east of Paradijs)	1796-1801	Samuel Is. Samuel L. Maduro	2,100		(OAC 1098, no. 208); 300(?) h
"	1801-28	Haim Gabriel da C. Gomez and his widow	1,500[52]	2[a]	[a] in 1828
"	1842	Samuel Cohen Henriquez			CEOE 172
"	1856	J. Naar			
LIGTENBERGH, near St. Michiel; see also Groot St. Michiel	1736-68	Jeosuah Henriquez and descendants	1,000		OAC 805, Oct. 9, 1736
"	1768	Benjamin Jeosuah Henriquez			OAC 904, May 31, 1768
LIGTENBERGH, a. Heronimo (near Hato), BENQ	1750-51	Moses Penso	15,000	6	OAC 828, May 11, 1753
LUFTEVREDEN, see Rust en Vrede	1870	Benjamin My. A. Correa			

48 The inventory lists among the livestock fifty fowl.

49 He bought it at auction with the small island in the Schottegat, "Het Schapen Eyland."

50 In 1828 the plantation had 31 slaves with those of the Noordkant; in 1863 there were only seven. In 1819 it was worth 4,230 pesos without the inventory (OAC 554, no. 62).

51 With an unnamed plantation.

52 Maduro exchanged his plantation for the parcels Stad-zee and Landzigt owned by Gomez. Each party estimated his holdings at 1,500 pesos.

M

Plantation or Garden	Year of ownership	Owner	Value	Slaves	Remarks
MADURO[53] (lots)	1719	Salomon L. Maduro			WICA 207, p. 581; WICA 217, p. 260
MAAY (lots near Zeelandia)	1805-09	Clara, wid. Gabriel Pinedo			OAC 1107, no. 173
MAHAAI, a. Rust, a. Bloemperk, MD, RQ	1803-18	Gabriel David da Costa Gomez and widow	12,000		OAC 1105, no. 18
"	1827	Isaac Cardoze			CGAR IV, Aug. 12, 1828
"	1828	Joseph Capriles			9 h
"	1836-67	Moses C. Henriquez and children			
"	1879	Manuel A. Correa Jr.	3,000		CGAK, Jan. 8, 1879
MALPAIS, a. Terburg, a. Texel; see also Groot and Klein	1739	Jeosuah Henriquez			OAC 1548, y. 1739; 25 h
Malpais, Daniel, Family Graves					
"	1744-64	Jeosuah Naar		30b	b In 1751 (OAC 1566, June 22, 1751; OAC 176, no. 89)
"	1768	Jacob Hisquiao Suares	12,400	26	Sold to †J. H. Ellis (OAC 904, April 9, 1768)
"	1807	Mord. de Rephael A. Correa			
"	1812	Abraham Naar		13	
"	1886	Abraham Delvalle [Henriquez]			
MANGELAS, RQ (lot)	1787	Moses Frois			
Mantancia, see Chango					
MARCHENA, JQ, a. Buena Esperansa; see Klein Marchena	1680(?)	De Marchena Family			
MA RETRAITE, see Gasparito					
MARIA ANTHONIA, BENQ (cunucu)	1789	Mordechay A. Correa			With cunucu Sablica Baddy (OAC 1095, no. 44)

Name	Year	Owner	Value	Slaves	Notes
MARIA MAAI					
MARIE PAMPOEN					38 h
MARTIJN (tuin)	1839				Known in 1713 as "east Steen Wijk" (WICA 205, p. 151)
MEEUWIJK	1849	Moses Aboab Osorio	1,000		Value in 1856
"	1862	Leah, d. Abm. Jesurun			
"		Jacob Abm. Jesurun			
MEIBERG (tuin), see also Hermanus	1842	M. A. Correa Jr.		37	With those of Oud St. Michiel; 454 h
MELANDER, see Paradijs					
MINGUILITO, see Dwars in de Weg					
MON REPOS, see Joontje					
MONTAGNE, OD	b1709-22	Moseh L. Maduro and his wid.		5	With those of Kl. St. Michiel (OAC 797, no. 306)
"	1722-36	Jeremiao and Is. M. L. Maduro			OAC 805, Feb. 27, 1736
"	1736	Is. L. Maduro and Jb. Henriquez			See Klein St. Michiel. (CEOE 172); 82 h
"	1846-47	Ribca Bueno Vivas	1,100		
"	1847-57	Hanah and Ribca, daughters of Manuel A. Correa	1,200		Sold with two slaves in 1857 for 3,500 fls.
"	1883	Jacob Is. de Castro	2,000		Sold to †F. W. Neuman in 1883
MONTE VERDE, see also Family Graves	1820	Jacob Senior			
MORGENSTER	1818-41	Aron Pinedo and his estate			CEOE 172
"	1842	David Abm. Jesurun	2,000		Value in 1853
MORGENSTER, MD	1853-55	Samuel da C. Gomez Jr.			
"	1825	J. Henriquez			Bt from †A. Mattey (CGAR II, Feb. 2, 1825)
"	1827	M. Pinedo			Bt from Henriquez (CGAR III, Jan. 24, 1827)
MORON, see Bloempot					

53 Near Ligtenbergh; originally known as Montje Maduro.

Plantation or Garden	Year of ownership	Owner	Value	Slaves	Remarks
MOUNT PLEASANT, see also Groot Malpais	1847-57	Alvares Correa Family	3,500	2	Value in 1857; 930 h
MOUNT VERNON, see Van Engelen					
MUNDO NOVO (cunucu), see also Family Graves	1801	Salomon de Castro			OAC 1009, no. 66
MUIJSBERGH (Muizenberg)	1711-20	David Dovale	4,400	15	Sold at auction for 521 pesos wi (WICA 574, p. 378); 258 h with Sint Jacob
N					
NAJOT [NAYOTH] BARAMA[54]	1741	Salomon M. L. Maduro		6	OAC 1144, Aug. 8, 1741
NEIDRUST, OD, see Cas Grandi					
NIEUWE WERELD, see Eensamhijd					
NEWPORT, a. Rust en Vrede					2.5 h
NOOIT GEDACHT (lots), BOQ, see also Brakkeput Ariba, Union, Blij en Heim	1730(?)-1748	Jacob Curiel and widow	1,950		Value in 1748 (OAC 819, May 28, 1748)
"	1792-1802	David L. Raphael	4,550	3	With a small island (OAC 1094, no. 149); in 1802 he had 39 slaves (OAC 1009, no. 12)
NOOIT GEDACHT, RQ	1789-92	Jb. Pinedo & Bros.	500		Bt and sold for the same price (OAC 1091, no. 95); 3.5 h
NOORDKANT, a. Suffisant	1660-1796	Dutch West India Co.			593 h
"	1828	Abraham Pinedo		38	With those of Koningsplein
O					
ONGEGUND	1762	Jacob Ho. Suares			OAC 1159, Apr. 30, 1762

ONVERWAGT, see Backer

	Years	Owner			References
OOST PUNT	1660-1796	Dutch West India Co.			
"	1806	Abm. Delvalle Henriquez			
"	1821-33	Haim Abinun de Lima	25c		c At his death in 1833 (CEOE 762, no. 215)
ORANGEBERG	1833-46	Haim aCohen			CEOE 172
"	1832	Joseph Fidanque			
"	1843	Elias Curiel et al.			
"	1845-85	Jeosuah Naar			
OUD SR. MARIE, see Hermanus, Meiberg					
OUD SR. MICHIEL, later St. Elizabeth; see also Blauw	1709-22	Isaac Maduro			WICA 203, p. 92b
"	1722-27	Isaac de Marchena		1,500	WICA 576, p. 674b
"	1727	Salomon L. Maduro		2,000	Sold to †A. Currie (OAC 798, no. 135)
"	1731-47	Elias Levy			OAC 818, June 26, 1747
"	1753	Jacob Elias Pareira	16	16,250d	d With Granatenberg (OAC 828, June 5, 1753)
"	1765	Jb. Hz. Fereira, Elias Hm. Pereira and Jb. Pereira	19e	15,000	e With those of Granatenberg (OAC 1558, no. 31)
"	1766-74	Mordechay Jb. Henriquez	20	12,000	OAC 900, no. 35
"	1774-78	David Jb. Henriquez	11	8,000	Sold to †G. C. Cobrol (OAC 919, no. 228)
"	b1796	Moses Frois			Sold to Rachel, wid. David Hz. Juliao
"	1796-1802	Rachel, wid. Dd. Hz. Juliao	1	4,000	OAC 1098, no. 93
"	1802-24	Abm. Dd. Henriquez Juliao and his descendants	1	4,000	OAC 1104, no. 71

54 Named after the biblical city in the time of Samuel and David (I Samuel 19:23).

Plantation or Garden	Year of ownership	Owner	Value	Slaves	Remarks
OUD ST. MICHIEL	1824-27	Leah Moses Haim Penso	19ƒ		CGAR II, Apr. 16, 1824; ƒ in 1827
"	1827	M. Pinedo			CGAR III, Dec. 28, 1827
P					
PANNEKOEK, see Klein Kloof					
PAPAYA					84 h
PARADERA					124 h
PARADERA, a. Slot van Uijtrecht					1,200 h with Sint Heronimus
PARADIJS, a. Paraiso, Melander, Onverwagt; see also Family Graves	1805	Abraham Delvalle			OAC 1107, no. 167
"	b1828	Moses Aboab Jr.			6 h
"	1828	Moses Penso			Bt from the Aboab estate
"	1840-55	Jeosuah Naar	4,500	2g	Value in 1855; g in 1842 (CEOE 172)
PARERA, a. Berg Carmel	1723(?)-45	Elias Pereira and estate			OAC 176, no. 86
"	1745	†Claas Schotborgh	3,500	1	Bt from Pereira's widow (OAC 816, no. 152)
"	1862-74	Jacob Abm. Jesurun			
"	1874-75	†M. B. Gorsira	20,000	1	Bt from Jesurun; sold in 1875 for only 10,000 fls.
PATIENTIE	1827	Haim aCohen			
PATRICK					388 h
PATTATE (tuin), BENQ	1796	Gabriel Pinedo			Sold to †Jacob Striddels
PENSO'S PARK, see Cas Cora					
PERSEVERENCIA, a. Welbedacht, a. Semi Koek (Symon Kok)	(?)	Penso Family			6 h

PISCADERA, see Groot and
Klein Piscadera, Weltevreden
PLANTATIONS, graves in the,
see Family Graves

PLANTERS, Jewish, whose plantations were unnamed:

1682   JACOB DA FONSECA

1683   ABRAHAM TOURO, Widow DAVID CARILHO, ISAQUE DE MARCHENA, DANIEL ABOAB CARDOZO, BENJAMIN CARVALHO, MANUEL DE PINA (a.k.a. Jacob Naar) in Scharloo, JACOB ULHOA, ELIAS DOVALE, JOSUAH ABOAB, Widow ESTHER MARCHENA (WICA 617, pp. 315, 319, 440)

1697   ABRAHAM ANTUNES PAREDES, 20 slaves; DAVID LEVY MENDES (ms., Ets Haim)

1709   MORDECHAY N. DE CRASTO, JACOB PRETTO (an island in the Schottegat), MANUEL ALVARES [CORREA] near Piscaderis (WICA 203, pp. 97-99, 281 v)

1713   Mrs. ABENDANA, SALOMON L. MADURO, ABRAHAM ISRAEL GOMEZ (WICA 205, pp. 533, 543, 545 v)

"   ABRAHAM PENSO whose plantation was situated near Fuik in 1723 (WICA 205, p. 526)

"   ABRAHAM HENRIQUEZ DE MESQUITA and ARON L. MADURO (WICA 205, p. 554)

1718   Estate of Dr. ISAAC DE ACOSTA (PJCAA, Dotar D, Sebat 20, 5490)

1721   SAMUEL L. MADURO, ABRAHAM DE MATTOS (WICA 576, p. 560)

1722   DAVID DE FONSECA, SELOMOH MOSEH L. MADURO, SELOMOH L. MADURO

1723   DAVID SENIOR, RAPHAEL ALVARES [Correa], ISAAC TOURO, MANUEL LEVY, JEOSUAH NAAR (WICA 208, p. 285)

1724   DAVID DE CRASTO & ELIAS PAREIRA who sold a plantation near Roodeweg to a Gentile for Ps. 3,021 wi (WICA 578, p. 55 v)

1732   ISAAC and JOSEPH TOURO who sold a plantation near Piscadera for Ps. 1,600 wi (WICA 580, p. 684)

1739   SALOMON MADURO, ISAAK JESURUN, MORDECHAY A. CORREA, ELIAS LEVY, "aan de Baaij Piscaderes" (OAC 1548, y. 1739)

1741   ARON HENRIQUEZ MORON who sold two plantations in RQ for Ps. 3,300 wi (WICA 588, p. 973 v)

"   Estate of ISAAC TOURO which sold a plantation for Ps. 1,450 wi (WICA 588, p. 971 v)

1741-46   BENJAMIN MORENO HENRIQUEZ whose plantation near Boca de Piscadera had eight slaves in 1741 and was sold in 1746 for Ps. 1,500 wi (OAC 817, no. 45; WICA 588, p. 971 v)

1742   ISAAC DA COSTA GOMEZ who bought a plantation in RQ (OAC 812, July 11, 1742)

"   DANIEL BELMONTE (OAC 812, Aug. 9, 1742)

1743   ISAAC NUNES REDONDO who sold his brother Selomoh a plantation in JQ (OAC 814, no. 297)

1744   ABRAHAM PIMENTEL who had six slaves working on his farm

Plantation or Garden	Year of ownership	Owner	Value	Slaves	Remarks
PLANTERS, Jewish, whose plantations were unnamed: (Cont.)					
	1757	Isaac Penso who sold his plantation with two lots in RQ and seven slaves to †Abraham Evertsz for Ps. 3,100 (OAC 834, no. 225)			
	1764	Rachel Touro, wid. Dr. Isaac Cardozo, whose plantation was near Vreeland (OAC 891, nos. 264-65)			
	1786	Mordechay Motta, David Naar			
	1787	Samuel Laguna, near Zeelandia (OAC 1090, no. 8)			
	1812	Aron Pinedo, Isaac Capriles, Isaac Cardozo, Widow Rephael Pinedo, Manuel Haim A. Correa, Abraham Is. Henriquez, S. J. Salom Delvalle, Manuel Pinedo, Mordechay Jeosuah Henriquez, Moses Henriquez Juliao, Gabriel Pinedo, Mordechay Benj. A. Correa, Hana A. Correa, Mother of Benjamin Henriquez, A. Naar, Mother of E. L. Maduro, Abraham Henriquez Juliao, David Capriles, Jacob de Castro[55] (OAC 484, Dec. 15, 1812)			
PLANTERSRUST	1713	Mordechay Namias de Crasto			
"	1737-53	Elias Levy	3,350	10h	OAC 806, March 1, 1737; h in 1749
PLEASANT VILLY [VALLEY], see Welgelegen					
POOS KABAAI, see also Suikertuintje	1742	David Lopez Laguna		8 h	
"	1745	Sarah da Costa Gomes	600 wi		WICA 592, p. 347v
"	1764-66	Moses Manuel A. Correa and his estate	3,800	1	Bt from †J. van Vilekens (OAC 891, no. 391)
"	1766	Manuel Moseh A. Correa	4,800	3	Sold to J. Maduro (OAC 895, no. 39)
"	1766-69	Jeremias Is. L. Maduro and his widow	4,100	6	Sold to †E. Houtschildt (OAC 906, June 9, 1769)
"	1805	†Suzanne Elizabeth van Schagen[56]			
"	1805	Abm. Samuel L. Maduro[56]	2,800	1	
"	1805	Salomon Cohen Henriquez	2,800	1	

1827-46	"	Esther, wid. Abm. Jb. Jesurun			‡ In 1828; ten in 1842
1846-55	"	Leah Jesurun Monsanto	9‡		CGAR IX, Sept. 28, 1846
1855	"	Elias S. L. Maduro		10,000	Value in 1855
1923	"	Manuel L. Maduro57			
1767	Popo, a. De Goede Hoop, BOQ	Elias Israel		2,625	With Zwarte Moriaan (OAC 901, Dec. 1, 1767); sold to †J. Loman
1773	"	David Jacob Henriquez			OAC 912, no. 114
1775	"	Abigail, wid. M. Penso		3,500	OAC 914, no. 26
1781	"	Widow Isaac Penso		1,400	OAC 933, no. 604
1789-91	"	Salomon de Castro			OAC 1091, no. 95
1791	"	Abm. Alexander Weiss	2	2,000	OAC 1093, no. 108
1792	"	Children of A. A. Weiss			OAC 1094, no. 127
1805	"	David Is. Henriquez	1	1,000	Bt from †N. Evertsz
1807	"	Abraham Bueno Vivas			
1815	"	Abm. [Roiz] Mendes			CGAR I, May 2, 1815
1839	"	Moseh Aboab Osorio (?)			35 h
1876-98	"	Jb. J. Naar and his estate			593 h
PORTO MARIE					
PRINCENHOFF, RQ					
1762-63		Isaac Mendes	4	2,600	OAC 917, no. 46
1826	"	J. de Sola			Sold to †P. F. de Haseth (CGAR II, Oct. 27, 1826)
1837-53	"	Elias Curiel and his estate	22ʲ		ʲ With those of Rust en Vrede in 1847 (CGANA, 1847, Apr. 12, 1847)
1853	"	Salomon E. L. Maduro		6,035	CGAT, 1853, no. 80

55 These nineteen planters petitioned Governor John Hodgson on December 8, 1812, to let their slaves work on the plantations Sundays since they rested on Saturday and on Jewish holidays. The petition was denied.

56 Widow of Dominie J. G. Muller. She sold it to Maduro who sold it the same day to Henriquez (OAC 1107, nos. 185, 188).

57 The documents contradict themselves. One of the cadastral documents of June 2, 1911, states that Poos Kabaai belonged to Lea Jesurun Monsanto and that she left it to her son Joseph in 1911.

Plantation or Garden	Year of ownership	Owner	Value	Slaves	Remarks
PRINCENHOFF, RQ	1923	Manuel L. Maduro			
PUERTO ESCONDIDO, JQ	1752	†J. Spadien	2,250	2	OAC 826, April 18, 1752
R					
RAFAEL, see Klein Piscadera					
RAMELJOSA, see Harmonie					
RAVENSLOT, a. Donkerberg, a. Jack Evertsz, a. Rust en Burgh, a. Bloem en Hoof	1827-57	Joseph My. Henriquez and his son Mordechay			122 h with Weltevreden
"	1857	†J. G. de Pool	2,000		Bt from My. J. Henriquez 714 h
RIF, a. Ste. Marie, WD, see also Family Graves	1660-1796	Dutch West India Co.			
"	1832-34	Joseph Capriles			CGAR IV, May 20, 1832
"	1843	Abraham Capriles		51	CEOE 172
"	1844-51	Esther, wid. Abm. J. Jesurun and her estate		50k	k In 1846 (CC, Feb. 27, 1846)
"	1851	Moses Abm. Jesurun		42	
"	1855	Leah Senior,[58] wid. Moses Jesurun		69[59]	CGAT, 1855, nos. 3-4
"	1855	Anjel Jb. Jesurun	52,650	69[59]	
"	1862	Jacob Abm. Jesurun	30,000 wi		
RIJKENBERG, OD	1828	J. de Solas			
RIJKENBERG, see Girouette					
RINCON	1737	Jeosuah Naar			
RIO MAGDALENA	1838	Marchena Family (?)			160 h
RONDE KLIP	1798-1807	Dr. Joseph Capriles[60]	38,000	50	Bt from †G. Erasmus (OAC 1100, no. 3); 825 h
"	1876-98	Jb. Jeosuah Naar and his estate	27,000		Bt from †H. N. Pietersz

	Years	Owner	No.	Value in 1898	References
"	1899	Herman Cohen Henriquez		25,600	
Rooi Canary[61] (Rio Canario)	1660-1750(?)	Dutch West India Co.	5	8,500[63]	OAC 1084, no. 29
Rooi Carootje,[62] see also Rust en Vrede	1780-82	Manuel Moshe A. Correa			
"	1818	Widow Raphael Pinedo		11,500wi	OAC 554, no. 428
"	1819-24	Jb. Salomon de Castro	6	12,000	OAC 1121, no. 73
"	1824-27	Jeosuah Jeudah Henriquez	26[1]		Sold to †Helena Raphael in 1827
"	1834-53	Elias Curiel and his estate	3	5,300	[1] In 1842 (CEOE 172)
"	1853-1923	S. E. L. Maduro and his estate			Bt from the Curiel estate
"	1923	Manuel L. Maduro		15,000	31.16 h
"	Since 1925	S. A. L. Maduro			
Roose Tak, JQ, see also Family Graves	1739	Isaac Aboab		1,000	OAC 1549, Oct. 6, 1739
"	1739-44	David Senior and son Jacob		3,500wi	WICA 591, p. 744v
"	1792	†Pierre Brion (?)			P. Brion's son-in-law
"	1803	†Joseph Foulke			
"	1803-07	Jb. Mordechay Henriquez		2,700	Bt from †Foulke (OAC 1105, no. 92)
Rozendaal	1756-58	Sarah, wid. Aron da C. Gomez	2	2,000	Sold for 2,600 ps. (OAC 837, July 4, 1758)

58 Grandmother of the Socialist Daniel de Leon.

59 The inventory also lists 87 cows, two horses, two mules, 48 donkeys, 352 sheep, 254 goats, 1,060 barrels of salt, two canoes, a pontoon, a boat, a corn mill, and so forth.

60 The deed was made in the name of Isaac Capriles although the true owner was his father, the physician. (See Dr. Capriles' will in Emmanuel, *Precious Stones*, p. 404; OAC 1023, no. 21.) In addition to the slaves the plantation had 1,000 sheep, 101 cows, six horses, 12 donkeys, a limekiln, and so forth (OAC 1100, no. 3).

61 Abraham Henriquez Moron fruitlessly tried buying it in 1709. Gabriel Levy rented it from the WIC in 1717 at a yearly rental of 291 pesos.

62 The "Statute of the Kingdom of the Netherlands" was drafted on this plantation in 1954 by the ministers of the Netherlands Antilles, and Surinam, respectively (Jan Hartog, *The Story of the Maduros* [Aruba, 1962], p. 122).

63 Correa bought it at public auction from the estate of †Isaac Paul van Schagen (son of Fiscal Jan van Schagen) in 1780 for 2,250 ps. (OAC 931, nos. 196-98).

Plantation or Garden	Year of ownership	Owner	Value	Slaves	Remarks
ROZENDAAL, see Ararat					
ROZENDAAL, JQ					
ROZENDAAL, RQ, near Rooi Catootje	1787-88	Hanah, d. Isaac Calvo	1,600	1	OAC 907, no. 74, y. 1770
"					OAC 1089, no. 31
"	1788-89	Moses Frois	1,600	1	OAC 1090, no. 36
"	1789	Salomoh Jb. L. Maduro	2,500	1	OAC 1091, no. 110
"	1789	Hanah Mordechay Calvo	2,000		OAC 1091, no. 168
"	1792	Salomoh Jb. L. Maduro	1,650		OAC 1094, no. 110
"	1794	†E. Weber			Bt from Maduro
"	1794-1805	Moses Cohen Henriquez Jr.			Bt from Weber (OAC 1095, no. 128)
"	1805	Ribca, wid. Joseph Curiel	1,900	3	OAC 1107, no. 157
RUST, see also Bloemperk, Mahaai	1828	Widow Aron Motta			4 h
RUST EN BURGH, near Piscadera	b1737	Elias Levy			OAC 806, March 6, 1737
"	1737-38	Jacob David Senior	3,000wi		WICA 584, p. 576v
RUST EN BURGH, form. Rust en Plant, a. Groot Kwartier, Vreeland, Vergenoeging	1737	Governor Johan van Collen[64]			22 h
"	1863-74	Daniel Jesurun Jr.			With Vreeland and an islet
"	1874	Jacob Salomon Senior	14,000		With Vreeland (CGAK, Aug. 23, 1874)
"	1874	Elias Jesurun Jr.	14,000		
	1900	Edward Jesurun	20,000		
RUST EN DORP, a. Kokote	1910(?)	E. Osorio			1.5 h
RUST EN HOFF (lot in Otrabanda)	1795	Salomon de Castro	2,745		OAC 1097, no. 171
RUST EN PAD, WD	1849	Jacob Jeosuah Naar			480h with Klein Sta. Martha and San Mango

Plantation	Date	Owner	Area	Slaves	Notes
RUSTENPAD, MD	1858	Joseph Jacob Henriquez			
"	1862	Henriquez & Naar			
RUST EN VREE, RQ[65]	1737-41	Aron Henriquez Moron[66]	3,000 wi		With the Uitzigt (WICA 584, p. 578v)
"	1741-43	†Jan Luls	9,000	15	OAC 814, no. 235
"	1743-54	Joseph da C. Gomez	5,500		OAC 871, no. 191
"	1754	†Samuel Striddels	8,550		With the Uitzigt (OAC 892, no. 264)
"	1764-65	Bn. Moses C. Henriquez[67]	9,000	6	OAC 899, no. 83
	Mar. 1766	Abraham Is. Senior and Mordechay Moseh Penso	6,492:4		Bt Senior's half interest (OAC 900, no. 53)
	Oct. 1766	Mordechay Moseh Penso			OAC 931, no. 196
RUST EN VREE, BOQ	1781	Manuel de Moses A. Correa	2,250		OAC 901, 84
"	1767-69	Abraham Is. Henriquez Moron	3,000	7	OAC 906, July 11, 1769
"	1769	†Hendrick de Pool	1,900	3	1.5 h
"	1815	Isaac Cardozo			CEOE 172
RUST EN VREDE	1842	David A. Jesurun	1,500		Sold to †J. Lammont
"	1846	Esther Abm. Jesurun's estate	3,000		
"	1853	David Pardo Jr.		1	41 h (OAC 555, no. 176)
RUST EN VREDE, a. Brakkeput Abao, OD	1818	Widow D. M. Henriquez	2,600 wi		
"	1840-47	Moses de Castro Jr.	2,500	4m	m In 1842 (CEOE 172)
"	1858	Samuel da C. Gomez Jr.	600		
"	1862	Abigail Bueno Vivas			

[64] Van Collen sold it to †G. Lixraaven for 22,000 ps. with 71 slaves (OAC 806, June 16, 1737).

[65] This plantation may have been known in the 19th century as Rust en Vrede.

[66] Moron bought it from †Jan Luls (OAC 807, Aug. 12, 1737). He had 15 slaves in 1737 (OAC 1144, March 9, 1741).

[67] Henriquez bought it from †Mathias Pabst in 1764 and sold it to †Pieter de Veer Vos, who later sold it to Senior and Penso.

Plantation or Garden	Year of ownership	Owner	Value	Slaves	Remarks
RUST EN VREDE, a. Karpata; see also Rooi Catootje	1811	Samuel Is. L. Maduro			(CGAR I, Jan. 8, 1811); 7(?) h
RUST EN VREDE, a. Luftevreden					4.75 h
RUST EN VREDE, a. Newport					2.5 h
S					
SABLICA BADDY, see Maria Anthonia					
SALINA ABAO, see Goed Heen Komen					
SALINA ARIBA, see Family Graves					
SAN MANGO, see Klein Sta. Martha					
SAN PEDRO (St. Pieter, St. Pierre)	1722	Rachel Naar, wid. Mordechay Ho. Henriquez			(WICA 603, p. 1366); 305 h
"	1757	Dominie Wigboldus Rasvelt and †the widow Van Uijtrecht		11	OAC 873, no. 19. See Asencion and Welgelegen.
"	1842-46	Widow Aron Motta		13	CEOE 172
"	1846-51	Bn. and My. A. Correa	2,020	2	Sold in 1851 for 3,900 ps. (CGAT, 1851, nos. 84-85)
"	1853	Abigail Motta, wid. Isaac de Castro	3,600		
"	1861	Jacob J. Naar	2,100	3	
STA. BARBARA,[68] BOQ	1751-58	Moses Penso and his estate	73,000	300[n]	n With those of the Fuik
"	1758	†Widow Willem Meyer	67,500	300	See Fuik; 1,202 h
"	b1875	Jacob Jeosuah Naar			
"	1875	†M. B. Gorsira	80,000[o]		o After discovery of its phosphate deposits
"	1876(?)	†J. Godden & Gorsira			

"	1912	†Hope & Co.	600,000p		p Only a half interest (OAC 892, no. 87); 604 h
STA. CATHARINA	1764-70	Isaac Mendes	29,000	466q	910 h
STA. CRUX (Sint Kruis), see also St. Jan, Family Graves					
SANTA MARIA MAGDALENA, JQ	1805	†Widow Victor Tessel	3,400q	4	q With inventory; sold to †Waters Forbes Apr. 5, 1805 (OAC 1107, no. 64)
SANTA MARTHA, see Groot and Klein Sta. Martha, St. Jan					
SANTA ROSA	1824-26	Moses Penso			Sold to †G. M. Ellis (CGAR II, March 8, 1824; III, Aug. 31, 1826)
SASSO (lots)	?	Sasso Family			
SAVAAN, BOQ, a. Kanga	1763	Jb. Elias Jesn Henriquez	3,000	4	Sold to †H. Evertsz (OAC 889, no. 62); 50 h
"	1774	Isaac Pardo & Sons			OAC 913, no. 69
"	1900?	J. R. da Costa Gomez			
SAVANA, near Steenen Coraal; see also Bona Vista	1715-17	Manuel A. Correa	550 wi		WICA 572, p. 754v
SAVONET (near Zorgvliet)	1717-41	Raphael A. Correa and his widow	675 wi		WICA 589, p. 85v; 712 h

68 Famed for its phosphate mines, the Santa Barbara merits a brief history. In 1668 it was jointly owned by Governor Mathias Beck and Government Secretary †Willem Juijst who sold his share to Beck in 1669 (WICA 208, pp. 227-8). Governor Jan Doncker owned it in 1677. His widow †Aletta Doman sold it to †Willem Meyer in 1705 with 101 slaves for 25,000 pesos. The deed was made out in 1708. After 1715 it was inherited by †Frederick Eck to whom it still belonged in 1724 (WICA 208, p. 151; WICA 577, pp. 828-49). The Santa Barbara again came into the possession of the Meyer family. They sold it to Penso with the Fuik plantation and a house on Breedestraat for 73,000 pesos (OAC 1566, June 1, 1751). Penso's heirs sold the two plantations to the Widow Meyer without the house. In 1763 it belonged to †Laurens de Mey Scholten and †Sara de Windt, widow of †Gijsbert Jan Vos. At the end of 1763 †F. W. Hermes bought it with 201 slaves for 60,000 ps. (OAC 889, no. 281; OAC 891, no. 79).

69 Besides the slaves there were 50 cows, 400 sheep, 250 goats, 10 horses, and so forth. After having sustained heavy losses at sea, Mendes was forced to sell his plantation at public auction in 1770. The Widow †Gerard Schonenboom bought it with four slaves for Ps. 16,201 (OAC 908, no. 27).

Plantation or Garden	Year of ownership	Owner	Value	Slaves	Remarks
SCHAPEN EYLAND	1766-68	Manuel and Moseh A. Correa	500		OAC 904, Sept. 6, 1768
SCHERPENHEUVEL, BOQ, see also Watervliet	1813-18	Jacob Lopez Penha	13,500 wi	6ʳ	Value in 1818 (OAC 554, no. 70); r in 1813
"	1827	Moses Henriquez Juliao		41	
"	1842-47	Manuel My. A. Correa and daughters			
"	1847-57	Jacob Abraham Jesurun	4,130	3	Bt from Correa (CGAR IX, April 19, 1847)
"	1857	†J. Ph. Evertsz	10,000		Bt from Jesurun
"	1875-85	Elias Dovale Mendes	20,000	7	Bt from †Ch. J. de Haseth with Watervliet, a. Gedachtenis
"	1891	Jesurun Penso			
"	b1892	M. E. Penso			
"	1892	Vicariate	24,000		Bt from the Penso estate together with the Watervliet
SCHRAALENBERG, BOQ	1794-1804	Widow Moses Henriquez			OAC 1096, no. 63; 1106, no. 66
SEBEL MANKOE (garden), MD	1843	The Pinedo estate			CEOE 172
SEMI KOEK (SYMON KOK), a. Welbedagt; see Perseverencia					
SERO FORTUNA, a. Sero Papaya (garden)	1805-[1847?]	Abraham Henriquez Juliao	7,240	1	Together with Zegening, a. Steenen Coraal (OAC 1107, no. 67); 64 h
"	1857	Aron Henriquez Juliao and Raphael N. de Crasto			
SIBERIE	1825	Manuel Pinedo Jr.			
SINT ELIZABETH, BENQ, see also Oud St. Michiel, a. Klein Blauw	1802-08	Wid. David Hz. Juliao and son			717 h with Fontein

"	1815-20	Gabriel Pinedo	7,000	18s	Value in 1820; s with those of Grote Blauw (OAC 1058, no. 82)
"	1841-43	Elias Penso	15,500	29t	t With those of Blauw (CEOE 172)
"	1879	Manuel Penso Curiel			226 h with Grote Blauw
St. Ention	1714	Mordechay Henriquez	4,000 wi		WICA 571, Sept. 21, 1714
St. Heronimos, a. Cabritenberg; see Barber, Family Graves					1,200 h with Paradera, a. Slot van Uijtrecht
St. Jacob	1716-28	Benjamin da Costa d'Andrade	1,200 wi		(WICA 572, p. 754v; 579, p. 379b); 258 h with Muizenberg
St. Jago (lots)	1790-98	Abraham (Antoine) Delvaille	1,201	68u	Bt from †G. R. Pletz (OAC 1092, no. 183); u with those of Coraal Tabak
"	1798	Emanuel da C. Gomez & Bros.	8,230		OAC 1100, no. 205
"	1798-1826	Haim Gabriel da C. Gomez and his widow			CGAR III, Oct. 27, 1826
"	1827 ?-1862	Abraham Hm. Senior and his descendants			
St. Jan[70]	1712	Elias Pareira	12,000	82v	v Including 20 children; 657 h

[70] Pareira bought the plantation from †Judith van Vilkens, widow of Apero van der Hoeven (co-Governor, 1685-86). The inventory also lists a sugar mill, a "house" for distilling sugar, etc., 47 cows, 302 sheep, 374 goats, 5 horses, a mule, and so forth (WICA 207, p. 711; WICA 577, pp. 162-65). It is not known how long Pareira or Pereyra kept the plantation. He died in 1744. Before 1770 it belonged to †Laurents de Mey who sold it in 1770 with fifteen slaves, animals and everything necessary for distilling sugar to †Gerard Striddels for 26,550 ps. (OAC 907, no. 19). In 1804 during the absence of her husband Albert Kikkert from Curaçao (governor from 1816-1819), †Maria Cornelia van Uijtrecht sold it to †Joseph Ellis de Veer, along with six slaves, various sugar mills, sugar distilling "house", blacksmith and carpentry workshops, for 21,500 ps. De Veer sold it to †Mathias Schotborgh in 1806 for 25,539:4:2 ps. with the same inventory (OAC 1108, no. 54).

In our opinion sugar was not distilled in Curaçao in great quantity in 1804. Sugarcane seems to have been cultivated fairly well in 1670 on the St. Kruis or Santa Crux plantation (Hamelberg, p. 84). From 1675-1689 the Curaçao Government shipped 274,092 lbs. of sugar to the directors of the WIC and very little from 1689-1712 (Verspreide W. I. Stukken 394, Reports on Curaçao [1675-1700]). There were sugar mills on the Piscadera plantation in 1715. According to Dominie Bosch, the Santa Crux and Santa Martha plantations, during Governor Kikkert's incumbency, grew small quantities of sugar which was used in the manufacture of rum (Bosch, I, p. 185). See also OAC 917, no. 111, y. 1777, about Klein Sta. Martha.

663

Plantation or Garden	Year of ownership	Owner	Value	Slaves	Remarks
Sr. Joris, a. Silberio; see also Groot and Klein St. Joris	1820-22	J. Henriquez and M. Cohen Henriquez			Bt from †G. M. Ellis (OAC 239, Aug. 6, 1822)
"	1822-25	†G. M. Ellis			Bt from Henriquez
"	1825-28	Manuel Pinedo Jr.		12[w]	[w] In 1828
Sr. Kruis, see Sta. Crux					
Sr. Michiel, see Groot- Klein- and Oud St. Michiel					
Sr. Nicolaas, BOQ	1803-12	Moses Henriquez Juliao	8,210	7[t]	OAC 1105, no. 40; 339 h with Casjoe Tuin 388 h
Sr. Patrick or Patrick					
Sr. Pierre, see San Pedro					
Sr. Pieter, see San Pedro					
Sr. Sebastiaan	1709-22	Jacob Ulhoa[72] and son Abm. Ulhoa Jr.			(WICA 203, p. 92a; WICA 576, p. 673b; OAC 797, no. 18); 180 h
Sr. Silvester, BENQ, see also Wacauw	1792	Gabriel Pinedo	9,100[x]	16	[x] With Wacauw and Bartholoolsche Kust
"	1802	Aron Gabriel Pinedo	36,000	72[y]	[y] With those of Wacauw (OAC 1104, no. 155)
Sr. Sioen	1719-30	Widow Mordechay Henriquez	1,300	40[z]	[z] In 1730 (OAC 1136, Jan., 1730; WICA 574, p. 422)
Ste. Marie, see Rif					
Slangenbaai, see Kl. St. Michiel, Weltevrede, Terra Royal and Takie-Takie					
'T (het) Slot van Uijtrecht, see Paradera					
See Kᵃᵉ, BENQ	1745-47	David Lopez Laguna	600		OAC 816, Jan. 21, 1745

	Years	Owner	Value		Reference
SOLEDAD, see Koedisje					
SONBY TUIN					
SOUAX, see Klein Malpais					
STADSRUST, BOQ	1660-1796	Dutch West India Co.			OAC 996, no. 205
"	1796	Salomon Samuel L. Maduro	4,500		Sold to †L. Booije (OAC 1100, no. 207)
"	1798	Abm. Samuel L. Maduro	4,650	6	Bt from †Booije with the lot Uytzigt (OAC 1107, no. 191)
"	1805	Salomon Salom Delvalle	6,200		
"	1870	Manuel Penso Curiel	6,000		
"	1875	Sarah, wid. Isaac Dovale	7,000		
"	1878	†J. Rojer	300		OAC 1098, no. 57
STAD-ZEE & LAND GEZICHT (lots near St. Jago)	1795-1801	Samuel Jesurun Pinto	300[73]		OAC 1103, nos. 53, 55
"	1801	David Leon de Meza	720		Bt from †Gerrit Specht (OAC 1102, no. 72)
STAD ZEE EN LAND ZICHT (near Parera's Garden); see also Family Graves	1800	Haim Gabriel da C. Gomez	1,500		See Lesch den Dorst (OAC 1103, no. 42)
"	1801	Samuel Is. L. Maduro			OAC 1074, no. 40b
"	1825	Grace, wid. Benj. Lindo			CGAR III, Oct. 6, 1826
STADSZICHT, see Deyn					
STARCKENBORGH, JQ, near Bleij en Heim					
STEENEN CORAAL, a. Zegening or Vrede	1805-62	Abraham Henriquez Juliao	7,240	37	See Sero Fortuna; 120 h.

[71] The inventory also lists 32 cows, 19 donkeys, 313 sheep, 47 goats, 2 horses and, very oddly, 20 pigs; fishing canoes, fishnets, and so forth.

[72] Ulhoa most probably owned it since 1683.

[73] De Meza sold his land the same day for 650 pesos.

Plantation or Garden	Year of ownership	Owner	Value	Slaves	Remarks
STEENRIJK, formerly Steen Wijk; see also Cher Asile, Family Graves	1804-09	Rachel, wid. Moses Frois	825		OAC 1106, no. 30
SUFFISANT, see Noordkant					
SUIKERTUINTJE,[74] see also Poos Kabaai, Family Graves	1754	Governor Faesch			OAC 1107, nos. 185, 187
"	1803-05	David Is. Henriquez	4,300	3	Bt from †B. L. Rappard (OAC 1105, no. 85)
"	1805-27?	Jacob Salomon de Castro	6,300	6	OAC 1107, no. 120
"	1827-62	Jacob Senior and his estate	14,000	2[a]	[a] In 1828 and in 1842
"	1901	J. Senior			
"	1902	M. B. de Marchena			
SUIKERTUINTJE, RQ	1805	Abm. Samuel L. Maduro	2,800		Bt from Dominie J. G. Muller (OAC 1107, no. 188)
"	1808	Widow Aron Aelion			
SUURZAK, see Zuurzak					
SUURZAK, RQ (lots)	1783-84	Sarah, wid. Eliao Hm. Pereira[75]	800[b]	1	[b] With Terra Secoe
"	1809	Widow Aron Aelion's estate			OAC 1027, no. 57
T					
TAKIE-TAKIE, BENQ, a. Slangenbaai; see also Weltevrede (lots)	1818	Samuel da Costa Gomez	2,000wi		OAC 554, no. 649
TERBURG A TEXEL, see Malpais					
TERRA ROYAL, a. Slangenbaai; see also Weltevrede	1740	Isaac Aboaff			
"	1741	Moses A. Correa			OAC 811, no. 365

TERRA SECOE, RQ	1783-84	Sara, wid. E. Hm. Pereira			See Zuurzak.
"	1809	Jacob Senior			
"	1852	Henry Nathan			
TEXEL, see Malpais					
THONY KOENTJE	1866-73	D. and Judith Jesurun Pinto			CGAR IX, March 3, 1873
TOEGIFT	1743	Joseph da Costa Gomez	2,000 wi		WICA 591, p. 86v
U					
UIJLENBURG, see Jan Zoutvat					
UITVLUGT, JQ (cunucu)	1789-90	Abm. Henriquez Melhado and Samuel de Casseres	1,350	1	OAC 1091, no. 27
UITZIGT, RQ, form. Zoutpan	1764	Benjamin Cohen Henriquez			See Rust en Vree.
"	1767	Leah, wid. Isaac Levy	1,500	2	OAC 901, no. 42
"	1848	Sarah da Costa Gomez			CGANA, 1848, II, no. 52
UNION,[76] BENQ	1819-43	Widow Rephael Pinedo and Benjamin A. Correa	26,000	36[c]	[c] In 1819; 37 slaves in 1843 when it belonged to Bn. A. Correa only
V					
VALENTIJN, a. Bragasmit, see Zorgvliet, Family Graves					

[74] Suikertuintje belonged to the WIC. In 1709 David Senior, owner of an adjoining plantation, offered the WIC 4,000 pesos for it but was turned down (letter of Governor Abraham Beck, Aug. 10, 1709, to the WIC [WICA 203, p. 139v]). According to Hamelberg (p. 89), this plantation was sold by Governor Bernagie's successor, Nicolaas van Beck (1700-04). This statement is erroneous because Suikertuintje still belonged to the WIC in 1709. Probably it was sold to David Senior by Jeremias van Collen (1710-15), a business partner of David's brother Philipe Henriquez.

[75] The widow Pereira sold it in 1784 with a slave for 1,150 ps. (OAC 1085, nos. 197-199; OAC 1086, no. 308).

[76] This plantation consisted of the plantations Westerveld, de Drie Gebroeders (a. Veeris), Eendracht and of the parcels Nooit Gedagt, Vergenoeging, de Lange Tuin, Dona Palia and Boca Chica. The Widow Pinedo and her son-in-law called it Union.

Plantation or Garden	Year of ownership	Owner	Value	Slaves	Remarks
VAN ENGELEN,[77] a. Engelenberg, Mount Vernon	1705-19	Salomon (Montje) L. Maduro			Bt from Governor van Engelen's widow
"	1719	Benjamin de Casseres	8,000 wi		Sold to †Mathias Brugman (WICA 575, p. 328; WICA 207, p. 721; WICA 571, p. 422v)
"	1840-75	Haim Cohen Henriquez and his estate		2[d]	[d] In 1842 (CEOE 172)
"	1875	Samuel Cohen Henriquez	6,000		
"	1936	Angel S. Cohen Henriquez			34 h
VARSE PUT	1743	Benjamin Vaz Faro	2,225:6	8	OAC 814, no. 199
"	1828	(Sebel) [Samuel?] Pereira		12	
"	1842	Benjamin Suares			CEOE 172
VEERIS,[78] see also Drie Gebroeders, Union	1828-50	Benjamin A. Correa	19,700[e]	20[e]	[e] With the Westerveld in 1850; 62 h
VERGENOEGD, OD	1817-21	Mordechay Raphael A. Correa	5,500 wi[f]		[f] In 1818 (OAC 554, no. 470)
VERGENOEGING, BENQ (cunucu), near Piscadera	1775-79	Abraham L. Henriquez	1,800	1	OAC 914, no. 146
"	1779	Manuel Raphael A. Correa	500		OAC 921, no. 91
VERGENOEGING					13 h
VERGENOEGING, near Brievengat, BOQ, see also Jan Jongbloed	1856-58	Moses Is. Henriquez Juliao	5,000		Bt from †N. Evertsz and sold to †C. Sprock in 1858 for 2,300 fls.
"	1900(?)	Rachel, wid. Bn. P. Brandao			
VERSALI, see Family Graves					
VER ZICHT, BOA (lots)	1802	Widow Aron Aelion	600		OAC 1104, no. 123
VISTON	1900(?)	E. M. Curiel			7 h
VREDE, BO	1765-68	Samuel Is. L. Maduro	4,800	6	OAC 1558, no. 72

668

Name	Date	Owner	Value	No.	Notes
"	1768	Rachel, wid. Salomon L. Maduro			Bt from Samuel (OAC 904, Jan. 12, 1768)
"	1768-82	Moses and Debora Henriquez	2,600	5	Bt from the Widow Maduro's estate
VREDE, BOQ	1842	J. Henriquez			CEOE 172
"	1787	Moses Frois			See Dwars in de Weg.
VREDE, see Cerito, Klein Kwartier					
VREDENBERG, a. Cunucu Abao, BOQ; see also Cas Cora, Jan Zoutvat	1767	Salomon Haim Calvo[79]	13,000	30	Bt from †J. Evertsz (OAC 901, no. 8)
"	1801	Isaac Cardozo	10,000	9	OAC 1103, no. 101; 66(?) h
VREDENBERG, JQ	1767-74	Josias de Casseres[80]	5,880	1	OAC 904, July 6, 1767
VREDENBERG, RQ	1774-79	Isaac Jb. L. Maduro	3,800	5	Bt from †M. de Pool (OAC 913, no. 138)
"	1779-81	David Henriquez[81]	1,625		Maduro's son-in-law (OAC 923, no. 719)
VREDENBERG, OD	1818	Mordechay R. A. Correa	12,000 wi		OAC 554, no. 470
"	1820	S. S. Delvalle			
"	1857-62	†J[an]. H[endrick]. Senior	3,000 wi		Value in 1862
VREDENBERG	b1860	Jacob Henriquez Juliao			
"	1860	Salomon E. L. Maduro			Bt from Juliao
VREELAND, RQ, see also Rust en Burgh	1764-70	Manuel Moseh A. Correa	8,700	12	OAC 891, nos. 264-65
"	1770-74	David Jb. Henriques	8,400	14[82]	OAC 907, no. 72
"	1774-78	Mordechay Jb. Henriquez	3,500	12	OAC 913, no. 147

[77] Planted by the co-Governor, Willem van Engelen, in 1686 (WICA 574, p. 424).

[78] Veeris and Union are almost synonymous.

[79] Calvo sold it ten months later with thirty slaves to †J. C. Hoevens for 12,000 pesos.

[80] Casseres sold it in 1774 with a small island and a slave to †F. Daal for 3,500 ps. (OAC 913, no. 166).

[81] His widow sold it to †J. Crison with a slave for 2,500 ps. (OAC 933, no. 643).

[82] The inventory also listed 120 sheep, 12 cows, 6 horses, 4 donkeys, much fowl, and so forth.

Plantation or Garden	Year of ownership	Owner	Value	Slaves	Remarks
VREELAND, RQ	1778	†Cornelis Stuyling	3,720	12	OAC 920, no. 336
"	b1874	Jacob Salomon Senior	14,000g		g With the Rust en Burgh
"	b1874	Daniel Jesurun Jr.			25 h with part of Gaito
"	1874	Elias Jesurun Jr.			Bt from the Daniel Jesurun estate
"	b1896	Abm. Benjamin Jesurun			
"	1900	Edward Jesurun	20,000		Bt from A. B. Jesurun
VREUGDE, see Vreugdendaal					
VREUGDENBERG, OD (garden)	1860	Abigail Bueno Vivas	700		
"	1873	Judith, wid. Gabriel Cohen Henriquez	1,450		Sold to a Gentile who in turn sold it to Dr. Capriles
"	1879	Hana, w. Dr. David Capriles	3,000		Sold in 1880 for 2,000 fls.
"	April 1881	Dr. David R. Capriles	1,050		
"	Dec. 1881	Moses Capriles	1,000		
VREUGENDAAL,[83] a. Vreugde, a. Damacór	1856	Salomon E. L. Maduro	1,600		Bt from †N. Evertsz
"	1923	Manuel L. Maduro			
VREUGENDAAL, RQ	Jan. 1770	David Jb. Henriquez	2,400	5	OAC 907, no. 24; 35 h
"	Apr. 1770-1781	Manuel M. A. Correa[84]	2,400	4	OAC 907, no. 73
"	1781	Daniel L. Penha	2,000	1	Bt from Correa (OAC 931, no. 337)
"	1789-1801	David Haim Dovale[85]	3,500	3	OAC 1103, no. 75
"	1825-28	Isaac Senior		20h	h In 1828; bt from †C. de Haseth
VREUGENDAAL, OD	1858	Jacob Henriquez Juliao	5,000		Bt from †N. Evertsz (CGAT, 1858, no. 35)
VRIENDENWIJK, form. Buena Vista, BOQ	1798-99	Judith, w. Samuel da C. Gomez	1,400		OAC 1100, no. 8

"	1799-1802	Haim Abinun de Lima	1,300		OAC 1101, no. 49
"	1802	†Jan Born	2,375	2	Bt from De Lima (OAC 1104, no. 149)
"	b1842	Wid. E. Jesurun Henriquez		27[i]	i In 1842 (CEOE 172)
"	1847	Jesurun Henriquez estate	3,000	2	CGAR IX, July 20, 1847
"	1889	David Ricardo	2,000		CEOE 172
VRIJ EN RUST	1842	Manuel Penso			
VRIJHEIJT, JQ	1749	Mordechay A. Correa	6,000		Sold to †Jan Hendricks (OAC 822, June 20, 1749); 35 h with Rust en Vrede and Goed Gezicht
VRISSENBURGH	1749-68	Jeosuah Raphael Henriquez and his descendants		50[j]	j With those of Groot St. Michiel (OAC 902, nos. 110, 114)
W					
WACAUW, BENQ	1792-1869	Gabriel Pinedo[86] and his descendants	9,100	16[k]	k In 1792; 1,019 h
"	1869	Gabriel Pinedo			
WASH TUIN, RQ	1729-41	Moses A. Correa[87]	1,500	12	OAC 1136, Aug. 5, 1729; OAC 804, no. 479; WICA 579, p. 809v
" (cunucu)	1741-45	David Lopez Laguna	600	1	OAC 813, no. 251

[83] In 1860 it belonged to Maduro and was assessed at 5,000 fls.

[84] Correa sold Henriquez his Vreeland plantation the same day for 8,400 pesos.

[85] Dovale bought it from †H. Nieuwkerk and sold it to †J. Corser with five slaves and another lot for 5,000 pesos.

[86] Pinedo bought it in 1792 at auction from the †Willem Martin estate together with St. Silvester, and Bartholsche Kust. In 1802 Aron Pinedo bought it from his father's estate for 36,000 ps. The inventory listed 72 slaves, 189 cows, 1,464 sheep, 813 goats, 46 horses, 29 donkeys, 3 mules, a large quantity of maize, lime, salt, two canoes, fishnets, two turtle nets (OAC 1104, no. 155). In 1818 the plantation was assessed at 36,000 ps. without the inventory (OAC 554, no. 624). The widow Aron Pinedo sold it in 1824 to her two sons Isaac and Moise (CGAR II, Feb. 27, 1824). In 1828 there were 49 slaves on the plantation. The Wacauw was one of the most fertile plantations on the island.

[87] Correa sold it in 1741 with Terra Royal to †Isaac Schoon with four slaves for Ps. 5,300 (OAC 811, no. 366).

Plantation or Garden	Year of ownership	Owner	Value	Slaves	Remarks
WATERLO, a. Land-zee-zigt					
WATERVLIET, a. Gedachtenis; see also Lange Tuin	b1842	Wid. Esther A. J. Jesurun			121 h
"					CEOE 172
"	1843-53	Jacob Abm. Jesurun	3,000		Sold to †J. Ph. Evertsz
"	1877	Elias Dovale			Bt from †De Haseth
"	b1891	Jeosuah A. Correa			
"	1891	Jesurun Penso	9,000		Bt from Correa
"	1892	The M. E. Penso estate			
"	1892	Vicariate	20,000		See Scherpenheuvel. 133 h
WEITJE, see Kl. Malpais					
WELBEDAGT, a. Semikoek, see Perseverencia					
WELGELEGEN[88] (HABAAI), a. Pleasant Villy [Valley], JQ; see also Family Graves	1713	Gaspar and Isaac Touro			
"	1713-23	Isaac David Senior			WICA 208, p. 110b
"	1723-32	Abraham Ulhoa Jr.	4,600 wi		l In 1739 (OAC 1142, July 7, 1739; OAC 808, no. 70; OAC 809, no. 476)
"	1738-40	Isaac Jesurun	2,000	9l	
"	1740	†Widow H. Winkler			Bt from Jesurun
"	1742-43	Moses Penso[89]	6,200	12	OAC 813, no. 367
"	1755	Dominie Wigboldus Rasvelt	2,200 wi	30m	m On his death in 1758 (WICA 218, Jan. 1, 1759; OAC 873, no. 20); see Asencion, San Pedro.
"	b1771	†J. H. Brugman			

"	1771-92	Moses, Isaac, Aron and Ribca, children of Jacob Gabay Henriquez	5,603		Bt from Brugman at public auction (OAC 908, no. 270)
"	1792-97	Governor Johannes de Veer Abmz.[90]	5,000	3	OAC 1094, nos. 71, 73, 80
"	1797-99	Jeudah Isaac de Solas	5,500	3	Bt from †De Veer (OAC 1099, no. 75)
"	1799-1802	†Henry Basden	7,500	6	Bt from De Solas (OAC 1101, no. 81)
"	1802-03	Moses Frois and his widow	13,000	22	Bt from Basden (OAC 1104, no. 152)
"	1803-44	†John Hero van der Meulen	9,000	4	Bt from the widow Frois (OAC 1105, no. 88)
"	1844-50	†R. F. Baron van Raders		16	With the lot Ruste (Maduro)
"	1850-51	†Widow John Hero v/d Meulen			
"	1851-56	Benjamin Alvares Correa	9,005	3	With the lots Ruste and Bijgelegen bt from v/d Meulen
"	1856	†Jean Blasini	22,000	9	
"	1864	Monseigneur Kistemaker for the "Vicariaat"			Bt from Blasini
WELGELEGEN, RQ, MD, near Suikertuintje	1782	Samuel Jos. da C. Gomez	11,500	5	Bt from †A. van Groot Davelaar (OAC 938, no. 93)
"	1783-1846	Da Costa Gomez Family	11,520 wi[n]		[n] In 1818 (OAC 554, no. 576)
"	1846	Widow Gabriel Dd. da C. Gomez			CGAT, 1846, I, no. 51
WELGELEGEN, OD	1827	Isaac Cardoze			
"	1828	Joseph Capriles			
"	1836-49	Samuel Cohen Henriquez		90	[o] In 1842 (CEOE 172)

88 The Welgelegen adjoined the cemetery "of the free negroes and mulattoes." It was De Solas who changed its name in 1799 in Pleasant Valley.
89 Penso sold it in 1743 with ten slaves to †N. Ellis for Ps. 7,500 (OAC 814, no. 206).
90 The plantation was sold by the parnassim Salomon de Castro and Jacob de Solas as sellers' representatives.

Plantation or Garden	Year of ownership	Owner	Value	Slaves	Remarks
WELGELEGEN, OD	1849-70	†J. Sterling	9,050	2	Bt from C. Henriquez
"	1870	Elias Jesurun Henriquez[91]	18,025		Bt from Sterling
"	1870-77	†R. R. Blanch[91]	15,600		Bt from C. Henriquez only three days later (CGANA, 1870, no. 99)
"	1877-82	Jacob Isaac Senior	27,000		
"	1882	M. de Castro	18,000		Bt from Senior
WELTEVREDE, MD, BENQ, a. Slangenbaai; see also Groot and Klein Piscadera, Terra Royal	1751-61	Is. Hm. Rz. da Costa	13,800		OAC 16, Sept. 26, 1751; 122 h with Ravenslot
"	1761-72	Moses D. and Jb. Dd. Lopez Henriquez	13,000	16	OAC 880, Feb. 20, 1761
"	1772-83	Raphael A. Correa	5,600		Bt from the M. L. Henriquez estate (OAC 911, no. 238)
"	1783-90	David Morales	15,000	11	With Terra Royal (OAC 1084, no. 138)
"	1790	Governor Johannes de Veer	4,000	2	OAC 1093, no. 37
"	1791-1802	Manuel Hm. A. Correa	4,400	2	Bt from †De Veer (OAC 1093, no. 40)
"	1802	†Joseph Foulke and †Louis Brion	6,000	7	OAC 1104, May 6, 1802
"	1818-28	Jeosuah de Sola	20,000	6[p]	Value in 1818 (OAC 554, no. 463); [p] in 1828
"	b1842-46	Joseph My. Henriquez		26[q]	[q] In 1843 (CEOE 172; *CC*, Oct. 9, 1846)
"	1847	Mordechay Jos. Henriquez			CGAR IX, March 8, 1847
WELTEVREDE, BOQ (lots)	1769	Abm. Is. Henriquez Moron	1,000	3	OAC 906, March 31, 1769
"	1818	Samuel da Costa Gomez	2,000 wi		OAC 554, no. 649

WESTERVELD, BENQ, see also Veeris, Union	1783	Mordechay A. Correa	11,000	11	OAC 1085, nos. 219, 221
"	1819-28	Wid. Raphael Pinedo and Benjamin A. Correa		38r	r In 1828; 62 h
WILHELMINA TUIN					7.5 h
Z					
ZAPATER, a. Buitenrust, OD	1845	Mordechay A. Correa		13	216 h
"	1846-53	Rachel de My. A. Correa	8,500	5	Sold to †Gravenhorst
"	1858	Jacob Jesurun Pinto	11,000	5	Bt from Gravenhorst
"	1859	Judith, orphan daughter of Jacob Jesurun Pinto	15,000		Gabriel Cohen Henriquez had received the plantation from Jn. Pinto as dowry estimated at 15,000 fls. (MIA, Ket. VIII, no. 168)
"	1869	Bn. A. Correa and Abigail Henriquez			
"	1915	†W. F. de Hart	10,000		Bt from Correa
ZEE- EN LANDSGEZICHT					40 h
ZEELANDIA, RQ, OD	1743	Joseph da Costa Gomez			39 h
"	b1781-87	Governor Jean Rodier[92] and his estate			
"	1787-1805	Jacob Gabriel Pinedo & Bros.	15,100	4	Bt from the Rodier estate (OAC 1090, nos. 7-9)
"	1805-09	Clara, wid. Gabriel Pinedo	12,500	12	Value with the lot Maay (OAC 1107, no. 173)

[91] Sterling probably owed money to Henriquez who accepted the plantation in payment and found it profitable to sell it at a loss to Blanch three days later.

[92] Married to Anna Elizabeth Ellis, widow of Government Secretary Aldert Pottey.

Plantation or Garden	Year of ownership	Owner	Value	Slaves	Remarks
ZEELANDIA, RQ, OD	1809-21	Raphael Jb. Pinedo and his widow	10,200		OAC 1059, no. 110; OAC 1062, no. 24
"	1821-22	Daniel da C. Gomez de la Penha			
"	Dec., 1822-38(?)	Dominie G. B. Bosch			OAC 295, Dec. 16, 1822
"	1855-62	Samuel L. Maduro Jr.	17,000	4	Bt from †G. W. Hellmund (CGAT, 1855, nos. 85-86)
"	1910	Sarah, wid. Salomon N. de Crasto			
ZEELUGT (near ZOUTPAN), RQ	b1737-42	Benjamin Motta	1,500		OAC 808, Nov. 4, 1737
"	1742-43	Joseph da Costa Gomez	2,000	1	Bt from Motta (OAC 814, no. 32) 31 h
(DE) ZEGENING, a. Cas Abau, see also Steenen Coraal					
ZEVENBERGEN					
ZEVENHUIZEN, see Jan Kok and Zorgvliet	1889-1902	Abraham Henriquez			
ZORGVLIET, a. Bragasmit, a. Valantijn, JQ; see also Family Graves	1730	†Hendrick de Wit			Member of the Government Council since 1718
"	1818-28	Aron Pinedo and his estate	14,000	19s	Bt from the Widow †Cambiaso with an island (OAC 1120, no. 63); s in 1828
ZORGVLIET, see Corporaal ZORGVLIET NEAR SAVONNET					
ZOUTPAN (GROTE ZOUT), see also Goed Heen Komen, Rif, Uitzigt, RQ	1738-41	Benjamin Motta			860(?) h OAC 1141, Jan. 22, 1738
"	1756	David Bueno Vivas and Henriquez Juliao			

ZUIKERTUINTJE, see
  Suikertuintje

ZUURZAK, BOQ, OD, see also
  Klein Zuurzak

1766-1803	Is. Hm. Rz. da Costa and his widow	31,000	30[93]	Bt from †H. Horst with Klein Zuurzak
1803-05	†Maria F. Hermes-Grading	13,030	5	OAC 1105, no. 94
1805-47	Abm. Is Henriquez[94] and his widow	12,350	5	OAC 1107, no. 162; he had 69 slaves in 1827, and 59 in 1838
1847-50	†J. H. Schotborgh & Co.	19,000	29	62 h
1850-60	Jb. Henriquez and Jb. J. Naar	29,000	50	CGAT, 1850, nos. 116-17
1860-62	Benjamin A. Correa	25,000	43	CGAT, 1860, no. 61

ZWARTE MORIAAN, see Popo

[93] The inventory also lists 50 cows, 8 bulls, 14 calves, 400 sheep, 16 horses and 16 donkeys (OAC 895, no. 224, y. 1766).
[94] Prince Henry (later king of Holland), on his visit to Curaçao in July, 1835, was the guest of Henriquez at the Zuurzak plantation.

FAMILY GRAVES ON THE PLANTATIONS

Although the Protestants were, and had a right to be, proud of their illustrious families — a number of them belonged to the Dutch nobility[95] — up to 1810 they did not always give their cemetery the same care that the Jews lavished upon their Beth Hahaim. Very often during the 18th century it was wantonly desecrated.[96] For this reason, among others, some families preferred burying their dear ones on their plantations, gardens or cunucus. The Jews too, for reasons set forth at pages 315-16, so interred two of their children. Below is a list of the plantations used as family graveyards with the names of several occupants as disclosed in divers records.[97]

Plantation	Name of Family	Remarks
ARARAT		
ALTENA	Pearse family	CGAR IV, Feb. 26, 1841
ASIENTO	Jonkheer Carel August Graaf de Larrij and other members of his family[98]	
BARON, east of Ararat		
BEVER, a. Bona Vista	J. Pietersz, 1694	
BEURS		
BLIJ EN HEIJM	The Lauffer family	See also Damasco.
BLAUW		
CHER ASILE	Child of T. D. Kock, 1818 (?)	
CARACASBAAI		
CUNUCU ABAO	Specht and †Jan Hendrick Senior families	
DAMASCO	The Lauffer family, 1847	See also Blij en Heijm (CEOE 163, May 26, 1847).
DANIEL		
GATO		
GROOT KWARTIER	Steenbergh, 1808	
HATO	G. K. Evertsz, 1807	In use in 1845 (CEOE 163, Jan. 29, 1845)

[95] See A. J. C. Krafft, *Historie en Oude Families van de Nederlandse Antillen* ('s Gravenhage, 1951).
[96] See Emmanuel, *Precious Stones*, pp. 52-53.
[97] See N. van Meeteren, "Het Kerkhof op 'Fo'i-Poorta'" in *Geschiedkundige Opstellen* (Curaçao, 1943), p. 54a.
[98] According to the will of his widow, Petronella Coerman Douairiere... Graaf de Larrij, done in Curaçao in 1836 and 1845 (CEOE 799, no. 39). The author had occasion to view these magnificent tombstones emblazoned with the family coat of arms.

Jalousie

Jan Zoutvat (Vredenberg) The Kikkert family, 1854 This cemetery appears in the records as late as 1898.

Juana Mateo †Maduro-Pelao families

Klein (Bloempot)
 [Bloemhoff]

Klein St. Michiel

Koningsplein Child of David Semah Valencia, 1821 During the Hazzan Piza affair, p. 316

Malpais

Manchie Irni (?), Berg Altena †Aldersina Cohen Pinedo, 1837 CEOE, 163, May 26, 1837

Monte Verde[99] The Nicolaas Evertsz Jr. family, 1816-52

Monte Verde W. Schmidt, 1819

Morgenstond Ex-Governor Johannes de Veer Abmz. He died on Dec. 26, 1796 (W. I. Comité 139, Journal of Governor Lauffer).

Mundo Novo The De Veer and Hellmund families[100]

Paradijs (Paraiso) The Brugman family, 1801 OAC 1103, no. 104

  " †Asilie, sister of †Chevalier Maduro CEOE 160, June 17, 1840

Rif

Rozentak (Roose Tak), JQ The Foulke and Brion families CEOE 163, Feb. 11, 1836

Salina Ariba The B. A. Canarijn family, 1837 CGAR V, July 1, 1837

St. Heronimus

St. Kruis (Sta. Crux)

Stad en Landzigh The P. F. Diedenhoven family[101]

Steenrijk

[99] Known as *Stuyvesant's Cemetery*. Tradition has it that Governor Peter Stuyvesant of New Amsterdam had his leg buried there. But W. Ch. de la Try Ellis has cogently disproved this claim. The cemetery bears the name Stuyvesant because in the early 19th century the land belonged to one Johannes David Stuyvesant who had inherited it from his wife Maria Gales. The graves belonged to the Evertsz family (W. Ch. de la Try Ellis, "De Gronden genaamed Stuyvesant," *Geschiedkundige Opstellen* [Curaçao, 1943], pp. 20-24).

[100] The Masonic Lodge Igualdad, during †Genereux de Lima's incumbency in 1868, bought this land of 7,340 square meters from †Henriette Catharina Raven, widow of Gotlob Wilhelm Hellmund (CGAR IX, Dec. 18, 1871). At that time the Catholic Church used to impede the burial of Catholic Freemasons. The Freemasons of Curaçao did not fight the Catholic Church, but helped, and do help, everyone without distinction as to race or religion.

[101] The real estate records distinctly mention the grave of Margaritha Elizabeth Sandtrock, widow of P. F. Diedenhoven, or refer to it as "P. F. Diedenhoven's cemetery" (CGAR III, Jan. 23, 1826). This cemetery was adjacent to the Jewish cemetery at Berg Altena. It is sad to think that the Government allowed a dry cleaning establishment to rise over these graves. Ironically Pieter Diedenhoven had lent the Government 40,000 pesos during its trying years.

SUIKERTUINTJE	Child of Isaac Levy Maduro, 1821	During the Hazzan Piza affair, pages 304-328
VALENTIJN	Governor P. B. van Starckenborgh [102]	CC, July, 1820
VERSALI		
WELGELEGEN (Habaai)	The Van der Meulen and Van Raders families, 1803-1851	CGAT, 1851, nos. 41-42
ZORGVLIET, a. Bragasmit	Hendrick de Wit in 1739, and his widow Magtilda van Kinswilder	OAC 822, April 28, 1749; OAC 907, no. 50, 1770

[102] Various dominies, as well as several governors and/or ex-governors, died in Curaçao. To the author's knowledge, nobody definitely knows of the graves of any of these dignitaries, at least of those who died before 1820.

NAVIGATION
1652-1919

A S EARLY AS 1652 the Jews of Curaçao were sailing the seas in their own
ships (pages 81-83, 215-22). Unfortunately, specific owners for the
early years cannot be supplied because of the lack of complete records for the
period. Yet, from time to time, Jews do appear as shipowners: Manuel Namias
de Crasto in 1674, followed shortly afterward by his cousin Manuel David Levy
Mendes. These kinsmen plied the Caribbean waters, mainly in the French
Antilles' area. Time and again Jewish shipowners are met in the annals of the
Dutch West India Company and in the Calendar of State Papers related to the
clandestine commerce of Curaçao with the islands. According to a letter of the
Curaçoan Jews to the Amsterdam Parnassim, February 17, 1721, the shipping
business was mainly a Jewish enterprise. This also was confirmed in 1726 by
eminent Gentiles who stated that the major part of Curaçoan navigation was in
Jewish hands. It is conservatively estimated that the Jews owned about 200
vessels during the first sixty years of their settlement in Curaçao. They armed
their vessels to defend themselves against pirates and privateers. Thus it comes
as no surprise to find the Spanish ambassador to the States General of Holland
charging that two Jewish-owned sloops were attacking Spanish shipping in the
waters of Santo Domingo.[1] The two lists following leave one amazed at the Jews'
prodigious activity as shipowners, or as captains of their own vessels or of others.
Also, they bring out the brisk changeover in ownership.[2]

All inconsistencies and discrepancies in the spelling of owners and ships are
rendered as they appear in the records. A cross before a name denotes Gentile.
The value of a ship or its cargo is expressed in pesos until January, 1827, and
thereafter in florins unless otherwise indicated.

[1] GAA 51, Burg: Lands- en geestelijk bestuur Brazilie... Curaçao.
[2] I had these lists ready in March, 1963, when I visited Curaçao with my manuscript. The late
Jossy M. L. Maduro, who also had consulted the old archives of Curaçao at The Hague, graciously
gave me another list. There I found an additional 105 boats and 14 captains — mostly for the years
1721 to 1780 — and these I have incorporated herein. The archivist Mr. R. F. W. Boskaljon was
good enough to give me, at my request, some records related to Curaçoan shipping between 1844
and 1875.

A. SHIPOWNERS

Vessel	Year	Owner	Value Pesos	Source	Remarks
ESTER	1681	Manuel de Pina, Benjamin Carvalho, Isaac de Marchena & Co.		WICA 617, p. 292	
DE VRIJHEID	1693	Philipe Henriquez, *alias* Jacob Senior			A well-armed slave ship which brought slaves from "Cap" (Africa); see p. 76
JUFFR. GEREBRECHT	1699	Philippe Henriquez, David Senior & Co.			Slave ship; see pp. 82-83
ST. FRANCISCUS	1701	Abraham Fundam		GAA 4775, p. 255	Rented to the WIC for the transportation of goods from Curaçao to Holland
HET WAPPEN VAN HOLLAND[3]	1701	Philippe Henriquez		WICA 1282	
NUESTRA SEÑORA DE CONCEPCION	1702	Philippe Henriquez		WICA 567, p. 317	
ANNA	1703	Moseh L. Maduro	518:7	WICA 200, p. 398	
	1703 to 1705	Philipe Henriquez, David Senior & Co., Mordechay N. de Crasto, Jacob Benjamin Jesurun Henriquez, Gabriel Levy & Co., Isaac Touro, Manuel Manases [Jn. Hz.], Moses Lopez Henriquez, Jacob de Crasto & Co.		WICA 200, p. 332 to 333b	Their ships and precious cargoes captured by the English between 1703 and 1705
FORTIJN	1706	Isaac Touro			
ST. JAN	1709	Philippe Henriquez & Co.		WICA 214	Armed vessel
LE GENEREUX	1709	Abraham Henriquez Moron	1,001	WICA 202, p. 222	

	Year		PJCAA[4]		
CATHARINA VAN CURAÇAO	1710	Mordechay, Manuel & Eliau N. de Crasto		27,500f	Value of this 40-ton vessel and cargo in florins
DE DOROTHEA	1713	Mordechay N. de Crasto			One-eighth interest
DE HOOP	1713	Manuel Alvares Correa	WICA 207, p. 82; Hamelberg D, p. 117		
DE DOROTHEA	1716	Gabriel Levy and David Ls. Dias	WICA 572, p. 373	6,300	Their vessels, valued at over 6,300 pesos, taken by the English in 1716
LA CONFIANÇA	1717	David Lopes Dias			
WYMOUT	1720	Isaac Senior & Co.	WICA 574, p. 474		
DE SOCIETYT	1720	Ferro & Neyra	Maduro's list		Seized by the Spaniards
JONGE ABRAHAM	1720	Daniel Moreno Henriquez	Ibid.		
JONGE DANIEL	1721	Ditto	Ibid.		
JONGE JACOB	1721	Ditto	Ibid.		
HANNA	1721	Widow Mordechay de Crasto	Ibid.		
JONGE MORDECHAY	1721	Ditto			
HELENA	1721	Isaac L. Henriquez, David & Isaac Senior	WICA 215		
DE BENJAMIN	1721	Daniel Moreno Henriquez	OAC 796, Sept. 30, 1721	1,000	
EENDRAGT	1721	Ferro & Neyra			Seized by the Spaniards
FORTUYN	1721	David Senior		350	
PHILIPPO QUINTO	1721	Elias & Manuel Touro			
SARA	1721	Salomo Vaz Faro	OAC 1564, Apr. 4, 1721		
ELISABETH	1722	Mordechay A. Correa	Maduro's list		
NUESTRA SEÑORA DE ROSARIO Y LAS ANIMAS	1722	Elias Jesurun Henriquez	Ibid.		
ZEEBLOM	1722	Ferro & Neyra	Ibid.		

³ The vessel belonged to the WIC and was chartered to Henriquez at 9,375 florins the trip to bring slaves from Africa (p. 77).

⁴ Correspondence Isaac Hoheb, letter of Nov. 26, 1710, to Joseph Fidanque of Curaçao.

Vessel	Year	Owner	Value Pesos	Source	Remarks
INDUSTRIA	1722	Ferro & Neyra	900	OAC 797, no. 64	
JONGE ABRAHAM	1722	Ditto			Same ownership in 1731
MARIA	1722	Jacob Belmonte & Daniel Moreno Henriquez			
JONGE ISAAC	1722	Gabriel Levy			
JOSEPH & BENJAMIN	1722	Ditto			
MARIA & FRANCIS	1723	Samuel Gomes		Maduro's list	
DE FORTUIN	1723	Jacob Belmonte		Ibid.	
GRACE & ELIZABETH	1723	David Levy		Ibid.	
DE LOYAL	1726	Ferro & Neyra			
LEA	1727	David Vaz Faro		OAC 2, no. 152	
LOYAL THOMAS	1727	Ferro & Neyra		OAC 2, no. 179	
DE INDUSTRY	1727	Elias Pareira, Isaac & Moses Penso	1,800	OAC 798, no. 104	
JONGE ISAAC	1727	David Aboab Cardozo		OAC 798, Sept. 23, 1727	
PACKET BOAT	1727	Mordechay A. Correa, Jb. Curiel & Jb. Abm. Hz. Moron		OAC 798, no. 137	Captured by a Spanish pirate
SANTA CLARA	1729	Isaac Monsanto		OAC 1136, Oct. 10, 1729	Mortgaged for 1,000 pesos
TWEE COUZIJNS	1729	Joseph Israel Touro & David Ulloa		OAC 799, Oct., 1729	
ELIZABETH EN MARIA	1729	Ditto		OAC 799, no. 47	
MARIA	1730	Abraham Campos Pereira		OAC 1137, Feb. 16, 1730	
ST. ANTHONY	1731	Abraham de Leon	1,460	WICA 580, p. 394	
OLIVE BRANCHE	1731	Ferro & Neyra	2,200	OAC 800, Jan. 1, 1731	
ROYAAL	1731	Ditto			
SUSANNA	1731	Francisco (alias Benjamin) Lopes Henriquez		OAC 800, Feb. 28, 1731	

Ship	Year	Owner	Reference	Tonnage	Interest
PAQUET BOOT		Moses Penso	OAC 800, March 17, 1731		
ROYAAL DE RIO DE LA HACHA	1731	Ditto			
ROYAAL v. CURAÇAO	1731	Ditto			
LA GRASIA	1731	Salomon L. Maduro Bros. & Co.	OAC 800, June 6, 1731	500	
KONING SALOMON	1731	Francisco Ls. Henriquez			
SARA	1733	Mordechay A. Correa	OAC 801, June 9, 1733	600	
PATACHE	1733	Benjamin Ls. Henriquez	OAC 1521, March 4, 1733		
LE CHEVAL VOLANT	1733	Abraham Sasportas	OAC 801, Oct. 24, 1733	1,050	
PAKETBOAT	1734	Abm. Jn. Hz., Joseph Is.¹ Touro & †Valentijn Pronk			
KONING DAVID	1734	Moses Penso, Aron Hz. Moron, Jb. Lopes Dias	OAC 803, May 31, 1734		Course: Curaçao-Amsterdam-Curaçao
JACOBUS EN ANNA	1734	David Senior & Sons			
JONGE ABRAHAM	1735	Mordechay Haim Senior			
ELISABETH	1735	Joseph Israel Touro & †Dirk van Uytrecht			
STA. CATHARINA	1736	Mordechay H. Senior			
DE EARK	1737	Mordechay A. Correa & Co.	OAC 807, Aug. 7, 1737	1,150	
GELENA	1737	Samuel de Casseres	OAC 807, Dec. 2, 1737		
ST. GOSSE	1737	Francisco Ls. Henriquez	Maduro's list		
ST. PIERRE	1738	Salomon Senior	OAC 842, no. 14		
KONINGIN ESTHER	1738	Joseph Fidanque	OAC, y. 1738	1,000	
FORTUYN	1738	Ditto		1,097	
PROVIDENS	1738	Ditto		229	One-eighth interest
FORTUYN	1738	Ditto		130	Ditto
COMERTIE	1738	Ditto		204	1/32 "
IMANUEL	1738	Ditto		876+	One-fourth "
CATHARINA	1738	Ditto		1,005+	Ditto "
ELIZABETH	1738	Ditto		857+	Ditto "
ANTJE	1738	Ditto		328+	One-half "

Vessel	Year	Owner	Value Pesos	Source	Remarks
JONGE ABRAHAM	1738	J. Fidanque & Daniel Moreno Henriquez	950		
NANNY	1738	Mordechay A. Correa	400	OAC 808, July 17, 1738	
CATHARINA-ELISABETH	1738	Abraham R. Sasportas & David Dias Arias	3,000	OAC, 842, Oct. 31, 1738	This ship and several others owned by Governor Van Collen & Co. were confiscated by Governor Gales in 1738.[5]
KONING DAVID	1738	Benjamin Vaz Faro		OAC 1141	
ST. JACQUES	1739	Manuel Lopez			
DE VRIENDEN	1739	Isaac Abarbanel		OAC 1548, March 12, 1739	Only a half interest
EXANGE	1739	David Dias Arias	1,800	OAC 1549, Sept. 18, 1739	
KONING DAVID	1739	Esther de Mord. Fundam			
NUESTRO SEÑOR	1739	Samuel & Benj. de Casseres	550	OAC 1549, Dec. 3, 1739	
ROYAL	1740	Benjamin de Casseres & Josias Pardo			Seized by the English in 1740 (p. 217)
SARA	1740	Jacob Salom			Ditto
DE HONEST	1740	Salomo Senior	220	OAC 809, no. 298	
SAMUEL	1740	Manuel Levy & Co.		OAC 1549, Dec. 23, 1740	
ELIZABETH	1740	Moses Penso		OAC 846, Aug. 10, 1740	
PAULINA	1740	Benjamin Ls. Henriquez		OAC 5, Sept. 6, 1740	
EL AMPARO	1740	Francisco Ls. Henriquez		OAC 846, Aug. 16, 1740	
ELIZABETH	1740	Francisco Ls. Henriquez		OAC 846, Oct. 27, 1740	
SAMUEL, die God Bewaart	1741	Manuel Levy			Seems to be the same "Samuel" of 1740
SUZANNA	1741	Mordechay A. Correa & Co.		OAC 847, no. 36	

686

230. DETAIL ON THE TOMBSTONE OF CAPTAIN ABRAHAM D. MORENO HENRIQUEZ, 1726

231. DETAIL ON THE TOMBSTONE OF CAPTAIN MOSSEH HENRIQUEZ COTIÑO, 1762

232. DETAIL ON THE TOMBSTONE OF CAPTAIN ISHAC H. DE
BENJAMIN MORENO HENRIQUEZ, 1767

233. DETAIL ON THE TOMBSTONE OF CAPTAIN AHRON DE
BENJAMIN MORENO HENRIQUEZ, 1778

Ship	Year	Owner	Amount	Reference	Notes
ANNA ELIZABETH	1741	Manuel Levy	2,100	OAC 847, no. 65	
L'AIMABLE	1741	Abraham Pimentel		OAC 847, no. 122	
DRIE GEBROEDERS	1741	Abraham and Aron Motta & Co.	14,586	OAC 842, no. 82	See p. 217.
HOOPWEL	1741	Moses Motta	700	OAC 847, no. 108	
FENCY OF BERMUDES	1741	Jacob David Senior	1,000	OAC 847, no. 28	
TRITON	1741	Jeosuah Henriquez Jr.			See p. 217.
JONGE MORDECHAY	1741	Moses Penso & a Gentile		OAC 854, no. 76	
JONGE ISAAC	1741	Abraham Dias Cotinho			
SARA	1741	Isaac da Costa Gomez & Co.		OAC 810, no. 53	
JUFFR. ELIZABETH	1741	†Willem Kock, Samuel and Benjamin de Casseres			
AMABLE ANNA	1741	Abraham Pimentel	600	OAC 811, p. 274	See p. 217.
ESTHER	1741	Ditto	1,209	OAC 811, no. 330	
SARA	1741	Benjamin Vaz Faro	870	OAC 811, July 7, 1741	
CURAÇAO GALLEY	1741	Isaac Abarbanel	1,400	OAC 811, no. 367	
GEERTRUIJDA	1742	Mordechay A. Correa			See p. 217.
VRIENDSCHIP	1742	Ditto			
RIBCA	1742	Jacob Cohen Henriquez			
SAMUEL AKATAN	1742	Mordechay L. Maduro, †David Redoch & †Juriaan de Pool de Jonge			See p. 217.
FORTUYN	1742	Aron Henriquez Moron			
CHARLES	1742	Jacob Cohen Henriquez & †Marten Hempel	1,375	OAC 1550, Jan. 25, 1742	
FORTUYN	1742	Daniel Belmonte	1,040	OAC 848, Jan. 30, 1742	
RIBCA	1742	Manuel Levy			
TRIALL	1742	Isaac Hz. Juliao & Co.	900	OAC 848, no. 143	Received in payment 200 gold pistoles

5 Jacob de Petersen, *Kort Vertoog aan de Edele... Bewinthebberen van... de W. I. Comp.* (no year or city of publication, but probably Amsterdam, 1740), p. 45.

Vessel	Year	Owner	Value Pesos	Source	Remarks
JONGE ISAAC	1742	Daniel Belmonte & Co.	2,100	OAC 848, no. 152	
ADRIANA ELISABETH	1742	Jacob Touro	3,000	OAC 812, Jan. 21, 1742	
DE DRIE CONFRATER	1742	Francisco Ls. Henriquez		OAC 813, Sept. 27, 1742	
TRUEJOKE (BERMUDA)	1742	Daniel Belmonte		OAC 848, no. 79	
MARIE	1742	Jeosuah Henriquez Jr.		OAC 848, no. 99	
JONGE JACOB, VICTORIA & ZEEBLOM	1742	†Estienne Picard, Abm. Dias Coutino, Samuel de Casseres & Co., and Francisco Ls. Henriquez		OAC 849, no. 8	
SEQUIRREL	1742	Abraham Monsanto & Co.		OAC 849, no. 123	
RELIEVE	1742	Mordechay A. Correa	2,022:4	OAC 849, no. 169	
DE HOOP	1742	Isaac Belmonte		OAC 812, Mar. 28, 1742	
FORTUYN	1742	Moses Motta & Co.	550	OAC 812, Mar. 29, 1742	
ANNA ELIZABETH	1742	Aron Henriquez Moron		OAC 814, no. 122	
SUCCES	1743	Abraham Motta & Joseph da Costa Gomez	2,850	OAC 850, no. 24	
DE BESTE IN AMERICA	1743	Aron Hz. Moron & Co.			
DE FANCEY	1743	Benjamin Motta & Co.	1,800	OAC 850, no. 69	
MARIA	1743	Abraham Diaz Coutinho, Elias Ulhoa & Co.	1,600	OAC 850, no. 79	One-fourth interest held by a Gentile
ANNA	1743	Moses Penso, Francisco L. Henriquez & Isaac Belmonte	1,400	OAC 850, no. 105	
TWEE GEBROEDERS	1743	Daniel Belmonte & Co.			
ANNA	1743	Isaac Suares & Co.	1,200	OAC 850, no. 130	
MARIANA	1743	Abraham J. Jeudah Leon, Samuel & Michael Jeudah Leon	1,600	OAC 850, no. 141	
MARIA EN JOSINA GALLEY	1743	Moses Penso		OAC 850, nos. 153, 169; OAC 852, no. 90	Only a 1/16 interest, the remainder of gentile owner-

Ship	Year	Owner	Tonnage	Reference	Remarks
GROOTE ZEEBLOM	1743	Aron Henriquez Moron & Co.		OAC 850, no. 156	...ship; an unusually large, costly vessel making the Curaçao-Amsterdam-Curaçao run
DICHOZA	1743	Abraham Diaz Coutinho & Co.		OAC 850, no. 204	
SEA FLOWER	1743	Jacob Lopez Dias	1,800	OAC 851, no. 15	
PATRIARCH JACOB	1743	Jacob Touro	3,000	OAC 851, no. 28	
REBECCA	1743	Abm. Hz. Coutinho & Co.	1,400		See p. 217.
SARA	1743	Abraham Henriquez Coutinho			
ESPERANSA	1743	Abraham Pimentel			
NOSTRA SEÑORA DEL ROSARIO	1743	Samuel Benj. D Costa d'Andrade	2,000	OAC 851, no. 95	
LA FLORA DE LA MAR	1743	Salomo Nunes Redondo		OAC 851, no. 102	
DE BESTE IN HET CHRISTENDOM	1743	Moses Penso & Isaac Belmonte		OAC 851, nos. 260, 105	Contemporaneously there was another ship of the same name which belonged to 23 Gentiles and 15 Jews. Penso & Blemonte probably bought out the others.
JONGE ABRAHAM	1743	Moses Penso & Aron Hz. Moron		OAC 850, no. 155	
DE GOEDE SUCCES	1743	Joseph da Costa Gomez		OAC 814, no. 254	
MARIA	1743	Abraham Motta	1,225	OAC 854, no. 78	
CATHARINA GEERTRUYDA	1743	Joseph da Costa Gomez		OAC 854, no. 117	
JONGE ISAAC	1743	David Jesurun, Mordechay de Crasto & Co.			
ESTER	1743	Moses Penso, Francisco L. Henriquez & Isaac Belmonte		OAC 853, no. 20; OAC 854, no. 123	Seized by the Spaniards
ANNA SOPHIA (formerly Nuestra Señora del Rosario)	1743	Isaac Abenatar, Josias Pardo & Samuel B. da Costa d'Andrade		OAC 855, no. 21	

Vessel	Year	Owner	Value Pesos	Source	Remarks
ANNA ELISABETH	1743	Moses Aboab		OAC 8, June 12, 1743	
PROPHEET MOSES	1743	Moses Motta		OAC 8, Nov. 12, 1743	
AURORA	1743	Aron Hz. Moron			
GLORIOSA	1744	Abraham Baruch Louzada	1,800	OAC 852, no. 160	Sold to Flores & Castro
LA MANSANA	1744	Samuel de Casseres	1,350	OAC 852, nos. 168, 175	One-half interest
DEN HELT JACOB	1744	Jacob David Senior	2,000	OAC 852, no. 178	
ZEEBLOM	1744	Joseph da Costa Gomez	900	OAC 852, no. 193	
MARIA	1744	Cohen Henriquez Jr. (= David Jeudah C. Hz.)	1,225	OAC 852, no. 227	
MARIA ROSA	1744	Abraham Belmonte & Co.	600	OAC 852, no. 264	
LA SOLEDAD	1744	Jeosuah Henriquez Jr.		OAC 854, no. 86	
KONINGIN ESTHER	1744	Benjamin Motta		OAC 854, no. 90	
FORTUYN	1744	Joseph da Costa Gomez		OAC 854, no. 125	
LA LEVINA	1744	Jeosuah Henriquez Jr.		OAC 854, no. 135	
SUZANNA	1744	Abraham Belmonte & Joseph da Costa Gomez			
INDEVOR	1744	Mordechay A. Correa		OAC 853, no. 252	
BLACK JOHE	1744	Moses de (Crasto) [Castro] & Co.		OAC 853, no. 256	
DE BRAVE	1744	Salomo Nunes Redondo		OAC 853, no. 277	
CATHARINA (Rio de la Hacha)	1744	Manuel A. Correa		OAC 853, no. 336	
ANNA SOPHIA	1745	Abraham Motta & Co.			
FORTUIN	1745	Jeosuah Henriquez Jr.			See p. 218.
JONGE ABRAHAM	1745	Aron Hz. Moron		OAC 854, no. 103	
NUESTRA SEÑORA DE CARME	1745	Jeosuah Henriquez Jr.		OAC 854, no. 172	

Ship	Year	Owner	Price	OAC reference	Notes
ROSARIO	1745	Francisco Ls. Henriquez & Manuel de Pina		OAC 854, no. 141	
VIOLANTE	1745	Mosseh Hz. Coutino & Co.		OAC 854, no. 235	
DIAMANT	1745	Mordechay A. Correa	1,400	OAC 857, no. 130	
PLAISIR (Vriendschap)	1745	Mordechay A. Correa	1,125	OAC 854, Jan. 25, 1745	
ST. ANTHONY Y ANIMAS	1745	Abraham Motta		OAC 855, no. 38	
ZEEBLOM CUMANERIS	1745	Moses Hz. Coutinho		OAC 857, no. 48	
LA GRANDE MARIA	1745	Salomo Nunes Redondo		OAC 857, no. 55	
MARGARITA	1746	Abraham Belmonte & a Gentile	2,000	OAC 861, no. 98	
DE POST VAN CURAÇAO	1746	Manuel de Britto		OAC 861, no. 73	
JONGE MORDECHAY	1746	Francisco L. Henriquez	650	OAC 861, no. 144	
CATHARINA	1746	Salomo Senior		OAC 866, no. 59	See p. 218.
JONGE MORDECHAY	1746	Moses Penso	7,000	OAC 858, no. 206	
JANE ANGELICA	1746	Aron Motta	750	OAC 858, nos. 273, 281	
NAPHTALI	1746	Aron Hz. Moron			
ABIGAEL	1746	Abraham Michael Roiz Mendes			
FORTUIN	1746	Abraham Nunes Redondo & Aron de Chaves		OAC 859, nos. 33, 124	
SARA	1746	Abraham Jesurun Henriquez			
MARIA GRANDE	1746	Salomo Nunes Redondo	2,300	OAC 859, no. 191	
FORTUYN	1746	Manuel de Pinedo	1,700	OAC 860, no. 98	
ESPERANSA (Thomas)	1746	Abraham L. Maduro	1,750	OAC 860, no. 226	The original price was 7,000 pounds or gourdes which were then worth four gourdes to the peso.
ZEBULUN	1746	Salomo Is. L. Maduro & Co.			Destination: Puerto Rico
ZEBULUN	1746	David de Castro			
ROYAL MARIA	1746	Isaac Suares			
KONINGIN ESTHER	1746	Joseph Jesurun Henriquez & Co.	800	OAC 817, no. 202	
JONGE BENJAMIN	1747	Isaac de Medina & Co.	1,975	OAC 863, no. 80	
REBECCA	1747	Isaac Jesurun & Co.	600	OAC 863, no. 240	

Vessel	Year	Owner	Value Pesos	Source	Remarks
JONGE JOHANNES	1747	Francisco L. Henriquez			See p. 218.
LA ESPERANZA	1747	Abraham Salomo Mord. L. Maduro			See p. 220.
ZEEBLOM	1747	Jacob Suares & Moses Henriquez Coutinho		OAC 862, no. 175	See p. 220.
VLIEGENDE VIS	1747	Moses Henriquez		OAC 863, no. 215	
MIRALDO	1747	Manuel de Campos [Pereira]		OAC 864, no. 106	
ST. EUSTATIUS POST	1747	Jacob Fermin [Ephraim Jn.] Henriquez		OAC 864, no. 148	
AVE MARIA	1747	Abraham Pimentel		OAC 865, no. 18	
DE JONGE HENDRIK	1747	†Christoffel Raphoen & Aron Hz. Moron		OAC 866, no. 92	
CONCORDIA	1747	Isaak Suares & Co.	1,250	OAC 864, no. 71	
VICTORIA	1747	Abraham Motta	2,300	OAC 864, no. 196	
EXPERIENTIE	1747	Jacob Senior			
PRINS VAN ORANJE	1747	Benjamin de Casseres & Co.		OAC 864, no. 41	
CONCORDIA	1747	Joseph de Pas	5,503	OAC 865, no. 30	
SARA	1747	Benjamin de Casseres & Co.		OAC 865, no. 63	
ABIGAIL	1747	Jacob Rz. Ribeiro of New York		OAC 865, no. 102	
REGOBOTH (DE GULLE)	1747	Jacob Suares & Moses Hz. Coutinho		OAC 865	The name is from Genesis 26:22.
PATACHE	1747	Benjamin de Casseres	1,100	OAC 865, no. 109	
DE HELD JOSUA	1748	Jacob Jeosuah Naar	5,800	OAC 866, no. 31	
MARIA	1748	Jeosuah Henriquez Jr.	3,600	OAC 866, no. 47	
FORTUYN	1748	Isaac Suares	429	OAC 866, no. 182	
MARIA LOUISA	1748	Abraham Motta	5,400	OAC 867, no. 67	
MARIA LOUISA	1748	Manuel de Campos Pereira		OAC 867, no. 26	
DE CATHARINA	1748	Salomon Senior		OAC 866, no. 59	

Ship	Year	Owner		Reference	Notes
St. Anthony de Padua	1748	Moses C. Henriquez	825	OAC 867, no. 120	
Renger	1748	Isaac Hz. Cautino & Co.		OAC 866, no. 44	
Maria	1748	Benjamin de Casseres	1,800	OAC 867, no. 121	
La Parfaict	1748	Abraham Motta		OAC 867, no. 134	
Maria	1748	Josias Dovale	2,200	OAC 869, no. 73	
Aurora de Curaçao	1748	Manuel Abm. A. Correa			See p. 221.
King David	1748(?)	Moses Penso & Co.			Well-armed ship with twelve cannon; destination: Amsterdam
Prins van Orange	1748	Ditto		OAC 822, Aug. 22, 1749 Ditto	
Curaçao	1748	Benjamin Naar & Co.		OAC 866, no. 143	
Jonge Jacob	1748	Francisco L. Henriquez & Co.			
Eunice	1748	Mordechay A. Correa		OAC 868, no. 108	
Jonge Willem	1749	Jacob L. Maduro	4,000	OAC 822, Feb. 3, 1749	
Maria	1749	Isaac Hz. Juliao	2,300	OAC 822, Feb. 17, 1749 One-half interest	
Dolphyn	1749	Francisco L. Henriquez	770	OAC 822, Apr. 15, 1749	
Lamiranda	1749	Moses Hz. Coutinho		OAC 822, Apr. 24, 1749	
Elizabeth	1749	Samuel Isaac Salom	1,600	OAC 822, Apr. 28, 1749	
Avontuur	1749	Abraham Fidanque		OAC 821, Nov. 14, 1749	
Buen Aventuur	1749	Benjamin Naar			
De Hoop	1749	Benjamin Naar and Manuel de Pina Jr.	1,200	OAC 822, May 13, 1749	
Postiljon	1749	Manuel Hisquiao Pinedo	600	OAC 822, May 18, 1749	
Hanna	1749	Josias Dovale		OAC 822, June 23, 1749	
Señora de la Concepcion	1749	Samuel Jb. Jeudah Leon		OAC 822, Sept. 5, 1749	
Pinchas	1749	Benjamin Suares			
Concordia Elizabeth	1749	Samuel Jb. Jeudah Leon		OAC 822, Nov. 11, 1749	
La Esperanza	1750	Ephraim Jesurun Henriquez, alias Fermin Henriquez			See p. 221.
Concordia	1750	Samuel Jb. Jeudah Leon			Apparently the same as the Concordia Elizabeth

Vessel	Year	Owner	Value Pesos	Source	Remarks
FLORA MELL	1750	Aron Hz. Moron		OAC 824, July 7, 1750	
FONTIJN	1750	Abraham Fidanque			
CONCORDIA	1750	Abraham Pimentel			
CLARA	1750	Benjamin Naar & Co.	2,000	OAC 16, y. 1751	Rented to Benjamin Vaz Faro for two months at the rate of 327 pesos the first month and 130 for the second
CATHARINA	1750	Jeosuah Henriquez Jr.		OAC 824, Nov. 9, 1750	
ANNA CORNELIA	1750	Moses Penso			
AVONTUUR	1750	Jeosuah Henriquez Jr.		OAC 824, July 28, 1750	One-half interest
FORTUYN	1750	Ditto		OAC 824, Aug. 5, 1750	
REAAL	1750	Aron Henriquez Moron	3,000	OAC 824, Aug. 19, 1750	
STA. RITA	1750	Jacob Jeudah Leon		OAC 824, Nov. 20, 1750	One-half interest See p. 221.
FORTUYN	1751	Isaac Vaz Faro	4,000		
SARAH	1751	Daniel Belmonte		OAC 1566, Feb. 11, 1751	
ST. BARBERA	1751	Daniel Peixotto		OAC 825, Jan. 8, 1751	
ST. JOSEPH	1751	Jeosuah Henriquez Jr.		OAC 825, Feb. 1, 1751	
JONGE WILLEM	1751	Jeosuah Henriquez Jr. & Co.	3,300	OAC 825, June 3, 1751	
PHENEIJ	1752	Isaac Hm. Rodriguez da Costa		OAC 827, y. 1752	Taken by a Spanish pirate
SUXES [SUCCESS]	1752	Manuel Abm. A. Correa		OAC 888, no. 228	
PRINSES CAROLINA	1752	Moses Penso		OAC 826, June 1, 1752	
D'HOOP	1752	Moses & David Hz. Juliao		OAC 827, July, 1752	
RESOLUTIE	1752	Abraham Jesurun Henriquez	700	OAC 827, Oct. 13, 1752	
NUESTRA SEÑORA DE AMPARO, alias Particulier	1752	Aron Henriquez Moron	1,800	OAC 827, Nov. 27, 1752	
PRINSES CAROLINA	1752	Moses Penso	5,400	OAC 826, June 1, 1752	

Ship	Year	Owner	Amount	Reference	Notes
DE JAGER	1753	Is. Hm. Rodriguez da Costa			
SPEEDWELL ELIZABETH	1753	Abraham Motta & Isaac Suares	625	OAC 828, Jan. 30, 1753	
ST. ANTONY	1753	Daniel Belmonte & Moses Henriquez	1,200	OAC 828, Feb. 2, 1753	
MARIAM	1753	Isaac Mendes	1,500	OAC 823, Feb. 13, 1753	
JONGE JACOB	1753	Abraham Motta			
DRIE SISTERS	1753	Isaac Henriquez Coutinho			
ESPERANSA (De Hoop)	1753	Abraham Jb. Jeudah Leon	1,200	OAC 870, no. 58	
ST. ANTHONY	1753	Isaac Belmonte & Moses Henriquez	1,200	OAC 870, no. 78	
DE SCHONE MORGEN STER	1753	Isaac Mendes	1,200	OAC 870, no. 95	
GEREGTIGHEIJT	1753	Daniel Belmonte and Moses Henriquez		OAC 870, no. 100	
JONGE ABRAM	1753	Ditto		Ditto	
VICTORIA	1753	Is. Hm. Rodriguez da Costa	6,000	OAC 870, no. 103	
SARA	1753	Ditto	3,500	OAC 870, no. 104	
RESOLUTIE	1753	Ditto	6,100	OAC 829, Oct. 2, 1753	
JONGE ALEXANDER	1753	Abraham Jb. Jeudah Leon		OAC 870, no. 146	
JOHANNA	1753	Isaac de Medina and Manuel de Pina		OAC 870, no. 175	
TRITON	1753	Michel Faro		GAA 51, Lands... Bestuur... Curaçao	
DE HOOP	1753	Salomo Motta, Jacob Ulhoa & Co.		OAC 829, Aug. 13, 1753	
COTO	1753	Isaac Hz. Coutinho		OAC 829, Sept. 3, 1753	
DRIE GEBROEDERS	1754	Manuel de Pina & Co.	1,700	OAC 871, no. 121	
JONGE MOSES	1754	Jacob Gabay Henriquez		OAC 871, no. 151	
COTTO	1754	Daniel Mendes de Castro & Co.			
REBECCA	1754	Manuel de Pina	725	OAC 871, no. 170	
CATHARINA	1754	Jeosuah Henriquez Jr.			One-half interest
L'FIDEL	1755	Isaac Mendes			
JONGE ABRAHAM (Victoria)	1755	Is. Hm. Rodriguez da Costa	1,201	WICA 218, July 29, 1755	Worth 6,000 pesos in 1753
PATACON	1755	Abraham Roiz Cunha			

Vessel	Year	Owner	Value Pesos	Source	Remarks
De Goede Sucses	1755	Abraham J. Jeudah Leon	600	OAC 832, Sept. 29, 1755	
St. Simon	1755	Francisco L. Henriquez		OAC 1553, May 18, 1756	
Sout Pan	1756	Isaac Dd. Roiz Monsanto	700	OAC 889, no. 61	See p. 218.
Geregtigheid	1756	Josua Henriquez Jr. & Michael de Leon			
Zebulun & Isachar	1756	Moses Hz. Coutinho		OAC 19, Mar. 5, 1756	So named — allusion to Midrash Raba, Genesis, sec. 72 — because Ribbi Jeosuah Cordova probably had a part interest in the vessel
Drie Vrienden	1756	Raphael Gomes, Joseph & Abraham Sasso	550	OAC 834, Dec. 12, 1756	
Vrij Metzelaar	1756	Jeosuah Henriquez Jr.		OAC 833, Oct. 4, 1756	Translation: Freemason
Nuestra Señora	1756	Manuel Hisquiao Pinedo		OAC 833, Sept. 9, 1756	
Klijne Pluton	1756	Aron Motta		OAC 833, Sept. 16, 1756	
Drie Vrienden (Leonora)	1756	Raphael Gomez, Abraham & Joseph Sasso	650	OAC 833, Nov. 4, 1756	
Dolphijn	1756	Aron Motta	500	OAC 833, Nov. 11, 1756	
Anna Cornelia	1756	Issac Jesurun	600	OAC 833, Nov. 19, 1756	
Maria	1756	Gomez Casseres & Co.	1,000	OAC 833, Dec. 6, 1756	
De Jonge Gose	1757	Abraham Hz. Coutinho		OAC 942, no. 129	
Paulina	1757	Daniel & David Gomes Casseres		OAC 834, June 6, 1757	
Richard en Robbert	1757	Jeudah Alva		OAC 835, Aug. 8, 1757	
Zegen & Vrede	1757	Isaac Levy & Co.		OAC 835, Aug. 3, 1757	
Charming Peggy	1757	Isaac Hz. Cotino & Elias Roiz Miranda			Two-thirds interest

Ship	Year	Owner(s)	Reference	Notes
JOHANNIS	1757	Isaac Mendes de Solas & Judah Cohen Henriquez	OAC 835, Aug. 12, 1757	
HET FORTUYN	1757	Isaac de Medina & Co.	OAC 835, July 26, 1757	
ADRIANA	1757	Jacob Hᵘ Suares & Co.	OAC 835, Sept. 1, 1757	
MAZAL	1757	Manuel de Pina	OAC 835, Sept. 20, 1757	Apparently identical with the "Masaltob" of the same year below
JONGE ISAAC	1757	Abraham Gomez	OAC 835, Oct. 10, 1757	
JONGE JACOB	1757	Jacob Lopez Dias & Samuel de Jb. Jʰ Leao	OAC 835, Oct. 20, 1757	
ZE(E)BULUN	1757	Moses Henriquez Cotino & Isaac Rz. Miranda	OAC 835, Oct. 20, 1757	
MARIA	1757	Francisco Lz. Henriquez	OAC 835, Oct. 24, 1757	
DRIE VRIENDEN	1757	Abm. de Jb. Jʰ Leon	OAC 835, Nov. 28, 1757	
JUFFR. RACHEL	1757	†Frederic Evertsz, Abm. & David de Jb. Lopez Dias & Mordechay Penso	OAC 835, Dec. 5, 1757	
CONTENT	1757	Aron Henriquez Moron	OAC 835, Dec. 9, 1757	
BERAHA VE SALOM	1757	Jacob de Crasto Manuelzon	OAC 835, Dec. 2, 1757	
DE HOOP	1757	Jacob de Elias Israel Jn. Henriquez and a Gentile	OAC 835, Dec. 5, 1757	
VRIJHEID	1757	David Gs. Casseres & Co.	OAC 835, Nov. 2, 1757	
ST. CHARLES	1757	Aron Motta	OAC 834, no. 87	
OLYFF TACK	1757	Manuel & Gabriel Pinedo	OAC 834, no. 227	
JONGE CORNELIS	1757	Moseh Hz. Coutinho	OAC 834, no. 249	See p. 218.
BRUTAAL	1757	David & Samuel Ricardo	OAC 834, no. 263	Two-thirds interest
MASALTOB	1757	Ditto	OAC 836, no. 365	Taken by French pirates (p. 220)
DE GOEDE HOOP	1757	Francisco L. Henriquez	OAC 834, no. 291	
FORTUYN	1757	Isaac Levy & Moseh Hz. Coutinho	OAC 834, no. 295	
DE TWEE BROEDERS	1757	Abraham Mendes		

697

Vessel	Year	Owner	Value Pesos	Source	Remarks
DE FLOUR MILL	1758	Aron Hz. Moron			Taken by the English in 1758 (p. 218)
JONGE DANIEL	1758	Isaac & Jacob Elias Jeudah Leon	2,100	OAC 873, no. 104	
JONGE ABRAHAM	1758	Aron Hz. Moron and a Gentile			
JONGE ABRAHAM	1758	Aron Hz. Moron (whole interest)		OAC 835, Sept. 14, 1757	Sold with ammunition to a Frenchman for 8,000 pesos
DE MARIA	1758	Aron Hz. Moron		OAC 837, Aug. 17, 1758	
BERAHA VESALOM	1758	Abm. Jb. Jʰ Leao & Co.		OAC 836, May 11, 1758	
KONINGIN ESTHER	1758	Abraham J. Jeudah Leon	1,800	OAC 836, Mar. 24, 1758	
LEONORA	1758	Ditto		OAC 836, Mar. 20, 1758	
JONGE ABRAHAM (Nuestra Señora del Carmer)	1758	Is. Hm. Rodriguez da Costa	2,000	OAC 836, Mar. 9, 1758	
DE PEARL	1758	Is. Hm. Rz. da Costa	1,202	OAC 836, no. 174	
CONCORDIA	1758	Abraham de Chaves	2,000	OAC 836, no. 118	
SARA	1758	Jacob Hm. Rz. Pareira	2,000	OAC 836, Mar. 30, 1758	
VRIENDSCHAP	1758	Isaac Hz. Coutinho		OAC 836, Mar. 31, 1758	
ANNA CAROLINA	1758	Manuel de Pina	700	OAC 836, Apr. 4, 1758	
SARA	1758	Isaac Hz. Coutinho	3,400	OAC 836, June 21, 1758	
FORTUYN	1758	Daniel & David Gomes Casseres		OAC 836, Apr. 5, 1758	
REBECCA	1758	Isaac Levy & Moses Coutinho		OAC 836, Apr. 26, 1758	
OLYFTAK	1758	Isaac & Jacob Elias Jeudah Leon		OAC 836, Apr. 21, 1758	
ELIZABETH	1758	Abraham de Chaves	3,450	OAC 836, May 5, 1758	
ARKE NOACH	1758	Abm. Mendes de Castro & Abm. & Joseph Sasso		OAC 836, no. 109	
JONGE ISAAC	1758	Abm. Rodriguez Pereira	1,200	OAC 837, July 24, 1758	
JONGE JOSEPH (St. Juan)	1758	Joseph Obediente	600	OAC 837, July 26, 1758	
JOSEPH	1758	Jacob Levy Maduro	2,500	OAC 837, July 27, 1758	Worth 1800 ps in Nov. 1758

Ship	Year	Owner	Pesos	Reference	Notes
SARA	1758	Daniel Gomes Casseres			
ELISABETH	1758	Jacob L. Maduro	2,000	OAC 837, Oct. 10, 1758	
CONVENTIE	1758	Isaac Pardo	3,000	OAC 836, no. 449	
JOHANNA	1758	Jacob L. Maduro	1,000	OAC 837, Dec. 12, 1758	
JONGE NAFTALI	1758	Semaya Bonan	1,500	OAC 837, Aug. 7, 1758	
SARA (Grenadier)	1758	Jos. da Fonseca Chaves	1,200	OAC 837, Aug. 23, 1758	
JONGE JACOB	1758	Jacob Mendes	1,800	OAC 837, Sept. 9, 1758	
LA SARA	1758	Abraham Pessoa		OAC 837, Sept. 11, 1758	
DE BEKEERDE JOOD (De Duyff)	1758	Moses Motta	1,016	OAC 837, Sept. 9, 1758	"The Converted Jew"; renamed Het Goed Succes when sold to †Claas Visser in 1759 for 1,500 pesos
JONGE ISAAC	1758	David Gomes Casseres, Rephael Molina Monsanto & Is. Lopes da Fonseca		OAC 837, Nov. 28, 1758	
TWEELINGEN	1758	Isaac Hz. Coutinho	1,500	OAC 837, July 28, 1758	
TWEE GEBROEDERS	1758	Isaac Mendes	1,050	OAC 837, Oct. 5, 1758	
AMSTERDAM	1758	Jacob Manuel de Crasto & Co.	1,230	OAC 837, Oct. 6, 1758	
KONINGIN ESTHER	1758	Manuel Moses A. Correa	2,800	OAC 837, Aug. 17, 1758	
VRIENDSCHAP	1758	Isaac Mendes	2,150	OAC 837, Sept. 9, 1758	
JUFFR. ADRIANA	1758	Ditto	1,400	Ditto	
JUFFR. CATHARINA	1758	Ditto	1,200	Ditto	
DE GOEDE HOOP	1758	Jacob L. Maduro	1,200	OAC 837, Nov. 10, 1758	
FORTUYN	1758	Isaac Pardo	2,250	OAC 837, Dec. 4, 1758	
JONGE JOHANNES	1758	Aron Hz. Moron		OAC 837, Dec. 15, 1758	
KONINGIN ESTHER	1758	Ditto	3,000	OAC 837, Aug. 18, 1758	
SUSANNA	1758	Abraham Hz. Moron		OAC 837, Dec. 13, 1758	
AURORA	1759	Isaac Pardo	2,000	OAC 1556, Jan. 4 and 8, 1759	Sold four days later to †Willem Lacrum for 3,000 pesos
JUFFR. JUDITH	1759	Manuel de Moses A. Correa		OAC 839, July 16, 1759	

Vessel	Year	Owner	Value Pesos	Source	Remarks
De Nancy	1759	Isaac de Medina & Manuel de Pina			
Jonge Moses	1759	Manuel Moses A. Correa	1,600	OAC 875, no. 254	
Jonge Moses	1759	Abraham Lopes Nunes		PJCAA[6]	Curaçao-bound; shipwrecked on leaving Amsterdam
Sta. Barba	1759	Jacob & David Suares		OAC 839, Aug. 17, 1759	
Elisabeth	1759	Abraham & Salomon Motta	1,001	OAC 839, Aug. 3, 1759; OAC 1567, Aug. 24, 1759	Mortgaged for 1,000 pesos, and sold a few months later for only 600 pesos
Vriendschap	1759	Michael de Leon	1,400	OAC 839, May 10, 1759	
Juffr. Angelica	1759	Abraham Hz. Moron	1,125	OAC 839, May 9, 1759	
Koningin Esther	1759	Isaac Levy		OAC 839, May 8, 1759	
Klijne Pluton	1759	Abraham Jb. Jeudah Leon	600	OAC 840, Nov. 9, 1759	See p. 219.
Elisabeth	1759	Rephael Molina Monsanto	1,000	OAC 839, Mar. 19, 1759	
Elisabeth	1759	Jeudah Alva	1,100	OAC 839, Mar. 21, 1759	
Curaçao	1759	Abraham Hz. Moron	1,400	OAC 839, June 7, 1759	
Concordia	1759	Moses Motta	540	OAC 839, July 24, 1759	
Johannes	1759	Jacob L. Maduro	670	OAC 839, July 24, 1759	
Uijtsigt	1759	Isaac Hz. Coutinho, Motta & de Crasto	600	OAC 839, Aug. 3, 1759	
Koning David (Maria)	1759	David Salom & Elias Fidanque	950	OAC 840, Sept. 11, 1759	
Rachel	1759	Jeudah Dd. C. Henriquez	700	OAC 840, Sept. 12, 1759	
Jonge Isaac	1759	Moses Hz. Juliao	950	OAC 840, Sept. 18, 1759	
Anna Maria	1759	Aron Hz. Moron			
Angelica	1759	Joseph Obediente	2,111	OAC 840, p. 88	
Jonge Abraham	1759	Isaac & Joseph Curiel	2,000	OAC 840, p. 120	
Dolphijn	1759	Manuel Moses A. Correa	1,200	OAC 840, Oct. 25, 1759	
Ana Catharina	1760	Abraham Hz. Moron			See p. 219

Ship	Year	Owner	Amount	Reference	Notes
KONINGIN ABIAGAILL	1760	Aron Hz. Moron			See p. 219.
OLYFTAK	1760	Jeosuah Henriquez Jr.			See p. 221.
ST. JOSEPH	1760	Benjamin da Costa de Andrade		OAC 877, Apr. 21, 1960	
JONGE MANUEL EN RACHEL	1760	Jacob Manuel de Crasto			See p. 219.
DE MAAGD	1760	Isaac Mendes	2,000	OAC 878, Aug. 7, 1760	
DE PEARL	1760	Jacob Jeosuah Naar	2,900	OAC 878, July 7, 1760	
EENDRAGT	1760	Aron Hz. Moron	1,400	OAC 878, July 2, 1760	
JAGER	1760	Isaac Pardo	600	OAC 878, Aug. 20, 1760	
VIGILANTE	1760	Jacob L. Maduro	1,000	OAC 877, June 20, 1760	
JONGE JOHANNES	1760	Aron Hz. Moron			Seized by the English (p. 219)
ABIGAIL	1760	Ditto			Ditto
DE DUIF	1760	Ditto			Ditto
LA PERLA	1760	Ditto			Ditto
ST. RAPHAEL	1760	Isaac Mendes	1,350	OAC 877, June 1760	
DE HOOP	1760	Michael de Leon	800	OAC 878, Sept. 4, 1760	
KONING DAVID	1760	Abraham Sasso		OAC 877, May 28, 1760	
DE HOOP	1760	Isaac Mendes		OAC 877, May 28, 1760	
'T FORTUYN	1760	Isaac Henriquez Julio		OAC 884, Jan. 4, 1762	
LA FORTUNA	1760	Jeosuah Henriquez Jr.	500	OAC 878, Sept. 24, 1760	
DE SCHOONE SARA	1760	Abraham Carillo Saldaña		OAC 878, Sept. 22, 1760	
ST. ANTONY	1760	Manuel Moses A. Correa	775		
DE HOOP	1760	Aron Hz. Moron			See p. 219.
MARIANA	1760	David Bueno Vivas			
JACOBA CHRISTINA	1760	Abraham Jb. Jeudah Leon & Abraham Hz. Coutinho	792	OAC 879, Oct. 10, 1760	
CATHARINA	1760	Jacob Mendes	10,000	OAC 879, Oct. 27, 1760	
DOLPHYN	1760	Jacob L. Maduro	1,200	OAC 879, Nov. 6, 1760	
CATHARINA	1760	Isaac Mendes	9,000	OAC 879, Dec. 22, 1760	

6 Resoluçoes do Mahamad, 5511-5527, meeting of Kislev 5, 5520.

701

Vessel	Year	Owner	Value Pesos	Source	Remarks
VRIENDSCHAP	1760	Isaac Mendes		OAC 882, July 7, 1761	
PATIENTIA	1760	Jacob Talavera	500	OAC 879, Dec. 12, 1760	
KONINGIN ESTHER	1760	Daniel Gomes Casseres & Daniel Mendes de Castro	1,000	OAC 879, Oct. 27, 1760	
DE BEMIDDELBAAR VAN DE VREEDE	1760	Joseph Buzaglo de Paz	30,000f	PJCAA[7]	Amount in florins; De Paz was from St. Eustatius; the ship's course: Dutch Antilles-Amsterdam
REINA ESTHER	1760	Ditto		Ibid.	
REINA ESTHER	1760	Jacobo Solas		OAC 880, Feb. 2, 1761	Solas was willing to pay a ransom of 3,000 pesos for his sloop seized by the English. See p. 219.
ADRIANA	1761	Jacob Hisquiao Suares & Manuel Lopez Jr.			
ST. PIER (PIETER)	1761	Aron Hz. Moron	1,000	OAC 883, Nov. 30, 1761	
HASARD	1761	Isaac Nunes Netto	1,800	OAC 884, no. 225	
JONGE ELIAS	1761	Jacob Eliao Jeudah Leon & Bros.	1,300	OAC 883, Dec. 17, 1761	
VRIJHEID	1761	Abraham de Chaves	1,700	OAC 880, Jan. 6, 1761	
ST. JOSEPH	1761	Samuel Bn. da Costa Andrade	450	OAC 880, Jan. 16, 1761	
CLARA	1761	Abm. de Jb. J^h Leon		OAC 880, Jan. 28, 1761	
MARIA	1761	Isaac Mendes	2,453	OAC 880, Mar. 17, 1761	
DE JONG ABRAHAM	1761	Aron Hz. Moron		OAC 880, Feb. 27, 1761	
AURORA	1761	Salomon Haim Calvo	2,500	OAC 881, Apr. 27, 1761	
AURORA	1761	Isaac Hz. Cautinho	450	OAC 880, Feb. 23, 1761	
MARIA	1761	Isaac Mendes	550	OAC 881, Apr. 17, 1761	
FORTUNA	1761	Ditto	400	OAC 881, June 5, 1761	

Ship	Year	Owner	Amount	OAC Reference	Notes
St. Joseph	1761	Medina & Pina	625	OAC 881, June 4, 1761	
Hanna	1761	Francisco L. Henriquez	700	OAC 882, Aug. 18, 1761	
De Wynanda	1761	Isaac Pardo	3,120	OAC 882, Sept. 8, 1761	
Las tres Hermanas (St. Jean Baptista)	1761	Abraham Carillo Saldaña	651	OAC 882, Sept. 10, 1761	
Elizabeth	1761	Jeosuah Henriquez Jr.	1,250	OAC 883, Nov. 13, 1761	
Jupiter	1761	Isaac Mendes	2,220	OAC 883, Nov. 24, 1761	
Jonge Elias (Nuestra Señora de Rosaria, alias St. Anthony)	1761	Jacob Eliau Jeudah Leao & Hermanos	1,300	OAC 883, Dec. 17, 1761	
Koning David	1761	Moses Morales, Abraham & Salomon Calvo	2,000	OAC 883, Dec. 18, 1761	
Adriana	1762	Aron Hz. Moron		OAC 888, no. 303	See p. 219.
Koningin Esther	1762	Daniel Lopes Castro & Manuel A. Correa			See p. 221.
Drie Patriarke	1762	Medina & Pina			
Vrij Metzelaar	1762	Abraham Hz. Moron		OAC 884, no. 88	
Mercurius	1762	Isaac Mendes		OAC 897, no. 99	
Koning David	1762	Raphael Molina Monsanto			
Nuestra Señora de los Dolores y las Animas	1762	Isaac Mendez	4,500	OAC 884, no. 25	
La Sirena	1762	Abraham Hz. Moron	5,000	OAC 884, no. 110	
Fortuyn	1762	Ditto		OAC 884, no. 180	
Soledad	1762	Ditto	1,000	OAC 884, no. 249	
De Hoop	1762	Abm. de Benjamin Naar		OAC 886, no. 55	See p. 219.
Juffr. Jannetje	1762	†J. A. K. Hendrikz & Manuel de Moses A. Correa		OAC 884, no. 39	
Kleine Oranje	1762	Abraham Hz. Moron		OAC 885, no. 29	

† Bundle, y. 1760, the Buzaglo Decedent's Estate Papers.

Vessel	Year	Owner	Value Pesos	Source	Remarks
DE VRIJHEID	1762	Jacob Monsanto	1,700	OAC 885, no. 3	Sold four months later for 3,600 pesos (OAC 886, no. 114)
ST. SUZANNA	1762	Daniel Lopez de Castro		OAC 886, no. 29	
KLYNE DRADER	1762	Abraham Hz. Moron	2,500	OAC 885, no. 37	
DE HOOP	1762	Moses Hz. Juliao		OAC 885, no. 105	
JONGE NICOLASS	1762	Manuel Moses A. Correa	500	OAC 885, no. 170	
ESPERANSA	1762	Joseph Touro	900	OAC 885, no. 194	
JONGE MORDECHAY	1762	Jacob Alvares & Co.		OAC 885, nos. 227-28	
AURORA	1762	Isaac Hz. Coutinho	2,400	OAC 885, no. 241	
DE HOOP	1762	Abraham Alvares		OAC 885, no. 148	
LA PROVIDENCIA	1762	Moses Motta	2,750	OAC 886, no. 110	
VRIENDSCHAP	1762	Isaac Pardo	950	OAC 886, no. 150	
DOLPHYN	1762	Hoheb & Mendes of St. Eustatius	3,200	OAC 886, no. 198	
DRIE SUSTERS		Abraham & Mordechay Motta			
VRIENDSCHAP	1762	Moses & David Hz. Juliao	5,800	OAC 886, no. 231	Taken by the English
LA REYNA ABIGAIL	1762	Aron Hz. Moron	550	OAC 886, no. 234	
SARA (ST. ANTONIO Y LAS ANIMAS)	1762	Coutinho, Victoria & Morales	1,300	OAC 886, no. 274	
DE HOOP	1762	Samuel Isaac L. Maduro	1,600	OAC 886, no. 286	
JONGE ANDRIES	1762	Manuel Moses A. Correa	550	OAC 887, no. 86	
DE WOLFF	1762	Aron Hz. Moron	1,200	OAC 887, no. 230	
NANCY (ZEPHYR)	1762	Isaac Mendes	4,500	OAC 887, no. 257	Sold in 1763 for 2,500 pesos (OAC 888, no. 281)
NEPTUNES	1762	Ditto	6,250	OAC 887, no. 268	
LA PALOMITA	1762	Abraham Benjamin Naar	400	OAC 887, no. 286	

Ship	Year	Owner	Amount	Reference	Notes
MARIA LOUISE	1762	Isaac Mendes	9,000	OAC 887, no. 289	An armed vessel
DE HOOP	1762	Raphael Molina Monsanto & David Morales	2,000	OAC 887, no. 307	
PERFECT	1762	Isaac Mendes	10,000	OAC 887, no. 308	
DE PIETER	1763	Aron Machoro			
CONSTANT	1763	Elias & Isaac Rz. Miranda	800	OAC 890, no. 114	
ANNA ELIZABETH	1763	Mordechay Motta		OAC 890, no. 117	One-third interest
ST. MARIA	1763	Isaac Pardo	19,000	OAC 890, no. 205	One-half interest
GOED BEGIN	1763	Abraham Motta			
VRIJDAG	1763	Moses Motta & Co.		Maduro's list	
FORTUYN	1763	Jacob Hz. Fereyra & Nagson Hz. Moron	700	OAC 890, no. 141	
PRUDENT	1763	Elias & Isaac Rz. Miranda	4,000	OAC 890, no. 155	
DOLPHYN	1763	Abraham & Salomon Calvo	4,000	OAC 890, no. 180	Sold in 1764 for 3,200 pesos (OAC 891, no. 102)
CONSTANT	1763	Moses Pereyra da Costa	1,200	OAC 890, no. 202	
VRIJHIJT	1763	Isaac Pardo	3,000	OAC 890, no. 230	
DE MERIANAS	1763	Isaac Mendes	5,000	OAC 890, no. 248	
DE HOOP	1763	Moses Vaz Nunes		OAC 890, no. 253	
FORTUYN	1763	Jacob Cohen Fereyra	600	OAC 890, no. 261	
CORNELIA	1763	Daniel & David Gomes Casseres		OAC 890, no. 196	Run: Curaçao-French Sto. Domingo-Bordeaux
PRIMO	1763	Abraham Lopez Peña	3,000	OAC 899, no. 60	
ST. CHARLES	1763	Isaac Hm. Rz. da Costa	6,000	OAC 889, no. 85	
DE HOOP	1763	Mordechay Isaac Calvo & Salomon Is. L. Maduro	2,000	OAC 889, no. 233	
DE SUPERBE	1763	Isaac Mendes	500	OAC 889, no. 304	
CHRISTMAS GALLEY	1763	Ditto	18,000cg	OAC 889, no. 342	Amount in Caroli guilders, i.e., florins
TWEE VRINDEN	1763	Isaac Mordechay de Crasto	2,400	OAC 889, no. 358	
MARIA MAGDALEENA	1763	Abraham Jb. Jeudah Leon		OAC 889, no. 392	

Vessel	Year	Owner	Value Pesos	Source	Remarks
DOLPHYN	1763	Abraham Hz. Moron	500	OAC 889, no. 119	
KONING DAVID	1763	David Morales & Rephael Molina Monsanto	725	OAC 890, no. 6	
SUBERBIA	1763	Aron & Abraham Hz. Moron			
LE BIEN VENU	1763	Isaac Nunes Netto	495	OAC 888, no. 92	
REBECCA	1763	Joseph Curiel	1,400	OAC 888, Feb. 7, 1763	
LA CANDELARIA, alias LA GARSA	1763	Isaac Pardo	5,500	OAC 888, no. 194	
JONGE ELIAS	1763	Isaac Elias Jeudah Leon	2,400	OAC 888, no. 213	
KONING DAVID	1763	Isaac Nunes Netto	900	OAC 888, no. 232	
SARA	1763	Cautinho, Victoria & Morales		OAC 888, no. 91	
MARLANDT	1763	Isaac Mendes		OAC 888, Apr. 20, 1763	
PENELOPE	1763	David Jacob Ho. Suares	1,160	OAC 888, no. 233	
LA VIOLANTE	1763	Isaac Nunes Netto	1,000	OAC 888, no. 247	
DOMIJN	1763	Manuel Moses A. Correa	460	OAC 888, no. 259	
LA NANCY	1763	Isaac Mendes	2,500	OAC 888, no. 281	
MARIANDS	1763	Ditto	7,360	OAC 888, no. 358	
MARIANDS	1763	Isaac & Jacob Jeudah Leon	1,500	OAC 888, no. 54	
INDUSTRIE	1764	Miguel de Leon		OAC 895, no. 59	
TWEE SUSTERS	1764	Robles & Miranda	1,950	OAC 892, no. 278	
JONGE ABRAHAM	1764	Michael de Leon	750	OAC 892, no. 299	Vessel of twenty Dutch last or ± 44 tons
ZEE VUÚR	1764	Isaac Mendes	2,500	OAC 896, no. 51	
ST. JOSEPH	1764	Manuel Moses A. Correa	750	OAC 896, no. 62	
SUBERBA	1764	Abraham & Salomon Hm. Calvo	4,000	OAC 896, no. 53	
DE HOOP	1764	Manuel Moses A. Correa	1,750	OAC 891, no. 14	Equipped with six cannon and divers munitions

Ship	Year	Owner	Amount	Reference	Notes
SARA	1764	Elias & Isaac Rz. Miranda	2,800	OAC 891, no. 41	
LALOS	1764	Manuel Moses A. Correa	1,300	OAC 891, no. 68	
JONGE MOSES	1764	Isaac Mendes	4,000	OAC 891, no. 131	
ROSARIA	1764	Isaac David Suares		OAC 891, no. 139	
SANTA CLARA	1764	Isaac Mendes	3,500	OAC 891, no. 145	
NIEUW FORTUYN	1764	Benjamin C. Henriquez Jr.	2,100	OAC 891, no. 161	
MARIANE	1764	Isaac Mendes	2,200	OAC 891, no. 203	
DE HOOP	1764	Moses Salomon L. Maduro	1,000	OAC 891, no. 212	
TWEE VRIENDEN	1764	Isaac Mord. de Crasto	2,413	OAC 891, nos. 238-39	Armed with seven cannon valued at 100 pesos each
KONING DAVID	1764	Isaac Hz. Juliao		OAC 891, no. 342	
LA DORADA	1764	Isaac Mendes	4,000	OAC 891, no. 395	
LA DORADA	1764	[Dr.] Joseph Caprille	800	OAC 892, no. 89	
DIAMANT	1764	Abraham de Chaves	1,000	OAC 892, no. 103	
MARIA LOUISA	1764	Ditto	5,000	OAC 892, no. 106	
FORTUYN	1764	Molina & Morales	595	OAC 891, no. 193	
DE FORTUYN	1764	David de Jacob Cohen Fereyra		OAC 892, no. 164	
LA MADRE SANTISIMA DE LA LUZ	1764	Isaac Abenatar			
TWEE ZUSTERS	1764	Robles & Miranda		OAC 892, no. 278	
REBECCA	1764	Manuel Moses A. Correa	1,900	OAC 892, no. 123	
PALMITA A ANNA SOPHIA	1764	Lea de Medina, Widow of Isaac Levy	650	OAC 892, no. 187	
DOLPHYN	1764	Abraham & Salomon Hm. Calvo	800	OAC 892, no. 198	
GEERTRUYDA	1764	Abraham Motta	800	OAC 892, no. 203	
VRINDSCHAP	1764	Robles & Miranda		OAC 892, no. 219	
SCHILDPAD	1764	Abraham de Chaves and a Gentile		OAC 892, no. 241	
LA REINA ESTHER	1764	Abraham de Chaves		OAC 892, no. 236	
JONGE BENJAMIN	1765	Mordechay Motta	1,400	OAC 897, no. 212	
SARA	1765	Joseph Calvo	1,000	OAC 897, no. 216	
VRIENDSCHAP	1765	Ishac Robles	2,500	OAC 1558, no. 104	

Vessel	Year	Owner	Value Pesos	Source	Remarks
DE MAAGT	1765	Abraham Motta	1,400	OAC 1558, no. 141	
KONINGIN VAN HUNGARIJEN	1765	David L. Raphael	600	OAC 1558, no. 154	Equipped with four cannon
ZEE VUÚR	1765	Isaac Mord. de Crasto		OAC 1558, no. 186	
VRIENDSCHAP	1765	Abraham de Chaves and a Gentile			
SARA	1765	Moses Motta	2,000	OAC 894, no. 22	
GOEDE VERVAGTING	1765	Abraham Motta		OAC 894, no. 76	
FORTUYN	1765	Isaac Rz. Miranda		OAC 894, no. 98	
MARIANA	1765	Isaac Mord. de Crasto		OAC 894, Sept. 6, 1765	
NUESTRA SEÑORA DEL ROSARIO	1765	Isaac Nunes Netto	600	OAC 894, nos. 158, 173	Sold fifteen days later in Jamaica for 1,100 pesos
REBECCA	1765	Joseph Curiel	2,251	OAC 894, no. 181	
JEREMIAS	1765	Abraham de Chaves		OAC 894, no. 11	
MARIA	1766	Isaac Pardo		OAC 895, no. 117	One-fourth interest
SOLEDA	1766	Nagson Hz. Moron	700	OAC 895, no. 148	
GEORGE	1766	Francisco L. Henriquez	2,000	OAC 895, no. 173	
MARIA LOUISA	1766	Abraham Hz. Moron	5,600	OAC 895, no. 184	Sold in 1767 for 6,500 pesos (OAC 1560, Oct. 20,1767)
DE HOOP (LA TRINIDAD)	1766	Isaac Pardo	1,450	OAC 898, no. 36	
RACHEL	1766	Jeudah Abraham Sasso	1,050	OAC 899, no. 58	
RACHEL	1766	Isaac Mord. de Crasto	1,500	OAC 899, no. 75	Bought for 1,050 pesos and sold a week later for 1,500 pesos
L' BASTAARD	1766	David Naar	2,200	OAC 900, no. 51	
PHANNIE	1767	Salomon Daguilar	500	OAC 1559, Jan. 2, 1767	
SARA	1767	Nahson Hz. Moron	900	OAC 1559, no. 117	
LA SALIES	1767	Jacob Manuel de Crasto		OAC 1560, Sept. 30, 1767	

Ship	Year	Owner		OAC reference	Remarks
St. Anna	1767	David da Costa Gomez & Co.			
Awa Pasaharina	1767	Manuel Ho. Pinedo	800	OAC 1560, Dec. 18, 1767	
Bastaard	1767	Raphael Molina Monsanto & David Morales	1,200	OAC 1560, Dec. 23, 1767	
Adriana	1768	Hoheb & Mendes	4,000	OAC 902, Jan. 1, 1768	
Broeder en Suster	1768	Jacob Hz. Fereira & Benjamin Cohen Henriquez		OAC 902, no. 9	
Soleda	1768	Moses Salomon L. Maduro	550	OAC 902, no. 97	
Goede Vrienden	1768	Isaac Pardo	1,300	OAC 902, no. 126	
Maria Ros	1768	Abraham Salsedo	600	OAC 902, no. 140	
Anna Catharina	1768	Joseph Curiel	2,400	OAC 903, Sept. 14, 1768	
St. Pedro	1768	Joseph Obediente and a Gentile		OAC 903, Sept. 2, 1768	
Formidable	1768	Abraham Hz. Moron	2,600	OAC 903, Oct. 21, 1768	Sold eight months later for Ps. 3,000 (OAC 905, June 22, 1769)
Dolphyn	1768	Elias & Isaac Rz. Miranda	2,500	OAC 903, Nov. 14, 1768	
Koningin van Bohemia	1768	Aron Hz. Moron & Co.		OAC 904, June 8, 1768	
Princesa Carolina	1768	Abraham Hz. Moron		OAC 906, Sept. 9, 1768	
Princesa Carolina	1769	Daniel Martinez			Captured with his vessel in 1769
De Jonge Joseph	1769	Joseph Obediente & Rachel, widow of David Bueno Vivas	500	OAC 905, Jan. 12, 1769	
Ressource	1769	Daniel Mendes de Castro	650	OAC 905, Mar. 16, 1769	
Jonge Haim	1769	Salomon Haim Calvo	2,000	OAC 905, May 18, 1769	Vessel taken by the Spaniards at Cartagena in 1772 (p. 225)
La Sebilana	1769	Joseph Jochem Alexander	400	OAC 905, June 22, 1769	Alexander (Ashkenazi with some Sephardic blood) also part owner of Curaçao's "De Vreede" corn mill

Vessel	Year	Owner	Value Pesos	Source	Remarks
LA SABILANA	1769	Benjamin C. Henriquez	600	OAC 905, Oct. 10, 1769	
MARIA LAMBERTA	1769	Jacob Manuel de Crasto	2,800	OAC 905, July 5, 1769	
SARA	1769	Raphael Molina Monsanto			
DE HOOP (Rosario)	1769	Salomon Samuel Hm. L. Maduro	200	OAC 905, Nov. 17, 1769	
ZEEBLOM	1769	Gabriel Pinedo			
DE HOOP	1769	Isaac Almeida	2,700	OAC 938, no. 20	
FORTUYN	1769	Rachel, widow of David Bueno Vivas	140		
KONING DAVID	1769	David Jb. Senior & David Fidanque	1,450	OAC 939, no. 114	
THERESA	1770	Isaac Pardo		OAC 940, no. 317	
NELLY	1770	Jacob Rz. Brandam	1,000	OAC 940, no. 137	
LA FORTUNA	1770	Ditto	300	OAC 907, no. 112	
TWEE SUSTERS	1770	David Morales	2,000	OAC 907, no. 135	
KONING DAVID	1770	Isaac Rz. Miranda			
L'INFORTUNE	1770	Moses L. Peña	300	OAC 907, no. 176	
LA ROSARIA	1770	Jacob Gomes Casseres	450	OAC 907, no. 216	
LA CHARMANTE MARIE	1770	Isaac Pardo	3,000	OAC 908, no. 58	
ESPERANSA	1770	Isaac Pardo		OAC 940, no. 399	
LA NELLY	1770	Mordechay & Elias Penso	920	OAC 941, no. 384	
L'ESPERANSA	1771	Moses Nunes Redondo	800	OAC 908, no. 92	
SULTAN	1771	Aron Hz. Moron	637	OAC 909, no. 211	
MEYBLOOM	1771	Benjamin C. Henriquez	3,000	OAC 908, no. 313	
JONGE ABRAHAM	1771	David Morales	4,100	OAC 908, no. 314	
LA MARIA, alias REBECCA	1771	Abraham Dias Coutinho		OAC 910, no. 23	Equipped with ten cannon
THOMAS & ROBERT	1771	Isaac Pardo		OAC 942, no. 14	
KONING DAVID	1771	Isaac Rz. Miranda		OAC 942, no. 19	
FORTUIN	1771	Salomon Is. L. Maduro		OAC 942, no. 43	

Ship	Year	Owner	Tonnage	Reference	Notes
KONINGIN ANNA	1771	Jacob Gomes Casseres		OAC 942, no. 50	
NUESTRA SRA DEL ROSARIO	1771	Gabriel Pinedo		OAC 942, no. 55	
CREOLE	1771	Jacob Gomes Casseres		OAC 942, no. 249	
CANDELARIA	1771	Isaac Pardo		OAC 943, no. 314	
HANNA PALLY	1771	Elias Rz. Miranda		OAC 943, no. 407	
SOLEDAD	1771	Isaac Pardo		OAC 943, no. 418	
ABIGAIL	1771	Isaac Robles		OAC 942, no. 432	
ST. JOSEPH	1771	Manuel da Costa Gomes & Bros.	1,500	OAC 910, no. 26	
FORMEDABEL	1771	Daniel L. de Castro & Co.	800	OAC 910, no. 42	
ST. ANNA	1771	Moseh Naar		OAC 942, no. 124	
TWEE GEBROEDERS	1771	Jacob Gomes Casseres		OAC 942, no. 185	
DOLPHYN	1771	Abraham Dias Coutinho	870	OAC 942, no. 216	
LA SOLEDA	1772	Abraham & Isaac de Marchena	250	OAC 911, no. 231	
DOMYN	1772	Jacob Aboab Cardozo	1,500	OAC 911, no. 293	
ST. ANDREU	1772	Josias de Casseres	1,000	OAC 911, no. 303	
ST. ANDREU	1772	Mosseh Flores			
JOLY	1772	†Jacob Francisco Maduro	2,000	OAC 944, no. 8	A half-Jew
HET GOED SUCCES	1772	Benjamin Jesurun	700	OAC 944, no. 31	
LA GUADALOUPE	1772	Salomon Vaz Faro	400		
FORTUYN	1772	Manuel d Costa Gomes & Brothers	600	OAC 944, no. 59	
DE HOOP	1772	Salomon Haim Calvo		OAC 944, no. 74	
RACHEL	1772	Isaac Abinun de Lima	500	OAC 944, no. 99	
DE JONGE ABRAHAM	1772	Gabriel Pinedo			
SOLIDAD	1772	Louzada & Hz. Coutinho		OAC 944, no. 131	
CLARA	7122	Rachel, wid. of David Bueno Vivas			
JONGE MANUEL	1772	Jacob Manuel de Crasto	1,500	OAC 945, no. 221	
LA SOLIDAD	1772	Rachel Jesurun Henriquez and a Gentile		OAC 945, no. 239	
ST. CARLOS	1772	Ester Penso de Aron Hz. Moron	3,200	OAC 945, no. 260	
MARGUERITA	1772	Manuel Ho. Pinedo	1,800	OAC 945, no. 324	

711

Vessel	Year	Owner	Value Pesos	Source	Remarks
PAULINA	1772	Daniel & David G. Casseres and David Taboada		OAC 942, no. 129	See p. 220.
DOROTHEA	1772	Samuel Salomon L. Maduro		OAC 201, no. 40	
EENDRAGT	1773	Jacob Nunes Redondo	400	OAC 912, no. 1	
L'ESPERANSA	1773	Isaac Pardo	3,000	OAC 912, no. 16	
MARYANA	1773	Ditto	6,000	OAC 912, no. 17	
KLYNE MARIANA	1773	Jacob Gomes Casseres	1,950	OAC 912, no. 71	
VIGILANTIE	1773	Jacob da Costa Gomez	1,000	OAC 912, no. 108	
DE JONGE JACOB (Nuestra Señora del Rosario)	1773	Jacob & Aron Pinedo	2,500	OAC 913, no. 32	
ST. ANTHOINE	1773	Isaac Mendes	1,125	OAC 946, no. 1	
HANNA PALLY	1773	Isaac Hm. de Jb. Senior	900	OAC 946, no. 9	
DOLPHYN	1773	Jacob Hz. Motta & Isaac L. Penha	600	OAC 946, no. 41	
FORTUYN	1773	Manuel d C. Gomez & Bros.	500	OAC 946, no. 46	
VIGILANT	1773	Gabriel Pinedo	4,000	OAC 946, no. 111	
DE HOOP (Lampario)	1773	Joseph Obediente Jr.		OAC 946, no. 152	
DE HOOP (Lampario)	1773	Jeosuah de Chaves		OAC 947, no. 220	Chaves' schooner seized by the Spaniards in 1773
DE HOOP	1773	Abraham David Jesurun & Raphael Penso	2,000	OAC 947, no. 245	
JONGE ABRAHAM	1773	Isaac Pardo & Sons	4,100	OAC 947, no. 351	
SANTANNA	1773	Ditto			
JONGE JACOB	1774	Gabriel Pinedo	2,000	OAC 949, no. 237	
LA DORADA	1775	Isaac Pardo & Sons		OAC 917, no. 72	
LA BONNE ESPERANSA	1776	Gabriel Pinedo			
DE HOOP	1776	Isaac Abm. de Marchena	2,100	OAC 954, no. 103	Armed with three cannon

Ship	Year	Owner	Value	Reference	Notes
PALLY	1776	Isaac Pardo & Sons		OAC 954, no. 155	Curaçao Destination: Amsterdam
PALLY	1776	Isaac Namias			
VIER GEBROEDERS	1776	David Abraham Sasso		OAC 916, no. 16	Seized by the Spaniards
DIAMANT	1776	Isaac de Marchena	2,500	OAC 916, nos. 300-301	Bought for 2,500 pesos and sold the same day for 3,000 pesos
STA. BARBERA	1776	Isaac Samuel L. Maduro & Co.	200	OAC 916, no. 303	
SARA	1776	David Pardo	240	OAC 916, no. 316	
FORTUYN	1776	Isaac de Marchena	3,600	OAC 916, no. 322	
LA HAZAR	1777	Isaac Pardo & Sons	2,750	OAC 955, no. 168	
DE GOEDE HOOP	1777	Ditto	650	OAC 918, no. 317	
CONCEPCION	1777	Joseph Pinhero (a Jew?)		OAC 918, no. 303	
DISPATCH	1777	Mordechaij Pardo & Co.		OAC 918, no. 358	
DE JONGE DANIEL	1778	Joseph Curiel	1,000		Captain-owner Curiel seized with his ship in 1778, taken to Havana and there detained for upwards of two years (p. 226)
SOLEDA	1778	Jacob Isaac Suares	100	OAC 919, no. 75	One-fourth interest
CATHARINA	1778	Elias Penso	400	OAC 920, no. 264	
CATHARINA	1778	Salomo Calvo	2,500	OAC 920, no. 330	
SOUPERBE	1778	David Cardoze & †Michiel Cambiaso		OAC 920, no. 379	
PAERLE	1778	David Morales		OAC 920, no. 419	
ZEEBLOM	1778	Cardoze & Cambiaso		OAC 920, no. 439	
GOED FORTUYN	1778	Ditto		OAC 920, no. 463	
TWEE VRIENDEN	1778	Manuel d Costa Gomez & Bros.	516	OAC 919, no. 56	
DE HOOP (St. Francisco i las Animas)	1778	Isaac Pardo & Sons	540	OAC 919, no. 60	

Vessel	Year	Owner	Value Pesos	Source	Remarks
JONGE ABRAHAM	1778	David Morales	4,100	OAC 956, no. 36	Value with its cargo
ST. JOSEPH	1778	Ditto	4,000	OAC 957, no. 177	Value of cargo only
ESPERANSA	1778	Abraham Calvo	5,000	OAC 956, no. 103	
JUFFR. RACHEL (Elisabeth)	1778	Salomo Is. L. Maduro	880	OAC 956, no. 104	
JUFFR. RACHEL	1778	Children of Samuel Is. L. Maduro	880	OAC 956, no. 133	
CATHARINA	1778	Elias Penso & Jacob P. Brandao		OAC 920, no. 475	
DE GOEDE HOOP	1779	Benjamin & Moses C. Henriquez		OAC 208, no. 202	
DE JONGE ISAAC	1779	Moses Monsanto		OAC 208, no. 124	
VROUW SARA	1779	Aron Pinedo			
CONCORDIA	1779	David Lopez Raphael	13,025	OAC 924, no. 1018	
EXPEDITIE	1779	Elias Penso & Abraham Dovale	4,641	OAC 924, nos. 1053-54	
TWEE GEBROEDERS	1779	David & Joseph L. Raphael	2,000	OAC 924, no. 1127	
JONGE ELIAS	1779	Benjamin Nunes Tavarez	3,500	OAC 924, no. 1138	
ZEEBLOM	1779	Isaac Pardo & Sons		OAC 921, no. 27	
ZEEBLOM	1779	Jacob Hz. Fereyra			
DE RESOLUTIE	1779	Jacob Carillo [Saldaña]		OAC 208, no. 157	
PRINS VAN ORANJE (Nuestra Señora de Candelaria)	1779	Benjamin Nunes Tavarez	4,781	OAC 924, no. 1235	
RWEE GEBROEDERS	1779	Dovale & Pardo		OAC 923, no. 804	
TACHEL	1779	Elias Rz. Miranda & Samuel Is. L. Maduro	1,600	OAC 921, no. 57	
SARA	1779	Benjamin Nunes Tavarez			
JONGE ABRAHAM [II]	1779	David Morales	1,900	OAC 924, no. 1339	
CAROLINA	1779	Isaac de Marchena & †Wm. Marten		OAC 924, no. 1389	
DE MARIANNA	1779	David Morales			

Ship	Year	Owner	Amount	OAC ref.	Notes
ABIGAEL	1779	Joseph Obediente Jr. & Jacob L. Penha		OAC 924, no. 1443	
ESTER	1779	Aaron Pimentel			
DOLPHIJN	1779	Moses Oliveira Isidro			
JONGE ISAAC	1779	Mordechay Jb. Henriquez	1,500	OAC 924, no. 1468	
JUFFR. SARA	1779	Jacob Jesurun Lindo		OAC 924, no. 1477	
DOROTHEA	1779	Jacob Jesurun Lindo		OAC 921, no. 208	
JONGE MOSES (St. Christo de Lazo)	1779	Jacob David Jesurun	1,300	OAC 921, no. 43	
ZEEBLOM	1779	Isaac Pardo & Sons		OAC 921, no. 44	
DE PEARL	1779	David Morales & Abraham Calvo		OAC 921, no. 47	
PERFECT	1779	David Montez	2,200	OAC 921, no. 77	
DE GOEDE HOOP	1779	Manuel d Costa Gomez & Bros.		OAC 921, no. 88	
KONINGIN ESTHER	1779	Isaac de Marchena		OAC 921, no. 144	
ELIZABETH	1779	Salomon & Jacob Moses de Castro		OAC 921, no. 130	
FORTUYN	1779	Salomon de Castro	990	OAC 921, no. 205	
ELISABETH	1779	Benjamin & Moses C. Henriquez		OAC 921, no. 210	
SAVANA	1779	David Morales		OAC 921, no. 213	
BORBON	1779	Ditto		OAC 921, no. 216	
JONGE JACOB	1779	Moses Mendes Monsanto		OAC 921, no. 237	One-half interest
DOLPHIJN	1779	Benj. & Moses C. Henriquez & †C. Visser			
CONCORDIA	1779	David Lopez Raphael	4,300	OAC 922, no. 336	
MARIANNA	1779	David Morales		OAC 922, no. 373	
ESTER	1779	Jacob Lopez Penha		OAC 922, no. 421	
MORGEN	1779	Jacob Abraham(s)		OAC 922, no. 426	Ashkenazi
CATHARINA	1779	Jacob de Sola and the widow of Jb. P. Brandam	1,200	OAC 922, no. 437	
RACHEL	1779	Isaac de Marchena	2,000	OAC 922, no. 438	Sold in 1780 for 3,000 ps. (OAC 928, no. 109)
JONGE JACOB (St. Joseph i las Animas)	1779	Jacob Jesurun Lindo	2,000	OAC 922, no. 440	Sold a few months later for 2,400 pesos

715

Vessel	Year	Owner	Value Pesos	Source	Remarks
JUDITH	1779	Benj. & Moses C. Henriquez		OAC 922, no. 456	
LA PARFAIT	1779	Moyse Oliveyra Isidro		OAC 922, no. 463	
PERFECT	1779	Daniel L. Penha	1,687	OAC 922, no. 473	
TWEE GEBROEDERS	1779	David & Joseph L. Raphael	1,840	OAC 922, no. 484	
CONCORDIA	1779	Jacob de Solas & Eliao Penso		OAC 922, no. 519	
TWEE GEBROEDERS (Bluto)	1779	Jacob Abraham	1,400	OAC 923, no. 712	
KONINGIN ESTER	1779	Abraham Calvo		OAC 923, no. 744	
JONGE GABRIEL	1779	Abraham Cohen Peixotto		OAC 923, no. 763	
STA. ANNA	1779	Jacob Jesurun Lindo	1,200	OAC 923, no. 799	Bought and sold the same day to Isaac Pardo & Sons for 1,000 pesos
STA. ANNA	1779	David Morales	650	OAC 923, no. 829	Bought in French Sto. Domingo in 1779
SARA	1779	Aron Pinedo		OAC 923, no. 845	
PERFECT	1779	David Morales		OAC 923, no. 846	
JONGE ABRAHAM	1779	Abraham Nunes Redondo	2,000	OAC 923, no. 874	
DE HOOP (Dorothea)	1779	Isaac Pardo & Sons	12,000	OAC 923, no. 884	
NUESTRA SEÑORA DE CARME	1779	David Morales	200	OAC 923, no. 885	
CATHALINA	1780	Jacob Mendes Henriquez	1,125	OAC 925, no. 266	
RACHEL	1780	Elias Rz. Miranda	4,000	OAC 925, no. 192	
JONGE GABRIEL	1780	Jacob & Abraham Cohen Peixotto	7,000	OAC 927, no. 879	
JONGE ARON	1780	Aron Gabriel Pinedo		OAC 925, no. 32	
ARIAANTJE	1780	Benjamin Suares	800	OAC 925, no. 67	
DE JONGE ISAAK (Nuestra Señora de Carme)	1780	Abraham de Leon Nunez	670	OAC 925, no. 86	
NEPTUNUS (St. Juan)	1780	David Morales	1,200	OAC 925, no. 249	

716

Ship	Year	Owner	Tonnage	Reference
Lea	1780	Rephael Jn. Sasportas	500	OAC 925, no. 250
De Hoop	1780	Jacob Jesurun Lindo		OAC 925, no. 256
Fortuyn	1780	David Lopez Raphael	1,100	OAC 925, no. 307
Zeeblom	1780	Isaac Pardo & Sons, David & Moseh Cardozo	10,000	OAC 926, no. 440
Expeditie	1780	Jacob de Sola and Eliao Penso	1,252	OAC 926, no. 442
Onverwacht	1780	†C. Visser & Benjamin C. Henriquez		OAC 930, no. 1521
Vriendschap	1780	Jacob & Abm. Cohen Peixotto		OAC 930, no. 1542
Sara	1780	Jacob Pinedo & Bros.	1,200	OAC 926, no. 453
Sara	1780	Benjamin Nunez Tavarez		OAC 926, no. 460
Morgenster	1780	Daniel L. Penha & Moseh Oliveyra Isidro	500	OAC 926, no. 482
Judith	1780	Josuah Mendez & Jacob de Sola	2,800	OAC 930, no. 1504
Het Goed Succes	1780	Benj. & Moses C. Henriquez		OAC 926, no. 647
Sara	1780	Gabriel Pinedo		OAC 927, no. 671
Koningin Ester	1780	David Morales	3,500	
Helena	1780	David Abinun de Lima	3,000	OAC 927, no. 756

Both ship and precious cargo were seized by the English during the American Revolution in 1780 (OAC 927, nos. 604, 648). Morales, the biggest merchant and shipowner of his time, lost his entire fortune apparently as a result of the French Revolution. His possessions in French Sto. Domingo seem to have been confiscated (WICA 616, no. 1, Feb. 12, 1791).

717

Vessel	Year	Owner	Value Pesos	Source	Remarks
JONGE SAMSON (St. George)	1780	Joseph Obediente Jr.		OAC 927, no. 767	
REBECCA	1780	Benj. & Moses C. Henriquez		OAC 927, no. 783	
JONGE JOSEPH	1780	Joseph Obediente Jr. & †C. Visser	2,680	OAC 927, no. 806	
JONGE ISAAK	1780	Dovale & Pardo		OAC 927, no. 843	
DE HOOP	1780	Moses Benjamin Jesurun	800	OAC 927, no. 870	
DE GOEDE INTENTIE	1780	Salomon Calvo		OAC 927, no. 873	
REBECCA	1780	David Montes		OAC 927, no. 924	
REBECCA	1780	Obediente & Penha	1,800	OAC 928, no. 1190	
CATHARINA	1780	Jacob da Costa Gomez	2,000	OAC 928, no. 1201	
DE HOOP	1780	Dovale, Pardo & David L. Raphael	1,800	OAC 928, no. 1240	
JOHANNA	1780	Raphael Molina Monsanto		OAC 929, no. 1328	
ST. ANNA	1780	Isaac Pardo & Sons	1,000	OAC 929, no. 1346	
ABIGAEL	1780	David Pardo	550	OAC 929, no. 1332	
ESTHER	1780	Jacob Lopez Penha	3,000	OAC 929, no. 1382	
PHENIX	1780	David L. Raphael, Dovale & Pardo	11,953	OAC 929, no. 1418	
JUFFR. SARA	1780	Jacob Abenatar & David Pardo		OAC 930, no. 1535	
PRINS VAN ORANJE	1780	David Morales		OAC 930, no. 1554	
GOEDE VRIENDSCHAP	1780	David Cardozo & Co.		OAC 929, no. 1423	
VIGILANTE	1780	Daniel L. Penha	2,700	OAC 929, no. 1446	
JUDITH	1780	Jacob de Sola	2,800	OAC 930, no. 1504	Sole owner
PRINCE VAN ASTURIAS	1780	David Morales	11,953	OAC 930, no. 1506	
DOLPHYN	1780	Daniel L. Penha	1,700	OAC 930, no. 1533	
CATHALINA	1780	Ditto	1,150	OAC 930, no. 1557	
JOHANNA NICOLINA	1780	Aron Machoro	1,625	OAC 930, no. 1577	
PORTLAND	1780	Josiau Naar	2,500	OAC 930, no. 1697	

718

Ship	Year	Owner	Value	Reference	Note
ESPERANSA	1780	Moses Benj. Jesurun			
FORTUYN (La Maria)	1781	D'Aguilar	3,000	OAC 931, no. 125	
FORTUYN (II)	1781	Moses Marache	600	OAC 931, no. 187	
JONGE DANIEL	1781	Moses Mendes Sexas		OAC 931, no. 296	
DE HOOP	1781	Abraham Salzedo	1,041	OAC 931, no. 304	
ST. TRINIDAD	1781	†Jan Claasz & Isaac Samuel L. Maduro			
JONGE THEODORE	1781	Moses Ceichas	350	OAC 932, no. 435	
JONGE ISAAC	1781	Abraham de Leao Nunes		OAC 932, no. 542	
TWEE GEBROEDERS	1781	David aCohen		OAC 932, no. 648	
ABIGAEL	1781	Isaac Pardo	625	OAC 933, no. 665	
ABIGAEL	1781	David aCohen		OAC 933, no. 676	
DOLPHYN	1781	David Morales			
RIBCA (St. Trinidad)	1781	Jacob Gabay Henriquez	1,400	OAC 933, no. 708	
FORTUYN	1781	Joseph L. Raphael & Abraham Dovale	3,000	OAC 934, no. 963	
VRIENDSCHAP	1781	David Morales & †H. E. Pletz	6,200	OAC 931, no. 86	
TWEE BROEDERS	1781	Isaac de Marchena		OAC 930, no. 1554	
L'HIBBÉ (De Hoop)	1781	Morales, †Cadiere & Robles	131,927g	OAC 959, nos. 418-19	Value in pesos, ±29,310 (the peso then worth between four and five gourdes); run of this well-armed ship: Curaçao-French Sto. Domingo-France
FLOR DE MAYO	1781	Joseph Obediente Jr.		OAC 931, no. 238	
RETROUVE	1781	David aCohen		OAC 933, no. 754	
ESPERANZA	1781	Jacob & Abm. Cohen Peixotto		OAC 934, no. 890	
JACK (Fontuin)	1781	Isaac Welcome		OAC 934, no. 893	
ZIEL(?) VAN KINGSTON	1781	David Montes		OAC 934, no. 1134	
RESOLUTIE	1781	David Morales			
REBECCA	1782	Abraham Salzedo		OAC 936, no. 126	

Vessel	Year	Owner	Value Pesos	Source	Remarks
NEUTRALITEIT	1782	Abraham Salzedo		OAC 936, no. 152	
REBECCA	1782	Issac Lopez	4,000	OAC 936, no. 197	
DE GOEDE INTENTIE	1782	Benjn & Moses Cohen Henriquez		OAC 938, Jan. 8, 1782	
DE HOOP	1782	Imanuel da Costa Gomez & Broeders		OAC 938, May 14, 1782	
KONING DAVID	1782	Ditto		OAC 938, Sept. 16, 1782	
TIEN TRADER	1782	Manuel Pinedo & Bros.	3,000	OAC 959, no. 480	
DE JONGE JACOB	1782	Manuel Pinedo		OAC 959, no. 524	
FORTUYN	1782	Abraham Athias	600	OAC 937, no. 98	
JONGE GABRIEL	1782	Manuel da Costa Gomez & Bros.	7,000	OAC 965, no. 24	
RESOLUTIE	1782	Abraham Dias Coutinho	4,000	OAC 965, no. 29	This vessel and the following three bought from Morales the same day
VRIENDSCHAP	1782	Ditto	9,000	OAC 965, no. 30	
BOURBON	1782	Ditto	5,000	OAC 965, no. 32	
DOLPHYN	1782	Ditto	8,000	OAC 965, no. 31	Apparently repurchased later by Morales
ST. JAN	1782	Ditto		OAC 965, no. 31	
ST. JUAN PAQUET	1782	Isaac Lopez	6,000	OAC 965, no. 47	
RUBIC	1782	David Morales		OAC 1084, no. 87	
LE ROI DAVID	1783	Ditto		OAC 959, no. 348	
MORGEN STAR	1783	Ditto	10,125	OAC 959, no. 533	
DE DOLPHYN	1783	Ditto	7,000	OAC 959, no. 534	
RACHEL	1783	Isaac Hm. Rz. da Costa	1,000	OAC 959, no. 535	
JONG ISAAC	1783	Lopez Raphael, Dovale & Pardo			
CONCORDIA	1873	Ditto	4,218:6	OAC 967, no. 511	
INTERPRIJS	1783	Moses Fernandes	647	OAC 967, no. 624	

Ship	Year	Owner	Tonnage	Reference	Notes
INTERPRIJS	1783	Abraham Calvo	2,550	OAC 967, no. 559	
INTERPRIJS	1783	Salomon & Jacob de Castro	800	OAC 967, no. 617	
ENTERPRISE	1783	Widow of Josuah G. Mendes		OAC 966, no. 268	
JONGE ISAAC	1783	Moses Fernandes		OAC 966, no. 353	
LA ESPERANZA	1783	D. Henriquez			
LA ESPERANZA	1783	M. Cohen Henriquez	1,500	OAC 966, no. 377	
JONGE ISAAK	1783	Elias Penso		OAC 1085, nos. 154-55	
JONGE MOSES	1783	Manuel Moses A. Correa		OAC 1084, no. 187	
DE HOOP	1783	David Morales		OAC 1085, no. 184	
LA CONCEPCION	1783	Joseph Athias	800	OAC 965, no. 36	
POSTILLON	1783	David Morales		OAC 1085, nos. 67-8	
REBECCA	1783	Jeosuah Mendes		OAC 967, no. 670	
CATHARINA	1784	Jacob Mendes Henriques		OAC 1086, no. 31	
REBECCA	1784	Moses Gabay Henriquez		OAC 1086, no. 155	
POMANIA	1784	David Morales		OAC 1086, no. 182	
NEPTUNES	1784	Isaac Gabay Henriquez		OAC 1086, no. 232	
ENDEAVOUR	1785	Selomo Isaac L. Maduro & Elias Dovale		OAC 970, no. 2	
REBECCA	1785	Salomon de Castro		OAC 970, no. 4	
SARA	1785	Abraham de Leon Nunes	700	OAC 970, no. 20	
DOLPHYN	1785	David Raphael	1,000	OAC 970, no. 30	
JONGE JACOB [II]	1785	Jacob G. Pinedo & Bros.	4,000	OAC 970, no. 70	
KONING DAVID (Nuestra Señora de Candelaria)	1785	David Isaac Suares	700	OAC 970, no. 73	
KONING SALOMON (Rome)	1785	Ditto	700	OAC 971, no. 32	
DOLPHYN [III]	1785	David Morales	1,300	OAC 971, no. 56	
DE TWEE VRIENDEN	1785	Raphael Molina & Abraham Daniel Gomes Casseres	2,200	OAC 971, no. 61	Bought in 1785 from an Englishman
LA MARIA (Sta. Rita)	1785	Isaac de Marchena	1,000	OAC 971, no. 96	
PRINS ROBERT	1785	Aron Ailyon	2,000	OAC 972, no. 66	

Vessel	Year	Owner	Value Pesos	Source	Remarks
VRIJ METZELAAR	1785	Moses Gabay Henriquez	1,125	OAC 972, no. 122	
LA VICTORIA	1785	Ditto	1,300	OAC 972, no. 109	
DE NANCY	1785	Moses Cohen Henriquez	1,500	OAC 972, no. 189	Sold a few months later for only 550 pesos
VROUW MARIA	1785	David Is. Suares	1,350	OAC 972, no. 63	
KONING SALOMON	1785	Jeosuah Cohen Peixotto	2,700	OAC 972, no. 64	
LA FORTUNA	1785	Moses Vaz Nunes	225	OAC 972, no. 95	
GOED FORTUYN	1785	Selomo Jacob Selomo L. Maduro	105	OAC 972, no. 121	
ESPERANSA	1785	Salomon Redondo		OAC 742, y. 1785	
LA SANTISIMA TRINIDAD	1786	Moses Vas Nunes		OAC 223, no. 117	
ADVONTUUR (Goed Succes)	1786	Aron Machoro & Co.	4,500	OAC 974, no. 307	
JONGE JACOB	1786	David Is. Suares	1,250	OAC 974, no. 338	
REBECCA	1786	Mordechay Pardo	4,500	OAC 975, no. 492	
LE PETIT MATHURIN	1786	Aron Motta	2,000	OAC 975, no. 511	
NIEUWE HOOP	1786	David Is. Suares	1,000	OAC 975, no. 604	
SALLY	1786	Isaac Rz. Miranda & Jacob Joseph Curiel	632	OAC 976, no. 757	
VROUW JUDITH	1786	Jacob de Casseres	250	OAC 976, no. 783	
DE GOEDE HOOP	1786	Abraham Minguel Roiz Mendez	200	OAC 976, no. 791	
RESOLUTIE	1786	Pardo Frères		OAC 214, no. 9	
DE GOEDE HOOP	1787	Abraham M. Roiz Mendes & †Paulina Suares	350	OAC 977, no. 35	
LA MARIA	1787	Andrade & Cohen Henriquez	300	OAC 977, no. 82	
JOSEPHUS	1787	Jacob Gabriel Pinedo & Bros.	8,437	OAC 977, no. 88	
COTORO	1787	Jesurun Brothers	240	OAC 977, no. 116	
SARA	1787	Isaac de Marchena	475	OAC 972, no. 182	

722

Ship	Year	Owner	Value	Reference	Remarks
CELIA	1788	Abraham Mord. Semag Aboab			
VRIENDSCHAP	1789	Jesurun Brothers	1,450	OAC 981, no. 36	
JONGE ABRAHAM	1789	David Hz. Juliao	150	OAC 981, no. 256	
JUFFR. RACHEL	1789	Abraham Athias	900	OAC 982, no. 39	
JUFFR. ANNA	1789	Jesurun Brothers	1,125	OAC 982, no. 47	
CARITAD	1789	David L. Raphael & Aron Pardo	2,250	OAC 982, no. 117	
GOED HOOP	1790	David Is. Suares	250	OAC 983, no. 37	
JUFFR. SARA	1790	Isaac Jesurun Sasportas	250	OAC 983, no. 82	
LOVELY ROSETTA	1790	Nathan Hart	850	OAC 983, no. 116	Schooner purchased during his visit to Curaçao, and sold on April 28, 1790, to †Jan Smith
EENDRAGT	1790	David Morales		OAC 148, p. 16	
ZEEBLOM	1791	Jacob Gab. Pinedo & Bros.			
SOLEDA	1791	David Abinun de Lima Jr. & Joseph Athias		OAC 133, no. 64	
ST. JOSEPH	1791	Gaspar David Henriquez	10,000	OAC 138, no. 19	Taken by the English
ELISABETH	1792	Jacob Mendes Henriquez		OAC 134, Jan. 24, 1792	
FURY	1792	Jesurun Brothers		OAC 134, Oct, 1792	
DIAMANT CRIOLLI	1793	Gaspar David Henriquez	40,000	OAC 138, no. 19	Value of ship and cargo
BETSY	1793	Ditto	20,000	OAC 138, no. 19	Ditto; laden with ammunition, the ship exploded at sea, bringing death to all, including Henriquez' brother.
EINDRACHT	1794	Raphael Pinedo		OAC 136, Apr. 8, 1794	
PEGGY	1794	David aCohen		OAC 221, no. 115	
LA RESSOURCE	1794	Isaac Rz. Miranda		OAC 221, no. 116	
TWEE GEBROEDERS	1794	Ditto		OAC 221, no. 116	Seized by the Spaniards
TWEE GEBROEDERS	1795	Benjamin Motta		W. I. Comité 139, Mar. 16, 1795	

Vessel	Year	Owner	Value Pesos	Source	Remarks
DE HOOP	1796	Abm. S^l Jeudah Leon		OAC 139, May 9, 1797	
GRACIA	1796	David de Isaac Henriquez		OAC 995, no. 207	
EL ROSARIO	1796	Benjn. de Mrdy. Henriquez		OAC 995, no. 208	
MARIE	1796	Raphael Jn. Sasportas		OAC 995, no. 215	
	1797	No record found for this year			
ACTIVE	1798	Isaac Cardozo		OAC 225, no. 19	
	1799-1802	No record found for these years			
JONGE JACOB	1803	Jacob Gabriel Pinedo	7,000p		Amount in *patintjes* (equivalent to 13,000 pesos); requisitioned by the Curaçao Government in 1803 because of its sore need for ships of that type
SARAH	1803	Isaac Jesurun Pinto		Amelunxem, p. 138	
	1804-10	No record found for these years			
CLYDE	1811	Benjamin Henriquez		OAC 483, no. 53	
JAN JAN	1812	Joseph Henriquez	550		
ELISA	1814	Isaac Cardoze	6,750	OAC 1563, no. 62	
TWO FRIENDS	1816	Isaac Penso		Koloniën 3740, 1816	Nineteen tons (included among the 14 vessels registered in Aruba in 1816)
CRIOOL	1816	Ditto		Ditto	Six tons; ditto
TWEE BROTHERS	1816	Mordechay Henriquez		Ditto	Ten tons; ditto
SOCIETEIT	1817	Isaac & Josiau Pardo		Koloniën 3615, no. 36	Seized by the Spaniards in Venezuelan ports
TWEELINGEN JOSEPH & BENJAMIN	1817	Salomon Pardo	1,300	OAC 1048, no. 92	

Ship	Year	Owner	Reference		Notes
LA MARIA	1817	Moses Elias Penso	OAC 1049, no. 6	1,100	
VENUS	1817	Aron Pinedo	OAC 1049, no. 31	1,200	
GOED HOOP	1817	Joseph Henriquez	OAC 1049, no. 114	650	
DELIGENCE	1818	Jeosuah de Sola & Son	OAC 1052, no. 19	2,300	
DELIGENCE	1819	Benjamin Mord. Henriquez	Koloniën 3621, Mar. 12, 1819		
LEONA	1819	Samuel Henriquez			Forty tons
DE HOOP	1821	Obadia Mendes da Costa	OAC 294, Aug. 3, 1821		
GOVERNOR VAN STARCKENBORGH	1821	Mathias Levy			Jewishness uncertain
ALEXANDRIA	1821	David Mord. Henriquez	OAC 294, no. 174		Taken by the Simon Bolivar Government (OAC 294, no. 154)
FANFAN	1821	Joseph de Mord. Henriquez			Ditto
UNION	1821	David Mord. Henriquez & Saul Haim Pardo			Ditto
TOEVALLIG	1821	Moses Elias Penso	OAC 294, Sept. 24, 1821		Ditto
DRIE VRIENDEN	1821	†Eman, †Oduber & Saul Haim Pardo			Ditto
TWEE VRIENDEN	1821	Moses de Elias Penso	OAC 294, no. 155		
PHILANTROPIA	1822	Saul Haim Pardo	OAC 294, Oct. 28, 1822		Ditto
ENTERPRISE	1822	Moses Abraham Jesurun	OAC 296, Sept. 1, 1822		Jesurun, grandfather of the Socialist Daniel de Leon, bought this American Revolutionary War schooner that had run aground at Klyn Curaçao.
HARMONY HALL	1823	Joseph P. Brandao			
JOSEPH EN ABRAHAM	1824	Ditto	OAC 1632, Dec. 14, 1824		20 tons
PERSEVERANCE	1825	David Gomes Casseres	OAC 1632, Jan. 1, 1825		32 "

Vessel	Year	Owner	Value Pesos	Source	Remarks
TWO RACHELS	1825	Jacob S. Delvalle & Eliao Curiel		OAC 1632, Jan. 7, 1825	18 tons
SARA	1825	Samuel Lyon		OAC 1632, Mar. 23, 1825	191 "
LA PROSPERA	1825	Mordechay Frois		OAC 1632, April 13, 1825	13 "
BERMUDIÁN	1825	David Mendes Monsanto		OAC 1632, July 1, 1825	101 "
TWEE GEBROEDERS	1825	Mordechay & Joseph Mord. Henriquez		OAC 1632, Sept. 14, 1825	24 "
GOUVERNOR CANTZLAAR	1825	Joseph Mord. Henriquez		OAC 1632, Dec. 28, 1825	44 "
WILLEM PRINCE	1825	Obadia Mendes da Costa			Taken by the Colombian Govt. (OAC 298, July, 1825)
HARMONIE	1825	Moses Marchena Jr.			
	1826	No record found for this year			
MATHILDE	1827	J. & A. H. Senior		K. H. Corporaal, p. 86	
	1828-34	No record found for these years			
DOROTEA	1835	David C. Henriquez		*Boletín del Archivo de la Nación*, vol. 35 (Caracas, 1948), p. 437	
	1836-42	No record found for these years			
DILIGENCIA	1843	Jacob Roiz Mendes		CEOE 791, no. 30	
LAFAYETTE	1843	Jacob Abraham Jesurun		CEOE 795, no. 19	
GRAN MARIA	1844	David Abraham Jesurun		CEOE 795, no. 19; CGANA, 1846, III, no. 92	70 tons
ESTER LINDA	1844	Jacob Rois Mendes		CGAMR, 1844, no. 348	
SUSANNA	1844	Mordechay Henriquez		CGAMR, 1844, no. 358	
VICTORIA	1845	David Abraham Jesurun		CEOE 795, no. 52	

N.B. - All amounts after January, 1827, are expressed in florins unless otherwise specified.

Name	Year	Owner	Value (doubloons/Pesos)	Reference	Steamer started its Curaçao-St. Thomas run in 1845; * value in gold doubloons
LA BEAUTÉ	1846	Moses & Haim C. Henriquez	2,375*	CGANA, 1846, I, no. 84	67 tons;
ESTER	1847	David Abraham Jesurun		CGANA, 1847, III, no. 33	
GRAN MARIA	1847	Gabriel Pinedo		CGAMR, 1847, no. 392	
RUDOLFINA	1848	Jacob & David A. Jesurun	8,000	CGANA, 1848, no. 53	101 tons
ESPERANSA	1848	Jacob Abraham Jesurun	500	CGANA, 1848, II, no. 70	47 „
ANGELIQUE	1848	Bn. (?) Suares		CGAMR, 1848, no. 100	
PACIENCIA	1848	Joseph I. Ricardo		CGAMR, March 3, 1848	
LAVINIA	1848	Jacob Abraham Jesurun	1,000*	CGANA, 1848, I, no. 59	* Pesos
PACIENCIA	1848	David Lopez Henriquez		CGAMR, 1848, no. 184	
GENERAL MONAGA	1848	Jacob Abraham Jesurun	200*	CGANA, 1848, II, no. 69	* Pesos
EMALIA	1848	Isaac Henriquez		CGAMR, 1848, no. 404	[$243^{0}/_{94}$ tons]
LEOCADIO	1849	David Lopez Henriquez		CGAMR, 1849, no. 218	
CLEMENCIA	1849	Isaac Henriquez		CGAMR, 1849, no. 541	
VICTORIA	1849	David A. Jesurun	1,000	CGANA, 1849, II, no. 31	40 tons
FERMEZA	1849	D. A. Jesurun	2,000	CGANA, 1849, II, no. 81	$50^{12}/_{94}$ tons
LAVINIA	1849	A. H. & J. Senior	2,000	CGANA, 1849, II, no. 62	51 tons
VICTORIA	1849	Mordechay Henriquez	6,000	CGANA, 1849, II, no. 58	$56^{72}/_{94}$ tons
ECLYPS	1849	Jb. & Dd. A. Jesurun	4,000	CGANA, 1849, II, no. 61	$83^{69}/_{84}$ „
TIRMERA	1849	Ditto			$50^{12}/_{94}$ „
HONTANDESA	1849	Ditto			$2^{1}/_{2}$ „
FFRMESA	1849	Ditto			40 „
ESTHER	1849	Ditto			72 „
ANITA	1849	David A. Jesurun	3,000	CGANA, 1849, I, no. 77b	$19^{3}/_{4}$ „
CITIS DOMINICANA	1849	Ditto	1,500	CGANA, 1849, I, no. 83	$52^{79}/_{95}$ „
JOANITA	1850	Ditto		CGANA, 1850, III, no. 26	21 „
FLEUR DE MARIE	1850	Jacob Abraham Jesurun	6,000	CGANA, 1850, III, no. 82	
CAROLINA	1850	David Lopez Henriquez		CGAMR, 1850, no. 289	

727

Vessel	Year	Owner	Value Pesos	Source	Remarks
Amable Helena	1850	David Lopez Henriquez		CGAMR, 1850, no. 335	
Sarah	1850	Moses R. Colman		CGAMR, 1850, no. 440	
Maria	1851	Jacob Abraham Jesurun	6,500	CGANA, 1851, I, no. 75	28 tons
Ana Maria	1851	Ditto	5,000	CGANA, May 5, 1851	59 "
Pietermaai	1851	Ditto		CGANA, 1851, no. 19	
Grenadina Lafayette	1851	Ditto	5,000	CGANA, 1851, nos. 25, 58	48
Morris	1851	Ditto	10,000	CGANA, 1851, no. 62	111 69/95 "
Gran Maria	1851	Ditto		CGANA, 1851, no. 92	"
Nina	1851	David A. Jesurun			57 "
Callao	1851	Isaac Rz. Miranda & Co.	6,500	CGANA, 1851, II, no. 25	83 75/95 "
Lafayette	1851	Isaac Pinedo Jr.	5,000	CGANA, 1851, III, no. 25	48 "
Esther	1851	Samuel L. Maduro Jr.	8,000	CGANA, 1851, III, no. 42	82 1/2 "
Morris	1851	David A. Jesurun	10,000	CGANA, 1851, III, no. 62	111 69/95 "
Lafayette	1851	Isaac Pinedo Jr.		CGANA, 1851, III, no. 61	48 "
Diana	1851	S. E. L. Maduro	4,000	CGANA, 1851, no. 103	110 50/90 "
Diana	1851	Isaac Dovale		CGANA, 1851, no. 384	"
Catharina	1852	David J[n]. Pinto		CGAMR, 1852, no. 24	[10 tons]
Silvania	1852	Abraham M. Capriles		CGAMR, 1852, no. 377	
Diamante	1852	David Abraham Jesurun	1,500	CGANA, 1852, I, no. 17	22 "
David en David	1852	Ditto		CGANA, 1852, II, no. 57	25 "
Amelia	1852	Abraham J. Jesurun	1,500	CGANA, Oct. 21, 1852	46 81/94 "
Clio	1853	David A. Jesurun	5,000	CGANA, 1853, I, no. 63	
Zeepaard	1853	Moise Penso		CGANA, 1853, no. 228	96 21/94 "
Florida Anita	1853	D. A. Jesurun	3,000	CGANA, 1853, II, no. 70	"
Mediateur	1853	David J. Pinto		CGANA, 1853, no. 338	
Anita	1853	Jacobus Henriquez	8,000	CGANA, 1853, I, no. 5	
Jabes Willems	1854	Mordechay Henriquez	10,000		

Name	Year	Owner	Price (florins)	Source	Tonnage	Remarks
CARLOTA	1854	Jose Curiel	4,000	CGANA, 1854, III, no. 28		
CIRO	1854	Benjamin Suares	8,000	CGANA, 1854, II, no. 39	[80 tons]	
CALLAO	1854	B. D. Jesurun, Miranda & Manuel A. Correa		CGAHV, 1854, no. 14	51	"
SILANIA [Silvania?]	1854	D. A. Jesurun		CGAHV, 1854, no. 15	7	"
MORRIS	1854	Ditto		CGAHV, 1854, no. 21	69	"
LAFAYETTE	1854	A. J. Jesurun		CGAHV, 1854, no. 24	56 1/2	"
AMICITIA	1854	†F. Vidal & D. A. Jesurun		CGAHV, 1854, no. 27	84	"
DIANA	1854	Jacob Rois Mendes		CGAHV, 1854, no. 29	62	"
DANTES	1854	Mordechay Henriquez	6,000[8]	CGAHV, 1854, no. 38	45(?)	"
CURAÇAOSCHE PAKKET	1854	D. A. Jesurun		CGAHV, 1854, no. 39	25	"
PRECILIA	1854	Ditto	2,000	CGANA, 1854, II, no. 19	$106^{20}/_{49}$	"
EL CURAÇAO	1854	Abm. Hm. & J. Senior		CGAHV, 1854, no. 42	57	"
ORIENTE [?]	1854	Ditto	8,000	CGANA, 1854, II, no. 32		
CUATRO DE MARZO	1854	Mordechay Henriquez			51	"
CLEOPATRA	1854	David A. Jesurun		CGAHV, y. 1854	72 tons	
PASEFON (?)	1854	Ditto		Ibid.	13	"
SARAH	1854	Jb. A. Jesurun & Son		Ibid.	68	"
DIANA	1855	Joseph Curiel	12,000	CGANA, 1855, III, no. 23		Bought from Jacob Rois Mendes
PORTEÑA	1855	Isaac Capriles	6,000	CGANA, 1855, I, no. 19	80 tons	
ROSALINDA	1855	David A. Jesurun		CGANA, 1855, I, no. 62		
SARA	1856	Jacob Abraham Jesurun	2,000	CGANA, Feb. 27, 1856	44	"
ESTHER	1856	Ditto			52	"
RICOT	1856	Dovale & Co. [= Abm. Jn. Dovale & L. L. Oliver]		CGANA, 1856, I, no. 58		328 tons; plying between Curaçao and Amsterdam and owned by a New York firm with a Curaçao branch

[8] According to CGANA, 1853, II, no. 51, M. Henriquez paid 6,000 florins for this boat of 83 58/94 tons.

Vessel	Year	Owner	Value Pesos	Source	Remarks
ANITA	1856	J. M. Curiel	3,000	CGANA, 1856, I, no. 53	52 tons
EL CORIANO	1856	Jeudah Senior	10,000	CGANA, 1856, I, no. 46	87³⁰/₉₄ tons
CLARA BORGES	1857	D. A. Jesurun & Co.	[15,000]	CGAHV, y. 1857	117 "
NUEVA AUSTRALIA	1857	J. A. Jesurun & Co.		CGAHV, y. 1857	70 "
TENOR	1858	Jb. Abm. Jesurun & Son	1,500		
GENERAL FALCON	1858	Ditto	3,000	CGANA, 1858, I, no. 33	43⁸⁰/₉₄ "
FLOR DE MARIA	1858	Ditto	2,000	CGANA, 1858, no. 136	12 "
ISABEL	1858	Ditto	10,000	CGANA, 1858, no. 184	182⁸⁹/₉₄ "
LA BEGEÑERA	1858	Dd. Abm. Jesurun & Co.	2,000	CGANA, 1858, Dec. 14, 1858	104 "
TACIA	1858	Ditto	6,000	CGANA, 1858, Aug. 20, 1858	102 "
ESTHER	1858	J. A. Jesurun & Son		CGAHV, y. 1858	60 "
ESTHER	1858	Ditto		Ibid.	52 "
ESTHER[9]	1858	Ditto		Ibid.	45 "
AMICITIA	1858	D. A. Jesurun & Co.		CGANA, 1858, II, no. 69	86 "
EL EX	1858	Jeosuah da Costa Gomez	$ 3,400	CGANA, 1858, II, no. 94	75 "
FLOR DE MARIA	1858	A. M. Capriles	2,000	CGANA, 1858, II, no. 136	12 "
FRATERNIDAD	1858	Gabriel Cardoze		CGANA, 1858, II, no. 138	10 "
PAQUETE DE TUCAENS	1858	Jeudah Senior	2,000	CGANA, 1858, II, no. 139	
ZEEPAARD	1858	Rebecca de Meza Meyerston	1,500	CGANA, 1858, III, no. 164	14⁴/₉₄ tons
SIMIS	1858	Jacob A. Jesurun		CGAHV, y. 1858	60 "
ECLIPSE	1858	J. A. Jesurun & Son		Ibid.	24 "
CARLOTA	1858	Moises & Haim J. C. Henriquez	3,000	CGANA, 1858, I, no. 34	23⁶⁴/₉₄ "
AGUILA	1858	Mordechay Henriquez		CGAHV, y. 1858	3 "
MARGARITA	1858	Jeosuah de Jeos. Henriquez		Ibid.	104 "
CAROLINA VICTORIA	1858	M. Cohen Henriquez	$ 8,000	CGANA, 1859, III, no. 255	80 "

Ship	Year	Owner	Reference		tons
ISABEL	1858	A. Cohen Henriquez	CGAHV, y. 1858		95
LUNITA	1858	D. A. Jesurun & Co.	Ibid.		75
DOS HERMANOS	1858	H. C. Henriquez	CGANA, 1858, I, no. 7	3,000	12
ROSEFINA	1858	A. M. Capriles	Ibid.		$6^{1}/_{2}$
FORTUNA	1858	Jeudah Senior	Ibid.		15
FACID (?)	1858	D. A. Jesurun & Co.	Ibid.		62
ELVIRA	1858	Ditto	Ibid.		12
ESTHER	1859	Jacob Abm. Jesurun			40
AMALIA	1859	J. A. Jesurun & Son	CGAHV, y. 1859		54
MAURICO	1859	Ditto	Ibid.		113
ADELICIA	1859	Jacob Rois Mendes	Ibid.		104
EDNIA	1859	Ditto	CGANA, 1859, I, no. 5	500	
FORTUNA (?)	1859	Gabriel Cardoze	CGAHV, y. 1859		5
ESSEX (?)	1859	J. A. Jesurun & Son and D. A. Jesurun & Co.	Ibid.		60
CASTOR	1859	Jeosuah da Costa Gomez	Ibid.		55
JOHN	1859	Jeudah Senior	CGANA, 1859, III, no. 262	4,000	$36^{93}/_{94}$
MAGDALENA	1859	Ditto	CGAHV, y. 1859		55
CLEOPATRA	1859	A. C[ohen]. Henriquez & Co.	Ibid.		66
AURORA	1859	Anjel J. Jesurun	Ibid.		17
MERY	1860	Jacob Abm. Jesurun	CGANA, Jan. 30, 1860	1,500	31
BRAN (?) RUBIS	1860	Jeudah Senior	CGAHV, y. 1860		17
DELIA	1860	Abraham Pinedo	Ibid.		80
CARMEL	1860	Isaac Pinedo Jr.	CGANA, 1860, II, no. 195		
SINORIA	1860	D. & M. de Castro	CGAHV, y. 1860		12
MAURICIO	1860	David de Moses de Castro	CGANA, 1860, I, 163	5,000	
MORRIS	1860	A. Pinedo & Co.	CGANA, 1860, III, no. 230		69
ROSALTA	1860	Rebecca de Meza Meyerston	CGANA, 1860, III, no. 292	2,000	$15^{42}/_{94}$

[9] Possibly, some of these boats are one and the same and there may be some discrepancy in the tonnage reported. Several appear in the name of J. A. Jesurun & Son just as often as they appear in the name of D. A. Jesurun & Co.

731

Vessel	Year	Owner	Value Pesos	Source	Remarks	
VENUS	1861	Salomon E. L. Maduro		CGANA, 1861, II, no. 119	249	tons
SARAH	1861	Jacob Abraham Jesurun			68	"
SEÑORITA DEL LAGO	1861	Ditto	19,500	CGANA, 1861, no. 29	55	"
MERY	1861	J. A. Jesurun & Son		CGAHV, y. 1861	15	"
MIDAS	1861	Jacob Rois Mendes		Ibid.	29	"
ROSA	1861	Isaac Pinedo Jr.		Ibid.	21	"
SEM	1861	J. A. Jesurun & Son		Ibid.	10$\frac{1}{2}$	"
ZUSTER	1861	A. Pinedo & J. M. Rubense		Ibid.	28	"
CARMITA	1861	J. A. Jesurun & Son		Ibid.	31	"
JULIA	1861	A. de Meza & M. Meyerston		Ibid.	7	"
ELEONOR	1861	J. & E. Jesurun Henriquez		Ibid.	39	"
CLARA[10]	1861	Jeosuah Mordechay Henriquez	50,000	CGAHV, y. 1861	87	"
NUEVA ERA	1862	Mordechay Henriquez		Ibid., y. 1862	32	"
DOS AMIGOS	1862	Gabriel A. Correa		Ibid.	104	"
VENUS [II]	1862	S. E. L. Maduro		Ibid.	193	"
CARMELITA	1862	Jacob Abm. Jesurun & Son		CGANA, 1862, II, no. 127	193^{74}/94	"
VICTORIA	1862	Abraham Pinedo	7,000	CGANA, 1861, II, no. 192	70	"
DOS AMIGOS	1862	Ditto		CGANA, 1862, I, no. 16	104	"
POLONIA	1863	J. A. Jesurun & Son		CGAHV, y. 1863	31	"
GAMBETI	1863	Ditto		Ibid.	111	"
ATALITA	1863	Isaac de Abm. Senior	[4,000]	Ibid.	12	"
ORIENTE	1863	Moses Jesurun	[3,000]	Ibid.	10	"
CHARM	1863	S. E. L. Maduro		Ibid.	19	"
GARRIBALDI	1863	J. A. Jesurun & Son		Ibid.	161	"
PRISCA ANTONIA	1863	Jeudah Senior	[4,000]	Ibid.	20$\frac{1}{2}$	"
NUEVA CLARA	1863	J. A. Jesurun & Son	[15,000]	Ibid.	50	"

Ship	Year	Owner	Value	Source	Tonnage
MISS	1863	Mordechay Henriquez and B. D. Jesurun		CGAHV, y. 1863	62 "
ISABEL	1863	Isaac Capriles	4,000	CGANA, 1863, II, no. 176	29
RAIJA	1863	Ditto	500	" , " II, " 177	9
ALFONSO	1863	Jb. Abm. Jesurun & Son	800	" , " III, " 385	16
MARISCAL DE AJECUCHO	1863	Ditto		" , " III, " 439	
MARISCAL	1864	Jacob Abraham Jesurun	Ps. 7,000	CGANA, 1864, no. 22	Apparently the same as the Mariscal de Ajecucho above
GALGO	1864	J. A. Jesurun & Son	10,000	CGAHV, y. 1863	82 tons
SIMON BOLIVAR	1864	Isaac de Bn. (?) Henriquez	16,000	CGAHV, y. 1864	68 "
CISNE	1864	Jeudah Senior	2,530	Ibid.	33 "
FILANTROPA	1864	J. A. Jesurun & Son	2,500	Ibid.	35 "
JOVEN CLAUDIA	1864	Moses Jesurun	18,000	Ibid.	11 "
VICTORIA	1864	Ditto	500	CGAHV, y. 1864	70 "
MARA	1865	David Moses de Castro	24,000	CGANA, 1865, no. 102	20 "
COQUETA	1865	Jacob Henriques		" " " 71	626⁷/₉₄ tons
ELLA FRANCES	1865	J. A. Jesurun & Son		" " " 85	22 "
PAJARO	1865	William Henriquez (a Jew?)		" " " 132	34 "
MATILDA	1866	David Abm. Jesurun		CC, Jan. 24, 1866	130 "
DOS HERMANOS	1866	Widow of Haim Josiau Cohen Henriquez		CGANA, 1866, no. 26	20 "
JULIE	1867	J. A. Jesurun & Son	Ps. 10,000	CGANA, 1867, no. 101	295 "
CERES	1868	Jacob Abraham Jesurun		CGANA, 1868, no. 42	125⁸⁸/₉₄ "
INES	1868	Benjamin Henriquez	1,700	" " " 55	97 "
MANUELITA	1868	David Haim Salas		" " " 101	291⁶/₉₄ "
ANITA	1868	Ditto	8,000	" " " 109	36 "
FILANTROPO	1868	Jesurun & Co.	Ps. 3,200	" " " 4, 7	35 "

[10] In 1861 this vessel and its cargo valued at 50,000 florins sank off the Venezuelan coast with its crew and 27 passengers (CC, Nov. 9, 1861).

Vessel	Year	Owner	Value Pesos	Source	Remarks
ESPERANZA	1868	Josias Judah Dovale	8,000	CGANA, 1868, no. 40	40 tons
CUMAREBO	1868	Jesurun & Co.	5,000	" " 92	7 "
SILANIA	1868	David Abm. Jesurun		" " 139	"
LA TRAVIATA	1868	Jesurun & Co.		" " 130	
DOS AMIGOS	1868	Ditto	9,000	" " 169	39 "
MINERVA	1868	David Abm. Jesurun		" 1869, I, no. 26	9 "
CISNE	1868	David Moses de Castro	16,000	CGANA, 1868, no. 127	44$^{16}/_{94}$ tons
ROBERT TODD	1688	Jacob A. Jesurun & Son			This steamer made the St. Thomas-La Guaira-Curaçao-Puerto Cabello-St. Thomas run.
JULIE	1869	J. A. Jesurun & Son		CGA, Death Register, 1869, pp. 70-71	275 tons
ADELAIDA	1869	Moises Salas			
ANNIE	1870	J. A. Jesurun & Son		CGANA, 1870, I, no. 89	91 "
NUEVA ERA	1870	J. A. Jesurun			65$^{85}/_{94}$ tons
ROSA	1870	A. Miranda & Co.	6,000		24 "
ANTONIA	1870	Isaac Haim Pereira	5,000		41 "
CIUDAD BOLIVAR	1870	Moses Salas	6,000	CGANA, 1870, no. 203	59 "
HONFLEUR (steamboat)	1870	J. A. Jesurun & Son	6,000	CC, Sept. 24, 1870	169 tons; run: Curaçao-La Guaira-Puerto Cabello-St. Thomas
CUMARIBO	1870	Jesurun & Co.	6,000	CGAK, June 1, 1870	32 tons
ANNIE	1870	Jacob Abraham Jesurun	6,500	CGANA, 1870, no. 19	59 "
FILANTROPOS	1870	Daniel Cohen Henriquez & Son	7,500	CGAK, June 11, 1870	35 "
PORTEÑA	1870	Ditto	17,000	CGANA, Feb. 2, 1870	39 "
DANKBAARHEID	1870	Jb. A. Jesurun & Son		CGANA, 1870, I, no. 89	

234. THE S.E.L. MADURO SAILBOATS: OCEAN BIRD, LEFT, AND VENUS, RIGHT

235. MANUEL PENSO CURIEL, 1831-1902, SHIPOWNER AND MEMBER OF COLONIAL COUNCIL

236. MOSES D. DE CASTRO, 1850-1921 (?), SHIPOWNER AND NOTED MERCHANT

237. MEDAILLON, S.E.L. MADURO & SONS, 100TH AND 125TH
ANNIVERSARIES, 1837-1937, 1837-1962

238. MEDALLION, EDWARDS, HENRIQUEZ & CO., 100TH
ANNIVERSARY, 1856-1956

Ship	Year	Owner	Florins	Source	Tons / notes
MARIE & SOPHIE	1870	Jb. A. Jesurun & Son		CGANA, 1870, I, no. 89	
TELEGRAFO	1862-71	Ditto	19,500	CGANA, 1862, I, no. 29	29 tons; sold in 1872 to †J. Godden for 10,000 florins
ZOILA	1871	Jesurun & Co.	8,500		62 tons
AMISTAD	1871	Manuel Penso Curiel	4,000	CGAK, Oct. 17, 1871	17 "
PANCHITA	1871	Samuel Curiel	4,000		28 "
MANARI	1871	Rachel Mordy. Henriquez Cadet	17,000		
CAROLINA	1871	Isaac Haim Pereira		CGAR, April 6, 1871	
LUMITA	1872	D. A. Jesurun & Co.	24,000	CGAK, June 5, 1872	75 "
URSULITA	1872	Jesurun & Co.	9,500	CGAK, Feb. 10, 1872	
NUEVA CLASA	1872	Jb. A. Jesurun & Son	15,000	CGAK, Feb. 1, 1872	$88^{16}/_{94}$ tons
MIDAS	1872	Ditto	9,000	CGAK, Feb. 3, 1872	29 "
SARAH	1872	Ditto	2,000	CGANA, 1856, I, no. 38	44 "
LA CREOLE	1872	Ditto	20,000	CGAK, June 25, 1872	17 "
ALMANIA VICTORIA	1872	Ditto			
ELVIRA	1872	Jesurun & Co.	10,000		45 "
BROTHERS	1872	Mord. Abinun de Lima	10,000	CGAK, Oct. 25, 1872	135 "
LA MIRTABELLA	1872	Ditto	16,000	" 16, "	32 "
PERSEVERENCIA	1872	Mordechay Henriquez Cadet	9,000	" Aug. 2, "	32 "
LA GRACIA DE DIOS	1872	Jeudah Senior	6,000		17 "
MISS	1872	Mordechay Henriquez			62 "
MAZA	1872	David Moses de Castro	10,000		40 "
DUTCH PRINCESS	1872	Joseph da Costa Gomez			
ISABEL	1872	Jacob Abm. Jesurun			92 "
COMERCIO	1872	Mord. Henriquez Cadet	25,000	CGAK, Oct. 8, 1873	74 "
TENTACION	1874	Ditto	4,000		41 "
CERES	1874	J. A. Jesurun & Sons	11,000	" Aug. 14, 1874	72 "
PROVIDENCIA	1875	R. Alvares Correa & Co.	5,000	" Feb. 2, 1875	$25^1/_2$ tons; bought in 1874 for 8,000 florins
COLIBRI	1875	The Jesuruns		K.H. Corporaal, p. 306	

Vessel	Year	Owner	Value Pesos	Source	Remarks
JULIA	1875	Abraham Jb. Jesurun	3,500	CGAK, March 8, 1875	35 tons
JULIETTE	1875	Dr. Mozes Jb. Jesurun	5,500	„ Aug. 2, 1875	49 „
RIGOLETTE	1875	Edwards, Henriquez & Co.	18,500	„ Sept. 16, 1875	75 „
PORTEÑA	1875	Daniel C. Henriquez	15,000	„ Dec. 28, 1875	39 „
CASTOR	1877	Jesurun & Co.			$83^{76}/_{100}$ tons
AMISTAD	1877	Gabriel Pinedo			$215^{81}/_{100}$ „
CONDOR	1877	J. A. Jesurun		CC, Sept. 29, 1877	
NUEVA	1878	Manuel Pinedo	6,000		$22^{07}/_{100}$ „
COMERCIO	1878	Benjamin Henriquez	20,000	CGAK, Dec. 7, 1878	$92^{84}/_{100}$ „
OTITIA	1878	David Leon	7,600		$32^{98}/_{100}$ „
TENTACION	1878	Mord. Henriquez Cadet	9,000	CC, Feb. 15, 1879	$55^{45}/_{100}$ „
CORNELIA	1879	J. A. Jesurun & Son	15,000		$118^{1}/_{2}$ „
CARMELITA	1880	Abraham Jb. Jesurun	6,100		$115^{42}/_{100}$ tons; Jesurun owned a $^4/_5$ interest in it.
ISABEL	1880	Ditto	15,000	CGAK, Aug. 11, 1880	92 tons
AMMI	1880	Ditto	6,500	„ Aug. 19, 1880	56 „
VENUS	1880	Jacob Jesurun Pinto	3,000	„ June 18, 1880	$316^{1}/_{100}$ tons
CURAÇAO	1880	Daniel Joseph Sasso	2,000	„ Feb. 18, 1880	$103^{5}/_{100}$ „
GOOD FAITH	1880	D. R. Pinedo	8,250		$85^{38}/_{100}$ „
EL TROVADOR	1880	David Raphael Pinedo	8,250		$60^{89}/_{100}$ „
OTITIA	1881	M. Alvares Correa			$32^{98}/_{100}$ „
VICTORIA	1881	Jeudah Senior & Son	8,000		$32^{04}/_{100}$ „
CLEOPATRA	1881	Manuel Penso Curiel[11]	5,000		$111^{43}/_{100}$ „
ISAAC OLIVER	1881	Elias M. Curiel	5,000		$246^{15}/_{100}$ „
TIGRE	1882	Ditto		CC, Jan. 28, 1882	
VENUS	1882	Manuel Penso Curiel		CC, Jan. 28, 1882	

Year	Ship	Owner		Registration	Tonnage / notes
1882	GOEVERNOR VAN DEN BRANDHOF	Daivd Raphael Pinedo	25,000	CGAK, Dec. 20, 1882	$77^{54}/_{100}$ tons
1882	ROSA	David Dovale Mendez	6,000		$35^{27}/_{100}$ "
1883	GRAN CANAL	Jacob Jesurun Pinto	3,000		
1883	GALGO	Jacob Abm. Jesurun	8,000		82 tons
1883	JULIO	Ditto	9,000		35 "
1883	GUILLERMINA	David Rephael Pinedo	11,000	CGAK, Jan. 10, 1884	$42^{47}/_{100}$ "
1884	AURORA	David Dovale Mendez	4,000	CGAK, Sept. 10, 1885	$14^{83}/_{100}$ "
1885	9 DE AGOSTO	Elias Penso Hijos & Co.	15,000		
1886	CARMELITA	Jacob Abm. Jesurun & Co.	12,000	CGANA, 1886, no. 3412	
1886	OSCAR	Ditto	1,000		
1886	JULIA	Ditto	3,000		$18^{40}/_{100}$ tons
1889	SARAH	S. E. L. Maduro & Sons			$6^{39}/_{100}$ "
1889	ZELIA	Jacob Jesurun	500		Mail, passenger and cargo schooner plying between Curaçao and Coro
1897	AURORA	Moses L. Maduro			
1897	9 DE AGOSTO	Edgar Senior & Co.			$78^{17}/_{100}$ tons
1901	SAETA	Maduro Jr. & Co.	18,375	CGAK, Nov. 20, 1901	$132^{36}/_{100}$ "
1901	LA INES	Moses David de Castro & Co.	13,000		$182^{36}/_{100}$ "
1901	FORTUNA	Mozes David de Castro	3,500		$146^{3}/_{100}$ "
1902	GALGO	David Haim Salas	6,000		$368/_{100}$ "
1903	AUGUSTA VICTORIA	Maduro Jr.	11,500	CGAK, Mar. 18, 1903	$55^{95}/_{100}$ "
1905	MARIA	Elias de Marchena	5,000		$214/_{100}$ tons; sold to Manuel Pinedo & Co.
1910	AMADORA	Benjamin J. de Castro		El Sol, Nov. 21, 1910	

11 In 1881 the [Jacob Rois] Mendes' shipyard built a schooner for the account of M. P. Curiel (CC, June 4, 1881).

737

Vessel	Year	Owner	Value Pesos	Source	Remarks
WILHELMINA[12]	1913	S. E. L. Maduro & Sons			27.83 tons — with motor
POCAHONTAS[12]	1913-16	Ditto			16.60 tons
DE RUYTER[12]	1913-16	Ditto			
TROMP[12]	1913-16	Ditto			
PRINCE HENDRIK[12]	1913-16	Ditto			
PIONEER	1919	Ditto		KV, 1919	1,590.67 tons
CARIBE	1919	Ditto			

[12] These vessels served to transport cargo within the Schottegat.

738

B. CAPTAINS

Year	Captain	Vessel	Source
1699	PHILIPPE HENRIQUEZ, *alias* JACOB SENIOR	Juffr. Gerebrecht	Pages 82-83 above
1703	MANUEL MANASES [Jesurun Henriquez]		WICA 200, p. 332a
1715	DAVID VAZ FARO		OAC 797, no. 4
1720	ANTHONIO FERERA HENRIQUEZ	Jonge Jacob	Maduro's list
1721	SAMUEL GOMEZ		WICA 577, p. 645
1721	JOSEPH NIETTO [1]	Nuestra Señora de Alta Gracia	
1722	JACOB TOURO		OAC 797, Mar. 6, 1722
1722	JOSEPH ABENDANA		WICA 577, p. 13
1731	MONCHE, *alias* SALOMON, L. MADORO		WICA 580, pp. 484v-85
1733	ABRAHAM SASPORTAS	Le Cheval Volant	OAC 801, Oct. 24, 1733
1739	SR. PIMENTEL	Reyna Esther	OAC 1549, July 19, 1739
1743	MANUEL GOMEZ	Fortuyn	OAC 850, no. 103
1745	DANIEL [COHEN] PEIXOTTO	Gloriosa	OAC 854, no. 114
1745	MANUEL LEVY JR.	't Fortuin	OAC 857, no. 53
1745	EPHRAIM ATIAS	Pacquet Boot	OAC 856, no. 139
1745	MANUEL LOPEZ	Maria Elizabeth	WICA 592, p. 580
1746	ABM. SALOMON L. MADURO [2]		OAC 858, no. 195
1746	ABRAHAM L. MADURO [2]	Esperansa	OAC 860, no. 226
1746	GILES, [*alias* ABRAHAM ?], SEMAH FERRO	Demoiselle Johanna	OAC 860, no. 34
1746	MOSSEH HENRIQUEZ		OAC 865, no. 129
1747	GARSON GARSIA	Regoboth (Genesis 26:22)	OAC 865, no. 112

[1] Jewishness uncertain.

[2] Abraham Salomon and Abraham seem to be one and the same person. He is also referred to as Capt. Abraham Salomon Moseh L. Maduro (OAC 9, y. 1746; OAC 864, no. 17). He registered his ship in St. Thomas to avoid payment of special taxes levied by the Danish Government on foreign vessels (OAC 862, no. 256).

Year	Captain	Vessel	Source
1748	MANUEL TOURO		OAC 867, no. 26
1748	ABRAHAM, *alias* BERNARDO, MOTTA	Guadaloupe	OAC 867, no. 81
1748	BERNARDO MOTTA	Maria Louisa	OAC 867, no. 94
1748	JACOB JESURUN	Catharina	
1748	MANUEL LOPEZ JR.	Jonge Jacob	OAC 867, no. 190
1749	MANUEL MANASSE [Jesurun Henriquez Jr.]	St. Anna	OAC 9, y .1749
1749	ABRAHAM PINEDO	Elizabeth	OAC 821, Oct. 15, 1749
1749	SALOMO CURIEL	Adventur	OAC 821, Nov., 1749
1750	SALOMO RIVERO	Anna Cornelia	OAC 14, Feb. 3, 1750
1750	MANUEL LOPEZ JR.	Zebulon	OAC 1551, Mar. 16, 1750
1751	MANUEL GOMEZ		OAC 183, no. 55
1752	ISAAC MOSEH ABOAB	Esther	OAC 826, May 30, 1752
1756	ISAAC HENRIQUEZ COUTINHO	Zebulun & Isachar	OAC 19, Mar. 5, 1756
1756	MORDECHAY MOTTA	Koningin Esther	OAC 833, Nov. 16, 1756
1756	DANIEL MENDES DE CASTRO	Buena Ventura	OAC 833, Dec. 8, 1756
1757	JOSEPH CURIEL	Triumph	OAC 836, no. 130
1759	MANUEL DE BRITO		OAC 840
1759	DAVID DIAS ARIAS	Texel	Comm., Rabbi B. W. Korn
1759	JACOB FRANCISCO MADURO[3]	Dolphyn	
1760	JOSEPH CRESPO	Eendracht[4]	OAC 882, Sept. 29, 1761
1760	JOSEPH DE CORDOVA (Jew?)	Esperansa	OAC 879, Oct. 13, 1760
1760	ELIAS DE MANUEL DE CRASTO	Jonge Manuel en Rachel[5]	OAC 878, July 28, 1760
1761	ISAAC Hz. JULIAO	Rey David	OAC 883, Nov. 26, 1761
1762	ISAAC NUNES NETTO	King David	OAC 888, nos. 204, 238, 246
1762	BENJAMIN SUARES		OAC 885, no. 31
1762	BENJAMIN COHEN HENRIQUEZ	De Hoop	OAC 885, no. 105
1762	JACOB ELIAS JH. LEON	Jonge Elias	OAC 885, no. 209
1762	MOSES MOTTA	Vrijheid	OAC 886, no. 154
1763	DAVID LOPEZ RAPHAEL	Mari-Bamba	OAC 888, no. 253
1763	BENJAMIN MOSSEH C. HENRIQUEZ	Domyn	OAC 888, nos. 191, 320
1763	ISAAC ARON Hz. MORON	Jonge Abraham	OAC 897, no. 88

[3] A half-Jew. Destination Mississippi. There were only a few Curaçoan Jews in Mississippi or New Orleans in 1759; among them: Manuel, *alias* David de Brito, and Isaac Roiz Monsanto (OAC 839, July 7, 1759). Maduro is also encountered as captain in 1763 (OAC 889, no. 305).

[4] Seized by Spanish pirates.

[5] Seized by English pirates and brought to Jamaica (Maduro).

Year	Captain	Vessel	Source
1763	PINHAS ISRAEL KEYSER[6]	De Hoop	OAC 889, nos. 129, 192
1764	DAVID JB. COHEN FEREYRA	Fortuyn	OAC 891, no. 141
1764	SALOMON HAIM CALVO	Dolphyn	OAC 891, no. 376
1764	BENJAMIN C. HENRIQUEZ JR.	De Nieuwe Fortuyn	OAC 891, no. 409
1764	MOSES MOTTA	'Slands Welvaaren	OAC 891, no. 432
1764	GABRIEL PINEDO	Jonge Jacob	OAC 896, no. 40
1764	SALOMON IS. L. MADURO	De Hoop	OAC 896, no. 69
1764	MORDECHAY DE ISAAC CALVO	De Hoop	OAC 193, no. 123
1765	MANUEL MONSANTO[7]	Vrijheid	OAC 1558, no. 237
1765	ELIAS PENSO	Jonge Abraham	OAC 894, Sept. 6, 1765
1766	DAVID MONTES		OAC 900, no. 56
1766	ABRAHAM RZ. MIRANDA	Soleda	OAC 895, no. 49
1768	ABRAHAM HZ. MORON	Sara	OAC 903, Oct. 17, 1768
1768	ABRAHAM CALVO	Dolphyn	OAC 904, June 8, 1768
1768	SALOMON L. MADURO	Rebecca	OAC 906, Sept. 21, 1768
1769	JOSEPH SANCHEZ[8]	Diana	OAC 939, no. 79
1769	ABRAHAM PENSO	Sara	OAC 939, no. 124
1770	ISAAC MENDEZ	Prins van Oranje[9]	OAC 941, no. 442
1770	ELIAS LOPEZ JR.	Zeeblom	OAC 941, no. 396
1770	DAVID FIDANQUE	Koning David	OAC 907, no. 147
1770	MICHAEL DE LEON	Sally	OAC 940, no. 50
1770	SALOMON SAMUEL L. MADURO	De Hoop	OAC 907, no. 113
1770	DAVID MORALES		OAC 909, no. 216
1770	DAVID SENIOR	Koning David	OAC 941, no. 396
1771	JACOB FRANKEN[10]	Los Dos Hermanos	OAC 908, no. 17
1771	JACOB FRANCISCO [Benjamin?] NAAR	La Feliz Maria	OAC 909, no. 178
1771	JACOBO DE CORDOVA[11]	El Successo	OAC 913, no. 48
1771	ISAAC NEYRA JR.	Pellegrina	OAC 942, no. 95
1771	JOSEPH BUENO VIVAS	Princesse de Lusanne	OAC 943, no. 334
1771	ISHAC ROBLES	Señora Abigail[12]	OAC 943, no. 432

[6] A Sephardi, *alias* Pichi, captain since 1753.

[7] Jewishness uncertain; Isaac L. Maduro was ship bookkeeper.

[8] Jewishness uncertain. Isaac Dias da Silva was ship clerk. The 36 slaves on board destined for French Santo Domingo were for the account of Elias and Isaac Roiz Miranda.

[9] Seized by Spanish pirates.

[10] Ashkenazi.

[11] Run: Curaçao-New York-England-Jamaica-Curaçao.

[12] Spanish corsairs took this schooner with her officers Jacob Moseh Salomon L. Maduro and Ephraim Jesurun Henriquez.

Year	Captain	Vessel	Source
1772	SAMUEL SALOMON L. MADURO	Dorothea	OAC 201, no. 40
1772	SALOMON CALVO	Fortuyn	OAC 201, no. 61
1772	BENJAMIN C. HENRIQUEZ	Zeeblom	OAC 201, no. 71
1772	ISHAC ROBLES	Maria Lamberta	OAC 911, no. 247
1772	JOSEPH OBEDIENTE JR.	Twee Vrienden	OAC 944, no. 89
1772	SAMUEL MOSEH L. MADURO	Sara	OAC 944, no. 161
1772	MOSES NUNES REDONDO	Goede Hoop [13]	OAC 944, no. 189
1773	ISAAC JACOB SENIOR	St. François	OAC 947, no. 189
1773	ELIAS LOPEZ JR.	Giertje	OAC 202, no. 13
1773	ABRAHAM NUNES REDONDO	Zeebloem	OAC 912, no. 87
1773	DAVID LOPEZ RAPHAEL	La Dame Abigail	OAC 912, no. 155
1774	SALOMON ABM. CURIEL	Ribca	OAC 949, no. 319
1774	MOSES [MENDEZ] MONSANTO	Anna Elisabeth [14]	WICA 610, Dagregister van te Curaçao inkomende en uitgaande schepen in het Jaar 1774
1774	ISAAC DIAS DA SILVA	Abigael	Ditto
1774	GABRIEL PINEDO	Amable	Ditto
1774	RAPHAEL MOLINA MONSANTO	Eendragt	Ditto
1774	NAGSON HZ. MORON [15]	La Perla	Ditto
1774	BENJAMIN C. HENRIQUEZ	Abigael	Ditto
1774	SALOMON CALVO	De Hoop	Ditto
1774	JOSEPH CURIEL	Jonge Daniel	Ditto
1774	JOSEPH PINEDO [16]	Candelario	Ditto
1774	ELIAS DAVIDS [17]	Catherina	Ditto
1774	JACOB ABOAB CARDOZO	Meyblom	Ditto
1774	BENJAMIN PINEDO	Constant	Ditto
1774	SALOMON ISAAC L. MADURO	Anna Elisabeth	Ditto

[13] Seized by pirates.

[14] This vessel and the next fifteen which arrived at or left Curaçao had come from or were going to the North, the Southwest, the West, Santo Domingo, the South or to St. Eustatius. They brought in coffee, sugar, tobacco, cacao, romwijn, butter, etc.

[15] His sloop was lost in a hurricane.

[16] Jewishness uncertain.

[17] Ashkenazi?

Year	Captain	Vessel	Source
1774	DAVID LOPEZ RAPHAEL	Clara	WICA 610
1774	BENJAMIN JESURUN	Fortuyn	Ditto
1774	ISAAC ABRAHAM SASSO	Elisabeth [18]	Ditto
1776	JOSEPH MONTES	La Bonne Esperansa	OAC 954, no. 91
1776	JACOB RZ. DELVALLE	Rebecca	OAC 954, no. 53
1777	MOYSE OLIVIE [OLIVEYRA] ISIDRO	La Dorada	OAC 917, no. 72
1777	JACOB L. MADURO	Mordogay	OAC 917, no. 81
1777	JOSEPH PARRERA [19]	Cristo	OAC 955, no. 206
1777	JOSEPH GUTTIERES	St. Joseph	OAC 955, no. 300
1778	JOSEPH MADURO [19]	Sarah	OAC 920, no. 373
1778	JACOB MOSES DE CASTRO	Elisabeth [20]	OAC 920, no. 402
1779	ABRAHAM NUNES REDONDO	Jonge Abraham	OAC 924, no. 1345
1779	Ditto	De Hoop	OAC 921, no. 77
1779	SAMUEL ISAAC L. MADURO	Rachel	OAC 921, no. 83
1779	MOSES MENDES MONSANTO	Jonge Jacob	OAC 921, no. 216
1779	JOSEPH LOPEZ RAPHAEL	Concordia	OAC 922, no. 337
1779	ISAAC, [alias JOACHIM], SASSO	Marianna	OAC 922, no. 373
1779	ABRAHAM CALVO	Koningin Esther	OAC 923, no. 744
1779	JEOSUAH COHEN PEIXOTTO	Jonge Gabriel	OAC 923, no. 764
1779	DAVID MONTES	Perfect	OAC 923, no. 846
1779	DAVID HENRIQUEZ	Twee Vrienden	OAC 923, no. 877
1779	JACOB ABOAB CARDOZO	Rachel	OAC 923, no. 889
1779	SALOMON [alias BERNARDO] MOSES L. MADURO	De Hoop	OAC 923, no. 914
1779	MOSES TABOADA	Jonge Isaac	OAC 208, no. 124
1779	JACOB HZ. FEREYRA		OAC 208, no. 149
1779	JEOSUAH MENDES	Resolutie	OAC 924, no. 1175
1779	ISAAC SALOMON CALVO	Sara	OAC 924, no. 1328
1779	MOSES C. HENRIQUEZ JR.	Goede Hoop	OAC 208, no. 202
1779	MOSES MOTTA	De Hoop	OAC 924, no. 1105
1779	MANUEL BELMONTE	Fortuin	OAC 924, no. 1029
1779	DAVID ABINUN DE LIMA JR.	Altona	OAC 924, no. 1123
1779	JOSEPH LOPEZ RAPHAEL	Zeeblom	OAC 924, no. 1212

[18] Last of the sixteen vessels listed in the *Dagregister* of 1774.
[19] Jewishness uncertain.
[20] In 1780 this vessel made stops at Haitian ports as well as at Providence and New York (OAC 925, nos. 166, 265).

Year	Captain	Vessel	Source
1779	SALOMON MOSEH L. MADURO	Marianna	OAC 924, no. 1428
1779	SELOMOH ISAAC L. MADURO	Rachel	OAC 924, no. 1286
1779	MATHIAS NIÑO	Sara	OAC 924, no. 1476
1779	MORDECHAY JB. HENRIQUEZ	Jonge Isaak	OAC 924, no. 1480
1779	NUNES GOMES	Savana	OAC 921, no. 210
1780	SAMUEL MOSEH L. MADURO	Esperanza	OAC 208, no. 22
1780	JACOB MORENO HENRIQUEZ	Johanna Nicolina	OAC 930, no. 1710
1780	ARON GABRIEL PINEDO	Jonge Jacob[21]	OAC 209, no. 8
1780	ISAAC SASSO	Neptunus	OAC 925, no. 394
1780	ABRAHAM DE LEON NUNES	Jonge Isaac	OAC 926, no. 448
1780	DAVID MONTES	Rebecca	OAC 927, no. 924
1780	JEOSUAH MENDES	Judith	OAC 926, no. 520
1780	SALOMON CALVO	De Goede Intentie	OAC 927, no. 873
1780	ABRAHAM RZ. MIRANDA	Catharina	OAC 928, no. 1201
1780	Ditto	Jonge Gabriel	OAC 930, no. 1742
1780	MOSES MARACHE	Vigilante	OAC 929, no. 1448
1780	DAVID ABINUN DE LIMA JR.	Dolphyn	OAC 930, no. 1707
1780	JACOB COHEN PEIXOTTO	Jonge Gabriel	OAC 925, no. 27
1780	JACOB ABRAHAMS[22]		OAC 209, no. 47 (Maduro)
1780	RAPHAEL BELMONTE	Sarah	OAC 930, no. 1535
1781	SALOMON L. MADURO	Herderin (?)	OAC 210, no. 132
1781	JOSEPH ATHIAS	De Hoop	OAC 931, no. 100
1781	JACOB ABENATAR	Abigael	OAC 933, no. 676
1781	SALOMON MOSES L. MADURO	Herderin	OAC 934, no. 991
1782	ABRAHAM CALVO JR.	De Hoop	OAC 938, no. 353
1782	JEREMIAS L. MADURO	Fortuyn	OAC 938, no. 374
1782	ABRAHAM ATHIAS	Fortuyn	OAC 1084, no. 73
1782	SAMUEL MOSEH L. MADURO	Ribca	OAC 1084, no. 87
1783	JEOSUAH COHEN PEIXOTTO	San Juan Paquet	OAC 966, no. 488
1783	ISAAC SASSO	Postillon	OAC 1085, no. 67
1783	JEREMIAS L. MADURO	Jonge Isaak	OAC 1085, nos. 154-55
1783	MANUEL PINEDO	Frea Freada	OAC 967, no. 601
1784	JACOB MENDES HENRIQUEZ	Catharina	OAC 1086, no. 31
1784	ABRAHAM CALVO		OAC 1086, nos. 160-61

[21] Seized by English corsairs (OAC 930, no. 1510).
[22] Ashkenazi.

Year	Captain	Vessel	Source
1784	ISAAC GABAY HENRIQUEZ	Neptunes	OAC 1086, no. 232
1785	JACOB FRANCISCO NAAR	El Rey Samuel	OAC 64, no. 117
1785	ABRAHAM SALZEDO	Postillon	OAC 973, no. 101
1786	ABRAHAM GARCIA	Postillon	OAC 973, no. 515
1786	DAVID HENRIQUEZ	Vriendschap	OAC 976, no. 763
1790	DANIEL CARDOZO	Vriendschap	OAC 148, y. 1790
1794	JACOB LOPEZ	Anna	OAC 221, Sept. 23, 1794
1795	DAVID LOPEZ DA FONSECA	Peggy	OAC 1096, no. 48
1796	ISAAC L. MADURO PEIXOTTO	De Hoop	OAC 996, no. 15
1796	JOSUAH SAMUEL JH. LEON	De Hoop	OAC 139, no. 60
1796	ISAAC CALVO	La Cabriolleur	W. I. Comité 141, Nov. 25, 1796
1796	JOSEPH COHEN PEIXOTTO	De Hoop	OAC 138, no. 72
1796	RAPHAEL JESURUN SASPORTAS[23]	Juf. Gracia	OAC 223, Mar. 12, 1796, no. 72
1797	ISAAC SALZEDO	De Hoop	W. I. Comité 141, Feb. 12, 1797
1797	JACOB JESURUN	Dolphyn	W. I. Comité 141, Apr. 3, 1797
1797	JEOSUAH ISAAC JH. LEON	David	W. I. Comité 141, Dec. 14, 1797
1800	ISAAC JESURUN PINTO	La Sainte Marie	OAC 1004, no. 25
1801	SALOMO ABRAHAM CURIEL	Christina	OAC 1005, Mar. 3, 1801
1817	DAVID JACOB HENRIQUEZ	Societeit	Koloniën 3615, 1817, no. 36
1819	SAMUEL HENRIQUEZ	Leona	*Correo del Orinoco*, Angostura, Apr. 24, 1819
1820	S[AMUEL] · D[AVID] · HOHEB	Nancy (76 tons)	OAC 1578, Apr. 12, 1820
1821	MATHIAS LEVY (Jew?)[24]	Gouvernor van Starckenborgh	Koloniën 3630, June 19, 1821
1826	JACOB ABENATAR	Amelia	OAC 1632, Mar. 17, 1826
1828	D. A. GOMES CASSERES	Gran Maria	K. H. Corporaal, p. 87
1840	JACOB ROIS MENDES		CEOE 784, no. 3
1844	JACOB ROIS MENDES	Ester Linda	CGAMR, 1844, no. 358

[23] He was charged by Governor Johannes de Veer Abmz. to go to Coro and bring some seamen deserters and slaves who had fled there (Maduro).

[24] David Gomes Casseres was agent for this vessel.

Year	Captain	Vessel	Source
1845	Jeosuah da Costa Gomez	Victoria	CGAMR, 1845, no. 84
1848	Bn. (?) Suares	Angelique	CGAMR, 1848, no. 100
1848	David Lopez Henriquez	Paciencia	Ibid., no. 184
1848	Isaac Henriquez	Emalia	Ibid., no. 404
1850	Abraham M. Capriles	David & David	CGAMR, 1850, no. 205
1850	Moses R. Colman	Sarah	Ibid., no. 440
1851	Isaac de J. Dovale	Diana	CGAMR, 1851, no. 384
1852	David J. Pinto	Catharina	CGAMR, 1852, no. 24
1852	Joseph de Meza	Bertha Harressowitz	Ibid., no. 134
1853	Mordechay Dovale	Johanna	CGAMR, 1853, nos. 42, 86
1853	Moise Penso	Zeepaard	Ibid., no. 228
1853	Jacob Rois Mendes	Diana	CGANA, 1853, no. 9
1862	Da Costa Gomez de la penha	Venus	CC, Feb. 22, 1862
1870	Jesurun	Honfleur	A steamboat (CC, Sept. 24, 1870)
1874	Jacob Sasso & Jeorge Marchena	Amistad	El Imparcial, Aug. 5, 1874
1881	[Daniel?] Sasso[25]	Curaçao	29 tons (CC, June 4, 1881)

[25] In 1883 Daniel Josef Sasso, a witness to the civil marriage of a Jewish couple, gave his profession as "sailor."

MISCELLANEOUS NOTES ON THE EARLY JEWS
OF CURAÇAO

A. RELATIONS BETWEEN JAN DE YLLAN AND THE
DUTCH WEST INDIA COMPANY

ONE "JAN DELIAN" sought a contract from the Dutch West India Company in 1668 for the purchase of salt from Bonaire, according to Hamelberg who did not know that De Yllan was a Jew.[1]

At their meeting of May 9, 1669, the directors of the Company took up "Jan Dilian's" claim for damages allegedly sustained in Curaçao. They decided to turn it over to the District Deputies for investigation and recommendations (OWICA 15, p. 100).

The Company directors decided at their meeting of September 7, 1673, to open negotiations with two Jews who had asked leave to fetch 500 African slaves for consignment to Cadiz, Spain. On October 9, 1673, they studied the conditions under which those slaves were to be brought and consigned to Cadiz for disposition by the Jewish merchants "N. & N. Delian" (OWICA 16, pp. 183v, 192).

On March 7, 1675, "Jan de Lion," in the name of his principals, wanted to negotiate with the Company for the delivery of 1,500-2,000 slaves from Rio Calabary. The directors decided to refer his request to the deputies in charge of slave traffic for their opinion (WICA 330, p. 113).

[1] Hamelberg, p. 45, referring to the Resolutions of the Chamber of Amsterdam, November 22, 1668.

B. RESOLUTION OF THE AMSTERDAM PORTUGUESE JEWISH COMMUNITY GRANTING ISHAC DA COSTA A SEPHER TORAH FOR CURAÇAO IN 1659

5419

Termo de Hun sefertora que en 18 de Iiar se entrego a Isack da costa guntamente Con aLgun ornamentos para leuar Consigo a Curasao =

Digo Heu IsacK da Costa que Recibi dos sses do Mahamad sefretorah de gebir [guebil] con seu aforo de taftan amareLo e huma faixa de damasco acul afLores Hema capade damasco vermello Con sua franga E Hún pano da taba de setin verde afLores. E Hun pano de tafetan narangado pa Cubir o sefreh I otra capa de sefre de damasco branco con galones de oro todo o cual se da por entrege para o Levar a Curasáo y querendo este K K que el dio aumente Lleaixan de pagar o que digeren os ssres do Mahamad y por ser ansy o firmey en Amsterdam A 18 de Iiar de 5419

Ishac da Costa
(PJCAA, Acordos, p. 457)

5419

Resolution made concerning a Scroll of the Law with some ornaments delivered to Isack da Costa on Iiar 18 to take with him to Curaçao

I, Isack da Costa, declare that I received from the gentlemen of the Mahamad a Sehper Torah of fine parchment with its yellow taffeta lining; a band of flowered blue damask; a cape of red damask with its fringe; a flowered green satin cloth for the reading desk; a cloth of orange taffeta to cover the Holy Scroll and another cloak of white damask with gold braid; all of which is given for delivery to Curaçao; and upon the request of this K[ahal]. K[ados]., which may God increase, the said gentlemen of the Mahamad are to be paid what they ask. In affirmation whereof I [have] signed it in Amsterdam on Iiar 18, 5419 (May 11, 1659).
[signed] Ishac da Costa [1]

The parnassim then were Abraham Pharar, Jacob Belmonte, Abraham de Prado, Selomoh Salom, Refael Atias, Abraham Franco Mendes and Ishac de Pinto, Treasurer. See I. S. Emmanuel, "Yedi'oth Ḥadashoth 'al hakehila Haportuguesith me-Amsterdam," *Ozar Yehudé Sefarad*, vol. VI (Jerusalem, 1963), pp. 173-182, for the list of Amsterdam's parnassim from 1619 to 1864.

[1] Cf. Emmanuel, *AJA*, 1955, p. 21.

C. COMMERCIAL RELATIONS BETWEEN THE JEWS
OF AMSTERDAM AND CURAÇAO, 1655-1680

As early as 1655 these Jews of Amsterdam were buying cacao from Curaçao: the brothers Emanuel [a.k.a. Hendrick] and Robert van der Star, a.k.a. Fernando Alvares and Antonio Correa de Mesquita, respectively; Pieter Cornelis Janssen, a.k.a. Rose Correa; A[br]aõ Jacobs, a.k.a. Martin Sobri; Jacques Smit, a.k.a. Daniel Perez; Manuel de Toralto, a.k.a. Albertos Dirksen; Isak Gabay Letob.[1]

In 1662 Joseph Frances, the Amsterdam merchant formerly of Brazil, bought 4,600 pounds of stockfish wood (logwood) from the Company. To "his nephew Jean d'Yllan" of Amsterdam he gave his authorization to receive the bill of lading for the shipment.[2]

Jonathan Levi — the son of Haham Saul Levi Morteira and brother-in-law of Haham Josiau Pardo — asked the Company for a permit to send a small seagoing vessel to Curaçao. This was granted under the customary terms, but not before Jan Pietersz had shipped his boat.[3] In 1671 Levi bought from Antonio [Isaac] Lopes Suasso the ship *De Koning van Sweden*. He renamed it *Het Huis Levy*.[4]

Abraham Drago appeared at a Company meeting to request passports for certain Portuguese [Jews] wishing to go to Curaçao, of course with fares prepaid. This was granted.[5]

Several years later Drago appeared at a Company meeting to ask for passports for himself and seven "free" families wishing to embark for Curaçao on the *Geertruidt*. The request was granted.[6]

Alvaro Pereira presented himself at a Company meeting to request a passport for himself for Curaçao and obtained it.[7]

---

[1] GAA 975B and 978, Not. Baddel, April 16 and Nov., 1655; GAA, Vaz Dias notes.
[2] GAA 2213, Not. Lock, Sept. 26, 1662; GAA, Vaz Dias notes.
[3] OWICA 15, meeting of Jan. 14, 1669, p. 79.
[4] GAA 2903, Not. Padthuysen, April 26, 1671.
[5] WICA 330, meeting of August 23, 1675, p. 182.
[6] WICA 335, meeting of March 14, 1680, p. 108.
[7] WICA 335, meeting of August 6, 1680, p. 189v.

MARRANOS IN CURAÇAO

SEVERAL MARRANOS, it was seen in the course of this work, migrated to Curaçao directly from Portugal or by way of Amsterdam. Some were so staunch in their faith that they sought, through their wills, to insure a relative's return to Judaism. Notably among these we encounter Jossias Gavay Ferro (more fully discussed below) and Joseph (a.k.a. Aron) Henriquez Medina. The latter specifically directed (in his will of September 14, 1716, made in Amsterdam) that his bequest of 40,000 guilders to his brother's son Jacob Henriquez Medina should not be paid unless his nephew professed Judaism and married a Jewess of Portuguese origin (PJCAA, no. 738).

A few Marranos had parents living in Portugal as late as 1762. This we know from the will of Isaac Nunes Lopes (widower of Rachel Nunes Lopes) made in Curaçao on August 1, 1762 (OAC 886, no. 103). To his father Joao Nunes Lopes and his mother Beatrix Nunes Lopes "in Portugal" he bequeathed "what the law allowed them." (The rest of the estate was to go to his brother Abraham Nunes Lopes of Amsterdam.) Interestingly, one of his executors in Curaçao — Jacob Mendes Monsanto — was born in Lisbon (GAA, DTB 730/97).

The last Marrano to arrive in Curaçao directly from Portugal was J. Fonseca. He came with his three children in 1822 (CEOE 310, May 14, 1822).

THE MARRANO JOSSIAS GAVAY FERRO

Jossias Gavay Ferro, among other Curaçoan Jewish testators, left a will naming relatives dwelling in the shadow of the Inquisition in Portugal and Brazil.[1] He was born in Spain in 1653. Although he visited Bayonne in 1675, he did not return to Judaism until 1689, probably in Amsterdam where he was well established. In 1692 he entered into a partnership agreement with David Bernal to go to Curaçao. Known as Henriquez & Francisco Henriquez, this partnership prospered. Bernal and Ferro were counted among Curaçao's richest Jews. In 1713 they paid a ransom of 2,000 pesos to the Frenchman Admiral Cassard.

Ferro's will,[2] drawn up in 1709, ranks high among old Curaçoan Jewry's more interesting and eloquent ones. After entrusting his soul to the "Almighty God of Israel" and asking Him to pardon his many sins (of which he had repented and therefore hoped God in his mercy would not take a "minute account of my

---

[1] Our *Precious Stones*, pp. 190, 249-50.
[2] OAC 1545, no. 221. This will was brought to my attention by the late Jossy M. L. Maduro.

numerous wrongs and errors"), he ordered the burial of his body in the "Beda-haim" of Curaçao or wherever "God in his judgment chooses to call me," and even supplied the epitaph to be engraved on his tombstone.

His will tells us that he had two brothers — Abraham Gavay in Amsterdam and Isaac Gavay in Bordeaux — and five sisters: four in Bayonne, and one deceased in Spain whose son Manuel Ferro was still living there. After leaving his kin specific bequests of precious jewels and money, including dowry for a niece, Ferro ordered the remainder of his estate to be distributed equally among his seven heirs. It is significant that his nephew Manuel was to receive only half of his legacy unless he returned to Judaism and underwent circumcision.

Jossias died in Curaçao on the 13th of Ab, 5483, or August 14, 1723. His partner and trusted friend David Bernal executed the will to the letter, down to the tombal inscription.[3]

[3] Our *Precious Stones*, p. 250; our Catalogue, no. C 1954.

TERRA SANTA

A. RECEIPT FOR MONEYS SENT BY THE CURAÇAO COMMUNITY FOR JERUSALEM[1]

We, the undersigned, parnassim and directors of this Holy Sephardic Community in the Holy City of Jerusalem, which may God rebuild and re-establish, hereby acknowledge receipt from the Haham Hashalem, the distinguished Ribbi Shimshon Gomez Pato, whom God protect, and from the able, exalted, venerable Ribbi Joseph Lopes, whom God protect, and of the exalted Haham Ribbi Sehid Bardah, whom God protect, the sum of fifty pieces of eight, full weight, which we have received and are empowered to use for the necessary expenses of this, our Holy Congregation. This [amount] is the fruit of the charity of our brothers, men of our salvation, of the Holy Congregation of Curaçao who remitted it through the intermediation of the parnassim and directors of the Holy Congregation of Amsterdam, whom God protect.

With the power of His Glory beyond our walls, may God bestow, for us, His eternal blessing on the said Holy Congregation [of Curaçao] and all those who help and occupy themselves with maintaining the City of God.

In witness whereof, we affix our true signatures hereto, in the Holy City of Jerusalem, which may God rebuild and re-establish, in the month of Kislev of the year 5463 of the Creation [Nov. 21–Dec. 19, 1702].

Signed: Haim 'Arukh
Mordechay Caerton[2]

[1] PJCAA, bundle. See p. 154 above.
[2] One of the signatures was deciphered by Meir Benayahu.

RECIBO DE DINERO DE קורסו
PARA JERUSALAIM.

מודים אנחנו הח״מ, פרנסי
ומנהיגי הק״ק ספרדים אשר
פע״הק ירושלם ת״ו, הודאה
גמורה איך אמת ויציב שקבלנו
מיד החכם השלם הדיין
המצויין כמה״ר שמשון גומץ
פאטו נר״ו והישיש נבון ונעלה
כה״ר יוסף לופיס נר״ו
והחכם הנעלה כה״ר סעיד
ברדע נר״ו סך חמשים
פייסאס די 8 די פיזו ובאו
לידנו ורשותנו משלם
לצורכי הוצאות הק״ק
עדתנו, וזה מפרי צדקת
אחינו אנשי גאולתנו אשר
בק״ק קוראסו אשר שלחו דרך
פרנסי ומנהיגי ואנשי מעמד
הק״ק אמשטרדם יע״א. ובכח
פני צדֵינו השוכן אחר
כותלנו ברכנו ברכה ערוכה
ושמורה לכוללות הק״ק הנ״ז ולכל
המשתדלים והעוזרים להעמיד עיר
האלקים סלה. ולראית האמת
כתבנו וחתמנו שמותנו פע״הק
ירושלם ת״ו בחדש כסליו משנת
התס״ג ליצירה וקים.
חיים ערוך
מרדכי קאירטן

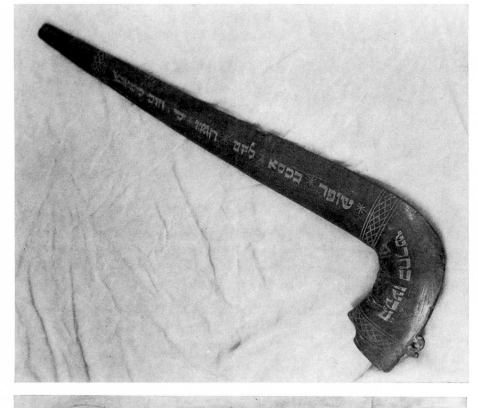

240. SHOFAR DONATED TO SYNAGOGUE MIKVE
ISRAEL, CURAÇAO, 1816

239. APPEAL OF THE HEBRON RABBIS FOR ASSISTANCE,
1872

241. THE TEN SONS BORN TO DAVID GOMES CASSERES AND RIBCA PEREIRA BRANDAO BETWEEN 1822 AND 1836: TOP ROW, FROM LEFT TO RIGHT, ABRAHAM, JOSEPH, JACOB; CENTER ROW, FROM LEFT TO RIGHT, MOISES, ELIAS, BENJAMIN, NAPHTALI; LOWER ROW, FROM LEFT TO RIGHT, ISAAC, JOSHUAH, GAD (GABRIEL), PAGE 261

B. RIBBI ABRAHAM SEROR, MESSENGER OF HEBRON
WHO DIED WHILE VISITING THE HAGUE

Ribbi Abraham Seror, one of Hebron's messengers to visit Holland in 1740, is described by Yaari (p. 499) as "Messenger of Hebron for Western Europe... not known from other sources." The unfortunate man died at The Hague on December 10, 1740, during his mission, according to David Franco Mendez. Two poets occupied themselves with writing the epitaph — David Franco Mendez and Daniel Cohen Rodriguez. The latter's epitaph was used. The Mendez tombal inscription, as found in his manuscript "Sucath David," p. 34 (Etz Haim Library, Amsterdam), follows.

מצבת קבורת הח" השלם כמוהר"ר אברהם צרור
שליח חברון תובב ונפטר בשליחותו באנא הבירה ביום
כֹּא כסליו שנת תהי נפשו צְרֹוֹרָֹה בצרור החיים
זכר צדיק לברכה Aᵒ 5501

זאת הקינה קננתי עליו להחקק על קברו בעט ברזל ועופרת ולא עלתה
בידי כי כבר קדמני נׄזׄי כהרֹ"ר דניאל הכהן רודריג במצבתו.

בכל מקום עבר אברהם ציר נאמן
בחוצה לארץ פה שמשו ש־קעה
יחידתו נקראת לשוב אל־יוצרה
ועינינו־ראות אותיות פורחות

שמו נדף כ צרור המור וכציץ שרון
ואמנם בארץ נקבר בשדה עפרון
לבית אביה עיר־עומדת על חברון
ושברי הלוחות מונחות בארון:

C. APPEAL BY THE RABBIS OF HEBRON TO CURAÇAO

The rabbis of Hebron apparently maintained contact with the community of Curaçao until 1872. Between 1869 and 1871 Hebron was plagued with a severe drought. Food was so scarce that the little available sold for ten times the normal value. Although the rains came in 1871, there was no easing of the famine, for the farmers had no seed to sow. The community was obliged to borrow money from non-Jews at exorbitant interest rates in order to buy wheat for their fold. Their leaders finally decided to send their eminent Chief Rabbi Eliau [Soliman] Mani to Egypt to obtain relief. At the same time they dispatched a printed appeal to various Jewish communities — including Curaçao. It described their plight and beseeched every Jew to contribute one grosh for Hebron. This appeal was written in Hebron at the end of Tebet, 5632 (early in January, 1872), and was signed by five prominent rabbis of the city: Moshe David Camhi, Nissim Baǧayo, David Polokhron Hasson, Ishac Rephael 'Azaria Zeebi (?), and Meir Yomtob Farhi. The appeal follows.

קול שועת

בני עמי הנאנקים והנאנחים על הלחם ופורש אין להם

ראשי אלפי ישראל העמודים והמכונות, רוזנים ומלכי ארץ העומדים בפרץ הפרתמים ושרי המדינות, אלה הם בני ישראל.

ראשי עם קדש הלולים הנה אלה חכמים מטע ה״ להתפאר, כל מעשיהם לשם שמים לשבחם אין די באר, אשריהם ישראל.

ראשי העדה שרי צבאות ישראל הגבירים הרמים, נדיבי עמים, די בכל אתר ואתר ישל״ע עד כי יבא משיח ישראל.

ראשי שורות האומ״ר המה נצבי״ם עומדים להתפלל אל אל נורא עלילה, מול מערת המכפלה, למען יאריכו ימים ושנות עולמים, ברוב הונים, תפארת ישראל, אנס״ו: הגדנו היום כי באנו אל האר״ש לפני שרי צבאות ישראל אשר בכל עיר מדינה ומדינה, שמעו מלכים האזינו רוזנים את כל דברי האגרת, אשר אמריה ממררת, כי זה שנתים הרעב בקרב הארץ ואל השלשה ל״ו בא, ועוד ידו נטויה להדאיבה ולהעציבה, על כן בצרה גדולה אנחנו, כי עוד לא נהיתה כרעה הזאת מכת יוקר השערים הגדול והנורא,׳ שוה זוז

754

למעלה מעשרה, דבר אשר לא היה לעולמים, ולא על הלחם לבדו נגזרה גזרה כי על כל
מאכל אשר יאכל עלה השער במעלה עקרבי״ם, ולא תדמה שמיעה לראיה את קול שועת
העניים ואנקת אביונים וצעקת יתומים ואלמנות במחנה העברים, זה הצועקים במר נפש רעבים
וגם צמאים. חשך משחור תארם וצפד עורם על בשרם מפני זלעפות רעב. ואמת יהגה חיכנו
כי שנה שעברה בשומעם אחינו אנשי גאולתינו היושבים בקר״ח את גודל צערנו נכמרו רחמיהם
עלינו ושלחו לנו מפרי צדקתם, ברם לא היה מספיק ואפי״ לשליש ולרביע, כי אין הקומץ
משביע, ואפי״ לחם שעורים, ולזאת הוכרחנו ללות ברבית אסור לב״ב ומשאינו בן ברית
לקנות בהם חטים כדי להעביר את השעה ולחלק לחם לפי הטף בצמצום גדול כדי פקוח
נפש בלבד, והן עתה עלו עלינו עול החובות המדאיבות, ובראותינו זאת כי הרבית אוכלת,
וגם כי עדיין לא נושענו מצרותינו מכת בצורת ורעבון, הוכרחנו במעשינו להוציא את מעלת
תהלת כתר תורה הרב המופלא בנסתר ובנגלה חק״ל ר״מ ור״מ דאתרא קדישא הדין
כמוהר״ר אליהו מני נר״ו לדפוק על פתחי נדיבים, ויצא ממחיצתו ומעבוד עבודתו תורתו
אומנתו, ללכת לקראת אחינו בני ישראל נדיבי עמים היושבים בעוב״י מצרים יע״א ונא אמן
יע״א ולדבר על לבבם את כל תוקף גודל צרתינו כי אמרנו אולי תעלה מקצת ארוכ״
למחלתינו, יען כי השתא הכא נפסקו צינורות השפע מכל המקומות באמרם כי בשנה הזאת
פקד ה׳ את עמו בגשמי רצון וכלה הרעב מן הארץ, האמנם הן לא נעלם מעיני כבודם כי בשנה
שעברה אף כי הי״ גשם על הארץ לא היה חטים לאכרים ולעובדי אדמה, על כן נשארה
הארץ שממה וגם חריש וקציר לא נראה בעליל ועל דבר זה היוקר יאמיר כאשר אמר בתחלה,
וביתר שאת, ואין ידינו משגת ואפי״ פת קיבר ולחם שעורים כדי להחיות נפש טפינו ועוללינו,
אשר המון דמעינו נוזלים בחיל מראות ברע העניים והאביונים צועקים במר נפש אצל מערת
אבותינו הקדושים זי״ע אבות העולם חמלו עלינו והתפללו בעדינו ולא נמות לעיניכם ברעב,
אחינו בני ישראל מי ראה מי שמע כאלה ומי יקרא סגור לבבו לי״ב קרעים, אף
השכינה מה הלשון אומרת קלני מראשי קלני מזרועי, ועל זאת תאבל הארץ כי שחה לעפר
נפשינו ותם לריק כחינו לא ידענו אנה נפנה לעזרה, והנה בעתה אנחנו מפילים חנותי״נו
במדב״ר בשפל קול התחנ״ה לפני מלכי ארץ השרים והסגנים נדיבי עמים אשר בכל תפוצות
ישראל ותנתן לנו נפשינו בשאלתינו, ויקנו אותנו ואת בני ביתינו לעבדים ולשפחות וחוסו וחמלו
על כל קהל עדת בני ישראל, כי דיני נפשות שנו כאן בזלעפות רעב וחמירא סכנתא כי
נפישי נפיחי כפן, וזאת עשו בכל עיר ועיר העמידו אנשים ויסובבו עיר מבית לבית משום
מצות **לחם לרעבים ופדיון שבויים** וזה יתנו לפחות גרוש אחד לנפש אשר דבר זה
מעט הוא אצלם ודבר גדול הוא בעיניגו, וימהרו לשולחם יפשא״ק [יפה שעה אחת קודם]
למען הציל נפשינו ממות ומבור שאול יעלונו, כי באמת שחה לעפר נפשינו, ואיש לרעיהו יאמר
חזק ונתחזק בעד עיר אלהינו עיר שחמדו לה אבות ראשונים זיע״א, וגאולה יתנו לארץ, כי
הן נודע את עיר הזאת נעמ״י עיר שכולה רשי״ם דלים ואומללים עניים במקום אחד עובדים
מאהבה, ואם ח״ו העלם יעלימו את עיניהם בימים דחוקים כאלו לתומכה ולסעדה, ידעו
נאמנה כי ח״ו חרבה עירנו עיר בתי אבות, ובמה יתרצה עבד אל אדוניו באומרם וזוכר חסדי

אבות, והן ידוע מ״ש בפענח רזא משם רבינו יהודה החסיד זצוק״ל כי מערת המכפלה יש
בה ס״ רבוא אמה כמספר בני ישראל להודיע שכל אחד מישראל יש לו אחיזה באתרא
קדישא הדין, ומכאן מוכח כי להם משפט הגאולה להכין אותה ולסעדה באמת ובצדקה רב
חנ״א ורב חסד״א להעמיד קהל ועדה העם היושב עליה, ואנן מהכא תפלתינו לפני משכן
אבותינו הקדושים אברהם יצחק ויעקב זי״ע בעדם ובעד כל המשתדל לקיום מקום
הקדוש הזה בעד חייהם ונוגה להם וגם לבניהם ולכל אשר להם למען יאריכו ימים ושנות
עולמים ויבלו בטוב ימיהם ובבנים ובני בנים ברוב הונים ואל ישמע שוד ושבר בארצם ומגן
אבות יגן עליהם כנה״ר וכנא״ה עמוסי התלאות, חותמים בדמע פעה״ק חברון ת״ו בש״א
לחדש טבת שנת התרל״ב בא סימן טוב לישראל ישוב ירחמנו לפ״ק דשו״ט ומעתירים
בעדם עתרת החיים והשלום.

משה דוד קמחי סֹט, נסים באגֹאלייו סֹט שוֹבֹ,* דוד פולוכרון חסון סֹט, יצחק רפאל עזריה
זאבי סט (?), מאיר יום טוב פרחי סֹט סט.**
*סופי טוב שלום וברכה.

** Some of the signatures were deciphered by Meir Benayahu.

LICENSED BROKERS

C ONSULS OF FRANCE AND ENGLAND accredited to Constantinople, Salonika and Smyrna during the 18th century stressed to their governments the difficulty for a European to conduct business without the services of the well-informed Jewish brokers. Their services were sought in other cities with a large Portuguese Jewish population: Amsterdam, later London, and cities in the Americas. Why? Because the Jewish broker with relatives and highly dependable connections scattered over the globe was kept abreast of local conditions and was thus in a better position to advise his clients.

As a matter of fact, the mayor of Amsterdam in 1614 granted broker's permits to a few Jews. By 1654 this number rose to twelve. That year with the influx of Jewish refugees from Brazil, the Parnassim prevailed upon the mayor to issue still more, as was done. Following the example of the rabbis in Turkey, the Parnassim protected the Jewish broker and his family from usurpation of his privilege. They saw to it that on a broker's death the permit went to the son. No Jew could apply for it to the son's detriment.[1]

The broker was not only a go-between, but an expert in judging merchandise and in appraising ships, houses, plantations, and so forth. His advice on a contemplated transaction was generally taken. He did not limit his services to negotiating the sale of merchandise, real estate or ships. He also went about interesting financiers to invest in mortgages or marine insurance. Very often the government of Holland, as of England, enlisted his services.

BROKERAGE ACTIVITY IN CURAÇAO

It is quite likely that among the Curaçao settlers of 1659 there was one or another ex-broker of Brazil with the necessary permit to continue in that field. In the absence of complete records for that era, it is impossible to furnish their names. The earliest broker we know of is Jacob Andrade who is first met in 1704.

Before practicing his profession, the broker had to take an oath before the governor to be "faithful, discreet and vigilant" (OAC 177, no. 24). During the 17th century and up to 1748 this business was held in high repute. Its prestige[2]

---

[1] On the death of the broker Ishac Hamis in 1647, the Amsterdam parnassim allowed no one but his son to fill his place (PJCAA, Acordos, 16 Sivan, 5407).

[2] Whereas Moses Penso voiced no objection in 1735 to officiating with broker Abraham Andrade as Bridegroom of the Law, he vehemently opposed this same Andrade's blowing the Shofar in the Synagogue on Rosh Hashanah, 1750 (letter of Feb. 3, 1750, of the Curaçao parnassim to those of Amsterdam [PJCAA, bundle]).

waned by 1764 when Curaçao boasted of as many as thirty-two Jewish brokers (WICA 604, p. 679). In time it ceased being lucrative either because of the large number of practitioners or of the marked decline in business. In 1775 the best among them barely realized 500 pesos annually and the less competent earned only 200 pesos.[3] Nevertheless, some families like the Andrades, Fidanques, Maduros, Lopez Penhas, and others, kept it up for three successive generations.

Jewish brokers in the second half of the 18th century outnumbered the gentile brokers by four or five times — possibly because business was mainly in Jewish hands. In 1794 Governor Johannes de Veer made a new ruling considerably limiting the number of brokers. It is estimated that there were some 200 Jewish brokers in Curaçao between 1660 and 1871. Following is a list of 150 of them culled chiefly from the records[4] in Holland and in Curaçao.

Year	Name	Source[5]
1704-31[6]	Jacob Andrade	WICA 200, p. 492v
1722	Abraham Ulloa	The Samson Papers, AJA
1722-41	Isaac Levy Maduro	WICA 580, p. 520; The Samson Papers, AJA
1723	Aron Cohen Rodriguez	OAC 169, July 30, 1723
1727-38	Joseph Fidanque	OAC 2, no. 224
1731-41	Jacob Dias Guadaloupe	OAC 800, Jan. 14, 1731
1731-42	Jacob Guadaloupe Andrade	OAC 800, Jan. 22, 1731
1732	M[ordechay]. Andrade	WICA 580, p. 520
1733-60	Abraham A. Correa	OAC 801, Feb. 3, 1733
1735-69	Abraham Andrade	WICA 604, p. 679
1736-58	Isaac Monsanto	OAC 864, no. 242
1737-69	Isaac Belmonte	OAC 847, no. 34
1737 (?)	Jacob de Isaac L. Maduro (?)	
1741	Efraim Castello	OAC 173, no. 34
1741-46	Moses Vaz Farro	OAC 173, no. 33
1742-45	Manuel Lopez	OAC 854, no. 45

[3] According to the sworn statement of fifteen brokers — twelve Jews and three Gentiles — made before Governor Rodier on June 26, 1778 (OAC 956, no. 135).

[4] The brokers' names also appear in lists of Curaçao officials formerly published in Amsterdam under the title *Naamlijst van.... der Regeeringe en Gequalificeerde Persoonen... op 't Eyland Curaçao.* The oldest *Naamlijst* consulted which had not yet included Jewish brokers is that of 1745 for the year 1744.

[5] Although the broker's name appears in various records, only one citation is given.

[6] The years are given as encountered in the archives. It is possible that the person acted as broker before or after the year here indicated.

LICENSED BROKERS

Year	Name	Source
1742	Isaac Lopez Dias	OAC 849, no. 14
1742-49	Isaac Hisquiao de Andrade	OAC 848, no. 61
1743	Benjamin d'Andrade	OAC 851, no. 104
1743-47	Abraham Belmonte	OAC 854, no. 70
1743-51	Josias Dovale	OAC 175, no. 20
1745	Garson Garcia	OAC 177, no. 24
1745-62	Isaac Villa Real	OAC 886, no. 243
1746-47	Daniel [Cohen] Peixotto	OAC 862, no. 19
1746-49	Daniel Ulloa	OAC 820, Jan. 14, 1749
1746-73	Jacob Mordechay Calvo	WICA 604, p. 679
1747	Elias Fidanque	OAC 818, no. 40
1747-74	Abraham Henriquez Coutinho	OAC 885, no. 80
1747-92	Jacob Fidanque	OAC 179, Feb. 28, 1747
1748	Aron Motta	
1749	Mordechay Fundam	OAC 821, July 22, 1749
1749-64	Jacob Manuel de Crasto	OAC 891, no. 57
1749-71	Moses Benjamin Jesurun	OAC 942, no. 232
1750	Benjamin Athias de Neyra (?)	OAC 874, no. 157
1750-60	Isaac Pardo	OAC 876, Jan. 25, 1760
1750-72	Ephraim Athias	WICA 604, p. 679
1751	Mordechay Raphael Halas	OAC 827, Sept. 11, 1752
1752	Elias Israel Jesurun Henriquez	OAC 827, Nov. 24, 1752
1753-59	Michael da Costa de Andrade	OAC 840, no. 252
1753-66	Moses Naar Henriquez	OAC 876, no. 39
1754-89	Raphael Gomez	OAC 890, no. 257
1754-89	Jacob Cohen Henriquez	WICA 604, p. 679
1755-89	Jacob Moreno Henriquez	WICA 609, p. 21
1755-92	Aron Machoro	OAC 930, no. 1591
1756-78	Manuel de Moseh Alvares Correa	OAC 941, no. 419
1756-89	Abraham de Isaac L. Maduro	OAC 889, no. 123
1758-89	Abraham Rodriguez Pereira	OAC 891, no. 327
1758-89	Jacob Monsanto	OAC 836, no. 238
1759	Isaac Andrade	OAC 874, no. 45
1759	Abraham Baruch Louzada (?)	OAC 874, no. 157
1759	Daniel Gomes Casseres (?)	OAC 874, no. 157
1759	Moses Motta (?)	OAC 874, no. 157
1759-72	Abraham Pessoa	OAC 911, no. 169
1759-80	Mordechay Motta	OAC 1086, no. 80

Year	Name	Source
1759-89	David Ricardo	OAC 887, no. 113
1760	David Lopez Raphael	OAC 191, July 25, 1760
1760	Benjamin da Costa Gomez	OAC 876, March 13, 1760
1760	Samuel da Costa Gomez	OAC 876, no. 79
1760-66	Isaac Jesurun	OAC 895, no. 155
1760-89	David Abinun de Lima Jr.	OAC 136, no. 133
1760-89	Isaac Cardozo da Costa	OAC 956, no. 135
1760-89	Raphael Monsanto	OAC 902, no. 165
1761	Benjamin Fidanque	OAC 890, no. 123
1761-89	Eliau David Namias de Crasto	WICA 609, p. 21
1762-99	Abraham Dias Coutinho, *alias* Serenie	OAC 141, no. 30
1762-89	Jacob Mordechay Andrade	OAC 920, no. 399
1762-89	Aron Ailion	OAC 972, no. 15
1763-89	Moses Salas	OAC 973, March 6, 1786
1764	Jacob Abraham Andrade	OAC 192, no. 7
1764-73	Isaac Andrade	WICA 609, p. 21
1764-73	Isaac Torres Pinto	OAC 891, nos. 264-65
1764-73	Benjamin Moses Motta	OAC 192, no. 5
1764-77	Benjamin Suares	OAC 918, no. 324
1764-89	Moses Naar	WICA 609, p. 21
1764-89	Salomon Motta	WICA 604, p. 679
1764-89	Abraham de Jacob Jesurun	WICA 604, p. 679
1764-89	David Ulloa	OAC 817, no. 76
1764-89	Jeudah Cohen Henriquez	WICA 609, p. 21
1764-89	David Abenatar	WICA 609, p. 21
1764-94	Jacob Haim Rodriguez Pereyra	OAC 935, no. 12
1765	Isaac Cardozo	OAC 894, no. 153
1765	Jacob da Costa Andrade	OAC 194, no. 3
1765-69	Jacob Henriquez Moron de Losena	OAC 194, no. 5
1765-86	Mordechay L. Maduro	OAC 976, no. 787
1765-90	David Jesurun Jr.	OAC 194, no. 2
1765-97	Daniel Cohen Henriquez	OAC 902, no. 43
1767	Isaac Jesurun Pinto	
1767	Samuel Aben (Habif) [Habib]	OAC 196, no. 14
1767-78	Aron Mendes de Solla	OAC 196, no. 8
1767-90	Jeosuah Guideon Mendes	OAC 196, no. 12
1767-95	Samuel Jesurun Pinto	OAC 196, no. 46
1768-74	Abraham Haim Vaz Nunes	OAC 950, no. 522

Year	Name	Source
1769-78	Benjamin Mordechay Motta	*Naamlijst*, y. 1774
1770	Isaac de Jacob Levy Maduro	
1770	David Henriquez Pimentel	OAC 907, no. 129
1770-74	Jacob de David Osorio Jr.	OAC 940, no. 213
1771-82	Abraham de Isaac Levy Maduro	OAC 936, no. 114
1772	Joseph Obediente	OAC 911, no. 178
1772-80	Abraham Salzedo	OAC 928, no. 1256
1772-82	Moseh Lopez Penha	OAC 205, no. 2
1772-90	Jacob Jesurun Sasportas	OAC 201, no. 56
1773	Jacob de Solas	OAC 946, no. 30
1777	Moses Cohen Henriquez	OAC 917, no. 70
1779-90	David Castillo	OAC 208, no. 77
1780	Daniel Belmonte	OAC 209, no. 28
1780	Abraham Haim Fidanque	OAC 209, no. 26
1780	Moses Abraham Sasso	OAC 937, no. 171
1780	Isaac Abinun de Lima	OAC 209, no. 132
1780	Isaac Hoheb	OAC 209, no. 227
1780-1819	Daniel Lopez Penha	Koloniën 3612, Sept. 9, 1816
1780-91	David de Moseh Cohen Henriquez	OAC 209, no. 164
1780-94	Moses [Mendes] Monsanto	OAC 937, no. 171
1781	Jacob de Manuel Abenatar Melo	OAC 932, no. 451
1781	Elias de Crasto	OAC 210, no. 5
1781-86	Jacob de Salomon Levy Maduro	OAC 210, no. 18
1781-94	Isaac Lopez Penha	OAC 931, no. 334
1781-99	Aron Ricardo	OAC 972, no. 151
1781-1816	Jacob Abinatar Jr.	W. I. Amerikaansche Read van Koloniën 179, p. 22
1782	Jacob Isaac Levy Maduro, *alias* Montje Bacoba	OAC 959, no. 303
1782	Abraham Jacob Lopez Penha	OAC 211, no. 219
1783	Mordechay de Salomo L. Maduro	OAC 965, no. 135
1783	Salomo de Jacob Levy Maduro	OAC 958, no. 205
1785-86	Raphael Jesurun Sasportas	OAC 971, no. 19
1786	Jacob Athias Robles	OAC 976, no. 804
1789	Abraham Andrade	*Naamlijst*, y. 1790
1790-95	Aron Jesurun d'Oliveyra	W. I. Comité, no. 136
1791	Jacob Pareira, *alias* Batist (?)	OAC 116, y. 1791
1791	Jacob Nunes Redondo	OAC 147, y. 1791

Year	Name	Source
1791-94	Elias Haim Sasso	OAC 116, y. 1791
1792	Abraham Cardozo da Costa	OAC 134, y. 1792
1792	Mosseh Jesurun Sasportas	OAC 134, y. 1792
1793-99	Judah de Leon Senior	OAC 1003, no. 44
1794	Abraham de Isaac Senior	W. I. Comité, no. 136
1794	Abraham Jesurun Lobo	OAC 136, no. 135
1794-1805	Salomo de Mordechay L. Maduro	W. I. Amerik. Raad v. Kol. 179, p. 22
1794-1816	Jacob Jesurun Sasportas	Koloniën 3611, July 5, 1816
1795	Isaac de Abraham Senior	W. I. Comité, no. 136
1795	Moses Vaz Nunes	W. I. Comité, no. 136
1795	Salomo Cohen Henriquez	W. I. Comité, no. 136
1795	Isaac Calvo Andrade	W. I. Comité, no. 136
1795	Raphael Namias de Crasto	W. I. Comité, no. 136
1795	David de Salomo de Meza	W. I. Comité, no. 136
1799	Elias Rodriguez Miranda	OAC 141, nos. 89-90
1800-16	Daniel Jesurun Lobo	W. I. Amerik. Raad v. Kol. 179, p. 22
1801-27	David [Haim de Jeudah] Cohen Henriquez	OAC 234, no. 133
1804-16	Isaac Haim Salas[7]	OAC 234, no. 141
1805	Jacob Haim Calvo	
1811	Jacob Senior	
1819	Moseh de Daniel Lopez Penha	OAC 235, no. 402
1824	Samuel Pereira	CC, Dec. 11, 1824
1856-71	Samuel da Costa Gomez	CGAR, 1862; MIA, loose papers of y. 1871
1868	Daniel da Costa Gomez de la Penha	

[7] Later on he was contracted by the government as *Lands Makelaar* or government broker.

JEWISH INCOME TAXPAYERS IN 1702 AND 1707
AND THEIR FAMILY STATUS IN 1709

I N 1702 THE GOVERNOR and his Council took the decision to levy an income
tax on the residents of the island. The Jewish taxpayers are listed below for
the years 1702 and 1707 with the amounts paid. It is noteworthy that of a total
of 4,002 pesos assessed in 1707 on Curaçao's 377 residents — including officials
and employees of the Dutch West India Company — 1,380 pesos or 34.5% of
the entire amount was contributed by 104 Jews. They represented only 27.75%
of the taxpayers.

The eight Jews in the top income tax bracket for the year 1707 were Manuel
Alvares Correa, 45 pesos; Jacob Namias de Crasto, 36; Philipe Henriquez
Senior, Mordechay Namias de Crasto, the Widow of David Carilho, Gabriel
Levy, Moses Lopez Henriquez and Abraham Lucena, each 34 pesos.

The eight Gentiles most highly taxed were Willem Meyer and the Widows
Kerckrinck, Jan Stoonhous and Apero van der Hoeven, each 50 pesos; the
Widows van der Straaten and Juan Moijaert, each 34; Johannes Goedvrind and
the Widow Tribier, each 32 pesos (WICA 201, pp. 94-100; WICA 567, pp.
365-72; WICA 572, pp. 369-75v).

Shortly afterward during the War of the Spanish Succession the Governor and
his Council, on Company orders, introduced the Family Tax. All white residents
twelve years and above had to pay a peso tax annually; children six to twelve,
a half peso. Only children under six were tax-exempt (WICA 203, p. 4v). This
list is combined with the preceding one in order to give an idea of the Jewish
population in 1709 (WICA 571, pp. 61-65).

As the Dutch were unfamiliar with the spelling of Portuguese names,
numerous corrections have been made, for example: Jacob Guardal en Andrade
to Jacob Guadalupe de Andrade or y Andrade; Frano Henriq & Bonal to
Francisco Henriquez & [David] Bernal; Jacob Henriquez Manase to Jacob de
Menaseh Jesurun Henriquez; the Widow Manasch to the Widow Menaseh
Jesurun Henriquez; and so on.

Taxpayer	Income Tax in pesos		Civil Status in 1709		
	1702	1707	Mar- ried	Single 12 yrs. & over	Children 6-12 yrs.
Mordechay de Crasto, wife & three children	32	34	2	2	1
Heirs of Manuel de Pina [*alias* Jacob Naar]	20				
Abraham Naar		12			
Isaac Galas, also Halas, and wife		6	2		
Philipe Henriquez [*alias* Jacob Senior]	32	34			
Widow Abendana	12	12			
Joseph Abendana and wife	2	2	2		
Salomo Vaz Faro and wife		6	2		
Samuel and Aron Gomes		20			
Samuel Gomes and two children			1		2
Aron Gomes and wife			2		
Eliau Pereira, wife and child	22	30	2		1
Jacob Pereira, wife and child	14	14	2		1
Benjamin de Casseres, wife (and sons) [son and cousin]	30	30	2	2	
Jacob Gutieres		10			
Widow [Esther David] Carilho	30	34	1		
Gabriel Levy	30	34			
Widow Esther Touro [1702]; Heirs of Esther Touro [1707]	20	20			
Widow D[avid]. Pardo	6(?)	6			
Jacob Guadalupe y Andrade } Apparently one	16				
Jacob Andrade } and the same person		16			
Isaac Abrahams		6			
Salomon L. Maduro, wife and child		4	2		1
Isaac [Mendes de] Gama, wife and three children	10	10	2	2	1
Widow [Benjamin] de Pas and sons Daniel and David	5	5	1	2	
Jacob Monsanto	10	8			
Juda Touro and three children	20	20	1	3	
Abraham de Pas		2			
Widow [David] Bueno Vivas, mother-in-law of Eliau Pereira	2				
David Bueno Vivas and wife; Isaac Bueno Vivas		12	2	1	
Isaac da Costa, Doctor	2	2			

JEWISH TAXPAYERS IN 1702 1707 AND THEIR FAMILY STATUS

Taxpayer	Income Tax in pesos		Civil Status in 1709		
	1702	1707	Married	Single 12 yrs. & over	Children 6-12 yrs.
David [Nunes] Fonseca and wife	6	6	2		
Jacob Ulhoa	12	12			
Abraham Lopes de Leon and wife		20	2		
Widow Balthazar de Leon and two sons	28	30	1	2	
Abraham de Chaves and son	20	25	1		1
Jacob de Crasto, wife and two children	28	36	2	1	1
Isaac Touro, wife and four children	12	12	2	2	2
Touron (Jewishness uncertain)		2			
Isaac Habillo		2			
Isaac Marchena	30	30	1		
Aron Marchena and wife	12	12	2		
Daniel Moreno [Henriquez], wife and two children	12	20	2		2
Daniel de Lyado		2			
Jacob Lucena		8			
Jacob de Menaseh Jesurun Henriquez		2		1	
Widow [Carlos] de Leon and five children	2	2	1	5	
Aron Levy Suares and wife	4	4	2		
Jacob [Semah] Ferro		20			
Salomo de Medina and wife		4	2		
Joseph [Athias] de Neyra		20			
David Levy Gato	12	12			
Aron Alvarin		10			
Isaac Ergas [Henriquez]	6	12		1	
David Vaz Faro and wife		6	2		
Jacob Vaz Faro	2				
Isaac Pardo Ciudad Real, brother-in-law of (Isaac) [Jacob] Molina	1				
Samuel Maduro, wife and child	2	2	2		1
Abraham Vaz Nunes	20				
Widow Abraham Vaz		2			
Moses Levy Maduro	16	16			
Widow Moses Maduro and son			1	1	
Isaac Levy Maduro and wife	6	6	2		
Jacob Molina, wife and two children	10	10	2		2

Taxpayer	Income Tax in pesos		Civil Status in 1709		
	1702	1707	Married	Single 12 yrs. & over	Children 6-12 yrs.
Henriquez and Francisco Henriquez, *alias* Josias Gabay Ferro and David Bernal	20	30		2	
Daniel Cohen Henriquez and son		3	1	1	
Moses Cohen Henriquez and wife			2		
Moses Pereira [Athias]	2				
Isaac Chaves, wife and two children	10	18	2	2	
David Lopes Dias		14			
Moses Lusada	6	6			
David Dias, wife and two children	12	12	2		2
Jacob Abenatar	6	10			
Joseph da Costa Andrade	20				
Widow Joseph da Costa Andrade and four sons		20	1	4	
David Senior, wife and two children	30	30	2	2	
Salomon Senior and wife	6	12	2		
Manuel & Jacob Vaz Nunes	8	20			
Manuel Vaz Nunes				1	
Abraham Vaz Nunes	20				
Isaac Baruch Lusada, wife and two children	12	12	2		2
Jacob Gaon and wife			2		
Abraham de Meza, cousin of Maduro the silversmith	7				
David Machoro	1				
Widow Motta	2	2			
Jacob Belmonte, wife and two children	6	6	2		2
Moses Meers	2	2			
Jeremias Maduro and wife	2	2	2		
Joseph Obediente, wife and three children	8	8	2	2	1
Abraham de David Ulloa	6	6			
Jacob Benjamin Jesurun Henriquez and wife			2		
Isaac Brandon		6			
Moses Lopez Henriquez	32	34			
Widow Moses Lopez Henriquez and four children			1	4	
Jacob Ephraim [Jesurun] Henriquez and wife		8	2		
Widow Vaz Martines and three children	1	2	1	3	
Abraham Gradis & Co.		10			
Abraham [Rois] Gradis, wife and five children			2	2	3

JEWISH TAXPAYERS IN 1702 1707 AND THEIR FAMILY STATUS

Taxpayer	Income Tax in pesos		Civil Status in 1709		
	1702	1707	Married	Single 12 yrs. & over	Children 6-12 yrs.
Daniel Lopez [Doctor], cousin of de Mattos	2				
Widow Fonseca	6	6	1		
Jacob Naar Henriquez and wife			2		
David Hoheb			1		
David de Leon		2			
Aron Maduro, wife and three children	6	6	2		3
Abraham Lucena	30	34			
Benjamin da Motta and wife		8	2		
Manuel Alvares Correa, wife and six children	32	45	2	4	2
Jacob Henriquez Moron	12				
Isaac Lopez Dias "van" [for] Abraham Marchena		26			
Widow and heirs of Abraham Marchena	12				
Abraham Rodriguez d'Aguilar				1	
Simha Israel and four children			1	2	2
Elias de Crasto and wife			2		
Abraham Penso, wife and five children	12	16	2	2	3
Widow Marache	1				
J[acob]. Dovale; his widow in 1707	12	12			
David Dovale		10			
Widow Menaseh Jesurun Henriquez	1		1		
Abraham Jesurun, wife and two children	12	20	2		2
? Jesurun		2			
Rachel Aboab		2			
Widow Aboab	2				
Widow Josuah Aboab and son	1		1	1	
Benjamin and Abraham Jesurun Henriquez		10			
Benjamin and Jacob Jesurun Henriquez	22				
Benjamin Jesurun Henriquez and two children			1	2	
Joseph Fidanque and wife	20	20	2		
Jacob Salom and wife			2		
David Pinheiro and daughter	1		1	(2) [1]	
Widow [David Raphael] de Mercado	6				
Isaac Netto	1				
Abraham Lopes and wife	2	6	2		
Daniel Delgado	2				

Taxpayer	Income Tax in pesos		Civil Status in 1709		
	1702	1707	Married	Single 12 yrs. & over	Children 6-12 yrs.
D[aniel]. Suares	1				
Isaac Nunes	2				
Heirs of Manuel Pinto		20			
Abraham de Mattos	10	10			
Abraham Henriquez de Mesquita and wife			2		
Josuah Henriquez	30				
Widow Josuah Henriquez [Leah Henriquez]		30	1		
Mordechay Henriquez [o] Mosso and wife	30	30	2		
Aron Cohen Rodriguez and wife			2		
Benjamin Carvalho	6	2			
Jacob Calvo, wife and two sons; in 1707 his widow and sons	8	8	1	2	
Daniel Aboab Cardozo, wife and child	6	6	2		1
Elishah Aboab, wife and five children	12	12	2	5	
Manuel Gomez, wife and three children	5	10	2	2	1
Salomo Levy Maduro Junior and wife	5	10	2		
David Aboab Cardozo				1	
Heirs of Manuel Netto	2				
Isaac Coutinho	6(?)				
Widow Abraham Touro	6				
Widow Molina	2				
Abraham Pereira	2				
Samuel Guer (i.e., Samuel the proselyte)	2(?)				
Widow Frois	1				
Esther Henriquez	3				
Total amount paid: Ps.	1,109	1,370			

JEWISH HOMEOWNERS IN WILLEMSTAD, 1715

PROVISIONAL GOVERNOR JONATHAN VAN BEUNINGEN had a census taken in March, 1715, of the privately owned houses in Willemstad or Punda, that is, of all the houses bordered by the city wall. Excluded from this census were the houses which belonged to the Dutch West India Company in the "Fort" area. The Jews possessed 85, and possibly 86, of the 218 privately owned dwellings in the city — or 39% (WICA 206, pp. 35-41). Below is a list of homes owned or occupied by Jews. The number opposite the homeowner's name is not his house number, since there were none at the time, but his place on the census list. That census makes it strikingly clear that Jews and Gentiles lived side by side. The only exceptions to this nearly perfect integration were the eight houses on Prinsenstraat (today's Madurostraat) and the fourteen houses south of Breedestraat exclusively owned by Gentiles. Where no tenant's name appears, the inference is that the premises were occupied by the Jewish owner.

"AEN DE WAETER KANT" — ALONG THE WATERFRONT
(Not to be confused with today's Handelskade which did not exist in 1715)
Three out of ten houses Jewish-owned

1. Abraham Henriquez Moron — occupied by †Zebaoth Callinghs
7. Henriquez & Francisco Henriquez — occupied by Jacob Preto
8. Gabriel Levy — occupied by a freed Negress — Isaac Abrahamsz lived at no. 4 owned by †Godfried Nieuwpagie.

"IN DHEERE STRAET AEN DE WEST ZIJDE" — AREA WEST OF HEERENSTRAAT
Nine out of sixteen houses Jewish-owned

11. David Lopes Dias
12. Salomon Senior — occupied by †Jan van Erpecum
13. Philipe Henriquez [Senior]
14. Gabriel Levy — occupied by Jacob Telles
15. Abraham Henriquez Moron — occupied by †Moijaert and †van Pruijsen
16. Elias Pereira
20. Elias Pereira — occupied by Abraham Lopes
21. Elias Namias de Crasto
22. Mordechay Namias de Crasto — occupied by Jacob Semach Ferro

"IN DITO STRAAT, AEN DE OOST ZYDE" — AREA EAST OF HEERENSTRAAT
Six out of seventeen houses Jewish-owned

28. Mordechay Namias de Crasto
30. Heirs of Manuel de Pina [Naar] — occupied partly by these heirs and partly by †Cornelis Bergh
31.[1] Widow Jacob Namias de Crasto
36. Isaac Touro
38. Manuel Gomes — occupied by Jacob Gaon
39. Jacob Andrade — occupied by †Freere & Otte

"IN DE BREED STRAAT AEN DE ZUIJDT SYDE" — AREA SOUTH OF BREEDESTRAAT
All fourteen houses exclusively Gentile-owned

Salomon Vaz Faro nevertheless lived at no. 51[2] together with the owner †Jan Dorcas, the Elder.

"OP DE BREED STRAEDT AEN DE NOORDT SIJDE" — AREA NORTH OF BREEDESTRAAT
Four out of eighteen houses Jewish-owned

69. Benjamin de Casseres
71. Widow [David] Carilho
72. Gabriel Levy
73. Widow [David] Pardo

"IN DE JOODESTRAET SOO AEN DE ZUIDT ALS NOORDT ZYDE — NORTH AND SOUTH JOODESTRAAT — MARCH 13, 1715
18, and probably 19, out of 22 houses Jewish-owned

76. Widow Balthazar de Leon
77. Abraham Henriquez Moron — occupied by Isaac Henriquez Coutinho
78. Abraham de Chaves
79. Isaac Mendes de Gama
80. Widow de Pas — occupied by Jacob Salom
81. Isaac Touro — occupied by Isaac Halas
82. [Belonging] "to the Jewish Church" — occupied by Abraham de Meza
83. Jacob Gaon — occupied by †Thomas Hobberts
84. Jacob Gaon — vacant
85. Abraham Ulloa
86. Isaac Marchena — occupied by Abraham de Leon

---

[1] Father Casedo lived at no. 32, house belonging to the heirs of the Widow Willem Kerckrinck.
[2] Father Schabel lived at no. 50, house belonging to the Widow Christiaen Boom.

87. Juda Touro
88. Daniel Moreno [Henriquez]
89. [Dr.] Isaac da Costa
91. Moses Athias Pereira
93. Jacob (Couro) [Touro] — occupied by †Grietje Willems
95. David Pinheiro — occupied by the Widow David Israel
98. Jacob Andrade — occupied by †Philip Waegebaer & Mordechay Calvo
107. Widow Isaac Netto

"INDE WINT STRAAT SOO AEN DE NOORDT ALS ZUYD SEYDE" — NORTH
AND SOUTH WIND STRAAT
Eight out of twenty-five houses Jewish-owned

115. Widow Andrade — occupied by †Gillis de Mel
116. Sarah Vaes
121. Samuel Maduro
125. Abraham Aboab — vacant
127. Widow Mordechay Henriquez — occupied by various people. This house belonged to the Henriquez family since 1660 (OAC 1534, no. 57) and, according to the late J. Maduro, since 1659.
129. Widow Carlos [Samuel Jeudah] de Leon
130. Widow Menase Jesurun Henriquez
132. David Levy Gato — occupied by various people
Isaac [Sant ?] Croes lived at no. 114 belonging to the Widow Dirk Leenders; Salomon de Medina lived at no. 120 belonging to Jacob van der Leijden.

"IN DE CEUKEN STRAET, SOO OOST ALS WEST" — EAST AND WEST
KEUKENSTRAAT
Four out of thirteen houses Jewish-owned

136. Widow Jacob Henriquez Moron & Aron Cohen [Rodriguez]
137. Benjamin Motta — occupied by †Margarita Niemant
138. Benjamin Motta
139. Joseph Fidanque

"IN DE PRINCE STRAAT" — PRINSENSTRAAT
Eight houses facing the city wall, all Gentile-owned

"IN DE JOOD [KERCK] STRAAT" — KERKSTRAAT
17 out of 26 houses (including the Synagogue and school) Jewish-owned

155. Widow Moises Maduro
156. Jacob Belmonte
158. Jacob Molina
161. Henriquez & Francisco Henriquez

771

162. Daniel Cohen [Henriquez]
163. Heirs of Moses Lopez Henriquez — occupied by various people
164. Isaac de Chaves — occupied by Samuel Pinto
165. David Lopes Dias — occupied by Moses Luzada
167. Widow Joseph da Costa [Andrade]
168. Jacob Andrade and David Dias — occupied by Andrade
170. David Senior
171. Widow Jacob da Fonseca
172. David Hoheb
174. [Belonging] "To the Jewish Church" — tenant's name not shown
175. Isaac Maduro — occupied by Deborah Nunes
177. "Being the Synagogue and a school"
178. "A school of the same"
    Abraham Penso lived at no. 157 owned by † Jan Drecx.

"DE KUYPERSTRAET" — KUIPERSTRAAT
10 out of 29 houses Jewish-owned

182. ⎱ Both belonging to the "Jewish Church"; one [to be] occupied by the
183. ⎰ Haham.
187. Widow Jeosuah Aboab
191. Manuel Alvares Correa
196. Isaac Abrahams(e) — occupied by Joseph Obediente
198. Abraham Henriquez Moron
199. Abraham Jesurun — occupied by † Fredrik Ecke
200. Jacob Jeudah Leon — occupied by Benjamin Jesurun
204. Isaac Maduro — occupied by Salomon Maduro
206. Isaac Lopes Dias

"DE SCHREYERSHOECK" — TOWN CRIER'S CORNER
All four houses Jewish-owned

209. Widow Martines
210. David Lopes Dias — occupied by Jacob Naar Henriquez
211. David Fonseca — occupied by Jacob Suares
212. Daniel Delgado

"EEN DWARSSTRAET BIJ DITTO" — A CROSS STREET BY SAME
(I.E., TOWN CRIER'S CORNER)
Two out of six houses Jewish-owned

214. Gabriel Levy — occupied by Abraham Salazar
218. Gabriel Levy — occupied by Isaac (Moyoro) [Machoro]

In our opinion, no Jews lived in any of the possible fourteen houses standing in Otrabanda in 1715.

772

THE OATH ADMINISTERED TO JEWS

D o you swear by the living God Almighty, who created heaven and earth, and by the law He gave Moses, honestly and truthfully to answer the questions put to you, as you are legally bound to do, and if you answer falsely or incorrectly, in whole or in part, that you should be plagued and punished now and forever with all the plagues that God visited upon Sodom and Gomorrah and also on Korah, Dathan and Abiram for their sins, and all such sufferings for falsely and rashly invoking God's name?

So may the Almighty, Omniscient God, Creator of heaven and earth, help or punish you.

The defendants at bar this day took the foregoing oath put to them.

N.B. This oath was given by Governor Du Fay and his Council on November 19, 1721, to Benjamin and Samuel de Casseres on the demand of Abraham de Pina, a.k.a. Naar (WICA 215, Nov. 19, 1721).

IMMIGRANTS TO CURAÇAO
AIDED BY THE AMSTERDAM PARNASSIM
1658-1792

IT WAS THE POLICY of the Amsterdam parnassim since 1639 to encourage the members of their community to leave Holland and settle in the colonies. They advanced the expenses of the trip. Between 1658 and 1660 they spent several thousand florins for the Jewish colonization of Essequibo. On Nisan 1, 5418 (1658), they disbursed 6,683:15 florins in fares, and so forth, for Jews migrating there.[1] Several days later they advanced 4,575 florins for the purchase of thirty adult slaves and a child that were to be distributed among "our brothers" bound for or already settled in Essequibo.[2] As these were not enough, a day later the community allocated 2,250 florins for the purchase of fifteen more slaves.[3]

As observed on another occasion, the parnassim also supplied the colonists with Scrolls of the Law.[4] Unfortunately, the colonization of Essequibo was a failure, and the Jews were compelled to return to Amsterdam or head for Cayenne. The parnassim spent 2,226:2:8 florins in 1661 for those fares.[5]

In spite of this disappointment the parnassim continued encouraging their members to emigrate, particularly to Cayenne and Curaçao. They spent 838:2 florins on Nisan 1, 1659, on persons who sailed for "Curasaó, Cayane and Salé;"[6] in 1664 and 1665, the sums of 424:10 and 90:11 florins, respectively, for fares to Cayenne.[7] There is no doubt that the parnassim helped the Curaçao-bound colonists of 1651 and of the intervening years to 1659. Unfortunately, the archives for these years do not always mention the beneficiaries by name. In 1667 one Mordechay Gabay Correa received 12:12 florins for his trip to Curaçao. The Aby Jetomim Brotherhood (Father of the Fatherless), sponsored by the parnassim, contributed toward the costs of the voyage from Amsterdam.[8] Their earliest recording of a Curaçao-bound settler, by name, is of the year 1697. The following is a list of Jews who migrated to Curaçao and other lands between 1697 and 1792, and the amounts they received in florins according to the Aby Jetomim Register and the Amsterdam Community's Books of Account.[9]

[1] PJCAA 174, pp. 252, 306.
[2] *Ibid.*, p. 272.
[3] *Ibid.*, p. 325.
[4] Emmanuel, NLEAJ, *AJA*, 1955, pp. 18-23, 63-64.
[5] PJCAA 174, p. 428. See also Emmanuel, *ibid.*, p. 23, regarding the failure of the colonization of Essequibo, Cayenne, Tobago and other islands.
[6] PJCAA 240, pp. 102-103.
[7] PJCAA 174, pp. 637, 685.
[8] PJCAA 1211.
[9] PJCAA 969, 970, 971, 978 and 1211.

Name	Amount	Year	Archives
Benjamin Abenatar	–	1697	PJCAA 1211, p. 18
Jacob Sanches	75	1705	„ „ 40
Abraham de Campos [Pereira]	50	1705	„ „ „
Benjamin Frois	150	1705	„ „ „
David Lopez Salzedo	150	1712	„ „ 46
Selomoh [Nunes] Redondo[10]	150	1713	„ „ 50
Isaac Lopes Penha	–	1730	969, „ 99
Semuel Pimentel	160	1730	„ „ „
Sarah Pimentel	50	1730	„ „ „
Daniel Pinto	40	1730	„ „ 100
Selomoh Fernandes	100	1730	„ „ „
Guideon Lopes Penha[11]	40	1732	„ „ 158
Isaac Fernandes Henriques	50	1732	„ „ 213
Abigail da Costa and family	200	1732	„ „ 214
Abraham Israel Dovale	80	1732	„ „ 213
Wid. Abm. de Meza and family	170	1733	„ „ „
Sarah Antunes and family	90	1733	„ „ „
Daniel Martines	160	1733	„ „ „
Samuel Gomes Silva	80	1734	„ „ ?
Mosseh Dias Fernandez	90	1735	1211, „ 131
Daniel Ribeiro	80	1735	970, „ 1
Abraham de Paz Cardozo	30	1735	„ „ „
Jeuda Touro[12]	130	1735	„ „ „
Abraham Gonsales	110	1736	„ „ 3
Benjamin Men[des?]. Quiros	30	1736	1211, „ 133
Benjamin Cortissos	35	1736	„ „ 134
Isaac Rodrigues[13]	15	1737	970, „ 5
Mordechay Lopes	25	1738	„ „ 7
Selomoh Henriques Obediente	20	1738	„ „ „
Jacob Rodrigues Miranda[14]	8	1738	„ „ „
Jeusua Cardozo	40	1738	„ „ „
Bin[jamin]. Falcao	60	1739	„ „ „
Son of Abraham Moreno	60	1739	„ „ „

[10] He repaid the community. See *Precious Stones*, p. 330.
[11] No destination given. He most probably went to Curaçao.
[12] No destination given.
[13] Went to "Karolinas."
[14] Destination not given, but he did go to Curaçao.

Name	Amount	Year	Archives
Mosseh Capriles [12]	10	1739	PJCAA 970 p. 8
Joseph de Isaac Lopes	70	1739	„ „ 9
Mosseh Frois	30	1739	„ „ 9
Raphael Molina Monsanto [14]	35	1739	„
Mosseh Lopes and a son of Samuel de Mercado	140	1741	„
Moses Martines	70	1741	„
Abraham Barzilay	15	1741	„
Isaac de Jb. Rodrigues Pereira and family	300	1741	„
Isaac Attias	15	1741	„
Daniel Rodrigues Nunes	200	1743	„
Abraham Moreno Delgado	160	1743	„
Jacob Fernandes	15	1743	„
Abraham de Selomoh Saruko	60	1745	„
Jeudith Lopes Mattos	55	1746	„
Samuel de Paz	60	1747	„
Son of Sabethay Ventura	40	1747	„
Orphan of Aron Cohen Delmonte	50	1747	„
Son (?) of Joseph Obediente	150	1747	„
Son of David de Souza Henriques	25	1747	„
Mordechay de Quiros	70	1747	„
Jacob de Matos Nobre	60	1747	„
A.º [= Aron?] Nunes Vaiz	90	1747	„
Isaac Pinheiro Nogueira [15]	100	1750	1211, p. 167
Joseph de Moseh Lopes	50	1751	970
Sarah Rodrigues Monsanto	120	1751	„
Daniel Hisq. Lopes de (Crasto) [Castro]	100	1751	„
David de Selomoh de Meza [11]	200	1751	971
Aron Lopes	51:4	1752	970
Abm. de Joseph Palache	45	1756	1211, p. 201
Abraham Nunes Vaz	90	1756	„ „ 204
Abm. de Jacob Rodrigues Miranda	60	1757	„ „ 207
Joseph da Fonseca Chaves	420	1757	970
Ishac Vas de Miranda	40 + 60	1758	970, pp. 207v, 211
Aquiba Nunes Rios	325	1759	970
Aron Mendes Solas	80	1759	978, p. 1

[15] Went to Jamaica, later to Curaçao as teacher (*Precious Stones*, p. 344).

776

Name	Amount	Year	Archives		
Abm. de Mordechay Lealtad, his wife and children Ester and Mosseh	350	1759	PJCAA	978, p.	3
Isaac Nunes Lopes and wife	275	1759	"	"	4
Daniel de Moseh Cortisos	100	1759	"	"	10
Joseph Levy Flores[16]	210	1759	"	"	5
Abraham Lopes Nunes	120	1759	"	"	10
Sarah, d. of Selomoh Nunes	130	1759	"	"	11
Daniel de Jacob Lopes Penha[17]	100	Nov. 19, 1759	"	"	12
Ishac de Abm. da Silva Curiel	120	1760	"	"	14
Rephael Carvalho de Lucena	150	1760	"	"	15
Jeudah de Moseh da Costa	90	1760	"	"	15
Jeudah de Moseh Uliel	100	1760	"	"	16
Ribca Nunes Carvalho, her husband Semuel de Porto and two children	300	1760	"	"	17
Daniel Levy de Barrios[18]	80	1760	"	"	18
Abm. Cohen da Silva, son [?] of Ribbi Hiya Cohen de Lara	100	1760	"	"	18
Esther de Benjamin Marache and mother	100	1761	"	"	19
Benjamin Jacob Taboada	100	1761	"	"	20
Baruch Guedelha	100	1761	"	"	20
Haim de Joseph Israel [Sant Croos?]	60	1761	"	"	21
Selomoh de Isaac aCohen Belinfante	100	1761	"	"	21
Isaac Camarino	62	1762	"	"	23
Selomoh Jeudah Leao Templo, wife and daughter (above, pp. 269-70)	300	1763	"	"	24
Sarah Sasso, wid. of Ebiatar Cohen da Silva, and two children	170	1763	"	"	24
Jacob de Cordova Jr., wife, three children and a stepchild, Rebecca de Selomoh Lopez Henriques	400	1763	"	"	26
Joseph Haim de Abm. de Paz	110	1763	"	"	27
David de Abraham Fidanque	200	1763	"	"	28
Isaac Nunes da Costa	80	1764	"	"	29
Jeosuah de Guideon Mendes	80	1764	"	"	30

[16] He went to New York via London.
[17] Above, p. 312; *Precious Stones*, pp. 424-26.
[18] Grandson of the poet De Barrios.

Name	Amount	Year	Archives
Abm. de Jeosuah Carilho de Matos	100	1764	PJCAA 978, p. 31
David de Moseh Rs. Nunes	80	1764	„ „ 33
Moseh Lopes Melhado and wife [19]	200	1765	„ „ 40
David de Mor[dechay]. Rs. Lopes [19]	140	1765	„ „ 43
Joseph Lopes Raphael, wife and four children	320	1765	„ „ 44
Jacob Machado Cardozo	120	1766	„ „ 49
Ishac de Baruch Guerman	70	1766	„ „ 52
Jacob Rodrigues da Costa and sisters Leah and Judith	300	1766	„ „ 55
Moseh Quiros, wife and child	250	1766	„ „ 57
Ishac de Jacob Lopes Penha	80	1766	„ „ 58
Moseh Mendes Solas	60	1766	„ „ 59
Selomoh de David Lopes Henriques	50	1770	„ „ 88
Isaac Nunes Ribeiro, wife and four children	380	1772	„ „ 101
Isaac de David Lopes Cardozo	120	1773	„ „ 110
Daniel de Isaac Cardozo da Costa	100	1773	„ „ 111
Aron de Jacob Lopes Penha [20]	100	1773	„ „ 117
Widow of Jacob Lopes Penha [20]	300	1774	„ „ 121
Jeudah de Isaac de Benjamin de Solas	100	1777	„ „ 134
Isaac de Mosseh Uliel	100	1777	„ „ 134
Isaac de Benjamin de Solas, [21] wife and four children	400	1777	„ „ 135
Matatia de Mosseh aCohen and wife	230	1780	„ „ 140
Abraham de Mosseh Abendana	70	1780	„ „ 141
Moseh Garsia Meneses, son of Jacob de Mosseh Garsia	110	1780	„ „ 142
Jacob de Isaac Semah Serano	100	1783	„ „ 146
Abraham de Ely Azuby [22]	150	1783	„ „ 147
Selomoh Gomes da Costa	250	1784	„ „ 149

[19] According to the WIC archives, the following left with Melhado and Lopes for Curaçao: Joseph Gallas, Elias Sasso, Joseph Israel [Sant Croos], Jacob de Leon, Don Salvador, Perez Carvalho, Isaac Henriques Coutinho and Moses Taboada. Like Coutinho, some were from Curaçao. Several settlers took their slaves along (WICA 420, pp. 138, 241).

[20] Aron was Daniel's brother. His mother, the widow of Jacob, must have arrived with other members of her family since she received 300 florins in assistance.

[21] Destination Surinam, but he went to Curaçao (*Precious Stones*, p. 415). Isaac, like Redondo above and Pinedo below, repaid the amount advanced for his trip.

[22] He went to Philadelphia.

Name	Amount	Year	Archives
Hisquiau Abm. Frois de Meza and wife	250	1785	PJCAA 978, p. 153
Moseh de David Levy Maduro	100	1785	„ „ 154
Rephael de Jeudah Penso, his wife and d. Rachel	200	1785	„ „ 155
Rachel, widow of Hanania Fano	125	1785	„ „ 156
Leah de Mosseh Garsia	100	1785	„ „ 157
Ribca de Abm. Morales and d. Sarah	200	1785	„ „ 157
Daniel de Abraham de Leon	100	1785	„ „ 158
Abraham de Isaac de Castro	70	1787	„ „ 164
David de Moseh de Semuel Pretto Henriques	120	1787	„ „ 165
Moseh de David de Tovar, his wife and son	250	1787	„ „ 165
Isaac Lopes Jesurun	100	1787	„ „ 168
David de Mehir aCohen, his wife and child	140	1788	„ „ 169
Abraham de Jacob de Abm. Israel [Sant Croos] (above, p. 422) and Jacob Isaac Sant Croos	120	1788	„ „ 169
David de Aron de Pinedo[23]	110	1788	„ „ 171
Rephael da Costa da Mesquita	130	1788	„ „ 172
Abraham de Isaac de Castro[24]	75	1789	„ „ 174
Jacob de Moseh Piza[25]	50	1789	„ „ 178
Selomoh de Baruch Alascar	100	1790	„ „ 183
David de Selomoh de Meza	200	1791	„ „ 186
Abraham Coronel Pereira, his wife and two children	300	1792	„ „ 187
David de Isaac de Jeudah Rodrigues (above, p. 439)	50	1792	„ „ 187
Jacob da Costa Pimentel	100	1792	„ „ 188

[23] He repaid the amount received.
[24] He seems to be the same person of the year 1787.
[25] Uncle of Hazzan Jeosuah Piza.

Between August, 1792, and 1814 no Jew received assistance from the Amsterdam Community to migrate to Curaçao. Many of the people so helped did not become radicated in Curaçao, and left for other parts. It is quite possible, too, that at the last moment, one or another of these voyagers changed his mind about proceeding to Curaçao and settled elsewhere. Some of these people, like members of the families Redondo, Rodrigues Pereira, De Sola, Lopez Rafael, Obediente, Lopes Penha, Molina Monsanto, Dovale, De Meza, Rodrigues Miranda, and others, succeeded in making a decent position for themselves and appear among Curaçao's boat and/or plantation owners. Others like Isaac Pinheiro de Nogueira, Selomoh Jeudah Leao Templo and David Rodrigues served as teachers. Still others like Abraham Moreno Delgado, Daniel Lopes de Castro and Abraham Israel Sant Croos became surgeons. In a general way, all of them helped Jewish transients in Curaçao and paid back, in some form or other, the assistance extended to them to reach Curaçao.

PARNASSIM AND BRIDEGROOMS OF THE LAW
5432-5728 (1671-1969)

THE LIST OF PARNASSIM serving between 5432 and 5559 (1671-1799) was compiled, in Portuguese, by members of the Senior family (ms., "Memorias Senior"). It was continued by members of the Curiel family (ms., "Memorias Curiel") and later, until 1941, by the late Jossy M. L. Maduro. The author brought it up to date to 1969, corrected some errors, filled in various omissions and the late Mrs. Emmanuel translated the material from the Portuguese.

Parnassim of the 17th and 18th centuries were chosen by the notables of the community from the affluent members among themselves before the Jewish New Year for a year's term. They constituted the "Mahamad" which was made up of a president, a vice president and a gabay or treasurer. After the Regulations of 1756 were enacted, two of these three regents were elected before the Jewish New Year and the president before Passover — all for a year. From Rosh Hashanah, 5524 (1763) to Rosh Hashanah, 5533 (1772), the Mahamad was increased to five members. Two parnassim and the treasurer were elected on Rosh Hashanah, and the other two on Passover. After Rosh Hashanah, 5533, the Mahamad reverted to being a three-man body, i.e., two parnassim and the gabay, until 1875. However, between 1810 and September, 1862, to the Mahamad of three were added six members to serve together in important matters. This nine-man body was called the "Congress." From 1875 to 1964, the Mahamad consisted of five parnassim. Three of them were chosen one year and the other two a year later so that every Mahamad would have at least two parnassim of the past year fully abreast of community affairs.

From 1820 onward, excepting the years 5615-5617 (1854-56), we could find no record of the Bridegrooms of the Law.

According to a regulation of 1688 the Hatan Torah could not be a bachelor.

This list does not always correspond with the parnassim who signed the marriage contracts through the years.*

---

* The inconsistant spelling of the names appears in the original.

RECORD OF THOSE PERSONS ELECTED IN THE HOLY CONGREGATION OF MIKVE ISRAEL AS PARNASSIM, GABAY AND BRIDEGROOMS OF THE LAW

[Key to symbols: P or Pr – president; 2d or VP – vice president; G – gabay or treasurer; B1 – Bridegroom of the law finishing the Torah; B2 – Bridegroom of the law starting the Torah; A1 – 1st Assessor; A2 – 2nd Assessor; *oro* – on the refusal of]

5432
Ishac Pereira	G

5433
No record of who served

5434
Ishac de Marchena	G

5435
Mordechay Henriquez	P
Joseph da Costa Andrade	G

5436
Eliao Namias	P
Jeosuah Henriquez	2d
Benjamin Aboab [de Paz?]	G
Mordechay Henriquez	B1
Joseph da Costa Andrade	B2

5437
Daniel Aboab [Cardozo]	P
Ishac de Marchena	2d
Benjamin Carvallo	G
David Abendana	B1
Jacob Naar	B2

5438
Mordechay Henriquez	P
Ishac Alvim	2d
Ishac Pereira	G
Abraham da Motta	B1
Mordechay Vieira	B2

5439
Eliao Namias	P
Jeosuah Henriquez	2d

Joseph da Costa Andrade	G
David Levy Mendez	B1
Manuel Alvares Correa	B2

5440
Daniel Aboab [Cardozo]	P
David Abendana	2d
Jacob Naar	G
Benjamin Jesurun Henriquez	B1
Abraham Aboab Cardozo	B2

5441
Mordechay Henriquez	P
David Carillo	2d
Abraham Aboab Cardozo	G
Eliao Namias	B1
Ishac Marchena	B2

5442
Jeosuah Henriquez	P
Ishac Marchena	2d
Benjamin Jesurun Henriquez	G
Ishac Drago	B1
Menaseh Jesurun Henriquez	B2

5443
Eliao Namias	P
Benjamin Aboab [de Paz?]	2d
Mosseh Lopez Henriquez	G
Daniel Aboab Cardozo	B1
Mosseh Henriquez Coutiño	B2

Re-election because of communal difficulties (p. 87)
David Bueno Vivas	P
Aron Nunes	B1
Elisah Aboab	B2

242. DR. ABRAHAM JEOSUAH NAAR, 1861-1905, NOTED PHARMACIST, PAGE 437

243. DANIEL (DAN DAN) JESURUN, BUSINESSMAN ACTIVE IN 1898

244. JACOB MOISES JESURUN, 1860-1942, BRITISH CONSUL FOR MANY YEARS

245. DAVID MOISES JESURUN, 1862-1936, NOTED MERCHANT

246. MORRIS CARDOZE JR.,
1855-1946, PHILANTHROPIST

247. JOSÉ D. PARDO, NOTED MERCHANT
IN 1887

248. ABRAHAM R. C. HENRIQUEZ, 1880-
1956, PRESIDENT OF THE TEMPLE FOR
MANY YEARS

249. MAURITS S. LANSBERG, 1859-1916,
JUDGE IN CURAÇAO

5444

Daniel Aboab Cardozo	P
Ishac Pereira	2d
Mosseh Henriquez Coutiño	G
Abraham de Marchena	B1
Benjamin Henriquez	B2

5445

Mordechay Henriquez	P
Joseph da Costa Andrade	2d
Jeudah Touro	G
Mosseh Lopez Henriquez	B1
Ishac Gaon	B2

5446

Eliao Namias	P
Jacob Naar	2d
Manuel Alvares Correa	G
Abraham Antunes Paredes	B1
Benjamin de Casseres	B2

5447

Jeosuah Henriquez	P
Ishac Marchena	2d
Abraham Antunes [Paredes]	G
Jacob Ulhoa	B1
[David?] (Jacob) Senior	B2

5448

Abraham Touro	P
Mosseh Lopez Henriquez	2d
Abraham Marchena	G
Abraham de Leao	B1
Abraham Penso	B2

5449

David Bueno Vivas	P
Benjamin de Paz	2d
Benjamin Henriquez	G
Jacob Touro	B1
Mordechay Namias	B2

5450

Ishac Marchena	P
Jacob Naar	2d

Mordechay Namias	G
Abraham Vas	B1
Ishac Touro	B2

5451

Mordechay Henriquez	P
Ishac Pereira	2d
Jacob Touro	G
Joseph Antunes Paredes	B1
Abraham de Lusena	B2

5452

Abraham de Leao	P
Manuel Alvares Correa	2d
(Jacob Senior) My lord father [i.e., David Senior]	G
Jacob Calvo	B1
Ishac da Gama	B2

5453

Mordechay Henriquez	P
Jeudah Touro	2d
Abraham Penso	G
Ishac Gaon	B1
Jacob Dovalle	B2

5454

Joseph da Costa Andrade	P
Mosseh Lopez Henriquez	2d
Ishac da Gama	G
. . . .	B1
. . . .	B2

5455

Ishac Marchena	P
Abraham Antunes Paredes	2d
Mordechay Henriquez	G
Gabriel Levy	B1
Jacob Carillo	B2

5456

Jeosuah Henriquez	P
Ishac Pereira	2d
Benjamin de Casseres	G
Ishac de Chaves	B1
Jacob de Molina	B2

5457

Mordechay Henriquez	P
Abraham Penso	2d
Abraham Henriquez Morao	G
Abraham Jesurun	B1
Mordechay Henriquez	B2

The members of the community convened on the 4th of Sivan to elect the following for four months, no reason for which is given:

Abraham Touro	
Ishac Gaon	
Ishac Touro	G

5458

Jacob Guadalupe	P
Jeudah Touro	2d
Ishac Touro	G
Jacob Andrade	B1
Daniel Moreno Henriquez	B2

5459

Ishac Marchena	P
Ishac Pereira	2d
Gabriel Levy	G
The worthy H : H : [Haham Lopez]	B1
Mosseh Levy Maduro	B2

5460

Benjamin Carvallo	P
Abraham de Chaves	2d
Jacob Crasto	G
Abraham Motta	B1
David Bernal	B2

5461

Joseph da Costa Andrade	P
(Jacob Senior) My lord father [i.e., David Senior]	2d
Eliao Pereira	G
Jacob Belmonte	B1
Manuel Levy	B2

5462

Mosseh Lopez Henriquez	P
Mordechay Namias	2d
Abraham Jesurun	G
Aron Marchena	B1
Jacob de Benjamin Jesurun Henriquez	B2

5463

Abraham Penso	P
Gabriel Levy	2d
Jacob Belmonte	G
Jacob de Crasto	B1
Ishac de Leao	B2

5464

Jeudah Touro	P
Abraham Orobio de Mattos	2d
Jacob Molina	G
Selomoh Senior on the refusal of (= oro) Eliao Pereira	B1
Jacob Efraim Jesurun Henriquez	B2

5465

Manuel Alvares Correa	P
Abraham Henriquez Morao	2d
Jacob Pereira	G
Joseph Abendana Pereira oro David Fonseca	B1
Abraham Naar	B2

5466

Ishac Marchena	P
Abraham Penso oro Isac de Chaves	2d
Eliao Bem Veniste	G
Gabriel Levy	B1
[Dr.] Daniel Ishac Lopez	B2

5467

Mosseh Lopez Henriquez	P
Abraham Jesurun	2d
Ishac Levy Maduro	G
The worthy Haham [Lopez] oro Joseph Athias de Neira	B1
My lord father [David Senior] oro David Bueno Vivas	B2

5468

My lord father [David Senior]	P
Jacob de Crasto	2d
Abraham Naar	G
Manuel Alvares Correa	B1
Ishac Lopez Dias	B2

5469

Abraham de Chaves	P
Mordechay Henriquez	2d
Selomoh Senior	G
[Dr.] Ishac da Costa	B1
David Lopez Dias	B2

5470

Abraham Penso oro	
Manuel Alvares Correa	P
Gabriel Levy	2d
Jacob Efraim Jesurun Henriquez	G
Mordechay de Crasto	B1
Eliao Pereira oro	
Jacob Semach Ferro	B2

5471

[Dr.] Ishac da Costa	P
Eliao Pereira	2d
Benjamin da Motta	G
Abraham Henriquez Morao	B1
Joseph Fidanque	B2

5472

My lord father [David Senior]	P
Mordechay de Crasto	2d
David Lopez Dias	G
Abraham de Chaves	B1
Eliao Namias	B2

5473

Abraham de Chaves	P
Mordechay Henriquez oro	
Abraham Henriquez Morao	2d
Joseph Fidanque	G
Mordechay Henriquez	B1
David Aboab Cardozo	B2

5474

Mordechay Henriquez	P
Ishac Touro	2d
David Aboab Cardozo	G
Ditto oro Aron [da] Costa Gomez	B1
Jacob Gaon	B2

This year they started electing four councillors to make up a council of seven members.

5475

Manuel Alvares Correa	P
Benjamin de Casseres	2d
Eliao Namias	G
David Vas Farro	B1
Jacob Jeuda Leao	B2

5476

Gabriel Levy	P
Jacob Belmonte	2d
Jacob Abenatar	G
Semuel Levy Maduro oro	
Abraham Rois Gradis	B1
Ishac Senior	B2

5477

Eliao Pereira	P
Jacob Efraim Jesurun Henriquez	2d
Jacob Jeudah Leao oro	
Jacob Semach Ferro	G
Ishac da Gama	B1
Ishac Henriquez Coutiño	B2

5478

Abraham de Chaves	P
David Lopez Dias	2d
David Vas Farro	G
Abraham Naar	B1
Ishac Bueno Vivas	B2

5479

Benjamin de Casseres	P
Abraham Naar	2d
David de Crasto	G

Jacob Efraim Jesurun Henriquez B1
David Aboab Cardozo *oro*
  Rafael Alvares Correa B2

5480

Gabriel Levy P
Jacob Jeudah Leao 2d
Ishac Bueno Vivas G
Abraham de Chaves *oro*
  Jacob Abenatar B1
David Lopez Dias *oro*
  Jeosuah Henriquez B2

5481

Eliao Pereira P
Jacob Efraim Jesurun Henriquez 2d
Isaac Henriquez Coutiño *oro*
  Semuel de Casseres G
Jacob Pinedo B1
Ishac Marchena B2

5482

Abraham de Chaves P
Jacob Abenatar 2d
Abraham [da] Costa Andrade G
Jacob de Benjamin Jesurun
  Henriquez B1
David Levy B2

5483

Eliao Pereira P
Ishac Levy Maduro 2d
Ishac Marchena G
Mordechay Alvares Correa B1
David de Crasto B2

5484

Gabriel Levy P
Ishac Bueno Vivas 2d
Eliao Jeudah Leao G
Eliao Jesurun Henriquez B1
Jacob Curiel B2

5485

My lord father [David Senior] P

Jacob Semach Ferro 2d
Eliao Jesurun Henriquez G
Daniel Aboab Cardozo B1
Semuel de Manuel da Costa Gomez B2

5486

David Lopez Dias P
Joseph Athias de Neyra 2d
Mordechay Senior G
Jacob Jeudah Leao B1
Mordechay Pereira B2

5487

Ishac Levy Maduro P
David Namias 2d
Jacob Curiel G
Mordechay Senior B1
Mosseh de Chaves B2

5488

Jacob Efraim Jesurun Henriquez P
Mordechay Alvares Correa 2d
Mordechay Pereira G
Mordechay Alvares Correa *oro*
  Eliao Jeudah Leao B1
Jeosuah Henriquez Junior B2

5489

Abraham Naar P
Abraham Costa Andrade 2d
Mosseh de Chaves *oro*
  Semuel [da] Costa Gomez G
Ishac Levy Maduro B1
Mordechay Alvares Correa *oro*
  Mosseh Alvares Correa B2

5490

Ishac Levy Maduro P
Ishac Marchena 2d
Jeosuah Henriquez Junior G
Abraham Jesurun Henriquez B1
Jacob Jesurun B2

5491

My lord father [David Senior] P

Eliao Jeudah Leao	2d
Semuel Idanha *oro*	
Mordechay de Crasto	G
Mordechay Alvares Correa *oro*	
Benjamin Costa Andrade	B1
Benjamin Lopez Henriquez	B2

5492

Jacob Efraim Jesurun Henriquez	P
Jacob Curiel	2d
Mosseh Penso	G
Jacob Senior	B1
Benjamin Naar	B2

5493

Abraham Naar	P
Mordechay Senior	2d
Jacob Levy Maduro	G
My lord father [David Senior]	B1
Jacob Efraim Jesurun Henriquez	B2

5494

David de Crasto	P
Mosseh de Chaves	2d
Benjamin Lopez Henriquez	G
Eliao Jeudah Leao	B1
Aron Henriquez Morao *oro*	
Joseph Touro	B2

5495

Eliao Jeudah Leao	P
Jeosuah Henriquez Junior	2d
Abraham Senior	G
Jacob Curiel	B1
David Lopez Henriquez	B2

5496

My lord father [David Senior]	P
Samuel Idanha de Casseres	2d
Jacob Lopez Dias	G
Mosseh Penso	B1
Abraham Andrade	B2

5497

Ishac Levy Maduro	P
Ishac Penso	2d

David de Isaac Senior	G
Isaac Penso *oro* Isaac Cardozo	B1
Joseph da Costa Gomez	B2

5498

Abraham Jesurun Henriquez	P
Benjamin Lopez Henriquez	2d
Mosseh de Isaac Levy Maduro	G
Mosseh de Chaves	B1
Abraham de David Senior	B2

5499

Jacob Senior	P
Mordechay de Crasto	2d
Jacob de Eliao Pereira	G
Jeosuah de Mordechay Henriquez	B1
Abraham de Isaac Senior	B2

5500

Eliao Pereira	P
Mosseh de Chaves	2d
Joseph Jesurun Henriquez	G
Mosseh de Isaac Levy Maduro	B1
Benjamin Rephael Henriquez	B2

5501

Ishac Levy Maduro	P
Jeosuah de Mordechay Henriquez	2d
Abraham de Ishac Senior	G
David Jesurun	B1
Abraham de Marchena	B2

5502

Jacob Curiel	P
Mordechay de Crasto	2d
Abraham de Marchena	G
Benjamin Lopez Henriquez	B1
Semuel de Jacob Jeudah Leao	B2

5503

Semuel Idanha de Casseres	P
Benjamin Lopez Henriquez	2d
Selomoh de Isaac Levy Maduro	G
Mordechay de Crasto	B1
David de Isaac Senior	B2

5504

Mordechay Haim Senior	P
Mosseh de Isaac Levy Maduro	2d
Selomoh Lopez Henriquez	G
Ishac Pereira	B1
Abraham Flores	B2

5505

Jeosuah Henriquez Junior	P
David Jesurun	2d
Abraham de Jacob Jeudah Leao	G
Jacob Henriquez	B1
Semuel de Eliao Jeudah Leao	B2

5506

Mosseh Penso	P
Abraham de David Senior	2d
Semuel de Isaac Levy Maduro	G
Jacob Levy Maduro	B1
Joseph Jesurun Henriquez	B2

5507

Mordechay de Crasto	P
Jacob Levy Maduro	2d
Ishac Motta	G
David Baruh Louzada	B1
Abraham Aboab Cardozo	B2

5508

Benjamin Lopez Henriquez	P
David de Isaac Senior	2d
Mosseh Henriquez Coutiño	G
Benjamin Rephael Henriquez	B1
Semuel Hoheb	B2

5509

Mordechay Pereira	P
Joseph Jesurun Henriquez	2d
Semuel Hoheb	G
Selomoh Lopez Henriquez	B1
Semuel de Isaac Levy Maduro	B2

5510

David Jesurun	P

Abraham de Marchena	2d
Aron Motta	G
Selomoh de Isaac Levy Maduro	B1
Ishac Motta	B2

5511

Selomoh Nunes Redondo	P
Abraham de Isaac Senior	2d
Jacob Fidanque	G
Mordechay Pereira	B1
Jacob de Isaac Levy Maduro	B2

5512

Abraham de David Senior	P
Jacob Lopez Dias	2d
Isac Haim Rodrigues da Costa *oro*	
Semuel de Eliao Jeudah Leao	G
The worthy Haham [De Sola] *oro*	
Isaac de Jacob Henriquez Fereira	B1
Isaac Haim Rodrigues da Costa *oro*	
Benjamin de Casseres	B2

5513

Jacob Levy Maduro	P
Selomoh Lopez Henriquez	2d
David da Costa Andrade	G
Joseph Jesurun Henriquez	B1
Jacob Fidanque	B2

5514

Mosseh Penso	P
Selomoh de Isaac Levy Maduro	2d
Michael de Eliao Jeudah Leao	G
Abraham de Marchena	B1
Ishac de Marchena	B2

5515

Jeosuah de Mordechay Henriquez	P
Aron Henriquez Morao	2d
Jacob de Mordechay de Crasto *oro*	
Eliao de Crasto	G
Abraham de Jacob Jeudah Leao	B1
Abraham de Chaves	

5516

David Jesurun	P
Semuel de Jacob Jeudah Leao	2d
Abraham de Chaves	G
David da Costa [Andrade] *oro*	
Manuel Alvares Correa	B1
Mordechay Henriquez	B2

5517
After the Regulation
[of 1756 was enacted].

Ishac Penso for six m[onth]s	P
Semuel de Eliao Jeudah Leao	2d
Isaac de Marchena *oro*	
Moseh Lopez Henriquez	G
Aron Henriquez Morao	B1
Isaac de Eliao Jeudah Leao	B2

On Passover

Mordechay de Crasto	P

5518
On Rosana (Rosh Hashanah)

Abraham de Jacob Jeudah Leao	2d
Isaac de Jacob Levy Maduro	G
Abraham de Isaac Senior	B1
Isaac de Jacob Jeudah Leao	B2

On Passover

Jacob Senior	P

5519
On Rosana

Ishac Henriquez Fereira	2d
Ishac de Eliao Jeudah Leao	G
Semuel de Eliao Jeudah Leao	B1
Abraham de David Jesurun	B2

On Passover

Benjamin Lopez Henriquez	P

5520
On Rosana

Ishac Haim Rodrigues da Costa	2d
Ishac de Jacob Jeudah Leao	G

Abraham Henriquez Fereira	B1
Jacob de Mordechay de Crasto	B2

On Passover

Jacob Levy Maduro	P

5521
On Rosana

Joseph Jesurun Henriquez	2d
Abraham de David Jesurun	G
Semuel Hoheb	B1
Abraham Henriquez Morao	B2

On Passover

Selomoh Lopez Henriquez	P

5522
On Rosana

Abraham de Isaac Senior	2d
Jacob de Joseph Jesurun Henriquez	G
Jacob Levy Maduro	B1
Isaac de Jacob Levy Maduro	B2

On Passover

David Jesurun	P

5523
On Rosana

Abraham de Marchena	2d
Abraham de Mordechay de Crasto	G
David Jesurun *oro*	
Jacob de Jeosuah Naar	B1
Jacob de David Jesurun	B2

On Passover

Aron Henriquez Morao	P

5524
[On Rosana]

Starting with [this] Rosana, with the approval of the directors of the [West India] Company, there have been and shall hereafter be elected two parnasims [and gabay] on Rosana and two on Passover.

Mordechay de Crasto
Benjamin Rephael Henriquez
Manuel de Moseh Alvares Correa
  oro Selomoh Curiel   G
Ishac Motta   B1
Jacob Namias de Crasto *oro*
  Michael Jeudah Leao   B2

On Passover

Abraham de Isaac Senior
David da Costa Andrade

5525
On Rosana

Benjamin Lopez Henriquez
Manuel Alvares Correa
Abraham Henriquez Morao *oro*
  Saul Idanha de Casseres   G
Isaac Haim Rodrigues da Costa   B1
Joseph Curiel   B2

On Passover

Joseph Jesurun Henriquez
Irmiao de Isaac Levy Maduro

5526
On Rosana

Benjamin Lopez Henriquez
Manuel de Rephael Alvares Correa
Joseph Curiel   G
Jacob de Joseph Jesurun
  Henriquez   B1
Ephraim de Joseph Jesurun
  Henriquez   B2

On Passover

Abraham de Marchena
Michael de Eliao Jeudah Leao

5527
On Rosana

Selomo Lopez Henriquez *oro*
  Jacob Levy Maduro
Abraham Curiel *oro*
  Jacob de Jeosuah Naar

Gabriel Pinedo   G
Ishac de Marchena   B1
Ishac de Abraham de Marchena   B2

On Passover

Semuel de Eliao Jeudah Leao
Isaac de Isaac de Marchena *oro*
  Benjamin de Casseres

5528
On Rosana

Jacob de Eliao Pereira
Abraham de Jeosuah Naar
Jeosuah de Mordechay de Crasto   G
Irmiao de Isaac Levy Maduro   B1
Abraham de Jeosuah Naar because
  of his brother David's
  Indisposition   B2

On Passover

Isaac de Marchena *oro* Isaac
  Henriquez Fereira and of Isaac
  Haim Rodrigues da Costa
Isaac de Eliao Jeuda Leao

5529
On Rosana

David Jesurun
Manuel de Moseh Alvares Correa
The worthy Haham [Da Fonseca] this
  year served as Gabay *oro* Semuel
  de Gabriel da Costa Gomez & of
  Semuel de Joseph da Costa
  Gomez   [G]
Michael de Eliao Jeuda Leao   B1
Abraham de Jacob Lopez Dias   B2

On Passover

David da Costa Andrade *oro*
  Benjamin Rephael Henriquez
Mordechay de Jeosuah Henriquez
  oro Isaac de Jacob Jeuda Leao

5530
On Rosana

Abraham Marchena   1st

Isaac Haim Rodrigues da Costa 2nd
Jacob de Mordechay Pereira G
Isaac Haim Rodrigues da Costa B1
David de Jacob Jesurun B2

On Passover

David da Costa Andrade for six
months

Mordechay de Jeosuah
Henriquez ditto

5531
On Rosana

Abraham de Marchena for six
months

Isaac Haim Rodrigues
da Costa ditto
Jacob de Jeosuah Naar for a year
Isaac de Jacob Jeuda Leao ditto
Jacob de Abraham Andrade G
Isaac de Jacob Jeuda Leao B1
Jacob de Abraham Andrade *oro*
Semuel Joseph da Costa Gomez B2

On Passover

Isaac Henriquez Fereira *oro* for six
Manuel de Rephael Alvares
Correa months
Ishac de Marchena for a year

5532
On Rosana

Joseph Jesurun Henriquez *oro*
Abraham Jesurun for a year
Jacob de Jeosuah Naar & Isaac de
Jacob Jeuda Leao until there is
a reply from the Messrs. Par-
nassim of Amsterdam in ac-
cordance with the resolution of
the Councillors and Elders of
said date.
Abraham de David da Costa
Andrade G
Mordechay Henriquez B1
David de Jacob Lopez Dias B2

On Passover

Ishac de Marchena P

5533
On Rosana

Gabriel Pinedo 2d
Isaac de Jacob Jeuda Leao G
in place of his brother-in-law
Isaac de Abraham de Isaac Senior
who is hereafter freed from
serving as Gabay G
Mordechay Penso B1
Isaac de Abraham de Isaac Senior B2

On Passover

Ishac de Marchena P

5534
On Rosana

Isaac de Jacob Levy Maduro 2d
David de Jacob Senior *oro*
Mordechay de Benjamin Lopez
Henriquez G
Abraham de David Jesurun B1
Jacob de Mordechay Pereira B2

On Passover

Manuel de Rephael Alvares Correa P

5535
On Rosana

Jacob Namias de Crasto 2d
Mordechay Motta G
Jacob de Manuel Namias de Crasto
oro Semuel de Joseph da
Costa Gomez B1
Rephael de Manuel Alvares Correa
oro Moseh de David de Moseh
Cohen Henriquez B2

On Passover

Benjamin de Rephael Henriquez
oro Abraham de Isaac Senior P

791

5536
On Rosana

Jacob de David Jesurun	2d
Jeosuah de Jacob de Jeosuah Naar	G
Jacob de David Jesurun *oro* Gabriel Pinedo	B1
David Henriquez	B2

On Passover

Abraham de Marchena	[P]

5537
On Rosana

Semuel de Joseph da Costa Gomez *oro* Semuel de Gabriel da Costa Gomez	2d
Moseh de Benjamin de Casseres *oro* Rephael Penso	G
Jacob de Mordechay Pereira	B1
Mordechay de Jeosuah Henriquez by lot *oro* Isaac de Abraham Henriquez Fereira & Semuel de Joseph da Costa Gomez, and elected on the first day of Tabernacles	B2

On Passover

Gabriel Pinedo *oro* Isaac de Jacob Jeudah Leao	[P]

5538
On Rosana

Jacob de Mordechay Pereira	2d
Moseh de David Cohen Henriquez *oro* Moseh Penso	G
Ishac de Marchena	B1
Moseh de Casseres *oro* Rephael Penso	B2

On Passover

Semuel de Joseph da Costa Gomez elected by lot on the Sabbath when Parasah Rehe Anochi is read, on the resignation of Ishac Haim Rodrigues da Costa in the month of Ab, & also *oro* Michael de Eliao Jeuda Leao   P

5539
On Rosana

Mordechay Motta	2d
Eliao Penso	G
Manuel de Rephael Alvares Correa by lot *oro* Semuel de Gabriel da Costa Gomez & David Gomez Casseres	B1
Selomoh de (Crasto) [Castro]	B2

On Passover

Gabriel Pinedo elected by lot *oro* Joseph Jesurun Henriquez and of Manuel de Rephael Alvares Correa   P

5540
On Rosana

Moseh Cohen Henriquez	2d
Benjamin Cohen Henriquez	G
Mordechay Motta	B1
David Morales	B2

On Passover

Mordechay Henriquez	[P]

5541
On Rosana

David de Jacob Jesurun	2d
David Morales	G
Doctor Capriles	B1
Jacob de Solas	B2
On the refusal of the above:	
Benjamin Cohen Henriquez	2d
Isaac de Abraham Henriquez Fereira	G
Benjamin Cohen Henriquez	B1
Moseh de David de Jeudah Cohen Henriquez	B2

On Passover

Abraham Jesurun	[P]

5542
On Rosana

David Morales *oro* Jacob de Joseph Jesurun Henriquez	2d
Selomo de Moseh de Castro *oro* Jacob de Solas	G
David Morales *oro* Moseh Cohen Henriquez	B1
Semuel de Gabriel da Costa Gomez by lot *oro* Jacob Henriquez Fereira & Moseh Penso	B2

On Passover

*Mordechay Motta	P

5543
On Rosana

David Morales	2d
David Dovale	G
David de Jacob Jesurun	B1
Jeosuah de Jacob de Jeosuah Naar	B2

David Dovale resigned in the middle of the year because of the Island Government Council's decision sentencing the Mahamad to pay the Abraham da Costa Andrade claim, & on the following Sabbath they elected as treasurer Jacob de Moseh de Castro who refused & in his stead, Isaac Henriquez Fereira [see pages 271-75].

On Passover

*Mordechay Motta	P

5544
On Rosana

David Morales	2d
Isaac de Abraham Henriquez Fereira	G

Abraham de Marchena by lot *oro* Aron Ajlion [Aelyon] & Jacob De Solas	B1
Ishac de Marchena by lot *oro* Isaac Vas de Oliveira & Daniel de Joseph Jesurun Henriquez	B2

On Passover

Mordechay Motta	P

5545
On Rosana

David Morales	2d
Isaac de Abraham Henriquez Fereira	G
Jeosuah Rephael Henriquez	B1
Jacob de Mordechay Henriquez	B2

On Passover

Mordechay Motta	P

5546
On Rosana

David Morales	2d
Isaac de Abraham Henriquez Fereira	G
Jacob de David Jesurun by lot *oro* Eliao Rodrigues Miranda & Abraham Henriquez Mellado	B1
Jacob de Joseph Jesurun Henriquez by lot *oro* Moseh Monsanto & Semuel Hisquiao de Casseres	B2

On Passover

Abraham de David Jesurun	P

5547
On Rosana

Doctor Joseph Capriles	2d
Moseh Monsanto	G
Jeosuah de Jacob de Jeosuah Naar	B1
David Dovale	B2

* After Mordechay Motta's name there is some illegible matter in the "Memorias Senior" followed by "...for his refusal on Passover, Isaac de Jacob Jeudah [Leao] [and on his refusal] Gabriel Pinedo."

On Passover

Ishac de Marchena P

5548
On Rosana

Abraham de Mordechay Senior 2d
Eliao de Ishac Jeudah Leao G
Selomoh de Moseh de Castro B1
Jacob de Moseh de Castro B2

On Passover

Moseh Cohen Henriquez *oro*
Gabriel Pinedo P

5549
On Rosana

Moseh de David de Judah Cohen
Henriquez *oro* Jacob de Solas 2d
Eliao Dovale G
Moseh de David de Judah Cohen
Henriquez B1
David Cohen Henriquez B2

In the middle of the year Moseh de David de Judah Cohen Henriquez resigned, and Abraham de David Jesurun was elected by lot as 2d.

On Passover

Ishac de Abraham de Marchena [P]

5550
On Rosana

Jeosuah de Jacob Naar 2d
David Haim Cohen Henriquez G
Moseh Cohen Henriquez by lot
oro Abraham de Mordechay
Senior & Rephael de Manuel
Alvares Correa B1
Daniel de David Gomez Casseres
oro Mordechay Alvares Correa B2

On Passover

David de Jacob Jesurun [P]

5551
On Rosana

Jeosuah de Jacob Naar 2d
David Haim Cohen Henriquez G
David de Abraham Senior *oro*
Isaac Abraham Senior B1
David Henriquez *oro* Jacob Pinedo B2

On Passover

Jacob de David Jesurun P

5552
On Rosana

David Abinun de Lima 2d
Daniel Gomez Casseres G
David Haim Dovale B1
Eliao Dovale B2

On Passover

Jacob de Solas by lot *oro* Semuel de Gabriel da Costa Gomez & Samuel de Joseph da Costa Gomez; and since David Abinun de Lima & Daniel Gomez Casseres resigned in the month of Nissan, they elected:
Selomoh de Castro 2d
Semuel de Benjamin de Casseres G

5553
On Rosana

Moseh de David de Judah Cohen
Henriquez by lot *oro* David
Dovale & Rephael Penso 2d
Abraham Haim Fidanque G
Daniel Lopez Penha *oro*
David Abinun de Lima B1
Ishac Calvo de Andrade B2

On Passover

David Abinun de Lima *oro* Jacob
de Joseph Jesurun Henriquez P

5554
On Rosana

Jeosuah Rephael Henriquez	2d
Abraham Haim Fidanque	G
Isaac Calvo de Andrade *oro*	
Abraham Lopez Penha	B1
Jacob de Isaac Suares	B2

On Passover

Rephael Alvares Correa *oro* Ishac de Abraham de Marchena	P

5555
On Rosana

Abraham Haim Fidanque	2d
Jacob de Isaac Suares *oro*	
Jacob Jesurun Sasporta	G
Isaac de Abraham de Marchena by lot *oro* Rephael Penso & Mordechay Alvares Correa	B1
Aron Pinedo	B2

On Passover

Selomoh de Castro by lot *oro* Rephael Alvares Correa & Jacob de Solas	P
Jeosuah de Jacob Naar by lot [on the resignation of] Jacob de Isaac Suares	G

5556
On Rosana

Mordechay Alvares Correa	2d
Semuel de David Hoheb *oro* Gabriel de David da Costa Gomez	G
Rephael Alvares Correa by lot *oro* Selomo de Casseres & Jacob Jesurun Sasporta	B1
Jeosuah Rephael Henriquez by lot *oro* Rephael de Manuel Pinedo & of Rephael Jesurun Sasporta	B2

On Passover

Abraham Haim Fidanque by lot *oro* Jeosuah de Jacob Naar & of Abraham Jesurun	P

5557
On Rosana

Jacob de Gabriel Pinedo	2d
Semuel de David Hoheb	G
Jacob de Gabriel Pinedo	B1
Abraham de Jacob Jesurun *oro* Gabriel de David da Costa Gomez	B2

On Passover

Mordechay Alvares Correa *oro* Moseh Cohen Henriquez & David Haim Dovale	[P]

5558
On Rosana

David Haim Cohen Henriquez	2d
Selomo Cohen Henriquez *oro* Moseh Cardoze	G
Jacob de Moseh de Castro	B1
Isaac Capriles *oro* Abraham Rodrigues Miranda	B2

On Passover

Jacob de Moseh de Castro	[P]

5559
On Rosana

David Haim Cohen Henriquez	2d
Selomo Cohen Henriquez	G
Abraham Haim Fidanque	B1
Semuel de David Hoheb	B2

On Passover

Jacob Pinedo by lot *oro* Selomo de Castro & of Rephael Penso	[P]

5560
On Rosana

David de Ishac Henriquez Bello	[P]
David Haim Cohen Henriquez by lot *oro* Ephraim Curiel and of Abraham de Jacob Jesurun	G
David de Isaac Henriquez Bello	B1
David Cohen Henriquez	B2

On Passover

Abraham Haim Fidanque *oro*
Jeosuah Rephael Henriquez   [P]

5561
On Rosana

Aron Pinedo   2d
David Haim Cohen Henriquez by
   lot *oro* Benjamin de Abraham
   Jesurun & of Abraham de Isaac
   de Marchena   G
   Because of circumstances it was
   resolved again to urge the said
   Mr. Cohen Henriquez to remain
   this year as treasurer and he
   agreed.
Aron Pinedo   B1
Abraham Pinedo   B2

On Passover

Abraham Haim Fidanque, at the
   request of the Parnassims and
   Councillors, agreed to serve this
   year as   P
On the 12th of Nissan the fol-
   lowing were elected to the
   Council of Seven:
Isaac Levy Maduro
Abraham de Mordechay Senior
Mordechay Alvares Correa &
David de Isaac Henriquez

5562
On Rosana

David de Abraham de Isaac Senior   P
Mordechay Haim Senior   G
   Ditto   B1
David Haim Dovale by lot *oro*
   Ephraim Curiel & of Selomoh
   Cohen Henriquez   B2

On Passover

Mordechay Alvares Correa   P

Elected to the Council of Seven:

Jacob de Joseph Jesurun Henriquez

5563
On Rosana

At the request of the Councillors [the following] were re-
elected:

David de Abraham de Isaac Senior   P
Mordechay Haim Senior   G

on condition that the President
shall be exampted from serving
as President of Passover and
the Treasurer as Treasurer of
Rosana, unless they seek re-
election.

Aron Pinedo by lot *oro* Semuel
   Hisquiao de Casseres & of
   Daniel de David Gomez
   Casseres   B1
Manuel de Rephael Alvares Correa
   oro Abraham de Isaac de
   Marchena   B2

On Passover

David Haim Cohen Henriquez   P

5564
On Rosana

Semuel Hisquiao de Casseres   P
Moseh Levy Maduro Peixotto   G
The worthy H: H: M: V: R:
   [Haham Jacob Lopez] da
   Fonseca]   B1
Gabriel de David da Costa Gomez B2

On Passover

David Haim Cohen Henriquez re-
elected by request   P

5565
On Rosana

Moseh Levy Maduro Peixotto *oro*
   Daniel de David Gomes
   Casseres   P

Abraham Salom Delvalle G
David Haim Cohen Henriquez *oro*
   Benjamin de Abraham Jesurun B1
Abraham Salom Delvalle at his
   request B2

Elected to the Council of Seven:

Mordechay Haim Senior and
Semuel Hisquiao de Casseres

On Passover

David Haim Cohen Henriquez P
and he having resigned, there
was elected [in his place] on
Menahem 20:

Aron Pinedo

5566
On Rosana

Mordechay Haim Senior by lot *oro*
   Benjamin de Abraham Jesurun
   and of Gabriel de David da
   Costa Gomez P
Selomoh Salom Delvalle *oro*
   David de Moseh de David
   Cohen Henriquez G
Abraham Pinedo *oro*
   Jacob Abenatar B1
David de Abraham de Isaac Senior
   by lot *oro* Abraham de Isaac
   Henriquez Bello and of Jacob
   de Jeosuah Naar B2

Elected to the Council of Seven:

David de Abraham de Isaac Senior
and Moseh Levy Maduro Peixotto

On Passover

David de Isaac Henriquez Bello P

Elected to the Council of Seven:

Jacob Abenatar in place of
   Abraham Haim Fidanque

5567
On Rosana

Ephraim Curiel *oro* Abraham
   Pinedo P
Selomoh Salom Delvalle at his
   request G
Ditto on the refusal of Moseh Levy
   Maduro Peixotto B1
Moseh Henriquez Juliao *oro*
   David de Moseh de David
   Cohen Henriquez B2

On Passover

Daniel de David Gomes Casseres
   oro Semuel Hisquiao de Casseres P

Elected to the Council of Seven:

Jeosuah Rephael Henriquez

5568
On Rosana

David de Moseh de David Cohen
   Henriquez *oro* Abraham de
   Jacob Jesurun P
Haim Gabriel da Gosta Gomez G
Daniel de David Gomez Casseres B1
Haim Gabriel da Costa Gomez B2

On Passover

Ephraim Curiel by lot *oro*
   Benjamin de Abraham Jesurun
   and of Abraham de Jacob
   Jesurun P

Elected to the Council of Seven:

Abraham Haim Fidanque
David Haim Cohen Henriquez and
Semuel Hisquiao de Casseres

5569
On Rosana

Rephael Pinedo P
David de Isaac de Crasto G
Abraham de Jacob Jesurun B1
David Capriles *oro* Moseh Hisquiao
   Jesurun B2

797

On Passover

Mordechay Haim Senior	P

5570
On Rosana

Moise Cardoze	P
Manuel Haim Alvares Correa	G
Ephraim Curiel	B1
Abraham de Jacob Jesurun Henriquez	B2

On the refusal of the Bride-grooms of the Law, [the following were] elected on the second ballot:

David Cohen Henriquez Junior	B1
Jeosuah de Solas	B2

And on [their] refusal there were elected by lot:

David de Isaac Henriquez	B1
Abraham Pinedo	B2

The Treasurer having resigned on Kislev 7, there was elected on the second ballot:

Moseh Hisquiao Jesurun

And the 2nd Treasurer having resigned on Kislev 20, [the following] was elected by lot on Sebath 13:

Abraham de Jacob Jesurun*

On Passover

Abraham Pinedo	P

5571
On Rosana

Moise Cardoze re-elected	P
Selomoh Senior	G
Mordechay Ricardo *oro* Selomo Cohen Henriquez	B1

David de Daniel Gomes Casseres *oro* Isaac de David Henriquez	B2

On Passover

Rephael Pinedo *oro* Gabriel de David da Costa Gomez	P

5572
On Rosana

Moise Cardoze	P
David Cohen Henriquez Junior by lot *oro* Abraham de Jacob Jesurun Henriquez and of Jacob de Jeosuah Naar	G
Moseh Henriquez Juliao	B1
Rephael Penso by lot *oro* Manuel Penso and of David Haim Abinun de Lima	B2

On Passover

My lord father [Ephraim Curiel] and, on his refusal, Jeosuah de Jacob Naar.	P

The election of the last incumbent took place in accordance with the old practice and established order because, on the termination of the Passover President's term, David Cohen Henriquez Junior & Moise Cardoze were serving and Abraham Salom Delvalle [of the Council] was related to the President.

5573
On Rosana

Selomoh Cohen Henriquez	P
David de Daniel Gomes Casseres	G
Daniel de David Gomes Casseres by lot *oro* Abraham de Isaac de Marchena and of Ishac Capriles	B1

* These resignations indicate that the Community was in financial difficulties in 1809.

Benjamin Jesurun by lot *oro*
Selomoh Senior and of Eliao
Jesurun Henriquez   B2

On Passover

Moise Cardoze *oro* Abraham
Salom Delvalle   P

5574
On Rosana

Manuel de Rephael Alvares Correa P
Semuel Hisquiao de Casseres by
lot *oro* Joseph de Mordechay
Henriquez and of Josiao de
David Dovale   G
Moise Cardoze   B1
David de Moise Cardoze   B2

On Passover

Moise Cardoze   P

5575
On Rosana

Daniel de David Gomes Casseres
by lot *oro* Abraham de Isaac de
Marchena and of Jeosuah de
Solas   P
Manuel Penso *oro* Eliao Jesurun
Henriquez   G
Benjamin Jesurun by lot *oro*
Abraham de Isaac Henriquez and
of Jacob de Jeosuah Naar   . B1
David de Moseh de David Cohen
Henriquez by lot *oro* Gabriel de
Jacob Pinedo and of Semuel da
Costa Gomez   B2

During the Feast of Tabernacles
Treasurer Manuel Penso re-
signed; elected by lot on Hosana
Raba:

Selomo Cohen Henriquez   [G]

On Passover

Moise Cardoze   P

5576
On Rosana

Jeosuah de Solas by lot *oro* Abra-
ham de Isaac Henriquez and of
Jacob de Jeosuah Naar   P
Semuel Hisquiao de Casseres by
lot *oro* Abraham de Benjamin
Jesurun and of David de David
Dovale   G
Aron Pinedo by lot *oro* Jacob Lopez
Penha and of Manuel Penso   B1
Gabriel de Aron Pinedo *oro* Joseph
de Mordechay Henriquez   B2

On Passover

Moise Cardoze   P

Elected by the Elders, he was
exempted from being chosen
by lot at a future term for
Treasurer. Those opposed were:

Rephael Penso
Manuel Haim Alvares Correa &
Selomoh Cohen Henriquez

5577
On Rosana

Jacob de Jeosuah Naar by lot *oro*
Moseh Henriquez Juliao and of
Abraham de Jacob Jesurun
Henriquez   P
Abraham de Jacob Jesurun Henri-
quez by lot *oro* David de Haim
Abinun de Lima and of Benjamin
de Selomo de Casseres   G
Manuel de Rephael Alvares Correa B1
Abraham de Isaac Henriquez by lot
oro Abraham de Jeosuah Naar
and of Josiao Dovale   B2
On Passover
Selomo Cohen Henriquez   P

5578
On Rosana

Moise Cardoze by lot *oro* Ishac

Capriles and of David Capriles   P
Abraham de Jacob Jesurun Henri-
quez by lot *oro* Benjamin de
Semuel Hisquiao de Casseres
and of Josiao Abinun de Lima   G
Moseh Henriquez Juliao by lot *oro*
Jeosuah de Sola and of Joseph
de Mordechay Henriquez   B1
Ephraim Curiel by lot *oro* Moseh
de Eliao Penso and of Gabriel
de Haim Gabriel da Costa
Gomez   B2

On Passover
Selomo Cohen Henriquez   P

5579
On Rosana
Moise Cardoze   P
Isaac de David Senior *oro*
Moseh de Eliao Penso   G
David de Daniel Gomez Casseres   B1
David Capriles by lot *oro* David de
David Dovale and of Benjamin
Alvares Correa   B2

On Passover
Moseh Henriquez Juliao   P

5580
On Rosana
Josiao Dovale   P
Selomo Cohen Henriquez by lot
oro Gabriel de Haim Gabriel da
Costa Gomez and of Isaac
Cardoze   G
Eliao Jesurun Henriquez   B1
Abraham de Benjamin Jesurun   B2

On Passover
Moseh Cardoze by lot *oro* Abraham
de Isaac Henriquez and of David
Capriles   P

* Later *assessor*.

5581
On Rosana
Josiao Dovale   P
Samuel Hisquiao de Casseres   G

On Passover
Aron Pinedo   P

5582
On Rosana
Mordechay Ricardo   P
David Namias* (Cashier) served as
Treasurer *oro* David Cardoze
and of Moseh Haim Cohen
Henriquez   G

On Passover
Ishac Capriles   P

5583
On Rosana
Moseh Eliao Penso   P
Abraham Haim Senior   G

On Passover
Ishac Capriles   P

5584
On Rosana
Eliao Jesurun Henriquez *oro*
Joseph Henriquez   P
David Semah de Valencia   G

On Passover
Jacob Naar *oro* Joseph Henriquez   P

5585
On Rosana
Eliao Jesurun Henriquez   P
Eliao Lopez   G

On Passover
Jacob Naar   P

5586
On Rosana

Eliao Lopez *oro* Benjamin
  Mordechay Henriquez   P
David Namias (Cashier) served as
  Treasurer *oro* Jeuda Haim
  Dovale and of Haim Josiao
  Cohen Henriquez   [G]

On Passover

Mordechay Ricardo   P

5587
On Rosana

Abraham Benjamin Jesurun   P
David Namias (Cashier)   G

On Passover

Mordechay Ricardo   P

5588
On Rosana

Haim Alexander Cohen *oro* Isaac
  Cardoze   P
David Namias (Cashier)   G

On Passover

Mordechay Ricardo   P

5589
On Rosana

Jacob Naar — ½ year   P
Eliao Jesurun Henriquez — ½ year   P
David Namias (Cashier)   G

On Passover

Mordechay Ricardo   P

5590
On Rosana

Ishac de Eliao Penso   P
Jeosuah de Jacob Naar *oro*
  Semuel Cohen Henriquez   G

On Passover

Haim Alexander Cohen *oro*
  Benjamin Mordechay Henriquez   P

President Cohen having resigned
on Rosana, there was elected
[in his place] by lot on Sabbath
Teshuba [i.e., the Saturday
between Rosh Hashanah and
Yom Kippur]:

Eliao Jesurun Henriquez   P

5591
On Rosana

Manuel Penso *oro* Moseh Haim
  Cohen Henriquez   P
Jacob de Abraham Jesurun *oro*
  Joseph Benjamin Pereira
  Brandao   G

On Passover

No election was held.

5592
On Rosana

Benjamin Alvares Correa   P
Eliao de Ephraim Curiel   G

On Passover

Abraham de Ishac Henriquez *oro*
  Eliao Lopez   P

5593
On Rosana

Eliao de Ephraim Curiel   P
Benjamin Suares   G

On Passover

Moseh Haim Cohen Henriquez   P

5594
On Rosana

Jeosuah de Jacob Naar *oro* Obadia
  Mendes da Costa and of Eliao de
  Moseh Penso   P

The Banca [i.e., the President and Vice President] assumed the duties of Treasurer.

In Kislev of the same year 5594 new Regulations arrived from Holland; under their terms the Director (Governor) of this Colony nominated the following:

Abraham Haim Senior	Pres.
Joseph de Benjamin Pereira Brandao	P
Moseh de Abraham de Marchena	G

to serve until Rosana 5596, and he dismissed the Mahamad then in office.

5596
On Rosana

Joseph Benjamin Pereira Brandao, Parnas, became	Pres.
Abraham de Isaac Henriquez by lot *oro* David Delvalle Henriquez	P
Moseh Hisquiao Jesurun	G

On Passover

Benjamin Suares	P

5597
On Rosana

Abraham de Benjamin Jesurun by lot *oro* David de David Dovale	P
Mordechay Frois	G

On Passover

Jacob Abraham Jesurun	P

5598
On Rosana

Jacob Moreno Henriquez	P
Eliao Benjamin Pereira Brandao	G

On Passover

Samuel Cohen Henriquez	P

5599
On Rosana

Moseh Hisquiao Jesurun	P
Moseh de Ephraim Curiel	G

On Passover

Obadia Mendes da Costa	P

5600
On Rosana

Eliao de Ephraim Curiel by lot *oro* Ishac Eliao Rodrigues Miranda	P
Benjamin de Abraham Jesurun	G

On Passover

Jeosuah Jacob Naar by lot *oro* Daniel Cohen Henriquez	P

5601
On Rosana

Jacob de David Senior	P
Daniel Abraham Jesurun	G

On Passover

Benjamin Alvares Correa *oro* David Abraham Jesurun	P

5602
On Rosana

Abraham Haim Senior by lot *oro* David Semah de Valencia	P
Ishac Eliao Rodrigues Miranda	G

On Passover

Jacob de Moseh Penso	P

5603
On Rosana

Benjamin de Abraham Jesurun	P
Joseph de Mordechay Fidanque	G

On Passover

Jacob de Jeosuah de Sola	P

5604
On Rosana

Abraham de Jacob Senior — P
Eliao de Moseh Penso by lot *oro*
David Abraham Jesurun — G

On Passover

Moseh de Ephraim Curiel — P

5605
On Rosana

Semuel Cohen Henriquez by lot
oro Mordechay de Mordechay
Alvares Correa — P
Joseph de Jacob de Joseph Curiel — G

On Passover

Selomoh de Eliao Levy Maduro — P

5606
On Rosana

Jeosuah de Eliao Jesurun
Henriquez — P
David de Josiao Pardo — G

On Passover

Manuel de Mordechay de Rephael
Alvares Correa [Jr.] — P

5607
On Rosana

Eliao de Eliao Jesurun Henriquez — P
Jacob de David Senior — G

On Passover

Daniel de Abraham Jesurun [Jr.] — P

5608
On Rosana

Benjamin de Benjamin de Casseres — P
David Semah de Valencia — G

On Passover

David de Selomo Cohen Henriquez — P

5609
On Rosana

Jacob Haim Jesurun [Jr.] by lot *oro*
Joseph de Mordechay Fidanque — P
Jacob Abraham Jesurun — G

On Passover

Moseh de David Cohen Henriquez — P

5610
On Rosana

David Delvalle Henriquez by lot
oro David de Josiao Pardo — P
Jeosuah de Eliao Jesurun Henriquez — G

On Passover

Rephael de Rephael Pinedo — P

5611
On Rosana

Moseh de Abraham Jesurun — P
Daniel de Selomo Cohen Henriquez — G

On Passover

Jacob de Joseph Henriquez — P

5612
On Rosana

Ephraim Edwards — P
Benjamin de Abraham Jesurun
next in turn by lot after the
refusal of Benjamin de Abraham
de Marchena — G

On Passover

Jeosuah de Eliao Jesurun Henriquez next in turn after the
refusal of Eliao Abinun de Lima — P

5613
On Rosana

Jacob de Benjamin Suares — P
Manuel de Mordechay de
Rephael Alvares Correa — G

On Passover

Isaac de Jacob Senior	P

5614
On Rosana

Jacob de Jeosuah Naar	P
David de Selomo Cohen Henriquez next in turn after the refusal of Eliao de Eliao Jesurun Henriquez	G

On Passover

Eliao de Benjamin Pereira Brandao next in turn after the refusal of Eliao de Moseh Penso	P

5615
On Rosana

Abraham de Haim Cohen Henriquez	P
Moseh de David Cohen Henriquez	G
Rephael de Rephael Pinedo	B1
Abraham de Jacob Haim Jesurun	B2

On Passover

Jeosuah de Abraham Naar	P

5616
On Rosana

Benjamin de Moseh Penso	P
David Delvalle Henriquez next in turn after the refusal of Abraham de Jacob Senior	G
Eliao de Benjamin Suares	B1
Manuel de Eliao Curiel	B2

On Passover

Benjamin Alvares Correa next in turn after the refusal of Joseph de Jacob Henriquez	P

5617
On Rosana

Mordechay de Joseph Henriquez	P
Isaac Namias de Crasto	G

The Reverend Haham Aron Mendez Chumaceiro	B1
Jacob de Jeosuah Naar	B2

On Passover

Selomo de Haim Cohen Henriquez	P

5618
On Rosana

Selomo de Haim Cohen Henriquez	Pr
Isaac Pinedo Jr.	VP
Manuel P. Curiel	G
Benjamin Alvares Correa	A1
Mordechay Henriquez	A2

On Passover

Isaac Pinedo Jr.	Pr
Jeudah Senior	VP
. . . .	G
Mordechay Henriquez	A1
Solomon Cohen Henriquez	A2

5619
On Rosana

Jeudah Senior	Pr
Eliao P. Suares	VP
Benjamin de Casseres	G
Solomon Cohen Henriquez	A1
Isaac Pinedo Jr.	A2

On Passover

Eliao P. Suares	Pr
Manuel de Mordechay Alvares Correa	VP
. . . .	G
Isaac Pinedo Jr.	A1
Jeudah Senior	A2

5620
On Rosana

Manuel de Mordechay Alvares Correa	Pr
Samuel Levy Maduro Jr.	VP
Joseph Jacob Henriquez	G
Jeudah Senior	A1
Eliao Penso Suares	A2

On Passover

Samuel Levy Maduro Jr.	Pr
Dr. Isaac Jacob Senior	VP
. . . .	G
Eliao Penso Suarez	A1
Manuel de Mordechay Alvares Correa	A2

5621
On Rosana

Dr. Isaac Jacob Senior	Pr
Efraim Curiel	VP
Samuel de Casseres	G
Manuel de Mordechay Alvares Correa	A1
Samuel Levy Maduro Jr.	A2

On Passover

Efraim Curiel	Pr
David A. Senior	VP
. . . .	G
Samuel Levy Maduro Jr.	A1
Dr. Isaac Jacob Senior	A2

5622
On Rosana

David A. Senior	Pr
Benjamin de Sola	VP
Samuel da Costa Gomez Jr.	G
Dr. Isaac Jacob Senior	A1
Efraim Curiel	A2

On Passover

Benjamin de Sola	Pr
Selomo David Cohen Henriquez	VP
. . . .	G
Efraim Curiel	A1
David A. Senior	A2

Sept. 16, 1862

Solomon Cohen Henriquez	Pr
Abraham Jacob Jesurun	VP
Benjamin Pereira Brandao	G

June 22, 1863

David Delvalle Henriquez	Pr
Benjamin de Casseres Jr.	VP
Jeudah Senior	)
Isaac Pinedo Jr.	) G

1864

Benjamin de Casseres Jr.	Pr
Isaac Pinedo Jr.	VP
Mordechay Senior	G

1865

Isaac Pinedo Jr.	Pr
Mordechay Senior	VP
Abraham D. Henriquez	G

1866

Isaac de Eliao Rodrigues Miranda	Pr
Abraham Delvalle Henriquez	VP
Moise Pereira	G

1867

Abraham Delvalle Henriquez	Pr
Moise Pereira	VP
Haim Lopez Penha	G

1868

Moise Pereira	Pr
Haim Lopez Penha	VP
Salomon Elias Curiel	G

1869

Haim Lopez Penha	Pr
Salomon Elias Curiel	VP
Mordechay Henriquez	G

1870

Salomon Elias Curiel	Pr
Mordechay Henriquez	VP
Isaac Capriles Az (son of Abraham)	G

1871

Mordechay Henriquez	Pr
Isaac Capriles Az	VP
Manuel Penso Curiel	G

1872

Isaac Capriles Az	Pr
Manuel Penso Curiel	VP
Samuel da Costa Gomez Jr.	G

1873

Manuel Penso Curiel	Pr
Samuel da Costa Gomez Jr.	VP
Mordechay Henriquez	G

1874

Samuel da Costa Gomez Jr.	Pr
Mordechay Henriquez	VP
Solomon E. Curiel	G

1875

Samuel da Costa Gomez Jr.	Pr
Mordechay Henriquez	VP
Solomon Elias Curiel	G
Solomon Moseh Lansberg	Pr
Manuel Penso Curiel	VP
Mordechay Henriquez	G
M. Alvares Correa Jr.	A1
M. D. Henriquez	A2

1876

Manuel Penso Curiel	Pr
M. D. Henriquez	VP
Mordechay Henriquez	G
M. Alvares Correa Jr.	A1
Solomon Moseh Lansberg	A2

1877

M. Alvares Correa Jr.	Pr
Benjamin de Casseres Jr.	VP
Solomon Moseh Lansberg	G
Manuel Penso Curiel	A1
Mordechay Henriquez	A2

1878

Solomon Moseh Lansberg	Pr
Manuel Penso Curiel	VP
Benjamin de Casseres Jr.	G

Eliao Jesurun Jr. ⎱	A1
Moses de Sola ⎰	
M. Alvares Correa	A2

1879

Manuel Penso Curiel	Pr
Moshe Haim Penso	VP
Murray Alvares Correa	G
Solomon Senior Jr.	A1
Haim M. Penso	A2

1880

Haim Lopez Penha	Pr
Murray Alvares Correa	VP
Haim M. Penso	G
Moise D. Henriquez	A1
Solomon Senior Jr.	A2

1881

Moise D. Henriquez	Pr
Haim Moshe Penso	VP
Haim Lopez Penha	G
Murray Alvares Correa	A1
Elias Jesurun Jr.	A2

1882

Elias Jesurun Jr.	Pr
Mordechay Solomon Levy Maduro	VP
Moise D. Henriquez	G
Haim Lopez Penha	A1
Jacob Maduro Lopez	A2

1883

Mordechay Solomon Levy Maduro	Pr
Manuel El Penso	VP
Elias Jesurun Jr. ⎱	G
Abraham B. Jesurun ⎰	
Jacob Maduro Lopez	A1
Isaac M. de Marchena	A2

1884

Jacob Maduro Lopez	Pr
Manuel Elias Penso	VP

250. MOSES S. L. MADURO, 1863-1911,
CAPTAIN OF THE CURAÇAO MILITIA AND
COMMUNITY PRESIDENT

251. SAMUEL M. DE SOLA, 1904-1940,
PRESIDENT OF THE COMMUNITY (1940)

252. MILTON L. MADURO, 1898-1948,
MANY TIMES PRESIDENT OF THE
COMMUNITY

253. LOUIS J. RICARDO, 1880-1968,
ADMINISTRATOR OF MIKVE ISRAEL OVER
30 YEARS; CONSUL OF BOLIVIA 46 YEARS

254. SILVER TRAY GIVEN HAHAM CHUMACEIRO BY THE
ST. THOMAS JEWISH COMMUNITY ON HIS VISIT IN 1858

Mordechay Solomon Levy Maduro G
Isaac M. de Marchena A1
Benjamin Mordechay
    Alvares Correa A2

1885

Manuel Elias Penso } Pr
Jacob E. Penso }
Mordechay Capriles VP
Benjamin Mordechay
    Alvares Correa G
Isaac M. de Marchena A1
Elias Solomon Levy Maduro A2

1886

Mordechay Capriles Pr
Benjamin Mordechay
    Alvares Correa VP
Moses de Castro G
Elias Solomon Levy Maduro A1
Joseph David Pardo A2

1887

Mordechay Capriles Pr
Manuel Penso Curiel VP
Morris Pinedo Jr. G
Joseph David Pardo A1
Moses de Castro A2

1888

Manuel Penso Curiel Pr
Mordechay Capriles VP
Manuel Elias Penso G
Isaac M. de Marchena A1
Morris Pinedo Jr. A2

1889

Manuel Elias Penso Pr
Manuel Penso Curiel VP
Benjamin Mordechay
    Alvares Correa G
Joshua Alvares Correa A1
Isaac M. de Marchena A2

1890

Benjamin Mordechay
    Alvares Correa Pr
Manuel Penso Curiel VP
Jeosuah Alvares Correa G
Samuel da Costa Gomez Jr. A1
Abraham M. de Marchena A2

1891

Benjamin Mordechay
    Alvares Correa Pr
Efraim Solomon Levy Maduro VP
Salomon de Casseres G
Abraham M. de Marchena A1
Samuel da Costa Gomez Jr. A2

1892

Solomon de Casseres Pr
Efraim Solomon Levy Maduro VP
Benjamin Mordechay
    Alvares Correa G
Manuel Elias Penso A1
Morris Elias Curiel A2

1893

Morris Elias Curiel Pr
Efraim Solomon Levy Maduro } VP
Josias Lopez Henriquez }
Moses Ephraim Curiel G
Manuel Elias Penso A1
Isaac M. de Marchena A2

1894

Josias Lopez Henriquez Pr
Moses Solomon Levy Maduro VP
David Delvalle Henriquez G
Moses Ephraim Curiel A1
Isaac M. de Marchena A2

1895

Moses Solomon Levy Maduro Pr
Elias de Marchena VP
David Delvalle Henriquez G
Josias Lopez Henriquez A1
Jacob Cardoze A2

1896

Elias de Marchena	Pr
Edward J. Henriquez ⎱	VP
Abraham David Capriles ⎰	
Jacob Cardoze	G
Josias Lopez Henriquez	A1
Moses Curiel	A2

1897

Moses de Castro	Pr
Abraham David Capriles	VP
Haim Moshe Penso	G
Efraim de Marchena	A1
Moses Curiel	A2

1898

Haim Moshe Penso	Pr
Efraim de Marchena	VP
Moses Ephraim Curiel	G
Abraham David Capriles	A1
Moses de Castro	A2

1899

Abraham David Capriles	Pr
David D. Henriquez	VP
Moses Ephraim Curiel	G
Moses Solomon Levy Maduro	A1
Morris Elias Curiel	A2

1900

David Delvalle Henriquez	Pr
Morris Elias Curiel	VP
Jacob Benjamin Delvalle	G
Moses Solomon Levy Maduro	A1
Solomon de Casseres	A2

1901

Jacob Benjamin Delvalle	Pr
Solomon de Casseres	VP
David Alvares Correa	G
Josias Lopez Henriquez	A1
Moses de Solas	A2

1902

Moses de Sola	Pr

David Alvares Correa	VP
Benjamin Jacob Delvalle	G
Josias Lopez Henriquez	A1
Mordechay Abraham de Marchena	A2

1903

David Alvares Correa	Pr
Mordechay Abraham de Marchena	VP
Jacob Isaac Pinedo	G
Benjamin Jacob Delvalle	A1
David Cardoze Cadet	A2

1904

Benjamin Jacob Delvalle	Pr
Jacob Isaac Pinedo	VP
David Alvares Correa	G
Elias M. de Marchena	A1
David Cardoze Cadet	A2

1905

Benjamin Jacob Delvalle	Pr
Elias de Marchena	VP
Jacob David Capriles	G
A. Alvares Correa ⎱	A1
Haim Mendes Chumaceiro ⎰	
Solomon de Casseres	A2

1906

Moises de Solas	Pr
Solomon de Casseres	VP
Haim Mendes Chumaceiro	G
Jacob David Capriles	A1
Silvanio Samuel Maduro Lopez	A2

1907

Moises de Sola	Pr
Silvanio Samuel Maduro Lopez	VP
Solomon Mordechay Levy Maduro	G
Manrique Capriles	A1
Solomon J. Delvalle	A2

1908

Solomon Mordechay Levy Maduro	Pr

Manrique Capriles	VP
Abram de Sola	G
Solomon Jacob Delvalle	A1
Arturo P. de Marchena	A2

1909

Abram de Sola	Pr
Arturo P. de Marchena	VP
Mortimer Alvares Correa	G
Haim Senior	A1
Solomon Elias Levy Maduro	A2

1910

Haim Senior	Pr
Abram de Sola	VP
Mortimer Alvares Correa	G
Arturo P. de Marchena	A1
Solomon Elias Levy Maduro	A2

1911

Mortimer Alvares Correa	Pr
Arturo P. de Marchena	VP
Julio Abinun de Lima	G
Abram de Sola	A1
Eleazar H. Levy Maduro	A2

1912

Manrique Capriles	Pr
Julio Abinun de Lima	VP
Mortimer Alvares Correa ⟩	G
Josef Cardoze	
Eleazar H. Levy Maduro	A1
Elias M. Penso	A2

1913

Elias M. Penso	Pr
David de Marchena Jr.	VP
Josef Cardoze	G
Manrique Capriles	A1
Montefiore Levy Maduro	A2

1914

David de Marchena Jr.	Pr
Solomon J. Delvalle	VP
Josef Cardoze	G

Montefiore Levy Maduro	A1
Julio Abinun de Lima	A2

1915

Solomon J. Delvalle	Pr
Julio Abinun de Lima	VP
Jacob David Capriles	G
Edward S. Lansberg	A1
Montefiore Levy Maduro	A2

1916

Edward S. Lansberg	Pr
Solomon de Casseres	VP
Jacob David Capriles	G
Montefiore Levy Maduro	A1
David de Marchena Jr.	A2

1917

Solomon de Casseres	Pr
Jossy Mordechay Levy Maduro	VP
Edward Alvares Correa	G
Edward S. Lansberg	A1
David de Marchena	A2

1918

Jossy Mordechay Levy Maduro	Pr
Benjamin Jacob Delvalle	VP
Edward Alvares Correa	G
David Cardoze Cadet	A1
Edward S. Lansberg	A2

1919

Benjamin Jacob Delvalle	Pr
Mordechay A. de Marchena	VP
David Cardoze Cadet	G
Edward Alvares Correa	A1
Solomon Morris Lansberg	A2

1920

Solomon Morris Lansberg	Pr
Mordechay A. de Marchena	VP
Solomon Abraham Levy Maduro	G
Solomon de Casseres ⟩	A1
Julio Abinun de Lima	
Edward Alvares Correa	A2

1921

Solomon Abraham Levy Maduro	Pr
Henry da Costa Gomez	VP
Michael Alvares Correa Jr.	G
Julio Abinun de Lima	A1
Elias Morris Curiel	A2

1922

Henry da Costa Gomez	Pr
Mordechay A. de Marchena	VP
Michael Alvares Correa Jr.	G
Elias Morris Curiel	A1
Abraham Ephraim Levy Maduro	A2

1923

Solomon Jacob Delvalle	Pr
Arthur de Sola	VP
Alex Curiel	G
Abraham Ephraim Levy Maduro	A1
Mordechay A. de Marchena	A2

1924

Solomon Jacob Delvalle	Pr
Manrique Capriles	VP
Solomon Abraham Levy Maduro	G
Arthur de Sola	A1
Alex Curiel	A2

1925

Manrique Capriles	Pr
Arthur de Sola	VP
Benjamin Jacob Delvalle	G
Mordechay A. de Marchena	A1
Solomon Abraham Levy Maduro	A2

1926

Arthur de Sola	Pr
Mordechay A. de Marchena	VP
Jacob David Capriles	G
Benjamin Jacob Delvalle	A1
Benjamin Levy Maduro	A2

1927

Benjamin Jacob Delvalle	Pr
Jacob David Capriles	VP
Moises Alvares Correa Jr.	G
Benjamin Levy Maduro	A1
Isidor Abinun de Lima	A2

1928

Benjamin Jacob Delvalle	Pr
Mordechay A. de Marchena	VP
Isidor Abinun de Lima	G
Moises A. Correa Jr.	A1
David Abraham Capriles	A2

1929

Solomon Abraham Levy Maduro	Pr
Mordechay A. de Marchena	VP
David Abraham Capriles	G
Egon Gerstl	A1
Alvin Delvalle	A2

1930

Solomon Abraham Levy Maduro	Pr
Moises Isaac de Marchena	VP
Alvin Delvalle	G
Isaac Haim Capriles	A1
Egon Gerstl } Michael Alvares Correa Jr. }	A2

1931

Solomon Jacob Delvalle	Pr
Moises Isaac de Marchena	VP
Michael Alvares Correa Jr.	G
Isaac Haim Capriles	A1
Solomon Abraham Levy Maduro	A2

1932

Solomon Abraham Levy Maduro	Pr
Isaac Haim Capriles	VP
Solomon Jacob Delvalle	G
Michael Alvares Correa Jr.	A1
Milton H. Levy Maduro	A2

1933

Isaac Haim Capriles	Pr
Milton H. Levy Maduro	VP
Solomon Jacob Delvalle	G
Samuel Maduro de Sola	A1
Victor Pinedo	A2

1934

Manrique Capriles	Pr
Samuel Maduro de Sola	VP
Victor Pinedo	G
Solomon Jacob Delvalle	A1
Solomon Mordechay Levy Maduro	A2

1935

Manrique Capriles	Pr
Solomon Jacob Delvalle	VP
Samuel Maduro de Sola	G
Victor Pinedo	A1
Solomon Mordechay Levy Maduro	A2

1936

Solomon Jacob Delvalle	Pr
Stanley Levy Maduro	VP
Samuel Maduro de Sola	G
Victor Pinedo	A1
Atilio de Marchena	A2

1937

Solomon Jacob Delvalle	Pr
Samuel Maduro de Sola	VP
Stanley Levy Maduro	G
Atilio de Marchena	A1
Benjamin Mendes Chumaceiro	A2

1938

Milton H. Levy Maduro	Pr
Samuel Maduro de Sola	VP
Solomon Jacob Delvalle	G
Benjamin Mendes Chumaceiro	A1
Morris David Cardoze	A2

1939

Milton H. Levy Maduro	Pr
Samuel Maduro de Sola	VP
Morris David Cardoze	G
Michael H. M. Pinedo	A1
Jossy Capriles	A2

1940

Samuel Maduro de Sola (Died in office) / Morris David Cardoze	Pr
Michael H. M. Pinedo	VP
Milton H. L. Maduro	G
Frank M. Chumaceiro	A1
Jossy A. Capriles	A2

1941

Milton H. L. Maduro	Pr
Victor Jesurun	VP
Morris D. Cardoze	G
Michael Alvares Correa Jr.	A1
Frank M. Chumaceiro	A2

1942

Milton H. L. Maduro	Pr
Victor Jesurun	VP
Morris D. Cardoze	G
Michael A. Correa Jr.	A1
Frank M. Chumaceiro	A2

1943

Milton H. L. Maduro	Pr
Victor Jesurun	VP
Morris D. Cardoze	G
Michael A. Correa Jr.	A1
Alfred Moron, Jr.	A2

1944

Morris D. Cardoze	VP
Alfred Moron Jr.	Pr
Benjamin M. Chumaceiro	G
Victor Jesurun	A1
Isaac Bloch	A2

1945

Morris D. Cardoze	Pr
David A. Capriles	VP
Victor Jesurun	G
Isidor Bloch	A1
Amilcar Namias de Crasto	A2

1946

Morris D. Cardoze	Pr
David A. Capriles	VP
Otto Senior	G
Isidor Bloch	A1
Amilcar Namias de Crasto	A2

811

1947

David A. Capriles	Pr
Amilcar Namias de Crasto	VP
Morris D. Cardoze	G
Isidor Bloch	A1
René Moreno	A2

1948

Morris D. Cardoze	Pr
Amilcar Namias de Crasto	VP
David A. Capriles	G
Isidor Bloch	A1
René Moreno	A2

1949

Otto Senior	Pr
Mordechay Salomon Levy Maduro	VP
Victor Pinedo	G
Isidor Bloch	A1
Moises Alvares Correa	A2

1950

Otto Senior	Pr
Mordechay Salomon L. Maduro	VP
Victor Pinedo	G
Isaac Bloch	A1
Morris D. Cardoze	A2

1951

Otto Senior	Pr
Mordechay Salomon L. Maduro	VP
Morris D. Cardoze	G
Isaac Bloch	A1
Ivan Moreno	A2

1952

Otto Senior	Pr
Mordechay Salomon L. Maduro	VP
Morris D. Cardoze	G
Isaac Bloch	A1
Ivan Moreno	A2

1953

Mordechay Salomon L. Maduro	Pr
Amilcar Namias de Crasto	VP

Morris D. Cardoze	G
Isaac Bloch	A1
Alfred Moron Jr.	A2

1954

Mordechay Salomon L. Maduro	Pr
Amilcar Namias de Crasto	VP
Morris D. Cardoze	G
Isaac Bloch	A1
Alfred Moron Jr.	A2

1955

Mordechay Salomon L. Maduro	Pr
Amilcar Namias de Crasto	VP
Morris D. Cardoze	G
Isaac Bloch	A1
Edmund Marius de Sola	A2

1956

Mordechay Salomon L. Maduro	Pr
Amilcar Namias de Crasto	VP
Edmund Marius de Sola	G
René Moreno	A1
Armando de Marchena	A2

1957

Mordechay Salomon L. Maduro	Pr
Edmund Marius de Sola	VP
Amilcar Namias de Crasto	G
René Moreno	A1
Armando de Marchena	A2

1958

Mordechay Salomon L. Maduro	Pr
Amilcar Namias de Crasto	VP
Otto Senior	G
Edmund Marius de Sola	A1
Alfred Moron Jr.	A2

1959

Otto Senior	Pr
Amilcar Namias de Crasto	VP
Morris D. Cardoze	G
Alfred Moron Jr.	A1
Jossy Capriles	A2

1960

Amilcar Namias de Crasto	Pr
Henry Levy Maduro	VP
Morris Cardoze	G
Norman Mendez Chumaceiro	
Jossy Capriles	A1
Ivan Moreno	A2

1961

Amilcar Namias de Crasto	Pr
Henry Levy Maduro	VP
Norman Mendez Chumaceiro	G
Jossy Capriles	A1
Ivan Moreno	A2

1962

Amilcar Namias de Crasto	Pr
Ivan Moreno	VP
Norman Mendez Chumaceiro	G
Otto Senior	A1
Jossy Capriles	A2

1963-64

Otto Senior	Pr
Ivan Moreno	VP
Norman Mendez Chumaceiro	G
William Cohen	A1
Lionel Capriles*	A2

1965
United Congregation Mikvé Israel-Emanuel

Otto Senior	Pr
Charles Gomes Casseres	VP
Lionel Capriles	G
Ivan Moreno	A1
William Cohen (officer)	A2
Georgo Brandao „	A3

Abram E. Salas   Honorary Secretary**

1966

Charles Gomes Casseres	Pr
Ivan Moreno	VP
Lionel Capriles	G
Frank Delvalle	Sec.
Abram E. Salas	A1
William Cohen	A2
Jaap de Vries	A3

1967

Charles Gomes Casseres	Pr
Ivan Moreno	VP
Lionel Capriles	G
Abram E. Salas	Sec
Frank Delvalle	A1
William Cohen	A2
Jaap de Vries	A3

1968

Frank Eliao Delvalle	Pr
Ivan Moreno	VP
Lionel Capriles	G
Abram E. Salas	Sec
Charles Gomes Casseres	A1
William Cohen	A2
Jaap de Vries	A3

1969

Frank Eliao Delvalle	Pr
Charles Gomes Casseres	VP
Jossy Capriles	G
Abram E. Salas	Sec
Dr. Jessy Jesurun	A1
Ivan Moreno	A2
Jaap de Vries	A3

---

* It was under the leadership of these gentlemen that *Mikvé Israel* merged with *Temple Emanu-El* as exposed in Chapter 25 of this work (pages 502-517).

** This title was given because the Regulations prohibit two brothers-in-law from taking part in the same meeting. René Maduro was the official secretary.

REPRESENTATIVES OF THE [JEWISH] NATION, 1719-1808

SINCE 1719 THE JEWS of Curaçao followed the practice of the Amsterdam community in electing at first two, then three, and later four notables to represent them before the government. Those men were known as "Attorneys or Representatives of the Nation." The records go up to 1808.

Feb.	3, 1719	Elias Pereira, Jacob Jeudah Leao[1]
Oct.	13, 1738	Samuel Idanha de Casseres, Mordechay Haim Senior[2]
Tammuz 25, 1745 (July 25, 1745)		Moses Penso in place of De Casseres who resigned (page 183)
1746		Jeosuah Henriquez Jr. in place of Penso who resigned (page 205)
July	24, 1747	Mordechay Haim Senior, Jeosuah Henriquez Jr.[3]
March	1, 1748	Selomoh Nunes Redondo together with Senior and Henriquez[3]
Sept.	16, 1750	Moses Penso by order of Prince Wilhelm IV (page 211), together with Redondo, Senior and Henriquez[4]
Elul (Aug.	19, 1755 26, 1755)	Jeosuah Henriquez, David Jesurun, Jacob Levy Maduro, Aron Henriquez Morao[5]
5541 =	1780-81	Isaac de Marchena, Abraham de David Jesurun, Mordechay Motta, David Morales
Dec.	13, 1803	David Haim Cohen Henriquez, David Haim Dovale who refused the honor; Aron Pinedo[6]
Jan.	23, 1805	Moseh Levy Maduro Peixotto, Abraham Salom Delvalle, together with Cohen Henriquez and Pinedo. At the same time Maduro served as parnas and Delvalle as treasurer of the community.[7]
March	11, 1806	Maduro and Delvalle resigned.[8]
Nov.	11, 1807	Aron Pinedo resigned.[9]
Tishri (Oct.	13, 1808 4, 1808)	Moises Cardoze, David Haim Cohen Henriquez[10]

[1] MS, Apoderados da Nacao.
[2] OAC 808, Oct. 13, 1738.
[3] OAC 867, no. 155.
[4] OAC 824, Sept. 16, 1750.
[5] MS, Elul 19, 5515.

[6] OAC 1012, no. 168.
[7] OAC 1016, no. 34.
[8] OAC 1018, no. 86.
[9] OAC 1023, no. 55.
[10] MS, Apoderados da Nacao.

DOCUMENTS CONCERNING THE GROUNDS OF THE SYNAGOGUE
AND COMMUNITY SCHOOLS, 1730-1732

A. RECEIPT FOR 800 PESOS

I, THE UNDERSIGNED, acknowledge receipt from the Messrs. Parnassim of the Jewish Community of the sum of Eight Hundred Pesos for the cost of building the City Wall in accordance with survey made by Jan Kock, Fortress Inspector, in connection with an agreement granting to said Parnassim the right to build their synagogue, said 800 pesos to cover those costs.
Fort Amsterdam, Curaçao, 30 June Aº 1730.
Signed: Jan Noach Du Faij
I repeat 800.–.–

I, the Secretary, affirm that this agrees with the Original in the hands of the Messrs. Parnassim of the Jewish Community of this city.
Curaçao, 5 9ber [November], 1732.

Jacob de Petersen
Secretary[1]

B. LETTER OF GOVERNOR VAN COLLEN TO THE COMPANY READ AT THE MEETING OF THE [COUNCIL OF] TEN ON NOVEMBER 7, 1733

Very Esteemed Noble Gentlemen:

[On the margin] The Parnassim of the Jewish Nation showed the Governor [Van Collen] a certain Obligation of Ps 800: signed by Jan Noach du Faij to demolish 20 feet of the City Wall in order to build a school there.

[Text] The Parnassim of the Jewish Community of this city have shown me a certain large obligation of p: 800:–:–, signed by the Hon. Jan Noach du Faij, Esq., for which sum (they say) Mr. Du Faij had granted them the right to demolish Twenty feet of the City Wall and to drain the water and fill it in so that a school for their children could be built on this [reclaimed] land. They have requested me to refund this money if I could not let them proceed. Since I found no entry in any ledger of the Noble West India Company showing that said 800 p: were brought to the Coffers of Your Noble, Honorable Worships, I denied the

---

[1] WICA 580, p. 953. See above, pp. 120-21, 138.

refund. They have doubtlessly addressed themselves to Your Noble, Honorable Worships on this occasion.

From Your Very Noble, Honorable Worships'
Most Obedient Servant
Van Collen[2]

Curaçao, the 17 December A? 1732.

C. LETTER OF THE PARNASSIM TO THE COMPANY

Very Noble, Honorable Gentlemen

Gentlemen:

With the deepest reverence we find ourselves obliged to inform you that our nation here, under the High Protection of Your Very Noble, Honorable Worships having increased, we have been forced to extend our synagogue[3] and for this purpose had to make use of our children's schoolrooms which were annexed [to the synagogue]. It was therefore imperative for us to look for a place for the children.

Since our synagogue is and was situated by the City Walls (in the direction of the Steene Pad) ending at Fort Orange, which fort and walls have been dilapidated for a long time and must be rebuilt, several sections thereof having cracks running from top to bottom, and since there have been discussions on different occasions of enlarging the city at this part and selling the lands [reclaimed] in order to pay for the cost of rebuilding the fort and City Walls,

Now, therefore, we, by virtue of the foregoing [facts], addressed ourselves to the Very Noble, Honorable Mr. Jan Noach Du Faij, Esq., then Governor of these islands, and having proposed to this Very Noble, Honorable Gentleman the foregoing, and because of the need for our schools (in order to inspire our children with Reverence for God), we explained and requested Your Very Noble, Honorable [Governor], since the City Walls have to be built, kindly to sell us a parcel of land of Twenty feet contingent to the side of our synagogue, especially since we are in great need of it for the continuation of our religious services.

Your Very Noble, Honorable [Governor] personally inspected [the area] with the "Equipaje" Master Jan Kock, who also is Inspector of Fortresses and Buildings. Your Very Noble, Honorable [Governor], after having deliberated on the matter, granted our request on condition that we paid him Eight Hundred Pesos to cover the cost of erecting the City Walls [anew], which sum we paid to the Very Noble, Honorable Mr. Jan Noach Du Faij, Esq., in accordance with the authentic copy of the receipt in full herewith enclosed.

For this reason Your Very Noble, Honorable [Governor], in time, permitted

[2] WICA 580, pp. 734, 738, 739.
[3] "Kerk" in the original — here translated as synagogue.

us to break the wall, according to our needs, up to 20 feet along the length of our synagogue wall. But when we saw that it was necessary to finish the synagogue first, we therefore took, at the time, approximately 10 feet on the front part of our synagogue and nothing to the rear. We reached to demolish only two to three feet of the wall to the bastion in order to open a passage, because the City Walls slant at that point.

But when we, with the grace of God, finished the synagogue and wanted to start tearing down the 20 feet of the City Wall to the rear [of the synagogue] and to extend the remaining ten feet on the front side, we were stopped from doing so.

Since the Equipaje Master and Inspector of Fortresses and Buildings was present with the Very Noble, Honorable Mr. Du Faij when we made the agreement and when he took the measurements as given in the receipt, we therefore addressed ourselves to the Very Noble, Honorable Governor Juan Pedro van Collen. We were told in reply that the Very Noble, Honorable [Governor Van Collen] did not find in any of the Company ledgers a credit by Mr. Du Faij for said 800 pesos and he could therefore make no decision.

For this reason, with humble Reverence and the deepest respect, we address ourselves to Your Very Noble, Honorable [Worships], to have the goodness to take this question under consideration and take us under your protection, under the wings of Your Very Noble, Honorable [Worships], submitting ourselves to Your Very Noble, Honorable [Worships'] wise judgment [on a matter] involving money of the synagogue and of the poor that is meant for the continuation of Religious services. [On the other hand] it is necessary to renovate the fort and the Walls, for which purpose the said 800 P^s were given to reduce the cost [of building the walls]. For all this, may Your Very Noble, Honorable [Worships] help us, ever your humble, loyal subjects, as we have always proven to be and shall always continue to be [at your service] with our fortunes and lives. Although we have paid said 800 P^s toward the construction of the walls, we shall not fail to contribute [more] toward the building of said fort and walls, as well as other municipal projects, with the rest of the citizenry.

In the hope that your Very Noble, Honorable Worships will care to favor us with our request, we wish for Your Very Noble, Honorable Worships and your beloved families the most Holy and Divine protection. With all humility and Reverence, we have the honor to be, Your Very Noble, Honorable [Worships], your humble subjects and ever obliging servants.

Abraham Naar
Mordechay Haim Senior
Jacob Levy Maduro, Treasurer[4]

---

[4] WICA 580, pp. 951-53. The petition is not dated. The signatures are those of the parnassim for the year 5493 (1732-33). See appendix 12, y. 5493.

APPENDIX 15

CONTRACTS FOR THE CONSTRUCTION OF THE SYNAGOGUE OF 1732

A. CONTRACT BETWEEN ELIAS AND MANUEL DE CRASTO JUNIOR AND HENDRIK SCHIELAGH

ON THIS 26TH DAY OF JULY, 1730, before me, Jan Barels, Notary admitted to the Court of Holland, residing in Amsterdam, in the presence of the witnesses hereinafter named, appeared the Messrs. *Elias and Manuel de Crasto Junior, merchants in this city*,[1] bearing written *instructions*[1] from the *Messrs. Parnassims and Treasurer of the Jewish Nation on the Island of Curaçao*,[1] parties of the first part, and Hend[ri]k Schielagh, master carpenter, also residing in this city, party of the second part, who mutually declared that they had entered into a contract and respectively agreed to do as follows.

That the party of the second part shall go to Curaçao on board the ship De Vogel Phenix, Captain Pieter Valck. His wife and child shall sleep in the ship's Cabin and he in the Constable's room; for the duration of the trip the family shall dine with the Captain in the Cabin. That the said second party shall be allowed to take along, free of freight charges, three cases of tools and other implements of his trade to be stored in the hold, a case and a bed with floss silk bed clothes [to be placed] in the Constable's room, and a bed and six chairs [to be put] in the Cabin. Food and fare shall be free.

That the said second party, immediately after his arrival in Curaçao on the said boat, shall enter into the service of the abovementioned Messrs. Parnassims and Treasurer of the Jewish Nation on the said Island and *help build for them*,[1] at a site to be indicated, *a Synagogue or House of Worship*,[1] under the orders and direction of Pieter Roggenburg, master carpenter, or his successors.

That the said second party shall be obliged not only to assist the above-mentioned master carpenter in planning the structure, drawing the ground plan, partitioning the said building and doing everything required to complete the same to perfection and according to the strict rules of architecture, for which the said second party declares he has the necessary skill, but also to help the master carpenter construct the building according to the blueprint and drawings already prepared. For this purpose he shall work daily without intermission, excepting only Saturdays and Sundays, as assistant carpenter, carefully and diligently following and executing the orders of the said Pieter Roggenburg until the said Synagogue is finished.

That the said second party shall receive for such work and services sixty guilders a month, and the parties of the first part, for and in the name of their

---

[1] Underscored in the original contract.

principals, promise to pay such wages starting from the day the ship sails from Texel and the ship's crew receives its wages, and thereafter *continuing until the said Synagogue is completed.*[1]

When the second party has finished his work to the complete satisfaction of the said Messrs. Parnassims [of Curaçao], he shall receive from them the sum of one hundred guilders as fare for his return trip to Holland or as a gift if he wishes to remain on the island.

In any event, the said second party shall have to provide board and lodging for himself and his family during his stay on said island.

It is further expressly stipulated that the said second party shall be cut down three guilders for each day, excepting Saturdays and Sundays, that he does not work because of illness or absenteeism.

It is also stipulated that the second party shall not contract for other work or go over to another service until the aforementioned Synagogue is completely finished, on pain of making good the wages already paid and still owing, in addition to a fine of two hundred fifty guilders to be imposed at the discretion of the said Messrs. Parnassims.

It is further stipulated that if it becomes evident on his arrival in Curaçao that the second party does not possess the skill necessary to perform the work or cannot work properly because of drunkenness or bad conduct, the said Messrs. Parnassims shall be free to dismiss him without any obligation whatsoever and shall hold him liable for costs and damages.

It is finally stipulated that the second party, while here [in Amsterdam], shall assist the first parties with the purchase and delivery of lumber, ironwork and other materials required for the construction of said building, for which he shall be paid two guilders daily as often as he is in their service.

The second party acknowledges the receipt from the first parties of the sum of one hundred twenty guilders for [the purchase of] necessary equipment, such amount constituting an advance on future monthly wages which he must earn before other payments are made to him.

Then appeared before us, Notary and witnesses, S. Claudius Schielag, wig maker residing here, and declared that he would stand as guarantor for his brother, the second party, under renunciation of the benefits of "ordinis et excussionis." After an explanation by me, the Notary, he promised to pay on demand the said F[lorins]. 120 as his personal debt if the said Hendrik Schielach did not embark on said ship.

The said parties mutually promised to carry out the provisions of this [contract] in good faith as bound by law.

Thus done in the said city of Amsterdam in the presence of Jan Gybel and Coenraad Ruysch as witnesses.[2]

[Signed:]		Elias & Manuel de Crasto Junior
Jan Gybel	Hendrik Schilag	J. Barels
Coenraad Ruysch	Cloudius Schilach	Notary (illus. 28)

[2] GAA 8817, Not. J. Barels, no. 451.

B. CONTRACT BETWEEN ELIAS AND MANUEL DE CRASTO JUNIOR AND JACOBUS DE WIT

Elias and Manuel de Crasto Junior, merchants in Amsterdam, [parties of the first part,] and Jacobus de Wit [also] merchant of Amsterdam, [party of the second part,] appeared [before me, Jan Barels, Notary Public, residing in Amsterdam].

The party of the second part promised the first parties to deliver the following lumber, at the prices listed below, on board the ship de Vogel Phenix, Captain Pieter Valck, within four or, at the latest, six weeks from [this] date.

13 Ribs of 4″ × 5″ × 22′		at 21 pennings[3] an inch
30 „ „ 4″ × 6″ × 20′		19 „ „ „
112 „ „ 5″ × 6″ × 19′		19 „ „ „
40 „ „ 5″ × 6″ × 20′		19 „ „ „
20 „ „ 5″ × 7″ × 22′		21 „ „ „
20 „ „ 5″ × 6″ × 18′		17 „ „ „
20 „ „ 5″ × 6″ × 23′		21 „ „ „
2 „ „ 10″ × 10″ × 22′		21 „ „ „
212 „ „ 3″ × 3″ × 20′		19 „ „ „
800 Fir Battens	1″ × 1½″ × 18′	f. 8½ the 100 battens
24 Timbers	4″ × 7″ × 18′	17 pennings an inch
10 Timbers	4″ × 12″ × 18′	17 „ „ „
30 Boards	1″ × 11″ × 20′	18 stuivers each
12 Boards	1½″ × 12″ × 18′	4 „ „
24 Foundation beams of Hamburg wood	4″ × 22″ × 26′	f. 8 each
26 Timbers	3″ × 7″ × 22′	21 pennings
6 Joists of Hamburg wood	13″ × 15″ × 29′	2 stuivers an inch
50 Ribs	3″ × 4″ × 18′	17 pennings
50 Ridge poles	2″ × 3″ × 18′	17 „
100 Double laths	1½″ × 2″ × 18′	4 stuivers each
10 Ribs	6″ × 7″ × 22′	21 pennings
2 Ribs of Hamburg wood	6″ × 7″ × 42′	3 stuivers each
31 „ „ „ „	5″ × 7″ × 22′	21 pennings
60 „ „ „ „	5″ × 7″ × 20′	19 „
450 Boards	2″ × 11″ × 18′	30 stuivers each

4 Thin masts, free from all defects, to make hoisting poles 40 feet long	f.	5
4 ditto to make ladders sawn through 40 feet long	f.	5

3 An old Dutch coin valued at 1/16 part of the stuiver.

Also the following items separately:

20	Beams	$6'' \times 8'' \times 20'$	19 pennings
70	Boards	$1\frac{1}{4}'' \times 11'' \times 18'$	20 stuivers each
25	Ribs	$4'' \times 5'' \times 20'$	19 pennings
6	Boards for wall plates	$3'' \times 14''\text{-}15'' \times 20'$	19 ,,
100	Double laths	$1\frac{1}{2}'' \times 2'' \times 20'$	5 stuivers
12	Ribs	$5'' \times 6'' \times 20'$	19 pennings

The wood must be delivered dry and properly conditioned without blue, brown or white sapwood, excepting only hard white sapwood, but as little as possible. The wood must also be free of heart-shake, of correct dimensions as sawn in this city, of the best and healthiest fir wood, square sawn, of Norwegian or Weijburger wood, without mixing any other sort, such to the satisfaction and judgment of two persons commissioned by the first parties to receive and inspect the abovementioned wood. They shall be at liberty to reject such wood as does not meet the abovementioned specifications, including the fixed length, thickness and breadth, for which the second party binds himself to deliver other wood of the same quality within the time fixed.

The first parties bind themselves to pay the second party immediately after delivery the price mentioned after each item less a discount of 1%.

It is further stipulated that, if the second party cannot make delivery within four to six weeks, the delivery date shall be extended fourteen days after the six weeks are up, and the second party shall compensate the first parties fifteen guilders for each and every day after the said six weeks until complete delivery is effected.

In the event that [the lumber is not delivered] within the said period of six weeks and fourteen days, the first parties are free to abide by the [terms of the] contract or to consider themselves released from it; however, the second party shall have to pay one thousand Caroli guilders as compensation and damages.

The said parties mutually promise to carry out the provisions of this [contract] in good faith as bound by law.

Thus done in the said city of Amsterdam in the presence of Jan ter Linde Junior and Coenraad Ruysch as witnesses.[4]

[Signed:]

Elias Namias de Crasto Junior
Jacobus de Witt

J. T. Linde Junior
C: Ruijsch

J. Barels, Notary[5]

[4] My thanks to S. E. L. Maduro & Sons' personnel, lumber department, for translating some technical lumber terms.

[5] GAA 8817, Not. Jan Barels, no. 416.

SETTLEMENT OF CURAÇOAN JEWS IN THE ANTILLES
AND THE AMERICAN MAINLAND

BARELY TWO YEARS after the settlement of Jews in Curaçao Spain saw fit in 1661 to dispatch a note "To the Governor and Captain General of the Province of Venezuela" about the "excessive trade carried on with the island of Curaçao."[1] This commerce was conducted chiefly with Jews who made regular calls at the Antilles and mainland ports (pages 73-74, 214-15). Sometimes they ran into difficulties with the Inquisition or fell victim to the fanaticism of some ardent Catholic. Despite these risks, we find Marranos since 1642[2] and other Jews established in the Spanish colonies — Santa Marta in the 1690s, and Tucacas in the early 18th century — and in one or another of the French colonies. Only after the liberation of Venezuela and Colombia in 1819 did the Curaçoan Jews begin installing themselves in different parts of these countries.

The Curaçoan Jewish newcomers found it hard to organize themselves into a congregational group like that of Curaçao. The frequent revolutions in Venezuela and in the Caribbean, the commercial instability of the Antilles, and the ardent desire to return to die in Curaçao hindered their settling down on a solid basis. Yet, several of these colonies in Venezuela were able to hold themselves together until the advent of Jews from Morocco and the Orient in the 1900s.

Here follow in alphabetical order several notes on the settlement of Curaçoan Jews in various ports and cities on the mainland and the Antilles.[3]

AU CAP (Cap St. François, now Cap Haitien), see French Santo Domingo.

AUX CAYES, see French Santo Domingo.

BARCELONA (Ven.). Abraham Henriquez Moron and Isaac Valencia were already established in B. in 1844. The children of Isaac Baiz — Jacob, David, Esther and Rebecca — were born here in 1845, 1848, 1853 and 1856, respectively.[4] H. Baiz[5] had been serving as U. S. Vice Consul in B. since 1851. Isaac Valencia[6]

[1] *Boletín del Archivo General de la Nación*, vol. 35, no. 140 (Caracas, 1948), p. 355.

[2] See below, "Caracas," "Maracaibo."

[3] Different archives consulted in Holland; CGA, Marriages from 1817 to 1962; CGA, Marriage Declarations with their supporting documents; CGA, Death Registers, vols. VII-XII; MIA and DJRCA, Marriage Registers and Correspondence.

[4] CGA, Marriages, 1874-76, 1879 and 1884.

[5] *The Occident*, vol. XIII, 1856, p. 603.

[6] CGA, Marriages, 1862, 1865.

255. KETUBAH OF ISAAC MOSES SALAS AND LEA JULIA DE
ISAAC BAIZ, BARCELONA, VEN., 1863

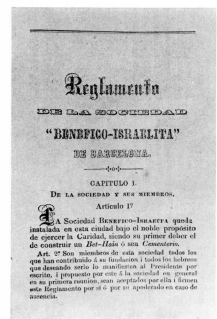

256. BYLAWS, CURAÇOAN JEWISH
CEMETERY OF BARCELONA, VEN.,
1874, FIRST PAGE

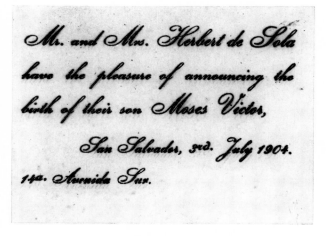

257. HERBERT DE SOLA, BIRTH
ANNOUNCEMENT, SAN SALVADOR, 1904

258. KETUBAH, MENASSE DE JOSE CAPRILES AND SARAH DE ABRAHAM SENIOR JR., PUERTO CABELLO, VEN., 1859, PAGE 857

259. KETUBAH, ABRAHAM P. DE MARCHENA AND LEAH MANUEL ALVAREZ CORREA, RIO HACHA, COL., 1874

was Dutch Vice Consul in 1855 and again in 1862. In 1856 Isaac Sasso made the trip from St. Thomas expressly to circumcise the sons of Isaac Baiz and of Jacob Jesurun Lindo. This Lindo,[7] a resident of Barcelona before 1847, officiated as cantor in 1855. Moises Salas[8] served in that capacity in 1863, and was sometimes assisted by Isaac Valencia.[9] As there was no Jewish cemetery in Barcelona, Isaac Valencia had to ship his wife's remains (d. 1856) to St. Thomas for burial. It was not until 1875 that the group organized a benevolent society, the Sociedad Benéfico Israelita, to erect a cemetery. For this purpose Salomon Pereira appealed to Congregation Mikvé Israel of Curaçao for a contribution[10] and received fifty florins while Guideon Salas and Levy Baiz addressed themselves to the Dutch Jewish Reform Community of Curaçao which donated 112 florins. Jacob Baiz, earlier mentioned, an influential merchant and army contractor, built the railroad projected in Venezuela. In 1892 the revolutionary troops took eighty tons of flour from Haim Gabriel da Costa Gomez[11] without paying him a farthing. The Curaçoan group maintained itself until the early 1900s when Sephardis from Morocco began arriving. Abraham Valencia of Curaçao officiated as cantor in 1904 at the marriage of one of these couples.[12]

BARQUISIMETO (Ven.). The vicar of this city forbade David Hoheb in 1841 from attending a Catholic burial.[13] Jews of this city contributed funds for the relief of Curaçoan hurricane victims of 1877. Jacob Salas[14] suffered property damages in 1902 during the siege of Barquisimeto by the revolutionaries. The Curaçoan poet David Dario Salas[15] celebrated his religious marriage here in 1903.

BARRANQUILLA (Col.). Isaac Rois Mendes[16] died in this city in 1841. Mordechay Alvares Correa Jr. and Moises Salas[17] are encountered here in 1844. Jacob Abraham Pinedo[18] died in B. in 1852 after a residence of several years. A Jewish cemetery was in existence since 1854. During the revolution of 1860 David Haim Dovale,[19] Dutch Vice Consul, distinguished himself by his hospitality and service to Colombian political fugitives and to Dutch subjects — mostly Jews.

---

[7] *Ibid.*, 1865.

[8] MIA, Ket. IX, no. 17.

[9] CGA, Marriages, 1863.

[10] MIA, Minutas de Parnassim, meeting of May 10, 1875; DJRCA, Actas, no. 5, 1875, Legajo no. 18 and Correspondencia, 1875-76.

[11] Corporaal, p. 362.

[12] MIA, Ket. XI, 1904; CGA, Marriages, 1862-1904; DJRCA, Marriages, no. 9.

[13] *CC*, Jan. 23, 1841.

[14] Corporaal, p. 415.

[15] DJRCA, Marriages, no. 54.

[16] *Precious Stones*, p. 442.

[17] CGA, Marriages, 1875, 1880 and 1882.

[18] *CC*, July 8, 1852.

[19] *CC*. Feb. 4, 1860. See also *CC*, April 17, 1862, about the Dutch colony of Barranquilla composed mainly of Curaçoan Jews and also for Dovale's splendid consular activity.

Isaac de Josias Pardo died here in 1862. David de Sola[20] collected more than 1,500 francs in 1864 for the Alliance Israélite Universelle of Paris. The Masonic Lodge[21] included several Curaçoan Jews as high dignitaries in 1866. Raphael Namias Curiel[22] officiated as cantor at a marriage in 1870 and again in 1878. The group organized itself as the Colombian Jewish Community on March 6, 1874, with the following individuals at the helm: A. J. Senior, president; David de Sola, secretary; J. A. Correa, treasurer; D. H. Dovale and D. H. Senior. In 1874 the community numbered 64 souls.[23] That year the mayor allotted a section of the city burial grounds to the Jews for their cemetery. About this time the Curaçoan Jews contributed to the foundation of the Banco de Barranquilla, to the industrialization of the city, and helped found the municipal waterworks. They maintained close contact with the two Jewish communities of Curaçao. In 1877 the Colombian Jewish community headed the list with a contribution of 500 pezos of the 8,000 pezos raised by Jews and Gentiles for the relief of Curaçao's hurricane victims of that year.[24] In 1881 the Colombian Government appointed David Lopez Penha Jr. director of the National Bank of Barranquilla. The poet Abraham Zacharias Lopez Penha published his *Revista Azul* in 1893.

Despite the liberalism shown by the authorities of the city, the public was still not mature enough to tolerate other religions. Because Moises de Eliezer Lopez Penha[25] of Curaçao had refused to kneel before a Catholic procession on June 13, 1878, he was held prisoner and assassinated that night by zealots who stormed his cell. The Curaçoan group maintained itself in Barranquilla until the arrival of Sephardi emigrés from Turkey. The Dutch Government very often appointed Curaçoan Jews to represent it in B (illus. 134).

CALLAO (Ven.). Dr. Haim Abraham de Casseres practiced medicine here between 1880 and 1890 and it is likely that other Curaçoan Jews lived in Callao at the time.

CAP FRANÇOIS or CAP ST. FRANÇOIS (a.k.a. Au Cap), see French Santo Domingo.

CARABOBO (Ven.). Curaçoan Jews settled in Carabobo in 1821. About 1843 Colonel Isaac (Juan) de Benjamin de Sola[26] was owner and publisher of *El Gaceta de Carabobo*.

[20] *Shemah Israel*, April 15, 1864, p. 28.

[21] See above, p. 368, footnote 67.

[22] MIA, Ket. IX, nos. 45, 70.

[23] DJRCA, Legajo no. 16, Correspondencia, 1874; MIA, Minutas de Parnassim, 1864-75; *Archives Israélites* (Paris, 1874), p. 305.

[24] *CC*, Nov. 17, 1877.

[25] According to the amplified Spanish version of the Lopez Penha Family Chronicle (manuscript in possession of the family of the late Julius L. Penha Jr.); communication of the late Jossy M. L. Maduro. See also *Precious Stones*, p. 455.

[26] See above, pp. 299-300, for more details about him.

CARACAS (Ven.). Several Marranos lived in Caracas between 1642-49, among them, Pedro de Campos, Gaspar Rodriguez, Enrique de Leon, Fernandez Amezquita and Luis Fernandez Angel. They left for Mexico only to run afoul of the Inquisition.[27] There is a possibility that some Curaçoan Jews started a settlement here directly after the independence of Greater Colombia in 1819. Aaron Mendes Monsanto died in C. in 1826. Six years later Samuel Hoheb published at his expense Menasseh Ben Israel's *Esperanza de Israel*. About the same period members of the Levy Maduro, Curiel and De Sola families[28] are met here. Between 1835 and 1854 Moises Frois Ricardo of Curaçao made sporadic visits to Caracas to circumcise the children. In 1845 Anjel J. Jesurun[29] published a small work on religious and moral instruction in Spanish. In 1848 a Jewish student was admitted to the University of Caracas.

The Jewish group formed a committee in 1838 to erect a cemetery. On June 13 they requested the Amsterdam community to make a collection to help them build their cemetery in Caracas where they "had established residence... for a long time."[30] In 1844 the municipality granted them a plot of land 190 feet by 72 feet. That year they started a Jewish Cemetery Fund[31] under the administration of an "economic assembly" composed of Moises Abraham Jesurun (treasurer), Samuel Hoheb, A. M. Seixas, M. Pardo Jr., Herman Cohen [Henriquez], A. Curiel, Frederico Nunes, Anjel J. Jesurun and Isaac Jacob Senior. They appealed to Mikvé Israel of Curaçao[32] for a contribution. The project was never realized: first, because of the political revolts which had been agitating the country since 1848 and, second, because at least 20,000 to 25,000 francs was required for the purpose. After the death of the treasurer M. A. Jesurun, his son Anjel took the matter up with M. Pardo Jr., the last member of the economic assembly in Caracas in 1854. It was decided to deposit this fund — then grown to 1,870 florins — with the Orphans Chamber of the Jewish community of Curaçao. This capital, with interest at $4\frac{1}{2}\%$, remained at the disposal of Curaçoan Jews who might wish to build a cemetery in Caracas. Meanwhile, the deeds to the property remained in the hands of the Dutch Consul General[33] at Caracas.

When order was restored in the country, the Jews returned to Caracas. There they founded large business firms.[34] However, they were unable to organize themselves into a community. Elias de Sola, on the marriage of his daughter

---

[27] Archivo Histórico de Madrid, Expediente 1, Legajo 1738, pp. 38, 51, 72. The document is entitled, "Certificación de la visita [en México] del Dr. don Pedro de Medina Rico de los procesos de fé" in 1656 (communication of Seymour B. Liebman; microfilm at AJA).

[28] CGA, Marriages, 1833, 1863, 1876; CGA, Mar. Documents, 1873; MIA, Birth Register B, 1835, 1842, 1849, 1850, 1854.

[29] See above, p. 456.

[30] Letter signed by M. A. Jesurun, Samuel Hoheb, M. Curiel Jr., Jacob Delvalle, Isaac Senior Jr., Isaac Delvalle, M. A. De Lima and M. Senior. The Amsterdam parnassim sent 20 florins (PJCAA, 74).

[31] *Archives Israélites*, 1844, pp. 807-808.

[32] MIA, Minutas del Mahamad, meeting of June 10, 1844.

[33] *CC*, July 29, 1854.

[34] *Ibid.*, Sept. 19, 1863.

Anna to Joshua E. Luria-Piza in 1889, was forced to act as hazzan, "there being no one invested with sacerdotal character." The governor[35] of the district attended the ceremony. This same De Sola again officiated as hazzan at a marriage in 1900. The Curaçoan Jewish colony of C. continued to exist until the arrival of Sephardis from Morocco. In 1918 Menahem J. Coriat[36] of Morocco acted as hazzan and was officially recognized as such.

CARORA (Ven.). David Curiel[37] was one of the pharmacists of this city. He was called to Coro where he rendered exceptional service during the cholera plague of 1855. Isaac Pereira died here in 1859 and was taken to Curaçao for burial. The Jews of Carora contributed funds in behalf of the Curaçoan victims of the hurricane of 1877.

CARTAGENA (Col.). About 1781 David Morales,[38] as "unofficial" agent of the Spanish Government in Curaçao, had business dealings with Cartagena. Several Jews of Curaçao settled in this city well before 1850. Samuel Pereira Jr. died here in 1858 and was taken to Curaçao for burial. Curaçoan Jews[39] who took up residence in C. included, among others, Joseph and Benjamin Pereira Brandao, Efraim and Jacob Delvalle, Abraham Salas, Elias Moreno, Elias de David Gomes Casseres, Mosseh Gomes Casseres and Isaac M. Penso. J. J. B. Moreno was the Dutch Vice Consul in 1874.

CHARLESTON (S.C.). Jacob Cohen Henriquez[40] traveled to Charleston in 1737. Jacob Motta[41] is encountered here in 1783. In 1816 the Jewish community of Curaçao contributed funds for the construction of the Charleston synagogue. Selomoh de Jeoshuah Cohen Peixotto[42] of Curaçao officiated as the hazzan from 1823 to 1835 and Joseph M. Chumaceiro as rabbi from 1867 to 1874.

CIUDAD BOLIVAR (Ven.). About 1820 Isaac (Juan) de Sola was on the editorial staff of the *Correo de Orinoco* in Angostura, Ciudad Bolivar. Customs duty receipts of this city were pledged to Jacob A. Jesurun & Son for their loan to the Venezuelan Government in 1865-66. Jacob Isaac Senior practiced dentistry in 1886 and Dr. Haim Abraham de Casseres medicine about the same period. Jewish merchants who settled in this city during the final quarter of the last century were unable to do a thriving business and were compelled to return to Curaçao.

35 MIA, Ket. XI, no. 2.
36 *Ibid.*, XII, no. 22; CGA, Marriages, 1897, 1902, 1913, 1929, 1935.
37 *CC*, May 19, 1855.
38 OAC 859, no. 374.
39 MIA, Birth Register B; CGA, Marriages, 1850, 1860 ,1862, 1890, 1901; Deaths, 1854.
40 OAC 820, March 27, 1749.
41 OAC 959, no. 355.
42 Malcolm H. Stern, *Americans of Jewish Descent* (Cincinnati, 1960), p. 171; manuscript notes of Selomoh Cohen Peixotto at the AJA.

COLON (Panama). Irmiau Levy Maduro[43] died in Colon in 1860.

CORO (Ven.). This was the largest Jewish center of Venezuela and perhaps one of the oldest too. The Jews enjoyed a certain measure of religious liberty, most probably since 1819. They had a house of worship which was attended regularly and led by one of their number as hazzan. Their cemetery[44] dates well before 1848. Joseph Curiel[45] served as their circumciser between 1829 and 1854. One D. Cohen Henriquez asked the Amsterdam parnassim if it was permissible to leave the back door of his pharmacy open on the Sabbath and for him to prepare and sell medicines.[46] In 1847 the Assessor Isaac Namias de Crasto was called to solemnize a marriage. In 1848 the Venezuelan Government pledged the customs receipts of Coro as security on a loan it obtained from Jacob and David Jesurun.[47] In 1848 the community counted some 160 souls. Many Jews fled to Curaçao during the Civil War of 1847-48.[48] They returned, but again were forced to quit Coro in 1855 (pp. 348-51). They returned in 1858. In 1864 various members became affiliated with the local branch of the Alliance Israélite Universelle of Curaçao. A year later they donated 290 florins for the construction of Temple Emanu-El of Curaçao. The government was ordinarily quite liberal toward the Jews who sometimes attained high positions in the administration of the municipality. For example: David Hoheb was mayor before 1840; David Lopez Fonseca,[49] secretary of the Departmental Assembly of Coro in 1875; Abraham Isaac Curiel,[50] secretary of the Miranda district in 1904, and José David Curiel was president of the Community Council of the City of Coro. Curaçoan Jews were still living in Coro as late as 1918.[51]

CUBA. On November 20, 1743, Don Joseph Ximenes, a Gentile of Havana, declared in Curaçao that he held "a general power of attorney from Martin de Harostigue, official mayor of the Holy Inquisition and president of the Compañia Real of that city and of the island of Cuba," to negotiate for the importation to Cuba of foodstuffs, slaves and materials needed for boat repairs.[52] Although business and shipping then were chiefly in Jewish hands, trade between Cuba and the Jews of Curaçao was very limited. Did the Inquisition wield a stronger club in Cuba than in the other Caribbean islands? Curaçoan Jews began settling in Cuba about 1880. One of these pioneers was Joseph Salomon de Jongh who

---

[43] MIA, Birth Register B.

[44] *The Occident*, vol. V, 1848, p. 318.

[45] MIA, Birth Register B.

[46] PJCAA 72, Correspondence with the Mahamad, 1829-1833.

[47] CGNA, 1848, I, no. 82; II; nos. 18, 30.

[48] *Archives Israélites*, 1848, p. 155.

[49] CGA, Marriages, 1891, no. 7.

[50] *Ibid.*, 1904, no. 42.

[51] MIA, Ket. IX, nos. 31, 57, 87, 91; XI, nos. 31, 58; DJRCA, Marriages, nos. 57, 67, 71; CGA, Marriages, 1846-1933.

[52] OAC 851, no. 282.

came in 1881. Early this century some Curaçoan Jews — among them Moises Benjamin de Marchena and the firm of S. E. L. Maduro later on — owned sugar plantations in Cuba. Religious marriages[53] among Curaçoan Jews took place in Havana in 1912, 1917, 1918, 1920 and 1936. David Mordechay L. Maduro served for many years as Consul General of the Netherlands in Cuba.

CUMANA (Ven.). Isaac Valencia was already established in Cumaná in 1857 when he lost a daughter who was taken to St. Thomas for burial. A religious marriage[54] was celebrated here in 1884.

CUMAREBO (Ven.). Isaac de Marchena died here in 1877.

FRENCH SANTO DOMINGO [HAITI] (= FSD). This includes "Au Cap," Aux Cayes, Boupou au Cap, Cap St. François ("Au Cap," now Cap Haitien), Chardonier, Fort Dauphin, Jacmel, Jeremie (Trou), Port au Prince and St. Louis. The oldest record extant of Jews trading with this colony dates back to 1708. One De la Peña[55] negotiated with the French Government to import slaves from Africa. Abraham Micael Rois Mendes[56] of Curaçao left for FSD in 1746. Manuel Lopez Jr.[57] had a home in Cap François in 1757. Jacob Rodriguez Campos died there in 1758. Joseph Hisquiau Rodriguez da Costa, Isaac Victoria, Josiau Naar and Isaac Jesurun Sasportas[58] sailed to "Cap" or FSD in 1758. Philip Waag and his wife Esther Benjamin of St. Eustatius had a large fortune in Fort Dauphin. Waag made his will there on February 6, 1762, and died a month later. The French judge confiscated all his wealth, whereupon Waag's heirs had the Amsterdam Parnassim[59] intervene in their behalf before the States General of Holland. Elias Israel[60] had business dealings in Boupou au Cap in 1763. About this year the French Government confiscated a ship with merchandise belonging to Abraham Alvares[61] of Amsterdam. Jacob Philip de Pas was in St. Louis in 1763. That year Moseh Henriquez Cotinho[62] of Curaçao transacted some business at this port. Joseph d'Aguilar,[63] who was born in [French] Santo Domingo, married in Curaçao in 1797.

Between 1775 and 1800 Jews of Curaçao settled in appreciable numbers in

---

[53] CGA, Marriages, 1881, 1912, 1918, 1922 and 1936.

[54] *Ibid.*, 1874, 1875; Marriage Documents, 1884; Jul. Margolinsky, *299 Epitaphs from the Jewish Cemetery in St. Thomas, W. I., 1837-1916...* (Copenhagen, 1957), in stencil, no. 99.

[55] In a PJCAA bundle there is a draft of two contracts made in 1708 and 1709 between De la Peña and the French Government.

[56] OAC 859, no. 19.

[57] OAC 906, Dec. 1, 1768, referring to the year 1757-58.

[58] OAC 834, no. 163; OAC 836, no. 111.

[59] PJCAA, bundle.

[60] OAC 890, no. 203.

[61] PJCAA, bundle.

[62] OAC 889, nos. 83, 109.

[63] OAC 1099, Nov. 12, 1797.

various parts of FSD, but mainly at Jacmel and Cap. St. François. Jacob Gabriel Pinedo[64] traded with Jeremie in 1775. Moses Lopez Penha[65] left for FSD in 1776. That year Gabriel Pinedo[66] shipped mules and donkeys from Curaçao to FSD. Pereira and Motta were merchants in FSD in 1777. Benjamin Jesurun Lindo lived at Au Cap in 1779 while his brother Jacob[67] ran a business in St. Louis. Imanuel da Costa Gomez & Bros.[68] had a business in Jacmel in 1778. David Morales and Rephael Molina Monsanto did a thriving trade with Au Cap in 1779. That year Benjamin and Moses Cohen Henriquez, Jacob and Isaac Haim Pereira, Isaac Pardo and Isaac Mendes transacted business at Au Cap.[69] This same Isaac Mendes,[70] having lost a lawsuit there, went to Paris in 1779 to appeal it. David Lopez Rephael left for Jacmel in 1779. Jacob de Castro sailed for Au Cap in 1780 where he met Isaac Molina, Mordechay Penso and Jacob Semah de Valensa.[71] Dr. Joseph Capriles traded with Au Cap in 1780. Abraham Dovale[72] is encountered at Aux Cayes in 1780. Benjamin Jesurun Lindo[73] met his death there the same year. Jacob, brother of David Morales, was already established in Port au Prince in 1780. Jacob Nunes Redondo and David Pardo left for Au Cap in 1781. Isaac de Molina Frères & Co.[74] had a flourishing business at Au Cap in 1782. Abraham Salzedo, Abraham Calvo, Salomo L. Maduro and Salomo de Jacob de Castro left for or had business dealings with Au Cap in 1783. Jacob Athias Robles and Eliau Rodriguez Miranda declared that they had attended the circumcision of Jacob,[75] son of Aron Sasportas and Rachel Alvares, done at Au Cap [about 1783]. Jacob Abenatar Jr. stated that he was at Au Cap on the death of Aron Sasportas who was buried according to Jewish rite. Moseh Cohen Henriquez, Moses Silva Leyba, Mosseh de Casseres, Isaac Haim Salas, David Cohen Henriquez, David Lopez Fonseca and Jacob Abenatar Jr. declared that Aron Sasportas[76] had all of his sons circumcised at Au Cap in accordance with Jewish Law. The firm of Cadieres (Gentile), Robles & Isaac Morales, merchants at Port au Prince, empowered David Morales[77] of Curaçao to purchase a brigantine for them in 1783. Esther, wife of Abraham Mendes Monsanto, was born at Cap Haitien in 1784 and died in St. Thomas[78] in 1856. Moses Julien,[79] born in Aux Cayes in 1788, settled in St. Thomas, and died in Curaçao in 1852. Abraham Suzarte[80] received from the Community Chest of Congregation Mikvé Israel, Curaçao, 16:7 pezos for provisions and fare to Au Cap.

[64] OAC 954, no. 22.

[65] OAC 954, no. 126.

[66] OAC 954, no. 91.

[67] OAC 921. nos. 6, 208.

[68] OAC 956, no. 14.

[69] OAC 923, no. 822.

[70] OAC 923, no. 1393.

[71] OAC 925, no. 305.

[72] OAC 926, no. 442.

[73] OAC 927, no. 829.

[74] OAC 959, no. 348.

[75] OAC 1047, no. 147.

[76] The declaration was made on Dec. 6, 1816, after Jacob de Aron Sasportas' death. The declarants must have lived at Au Cap between 1785 and 1795 (OAC 1047, no. 148).

[77] OAC 959, no. 418.

[78] Margolinsky, no. 105.

[79] CGA, Death Register, 1852.

[80] MIA, loose papers.

Trade between Curaçao and Haiti was very brisk between 1789 and 1795.[81] The Curaçoan Jewish colony at Cap St. François had grown so large in 1790 that it was found necessary to engage the services of Dr. Isaac Cardozo[82] of Curaçao. Jacob Gaspar Henriquez,[83] owner of the *St. Joseph* which was lost at sea, was in Juaquim (Aquin?) with his family in 1791. David Lopez Raphael, Joseph Cohen Peixotto, Salomon Calvo and David and Abraham Jesurun are encountered at Jacmel about 1794.

A report of the Curaçoan Government to Holland on the trade with Haiti from 1781 to 1818 reveals that the Haitian revolution of 1795-96 "ruined many needy residents and reduced entire families to beggary."[84] Among those severely hit was Gaspar David Henriquez[85] whose large fortune was confiscated by the French Government of Jeremie in 1795. In 1797 Henriquez owned a plantation with 240 slaves, a house in Aquim (Aquin), and moneys due him in Jacmel — all of which was lost during the French Revolution.[86] Isaac Jesurun Sasportas was an ardent revolutionary in 1799 (pp. 284-85). David Abinun de Lima died in Jacmel in 1826. Sigismund Rotschild lived with his family in FSD in 1829. Most of the dignitaries of the Masonic Lodge at Port au Prince in 1847 were Jews: David Leon, venerable master; J. Naar Jr., Raphael de Marchena, Ralph Wolff, H. L. Penha, Jacob Naar, Alexandre Victoria, Général de Marchena, Gérard de Marchena, Abraham Gomes Casseres, E. Benlisa, E. de Pinna, Benjamin de Marchena and E. Wolff.[87]

Curaçoan Jews are found at Chardonier[88] as late as 1851. As a result of the frequent revolutions which rocked FSD or Haiti during the second half of the 19th century, Curaçoan Jews left the island.

GUADELOUPE (Fr. Antilles). In 1838 David L. Cardoze was established at Pointe-a-Pitre, chief seaport of G., where his son Samuel[89] was born.

GUARICO (Ven.). The Community Chest of Congregation Mikvé Israel of Curaçao paid Rachel Rodriguez da Costa[90] 56:2 pezos on April 20, 1789, for provisions and fare to Guarico for herself and four children.

HAITI, see French Santo Domingo.

JACMEL, „ „ „ „

JEREMIE, „ „ „ „

[81] CGA, Koloniaal Verslag, 1818 (?).
[82] OAC 133, no. 56; see above, pp. 419-20.
[83] OAC 497, Oct. 17, 1825, referring to the events of the past thirty years.
[84] CGA, Koloniaal Verslag, 1818 (?).
[85] OAC 138, no. 19.
[86] OAC 140, no. 102.
[87] *Archives Israélites*, 1847, pp. 861-63.
[88] CGA, Not. Acts, 1851, no. 51.
[89] Margolinsky, no. 58.
[90] MIA, loose papers.

260. KETUBAH, JACOB M. SENIOR AND ESTHER B. DE MARCHENA, BARRANQUILLA, COL., 1878

261. KETUBAH, JOSHUA ERNEST BENJAMIN LURIA AND ANNA ELIAS DE SOLA, CARACAS, VEN., 1889

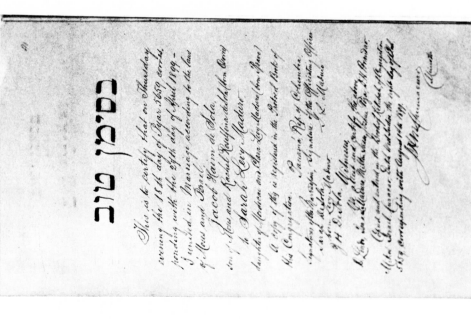

263. LETTER OF SAMUEL HOHEB JR. ASKING THE
CURAÇAO PARNASSIM TO RETURN THE REPAIRED
SCROLLS OF LAW ST EUSTATIUS 1772

262. KETUBAH, JACOB HAIM MOSES DE SOLA AND
SARAH MORDECAI LEVY MADURO, PANAMA, 1899

LA GUAIRA (Ven.). One David Levy Maduro died in this city in 1819. Samuel Abraham Curiel was born here in 1836 and Isaac M. Pardo in 1842. The Jews of this port gave 75 pezos toward the construction of Temple Emanu-El of Curaçao in 1865 and later contributed in behalf of the Curaçoan hurricane victims of 1877. A. M. Seixas & Co. (= Elias de Sola) was one of La Guaira's outstanding business houses in 1866. One quarter of the customs duty receipts of this port was pledged to J. A. Jesurun & Son against a loan floated by this Curaçoan firm to the Venezuelan Government in 1865-66. Commerce between Curaçao and La Guaira expanded when J. A. Jesurun & Son opened a sailing line plying between Curaçao-La Guaira-Puerto Cabello-St. Thomas-Europe.[91]

MARACAIBO (Ven.). Here too we find several Marranos between 1642 and 1649, among them, Gaspar Andres, Francisco de la Cerda, Benito Henriquez and Manuel de Zerda. Later they are encountered in Mexico in trouble with the Inquisition.[92] We find the Curaçoan Jewish merchants Isaac and Josias Pardo established at this port in 1820. David Abensur of Mogador lived in M. in 1838; Jacob M. de Castro and Abraham de Castro before 1854. David de David Henriquez Juliao[93] was assassinated here in 1855. As there was no Jewish cemetery, the Jews had their dead buried either in the English cemetery of M. or in Curaçao. In 1848 the Venezuelan Government pledged part of its customs duty receipts to J. and D. Jesurun; in 1865-66, 25%.[94] D. A. Jesurun had a business firm there in 1870. Benjamin Henriquez was Dutch Vice Consul at M. in 1874. Haim da Costa Gomez founded an important business which continued operating until the end of the last century. He was consul of Belgium until 1881 and had charge of the affairs of the Dutch Consulate. The fact that there was a Dutch Consul from 1874 to 1881 leads one to believe that Maracaibo had a large number of Curaçoans, including Jews. Various documents[95] show that Curaçoan Jews took up residence there sporadically until 1935.

MARTINIQUE (Fr. Antilles). Through the "Lettres Patentes" granted to them by the kings of France in 1550, 1574, 1580, 1656 and 1722, the Portuguese Jews had the privilege of settling in all lands under French dominion. Some took up residence in Martinique[96] before 1654, only to be cast out in 1683. Most of the emigrés flocked to Curaçao (p. 88). Although Curaçoan Jews traded with Martinique after their expulsion,[97] it is not certain when they returned to

[91] CC, March 12, 1819; April 10, 1851; June 2, 1866; April 9, 1870; CGA, Rechtsbank, 1866; CGA, Marriages, 1860, 1870, 1897; MIA, Birth Register B.

[92] Archivo Histórico de Madrid, ibid., pp. 44, 51, 77 (courtesy S. B. Liebman). See note 27 above.

[93] MIA, Birth Register B, letter D.

[94] CGNA, 1848, II, no. 30.

[95] CC, March 15, 1851; June 2, 1866; CGA, Marriages, 1890, 1891, 1896, 1905, 1906, 1918, 1921, 1922, 1928, 1929, 1935.

[96] Emmanuel, "New Light on Early American Jewry," AJA 7:22.

[97] Emmanuel, "Les Juifs de la Martinique et leurs coreligionnaires d'Amsterdam au XVIIe siècle," Revue des Etudes Juives, vol. CXXIII, 1964, pp. 515-16.

settle on a permanent basis. In 1785, a century later, we find the Community Chest of Congregation Mikvé Israel of Curaçao lending Moses Ramos 16:4 pezos for his fare to Martinique.[98]

MOMPOS (Col.).   Mordechay A. Correa Jr. settled in Mompos with his family between 1846 and 1847. His sons were born in M. — Julio in 1846 and Jacob in 1847 — and his wife died there.

MONROE (Mich.).   Obadia Mendes da Costa declared in his will of 1848 that he owned 160 acres of land in Monroe, Michigan.[99]

NEW ORLEANS (Miss. [Ter.]).   David Dias Arias, former son-in-law of Haham Jesurun, died in N.O. in 1759.[100] Manuel de Britto, Isaac Roiz Monsanto and Isaac Mendes were merchants[101] of this city in 1760. In 1764 [Isaac] Fastio & [Manuel] Monsanto of Curaçao imported wines and liquors in exchange for timber.[102] The De Meza family of Curaçao resided in N. O. since 1846.[103] The Reverend Joseph M. Chumaceiro of Curaçao officiated here as preacher of Congregation Nefusoth Yehudah (1874-80), and edited *The Jewish South* (1879-83).

NEW YORK.   Three cantors of New York's Congregation Shearith Israel came from Curaçao: Saul Pardo,[104] Mosseh Lopez da Fonseca[105] and Moseh Levy Maduro Peixotto.[106] From the earliest times Jews of Curaçao had family ties in New York.[107] The widow Rachel Luis of New York[108] was in correspondence with the Curaçao parnassim regarding the estate of her brother who died in Curaçao in 1724. Daniel Gomez of New York, widower of Rebecca Torres and father of the youngsters Moses and Joseph, went to Curaçao in 1733 to marry Ester de Gabriel Levy from whom he received a dowry of 3,640:5:2 pesos. Before this second marriage, he declared to having assets of 10,000 pesos. He set aside 5,000 pesos of this amount in favor of the minor sons in his custody and named as their guardians the Messrs. Mordechay and David Gomez and Moses Michal of New York and Jacob Curiel of Curaçao. As security for that amount, he gave a mortgage on his New York house situated at "Smith Vlyt" or Vlij and on some land at "Husten Revuir" [Hudson River] with its four slaves.[109]

98 MIA, loose papers.
99 CGNA, 1848, no. 62.
100 Communication of Rabbi Bertram W. Korn.
101 Resolutions of the States General of Holland, y. 1761, p. 627; OAC 879, Aug. 12, 1760.
102 OAC 892, no. 223.
103 CGNA, 1846, vol. I.
104 *Precious Stones*, pp. 198-99.
105 *Ibid.*, pp. 315-17; see above, p. 131.
106 David De Sola Pool, *Portraits Etched in Stone*, pp. 428-32; see above, p. 425.
107 *Precious Stones*, pp. 149, 199, 235, 327, 339, 418, 428.
108 MIA, loose papers.
109 OAC 901, no. 240, Aug. 4, 1733.

The records of the Mikvé Israel of Curaçao disclose that the Community Chest either paid or advanced the fare to New York to the following travelers: Joseph Nathan and son, 44:3:3 pezos; David Porto, 21:5:5 and Ishac Saldaña, 21:5:4 in 1766; Moses Valença Callo, 37:4 in 1770; David Moses Copels, 22:4 in 1771; Isaac de David Lopez Cardozo, 22:4 in 1774; David Rodriguez Pimentel, 33:6 pesos in 1789 on condition that he did not return to Curaçao for six years; Isaac Ribeiro, 59 pezos in 1793 and Jacob da Costa Pimentel, 43 pezos in 1802.[110]

Among the New Yorkers who settled in Curaçao was one Samuel Lyon of the firm of Lyon Bros. He made a will in Curaçao on April 3, 1818, naming a brother Philip in New York.[111]

In the same period several Curaçoan families settled in New York: Maduro Peixotto, De Meza, Dovale, De Sola, A. Correa, Da Costa Gomez, Cohen Henriquez, Baiz, Senior, Mendes Monsanto, and others. During the first half of the 19th century several Curaçoan families with large business interests in New York — De Lima, Senior, Capriles, Jesurun, among others — sent their sons to study medicine there. Various firms of Curaçoan Jews — notably Dovale & Co., D[avid]. A[binun]. de Lima & Co., De Sola, Lobo & Co. — are encountered in New York in the second half of the 19th century. They conducted a prodigious business with their representatives and relatives in Curaçao, in the Caribbean and in Venezuela. The export figures on U.S. goods to Curaçao attest to this commercial activity. In 1894 this amounted to $1,266,192; in 1896 to $1,185,066 and the same for 1897. "Of all goods exported from America to Curaçao between 1894 and 1897, D. A. de Lima & Co. shipped fully one-half."[112] On his death in 1891, David Abinun de Lima's three sons (all native-born Curaçoans) took over the business. They also carried on an extensive trade with Venezuela, Colombia, Jamaica, Barbados and other islands of the West Indies. De Sola, Lobo & Co. exported large quantities of merchandise to Curaçao, Venezuela and Central America. S. E. L. Maduro & Sons, who had been trading with New York since 1840, opened their New York branch in 1917 under the style of Selma Mercantile Corp.[113]

Curaçoan Jews established in New York usually became members of Congregation Shearith Israel, the Portuguese Jewish community. In 1930 when the Shearith Israel celebrated the 200th anniversary of her synagogue, the Mikvé Israel commemorated the event with a special synagogue service on the seventh day of Passover, and also sent a board member, I. H. Capriles, to represent her in the bicentenary ceremonies.

PANAMA.   Curaçoans and some Jews of St. Thomas, mostly of Curaçoan origin, founded a Hebrew Benevolent Society in this city in 1852.[114] Because of the

---

[110] MIA, Libro del Tezorero, y. 5526, p. 27; loose papers.
[111] OAC 1051, no. 90.
[112] *The Monthly Illustrator*, vol. XVI, no. 1 (New York, June 1898), p. 28.
[113] Selma stands for S. E. L. Maduro.
[114] *The Occident*, vol. X, 1852, p. 175.

membership's Dutch origin (i.e., Curaçoan), the Panama community is generally referred to as "Los Holandeses." The frightful earthquake of St. Thomas in 1867 sent various Jews of that island scurrying to Panama. Other Curaçoan Jews joined them during the early attempts to build the canal. Some of the disillusioned went home. The Panama community nevertheless grew so fast that in the early 1900s they found it necessary to ask the Mikvé Israel of Curaçao for an "imperfect" Scroll of the Law. This was refused, surely because a defective Torah cannot be used unless corrected. Despite some opposition by the conservative element among the Curaçoans, the Reform ritual was adopted but with Sephardic pronunciation. S. Levy Maduro served as their hazzan in 1899 and Moses de David Cardoze in 1915 (illus. 262).

The community is well organized and numbers some 400 souls.[115] It has a cemetery, a fine synagogue and a meeting room. It enjoys an honorable reputation among the people of the city. For more than seventy years the Dutch Government has entrusted its consular service to a native Curaçoan Jew or to his descendants.[116] The Jewish community[117] of Panama is the only one of all the communities and societies founded by Curaçoan Jews that has been able to maintain itself since 1850.

PORT AU PRINCE, see French Santo Domingo.

PUERTO CABELLO (Ven.). Curaçoan Jews lived in PC since 1835. David Lobo lived there in 1846. In his letters to the Amsterdam parnassim he wrote that the colony was too small to form a congregation. M. F. Nunez, a layman, performed a marriage in 1853. On the Day of Atonement that year (Yom Kippur, 5614), Samuel Jesurun Pinto[118] officiated as hazzan. The services were held in David Lobo's home for fourteen men and seven women. A circumciser from Curaçao would visit PC from time to time between 1847 and 1864 to circumcise the children sometimes as old as three years. Dr. Salomon Lobo was one of PC's most prominent Jews in 1864. The following year 20% of the customs duty receipts were pledged by the government to J. A. Jesurun & Son. The Jews of this city contributed funds in behalf of the Curaçoan victims of the hurricane of 1877. As this small group did not have a hazzan in 1890, Raphael Polly officiated as such at the marriage of his daughter Abigail to Jacob M. Jesurun of Curaçao.

---

[115] Besides Congregation Kol Sharith Israel (a.k.a. Los Holandeses), there are two other Jewish communities: the Cheveth Ahim, with the largest number, made up chiefly of Sephardis from Syria; and the Beneficencia Israelítica of the Ashkenazis who migrated to Panama since 1930. Both communities have a social club and a synagogue. The Cheveth Ahim also has its own cemetery and ritual slaughterer, both facilities being used by the Ashkenazis too. The author is happy to state that during his rabbinate of the Cheveth Ahim in 1946-48, there was, and still continues, a perfect understanding among the three congregations.

[116] Herbert De Sola was the Dutch Consul in 1894 and Abraham Jesurun Jr. in 1899 (CGA, Marriages, 1895, no. 4; 1899, no. 53). Today this office is filled by David (?) Sasso.

[117] MIA, Ket. XI, no. 40; XII, no. 29; DJRCA, Marriages, nos. 40, 43.

[118] The Occident, vol. V, 1848, pp. 615-16; vol. XI, 1854, pp. 79, 534-35.

The Jews of PC would apply for religious assistance either to Congregation Mikvé Israel or Temple Emanu-El of Curaçao in accordance with their religious tendencies.[119] Curaçoan Jews remained in PC until 1926 (illus. 258).

PUERTO PLATA, see Santo Domingo.

PUERTO RICO. David de Castro of Curaçao obtained a permit from the governor of Puerto Rico in 1746 to navigate in her waters. Jews of Curaçao traded with the island in 1771. Sarah Nunes Mercado died in Guayanilla in 1805. Isaac de Sola is encountered in PR in 1828. Elias de Jeosuah de Sola was living there in 1839. Dr. Isaac Abinun de Lima practiced medicine in Mayaguez in 1840. The Jesuruns had Jewish agents in PR in 1846. Selomoh Haim Senior died in Aguadilla in 1849 and was taken to Curaçao for burial. Solomon Pardo lived in Mayaguez in 1856. Curaçoan Jews continued migrating to Puerto Rico up to 1943.[120]

RIO HACHA (Col.). Curaçoan Jews had been exporting timber to Rio Hacha ever since 1700. In 1766 David Morales brought in mules purchased from the French colonies. Salamo Haim Calvo of Curaçao was providentially skirting the seacoast in his sloop *De Jonge Haim* in 1770 when the Indians tried to seize this city. On the demand of RH's governor, Calvo put his artillery to use and successfully routed the invaders. The governor ordered him to bring more arms. Calvo went to Kingston. On the way back he was captured by a Spanish corsair and taken to Cartagena. In 1772 Gabriel Pinedo was given the privilege of importing foodstuffs and supplies to RH. In 1773 David Morales and Abraham Calvo had business dealings in this city. In 1783 Salomon de Moses L. Maduro (a.k.a. Bernardo Maduro) settled there with his family. The colony was very prosperous between 1840 and 1843. During this period the office of cantor was most probably filled by Moises Salas. Isaac Pinheiro de Nogueira lost his wife in 1846; Isaac Pinedo Jr. and Moises Salas attended the burial. As the Jews of RH did not have a circumciser in 1846 and 1848 when Jacob de David Henriquez and Guideon de Moises Salas were born respectively, the boys were taken to Curaçao for the circumcision. At the settlers' request, the Jewish community of Curaçao sent a contribution of a hundred florins for the erection of a cemetery.

The number of Dutch subjects, mostly Jews, must have been quite large to warrant the accreditation of a Dutch Vice Consul. This office was filled since 1856, and perhaps earlier, by a member of the Pinedo family. During the Colombian revolution of 1860 when Eli Pinedo was Dutch Vice Consul at RH, Curaçao sent the battleship *Schorpioen* to protect her subjects. Jacob Pinedo was Dutch Vice Consul here in 1871.

[119] PJCAA, 77; CGA, Deaths, 1832; Marriages, 1844, etc., 1891, 1908, 1926; DJRCA, Legajo no. 28, 1885; Marriages, no. 36; CC, Oct. 29, 1864.

[120] PJCAA, bundle; OAC 944, nos. 55-56; OAC 1077, no. 74; CGA, Not. Acts, 1846; Marriages, 1911, 1943; CEOE 779, no. 63; *Precious Stones*, p. 137.

Samuel de Casseres and Mordechay A. Correa officiated as hazzanim at marriages, the former in 1857 and the latter in 1874. Morris Pinedo Jr. "sanctified" a marriage in 1898 "with the authorisation of the minister[121] of the Portuguese Jewish Community Mikve Israel of Curaçao." See illustration 259.

The Jews suffered greatly as a result of the uprisings of August, 1865, and April 1875, — the latter headed by Manuel Gunaga. Imprisoned, Cheri M. Leon and Mordechay A. Correa were released only after the payment of a staggering sum to the revolutionaries who also extorted the sum of 10,000 pezos cash from Correa Bros., Abraham de Marchena, and Samuel, Morris and Jacob Pinedo.[122]

The colony broke up a little after 1913.[123]

ST. CHRISTOPHER, see St. Kitts.

ST. CROIX or SANTA CRUS (formerly Danish West Indies).
Aron de Mattos Gutieres died here in 1762. His son Abraham owed money to merchants of Curaçao. At the request of the St. Croix parnassim, Congregation Mikvé Israel of Curaçao sent Jeudah de Abraham Sasso as hazzan in 1765 and paid his fare of 45 pezos. The same year the Mikvé Israel donated 200 pezos toward building the SC synagogue. In 1766 Abraham Henriquez asked the Amsterdam parnassim for a Scroll of the Law for the "Holy Congregation Santa Crux in America." One without ornaments was given, but returned as Henriquez had meanwhile obtained another elsewhere. In 1770 the Community Chest of Mikvé Israel, Curaçao, paid the fare to Santa Crus for Hannah Lealtar and her five children. David de la Motta lived there in 1784, Joseph Levy in 1785, Solomon de Leon and family in 1809, and Abraham L. Maduro and family in 1813. Elias Mendes Monsanto and Judith de Sola were married in Santa Crus in 1817 by Hazzan Abraham de Samuel Jesurun Pinto in the presence of David Levy Jr. (Levy died in Curaçao in 1832.) Aron de Sola resided in SC in 1818. Salomo de Benjamin Lindo was living there in 1825 when his mother died in Curaçao. Aimé, wife of Jacob Pereira, was born in Christiansted in 1825. Isaac Levy's wife Rachel died in SC in 1840. Isaac Haim de Sola's daughter Hannah was born there a little before 1844.[124] David de Leon died there about 1863.

[121] He was the preacher Joseph Mendes Chumaceiro (pp. 403-410; MIA, Ket. XI, no. 35).

[122] CGNA, 1865, nos. 157-58; El Imparcial, Curaçao, April 10, 1877; CC, April 14, 1877.

[123] OAC 899, no. 14; PJCAA, Copiador de Cartas, 1764-1773, letter of the Amsterdam parnassim to the King's attorney general; estate papers of Mercado-Delvalle, PJCAA bundle; OAC 944, no. 121; OAC 947, no. 327; OAC 959, no. 370; MIA, Minutas de Parnassim, Aug. 15, 1850; Ket. VIII, no. 153; IX, no. 67; CGA, Rechtsbank, 1868; Marriages, 1856, etc., 1879, etc., 1901, 1913; Deaths, 1862; CC, June 23, 1860.

[124] OAC 886, no. 146; OAC 1558, no. 229; OAC 898, no. 28; OAC 970, 115; OAC 497, no. 40; MIA, Libro del Tezorero, 1755-1764, pp. 29, 46; loose papers; PJCAA, Rezoluçoems dos Sres do Mahamad, 5511-5527, 5527-5533, meetings of 19 Menahem, 5526, and 2 Hesvan, 5527; photostat of the Monsanto-De Sola ketubah, courtesy AJA; Margolinsky, nos. 24, 233; Precious Stones, pp. 430, 436.

ST. KITTS or ST. CHRISTOPHER (Brit. Antilles). Curaçoan Jews had been trading with St. Kitts since 1713. Abraham Melado, who had a brother in Curaçao, lived there in 1732. Joseph Sasso sailed to SK in 1738. Sara Mendes Solas and Joseph Nunes Netto, natives of SK, married in Curaçao, the former in 1756 and the latter in 1763. Abraham Abendanone was born in SK in 1747 and died in St. Eustatius in 1792. Gracia de Leon, who was born in SK in 1767, married Benjamin Lindo in St. Eustatius in 1791, dwelled for a long while in St. Thomas and died a widow in Curaçao in 1825. Zippora de Leon, born in SK, married in St. Eustatius in 1787. Mary Ann and Gratia Abendanone, who were born in SK in 1772 and 1774, respectively, married in St. Eustatius in 1792.[125]

ST. LOUIS, see French Santo Domingo.

ST. THOMAS (formerly Danish West Indies). Curaçoan Jews had been trading with St. Thomas since 1713 and possibly earlier. Jacob Gaon's wife Esther Marchena left Curaçao for ST in 1722. Manuel Vaz Nunes and Juda Obediente of ST owed monies in 1722 to Joseph Fidanque of Curaçao. Moses Motta resided there in 1741. Curaçoan Jewish merchants who settled there counted among them Abraham Rosetto in 1743, Joseph Sasso in 1747 and Jacob de Leon in 1750. Esther de Moses Motta and Benjamin Motta, natives of ST, married in Curaçao in 1764 and 1768, respectively. Captain Abraham de Salomon L. Maduro became a citizen of St. Thomas in 1747 and was thereby exempted from paying the tax imposed on captains manning vessels of foreign registry. He entered Curaçao with naturalization papers of ST. In 1782 during the American War of Independence, some Curaçoan merchants purchased sailing vessels registered in ST. Isaac de Marchena lived in ST in 1782. Mosseh Rodrigues da Costa of Curaçao went insane in 1785 from the shock of losing his huge fortune in ST. His creditors were paid 30% on their claims. During the Napoleonic wars, and especially in 1797, Curaçao did a flourishing trade with ST. One Gaspar David Henriquez invested over 150,000 pezos in St. Thomas in 1797. Salomon de Abraham Curiel, captain of the *Christina*, lived there in 1801. That year Ester de Isaac Senior of Curaçao wished to leave for ST with her six daughters. In 1803 the following Curaçoan Jews resided in ST: Moses Henriquez Juliao, Jacob M. Monsanto, Isaac Monsanto, Benjamin de Mordechay Motta, Aron Gabay Henriquez, Samuel de Josiau de Casseres, David Semah Valensa and Jacob de Neyra. The Jewish community of ST then numbered 22 families. In 1819 its officers were Moses d'Azevedo, president; Levy Fils aîné, vice president; David Pardo, treasurer. That year Meza & Delvalle of Curaçao had business dealings in ST.

Between 1796 and 1833 Congregation Mikvé Israel of Curaçao contributed funds for the construction of the St. Thomas synagogues.[126] The cantors who

---

[125] WICA 206, p. 13; MIA, loose papers; OAC 846, nos. 6, 10; OAC 1555, y. 1756; OAC 888, no. 141; Old Archives St. Eustatius, no. 245; see appendix 24, B and C.

[126] The synagogue burned down in 1804, was rebuilt in 1812 and made way for a larger one in 1823. Fire destroyed it in 1831 and another was constructed in 1833.

served this community between 1824 and 1890 were either natives or residents of Curaçao: Jeosuah Piza, Abraham Jesurun Pinto, Samuel Levy Maduro Jr., Moseh Levy Maduro and David de Isaac Cardoze. St. Thomas had two Jewish congregations in 1840: that of the German Jews (Ashkenazis) and the other of the Portuguese Jews. B. C. Carion was rabbi of the Portuguese community. He favored religious reforms, but met with the opposition of the orthodox element. The community council of 1842 was composed of A. Wolff, president; P. Isaacson, vice president, and J. C. d'Azevedo, treasurer. In 1851 these offices were filled by J. H. Osorio, P. Isaacson and P. H. Simmonds. In 1858 Jacob Mendes Monsanto was vice president and B. Luria treasurer. In 1871 Salomon L. Maduro was president and Benjamin Delvalle one of the parnassim.

The cholera epidemic of 1853 which wiped out 1,500 of a population of 13,666 and the devastating earthquake of November 18, 1867, caused several Jewish families to return to Curaçao or to migrate to Panama.[127] Curaçoan Jews account for almost a sixth of the 299 tombstones in the Jewish cemetery of St. Thomas copied by Margolinsky.

SAN JOSE (Costa Rica). The late Milton Haim de Samuel L. Maduro, an ex-president of Congregation Mikvé Israel of Curaçao, was born in San José in 1898. Isaac David Sasso officiated as hazzan at a marriage in 1909. The Curaçoan group has maintained itself to this day.[128]

SANTA CRUS, see St. Kitts.

SANTA MARTA (Col.). Surprising as it may seem, a small Jewish settlement existed in Santa Marta at the end of the 17th century (pp. 82-83). Moses de Abraham Gonzales, born in SM, married in Curaçao in 1762. The Pinedos did business with this city since 1785 and probably before then. David Morales and Abraham Garcia had business interests in SM in 1783. Isaac (a.k.a. Joachim) Sasso traded with this city in 1783. As there was no Jewish cemetery, the deceased were taken to Curaçao for burial. Josiau Dovale, who passed away in 1844, was interred in Santa Marta's Catholic cemetery. This aroused much comment among the Curaçoan Jews and spurred them to found their cemetery that year. In 1865 they contributed 300 florins toward the construction of

---

[127] WICA 206, p. 13; OAC 797, no. 61, July 27, 1722; OAC 847, no. 66; OAC 850, no. 182; OAC 847, no. 106; OAC 853, nos. 246-47; OAC 891, no. 199; OAC 904, Oct. 16, 1768; OAC 862, no. 256; OAC 872, no. 65; OAC 959, no. 480; OAC 140, no. 55; OAC 143, nos. 51, 53; OAC 1105, no. 15; PJCAA, bundle; Lopez Penha Chronicle in manuscript; Archives of the Penha Beth Din in this author's possession; MIA, Ket. VIII, nos. 60, 122; CC, Feb. 24, 1827; CC, Nov. 7, 1840 — article by Carion; CC, May 29, 1841 — reply to Carion by the rabbi of Ancona; St. Thomas Courant, Jan. 15, 1842 — article by Carion; CC, March 5, 1842, and Jan. 28, 1854; CGA, Marriages, 1863, 1864, no. 72, 1867, no. 59; Marriage Documents, 1871; Records in AJA. See above, p. 357, regarding Haham Chumaceiro's visit to St. Thomas and St. Thomas Rabbi Meyer's return visit to Curaçao, p. 357.

[128] MIA, Ket. XI, no. 70; CGA, Marriages, 1890, 1911, 1930, 1932.

Temple Emanu-El in Curaçao. D. H. Senior was the Dutch Vice Consul at Santa Marta[129] in 1873.

SANTO DOMINGO. Trade between 18th century Santo Domingo and Curaçao was active. In 1783 Joseph Obediente did a large volume of business with this island where his cousin Aron Pimentel lived. In this period Salomoh Curiel and David Gomes Casseres conducted a brisk trade between Curaçao and SD. One Isaac Monsanto was established in Puerto Plata (SD) in 1828. Other Curaçoan Jews lived in the capital city about the same time. In 1837 Santo Domingo's Jews sent 27 pesos to the Curaçao community. By 1846 there were over a hundred Jews in SD.[130] Mordechay Cohen Henriquez died there that year and was taken to Curaçao for burial. Thanks to the treaty of commerce and navigation signed by Holland and SD in 1856, the Curaçoan Jewish colony grew substantially. In 1858 David Leon was the Dutch Consul at SD; Abraham Cohen and later Jesurun, SD's Consul in Curaçao. Between 1850 and 1880 the Curaçoan Jews Senior, Lopez Penha, Marchena and Namias de Crasto were among SD's prominent families. J. A. Jesurun & Son opened a sailing line between SD and Curaçao in 1869. During this period S. E. L. Maduro had an agency in SD. Levy Baiz and Sol Senior Jr. ran a large business at SD in 1883; it was continued by Senior's son, SD's Danish Consul in 1898.

The Curaçoan group was never organized into a community. Ordinarily one of their number officiated as hazzan. Raphael Namias Curiel acted as hazzan of marriages in 1881, 1884 and 1898.[131]

TUCACAS (Ven.). Corcos[132] tells us that there was a Jewish community in Tucacas in the early 18th century and that it was helped by Congregation Mikvé Israel of Curaçao.

VALENCIA (Ven.). Several Curaçoan Jewish families settled in Valencia during the 19th century. Abigail de Sola Leon died there in 1837. Isaac (Juan) de Sola published *El Patriota* in V. about that time. The frequent political upheavals forced the Jews to leave.[133]

---

[129] OAC 885, April 16, 1762; OAC 64, no. 33, March 17, 1785; OAC 959, nos. 371, 375; CEOE 775, no. 110. Some thought that Dovale's burial in a Catholic cemetery meant that he had died a Catholic and for that reason they hesitated to say memorial prayers for him. The fact that a Jewish cemetery was erected that year in Santa Marta would point to his having died a Jew and having been buried where he was because there was no Jewish cemetery (MIA, Minutas del Mahamad, meeting of April 26, 1844). Also, DJRCA, Actas, no. 3, y. 1865; CGA, Marriages, 1835 and 1887; *Precious Stones*, p. 137.

[130] *The Occident*, vol. IV, 1846, p. 58.

[131] OAC 970, no. 50; CGA, Deaths, 1844, 1862; Marriages, 1829, etc., 1860, etc., 1889, etc., 1900, etc., and 1914; MIA, Ket. IX, nos. 81, 86; *ibid.*, XI, no. 52; CC, Sept. 6, Dec. 31, 1856 and Feb. 13, 1869; *Precious Stones*, p. 137; CEOE 779, no. 95; *ibid.*, 794, no. 23.

[132] Corcos, *ibid.*, p. 19.

[133] CGA, Marriage Documents, 1883.

Most of the settlements already discussed had an ephemeral existence. There are records of some isolated Curaçoan Jews in the following spots: Bogota (Col.) in 1867, 1878 and 1885;[134] Callao (Peru) in 1875;[135] Carmen (Ven.) in 1874;[136] Cinelejo (Col.) in 1878; Cúcuta in 1900; Cunaga (Col.) in 1881; Encontrados (Ven.) in 1899;[137] Juntagne (Ven.) in 1866; Nueva Grenada, i.e., Colombia, 1863; Paraguana (Ven.) about 1835; San Felipe (Ven.) in 1880, and San Salvador (C. A.) from 1912 to 1960.

[134] CGA, Transport, 1878; Marriages, 1901; *El Ensayo*, Curaçao, Dec. 10, 1885.
[135] CGA, Marriage Documents, 1875.
[136] *Ibid.*, Marriages, 1907.
[137] Corporaal, p. 386.

MARRIAGES

D R. JACOB R. MARCUS, director of the American Jewish Archives, gave so much importance to the genealogy of the old American Jewish families that he entrusted Malcolm H. Stern with the compilation and publication of those genealogies* before they were lost to posterity. For the same reason the author took great pains to compile the marriages of the Curaçoan Jews from as far back as the beginning of the 17th century up to now.

The following records were consulted for this purpose:

1. The A. M. Vaz Dias manuscript notes (at the Municipal Archives of Amsterdam) for the Portuguese Jewish marriages of the 17th century;
2. The Marriage Registers (Ketuboth) of the Portuguese Jewish Community of Amsterdam since 1673;
3. The Old Archives of Curaçao at The Hague and those dating from 1818 at Curaçao; also, the archives of the Dutch West India Company in Holland;
4. The Marriage Registers (Ketuboth) of the Mikvé Israel since 1782 and of the Emanu-El community since 1864; and
5. Many notes given to the author by the late Jossy M. L. Maduro.

The mixed marriages have been deliberately omitted, especially since assimilation during the past few years has reached alarming proportions in Curaçao.

In the early years of the community, a girl could not marry without a dowry. Exhaustive investigations were made to unearth those dowries. Most of them were culled from notarial records of antenuptial agreements, wills and the distribution of decedents' estates. Others were obtained from court records of lawsuits, and also from the Ketuboth Registers of the Mikvé Israel community from February 29, 1782 to 1863. Many of the dowries given since 1817 were taken from the Register of Matrimonial Conditions located at the Department of Justice in Curaçao.

Thanks to these dowries we can trace the economic development of the families. For example, a family who settled a modest dowry of 200 pesos on their daughter in 1813, reached to give the smashing record of 513,365.41 florins 120 years later.

In order to save space, the marriages of the daughters have been omitted. The bride's full name appears under the family of her husband, and at the foot

* Malcolm H. Stern, *Americans of Jewish Descent* (Cincinnati: Hebrew Union College Press, 1960), pp. 307, in folio — an important book for every old American Jewish family.

of every family there is a cross-reference to the families of all the women married into it. However, in the few instances where a daughter is the only representative of her family, her name appears in the bridegroom's column.

From time to time we have listed the children of a couple whose family still exists in Curaçao or Panama in order to make it easier for one to determine his genealogy. Other genealogical material of the families is available in our *Precious Stones of the Jews of Curaçao* (biographies, pp. 143-488; catalogue, pp. 495-548).

ABADY

Marriage Date	Bridegroom	Bride	
May 21, 1955	Joseph de Salvador y Husney	Margot de David Lucy y Gamus	
Nov. 15, 1964	Maurice Abm de Aron y Aboud	Blima de Herbert Lobel y Leah Hleap	
Aug. 10, 1965	Victor de Aron y Aboud	Viviane de Ezra Laniado y Victoria Sendler	Married in Italy

ABARBANEL, see Abravanel.

ABAS, see Curiel, Ricardo.

ABENATAR

Marriage Date	Bridegroom	Bride	
About 1710	Jacob	Esther Pereira	
1746	David de [Jacob ?]	Sarah de Abm Lz da Fonseca y Jn Henriquez	1,180 fls. plus
1746	Isaac de [Jacob ?]	Abigail de Abm Lz da Fonseca y Jn Henriquez	
March 4, 1753	Manuel de [Jacob ?] Melo	Esther de Is Hm Calvo y L. Maduro	
March 12, 1775	Jacob de Is y [Lz da Fonseca ?]	Ribca de Saml Sº L. Maduro y Keizer	
Sept. 22, 1776	Jacob Jr. de Imanuel	Gracia de Benj Vaz Faro y A. Correa	
Before 1782	Jacob Jr.	Simha Vaz Faro	
„ 1783	Jacob de Isaac	Clara Levy Maduro	
May 31, 1795	Jacob Jr. de Imanuel, widower	Violanta de Gl Ml aLevy y Belmonte	1,249 : 4 pesos
Nov. 25, 1804	Imanuel de Jb Imanuel y aLevy	Abigail de Jb Is Abenatar y L. Maduro	2,200 pesos
About 1830	Isaac (of Coro)	Jochebed Levy Maduro	
About 1840 (?)	Isaac de Emanuel	Ribca de Abm L. Maduro y Athias Robles	

843

Marriage Date	Bridegroom	Bride	Dowry and/or Remarks
See allied families:	Curiel, Lopez Fonseca, Hoheb, Levy Maduro, Monsanto, Pardo.		
	ABENDANA, see Alvares Correa, Piza.		
	ABENDANON, see Julien.		
	ABEN DENAN, see Cohen Peixotto.		

ABEN HABIB

Marriage Date	Bridegroom	Bride	Dowry and/or Remarks
Jan. 10, 1762	Samuel	Sarah de Daniel Israel RICARDO y ABAZ	
	ABENSUR, see Cohen Peixotto.		

ABOAB

Marriage Date	Bridegroom	Bride	Dowry and/or Remarks
Before 1729	Jeosuah	Rachel NETTO	
June 28, 1736	Abraham	Sarah PRETTO, widow of Abm de MEZA	
Before 1743	Samuel	Lea	
„ 1743	Moses	Sarah	
„ 1746	Moses	Ribca COHEN HENRIQUEZ	
„ 1761	Isaac	Esther NETTO	
„ 1769	Isaac	Esther LETOB	
Feb. 23, 1794	Moses Jr. de Samuel	Sarah de Abm Michael ROIZ MENDES y CAMPOS PEREIRA	
See allied families:	Gomez, Cohen Henriquez, Naar, Cohen Peixotto, Carillo Saldaña, Rodrigues, Touro.		
	SEMAH ABOAB, see Ricardo, Senior.		
	ABRAHAMS, see Eisenburg.		

ABRAVANEL

Marriage Date	Bridegroom	Bride	Dowry and/or Remarks
1746	Isaac ABARBANEL	Abigail MONSANTO	

844

AELION

| Sept. 30, 1759 | Moses de Jacob | Sarah de Abm Monis y Moron Telles |
| July 20, 1766 | Aron de Jacob | Hanah de Daniel Israel Ricardo y Abas |

D'AGUILAR

| Nov. 12, 1797 | Joseph de Mordechay | Sarah de Abm Lz Salzedo y Nunes Redondo |

ALASCAR

| Dec. 10, 1784 | Salomon de Baruch | Judith de Samuel Israel Ricardo | Separated |

ALBERGA

| About 1890 | Abraham Samuel | Helene D'Fonseca |
| June 9, 1912 | Arthur de Abm Samuel y Fonseca | Mathilde Judith de Abm de Vries y Rusten |

Jesurun Alcobasa, see Ricardo.
Aletrino, see Delvalle, De Leon.

D'ALMEIDA

| Before 1844 | Jacob Edward de Abraham | Esther de David Pretto y Pereira |

Alpron, see Naar.

ALVA

| July 3, 1721 | Moseh Haim de Jeudah | Ribca de Ishac Gomes Silva | 400 fls.; mar. in A'dam |

Marriage Date	Bridegroom	Bride	Dowry and/or Remarks
		ALVA (cont.)	
Aug. 8, 1756	Jeudah de Moseh y GOMES SILVA	Hanah de Isaac (?) CALVO y L. MADURO (?)	
See allied families:	Calvo, Gomes Casseres, Dovale, Dias Guadalupe, Molina Monsanto, Rodriguez Nunes.		
	ALVARES, see Lopez Henriquez.		
	HENRIQUEZ ALVARES, see Henriquez Fereira, Pinto.		
	JESURUN ALVARES, see Pinto.		
	LOPES ALVIN, see Vaz Martines.		
	AMADIOS, see Ricardo.		
		AMIEL	
June 15, 1963	Maurice de Victor y Victoria COHEN	Edith Esther de Amilcar NAMIAS DE CRASTO y CURIEL	
		AMON	
June 28, 1919	Jacob de Nissim y DANON	Rose de Abm de MARCHENA y Lz PENHA	Two houses
		ANDRADE	
June 10, 1661	Mordechay	Sarah GALLAS	
1667	Ditto, widower	Rachel GALLAS	*Precious Stones*
			[= Pr. St.], p. 155
Before 1729	Abraham	Ribca de CHAVES	

264. THE OLDEST MARRIAGE CONTRACT EXTANT IN CURAÇAO, MAY 29, 1782
(SAMUEL DE CASSERES AND LEA DE ABRAHAM HENRIQUEZ MELHADO)

265. COAT OF ARMS, NAMIAS DE CRASTO (CF. PSALM 91 : 2)

266. COAT OF ARMS,
MENDES GAMA, 1767

267. COAT OF ARMS,
DA COSTA GOMEZ,
1761

268. COAT OF ARMS,
DE SOLA (PSALM 23 : 1)

	Mordechay de Jb Israel y GUADALUPE	Rachel de Isaac de CHAVES y LEVY	
Before 1730			
" 1742	Abraham	Esther CHAVES	
" 1744	Isaac Hisquiau	Rachel ULLOA	
" 1759	Jacob de Abm y CHAVES	Sarah de Mordechay ANDRADE	
" 1769	Jacob de Mordechay	Sarah de Abm ANDRADE	
Dec. 5, 1773	Isaac CALVO	Ribca de Benj Lz FONSECA [y B. LOUZADO ?]	
Before 1784	J. D. ANDRADE	Sarah DA COSTA ANDRADE	
June 5, 1796	Abm de Jb Mord Israel y ANDRADE	Clara de Ishac de Sam. L. MADURO	500 pesos

See allied families: Da Costa Andrade, Calvo, Aboab Cardozo, Alvares Correa, Dias, Lopez Fonseca, Hoheb, Motta, Santcroos.

DA COSTA ANDRADE

Before 1675	Joseph	Sarah ABOAB CARDOZO	Pr. St., pp. 200-202
" 1677	Benjamin	Luna D'OLIVEIRA	2,000 fls.; mar. in Martinique
1685	Abraham de David	Leah de David CURIEL	15,000 fls.
1694	David	Sarah de Benj DA COSTA D'ANDRADE	
1699	Benjamin, wid. of L. D'O.	Esther BARUH CARVALHO	
Before 1714	Benjamin de Joseph y ABOAB CARDOZO	Rachel de Samuel JEUDAH LEON y GAON	
" 1735	Abraham de Joseph y ABOAB CARDOZO	Ribca de Samuel JEUDAH LEON y GAON	
Feb. 22, 1747	David de Abm de Benjamin y LEON	Esther ANDRADE	
Before 1751	Jacob	Sarah GUADALUPE	
May 28, 1769	Abraham Jr. de David y ANDRADE	Gracia de Sam. Jb JEUDAH LEON y A. CORREA	
Nov. 25, 1795	Moshe de David y ANDRADE	Ribca de Moshe COHEN HENRIQUEZ	1,500 pesos

Marriage Date	Bridegroom	Bride	Dowry and/or Remarks
		DA COSA ANDRADE (cont.)	
Oct. 22, 1823	David de Moshe y [Cohen Hz?]	Sarah de Mord Fidanque y Hz Fereyra	1,400 pesos
See allied families: Andrade, Athias, Carvalho, Curiel, Jesurun Henriquez, Levy Maduro, Suares.			
	Frois d'Andrade, see Frois.		
	Arari, see Cohen Henriquez, Cohen Peixotto.		
		DIAS ARIAS	
March 11, 1739	David	Gracia de Rephael Jesurun y Sasportas	£416; divorced
	Lopes Arias, see Mendes Chumaceiro.		
	Arons, see Herris.		
		ASCOLI	
About 1880	Marcus	Miriam de Salomon Sam. L. Maduro y Piza	
See Piza.			
		ATHIAS ROBLES	
Before 1744	David	Branca (Marces) [Marques]	
June 9, 1745	Ephraim de David y Branca Marques	Esther de Jacob Barzilay Robles	
March 24, 1771	Jacob Robles de Ephraim y B. Robles	Ribca de Joseph da Costa Andrade	
Feb. 25, 1781	Joseph de Ephraim y B. Robles	Esther da Costa Andrade	

Oct. 26, 1841	Jacob de Ephraim de Jacob	Rachel de Mord ABINUN DE LIMA y C. PEIXOTTO	
June 22, 1858	Jacob de Ephraim de Jacob, widower	Esther de Mordechay SASSO y JN LINDO	
Nov. 23, 1864	Ephraim de Jacob y ABINUN DE LIMA	Rebecca de Isaac L. MADURO	
Before 1866	Mordechay (Mauricio) de Jb y ABINUN DE LIMA	Esther de Isaac SASSO	
About 1885	Abraham de Jacob y SASSO	Alice SASSO	
„ 1890	Joseph de Jacob y SASSO	Consuelo de David de Isaac CARDOZE	
„ 1890	Elias de Jacob y SASSO	Adela SASSO	
„ 1910 (?)	Elias de Jacob y SASSO, widower	Anita LEVY	
„ 1918	Jacob Bertie de Elias y SASSO	Rachel de Daniel David DE CASTRO y FIDANQUE	

See allied families: De Castro, Delvalle, Abinun de Lima, L. Maduro, De Meza, Salas, Sasso.

PEREIRA ATHIAS

Before 1702	Moses	Rachel VAZ DE OLIVEIRA	4,000 fls.

See Calvo, Pinto.

AUBI, see Piza.

AZULAY, see Piza.

BAESSA, see Piza.

BAIZ

About 1806	Jacob (b. Bayonne, 1779; d. St. Thomas, 1857)	Lea OLIVEIRA ISIDRO
Before 1844	Isaac [de Jacob y O. ISIDRO ?]	Rachel PEREIRA
„ 1848	Abraham de Jacob y O. ISIDRO	Sarah de David NAAR y C. d'AZEVEDO

Marriage Date	Bridegroom	Bride	Dowry and/or Remarks
		BAIZ (cont.)	
Before 1854	Moses	Hermine DEBLEINE (Jewish ?)	
June 6, 1874	Jacob de Isaac y PEREIRA	Rebecca de Jb Jeosuah NAAR y HENRIQUEZ	8,000 fls.
Dec. 20, 1882	Levy de Moises y DEBLEINE	Nanette de Isaac BAIZ y PEREIRA	
Dec. 10, 1884	David de Isaac y PEREIRA	Abigail de Josias Lz HENRIQUEZ y VALENCIA	15,000 "
Aug. 28, 1889	Prospero de Isaac y PEREIRA	Julia de Benj PEREIRA BRANDAO y A. CORREA	8,000 "
Jan. 15, 1890	Henry de Isaac y PEREIRA	Emma de Murray A. CORREA y JESURUN	
Apr. 9, 1892	Daniel Moises de Isaac y PEREIRA	Rose de Moses PINEDO y A. CORREA	7,000 (?) fls.
Dec. 18, 1912	Isaac de David y LOPEZ HENRIQUEZ	Alicia de Raphael COHEN Hz y DELVALLE Hz	
June 1, 1918	Isaac Edgar de Prospero y P. BRANDAO	Lelia de Moises Bn de MARCHENA y MARCHENA	50,000 fls.
About 1918	Margot de Daniel Moises y A. CORREA	David SOBERHEIM (of New York)	
June 24, 1940	Egon David de Is y COHEN HENRIQUEZ	Olga de Julius Lz PENHA Jr. y L. MADURO	Divorced
June 10, 1946	Ditto	Blanche de Martin HALPERIN y PERLMUTTER	

See allied families: Gomes Casseres, Curiel, Da Costa Gomez, Henriquez, Levy Maduro, Henriquez Moron, Naar, Salas, Senior.

Genealogy: [Jacob = Lea ?] → Isaac = Rachel P. → David = Abigail Lz Hz → Isaac = Alicia C. Hz →
Egon David = Blanche H. → Gary, b. 1950.
MENDES BALBORDA, see Sasso.
LEVY BARRIOS, see Dias Fernandez, Nunes Redondo.

SEMAH BARRIOS

Before 1741	Samuel	Judith de Rephael JESURUN y SASPORTAS
„ 1748	Manuel	Rachel

See Henriquez Moron.

BARUCH, see Pardo.

BARZILAY, see Henriquez, Jesurun, Moreno Henriquez.

BEHAR

Apr. 19, 1960	Gabriel de Moise y COHEN	Paulette de Jacques BEHAR y Sultana PERMITCHI
May 11, 1960	Henry de Ezra Haim y BENAROYA	Caden de Moshe SARFATTI y ROMI, widow

DE LA BELLA, see Mendes de Sola.

MENDES BELISSARIO

Aug. 18, 1862	Henry	Esther de Jeosuah PIZA y SASSO

BELMONTE

1662	Abraham, a.k.a. Miguel Rz NUNES	Violanta de Isaac ERGAS, a.k.a. Sebastian DA CUNHA	
About 1698	Jacob de Abraham y ERGAS	Rachel de Abm ABOAB CARDOZO y Baruch CARVALHO	
Jan. 6, 1734	Abraham de Jb y ABOAB CARDOZO	Ribca de Jeosuah NAAR	
Before 1739	Daniel de Jacob y ABOAB CARDOZO	Jael de Raphael A. CORREA y ROIS MONSANTO	3,400 pesos

Marriage Date	Bridegroom	Bride	Dowry and/or Remarks
		BELMONTE (cont.)	
Feb. 13, 1742	Isaac de Jacob y ABOAB CARDOZO	Rachel de Raphael A. CORREA y ROIS MONSANTO	3,650 pesos
Oct. 14, 1770	Jacob de Isaac y A. CORREA	Ribca de Moses A. CORREA y SEMAH FERO	
Jan. 31, 1796	Jeosuah de Abraham y NAAR	Esther de Daniel BELMONTE y A. CORREA	2,949 : 4 ,,
See allied families: Alvares Correa, Levy, Henriquez Moron, Vaz d'Oliveira, Penso, Senior. ABENDANA BELMONTE, see Pardo.			
		BLOCH	
June 26, 1938	Isaac de Marcus Andre y LEEUW	Xenia de Jeudah ABINUN DE LIMA y COHEN HENRIQUEZ	10,000 fls. and two houses
		BENVENISTE	
Before 1744	Eliau	Hanah ABOAB DE PAZ	
June 26, 1781	Moses de Daniel Benjamin	Rachel de Joseph DE LEMOS, a.k.a. BENVENISTE	
See allied families: Lopez Fonseca, Henriquez, Lopez Henriquez. NUNES BERNAL, see Piza.			
		BONAN	
Before 1740	Joseph	Hanah de Samuel IDANHA DE CASSERES y PARDO	
See Lopez Dias.			

852

RODRIGUEZ BRANDAM

| Before 1775 | Jacob | Hanah de Jacob de Chaves y Chaves | |

PEREIRA BRANDAO

Date	Groom	Bride	Amount
Nov. 4, 1753	Joseph de Jacob	Leah de Elias Levy y Touro	
May 28, 1775	Jacob de Joseph y Levy	Ribca de Benj Vaz Faro y A. Correa	
Nov. 16, 1794	Joseph de Jacob y Vaz Faro	Hanah de Abm Hm Calvo y Lz Penha	400 pesos
Nov. 16, 1794	Benjamin de Jacob y Vaz Faro	Rachel de Abm Hm Calvo y Lz Penha	400 "
	(Children: Jacob, Abraham, Eliao, Joseph, Ribca, Ishac, Selomoh, Esther and Samuel)		
Oct. 23, 1822	Joseph Jr. de Benjamin y Calvo	Miriam de Moshe Eliau Penso y Suares	6,000 "
Jan. 28, 1824	Eliau de Benjamin y Calvo	Ribca de Salomoh Cohen Hz y Casseres	
June 11, 1828	Joseph Jr. de Benj y Calvo, wid.	Jael de Moshe Eliau Penso y Suares	10,670 fls.
Oct. 31, 1838	Selomoh de Benjamin y Calvo	Abigail de Abm de Meza y Athias Robles	10,000 "
June 12, 1867	Elias de José y Penso	Alcida de Mose Cohen Hz y Jesurun	32,500 "
Nov. 9, 1870	Benjamin Jr. de Joseph y Penso	Rachel de Manuel A. Correa y Jn Sasportas	8,000 "
Before 1865	Jacob de Joseph y Penso	Henriette de Samuel Bn Nones y Isacson	
Dec. 5, 1894	Sam. Benj de Jb y Nones	Hanah de Mord Cohen Hz y Jn Henriquez	10,000 "
Aug. 11, 1897	Joseph Wm de Benj y A. Correa	Sarah de Jb Benj Delvalle y Jn Henriquez	7,000 "
Jan. 5, 1902	Mauritz de Elias y Cohen Hz	Delia de Sam. A. Correa y Gomes y Casseres	10,000 "

Marriage Date	Bridegroom	Bride	Dowry and/or Remarks
		PEREIRA BRANDAO (cont.)	
March 28, 1928	Frank de Mauritz y A. Correa	Sarah de Moses L. Maduro y Naar	Share in two sugar plantations in Cuba
Feb. 26, 1930	Jacob Herbert de Joseph Wm y Delvalle	Olga de Mozes Michael Pinedo y Curiel	
Nov. 1, 1936	Victor de Mauritz y A. Correa	Else de David Mord L. Maduro y Marchena	25,000 fls.
Sept. 20, 1956	George de Jacob Herbert y Pinedo	Marlene de Hector Henriquez y Salas	

See allied families: Baiz, Capriles, Gomes Casseres, Da Costa Gomez, Cohen Henriquez, Moreno Henriquez, Levy Maduro, Naar, Nones, Suares, Valaencia.

Genealogy:
Joseph = Leah L. → Jacob = Ribca V. F. → Benjamin = Rachel C. →
Miriam P. ↘
Joseph = Jael P.   Elias = Alcida C. H. → Mauritz = Delia A. C. →

Victor = Else L. M. → Victor Sergio.

		BRANDON	
About 1882	David	Judit de Salomon Sam. L. Maduro y Piza	

See allied families: Hoheb, Levy Maduro, Namias de Crasto.
Fonseca Brandon, see Mendes da Costa.
Bravo, see L. Maduro.
Brichta, see Valencia.
Burgos, see Suares.

		SOUZA BRITTO	
1746	David, a.k.a. Manuel	Lea Ulloa	

	Moses	Rachel de Aron Israel
		Santcroos y Moreno Hz
Mar. 24, 1771	Gabriel	Clara de Mordechay ABINUN DE LIMA y HALAS

See Salas.

BUENO

Before 1717	Abraham de Isaac	Sarah PINTO

BUENO VIVAS

About 1678	David	Rachel
Before 1713	David	Esther
„ 1741	Isaac	Esther TOURO
Nov. 13, 1746	Abraham de David	Sarah Baruch LOUZADA
Nov. 9, 1749	David de Isaac	Rachel de Abraham HENRIQUEZ JULIAO
April 15, 1753	Joseph	Batsebah ULLOA
Sept. 23, 1798	Abraham de David	Jeudith de Aron MENDES SOLA y GOMEZ	982 pesos

See allied families: Calvo, De Castro, L. Maduro, Leon Nunes, Pessoa, Touro.

CALVO

About 1691	Jacob	Esther
Before 1712	Mordechay	Esther d'ANDRADE
„ 1726	Isaac Haim	Hanah Ribca (?) de Moses NUNES (REDONDO) y L. MADURO
June 19, 1729	Ditto, widower	Sarah de Samuel L. MADURO y VIEYRA
April 18, 1742	Jacob de Mordechay [y ANDRADE ?]	Esther de Moses PEREIRA ATHIAS y VAZ DE OLIVEIRA

CALVO (cont.)

Marriage Date	Bridegroom	Bride	Dowry and/or Remarks
Oct. 16, 1759	Mordechay de Isaac Haim y L. MADURO	Esther de Isaac Samuel L. MADURO y L. MADURO	
Before 1760	Salomo Haim [de Isaac Haim y L. MADURO ?]	Sarah LEVY MADURO	500 pesos
„ 1761	Samuel [de Isaac Haim y L. MADURO ?]	Esther de Jacob L. MADURO	
April 12, 1761	Salomo Haim [de Is Hm y L. MADURO ?], widower	Simha de Moses L. MADURO	
Before 1764	Abraham de Isaac Haim y L. MADURO	Simha de Moseh ALVA y GOMES SILVA	
Sept. 1, 1765	Ditto, widower	Esther de Abraham LOPEZ PENHA y Rz MIRANDA	
Before 1766	Mordechay de Jb de Mord y Pa. ATHIAS	Clara TABOADA	
Dec. 5, 1784	Ishac de Salomo Haim y L. MADURO	Rachel de Michael Elias JEUDAH LEON y HENRIQUEZ	6,600 „
Nov. 11, 1788	Jacob de Mordechay Haim	Ribca de David BUENO VIVAS y Hz JULIAO	1,000 „

See allied families: Abenatar, Alva, Pereira Brandao, Abinun de Lima, Levy Maduro, De Mercado, Senior, Taboada.

RODRIGUEZ CAMPOS, a.k.a. LOPEZ PENHA

Marriage Date	Bridegroom	Bride	Dowry and/or Remarks
Feb. 12, 1749	Jacob, born in Lisbon	Rachel, a.k.a. Kiña, de Joseph FIDANQUE y JN HENRIQUEZ	1,500 (?) pesos

ISRAEL CAMPANAL, see Sasso.

CAPRILES

Date	Groom	Bride	Dowry
Oct. 28, 1784	Dr. Joseph, widower	Rachel de Aron Henriquez Moron y Penso	
Jan. 21, 1795	Isaac de Joseph y Hz Moron	Sarah de Haim David Dovale y Alva	7,400 "
March 21, 1795	David de Joseph y Hz Moron	Sarah de Is Abm Hz Fereyra y Hz Moron	1,300 "
Nov. 2, 1825	Joseph de Isaac y Dovale	Batsebah de Mord Ricardo y Frois Andrade	4,005 "
June 22, 1831	Abraham de Isaac y Dovale	Rachel de Mord Ricardo y Frois Andrade	4,860 fls.
	(Children: Isaac, Mordechay, Joseph Jr., Moses, Benjamin Jr., Elias, Dr. David R., Salomon, Sarah, Jacob, Aron and Daniel)		
Sept. 7, 1859	Dr. David Ricardo de Abm y Ricardo	Hanah de Abm Jb Senior y Senior	3,500 fls.
Oct. 19, 1859	Menasse de Joseph y Ricardo	Sarah Cecilia de Abm Senior y Calvo	4,000 pesos
	(They married in Puerto Cabello. Haham Chumaceiro did not record this marriage in the Ketuboth Register since they married on Hosha'na Rabbah. Menasse Capriles is the only member of his family buried in the Jewish Reform Cemetery.) See illus. 258, 283.		
Aug. 28, 1861	Mordechay de Abraham y Ricardo	Esther de Abm Jacob Senior y Senior	3,500 fls.
June 13, 1866	Joseph Jr. de Abm y Ricardo	Rachel de Gabriel Pinedo y Delvalle	9,000 "
Sept. 1, 1875	Elias de Jose y Ricardo	Sarah Maria de Abm Meyerston y Abinun de Lima	
Dec. 4, 1889	Abraham de David Ricardo y Senior	Rachel de Abm Ms Chumaceiro y Lz Henriquez	
June 24, 1891	Jose de Menasse y Senior	Ana de Mordechay Capriles y Senior	
March 15, 1891	Abraham Senior de Menasse y Senior	Enriquetta de David Ricardo y de Jongh	10,000 "

CAPRILES (cont.)

Marriage Date	Bridegroom	Bride	Dowry and/or Remarks
Nov. 12, 1902	Jacob de David Ricardo y SENIOR	Rebecca de Julius Lopez PENHA y NAAR	33,000 fls.
March 27, 1904	Manrique de David Ricardo y SENIOR	Amy de Gad GOMES CASSERES y NAAR, illus. 272	
Oct. 21, 1905	Julio Cesar de Menasse y SENIOR	Alicia de Elias CAPRILES y MEYERSTON	
Feb. 7, 1914	Manases de Elias y MEYERSTON	Deborah de David Lz FONSECA y MORENO	
Nov. 9, 1927	Isaac Haim de Abm y Ms CHUMACEIRO	Hilda de Alvares Correa PINEDO y MORENO	4,000 „
Nov. 14, 1928	Donald de Manrique y Gs CASSERES	Ena de Jacob CAPRILES y Lz PENHA	4,000 „ ; divorced
April 10, 1929	Dick de Jacob y Lz PENHA	Hanah Helène de Jb Wm P. BRANDAO y DELVALLE	5,000 „
July 16, 1939	Edwin de Manrique y Gs CASSERES	Florence HALPERN	Divorced
July 20, 1940	Jossy de Abraham y Ms CHUMACEIRO	Nora de Moises de MARCHENA y SALAS	
Feb. 2, 1950	Donald de Manrique y Gs CASSERES, divorcé	Ruth Senior de Benj. S. DELVALLE y MADURO LOPEZ (divorced L. Maduro)	Divorced
March 4, 1951	Fred de Manrique y Gs CASSERES	Magda de †Horacio Eugenio LEYBA y PINEDO*	Divorced
Aug. 9, 1958	Lionel de Isaac Haim y PINEDO	Diane Monique de Max Frederic [COHEN] Hz y A. CORREA	

* Since the bride's mother was Jewish, the religious marriage was recorded.

858

CASSERES, divorcé   COHEN Hz

July 10, 1967   Josette de Jossy y MARCHENA   Louis Harvey de Jacob GOLDISH y GLICK

See allied families: Cardoze, Charlonis, Mendes Chumaceiro, Delvalle, Dovale, Da Costa Gomez, Jesurun, Levisson, Levy Maduro, Marchena, Meyerston, Moreno Henriquez, Ricardo, Spritzer, Nunes Vaz.

Genealogy:

Dr. Joseph = Esther U. / Rachel H.M. ↗   Isaac = Sarah D. → Abraham = Rachel R. → Dr. David R. =

Hanah S. → Abraham = Rachel M. C. → Isaac H. = Hilda P. → Lionel = Diane Monique C. H.

CARDOZE

Sept. 1, 1765	David Pereira	Abigail de Abm Lopez PENHA y Rz MIRANDA	
Dec. 24, 1786	Moise de David y Lz PENHA	Esther de Joseph CAPRILES y ULIEL	6,500 pesos

(Moise Cardozo modified his name from Cardozo to Cardoze. Haham Da Fonseca did not recognize this modification and inscribed the name in the Ketuboth Register as Cardozo.)

Dec. 6, 1809	David de Moise y CAPRILES	Rachel de Moshe Ms MONSANTO y Lz PENHA	3,000 pesos
May 15, 1814	Isaac de Moise y CAPRILES	Batsebah de Mord FIDANQUE y Hz FEREYRA	13,500 patacas
Aug. 25, 1847	Gabriel de Isaac y FIDANQUE	Batsebah de Moseh David de CASTRO y BUENO VIVAS	1,000 fls.
May 19, 1850	David de Isaac y FIDANQUE	Rachel de Rephael de MEZA y de CASTRO	Mar. in St. Thomas
Before 1873	Mordechay Morris de Gabriel y CASTRO	Esther FINSI	
June 6, 1883	Moises de Gabriel y CASTRO	Hanah de David Moses de CASTRO y HENRIQUEZ	6,000 fls.
June 19, 1889	Jacob de Gabriel y CASTRO	Arabella (Abigail) de Murray PINEDO y A. CORREA	2,000 „

859

Marriage Date	Bridegroom	Bride	Dowry and/or Remarks
		CARDOZE (cont.)	
About 1900	Ignacio (Isaac ?)	Rosa SIMONSON	
March 14, 1907	David de Morris Mord y FINSI	Rebecca de Benj CURIEL y NAMIAS de CRASTO	

See allied families: Fisher, Cohen Henriquez, Mendes Monsanto, Osorio.

Genealogy: David = Abigail L. P. → Moise = Esther C. → Isaac = Batsebah F. → Gabriel = Batsebah C. →
Morris = Esther F. → David = Rebecca C. → Morris.

		CARDOZO	
Before 1733	Dr. Isaac	Rachel de Isaac TOURO y ULLOA	
1761	Dr. Isaac de Isaac y TOURO	Rachel Abigael de Bn MORENO Hz y TOURO	
June 2, 1771	Jacob, b. Bordeaux	Sarah LOPEZ RAPHAEL	

See allied families: Cardoze, Da Costa, Moreno Henriquez, Namias de Crasto, Touro.

		ABOAB CARDOZO	
About 1678	Abraham	Abigail Baruch CARVALHO	Pr. St., pp. 167-68
" 1683	Daniel	Rahel	Cat. 1203-1204
Before 1716	Daniel	Esther TOURO	
" 1730	Ditto, widower	Ribca DE MARCHENA, widow of A. de Marchena	
" 1730	Abraham de Daniel	Leah GAON	
About 1734	Ditto, widower	Rachel GAON	
Before 1737	Abraham	Abigail (Cat. 1168)	
Aug. 9, 1746	Abraham de Daniel, widower	Deborah de Moseh NUNES (REDONDO) y I. MADURO	

Before 1748	David	Ribca de Jacob ANDRADE
„ 1759	Daniel	Sarah de Jacob GUADALUPE D'ANDRADE
April 4, 1762	Jacob	Ribca de Manuel LEVY y BELMONTE
About 1782	Jacob	Ribca de Abraham NAAR y TOURO

See allied families: Andrade, Belmonte, Da Costa, Rodriguez da Costa, Levy Maduro, Nunes Redondo, Ulloa, Valencia, Senior.

ATHIAS CARDOZO, see Moreno Henriquez.

DA COSTA CARDOZO, see Penso.

JESSURUN CARDOZO, see Linder.

LOPEZ CARDOZO, see Mendes Chumaceiro.

MENDES CARDOZO, see Mendes.

PEREIRA CARDOZO, see Cardoze.

UZIEL CARDOZO

Before 1732	David Jr.	Esther de Abm Israel ULLOA
Dec. 16, 1743	Ditto, widower	Judith ULLOA
June 12, 1752	Aron de David y ULLOA	Ribca DIAZ COUTINHO
Dec. 27, 1801	Isaac de Aron y DIAZ COUTINHO	Ribca de David Ishac HENRIQUEZ

(The bridegroom signed his Ketubah as "Isaac Cardozo," dropping "Uziel.")

See allied families: Gomes Casseres, Rodriguez da Costa, Moreno Henriquez.

CARILHO

About 1681	David	Esther	
Before 1766	David, resident of Surinam	Ribca de Benjamin HENRIQUEZ MORON	22,000 fls.; Pr. St., p. 164

See allied families: Lopes Dias, Jesurun Henriquez, Marchena, Pereyra, Namias de Crasto.

Marriage Date	Bridegroom	Bride	Dowry and/or Remarks
		CARVALHO	
Before 1704	Isaac	Ribca de Bn da Costa d'Andrade y Oliveira	
„ 1740	Isaac	Rosa Athias de Neyra	
„ 1741	Isaac	Rachel Athias de Neyra	

See allied families: Costa d'Andrade, Cohen Henriquez, Vaz Farro, De Medina.

Baruch Carvalho, see Aboab Cardozo, Frois, Henriquez Moron.

Marriage Date	Bridegroom	Bride	Dowry and/or Remarks
		CASSERES	
June 2, 1650	Samuel de Daniel	Miriam de Michael Spinoza y Senior	Pr. St., pp. 193-95
April 14, 1679	Daniel de Samuel y Spinoza	Judica Moreno [Henriquez ?]	3,600 fls.; divorced
About 1685	Benjamin de Samuel y Spinoza	Esther [de Eliau ?] Dovale	
Before 1721	Samuel de Benjamin y Dovale	Abigail de Saul Josiau Pardo	
Feb. 3, 1743	Ditto, widower	Rachel de David Dovale	6,000 pesos
About 1743	Benjamin Hu de Samuel y Pardo	Sarah Dovale	
Aug. 26, 1764	Josias de Samuel y Dovale	Abigael de Benjamin de Casseres y Dovale	6,500 „ ; separated
March 24, 1771	Moses de Benjamin y Dovale	Ribca de Isaac Hz Coutinho y L. Maduro	
July 6, 1777	Salomon de Benjamin y Dovale	Sarah de Is Pinheiro de Nogueira y Hz Melhado	
May 29, 1782	Samuel de Benjamin Hu y Dovale (This is the oldest Ketubah in the MIA. See illus. 264.)	Leah de Abm Hz Melhado y Suarez	9,050 „
Nov. 22, 1782	Samuel de Josiau y Casseres	Leah de Aron Mendes de Sola y Gomez	5,350 „

270. KETUBAH, DR. ISACK GOMES CAÇERES AND
RIVKA GOMES DE CAÇERES, SIGNED ALSO BY
HAHAM ABOAB, 1690, PAGE 417

269. KETUBAH, ABRAHAM ISAAC DE MARCHENA AND
SARAH MORDECHAY DE CRASTO, SIGNED ALSO BY
HAHAM ABOAB, AMSTERDAM, 1682

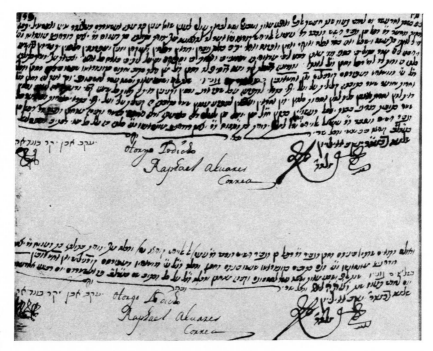

271. KETUBAH, RAPHAEL MANUEL ALVARES CORREA AND JUDITH ISAAC RODRIGUEZ
MONSANTO, SIGNED ALSO BY HAHAM AELYON, AMSTERDAM, 1716

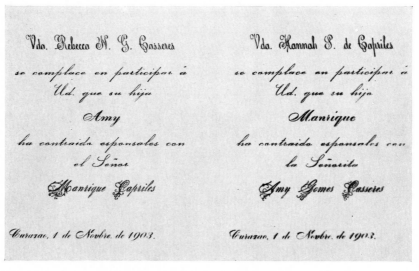

272. ENGAGEMENT, AMY GOMES CASSERES TO MANRIQUE CAPRILES, CURAÇAO, 1903

Date	Name	Spouse	Notes
March 6, 1816	Benjamin de Selomoh y PINHEIRO DE NOGUEIRA	Sarah de Sam. de CASSERES y Hz MELHADO	4,000 "
Sept. 11, 1816	Benjamin de Samuel y Hz MELHADO	Rebecca de Daniel Lz PENHA y Lz PENHA	4,000 "
Jan. 28, 1847	Samuel de Benjamin y Lz PENHA	Jeudith de Samuel DA COSTA GOMEZ y PINEDO	4,000 fls.
Feb. 15, 1849	Benjamin de Benj Sam. y Lz PENHA	Sarah (Sally) de Abm Hm SENIOR y COHEN Hz	4,000 "

See allied families: Idanha de Casseres, Alvares Correa, Curiel, Lopez Fonseca, Henriquez, Cohen Henriquez, Lopez Henriquez, De Mercado, Piza, Senior.

Genealogy:

Samuel = Miriam S. → Benjamin = Esther D. → Samuel = Abigail P. / Rachel D. → Benjamin = Sarah D. →

Samuel = Leah H. M. → Benjamin = Ribca L. P. → Benjamin = Sarah S.

GOMES CASSERES

Date	Name	Spouse	Notes
Oct. 1, 1690	Dr. Isaac	Ribca de Dr. Manuel GOMEZ DE CASSERES, illus. 270	Pr. St., pp. 185-86
About 1720	Abraham	Sarah de Dr. Isaac Gs CASSERES y Gs DE CASSERES	
" 1720	Antonio	Ana FROIS MONIS	Marranos, married and residing in Portugal
1746	Jacob de Antonio y FROIS MONIS	Leah de Moseh ALVA y GOMES SILVA	750 pesos; mar. in Curaçao
(1755) 1749	David de Antonio y FROIS MONIS	Abigail de Moseh ALVA y GOMES SILVA	750 pesos; mar. in Curaçao
Before 1756	Isaac	Sarah GOMEZ CASSERES	
" 1762	Daniel	Esther [GOMES CASSERES ?]	
Sept. 12, 1762	Jacob de David	Abigail de Daniel GOMES CASSERES	
Jan. 27, 1782	Daniel de David y ALVA	Sarah de Abm David Abm JESURUN y Lz HENRIQUEZ	1,300 pesos

863

GOMES CASSERES (cont.)

Marriage Date	Bridegroom	Bride	Dowry and/or Remarks
May 21, 1786	Abm de Rephael, b. Portugal	Rachel de Aron Uziel Cardozo y Dias Coutinho	500 pesos
Oct. 11, 1801	David de Daniel David y Jesurun	Rachel de Jb de David Jesurun y Crasto	1,000 "
Sept. 19, 1821	Ditto, widower	Ribca de Joseph Jb Pereira Brandao y Calvo	
	(This marriage is not recorded in the Ketuboth Register of Mikvé Israel since it took place during the Piza affair, Chapter XV.)		
April 6, 1851	Jose de David y Pereira Brandao	Dilia Deborah de Bn S. Delvalle y Castro	
	(Children: Rebecca, David, Benjamin Delvalle, Abraham Brandao, Judith, Esther, Daniel, Sol and Dilia)		
Nov. 25, 1863	Elias de David y Pereira Brandao	Rachel de Jacob Jesurun y Lopez Penha	
April 17, 1872	Jeosuah de David y Pereira Brandao	Abigail Amelia de Moses A. Jesurun y Senior	4,000 fls.
Dec. 17, 1873	José de David y Pereira Brandao, widower	Rachel de Eliao Pereira Brandao y Cohen Hz	1,500 "
June 20, 1877	Gad de David y Pereira Brandao	Ribca de Jeosuah Jr. de Abm Naar y P. Brandao	
July 12, 1879	Isaac de David y Pereira Brandao	Rachel de Jeosuah Jr. de Abm Naar y P. Brandao	
June 8, 1892	Daniel de Joseph y Delvalle	Silvia Beatrice de Abm Salomon da Costa	
Aug. 17, 1904	Gabriel de Gad y Naar	Angela de Jacob Baiz y Naar	25,000 (?) fls.
Sept. 26, 1912	Benjamin de Gad y Naar	Sefora de Isaac Cohen Hz y Jesurun Hz	6,000 fls.

June 25, 1945	Charles de Benjamin y COHEN Hz	Ruth de Arnold Jb SALAS y DE JONGH	
See allied families:	Capriles, Castro, Mendes de Castro, Mendes Chumaceiro, Alvares Correa, Jesurun, De Leon, Naar, Lopes Pereira, Jesurun Sasportas.		

Genealogy:

Antonio = Ana F. M. → David = Abigail A. → Daniel = Sarah J. → David =
Rachel J. ↗ Gad = Ribca N. → Benjamin = Sefora C. H. → Charles = Ruth S. →
Ribca P. B. ↗
Ronald, born 1946.

IDANHA DE CASSERES

Jan. 11, 1675	Isaac de Abraham (without "Casseres")	Hanah de Samuel Danl de CASSERES y SPINOZA	
About 1717	Samuel de Isaac y CASSERES	Simha de Saul Josiau PARDO	Pr. St., pp. 325-27
Before 1746	Isaac de Samuel (without "Casseres") y PARDO	Benvenida LEDESMA	
Oct. 17, 1762	Josiau de Samuel y PARDO	Simha de Isaac Sam. IDANHA DE CASSERES y LEDESMA	
Oct. 17, 1762	Saul de Samuel y PARDO	Sarah de Moses Lz Dias y IDANHA DE CASSERES	
Dec. 27, 1801	Samuel de Rephael Saul	Ribca de David Jb Lz FONSECA y Hz FEREYRA	650 pesos
See allied families:	Bonan, Lopez Dias.		

CASTILLO

June 30, 1748	David de Ephraim	Hanah [de Benjamin y B. Hz. ?]

DE CASTRO

About 1742	Moses	Judith de Jb ATHIAS DE NEYRA y CHAVES

DE CASTRO (cont.)

Marriage Date	Bridegroom	Bride	Dowry and/or Remarks
Oct. 12, 1777	Salomo de Moses y Athias de Neyra	Ribca de David Gomes Casseres y Alva	
March 3, 1782	Jacob de Moses y Athias de Neyra	Esther de Isaac Gomez y Jesurun	
Oct. 4, 1797	David de Haim Moses y A. de Neyra	Batsebah de David Jb Senior y Fidanque	2,500 pesos
Oct. 22, 1800	Jacob de Salomo y Gomes Casseres	Rachel de Jb Jesurun Sasportas y Cohen Peixotto	4,000 "
Jan. 27, 1805	David de Salomo Hm y Gs Casseres	Rahel de Jacob de Castro y Gomez	600 "
Sept. 19, 1823	Mose Jr. de David y Senior	Hanah de Abm Hm Bueno Vivas y Mendes Sola	
July 4, 1827	David de David de Hm Moses y Senior	Esther de Moses Hz Juliao y Ms Sola (?)	
Dec. 12, 1827	David de Jacob y Gomez	Gracia de Moses Aboab Osorio y Fereira	1,333.33 fls.; they had seven children
Sept. 3, 1828	Ishac de Jacob y Gomez	Abigail de Aron Motta y Cohen Hz	
April 3, 1844	Jacob de David Moses y Senior, illus. 274	Sarah de Moses Aboab Osorio y Hz Fereyra	
Jan. 16, 1850	David de Moses y Bueno Vivas	Ribca de Jeosuah Henriquez y Pinedo	
About 1850	Moses Osorio	Esther de Sam. Salomo L. Maduro y Sasso	
1852	Jacob Osorio	Hanah de Is Hm de Sola y Hoheb	
June 20, 1855	Isaac de Moises y Bueno Vivas	Ragel de David de Castro y Osorio	
Feb. 11, 1857	Jacob de Isaac y Motta	Leah de Daniel Jn Sasportas y Gs Casseres	6,025 fls.

Date	Name	Spouse	
About 1860	David de David y Hz Juliao	Miriam de Daniel Jn Sasportas y Gs Casseres	
Jan. 23, 1884	Moises de David y Henriquez	Clara de Benj A. Correa y Henriquez	22,050 "
About 1890	Daniel de David y Hz Juliao	Rebecca de Miriam Jb Fidanque y S. Delvalle	
April 4, 1894	Jeosuah Hz de David y Henriquez	Sarah de Isaac Lz Henriquez y Lz Henriquez	
About 1894	Moses de David y Jn Sasportas	Leonor Sasso	
About 1916 (?)	David de Moses y Sasso	Vivienne de Elias Athias Robles y Sasso	
March 23, 1918	Benjamin de Jacob y Jn Sasportas	Sarah Selina de Josiau Pardo y A. Correa	8,570 "
Dec. 9, 1943	Max de Benjamin y Pardo	Elvira de Max Kywi y Andree	Divorced

See allied families: Athias Robles, Cohen, Curiel, Delvalle, Henriquez, Cohen Henriquez, Jesurun, Henriquez Juliao, Leao, De Meza, Namias de Crasto, Lopez Penha, Sasso, Senior, Serphos.

Genealogy: Moses = Judith A.N. → Jacob = Esther G. → Isaac = Abigail M. → Jacob = Leah J.S. → Benjamin = Sarah Selina P. → Max.

LOPES DE CASTRO

May 13, 1753	Daniel, b. Portugal	Abigail de Abm A. Correa y Andrade

MENDES DE CASTRO

Aug. 8, 1756	Daniel de Isaac	Esther de Daniel Gomes Casseres, b. Portugal
Sept. 12, 1762	Ditto, widower	Rachel Gomes Casseres, b. Portugal
Jan. 4, 1767	Ditto, widower	Leah de Benjamin Athias de Neyra y Naar

Marriage Date	Bridegroom	Bride	Dowry and/or Remarks
OROBIO DE CASTRO			
Sept. 26, 1721	Isaac	Esther de Abraham Hz Moron	
CALLO or CAYO			
Much before 1797	Benjamin	Ribca de Jacob Levy Maduro	
DIAS CAUTINHO			
Dec. 6, 1733	Abraham, b. Seville	Rachel de Abm Israel Ulloa	4,500 pesos
1744	Ditto, widower	Sarah de Salomo Medina y Carvalho	1,600 "
Before 1764	Abraham Jr.	Sarah de Abm Dias Cautinho y Ulloa	
See Uziel Cardozo.			
HENRIQUEZ CAUTINHO, also COTINHO			
June 17, 1682	Moseh de Isaac	Rachel de Isaac Henriquez Morao	
Before 1713	Isaac de Moseh y Hz Morao	Ribca de Jacob Dovale y Hz Morao	
" 1744	Jacob de Isaac y Dovale	Rachel	
" 1749	Abraham de Isaac y Dovale	Rachel de Benjamin Motta y Baruch Henriquez	
Nov. 8, 1750	Isaac de Isaac y Dovale	Esther de Moses Samuel Levy Maduro	
Before 1754	Moses de Isaac y Dovale	Esther Lopez	
Aug. 31, 1755	Ditto, widower	Judith de Benjamin Motta y Baruch Hz, widow of Moses Cohen Hz	3,000 "
Jan. 14, 1781	Isaac de Moses, b. Surinam	Judith de Jacob [Mendes ?] Monsanto	
Feb. 10, 1782	Isaac Sebastiaan	Sarah de Moses Jesurun	
March 24, 1782	Isaac de Moses, widower	Leah Mendes Solas	

868

See allied families: Casseres, Lopez Fonseca, Henriquez, Gabay Henriquez, Henriquez Junao, Motta, Pereira.

MENDES CAUTINHO, see Mendes de Sola.

CHARLONIS

| Oct. 29, 1890 | Andries de Daniel y Arias | Sarah de Mordechay Capriles y Senior | |

CHAVES

Before 1695	Isaac	Esther de David Levy Mendes y Brandon	1,600 fls.
About 1699	Abraham	Rachel de Manuel A. Correa y Abendana	
Before 1727	Moses de Abraham y A. Correa	Ribca de Mord Henriquez y Naar	
Jan. 6, 1734	Ditto, widower	Esther de Mord Henriquez y Naar	
About 1731	Jacob	Sarah de Isaac Chaves y Levy Mendes	
Nov. 17, 1743	Aron, b. London	Rachel de Gabriel Levy y Touro	
Before 1749	Moses de Abraham, widower	Leah de Jeosuah Henriquez y Lz Henriquez	3,500 pesos
Sept. 5, 1751	Abraham de Moses	Rachel Ribca de Jeosuah Henriquez Jr. y Lz Henriquez	

See allied families: Andrade, Rodriguez Brandam, Henriquez, Leon, Motta, Athias de Neyra.

CHILON, see Naar.

MENDES CHUMACEIRO

| Before 1669 | Abraham | ? ? | |
| Dec. 4, 1693 | Ditto, widower | Benvenida de Aron Jesurun [y Campos ?] | Mar. in Seville 400 fls.; mar. in Amsterdam |

869

MENDES CHUMACEIRO (cont.)

Marriage Date	Bridegroom	Bride	Dowry and/or Remarks
May 30, 1704	Jacob de Abraham, b. Seville	Rachel de Shemtob aCohen y Luria	800 fls.
Before 1735	Abraham de Jacob y aCohen	Leah Castro Lara	
May 7, 1764	Aron de Abm de Jacob y Castro Lara	Esther de Joseph Siprut de Gabay y Orobio Furtado	
Sept. 26, 1806	Jacob de Aron y Siprut de Gabay	Simha de Eliezer Ferrares y Cohen Belinfante	
Feb. 27, 1833	Aron de Jacob Jr. y Ferrares	Abigail de Jacob Lz Cardozo y Hz Coelho	
Sept. 3, 1862	Abraham de Aron y Lz Cardozo, illus. 154-155	Abigail de Josiau Lz Henriquez y Namias de Crasto	5,500 „
(Children: Josias Haim, Jacob, Isaac Haim, Rachel, Simha, Abigail, and Leah Leonie)			
Aug. 17, 1871	Aron de Jb Jr. y Ferrares, wid.	Sarah de Aron de Jacob Vaz Dias y Barzilay	
About 1871	Joseph Haim de Aron y Lz Cardozo	Eudora Rachel Sampson, widow of Abrahams	
April 11, 1894	Josias Haim de Abm y Lz Henriquez	Sarah de Benj de Marchena y L. Maduro	17,000 „
Sept. 4, 1895	Jacob de Abraham y Lz Henriquez	Isbelia de Elias Capriles y Meyerston	
July 4, 1896	Isaac Haim de Abm y Lz Henriquez	Abigail de Julius Lz Penha y Naar	
June 18, 1930	Benjamin de Josias y Marchena	Thelma de Isaac A. Correa y Curiel	3,200 „
March 13, 1938	Frank de Isaac Hm y Lz Penha	Estella de Benjamin Gomes Casseres y Cohen Hz	

See allied families: Capriles, Delvalle, Marchena, Salas, Santcroos, Sasso.

Genealogy: Abraham → Jacob = Rachel aC. → Abraham = Lea C.L. → Aron = Esther S.G. → Jacob

274. KETUBAH, JAHACOB DAVID DE CASTRO AND
SARAH MOSSEH ABUAB OSORIO, CURAÇAO, 1844,
IN PORTUGUESE

273. SALOMON DE ISAAC ABINUN DE LIMA,
1834–1898. AND HIS WIFE SILVIA SARAH MOSES
JESURUN, 1837–1910

276. ISAAC M. C. HENRIQUEZ AND HIS WIFE REBECCA JESURUN HENRIQUEZ, M. 1880

275. AARON M. A. CORREA, 1848-1915, NOTED MERCHANT, AND HIS WIFE ESTER JESURUN HENRIQUEZ

L.P. → Frank = Estella G.C. → Fred, b. 1951.

HENRIQUEZ COELHO

May 23, 1802 — Moses de David — Esther de Aron Mendes de Sola y Gomez

Coen, see Osorio.

COHEN

Nov. 30, 1806	Moses de Aron Moses	Batsebah de Abm Haim Fidanque y Fidanque	600 pesos
Nov. 1, 1818	Haim (Hyman) de Alexander Abraham	Sarah de Abm Pineiro de Nogueira y Lz Fonseca	3,650 "
Aug. 16, 1939	Marcos Maurits Abrahams de Andreas Salomon Abrahams y Salomons	Ena de Benjamin de Castro y Pardo	Divorced
May 10, 1932	Vitali de Gabriel y Eugenie Mandil	Vida Victoria Bitchadji	6,000 fls.

See allied families: Salas, De Sola, Mendes de Sola.

Cordova, see Lopez Henriquez.

Correa, see Fonseca.

ALVARES CORREA

| June 9, 1673 | Manuel | Sarah de Rephael Abendana and Rachel Mendes, illus. 16 | 1,103 " |
| April 10, 1691 | Ditto, widower | Esther de Isaac Febos, widow of Mord Abendana | 2,000 " |

871

ALVARES CORREA (cont.)

Marriage Date	Bridegroom	Bride	Dowry and/or Remarks
July 3, 1699	Gabriel de Manuel y ABENDANA	Rachel de Isaac FEBOS and Sarah ABARBANEL	See illus. 271
July 1, 1716	Raphael de Manuel y ABENDANA	Judith de Isaac RUIS MONSANTO	
Before 1718	Abraham de Manuel [y FEBOS ?]	Esther d'ANDRADE	
June 15, 1721	Mordechay de Manuel y ABENDANA	Sarah de Mord NAMIAS DE CRASTO y CARILHO, widow of Elias Manuel Namias de Crasto	38,000 pesos
Before 1731	Isaac de Manuel y FEBOS	Rachel ISRAEL	
" 1736	Moses de Manuel y FEBOS	Esther de Jacob SEMAH FERRO y A. CORREA	
" 1741	Manuel de Raphael y RUIS MONSANTO	Hannah de Jacob SEMAH FERRO y A. CORREA	
Sept. 5, 1745	Mordechay de Manuel y ABENDANA, widower	Abigail de Raphael A. CORREA y RUIS MONSANTO	14,000 "
Aug. 29, 1756	Manuel de Moses y SEMAH FERRO	Judith de Abm A. CORREA y ANDRADE	2,000 "
May 24, 1761	Rephael de Manuel y SEMAH FERRO	Leah de Benjamin LZ HENRIQUEZ y NAAR	
May 18, 1766	Ditto, widower	Rachel de Joseph JESURUN HZ y DA COSTA d'ANDRADE	
June 4, 1768	Manuel de Moses y SEMAH FERRO, widower	Judith de Isaac BELMONTE y A. CORREA	1,709 fls. plus
April 16, 1783	Mordechay de Iml RL y SH FERRO	Hannah de Rephael Iml A. CORREA y BELMONTE	5,000 pesos
June 16, 1790	Imanuel Hm de Rephael y JN HENRIQUEZ	Sarah de Benj COHEN HENRIQUEZ y CASTRO	7,000 "
June 21, 1795	Moises Hm de Imanuel y	Rachel de Jacob IS HZ FEREYRA [y PEREYRA ?]	700 "

Date	Husband	Wife	Amount	Notes
Sept. 3, 1806	Mordechay de Rephael y Jn Henriquez	Clara de Jacob Gl Pinedo y Marchena	4,000 "	
March 20, 1814	Imanuel de Mordechay y A. Correa	Esther de Jacob Gl Pinedo y Marchena	2,500 "	
Feb. 22, 1815	Benjamin de Imanuel Hm y Cohen Hz	Sarah de Rephael Pinedo y Penso	6,500 "	
Before 1825	Emanuel de Moshe Hm y Hz Fereyra	Judith de Abraham Julien		(Children: Rachel, Moses, Abraham, Jacob and Gabriel [CGANA, 1847, no. 165])
Oct. 20, 1830	Mordechay de Mordechay y A. Correa	Rachel de Mord Rephael A. Correa y Pinedo	1,000 fls.	(Children: Mordechay, Hana, Manuel, Clara, Esther, Julia and Haim)
June 30, 1835	Imanuel Jr. de Mordechay y Pinedo	Ribca de Daniel Jn Sasportas y Gs Casseres	3,000 "	(Children living in 1880: Jacob, Murray, Mozes Marius, Refael Raymond, Daniel, Aron, Abraham, Isaac, Clara, Miriam, Sarah, Rachel, Grace and Hanny. Two others died in infancy.)
(?)	Jacob de Mordechay y Pinedo	Rachel Pinto		According to H. M. A. Correa, p. 34
Sept. 13, 1837	Rephael de Mordechay y Pinedo	Ribca de Moises Aboab Osorio y Hz Fereyra	1,500 fls.	
Feb. 7, 1838	Mordechay Jr. de Imanuel y Pinedo	Esther de Samuel da Costa Gomez y Pinedo	1,400 "	
Aug. 18, 1840	Mordechay de Rephael y Jn Henriquez, widower	Clara de Moises Hz Juliao y Mendes de Sola	1,250 "	
June 27, 1855	Benjamin de Manuel Hm y Cohen Hz, widower, 62	Abigail de Jeosuah Rephael Henriquez y Pinedo, 21	4,000 "	
Dec. 21, 1859	Mordechay (Murray) de Manuel y Jn Sasportas	Deborah de Moises A. Jesurun y Senior	4,000 "	
May 7, 1863	Raphael (Raymond) de Iml y Jn Sasportas	Julia de Moises Rois Mendes y Jn Sasportas	2,285 "	

ALVARES CORREA (cont.)

Marriage Date	Bridegroom	Bride	Dowry and/or Remarks
About 1864	Murray (Mordechay) de Rephael y ABOAB OSORIO	Esther Ellen de Jb Hm de Moses ABOAB OSORIO y Hz FEREYRA	
Sept. 13, 1865	Manuel de Mord y DA COSTA GOMEZ	Abigail de Manuel A. CORREA y PINEDO	9,000 fls.
		(This marriage, forbidden by Jewish Law because the bride was the bridegroom's paternal aunt, is recorded in the Government Marriage Register only, since neither the Reform nor the Orthodox Jewish Community would perform it. See Herbert C. Zafren, *ibid.*, pp. 322-23; above, p. 389.)	
Aug. 22, 1866	Benjamin de Mordechay y Hz JULIAO.	Hanah de David DELVALLE Hz y PENSO	3,000 „
June 5, 1872	Marius Mozes de Manuel y JN SASPORTAS	Rebecca Rosalind de Isaac SEMAH VALENCIA y ABINUN DE LIMA	14,500 „
Jan. 15, 1873	Aron de Manuel y JN SASPORTAS	Esther de Jeosuah JN HENRIQUEZ y COHEN Hz, illus. 275	19,399 „
June 23, 1875	Samuel de Mord y DA COSTA GOMEZ	Rachel de Samuel DE CASSERES y D. C. GOMEZ	2,000 „
March 3, 1880	Jeosuah de Benjamin y HENRIQUEZ	Ricot de Isaac PINEDO Jr. y PINEDO	15,000 „
May 1, 1880	Samuel de Mord y D. C. GOMEZ, widower	Judith de Jose Gs CASSERES y DELVALLE	20,000 „
Aug. 22, 1883	Isaac de Manuel y JN SASPORTAS	Rose de Eliau M. CURIEL y A. CORREA	3,000 „
Before 1885	Alejandro	Rebecca CORTISSOZ	
Jan. 12, 1898	David de Benjamin y DELVALLE Hz	Nanette Sophie Rosine de Edward Is van LIER y SALOMON	
Sept. 10, 1902	Dr. Manuel Michael de Moses y VALENCIA	Rosabella de Jacob Elias PENSO y A CORREA	

874

About 1906   Isaac James de Marius Moses y   Carina de Jacob Elias Penso y
              VALENCIA   A. CORREA

Jan. 3, 1906 Mortimer de Samuel y CASSERES   Henriette de Moses LOPEZ DE LEAO
                                                LAGUNA y OUDS

June 20, 1912 Joseph de Samuel y Gs CASSERES   Sarah de Mord L. MADURO y   25,000 „
                                                Lz PENHA

June 3, 1925 Moises de Jeosuah y PINEDO   Rose de Morris E. CURIEL y SENIOR 10,000 „

May 22, 1926 Mortimer de Samuel y CASSERES,   Ofelia de Isaac Hz MORON y PINEDO
              widower

July 10, 1941 Moises de Jeosuah y PINEDO,   Rachel de Haim DA C. GOMEZ y
              wid.   COHEN Hz

Aug. 10, 1946 Jacob Constant de Manuel   Sybil Lois de Jeosuah L. MADURO
              Michael y PENSO   y L. MADURO

See allied families: Baiz, Belmonte, Pereira Brandao, De Castro, Lopez de Castro, Chaves, Mendes Chumaceiro,
Rodriguez da Costa, Curiel, Delvalle, Vaz Farro, Semah Ferro, Lopez da Fonseca, Cohen
Henriquez, Lopez Henriquez, Jesurun, Lansberg, Leon, Levy Maduro, Marchena, Moreno,
Motta, Naar, Namias de Crasto, Osorio, Pardo, Penso, Pinedo, Senior, De Sola, Valencia, Ulloa.

GENEALOGY

1st Branch: Manuel = Sarah A.   Raphael = Judith R.M. → Imanuel = Hanah S.F. → Rephael =
                     = Esther F. ↗

              Leah L.H.   Clara P. ↘
              Rachel J.H. ↗ Mordechay =   Manuel Jr. = Ribca J.S. → Moses = Ribca R.V.
                                Clara H.J.
              → Dr. Manuel Michael = Rosabella P. → Jacob Constant = Sybil L. M. → George Maduro,
              born 1947.

                                                    Sarah P.
2nd Branch: Rephael = Rachel J.H. → Manuel = Sarah C.H. → Benjamin =   Abigail H. → Jeosuah =

              Rose C.
              Ricot P. → Moises = Rachel d. C.G. ↗ John Henry.

875

Marriage Date	Bridegroom	Bride	Dowry and/or Remarks
		CORTISSOZ	
Before 1820	Imanuel	Rebecca Hoheb	
June 26, 1844	Joseph de Imanuel y Hoheb	Esther de Jacob Jn Pinto y Cohen Hz	
About 1881	Aron	Judith de Salomon B. Delvalle y Piza	

See allied families: Alvares Correa, Cardozo da Costa, Lobo, Senior.

CRASTO, see Gaon, Jn Henriquez, L. Maduro, Marchena, Namias de Crasto, Pinto.

Marriage Date	Bridegroom	Bride	Dowry and/or Remarks
		DA COSTA	
Before 1702	Dr. Ishac	Ribca Cardoso	Pr. St., p. 233
„ 1828	Jacob	Esther de Isaac Gomez	

See allied families: Henriquez Moron, Ricardo.

Marriage Date	Bridegroom	Bride	Dowry and/or Remarks
		CARDOZO DA COSTA	
Oct. 4, 1778	Abraham, b. England	Esther de Jacob de David Suares	
July 16, 1780	Ditto, widower	Sarah de Jacob de David Suares	
Feb. 19, 1809	Daniel de Abraham y Suares	Jeudith de Eliau Haim Sasso	
Aug. 24, 1884	Daniel de Abraham y Rodriguez	Sarah de Jose Cortissoz	

See allied families: De Meza, Rodriguez, Salas, Sasso.

Marriage Date	Bridegroom	Bride	Dowry and/or Remarks
		MENDES DA COSTA	
Before 1827	Obadia de Hananel y Lindo	Eliza de Jacob da Fonseca Brandon y Mendes da Costa	

See allied families: Cohen Peixotto, Lopez Penha, De Sola, Senior.

Nunes da Costa see Baruch Louzada, De Sola.

RODRIGUEZ DA COSTA

May 4, 1750	Isaac de Mosse y CAPADOCE	Sarah de Mord A. CORREA y NAMIAS DE CRASTO	40,000 pesos
Before 1781	David Rois	Rachel de Rephael UZIEL CARDOZO	
Jan. 8, 1786	Mordechay de Ishac Haim y A. CORREA	Sarah de Jb David JESURUN y NAMIAS DE CRASTO	3,150 "

See allied families: Henriquez Fereira, Jesurun Lobo, Pinedo.

TELLES DA COSTA, see Da Costa Gomez.

VAZ DA COSTA

| May, 1753 | Joseph | Judith de David GARCIA DE PAZ | |

See Garcia, Sasso.

RODRIGUEZ CUNHA

| Mar. 16, 1742 | Abraham, b. Bordeaux | Judith LOPEZ, b. Amsterdam | |

See Semah Ferro, Levy Maduro.

CURIEL

Before 1587 About 1617	Dr. Jeronimo Nunes Ramirez Jacob CURIEL de Jeronimo y DA FONSECA	Maria de Dr. Lopo DA FONSECA Leah ABAS	Mar. in Portugal Pr. St., pp. 284-88
Before 1662	Salomon de Jacob y ABAS	Sarah (?)	
May 14, 1685	Abraham de Salomon de Jacob	Ribca de Jacob FRANCO DA SILVA y FRANCO DE SILVERA	
Feb. 22, 1722	Jacob de Abm y F. DA SILVA	Ribca de Isaac MENDES DE GAMA y PINHEIRO	24,000 fls.
Before 1725	Salomon de Abm y F. DA SILVA	Sarah CURIEL (?)	A half interest in a house on Joodestraat

Marriage Date	Bridegroom	Bride	Dowry and/or Remarks
		CURIEL (cont.)	
Feb. 22, 1747	Abm de Salomon Abm, b. Jamaica	Sarah de Jacob Curiel y M. Gama	2,000 pesos
Oct. 17, 1751	Abraham de Jb y M. Gama	Leah de Joseph Fidanque y Jn Henriquez	2,500 (?) pesos
Before 1756	Isaac de Jacob y M. Gama	Ribca de Abm Lz da Fonseca y Jn Henriquez	
Nov. 28, 1756	Isaac de Jb y M. Gama, widower	Jael de Joseph Fidanque y Jn Henriquez	3,500 (?) "
Oct. 21, 1759	Salomoh de Jacob y M. Gama	Rachel de Ephraim Jn Henriquez y Gaon	
May 23, 1762	Isaac Jr. de Sal. Abm, b. Amsterdam	Hanah Jesurun Henriquez	
June 27, 1762	Joseph de Jacob y M. Gama	Ribca de David da Costa Andrade y Andrade	
June 27, 1779	Salomon de Abraham y Curiel	Clara de Abraham Monis y Moron Telles	
Aug. 27, 1780	Jacob de Abraham y Curiel	Rachel Nunes (Machuca) [Machorro]	
Aug. 25, 1784	Jacob Haim de Abm Jb y Fidanque	Sarah de David Hu Suares y Hz Fereyra	250 pesos
Aug. 25, 1784	Joseph de Isaac Jb y Fidanque	Ribca de Abraham Curiel y Fidanque	1,300 "
May 30, 1797	Benjamin de Is Jb y Fidanque	Esther de Jb Eliau Israel Jn Henriquez y Namias de Crasto	2,700 "
Jan. 31, 1798	Ephraim de Selomoh y Jn Henriquez	Ribca de Eliau Penso y [Belmonte ?]	850 "
Aug. 22, 1798	Jacob de Joseph y da Costa Andrade	Leah de Moses Cohen Hz y Lz Henriquez	1,500 "

June 18, 1817	Abraham de Salomoh y Jn HENRIQUEZ	Esther de Samuel DE CASSERES	3,000 pesos; separated
Dec. 19, 1819	Joseph de Jacob Haim y SUARES	Deborah de Salomoh L. MADURO y Lz FONSECA	
	(This marriage is not recorded in the MIA Ketuboth Registers since it took place during the Piza Affair, Chapter XV.)		
Nov. 6, 1822	Isaac de Jacob Haim y SUARES	Leah de Jb HENRIQUEZ y Jn HENRIQUEZ	5,300 pesos; separated
Feb. 12, 1823	Eliau de Ephraim y PENSO	Rachel de Manuel PENSO y A. CORREA	8,000 pesos
	(Children: Ephraim, Manuel Penso, Ribca, Salomon, Ester, Moise, Jael and Sarah)		
March 4, 1829	Jacob de Benjamin y Jn HENRIQUEZ	Sarah de Rephael NAMIAS DE CRASTO y L. MADURO	1,866.66 fls.
Oct. 20, 1830	Moises de Ephraim y PENSO	Esther de Mord FIDANQUE y Hz FEREYRA	
	(Children: Ephraim, Ribca, Mordechay Fidanque, Elias, Rachel, Batsebah and Jacob)		
Before 1832	Salomoh Haim de Ephraim y PENSO	Judith de Jb DE CASTRO y Jn SASPORTAS	See above, p. 340
March 13, 1833	Eliau de Benjamin y Jn HENRIQUEZ	Leah de Aron Jn de OLIVEYRA y PENSO	
June 26, 1833	Abraham Jr. de Jb Hm y SUARES	Ribca de Samuel HOHEB y COHEN Hz	7,048 fls.
Feb. 17, 1836	David de Jb Hm y SUARES	Clara de Moshe ABOAB OSORIO y Hz FEREYRA	
Nov. 25, 1839	Jacob de Ephraim de Sal. y PENSO	Sarah de Daniel Jn SASPORTAS y Gz CASSERES	
About 1850 (?)	David de Joseph y L. MADURO (?)	Celinda ABENATAR	
Jan. 28, 1852	Benjamin de Jacob y NAMIAS DE CRASTO	Hanah de Selomoh NAMIAS DE CRASTO y CASTRO	2,000
Jan. 12, 1853	Manuel Penso de Eliau y PENSO	Ribca de Moses CURIEL y FIDANQUE	2,000 „

CURIEL (cont.)

Marriage Date	Bridegroom	Bride	Dowry and/or Remarks
Feb. 2, 1853	Ephraim Jr. de Moises Ephraim y FIDANQUE	Esther de Eliau CURIEL y PENSO	2,000 fls.
July 13, 1853	Ephraim de Eliau Ephraim y PENSO	Sarah de David DELVALLE Hz y PENSO	3,000 "
Feb. 20, 1861	Ephraim Jr. de Moises Ephraim y FIDANQUE, widower	Rebecca Judith de Jacob FIDANQUE y Ms MONSANTO	Mar. in St. Thomas
Dec. 23, 1857	Selomoh de Eliau Ephraim y PENSO	Esther de David DELVALLE Hz y PENSO	3,000 fls.
Sept. 22, 1858	Rephael Namias de Jacob y NAMIAS DE CRASTO	Esther de Selomoh NAMIAS DE CRASTO y CASTRO	
March 5, 1862	Eliau de Moises y FIDANQUE	Clara de Rephael A. CORREA y OSORIO	
Dec. 23, 1863	Jacob de Abm de Jb y HOHEB	Sarah de David CURIEL y OSORIO	600 "
Aug. 16, 1865	Isaac de Abm Jb y HOHEB	Deborah de Isaac ABENATAR y L. MADURO	
March 28, 1866	Mordechay Fidanque de Moises y FIDANQUE	Esther de Isaac Rz MIRANDA y JESURUN	12,000 "
April 13, 1870	Samuel de Abm Jb Hm y HOHEB	Hanah de Samuel [Rz] PEREIRA y Lz PENHA	
Sept. 6, 1876	Moises de Ephraim Jr. y CURIEL	Rachel de Manuel CURIEL y CURIEL	3,000 "
Dec. 17, 1884	Elias de Ephraim y DELVALLE Hz	Rosaline de Raymondo A. CORREA y ROIS MENDES	
Aug. 15, 1888	Morris de Elias y A. CORREA	Abigail de David SENIOR Jr. y COHEN Hz	12,000 "
Dec. 14, 1898	Jacob de Rephael NAMIAS DE CRASTO y NAMIAS DE CRASTO	Julia NAMIAS CRASTO	
About 1904	Joseph de Ephraim Moses y FIDANQUE	Rebecca de Samuel Mord SASSO y CASTRO	

July 31, 1918	Elias de Morris y SENIOR	Raquel Reneta de Henry BAIZ y A. CORREA	Divorced
July 8, 1920	Alex de Morris y SENIOR	Zelma de Moises Benj DE MARCHENA y MARCHENA	
May 21, 1930	Ephraim de Joseph y SASSO	Romelia de David Hm Lz PENHA y CASTRO	

See allied families: Da Costa Andrade, Cardoze, A. Correa, Delvalle, Lopez Fonseca, Cohen Henriquez, Moreno Henriquez, Lopez, L. Maduro, Marchena, Hz Moron, Namias de Crasto, Leon Nunes, Osorio, Lz Penha, Pinedo, Querido.

GENEALOGY

1st Branch: Dr. Ramirez = Maria d.F. → Jacob = Leah A. → Salomon → Abraham = Ribca F.S. →
Jacob = Ribca M.G. → Salomon = Rachel J.H. → Ephraim = Ribca P. → Moises =
Esther F. → Eliau = Clara A.C. → Morris = Abigail S. → Elias = Raquel R.B. → Morris.

2nd Branch: Moises = Esther F. → Ephraim Jr. = Esther C.
Rebecca Judith F. ↗ Joseph = Rebecca S. → Ephraim =
Romelia L.P. → Donald, born 1933.

DEBLEINE, see Baiz.

COHEN DEITELZWEIG, see Senior.

SALOM DELVALLE, DELVALLE HENRIQUEZ, DELVALLE

April 9, 1694	Jacob de Ishac SALOM D.	Sarah de Jacob ISRAEL	2,550 fls.; mar. in A'dam
May 23, 1708	Mordechay de Ishac S. D.	Rosa de Ishac DE MEDINA	Mar. in A'dam
Sept. 9, 1761	Jacob de Mordechay [y MEDINA ?]	Esther de Ishac DE MERCADO	Ditto
Jan. 21, 1795	Abraham de Jacob y MERCADO	Hanah de Dr. Joseph CAPRILES y Hz MORON	6,500 pesos; mar. in Curaçao; separated

SALOM DELVALLE (cont.)

Marriage Date	Bridegroom	Bride	Dowry and/or Remarks
Oct. 16, 1796	Salomoh de Jacob y Mercado	Deborah de Isaac Haim Motta y Hz Moron	6,000 pesos
	(Children: Esther, Jacob, Abigail, Hannah, Sarah, Isaac, David, Abraham and Benjamin)		
About 1807	Isaac	Sarah	Mar. in St. Thomas
March 29, 1807	Elias de David Delvalle, b. France	Rachel de Jacob Pinedo y Marchena	4,000 pesos
Jan. 12, 1812	Abraham de Jacob y Mercado, widower	Siporah de Abm de Meza y Athias Robles	3,000 ,,
June 18, 1823	Jacob de Salomoh y Motta	Rachel de Ephraim Curiel y Penso	5,500 ,,
Aug. 24, 1831	David de Salomoh y Motta	Abigail de Manuel Penso y A. Correa	13,333.33 fls.
Sept. 27, 1833	Benjamin de Salomoh y Motta	Judith de Jb de Castro y Jn Henriquez, widow	See above, p. 340
Aug. 24, 1856	Abraham de David y Penso	Hanah de Mord A. Correa y A. Correa	4,000 fls.
July 25, 1857	Abraham Curiel de Jb y Curiel	Esther de David Hz Juliao	
Oct. 22, 1858	Manuel Penso de David y Penso	Rebecca de Benjamin S. Delvalle y Castro	
Feb. 1, 1860	Ephraim Curiel de Jacob y Curiel	Esther de Mord de Marchena y Curiel	1,000 ,,
About 1860	Salomoh de Benj y Castro	Rachel de Jeosuah Piza y Sasso	They had 14 children.
Dec. 5, 1866	Moises de David y Penso	Miriam de Eliau Penso y Penso	5,000 fls.
Before 1867	Isaac de Benjamin y Castro	Emily de Jacob Lindo y Piza	
June 7, 1871	Jacob de Benjamin y Castro	Hanah de Jeosuah Jn Henriquez y Cohen Hz	19,300 ,,
Before 1876	David de Benjamin y Castro	Grace [Cardoze ?]	

Date	Groom	Bride	Amount
Dec. 11, 1889	Jacob de Ephraim Curiel y MARCHENA	Simha de Abm Ms CHUMACEIRO y Lz HENRIQUEZ	
March 26, 1890	David de Abraham y A. CORREA	Clara de Benj Mord A. CORREA y DELVALLE Hz	
June 4, 1890	Manuel de Abm y A. CORREA	Judith de Jacob LEVY MADURO	
June 10, 1900	Benjamin de Jacob y JN HENRIQUEZ	Serafina de Jacob MADURO LOPEZ y SENIOR	5,000 "
Feb. 20, 1901	Elias Penso de Moises y PENSO	Sarah de Moises E. PENSO y L. MADURO	25,000 "
June 29, 1910	Arturo de Moises y PENSO	Rachel Amelia de Abm Sal L. MADURO y LOPEZ PENHA	25,000 fls.
Dec. 10, 1924	Alberto de Manuel y L. MADURO	Zoroya de Rephael COHEN Hz y DELVALLE Hz	
Nov. 12, 1933	Max de Arturo y L. MADURO	Yvonne de Joseph A. CORREA y L. MADURO	30,000 "
March 4, 1936	Eric de Arturo y L. MADURO	Abigail Judith COHEN Hz y DELVALLE Hz	
March 4, 1952	Cecil Lopez de Benj y MADURO LOPEZ	Florence HALPERN, divorcée Capriles	
March 22, 1953	Frank de Eliau y PENSO	Rebecca de Jb Bertie ATHIAS ROBLES y CASTRO	

See allied families: Pereira Brandao, Capriles, Gomes Casseres, Alvares Correa, Cortissoz, Curiel, Fidanque, Lopez da Fonseca, Henriquez, Cohen Henriquez, Moreno Henriquez, De Jongh, Lindo, Levy Maduro, Marchena, De Meza, Pinheiro de Nogueira, Osorio, Penso, Pinedo, Piza.

Genealogy: Mordechay = Rosa M. → Jacob = Esther M. → Salomoh = Deborah M. → David = Abigail P. → Moises = Miriam P. → Elias = Sarah P. → Frank = Rebecca A.R. → Sheila Ann.

DIAS

About 1705	David	Judith RODRIGUEZ GUADALUPE
Dec. 6, 1733	Abraham	Abigail ANDRADE

Marriage Date	Bridegroom	Bride	Dowry and/or Remarks
		DIAS (cont.)	
Before 1742	Isaac de Jacob	Rachel Vaz de Oliveyra	
„ 1776	Isaac	Ribca Vaz de Oliveyra	
See Levy Maduro.			
		LOPEZ DIAS	
About 1705	Isaac	Sarah Carillo	22,000 fls.
Before 1709	David	Hanah	Pr. St., p. 227
Before 1732	Jacob de Isaac	Rachel de Abraham Penso y Pereira	
April 10, 1738	Mozes, b. Lisbon	Esther de Samuel Idanha de Casseres y Pardo	
April 27, 1744	Abraham de Isaac	Rachel de Abm Jn Henriquez y Rz Gradis	1,300 pesos
Before 1764	Abraham de Jacob	Ribca de Abm Isaac Senior y Penso	
Dec. 2, 1764	Abm. de Jb, widower of Ribca Jn Henriquez	Sarah de Mord Haim Senior y Jesurun	
Sept. 14, 1766	Abraham de Mozes y Id. de Casseres	Esther de Joseph Bonan y Idanha de Casseres	
Feb. 27, 1767	David de Jacob y Penso	Rachel de Abm Jb Hz Fereyra y Lopez Dias	
Sept. 18, 1768	Abm de Jb, widower of Sarah S.	Leah de Moses Is L. Maduro y Lopez Dias	
Sept. 7, 1806	Moses de Abm Moses	Deborah de Jb Samuel L. Maduro [y Curiel ?]	200 „

See allied families: Idanha de Casseres, Henriquez Fereyra, Jesurun, Levy Maduro, Senior.

Vaz Dias, see Mendes Chumaceiro.

884

DOVALE

Date			Amount
About 1692	Jacob	Esther de Isaac (?) Henriquez Morao	
June 30, 1748	Josiau de David	Sarah de Abraham Ulloa	
Jan. 19, 1777	David Haim de Josiau y Ulloa	Ribca de Jeudah Alva y Calvo	
March 26, 1783	Eliau de Josiau y Ulloa	Clara de Mord Motta y L. Maduro	4,050 pesos
Feb. 12, 1812	David de David Haim y Alva	Rachel de Isaac Capriles y Dovale	7,300 "
	(Children: Rebecca, Esther, Hannah, Dilia, David Haim, Abraham Jesurun and Julia)		
May 13, 1812	Josiau de David Haim y Alva	Sarah de Abm Jb Jesurun y Henriquez	11,000 "
Sept. 28, 1814	Josiau Jr. de Eliau y Motta	Rachel de David de Mord Abinun de Lima	2,000 "
Dec. 18, 1822	Jeudah Haim de David Hm y Alva	Rachel de Moises Abinun de Lima y de Sola	1,500 "
Sept. 13, 1854	Isaac de Josias y Abinun de Lima	Sarah de David Abinun de Lima y Salas	1,260 fls.
June 18, 1856	Abraham Jesurun de David y Jesurun	Ribca Ricot de Jb Jesurun y Pinedo	14,500 "
Sept. 30, 1857	David Jr. de Josiau Jr. y A. de Lima	Leah de Abm David Senior y Calvo	2,000 "
Sept. 11, 1876	David Dovale Mendez de Isaac y A. de Lima	Leonor de David Moses Jesurun y Pinedo	3,000 "
	(David, who was adopted by Jacob Rois Mendez, assumed the name Dovale Mendez, as the family is known to this day in Puerto Rico.)		

See allied families: Capriles, Casseres, Henriquez Cautinho, Jesurun Henriquez, Jesurun, Abinun de Lima, Pardo, Pinedo.

Genealogy: David → Josiau = Sarah U. → Eliau = Clara M. → Josiau = Rachel A. d. L. → Isaac = Sarah A. d. L. → David D. M. = Leonor J. → Jacinto.

Marriage Date	Bridegroom	Bride	Dowry and/or Remarks
		EDWARDS	
Sept. 5, 1849	Sevi Hirsch de Ephraim y NEWFELD	Esther de Abm Hm SEBNIOR y COHEN Hz	16,500 fls.
		EISENBURG	
Nov. 27, 1889	Eliezer Lazarus de Moses y BLUMENTHAL	Katie S. de Jb Melvin ABRAHAM y SAMPSON	
	ERGAS, see Belmonte.		
		ETTEDGUI	
Dec. 2, 1908	Salomon de Abraham y ETTEDGUI	Leah Lilian de Moises DE SOLA y OSORIO	
		EZRA	
About 1800	Michael	Miriam de Jeosuah NAAR y L. MADURO	Separated
		HENRIQUEZ FARRO	
March 11, 1707	Jacob	Sarah de Ishac GOMEZ DE MESQUITA	1,500 fls.
Oct. 11, 1734	Haham Ishac de Jacob y Gz de MESQUITA	Ribca de Moshe GOMEZ DE MESQUITA y FERNANDEZ MEDINA	Pr. St., p. 346

See Lopez Henriquez.

VAZ FARRO

Before 1709	David Israel Salomoh	Raghel Carvalho	
" 1709	Salomoh	Sarah de Benjamin Aboab Furtado	Pr. St., p. 245
" 1737	Mosseh Hu de Salomoh y A. Furtado	Ribca de David Vaz Farro y Carvalho	
Nov. 13, 1746	Ditto, widower	Abigail de David Vaz Farro y Carvalho	1,050 pesos
1746	Benjamin de David y Carvalho	Esther de Abraham A. Correa y Andrade	
June 30, 1748	Ditto, widower	Sarah de Abraham A. Correa y Andrade	
Much before 1756	Aron de Salomoh y A. Furtado	Abigail Miranda	
May 18, 1766	Salomoh de Moses y Vaz Farro	Sarah de Isaac Pardo y Vaz Farro	Above, pp. 271-75

See allied families: Abenatar, Pereyra Brandam, Fundam, Guedalia, Halas, Keyzer, Abinun de Lima, Levy Maduro, Monsanto, Naar, Pardo, Lopez Penha.

DE LA FAYA, see Cohen Peixotto, Ricardo.

FEBOS, see Alvares Correa, Rodriguez Monsanto.

HENRIQUEZ FEREYRA

Nov. 17, 1719	Jacob de Isaac (?)	Rachel Henriquez Alvares	Mar. in A'dam
Before 1744	Isaac de Jacob	Esther de Jb Ephraim Jn Henriquez y Carilho	
1746	Isaac de Jb de Is y Alvares	Esther de Elias Namias de Crasto y Namias de Crasto	15,000 pesos
May 26, 1748	Abm de Jb y Alvares, b. A'dam	Sarah de Jb Lopez Dias y Penso	6,000 "
Before 1752	Isaac de Abraham	Gracia Hz de Mesquita y Franco de Castro	

887

Marriage Date	Bridegroom	Bride	Dowry and/or Remarks
		HENRIQUEZ FEREYRA (cont.)	
Nov. 6, 1763	Jacob de Isaac y NAMIAS DE CRASTO	Clara de Jb PEREIRA y JEUDAH LEAO	
May 28, 1775	Isaac de Abm y LOPEZ DIAS	Ribca de Abm Aron Hz MORON y PENSO	
Jan. 18, 1778	Jacob de Isaac y NAMIAS DE CRASTO	Esther de Isaac Rz DA COSTA y A. CORREA	14,000 „
Before 1828	Joseph de Jacob y Rz DA COSTA	Abigail DE CRASTO	
See allied families: Capriles, Alvares Correa, Lopez Dias, Fidanque, Lopez Fonseca, Da Costa Gomez, Osorio, Suares.			
FERNANDEZ, see Lopez da Fonseca.			
		DIAS FERNANDEZ	
Sept. 9, 1764	Abraham, b. Jamaica	Deborah LEVY BARRIOS, b. A'dam	
FERRARES, see Mendes Chumaceiro.			
FERRO, see Da Costa Gomez.			
		NUNES FERRO	
About 1760	Daniel	Rebecca de Jacob HENRIQUEZ MORON	
		SEMAH FERRO	
Oct. 30, 1671	Jacob de Abm, b. Portugal	Esther Israel DE TORRES	Mar. in A'dam
About 1702	Jacob de Jacob y TORRES	Gracia de Manuel A. CORREA y ABENDANA	

May 8, 1749	Ditto, widower	Deborah Jesurun da Cunha y Curiel	
Before 1756	Isaac	Gracia de Moses A. Correa y Semah Ferro	

See allied families: Alvares Correa, Lopez Henriquez, Namias de Crasto.

FIDANQUE

Before 1670	Benjamin	Hanah Leah	
June 10, 1703	Joseph de Benjamin	Sarah de Benj Jn Henriquez y Namias de Crasto	2,812:4 pesos; Pr. St., pp. 289-91
Aug. 16, 1746	Jacob de Joseph y Jn Henriquez	Batsebah de Abm Jn Henriquez y Rois Gradis	
Oct. 17, 1751	Elias de Joseph y Jn Henriquez	Batsebah de Elias Jn Henriquez y Namias de Crasto	
Sept. 30, 1781	Abraham Hm de Jacob y Jn Henriquez	Sarah de Elias Fidanque y Jn Henriquez	
June 28, 1797	Mordechay de Jacob y Jn Henriquez	Ribca de Jacob Ishac Hz Fereyra	900 pesos
About 1830	Jacob Jr., b. Curaçao	Rebecca Mendes Monsanto	
March 23, 1831	Joseph de Mordechay y Hz Fereyra	Rachel de Josiau Pardo y Abinun de Lima	2,000 "
	(Children: Rebecca, Sarah, Josias, Gabriel and David)		
About 1858	Morris de Jacob	Rachel de Benjamin S. Delvalle y Castro	
July 21, 1869	Gabriel de Joseph Mord y Pardo	Rachel de David Osorio y Cardoze	
Before 1872	Mordechay	Rachel	
About 1890 (?)	Jacob de Morris	Rebecca Sasso	

See allied families: Da Costa Andrade, Rodriguez Campos, Cardoze, Castro, aCohen, Curiel, Henriquez, Hoheb, Levy Maduro, Osorio, Lopez Penha, Senior. Figueroa, a.k.a. Spinoza, see Cohen Henriquez.

Marriage Date	Bridegroom	Bride	Dowry and/or Remarks
	LOPEZ FINCHY, a.k.a. FINSY, without "Lopez"		
Before 1789	Nissim Haim Lopez	Rachel de I. MARACHE DE LEON	
See Cardoze, Porto.			
		FISCHER	
Dec. 16, 1939	Siegmund de Alois y POLLAK	Nellie de Ignacio CARDOZE y SIMONSON	
		FLORES	
Before 1741	Moses	Esther de Benjamin ATHIAS DE NEYRA	
Aug. 12, 1742	Abraham, b. Bayonne	Esther de Jacob ATHIAS DE NEYRA y CHAVES	
See Keyzer, Rodriguez.			
		FONSECA	
1712	Jacob	Ribca GABAY CORREA	
(Most probably Jacob's family name was Nunes da Fonseca. See *Precious Stones*, p. 144.)			
See allied families: Alberga, Curiel, Henriquez Moron.			
GOMEZ FONSECA, see Jesurun Pinto.			
HABILIO DA FONSECA, see Touro.			
		LOPEZ DA FONSECA	
Oct. 21, 1676	Haham Eliau LOPEZ (without "Da Fonseca")	Rahel de David NUNES DA FONSECA	Mar. in A'dam

Date	Groom	Bride	Dowry / Notes
About 1708	Abraham de Eliau y Nunes da Fonseca	Rachel de Menasseh Jn Henriquez y Pereyra	A half interest in a house on Windstraat
Feb. 26, 1722	Jacob de Eliau y Nunes da Fonseca	Ribca de Eliau Benveniste y Aboab de Paz	Mar. in New York
About 1722	Moseh de Eliau y Ns da Fonseca	Miriam de Isaac Naftali	
Before 1735	Aron de Eliau y Ns da Fonseca	Leah Andrade	
August, 1736	Moseh de Eliau y Ns da Fonseca, widower	Rachel Israel, widow of Is A. Correa	
About 1748	Eliau de Jacob y Benveniste	Esther de Samuel Mendes de Sola y Henriquez	
Nov. 26, 1755	Jacob de Aron y Andrade	Rachel de Samuel Mendes de Sola y Henriquez	1,450 pesos
About 1756	Benjamin de Jacob y Benveniste	Esther Baruch Louzado	
May 23, 1762	David de Jacob y Benveniste	Leah Henriquez Fereyra	
Oct. 28, 1764	Jacob de Aron y Andrade, wid.	Sarah de Samuel Fernandez y Lopez Rodriguez	3,000 "
Oct. 26, 1766	Eliau de Jacob y Benveniste, widower	Simha de Moseh Lz da Fonseca y Naffali, b. New York	
Oct. 26, 1766	Elias Jr. de Moseh y Naffali, b. New York	Leah de Jeosuah Touro y Lz da Fonseca	
May 26, 1771	Eliau de Aron y Andrade	Sarah de Jeudah Cohen Hz y Lz da Fonseca	
Aug. 3, 1785	Samuel Haim de Jacob y Fernandez	Gracia de Imanuel Hu Pinedo y Hz Moron	1,850 "
Nov. 11, 1798	Moshe de Jacob y Fernandez	Sarah de Selomoh de Casseres y Pinheiro de Nogueira	
March 14, 1802	David Hu de Eliau y Ms de Sola	Rachel de Isaac Abm Hz Cotinho	2,000 "
About 1810	Imanuel de Samuel Hm y Pinedo	Charlotte de Samuel Prado	1,400 "
June 26, 1833	Isaac de David	Batsebah de Imanuel Lopez Fonseca y Prado, b. Jamaica	15,592.33 fls.

891

Marriage Date	Bridegroom	Bride	Dowry and/or Remarks
	LOPEZ DA FONSECA (cont.)		
About 1839 (?)	Eliau de David y Hz Cotinho without "Da Fonseca"	Sarah de Joseph Curiel y L. Maduro	Mar. in Coro
„ 1875 (?)	David de Eliau y Curiel	Johebed de Isaac Moreno Hz y L. Maduro	
„ 1876 (?)	Isaac de Eliau y Curiel	Abigail de Ephraim Curiel y Delvalle Hz	
1877	Joseph de Eliau y Curiel	Abigail de Manuel Delvalle Hz y Salom Delvalle	
1884	Salomoh de Eliau y Curiel	Gracia de Rephael A. Correa y Roiz Mendez	
1888	Jacobo de Eliau y Curiel	Judith de Manuel Delvalle Hz y Salom Delvalle	
About 1890 (?)	Abraham de Eliau y Curiel	Abigail de David Curiel y Abenatar	

See allied families: Abenatar, Andrade, Capriles, Idanha de Casseres, Curiel, Cohen Henriquez, Lopez Henriquez, Leon, Lopez, Levy Maduro, Namias de Crasto, Pinheiro de Nogueira, Piza, Sasportas, Mendes de Sola, Taboada, Touro.

Marriage Date	Bridegroom	Bride	Dowry and/or Remarks
	NUNES DA FONSECA		
Before 1705	David	Abigail	

See Lopez da Fonseca.

Marriage Date	Bridegroom	Bride	Dowry and/or Remarks
	FONTEIN		
Feb. 28, 1960	Bernard Anton de Hyman y Sonepouse	Stella de Jacob Arnold Salas y de Jongh	

FRANCES

Before 1765   Isaac   Judith PRETTO

FRANCO, see Moreno Henriquez.

FRANKEL

Jan. 31, 1762   Moses Haim, b. Westburg, Ger.   Leah de Aron MENDES MACHADO

FROIS

July 5, 1696   Mosseh de Abraham   Judith de Abm BARUCH CARVALHO   Mar. in A'dam

See Salas and the following family.

FROIS D'ANDRADE (known as FROIS)

Aug. 5, 1781   Moses, b. Bayonne   Rachel de Isaac DE SOLA y NUNES DA COSTA

See Ricardo.

FUNDAM

Aug. 24, 1686   Abraham de Jacob   Rachel de Mordechay SENIOR y LOPEZ SUASSO   8,000 fls.

Dec. 21, 1734   Mordechay de Abm y SENIOR   Esther de David VAZ FARRO y CARVALHO

See allied families: Naar, Pardo, Senior.

ABOAB FURTADO, see Vaz FARRO.

RIBEIRO FURTADO, see De Solas.

GABAY, see Piza.

SIPRUT DE GABAY, see Mendes Chumaceiro.

GALLAS, see Halas.

893

Marriage Date	Bridegroom	Bride	Dowry and/or Remarks
		MENDES DA GAMA	
About 1691	Isaac	Sarah Pinheiro	
Before 1726	Abraham de Isaac y Pinheiro	Leah de Abm Jb Jesurun y Levy	
See Curiel.			
	Gamis, see Namias de Crasto, Cohen Peixotto.		
		GAON	
July 22, 1676	Isaac de Jacob y Ribca Linda	Rachel de Mordechay de Crasto	4,500 fls.
Before 1709	Jacob	Esther de Abraham de Marchena	
See allied families: Aboab Cardozo, Jesurun Henriquez, Leon, Senior.			
		GARCIA	
Before 1737	Garson	Sarah Iftagh	
Aug. 23, 1731	Jacob	Esther de Benjamin Marache, b. The Hague	
Jan. 20, 1771	Abraham, b. Barbados	Abigail de Joseph Vaz da Costa	
March 26, 1783	Abraham de Benj, b. A'dam	Rachel de Mordechay Motta y Levy Maduro	
See allied families: Leon, Sanches, Suares.			
		VAN GELDER	
April 4, 1888	Dr. Jacob de Gerson	Rachel Reneta de Isaac Salas y Baiz	Mar. in Trinidad
	Gersh, see Maduro.		

894

GERSIL

Oct. 16, 1895	Dr. Moses de Sem. y ROSENTHAL	Serafina de Manuel PENSO y A. CORREA	25,000 fls.
June 12, 1932	Egon de Moses y PENSO GOLDISH, see Capriles.	Georgette GERÖ	

GODSCHALK

June 3, 1951	Hartogh de Moses y VAN KLUF	Elaine de Benj HENRIQUEZ y SALAS

GOMEZ

Before 1697	Ymanuel	Gracia ABOAB	
Feb. 10, 1724	Daniel, b. France	Ribca de Joseph TORRES	5,000 (?) pesos
June 17, 1733	Ditto, widower	Esther de Gabriel LEVY y TOURO	3,640:5:2 pesos
Aug. 25, 1748	Isaac Jr.	Ribca de Jacob Abm JESURUN y LOPEZ DIAS	
March 27, 1768	Moses de Rephael	Sarah RODRIGUEZ	

See allied families: Castro, Da Costa, Henriquez Juliao, Melo de Leon, Levy Maduro, Frois de Meza, Campos Pereira, Mendes de Sola.

DA COSTA GOMEZ

Before 1689	Imanuel, b. Lisbon	Rachel	Both died in A'dam
" 1705	Samuel de Imanuel	Hanah Abigail	
Aug. 3, 1705	Samuel de Abraham	Hanah de Abraham LOPEZ LAGUNA	4,000 fls.
Aug. 3, 1705	Aron de Abraham	Ribca de Abraham LOPEZ LAGUNA	4,000 "
Aug. 3, 1705	Mosche de Abraham	Simha de Abraham LOPEZ LAGUNA	4,000 "

(These three couples were born in Lisbon to Marranos who adopted the name Abraham on returning to Judaism. They arrived in Amsterdam married, but remarried there according to Jewish Law [PJCAA, Ket., vol. VI, nos. 107-109].)

DA COSTA GOMEZ (cont.)

Marriage Date	Bridegroom	Bride	Dowry and/or Remarks
June 23, 1706	Aron, widower of Ribca L. L.	Sarah de Imanuel DA COSTA GOMEZ	Mar. in A'dam
Nov. 18, 1717	Imanuel de Abraham, wid. of Rachel	Esther LOPEZ LAGUNA y DA FONSECA, wid. of Is Medina Pereira	
	(Both were born in Lisbon and married in Amsterdam.)		
Nov. 25, 1721	Samuel de Imanuel	Esther de Samuel DA COSTA GOMEZ	2,000 pesos
	(Both were born in Lisbon and married in Curaçao.)		
Jan. 5, 1729	Gabriel de Imanuel	Rachel de Daniel DE LA PENHA y DE CASTRO	Mar. in A'dam
	(Children: Daniel, Joseph, Imanuel, Judith, Isaac, Samuel and David)		
Dec. 6, 1733	Joseph, b. Lisbon	Hanah LOPEZ LAGUNA	Mar. in Curaçao
May 21, 1734	Joseph de Imanuel	Sarah de Is MEDINA PEREIRA	Mar. in A'dam
June 2, 1734	Isaac de Mosseh y LOPEZ LAGUNA	Rachel DA COSTA GOMEZ, b. Portugal	
After 1735	Gabriel de Imanuel, widower	[Daughter of Daniel DE LA PENHA ?]	
April 18, 1742	Joseph, wid. of Hanah L. L.	Rachel LOPEZ LAGUNA	
Aug. 7, 1763	Samuel de Joseph y LOPEZ LAGUNA	Judith de Gabriel DA COSTA GOMEZ [y DE LA PENHA ?]	
Aug. 7, 1763	Samuel de Gabriel y DE LA PENHA	Sarah de Isaac PEREIRA y PENSO	
Aug. 7, 1763	David de Gabriel y DE LA PENHA	Ribca de Isaac PEREIRA y PENSO	
Nov. 23, 1775	Daniel de Gabriel y DE LA PENHA	Esther de Moses TELLES DA COSTA	
March 13, 1788	Gabriel de David y PEREIRA	Esther de Jacob Hz FEREYRA y PEREIRA	600 pesos
May 5, 1790	Haim Gabriel de Samuel y PEREIRA	Sarah de Gabriel PINEDO y Hz MORON	10,000 „
May 26, 1793	Ditto, widower	Esther de Gabriel PINEDO y Hz MORON	10,000 „
Dec. 2, 1802	Joseph DE LA PENHA, b. Curaçao	Angela de Abraham (FAERO) [FERRO], widow of Isaac Levy Flores	Mar. in A'dam

Date	Groom	Bride	Amount
March 19, 1812	Samuel de Haim Gabriel y PINEDO	Rachel de Jacob Gabriel PINEDO y MARCHENA, wid. of Elias Delvaille	1,000 pesos
April 3, 1816	Gabriel de Haim Gabriel y PINEDO	Rachel de Jeosuah Rephael HENRIQUEZ y CHAVES	3,000 "
Sept. 16, 1829	Daniel de Haim Gabriel y PINEDO	Sarah de Isaac Hz MORON y L. MADURO (The bridegroom signed the Ketubah as "Daniel Da Costa Gomez de la Penha.")	
March 29, 1843	Jeosuah de Gabriel y HENRIQUEZ	Sarah de Joseph ENRIQUEZ y PARDO	
June 26, 1849	Samuel Jr. de Gabriel y HENRIQUEZ	Ribca de Mordechay HENRIQUEZ y HENRIQUEZ	5,100 fls.
Jan. 29, 1873	Aron de Haim Gabriel y PINEDO, 65	Clara de Moses Hz JULIAO y MENDES DE SOLA, widow of Mordechay A. Correa, 57	
April 6, 1892	Haim Gabriel de Jeosuah y HENRIQUEZ	Aurora de Herman COHEN Hz y NAAR	2,500 "
March 14, 1894	Mordechay de Samuel y HENRIQUEZ	Esther de Haim ABINUN DE LIMA y HENRIQUEZ	
June 6, 1917	Henry de Haim Gabriel y COHEN Hz	Deborah Rebecca de Elias S. L. MADURO y JN HENRIQUEZ	14,000 "
Feb. 9, 1918	Jeosuah de Haim Gabriel y COHEN Hz	Adela Rachel de Prospero BAIZ y P. BRANDAO	
March 6, 1948	Frank de Jeosuah y BAIZ	Marjorie de Frank PEREIRA BRANDAO y L. MADURO	
April 4, 1951	George de Jeosuah y BAIZ	Joan de Ishac Haim CAPRILES y PINEDO	

See allied families: Casseres, Alvares Correa, Cohen Henriquez, Lopez Laguna, Pinedo.

Genealogy:

Imanuel = Rachel → Gabriel = ? D.L.P. → Samuel = Sarah P. → Haim Gabriel = Esther P° → Gabriel = Rachel H. → Jeosuah = Sarah H. → Haim Gabriel = Aurora C.H. → Jeosuah = Adela R.B. → George = Joan C. → Anthony, b. 1962.
Rachel D.L.P.

Marriage Date	Bridegroom	Bride	Dowry and/or Remarks
	GONZALES		
April 16, 1762	Moses de Abm, b. Sta. Marta	Abigail GUERMAN, b. A'dam	
	RODRIGUEZ GRADIS		
Before 1697	Abraham	Esther	
See Jesurun Henriquez.			
	GRANADA, see Piza.		
	GUADALUPE, see Da Costa Andrade.		
	DIAS GUADELUPE		
About 1749	Jacob	Sarah de Moses ALVA y GOMES SILVA	
	RODRIGUEZ GUADELUPE, see Dias.		
	GUEDELIA		
May 19, 1776	Baruch, b. A'dam	Rachel de Benjamin VAZ FARRO y A. CORREA	
	LEON GUEDES, see Vaz Martinez.		
	GUERMAN, see Gonzales.		
	HABIB, see Aben Habib.		
	HALAS		
Before 1707	Isaac	Rachel ANDRADE	

Jan. 4, 1750	Mordechay Rephael	Judith de David Vaz Farro y Carvalho	1,650 pesos
Before 1764	David	Leah de Haim Abinun de Lima y Halas	

See allied families: Andrade, Abinun de Lima, Touro.

HALMAN

Before 1837	Samuel	Hannah Sasso	
About 1860	Abraham de Samuel y Sasso	Abigail de Mordechay Sasso y Jn Lindo	

See Cohen Henriquez.

HALPERIN, see Baiz.

HALPERN, see Capriles, Delvalle.

HENRIQUEZ

Before 1636	Mordechay Hu the Elder	Ribca	Pr. St., pp. 151, 197-98
About 1659	Jeosuah	Leah [de Benjamin ?] Barzilay	Pr. St., pp. 203-204
Before 1688	Benjamin de Jeosuah y Barzilay	Leah Namias de Crasto	
" 1697	Mordechay O Moso de Jeosuah y Barzilay	Rachel de Jacob Naar y Henriquez	
About 1711	Jeosuah Rephael de Mord	Esther de Moses Lopez Henriquez y Henriquez	
" 1720	Eliezer (Elias), an Ashkenazic soldier	Dina Obediente	See above, pp. 110-11.
Before 1728	Jeosuah Jr. de Mordechay y Naar	Ribca de Moses Lz Henriquez y Henriquez	2,500 pesos
June 12, 1735	Benjamin Rephael de Mord y Naar	Rachel Hanah de Jeosuah Henriquez y Lz Henriquez	2,000 "

HENRIQUES (cont.)

Marriage Date	Bridegroom	Bride	Dowry and/or Remarks
1736	Jacob de Mord y Naar	Leah de Isaac Moises Levy Maduro y Touro	6,200 pesos
About 1741	Salomo de Eliezer (Elias) y Obediente	Esther Lobato	
Jan. 18, 1743	Moses de Jeosuah y Lz Henriquez	Esther de Samuel Benjamin de Casseres y Pardo	6,000 „
Aug. 25, 1748	Jacob de Mord y Naar, wid.	Sarah de David Namias de Crasto y Marchena	
June 6, 1751	Mordechay de Jeosuah y Lz Henriquez	Sarah de Jb Dd Senior y Henriquez	House on Joodekerkstraat
April 10, 1760	Benjamin Rephael de Mord y Naar, widower	Esther de Jeosuah Henriquez y Lz Henriquez	
Sept. 22, 1762	Mordechay de Jacob y L. Maduro	Leah de Jb Dd Senior y Henriquez	
Nov. 25, 1764	Moses de Jeosuah y Lz Henriquez, widower	Deborah de Aron Israel Santcroos y Moreno Hz	3,666 pesos
May 14, 1769	David de Jacob Namias de Crasto	Hanah de Is Jacob L. Maduro y Henriquez	
Before 1775	Isaac de Gaspar, b. Lisbon	Ribca da Costa	
May 28, 1775	Ditto, widower	Esther de Abm Hz Cotino y Motta	
Aug. 31, 1777	Jeosuah Rephael de Mord y Senior	Ribca de Abm Moses de Chaves y Henriquez	
	(Children: Sarah, Mordechay, Rachel, Leah, Jeosuah and Esther)		
June 12, 1782	Jacob de Mord Jeosuah y Senior	Ribca de Jb Jos. Jn Henriquez y Senior	2,800 „
Sept. 29, 1784	David de Isaac, b. France	Esther de Moses de Castro y Athias de Neyra	2,100 „
May 28, 1797	Abraham de Isaac y Hz Cotino	Sarah de David Morales y Hz Moron	4,800

Date	Groom	Bride	Amount
June 26, 1799	Jacob de David	Esther de Samuel Jn Pinto y Monsanto	1,000 „
Aug. 16, 1809	Joseph de Mord Jacob	Leah de Josias Pardo y Henriquez	5,027:4 „
July 1, 1810	Isaac de David y Castro	Rachel de Moses Hu Benveniste y Benveniste	3,800 „
Oct. 23, 1811	Benjamin de Mord Jacob	Sarah de Jeosuah Rephael Henriquez y Chaves	4,000 „
Oct. 8, 1813	Mordechay de Jeosuah Rephael y Chaves	Abigail de Jacob Henriquez y Jn Henriquez	5,000 „
June 1, 1814	Jeosuah de Mord Jacob	Leah de Rephael Namias de Crasto y L. Maduro	260 „
Feb. 7, 1819	Benjamin de Isaac	Rachel de Moses Hz Juliao y Mendes de Sola	3,350 „
Aug. 15, 1823	Jeosuah de Jeosuah Rephael y Chaves	Clara de Rephael Pinedo y Penso	3,050 „
March 28, 1824	Mordechay de Mordechay	Rachel de Mordechay L. Maduro [y Namias de Crasto ?]	1,000 „
Oct. 6, 1824	Joseph de Jacob	Sarah de Benjamin Jesurun [y de Sola ?]	4,000 „
Before 1830	David de Jacob	Branca de Jacob Jn Lindo y L. Maduro	
Oct. 10, 1834	Abm de Isaac y Hz Cotino, wid.	Esther de Salomoh Salom Delvalle y Motta	
Jan. 28, 1847	Jacob de Joseph y Jesurun	Sarah de Jeosuah Jb Naar y Jesurun	8,000 fls.
Nov. 5, 1851	Mordechay Cadet de Joseph y Jesurun	Rachel de Jeosuah Jb Naar y Jesurun	8,000 „
Sept. 5, 1855	Benjamin de Joseph y Jesurun	Ragel de Daniel Cohen Hz y Monsanto	4,000 „
May 1, 1861	Mordechay de Jeosuah Rephael y Pinedo	Leah de Daniel Jesurun y Henriquez	3,000 „

901

Marriage Date	Bridegroom	Bride	Dowry and/or Remarks
		HENRIQUEZ (cont.)	
Jan. 29, 1862	Benjamin de Joseph y JESURUN, widower	Judith de Daniel COHEN Hz y MONSANTO	4,000 "
May 27, 1885	Joseph de Benjamin y COHEN Hz	Aminta de Haim ABINUN DE LIMA y COHEN Hz	4,000 "
Before 1887	Edward Joshua	Zilla de Morris Jb FIDANQUE y SALOM DELVALLE	
Oct. 8, 1890	Jacobo de Mordechay Cadet y NAAR	Abigail de Benjamin HENRIQUEZ y COHEN Hz	2,000 "
April 5, 1903	Jacob de Benjamin y COHEN Hz	Rachel de David BAIZ y Lz HENRIQUEZ	8,000 "
Jan. 30, 1929	Benjamin de Jacob Mord y HENRIQUEZ	Atala de David Haim SALAS y ABINUN DE LIMA	14,900 "
Jan. 8, 1933	Hector de Jacob y BAIZ	Gladys de Arnold Jacob SALAS y DE JONGH	

See allied families: Pereira Brandao, Uziel Cardozo, Castro, Chavez, Alvares Correa, Curiel, Godschalk, Da Costa Gomez, Cohen Henriquez, Lopez Henriquez, Jesurun, Henriquez Juliao, Lansberg, Leon, Abinun de Lima, Jesurun Lobo, Levy Maduro, Marchena, Motta, Naar, Namias de Crasto, Pardo, Lopez Penha, Pinedo, Jesurun Pinto, Salas, Senior, Mendes de Sola, Valencia.

Genealogy: Jeosuah Rephael = Esther L.H. → Mordechay = Sarah S. → Jacob = Ribca Jn H. → Joseph = Sarah J. → Mordechay Cadet = Rachel N. → Jacob = Abigail H. → Benjamin = Atala S. → Elaine = Hartog Moses Godschalk.

BARUCH HENRIQUEZ, see Motta.

COHEN HENRIQUEZ

Before 1610	Abraham, a.k.a. Francisco Vaz de Leon	Esther	Pr. St., pp. 272-78

277/278. ELIAS DANIEL JESURUN, NOTED MERCHANT, AND HIS WIFE
RACHEL JESURUN HENRIQUEZ, M. 1868

279. JOSIAS A. M. CHUMACEIRO,
MERCHANT ACTIVE IN 1900

280. MORDECHAY MOSES C. HENRIQUEZ,
MEMBER OF GOVERNMENT
COUNCIL, 1909-19

281. MANUEL ELIAS PENSO, 1835-1908,
PRESIDENT OF THE COMMUNITY

282. MOSES HAIM E. PENSO, 1841-1924,
PROMINENT MERCHANT

283. MENASES J. CAPRILES, 1837-1894,
NOTED MERCHANT (BUST ON HIS
TOMBSTONE, REFORM CEMETERY)

284. ARON ABRAHAM CAPRILES,
1848-1912, PHARMACIST

Date	Groom	Bride	Notes
March 25, 1630	Jacob de Abraham	Judith de David Arari	16,000 lls.
Jan. 8, 1631	Moseh de Abraham	Rachel de Abm Figueroa, *alias* Spinoza (?)	
Before 1649	David	Leah	
" 1696	Daniel de David y Leah	? ?	Daniel died in Curaçao in 1725
March 8, 1702	Jeudah de David	Ribca de Isaac Carvalho	Mar. in London
Sept. 25, 1706	Moseh de David y Leah	Leah de Daniel Cohen Henriquez	A half interest in a house on Joodekerk-straat
Nov. 4, 1707	Daniel de David, b. A'dam	Benvenida de Mordechay Rodriguez	Mar. in A'dam
Jan. 4, 1735	David de Jeudah y Carvalho, a.k.a. Cohen Henriquez Jr.	Sarah de Benjamin Motta y Baruch Henriquez	
May 27, 1736	Moseh de David, widower Leah	Judith de Benjamin Motta y Baruch Henriquez	
Before 1741	Jacob de Jeudah y Carvalho	Esther de Moses Aboab	
1746	David de Moseh y Cohen Hz	Esther de Abm Lopez da Fonseca y Jn Henriquez	
About 1750	Moses	Leah de Abm Lopez da Fonseca y Jn Henriquez	
Aug. 20, 1755	Jeudah de David y Motta	Rachel de Aron Lopez da Fonseca y Andrade	
May 24, 1761	Benjamin de Moseh David y Motta	Ribca de David Jeudah Cohen Hz y Motta	
May 18, 1766	Moses de David y Lopez da Fonseca	Rachel de Salomoh Lz Henriquez y Semah Ferro	
Sept. 15, 1771	Moses Jr. de David Jeudah y Motta	Ribca de Aron Motta y Hz Cotino	
Before 1772	Benjamin de David Jeudah y Motta	Rachel de Moses de Castro y Athias de Neyra	

903

COHEN HENRIQUEZ (cont.)

Marriage Date	Bridegroom	Bride	Dowry and/or Remarks
March 26, 1783	David Haim de Rephael Jeudah David y LOPEZ DA FONSECA	Esther de Mordechay MOTTA y L. MADURO	4,700 pesos
March 30, 1791	Salomon de Moses David y Lz HENRIQUEZ	Sarah de Josias DE CASSERES y CASSERES	2,600 ,,
June 3, 1804	David de Moses David [y MOTTA ?]	Abigail de Rephael PENSO y MARCHENA	2,500 ,,
March 31, 1819	Jeudah de David Haim y MOTTA	Sarah de Aron PINEDO y Rz DA COSTA	7,000 ,,
Dec. 8, 1819	Mordechay de David y MOTTA	Leah de Jeosuah DE SOLA y MONSANTO (This marriage is not recorded in the Ketuboth Registers since it took place during the Piza Affair, Chapter XV.)	
Nov. 17, 1820	Moises Haim de Salomoh y CASSERES	Deborah de Abm Jb JESURUN y HENRIQUEZ	10,000 ,,
Feb. 11, 1824	Haim Josiau de Salomoh y CASSERES	Rachel de Abm Jb JESURUN y HENRIQUEZ	12,470 ,,
March 9, 1825	Samuel de Salomoh y CASSERES	Sarah de Haim Gabriel DA COSTA GOMEZ y PINEDO	27,711:2 ,,
Sept. 9, 1829	Daniel de Salomoh y CASSERES (Children: Salomon, Sarah, Rachel, Rebecca, Abigail, Leah, Judith and Hanah)	Esther de Isaac MONSANTO y PINEDO	5,666.66 fls.
Jan. 1, 1840	Moises de David y PENSO	Hanah de Mord Rephael A. CORREA y PINEDO	1,500 fls.
March 17, 1841	David de Salomoh y CASSERES	Esther de Moises ABINUN DE LIMA [y CALVO ?]	Mar. in Coro
Oct. 10, 1855	Salomoh de Haim Josiau y JESURUN	Esther de Moises COHEN Hz y JESURUN	14,000 fls.
Nov. 5, 1856	Abraham de Haim Josiau y JESURUN	Sarah de Jacob Abm JESURUN y PINEDO	14,500 ,,

904

Date	Groom	Bride	Amount
Jan. 20, 1858	Salomon de Daniel y Monsanto	Esther de Joseph Henriquez y Jesurun	8,000 "
Before 1859	Gabriel Edmond de Jeudah David y Pinedo	Batsebah de David de Castro y Hz Juliao	
Aug. 24, 1859	Ditto, widower	Judith de Jb Haim Jn Pinto y Cohen Hz	15,000 "
June 3, 1868	Dr. Abraham de Moises y Jesurun	Rebecca de Rephael Wolff y Jesurun Pinto	
Jan. 13, 1869	Haim Herman de Moises y Jesurun	Rachel de Jacob Jeosuah Naar y Henriquez	8,000 "
July 6, 1871	Jacob de Haim Josiau y Jesurun	Rachel de Jeosuah Elias Jn Henriquez y Cohen Hz	19,398 "
Sept. 22, 1875	Samuel de Haim Josiau y Jesurun	Leonor de Anjel Jacob de Moises Jesurun y Jesurun	
March 29, 1876	Salomoh de Daniel y Monsanto, widower	Sarah de Salomon Andries Willing y Benjamin	
April 5, 1876	Mordechay de Moises David y A. Correa	Delia de Jeosuah Elias Jn Henriquez y Cohen Hz	20,000 "
Jan. 16, 1878	Rephael de Moises David y A. Correa	Abigail de Abm Delvalle Hz y A. Correa	1,000 "
Dec. 11, 1880	Isaac de Moises David y A. Correa, illus. 276	Rebecca de Jeosuah Elias Jn Henriquez y Cohen Hz	19,398 (?) fls.
Jan. 18, 1905	Morris de Rephael y Delvalle Henriquez	Dalia de Mozes (Marius) A. Correa y Valencia	
About 1905	Herman de Samuel y Jesurun	Sipporah de Moses Halman	
March 14, 1906	Jacob Naar de Herman y Naar	Sarah de Aron A. Correa y Jn Henriquez	
April 8, 1908	Maurice de Mordechay y Jn Henriquez	Ida de Jacob Maduro Lopez [Hz] y Senior	
June 22, 1910	Abraham de Rephael y Delvalle Hz	Rachel de Jacob B. Salom Delvalle y Jn Henriquez	7,500 fls.

COHEN HENRIQUEZ (cont.)

Marriage Date	Bridegroom	Bride	Dowry and/or Remarks
June 25, 1910	Moises de Isaac y Jn Henriquez	Rosaura de David Moises Jesurun y Cohen Hz	Mar. in Coro
March 22, 1911	Jeosuah de Mordechay y Jn Henriquez	Agnes de Morris E. Curiel y Senior	5,000 fls.
Oct. 25, 1911	Julio de Rephael y Delvalle Hz	Belinda de Jacob Cardoze y Pinedo	35,500 " ; divorced
Nov. 16, 1916	Jeosuah de Mordechay y Jn Henriquez, widower	Olga de Morris E. Curiel y Senior	7,500 "
Aug. 31, 1918	Daniel de Benjamin y Cohen Hz	Elene de David Lopez Fonseca y Moreno [Hz]	Mar. in Coro
Nov. 4, 1919	Eugene de Rephael y Delvalle Hz	Ana de Manuel Delvalle Hz y L. Maduro	Mar. in Panama
March 12, 1921	Mario de Isaac y Jn Henriquez	Daisy de Samuel Benj Jb Pereira Brandao y Cohen Hz	5,000 fls.
Feb. 27, 1929	Josua de Isaac y Jn Henriquez	Mildred de Samuel Benj Jb Pereira Brandao y Cohen Hz	25,000 "
April 14, 1929	Julio de Rephael y Delvalle Hz	Camila de Alvares Correa Pinedo y Moreno [Hz]	4,000 "
March 26, 1930	Anjel Jacob de Samuel y Jesurun	Estela de David Haim Salas y Abinun de Lima	6,000 "
Aug. 13, 1933	Richard de Abraham y Delvalle	Emma de Salomoh Mord L. Maduro y L. Maduro	77,300 "
Nov. 6, 1935	Max Frederic de Morris y A. Correa	May de Joseph A. Correa y L. Maduro	30,000 "
Dec. 10, 1948	Ernest de Jeosuah y Curiel	Ina de Alex Curiel y Marchena	Divorced

See allied families: Aboab, Da Costa Andrade, Baiz, Pereira Brandao, Capriles, Gomez Casseres, Curiel, Delvalle, Lopez Da Fonseca, Da Costa Gomez, Henriquez, Jesurun Henriquez, Lopez Henriquez, Hoheb, Jesurun, Lansberg, Abinun de Lima, Levy Maduro, Motta, Lopez Penha, Pinedo, Jesurun Pinto, Saldaña, Senior, De Sola, Weinstein.

GENEALOGY

Amsterdam Branch: David = Leah → Moses = Leah C.H. ↘ David = Esther L.F. → Moises = Rachel L.H. →
Judith M.

Salomon = Sarah C. → Haim Josiau = Rachel J. → Samuel = Leonor J. → Herman =
Siporah H. → Milton.

London Branch: Jeudah = Rebecca C. → David = Sarah M. → Moses = Ribca M. → David = Abigail P. →

Moises = Hanah A.C. → Mordechay = Delia J.H. → Jeosuah Jossy = Agnes C.
Olga C. ↗ Ernest =

Ina C. → André, born 1954.

GABAY HENRIQUEZ

May 18, 1749	Jacob, born in Amsterdam	Rachel de Isaac Hz Juliao y Gomez	2,000 pesos
Before 1792	Isaac de Jacob y Hz Juliao	Rachel Henriquez Cotinho	
June 1, 1794	Aron de Jacob y Hz Juliao	Esther de Samuel Salomoh L. Maduro y Keyzer	800 ,,

See Naar, Sasso.

JESURUN HENRIQUEZ

Before 1671	Ephraim	Esther	
About 1680	Benjamin de Jacob	Batsebah de Eliau Namias de Crasto y Brandon	
Before 1681	Menaseh	Esther Pereira	
,, 1702	Jacob de Benjamin y Namias de Crasto	Leah de David Carilho	
,, 1704	Jacob de Ephraim	Rachel de Joseph da Costa Andrade y Aboab Cardozo	
May 27, 1721	Elias de Benjamin y Namias de Crasto	Esther de Jacob de Crasto	1,500 fls.

JESURUN HENRIQUEZ (cont.)

Marriage Date	Bridegroom	Bride	Dowry and/or Remarks
Before 1729	Abraham de Benjamin y Namias de Crasto	Sarah de Abm Rodriguez Gradis	
" 1733	Ephraim	[Daughter of David de Crasto ?]	
Dec. 6, 1733	Joseph de Jacob y da Costa Andrade	Esther [de Benjamin ?] da Costa Andrade	
Before 1740	Ephraim de Jacob y da Costa Andrade	Sarah Gaon	1,000 pesos
" 1753	Abraham de Benjamin	Sarah	
May 25, 1755	Jacob de Joseph [y da Costa Andrade ?]	Sarah Hanah de Abm Senior [y Jn Henriquez ?]	
Nov. 2, 1755	Benjamin de Elias Israel y de Crasto	Ribca de Jacob Pinedo y A. Correa	
June 27, 1756	Jacob de Elias y de Crasto	Esther de David Namias de Crasto y Marchena	
May 25, 1760	Ephraim [de Joseph ?]	Ribca de David Namias de Crasto y Marchena	
About 1775	Jeosuah de Elias y de Crasto	Hanah Leah de Samuel Hoheb	
June 12, 1782	Daniel de Joseph y da Costa Andrade	Esther de Jacob Jn Henriquez y Senior	2,800 "
Jan. 5, 1791	Abraham de Benjamin y Pinedo	Esther de Moseh Israel Naar	2,250 "
March 26, 1806	Abraham de Jacob y Senior	Rachel de Abm Mord Hm Senior y Senior	1,400 "
May 17, 1809	Eliau de Jeosuah y Hoheb	Rachel de Eliau Lopez Penha y Vaz Farro	6,000 "
May 27, 1846	Jeosuah de Elias y Lopez Penha	Sarah de Moises Cohen Hz y Jesurun	14,000 fls.
March 24, 1847	Eliau de Eliau y Lopez Penha	Deborah Dilia de David Dovale y Jesurun	4,000 "

See allied families: Alvares Correa, Curiel, Delvalle, Lopez Dias, Fidanque, Lopez Da Fonseca, Henriquez, Cohen Henriquez, Jesurun, Levy Maduro, Rodriguez Miranda, Henriquez Moron, Pereira, Senior, De Sola, Valencia.

LOPEZ HENRIQUEZ

			Pr. St., pp. 207-208
			Mar. in A'dam
About 1684	Moses [de Salomoh ?]	Rachel de Jeosuah HENRIQUEZ y BARZILAY	
Aug. 25, 1689	Salomoh	Ribca HENRIQUEZ FARRO	
Before 1716	Ishac de Salomoh	Ribca de Abraham VAZ NUNES	
" 1719	David de Moses y HENRIQUEZ	Rachel de Jacob SEMAH FERRO y A. CORREA	
About 1721	Salomoh de Moses y HENRIQUEZ	Ribca de Jacob SEMAH FERRO y A. CORREA	
Before 1726	David	Deborah Sarah, d. 1726 (C 1032)	
" 1731	Benjamin, a.k.a. Francisco, de Moises, y HENRIQUEZ	Ribca de Abraham NAAR y Lz HENRIQUEZ	
" 1741	David de Salomon	Rachel BENVENISTE	
" 1742	David	Rachel LOPEZ DA FONSECA	
" 1751	Moseh de Benjamin y NAAR	Leah de Benjamin NAAR y NAAR	
Feb. 19, 1751	Joseph Alvares, alias Lopez Henriquez	Rachel PIMENTEL	
May 13, 1759	Abraham de Benjamin y NAAR	Deborah de Jeosuah NAAR y LOPEZ HENRIQUEZ	
Dec. 7, 1760	Moses de David y SEMAH FERRO	Gracia de Mord DE CRASTO y SEMAH FERRO	
May 24, 1762	Mordechay de Benjamin y NAAR	Judith de Manuel A. CORREA y SEMAH FERRO	
Feb. 9, 1766	Jacob de David y SEMAH FERRO	Rachel de Mord DE CRASTO y SEMAH FERRO	

LOPEZ HENRIQUEZ (cont.)

Marriage Date	Bridegroom	Bride	Dowry and/or Remarks
May 18, 1766	Jacob de Salomoh y SEMAH FERRO	Leah de David COHEN Hz y LOPEZ DA FONSECA	3,000 pesos
Before 1779	Salomoh de David y BENVENISTE	Simha de CORDOVA	
Nov. 9, 1800	David de Jacob y CRASTO	Rachel de Josiau DE CASSERES y CASSERES	3,300 ,,
Nov. 26, 1823	Jacob de David y CASSERES	Abigail de Ishac Abm SENIOR [y LEVY ?]	2,385 ,,
Jan. 25, 1842	Josiau de David y CASSERES	Abigail de David NAMIAS DE CRASTO y LOPEZ DA FONSECA	
	(Children: Rachel, Abigail, Sarah, David, Leah, Jacob, Ribca, Esther and Hana)		
June 2, 1855	Josias Jr. de Jacob y SENIOR	Rachel de David VALENCIA y SENIOR	Mar. in Venezuela
Aug. 5, 1863	Isaac de Jacob y SENIOR	Sarah de Josias Lz HENRIQUEZ y NAMIAS DE CRASTO	Mar. in Coro
Sept. 5, 1866	Ditto, widower	Abigail Amethist de Isaac ABINUN DE LIMA Jr. y COHEN Hz	Ditto
Feb. 2, 1872	David Jr. de Josias y NAMIAS DE CRASTO	Julia de Mord HENRIQUEZ Cadet y NAAR	5,000 fls.
Sept. 4, 1872	Jacob de Josiau (a.k.a. Jacob Maduro Lopez) y NAMIAS DE CRASTO	Rachel de Isaac Jb SENIOR y MENDES DA COSTA	4,000 ,,
	(Jacob was adopted by Samuel Levy Maduro Jr. and assumed the name "Maduro Lopez.")		
June 8, 1887	Isaac de Josiau y NAMIAS DE CRASTO	Julia de Abraham SALAS y VALENCIA	
June 3, 1896	Jacob de Isaac y ABINUN DE LIMA	Sarah de Mord L. MADURO y ABINUN DE LIMA	
Dec. 12, 1897	Silvanio Samuel de Jacob (Maduro Lopez) y SENIOR	Eveline de David SENIOR Jr. y COHEN Hz	

910

Date	Groom	Bride	Notes
Aug. 17, 1921	Emilio de David Josiau y HENRIQUEZ	Sarah Esther de Is Jorge SALAS y ABINUN DE LIMA	5,000 fls.
Jan. 14, 1922	Julio de David Josiau y HENRIQUEZ	Adelaida de Julius Jacob SEMAH DE VALENCIA y LOPEZ PENHA	15,000 "

See allied families: Baiz, De Castro, Alvares Correa, Mendes Chumaceiro, Delvalle, Henriquez, Cohen Henriquez, Jesurun, Abinun de Lima, Baruch Louzada, Cohen Peixotto, Rodriguez Pereira, Rodriguez Pimentel, Naar, Namias De Crasto, Salas, Senior.

Genealogy: Moses = Rachel H. → David = Rachel S.F. → Jacob = Rachel de Cr. → David = Rachel de Ca. → Josiau = Abigail N.d.C. → David = Julia H. → Emilio = Sarah S. → David.

MENDEZ HENRIQUEZ

Date	Groom	Bride
April 8, 1780	Jacob, a.k.a. Gaspar	Rachel RICARDO

MORENO HENRIQUEZ

Date	Groom	Bride	Notes
1650	Aron	Sarah FRANCA	Mar. in A'dam
April 14, 1662	Aron	Batsebah de LEON	Ditto
April 23, 1694	Abraham de Moses	Ribca de Abraham MORENO HENRIQUEZ	Ditto
About 1695	Daniel de Aron	Rachel de Jacob ULLOA	
Aug. 28, 1716	Aron de Daniel y ULLOA	Batsebah de Daniel ATHIAS CARDOZO	Ditto
About 1720	Benjamin de Daniel y ULLOA	Ribca de Isaac TOURO y ULLOA	
April 1, 1722	Aron de Daniel y ULLOA, wid.	Judith de Isaac MENDEZ	Ditto
About 1724	Jacob de Daniel y ULLOA	Esther de Isaac TOURO y ULLOA	
July 9, 1732	Joseph de Daniel y ULLOA	Benvenida de Isaac BARZILAY	
May 13, 1770	Aron de Benjamin y TOURO	Leah de Isaac CARDOZO y TOURO	Ditto
June 29, 1777	Aron de Jacob y TOURO	Leah de Joseph Israel TOURO y ULLOA	
Aug. 17, 1777	Isaac de Jacob y TOURO	Esther de Aron UZIEL CARDOZO y Hz COTINHO	

MORENO HENRIQUEZ (cont).

Marriage Date	Bridegroom	Bride	Dowry and/or Remarks
May 18, 1817	Jacob de Isaac y Uziel Cardozo (Children: Isaac, Esther, Rachel and Benjamin)	Jael de Eliau Penso y Belmonte	4,000 pesos
About 1843 (?)	Isaac de Jacob y Penso	Sarah de Isaac L. Maduro y Abenatar	Mar. in Coro
Jan. 14, 1859	Eliau Penso de Jacob y Penso	Miriam de Joseph Pereira Brandao y Penso	5,000 fls.
?	Aron, b. 1789	Rachel Levy	
Aug. 10, 1881	Jacob de Isaac y L. Maduro	Rachel de Rephael Wolff y Jn Pinto	
July 3, 1890	Jacob de Elias Penso y P. Brandao	Alice de Jacob P. Brandao y Nones	
March 20, 1918	Elias Rephael Adolfo de Jacob y P. Brandao	Henny Haydee de David Delvalle Hz y A. Correa	
Jan. 27, 1945	Ivan de Elias R. A. y Delvalle Hz	Irene de Manrique Capriles y Gs Casseres	
July 3, 1946	Rene de Elias R. A. y Delvalle Hz	Norma de Alex Curiel y Marchena	

See allied families: Cardozo, Casseres, Lopez da Fonseca, Henriquez Juliao, Namias de Crasto, Israel St. Crus, Suares.

Genealogy: Daniel = Rachel U. → Jacob = Esther T. → Isaac = Esther U.C. → Jacob = Jael P. → Eliau = Miriam P.B. → Jacob = Alice P.B. → Elias = Henny D.H. → René = Norma C. → René, born 1952.

Naar Henriquez, see Naar.

Nunes Henriquez, see Naar, Sasso.

PRETTO HENRIQUEZ

Marriage Date	Bridegroom	Bride	Dowry and/or Remarks
Before 1770	Jacob	Sarah de Meza	

HERRIS

Feb. 22, 1778	Nathan, b. Hamburg	Penina de Jacob ARONS, b. St. Eustatius	

HOHEB

July 20, 1701	David de Samuel	Sarah de Simhon JESURUN	780 fls. plus; mar. in Hamburg
July 4, 1710	Ditto, widower	Jael de Benjamin FIDANQUE	
Before 1740	Samuel de David y [JESURUN ?]	Hanah Leah de Joseph FIDANQUE y JN HENRIQUEZ	2,500 pesos
After 1740	Ditto, widower	Esther de Joseph FIDANQUE y JN HENRIQUEZ	
June 19, 1765	Samuel de Samuel of St. Eustatius	Jael de Samuel y Esther FIDANQUE	3,000 "
May 18, 1766	David de Samuel y FIDANQUE	Leah de Moseh COHEN Hz y MOTTA	
March 12, 1782	Joseph Hu de Samuel y FIDANQUE	Sarah ANDRADE, wid. of Benj Motta	
Jan. 22, 1786	Samuel de Jacob d'Ancona	Jael de Jacob Eliau NAAR y A. CORREA	Both born in A'dam
March 30, 1791	Samuel de David y COHEN Hz	Esther de Moshe COHEN Hz y Lz HENRIQUEZ	1,100 pesos
About 1795	Samuel de Isaac	Hanah de Mordechay CALVO	
Aug. 16, 1795	Isaac de Samuel y FIDANQUE	Ribca de David ABENATAR	
Dec. 21, 1817	David de Samuel	Sarah de Rephael PENSO [y MARCHENA ?]	
May 13, 1827	Jeudah de Benjamin Haim	Rachel de Mosseh DA COSTA ANDRADE	

See allied families: Brandon, Cortissoz, Curiel, Jesurun Henriquez, Levy, Namias de Crasto, Van Praag, De Sola, Suares.
IFTAGH, see Garcia, Marache.
ISACSON, see Nones.

OLIVEYRA ISIDRO

Marriage Date	Bridegroom	Bride	Dowry and/or Remarks
Sept. 15, 1771	Moises, b. Bayonne	Rachel de Jacob Campos de Leon [y Garcia de Paz ?]	
See Baiz.			

ISRAEL

Marriage Date	Bridegroom	Bride	Dowry and/or Remarks
Jan, 14, 1759	Moses, b. Spain	Sarah Tores Pinto, b. Jamaica	
See allied families: Alvares Correa, Delvalle, Lopez da Fonseca, Ricardo, Santcroos.			

JESURUN

Marriage Date	Bridegroom	Bride	Dowry and/or Remarks
Oct. 28, 1655	Jacob, b. Lisbon in 1634	Judith de Jacob Barzilay y Rachel Jesurun, b. A'dam in 1635	Mar. in A'dam
May 17, 1658	Ditto, widower	Ribca de Jacob Barzilay y Rachel Jesurun, b. A'dam in 1639	Ditto
(Children: Salomoh = Sarah Aboab in 1680; Isaac, a.k.a. De Jonge, = Esther Jesurun; Aron, Abraham, Benjamin and David. The last three died in Curaçao — David and Benjamin childless.)			
Nov., 1694	Abraham de Jacob y Barzilay	Ribca de David Levy Mendes y Brandon	4,000 fls.; mar. in Curaçao
(Children: Jacob; Ribca = Isaac Gomez; Isaac; Leah = Abraham Mendes de Gama Sarah = David de Gabriel Levy; Rachel = Mordechay Haim Senior; Rachel = Abraham Lopes Dias)			
Oct. 20, 1708	Haham Rephael de Moshe	Rachel de Abm Jb Sasportas, illus. 35	4,800 fls.; mar. in A'dam
May 27, 1722	Ditto, widower	Esther de Jacob Vaz Martines y Leon Guedes	1,200 pesos

914

Date	Groom	Bride	Notes
Before 1730	Jacob de Abraham y LEVY MENDES (Children: Abraham, Aron and David Jr.)	Esther de Isaac LOPEZ DIAS	6,000 "
March 22, 1730	David de Abraham y LEVY MENDES (Children: Abraham and Jacob.)	Sarah de [Jacob ?] NAMIAS DE CRASTO	
Jan. 6, 1734	Moses de Rephael y SASPORTAS	Leah de Samuel PINTO y JESURUN ALVARES	2,400 pesos
Before 1738	Benjamin de Jacob y BARZILAY (Sarah Israel was a widow. The children of her first marriage — Moses, Sarah and Ribca — assumed the name Jesurun.)	Sarah ISRAEL	Mar. in Curaçao
1739	Isaac de Abraham y LEVY MENDES	Sarah de Rephael A. CORREA y Rz MONSANTO	4,000 pesos
1746	Ditto, widower	Esther de Jacob ABENATAR	He died childless.
Dec. 2, 1746	Moses de Benjamin	Sarah de Jacob LINDO, b. Barbados	
Before 1756	Jacob de David y NAMIAS DE CRASTO	Leah de Mordechay DE CRASTO	1,000 pesos
" 1758	Abraham de David y NAMIAS DE CRASTO (Children: Sarah = Daniel David Gs Casseres; Ribca; Leah = Jeosuah Jb Naar; Esther, David, Benjamin and Rachel)	Rachel de Benjamin Lz HENRIQUEZ y NAAR	
" 1762	Abraham de Jacob y LOPEZ DIAS	Clara de Jacob JEUDAH LEAO y PEREIRA	
April 1, 1764	Jacob de David y NAMIAS DE CRASTO, widower (Children: From the first wife — Sarah; from the second — Abraham, Ribca, Isaac, Leah, Abigail, Moses; Rachel = David Daniel Gs Casseres)	Sarah de Moses PENSO y NAMIAS DE CRASTO, wid. of Jacob Namias de Crasto	10,000 pesos
Jan. 27, 1765	Benjamin de Moses y LINDO	Rachel de Abraham BARUCH LOUZADA	

915

JESURUN (cont.)

Marriage Date	Bridegroom	Bride	Dowry and/or Remarks
March 22, 1766	David de Jacob y Lopez Dias	Abigail de Jacob Lz Dias y Penso	
March 9, 1791	Benjamin de Abraham y Lz Henriquez	Abigail de Jacob de Sola y Jn Henriquez	6,000 pesos
April 17, 1791	David de Abraham y Lz Henriquez	Sarah de Moseh de Castro y Athias de Neyra	2,250 "
Dec. 27, 1795	David Jr. de Isaac, b. A'dam	Leah de Samuel Jn Pinto y Monsanto	1,300 "
June 8, 1796	Abraham de Jacob y Penso	Esther de Moseh Henriquez y Israel St. Crus	10,000 "
July 30, 1806	Moises de Jacob y Penso	Leah de Moseh L. Maduro [Peixotto] y Lopez Salzedo	5,000 "
	(Children: Jacob, Moses, Sarah, Rachel, Judith, Abigael, Gracia, Esther and Ribca).		
Jan. 29, 1812	Abraham de Benjamin y de Sola	Rachel de Daniel Gs Casseres y Jesurun	6,000 "
Jan. 2, 1822	Moises de Abraham y Henriquez	Leah de David Abm Senior	2,143 "
	(Children: Anjel Jacobo, Ester, David, Sarah, Dilia, Abigail and Rachel)		
Aug. 28, 1829	Jacob Haim de Abraham y Henriquez	Clara de Abraham Pinedo y Marchena, illus. 105-106	8,666.66 fls.
July 4, 1832	David de Abraham y Henriquez	Sarah de Moshe Hu Jesurun y L. Maduro Peixotto	
Feb. 10, 1836	Daniel de Benjamin y de Sola	Leah de Joseph Henriquez y Pardo	4,500 "
March 23, 1836	Benjamin Jr. de Abm y Gs Casseres	Leah de Abm de Marchena [y De Sola ?]	6,000 "
Before 1838	Elias de Benjamin Abm y de Sola	Hannah de [Isaac ?] Capriles [y Dovale ?]	
Jan. 10, 1838	Daniel Jr. de Abm y Gs Casseres	Ribca de Eliau Rz Miranda y Rz Miranda	5,500 "

(Children: Abraham, Elias Jr., Rachel and Esther)

Date	Groom	Bride	Amount
Aug. 7, 1844	Jeosuah de Benjamin y DE SOLA	Abigail de Abm JESURUN y Gs CASSERES	6,000 "
Feb. 18, 1846	Jacob Jr. de Abm y Gs CASSERES	Ragel de Jacob Lz PENHA y COHEN Hz	2,300 "
Nov. 19, 1851	Anjel Jacob de Moises y SENIOR	Esther de Jacob JESURUN y PINEDO	14,500 "
June 25, 1856	David de Moises y SENIOR	Abigail de Rephael PINEDO y A. CORREA	10,000 "
March 18, 1857	Abm de Jacob Abm y PINEDO	Esther de David Abm JESURUN y JESURUN	
April 1, 1857	Jeosuah de Benjamin y DE SOLA, widower	Miriam de Isaac Elias PENSO y SUARES	7,000 "
Aug. 25, 1858	Moises de Moises y L. MADURO PEIXOTTO	Luna de Rephael PEIXOTTO y HENRIQUEZ	
Jan. 20, 1859	Dr. Moises de Jacob Hm y PINEDO	Julia de David DOVALE y JESURUN	4,000 "
Feb. 9, 1859	Benjamin Jr. de Abm y Gs CASSERES, wid.	Sarah de David PARDO y PENSO	2,000 "
June 13, 1864	David de Moises Abm y SENIOR, wid.	Rachel de Moises David COHEN Hz y A. CORREA	
May 16, 1866	Abraham de Benjamin Jr. y MARCHENA	Rachel de Daniel JESURUN Jr. y Rz MIRANDA	12,500 "
June 10, 1868	Elias Jr. de Daniel y Rz MIRANDA, illus. 277-278	Rachel de Elias Jn HENRIQUEZ y DOVALE	19,000 "
Aug. 30, 1876	Anjel Jacob de Moises y SENIOR wid.	Esther de Jacob Jeosuah DE SOLA y COHEN Hz	2,500 "
Dec. 8, 1880	Abraham de Daniel Jr. y Rz MIRANDA, illus. 137-138	Rachel Rose de David Ricardo CAPRILES y SENIOR	15,000 "
Jan. 8, 1890	Abraham Jr. de Jacob y Lz PENHA	Delia de David Lz PENHA y HENRIQUEZ	

JESURUN (cont.)

Marriage Date	Bridegroom	Bride	Dowry and/or Remarks
June 4, 1890	Jacob de Moises y Dovale	Abigail de Rephael Polly y Senior	Mar. in Puerto Cabello
June 7, 1911	Willy de Moises Jacob y Dovale	Esterlinda de David Dovale Mendez y Jesurun	
Dec. 6, 1911	Charles de Moises Jacob y Dovale	Solita de David Abinun de Lima y Cohen Hz	6,000 "
March 2, 1921	Victor de Abraham Jr. y Lz Penha	Emma de Julio Valencia y Lz Penha	6,000 "
April 6, 1949	Dr. Jessy de Charles y Abinun de Lima	Sybil de Manfredo Abinun de Lima y Valencia	
Feb. 14, 1951	Abraham de Victor y Valencia	Gloria de †Horacio Leyba y Pinedo	

(Since the bride's mother was Jewish, the religious marriage was recorded.)

See allied families: Dias Arias, Semah Barrios, Gomes Casseres, Ms Chumaceiro, A. Correa, Rodriguez da Costa, Henriquez Cotinho, Dovale (Mendez), Mendes Gama, Gomez, Henriquez, Cohen Henriquez, Hoheb, Leon, Levy, Abinun de Lima, Levy Maduro, Marchena, Monsanto, Mendez Monsanto, Naar, Penso, Piza, Robles, Sasso, Senior, Simmonds, De Sola.

See also Jesurun Pinto and Jesurun Sasportas.

Genealogy:
Jacob = Judith B. ↗ Abraham = Ribca L. M. → David = Sarah N. d. C. → Jacob = Leah d. C.
Ribca B. ↗ ⟶ Sarah P. →
Abraham = Esther H. → Jacob = Clara P. → Moises = Julia D. → Charles = Solita
A.d.L. → Jessy = Sybil A. d. L. → Aida, born in 1955.

DE JONGH

Marriage Date	Bridegroom	Bride	Dowry and/or Remarks
Aug. 23, 1837	Selomoh de Joseph Levy	Ribca de Abm Salom Delvalle y de Meza	

918

DELVALLE

See Ricardo, Salas.

HENRIQUEZ JULIAO

Date	Name	Spouse	Dowry
Before 1720	Isaac	Esther de Manuel GOMEZ	
" 1736	Abraham Haim	Rachel de David BUENO VIVAS, wid. of Abm Pessoa	
" 1742	David de Abraham y BUENO VIVAS	Esther de Samuel L. MADURO	
" 1762	Moseh de Abraham	Jeudith ROIZ MONSANTO	
Aug. 14, 1768	David de Abraham y BUENO VIVAS, wid.	Rachel de Abraham Hz COTINHO	
Aug. 23, 1795	Abraham de David	Ribca de Aron MENDES DE SOLA y GOMEZ	2,100 pesos
Dec. 27, 1795	Isaac de David	Abigail de Isaac HENRIQUEZ	1,400 "
Sept. 11, 1796	Moises de David	Rachel de Aron MENDES DE SOLA y GOMEZ	1,550 "

(Children: Rachel, Aron, David, Abraham, Hanah, Esther, Rephael, Isaac and Leah)

Date	Name	Spouse	Dowry
About 1790	Moses, b. 1770	Esther de CASTRO	
Feb. 15, 1807	David de David	Esther de Samuel L. MADURO PEIXOTTO	1,900 pesos; separated
Sept. 1, 1814	Moises de David, wid.	Judith de Aron MENDES DE SOLA y GOMEZ, wid. Abraham Bueno Vivas	302 pesos

(With her dowry Judith brought seven daughters. She bore a son and daughter to Moises, who already had nine children from his first marriage.)

Date	Name	Spouse	Dowry
Sept. 5, 1819	David de Abraham y MENDES DE SOLA	Esther de Rephael NAMIAS DE CRASTO y L. MADURO	
May 4, 1823	David de Moises y MENDES DE SOLA	Esther de Abm Haim BUENO VIVAS y Ms DE SOLA	600 pesos

HENRIQUEZ JULIAO (cont.)

Marriage Date	Bridegroom	Bride	Dowry and/or Remarks
June 27, 1827	Aron de Abraham y Mendes de Sola	Hanah de Moises Hz Juliao y Ms de Sola	
May 12, 1830	Isaac de Moises y Mendes de Sola	Leah de Abm Haim Bueno Vivas y Ms de Sola	
Jan. 25, 1837	David de David	Sarah de Abm Roiz Mendes [y Hz Moron ?)]	
Jan. 20, 1858	Jacob de Moises y Mendes de Sola	Rachel de David Hz Juliao y Bueno Vivas	
Oct. 29, 1862	Abraham de Isaac y Bueno Vivas	Abigail de Jacob Moreno Hz y Penso	10,500 fls.
Oct. 6, 1920	Samuel de Samuel	Sarah de Daniel Joseph Sasso y L. Maduro	

See allied families: Bueno Vivas, De Castro, A. Correa, Delvalle, Da Costa Gomez, Henriquez, Gabay Henriquez, Namias de Crasto, Lopez Penah, Senior.

JULIEN

Marriage Date	Bridegroom	Bride	Dowry and/or Remarks
About 1790 (?)	Moses	Hanah Abendanon	
„ 1810 (?)	Abraham de Moses y Abendanon	[Clara Mendes Monsanto ?]	
„ 1830 (?)	Ditto, widower	Rachel Lopez Diaz	

See Alvares Correa.

KEYSER (Sephardi)

Marriage Date	Bridegroom	Bride	Dowry and/or Remarks
Jan. 6, 1734	Moses Israel, b. Smyrna	Esther de Salomon Vaz Farro y Furtado	
Oct. 2, 1763	Salomoh de Moses Israel y Vaz Farro (?)	Leah de Abm Flores y Athias de Neyra	

See L. Maduro, De la Rosa.

KYWI, see De Castro.

LABADIA, see Carvalho.

LEAO LAGUNA

June ?, 1869   Moises Lopez   Catharina Ouds   Mar. in Holland

See Alvares Correa, Henriquez Moron.

LOPEZ LAGUNA

Oct. 8, 1710   Jacob de Leonore Da Fonseca, 21   Sarah de Samuel DA COSTA GOMEZ, 15   Mar. in A'dam
(Born in Lisbon, both settled in Curaçao.)

See Da Costa Gomez.

LANSBERG

Nov. 17, 1858   Dr. Selomoh de Moises Nathan y BRONNET   Esther de Haim Josiau COHEN Hz y JESURUN   12,000 fls.

Aug. 3, 1887   Maurits de Salomoh y COHEN Hz   Sarah de Salomoh COHEN Hz y COHEN Hz

July 26, 1899   Edward Eliezer de Salomoh y COHEN Hz   Jane Judith de Moses A. CORREA y VALENCIA

Oct. 28, 1916   Salomoh Moses de Mauritz y COHEN Hz   Albertina de Alberto HENRIQUEZ y SENIOR

See Pinedo.

CASTRO LARA, see Mendes Chumaceiro.

COHEN DE LARA, see Cohen Peixotto.

BARUCH LATES, see Cohen Peixotto.

LEDESMA, see Idanha de Casseres.

Marriage Date	Bridegroom	Bride	Dowry and/or Remarks
		LEEZER	
May 11, 1895	Lezer Moses de Israel y SALOMONS	Rachel Reneta de Isaac SALAS y BAIZ, wid. of Jacob van Gelder	
	DE LEMOS, see Benveniste.		
		DA COSTA LEMOS	
Before 1762	Moses	Rachel MORALES	
		DE LEON	
Before 1675	Abraham, a.k.a. Balthazar	Blanca DIAS	Mar. in Portugal; Pr. St., pp. 189-92
About 1687	Ditto, widower	Isabel (Sarah) GOMEZ CASSERES y DE LA PAS	
Sept. 8, 1788	Samuel Haim, b. Hamburg	Esther de Abraham RODRIGUEZ MIRANDA [y CAMPOS DE LEON ?]	600 pesos
Jan. 28, 1821	Daniel de Selomoh	Rachel de Isaac ALETRINO	
June 17, 1829	Ditto, widower	Esther de Joseph ISRAEL RICARDO	
About 1830	David	Abigail DE SOLA	
Before 1846	David	Esther GARCIA	
Oct. 8, 1851	Dr. Salomoh de Daniel y ALETRINO	Sarah de Moises JESURUN y SENIOR	A contingent annuity of 600 fls.
Jan. 18, 1871	Cheri Moses de David y GARCIA	Leah de Mordechay DE MARCHENA y CURIEL	2,500 fls.

(Very surprisingly this marriage is not recorded by the Curaçoan Jewish Communities.)

Date	Groom	Bride	Amount
May 3, 1876	David de David y de Sola	Rachel Rosefina de Mord	
		A. Correa y da Costa Gomez, wid. of Elie Pinedo	
Aug. 2, 1882	Daniel de Salomoh y Jesurun, illus. 158-159	Sarah de David Salomoh Lobo y Senior	

See allied families: Moreno Henriquez, Silva Leyba, Jesurun Lindo, Marchena, Salas, Tavares.

CAMPOS DE LEON

Date	Groom	Bride	Amount
1747	Jacob	Abigail de David Garcia de Paz	

See Isidro, Rodriguez Miranda.

JEUDAH LEAO, a.k.a. LEON

Date	Groom	Bride	Amount
Dec. 5, 1681	Samuel	Esther de Jacob Gaon	
Before 1714	Jacob de Samuel y Gaon	Clara de Abraham Hz Morao	18,000 fls.; Pr. St., p. 335
" 1718	Eliau de Samuel y Gaon	Rachel de Abraham Hz Morao	9,000 fls.
" 1721	Ditto, widower	Abigail de Abraham Penso y Pereira	5,000 (?)
July 15, 1727	Jacob de Samuel y Gaon, wid.	Ribca de Isaac Pereira	5,000 "
Nov. 4, 1739	Abraham de Jacob y Hz Morao	Ribca de Abraham Penso y Pereira	
Nov. ?, 1740	Samuel de Jacob y Hz Morao	Leah de Elias Pereira y Bueno Vivas	3,500 pesos
About 1745	Ditto, widower	Gracia de Rephael A. Correa y Rz Monsanto	3,650 "
Before 1747	Samuel de Elias y Penso	Sarah de Jeosuah Rephael Henriquez y Lz Henriquez	2,500 "
Nov. 2, 1755	Isaac de Jacob y Pereira	Rachel de Abm Isaac Senior y Penso	

JEUDAH LEAO, a.k.a. LEON (cont.)

Marriage Date	Bridegroom	Bride	Dowry and/or Remarks
Before 1760	Michael de Elias y PENSO	Abigail Hanah de Jeosuah Rephael HENRIQUEZ y Lz HENRIQUEZ	4,000 pesos
About 1760	Isaac de Elias y PENSO	Leah de Jeosuah HENRIQUEZ Jr. y Lz HENRIQUEZ	
May 11, 1760	Michael de Elias y PENSO, wid.	Rachel de Moses de Abm DE CHAVES	2,500 "
June 12, 1782	Elias de Isaac Elias y HENRIQUEZ	Leah de Mord Jeosuah HENRIQUEZ y SENIOR	2,800 "
Oct. 31, 1790	Elias de Samuel Elias y HENRIQUEZ	Leah de Moseh Hm DE CASTRO y ATHIAS DE NEYRA	2,100 "
Feb. 18, 1798	Jacob de Isaac Jb y SENIOR	Leah de Eliau Aron LOPEZ DA FONSECA y COHEN Hz	804:4 "
Dec. 10, 1809	Abraham Haim de Is Jb y SENIOR	Batsebah de Nachson Hz MORON y BELMONTE	1,100 "
See Leon.			
See allied families:	Da Costa Andrade, Calvo, Jesurun, Pereira.		

LOPEZ DE LEON

March 25, 1705	Abraham	Sarah de Jacob ULLOA y ABOAB	3,250 "

MACHORRO DE LEON

1681	David	Ribca de Selomoh LEVY MADURO y CRASTO	

MELO DE LEON

Before 1727	Abraham	Reyna GOMEZ	

LETOB, see Aboab.

GABAY LETOB, see Vaz Martin.

LEVATON, a.k.a. LEVANTOU

Nov. 18, 1943	Isidoro (Nissim) de Yomtob y ALMOSNINO	Caden de Moises SARFATTI y ROMI	

LEVY

About 1630	Gabriel de Manuel LEVY, a.k.a. DOVALE, 55	Leonore de PAZ, 40	

(They registered their marriage in Amsterdam only in 1649.)

Dec. 1, 1662	David de Gabriel, a.k.a. DOVALE MENDES, y DE PAZ	Leah de David BRANDON, a.k.a. HOHEB	
1694	Gabriel de David y BRANDON	Ribca de Eliau TOURO y MARCHENA	6,000 fls.
Before 1730	Elias de Gabriel y TOURO	Ribca TOURO	
About 1737	Manuel de Gabriel y TOURO	Violanta de Jacob BELMONTE y ABOAB CARDOZO	
Before 1737	David de Gabriel y TOURO	Sarah de Abraham JESURUN y LEVY	
Nov. 17, 1743	Isaac de Gabriel y TOURO	Abigail de Elias PEREIRA y BUENO VIVAS	2,000 pesos
About 1745	Ditto, widower	Leah de Salomoh de MEDINA y CARVALHO	
Before 1746	Abraham de Gabriel y TOURO	Sarah de Elias LEVY y TOURO	
June 4, 1769	Gabriel de Manuel y BELMONTE	Sarah de Isaac y A. CORREA	1,709 pesos plus
June 3, 1770	Joseph Simon, b. London	Sarah de Joseph SASSO y JESURUN	
Jan. 22, 1797	David de YOMTOB, b. Constantinople	Leah de Moses Is L. MADURO y Lz DIAS, wid. of Abm Jb Lz Dias and of Jeosuah Jb Abm Naar	1,550 pesos

Marriage Date	Bridegroom	Bride	Dowry and/or Remarks
		LEVY (cont.)	
About 1815	David Jr.	Sophia Mendes	
Oct. 27, 1824	Jehezquel de Is Levy, a.k.a. Levin a.k.a. Levison	Rachel de Abm Pinheiro de Nogueira y Lopez da Fonseca	4,360 pesos
About 1834	David	Esther de Abm L. Maduro y Athias Robles	

See allied families: Abenatar, Pereira Brandao, Aboab Cardozo, Chavez, Gomez, Moreno Henriquez, Henriquez, Moron, Naar, Athias de Neyra, Senior, Touro.

Marriage Date	Bridegroom	Bride	Dowry and/or Remarks
		LEVISSON	
Feb. 4, 1943	Benno Mozes de Levie	Maud de Jacob David Capriles y Lz Penha	

See Levy.

Marriage Date	Bridegroom	Bride	Dowry and/or Remarks
		DA SILVA LEYBA	
Before 1811	Moses de David, b. Barbados	Hannah Leon	
Dec. 19, 1811	Ditto, widower	Esther de Isaac Motta y Chaves, wid. of Isaac Hz Moron	

Marriage Date	Bridegroom	Bride	Dowry and/or Remarks
		VAN LIER	
April 27, 1860	Edward de Isak y Nanette Polak	Sarah de Simon Salomon y Sophie van Bienna	
Feb. 19, 1896	Isidor de Edward Isak y Salomon	Sila de † Louis Oduber y Julia Pardo	(Although the bride's mother was Jewish, the marriage was not recorded by the Curaçoan Jewish Communities.)

See Alvares Correa.

ABINUN DE LIMA

Date	Groom	Bride	Mar. in A'dam
Aug. 26, 1699	David de Haim, b. Venice	Leah de Mord Halas y Clara Montezinos	
Before 1724	Haim de David y Halas	Sarah Halas	
Dec. 6, 1733	Ditto, widower	Clara [de Isaac ?] Halas [y Andrade ?]	
Before 1744	Mordechay de David y Halas	Leah Halas	
Jan. 4, 1750	Haim de Moseh, b. Barbados	Leah de David Vaz Farro	
Before 1765	Haim	Ribca Monsanto	
March 24, 1765	David Jr. de Mordechay y Halas	Hanah [de Isaac ?] Calvo [y. Maduro ?], wid. of Jeudah Alva	
Oct. 10, 1769	Isaac de Mordechay y Halas	Rachel de Moses de Selomoh Levy Maduro	
Dec. 17, 1786	Haim Jr. de David y Calvo	Esther de Josias Dovale [y Ulloa ?]	3,000 pesos
	(Children: Hannah, David, Josias, Abraham, Sarah, Jeudah, Elias and Dr. Isaac)		
Aug. 23, 1795	Mordechay de David Mordechay	Gracia de Jeosuah Cohen Peixotto	1,300 "
April 6, 1803	Moises de Isaac [y L. Maduro ?]	Sarah de Isaac de Sola y Nunes da Costa	1,500 "
Feb. 14, 1808	Moseh Haim de David Mordechay y Calvo	Clara de Jacob Haim Calvo [y Bueno Vivas ?]	3,400 "
May 30, 1810	David de Haim y Dovale	Hanah de David Haim Dovale y Alva	10,300 "
May 19, 1813	Josias de Haim y Dovale	Abigail de Abm Jesurun Lobo y Rz da Costa	15,950 "
Jan. 4, 1815	Abraham Galas de Haim y Dovale	Hanah de Moseh Hu Monsanto y Taboada	6,000 "
Feb. 26, 1823	David [de Mord y C. Peixotto ?]	Clara de Isaac Haim Salas y Souza Britto	1,100 "
July 8, 1829	Eliau de Haim y Dovale	Esther de Salomoh Cohen Hz y Casseres	6,500 fls.

ABINUN DE LIMA (cont.)

Marriage Date	Bridegroom	Bride	Dowry and/or Remarks
Dec. 30, 1829	Jeudah de Haim y DOVALE	Clara de David SENIOR	1,198 fls.
March 21, 1832	Dr. Isaac de Haim y DOVALE	Esther de Jeosuah DE SOLA y ABINUN DE LIMA	3,500 „
Before 1836	Isaac Jr. de Moses y SOLAS (Children: Amethist, Salomé, Rachel, Rodolfina, Hanah and Jeudah)	Sarah de David COHEN Hz y PENSO	Mar. in Coro
Jan. 16, 1856	Haim de Eliau y COHEN Hz	Sarah de Daniel COHEN Hz y MONSANTO	4,000 fls.
Feb. 29, 1860	David de Eliau y COHEN Hz	Sarah de Rephael WOLFF y JN PINTO	
Nov. 20, 1861	Salomoh de Eliau y COHEN Hz	Sylvia de Abm Haim SENIOR y COHEN Hz	14,000 „
Aug. 12, 1863	Jeudah de Eliau y COHEN Hz	Leah de Daniel COHEN Hz y MONSANTO	4,000 „
Dec. 11, 1872	Moise de Isaac y COHEN Hz	Rachel de David COHEN Hz y ABINUN DE LIMA	
Nov. 19, 1873	David de Isaac y COHEN Hz	Sarah de David COHEN Hz y ABINUN DE LIMA	
Jan. 4, 1888	Jeudah de Isaac y COHEN Hz	Abigail de Isaac Lz HENRIQUEZ y ABINUN DE LIMA	
Feb. 4, 1891	Salomoh de Isaac y COHEN Hz, illus. 273	Sarah de Moses J. JESURUN y DOVALE	
June 20, 1894	Salomon H. de Haim y COHEN Hz (Married in Panama; divorced in Curaçao in 1903)	Emeline de Morris Osorio y COEN	
April 14, 1897	Jeudah de Isaac y COHEN Hz, widower	Zoraida Serafina de Herman COHEN Hz y NAAR	4,500 „
Oct. 18, 1905	Manfredo de David y COHEN Hz	Ribca de Isaac Lz HENRIQUEZ y ABINUN DE LIMA	

Oct. 25, 1905	David de Moise y COHEN Hz	Emma de Benjamin HENRIQUEZ y COHEN Hz	
June 8, 1912	Manfredo de David y COHEN Hz, widower	Clara de David VALENCIA y A. CORREA	
Aug. 31, 1921	Melecio de David y COHEN Hz	Deborah Delia de David VALENCIA y A. CORREA	5,000 fls.
Dec. 23, 1939	Isidore de Jeudah y COHEN Hz	Edith de Morry Isaac SENIOR y ABINUN DE LIMA	
Jan. 6, 1943	Hector de Manfredo y VALENCIA	Iraida de Charles JESURUN y ABINUN DE LIMA	
Aug. 28, 1948	Ralph de Melecio y VALENCIA	Doris de Jacob B. ATHIAS ROBLES y CASTRO	

See allied families: Bloch, Souza Britto, Dovale, Da Costa Gomez, Halas, Henriquez, Cohen Henriquez, Lopez Henriquez, Jesurun, Levy Maduro, Meyerston, Pardo, Pereira, Salas, Senior, De Sola, Valencia.

Genealogy: Haim → David = Leah H. → Mordechay = Leah H. → Isaac = Rachel L. M. → Moises = Sarah de S. → Isaac Jr. = Sarah C. Hz. → David = Sarah C. Hz. → Melecio = Delia V. → Ralph = Doris A. R.

LINDER

Aug. 7, 1955	Salo de Elias y KLEINMAN de LISZ	Elisabeth Johanna de David Jn CARDOZO y LIERENS

LINDO and JESURUN LINDO
(apparently the same family)

Before 1738	Benjamin de Jb JESURUN y BARZILAY	Sarah ISRAEL

(Sarah was a widow. Though her children Moses, Sarah and Ribca were known as Jesurun, they were not Benjamin's but were probably adopted by him.)

LINDO and JESURUN LINDO (cont.)

Marriage Date	Bridegroom	Bride	Dowry and/or Remarks
Dec. 2, 1746	Moseh de Benjamin y ISRAEL	Sarah de Jacob LINDO, b. Barbados	
Aug. 28, 1791	Jacob de Moses y LINDO, known as Jesurun Lindo	Judith de Samuel Moseh L. MADURO	400 pesos
Before 1800	Benjamin	Grace DE LEON	
„ 1814	Jacob	Judith SASSO	
About 1820	Raphael	Hannah HOHEB	
„ 1825	Jacob	Esther	
Sept. 25, 1844	Jacob de Moses	Benvenida de Jeosuah PIZA y SASSO	
April 8, 1857	Moises de Rephael y HOHEB	Ribca de Abraham SENIOR y CALVO, wid. of Mord Haim Senior	5,000 fls.
About 1885	Sam	Delia de Salomon Benj DELVALLE y PIZA	

See allied families: Delvalle, Nathan, Rodriguez Pereira, Sasso, Valencia.

LOBATO, see Henriquez.

LOBO and JESURUN LOBO (apparently the same family)

Marriage Date	Bridegroom	Bride	Dowry and/or Remarks
July 25, 1704	Daniel	Sipporah FRANCO MENDES y Rachel MOCATTA	Mar. in A'dam
June 5, 1750	Joseph de Daniel y FRANCO MENDES	Abigail de Moshe Rz DA COSTA y CAPADOCE	Ditto
June 5, 1750	Isaac de Daniel y FRANCO MENDES	Esther de Moshe Rz DA COSTA y CAPADOCE	Ditto
May 12, 1784	Abraham de Joseph y Rz DA COSTA	Abigail de Isaac Hm Rz DA COSTA y A. CORREA	14,000 pesos

About 1833	Jacob (without "Jesurun")	Leah HENRIQUEZ	
" 1854	David	Sarah CORTISSOZ	
June 13, 1860	David Selomoh de David	Clara de Jacob Haim SENIOR y PARDO	1,500 fls.

See allied families: De Leon, Meyer, Polly.

MEDINA LOBO, see Saporta.

LOPEZ

Oct. 21, 1676	Eliau, see Lopez Da Fonseca.		
About 1702	Dr. Daniel de Isaac	Leah de Jacob NAAR y HENRIQUEZ	See above, pp. 103-104.
Before 1709	Abraham	Simha COHEN RODRIGUEZ	
Jan. 17, 1731	Benjamin de Daniel y NAAR, known as Naar	Rachel de Abm NAAR y Lz HENRIQUEZ	
Before 1743	Manuel, a.k.a. Gabriel	Sarah de Moses NUNES (REDONDO) y L. MADURO	
About 1839 (?)	Elias	Sarah de Joseph CURIEL y LEVY MADURO	

See allied families: Henriquez Cotinho, Cunha, Levy Maduro, Henriquez Moron, Rodriguez Pimentel, Senior.

MADURO LOPEZ, see Lopez Henriquez.

DIAS LORENSO

| Before 1765 | Benjamin | Rachel NUNES NETTO |

BARUCH LOUZADA

| Before 1705 | Isaac | Esther DA MOTTA |
| " 1715 | Moseh | Sarah de Moseh Lz HENRIQUEZ y HENRIQUEZ |

Marriage Date	Bridegroom	Bride	Dowry and/or Remarks
		BARUCH LOUZADA (cont.)	
Aug. 19, 1729	David de Moseh	Hanah ISRAEL	
March 16, 1742	Abraham	Abigail NUNES DA COSTA, b. A'dam	
Before 1747	Isaac de Abraham	Esther de David BARUCH LOUZADA	
May 22, 1774	David	Ribca de Abraham SASSO y CAMPANAL	
See allied families:		Bueno Vivas, Lopez Da Fonseca, Jesurun, Molina.	
	LUCENA, see Henriquez Moron.		
		LURIA	
1856	Benjamin	Leah de Jeosuah PIZA y SASSO	
1857	Aaron	Rebecca de Jeosuah PIZA y SASSO	
June 9, 1889	Joshuha Ernest de Benjamin y PIZA, illus. 261	Anna de Elias DE SOLA y SENIOR	
See Levy Maduro.			
	MENDES MACHADO, see Frankel, Marache.		
		MACHORRO	
About 1715 (?)	Simon	Judith de Abm ANTUNES PAREDES y LEVY	
Before 1728	Isaac de Salomoh	Ribca de David ISRAEL	
See Marache.			
	NUNES MACHORRO, see Curiel.		

LEVY MADURO

Date	Groom	Bride	Notes
1619	Moshe Levy	Rachel de Antonio Rz Maduro y Rodriguez	Mar. in A'dam
Oct. 27, 1648	Salomon de Moshe L. M. y Maduro	Hanah de Samuel de Crasto	Ditto; Pr. St., p. 210
1654	David y Maduro	Judiqua Peres (PJCAA, Dotar, y. 5395, p. 27a)	Mar. in A'dam
Sept. ?, 1662	Ditto, widower	Deborah Gomez	Ditto
June 27, 1670	Mosseh de Salomon y Crasto	Esther Dias Sardo	Ditto
Sept. 6, 1679	Isaac de Salomon y Crasto	Esther de Jacob Rodriguez	1,000 fls.; mar. in A'dam
Before 1697	Samuel de Mosseh y Sardo	Esther Vieyra	
About 1700	Aron de Salomon y Crasto	Ribca de Abm Hz de Mesquita	
„ 1700	Isaac de Mosseh y Sardo	Sarah Touro	
„ 1701	Irmiau Rephael de Salomon y Crasto	Sarah Machorro de Leao	
Before 1709	Salomon de Mosseh y Sardo	Deborah	
„ 1717	Salomon de Samuel	Rachel Calvo	
June 12, 1729	Salomon de Aron y Hz de Mesquita	Rachel de Jacob Salom y Hz de Mesquita	1,500 pesos
About 1730 (?)	Moses de Aron y Hz de Mesquita	[Maria Gomez of New York ?]	
1730 (?)	Moseh de Isaac y Touro	Sarah de Isaac Lz Dias y Carilho	6,000 „
Before 1731	Irmiau Haim de Mosseh y Sardo	Abigail de Daniel Aboab Cardozo	6,000 „
„ 1731	Salomon de Mordechay	? ? His child died in 1731 (C 819)	
„ 1731	Samuel de Mordechay	? ? His child died in 1731 (C 819a)	
Dec. 6, 1733	Abraham de Salomon de Mosseh y Deborah	Esther de David Rephael Dias y Guadalupe	
Dec. 6, 1733	Salomon de Samuel [y Vieyra ?]	Ribca Calvo	Pr. St., p. 337
Before 1737	Isaac de Samuel y Vieyra	Esther de Salomon Mosseh L. Maduro y Deborah	

LEVY MADURO (cont.)

Marriage Date	Bridegroom	Bride	Dowry and/or Remarks
Before 1741	Mordechay	Ribca L. MADURO	
„ 1741	Jacob de Salomoh	Hanah de Samuel L. MADURO y VIEYRA	
Before 1742	Moses de Salomon de Mosseh y Deborah	? ? He had six children in 1753	
1743	Abraham de Selomoh Samuel	Rachel de Jacob Rz MARQUES y L. MADURO	
Before 1744 (?)	Jeremias de Isaac y TOURO	Esther de Abm DA COSTA ANDRADE y LEAO	3,750 pesos
„ 1746	Selomoh Hu de Isaac y TOURO	Deborah de MEDINA	
„ 1746	Samuel Hu de Isaac y TOURO	Rachel BUENO VIVAS	
„ 1746	Moses de Samuel [y VIEYRA ?]	Rachel LOPEZ	
Nov. 9, 1749	Abraham de Isaac y TOURO	Ribca BUENO VIVAS	House in Altena
Before 1750	Jacob de Isaac y TOURO	Hanah	
„ 1751	Jacob de Selomoh	[Esther de Jacob PEREIRA ?]	
May 13, 1753	Abm de Is y TOURO, widower	Rachel de Abm DA COSTA ANDRADE	1,200 pesos
May 30, 1756	Samuel de Salomon	Sarah de Moseh Israel KEYZER y VAZ FARRO	1,300 „
Before 1760	Abm de Salomon de Samuel	Rachel de Abm de Salomon L. MADURO	1,250 „ ; separated
May 31, 1761	Samuel de Isaac Samuel y L. MADURO	Esther de Benjamin VAZ FARRO y A. CORREA	800 „
Sept. 6, 1761	Salomon de Jacob de Salomon	Rachel de Isaac Sam. L. MADURO y L. MADURO	
Before 1762	Mordechay	Esther de Jacob Mord CALVO y PEREIRA ATHIAS	4,000 „
Feb. 20, 1763	Samuel de Salomon, widower	Judith KEYZER	

934

Date	Groom	Bride	Notes
Aug. 21, 1763	Isaac de Samuel, widower	Sarah de Salomon Mossen Mosseh L. MADURO y Deborah, wid. of David Motta	
1764	Salomon de Mosseh	Sarah de Jacob L. MADURO	
Feb. 12, 1764	Abm de Is y TOURO, widower	Sarah de Moses Is L. MADURO y Lz DIAS	
1765	Samuel de Is y L. MADURO, wid.	Deborah de Abm L. MADURO y DIAS	
Aug. 18, 1765	Samuel de Moses de Samuel	Leah de Daniel COHEN PEIXOTTO y CAMPOS PEREIRA	
Aug. 25, 1765	Abraham de Is y TOURO, wid.	Rachel de Moses L. MADURO	His fourth marriage
Feb. 7, 1768	Salomo de Abraham y Rz MARQUES	Rachel de Jacob de Salomoh L. MADURO	
Oct. 30, 1768	Samuel de Salomon, widower	Deborah KEYZER	
Before 1769	Isaac de Jacob y Hanah	Rachel HENRIQUEZ	
Sept. 30, 1770	Jacob de Moses de Salomon	Branca de Ephraim ATHIAS y ROBLES	
Nov. 4, 1770	Salomon de Jacob	Leah de Samuel Hu L. MADURO	
Sept. 26, 1773	Moses de Salomon	Esther de Moses SALAS y MENDES	
Jan. 29, 1775	Mordechay de Moses Salomon	Esther de Abraham SASSO y CAMPANAL	
Jan. 11, 1778	Jacob de Abraham y Rz MARQUES	Deborah de Jb David SUARES y Hz MELHADO	
About 1780	Salomoh de Mordechay	Judith	
Oct. 8, 1780	Jacob de Samuel	Esther de Abm Salomon CURIEL y CURIEL	
Before 1781	Samuel	Hanah de Abraham SASSO y CAMPANAL	
April 8, 1781	Salomon de Moses	Rachel ABOAB CARDOZO	
May 27, 1781	Jacob de Salomon	Hanah de Joseph SASSO	
May 25, 1784	Abraham de Abm Isaac y L. MADURO	Rachel de David DA COSTA ANDRADE y ANDRADE	1,400 pesos
Before 1787	Moses	Esther de Joseph ATHIAS ROBLES y DA COSTA ANDRADE	
March 4, 1787	Selomoh de Mordechay y CALVO	Judith de Samuel Haim L. MADURO	1,100 "

935

LEVY MADURO (cont.)

Marriage Date	Bridegroom	Bride	Dowry and/or Remarks
Sept. 7, 1789	Moses de Samuel y COHEN PEIXOTTO, a.k.a. Moses Levy Maduro Peixotto	Rachel de Isaac JN SASPORTAS y Lz DA FONSECA	1,400 pesos
Nov. 25, 1792	Abm de Samuel Isaac y L. MADURO	Rachel de Jeosuah TOURO y Lz DA FONSECA	1,625 "
May 16, 1793	Irmiau de Jacob	Leah de Isaac Jb L. MADURO y HENRIQUEZ	1,500 "
March 16, 1794	Selomoh de Samuel Isaac Samuel	Jochebed de Eliau Lz DA FONSECA y TOURO	1,300 "
April 19, 1797	Moses de Samuel y COHEN PEIXOTTO, widower	Judith de Samuel de Isaac LOPEZ SALZEDO y MENDES PENJA	Mar. in A'dam
Aug. 24, 1796	Mordechay de Isaac de Jacob y HENRIQUEZ	Miriam de Ishac David NAMIAS DE CRASTO y HENRIQUEZ	400 pesos
May 20, 1798	Selomoh de Is de Jb y HENRIQUEZ	Hanah de Ishac David NAMIAS DE CRASTO y HENRIQUEZ	400 "
Feb. 20, 1800	Abm de Samuel Is Samuel y L. MADURO, widower	Clara de Mordechay MOTTA y L. MADURO, wid. of Elias Dovale	1,500 " ; separated
May 13, 1804	Jacob de Selomoh de Jacob	Esther de Mosseh MARACHE y SASSO	
June 2, 1805	Isaac de Samuel y COHEN PEIXOTTO, a.k.a. Isaac Levy Maduro Peixotto	Sarah de David Jb Lz DIAS y Hz FEREYRA	2,000 "
About 1810	Mozes	Esther de Joseph ATHIAS ROBLES y DA COSTA ANDRADE	
Dec. 18, 1811	Jacob de Salomoh Jb, widower	Rachel de Mosseh MARACHE y SASSO	
About 1812	Abm de Abm y DA COSTA ANDRADE	Sarah de Jb ATHIAS ROBLES y DA COSTA ANDRADE	
Feb. 17, 1813	Samuel de Selomoh Hu y Lz DA FONSECA	Deborah de Abm Semuel L MADURO y TOURO	200 "

Date	Groom	Bride	Amount
Feb. 17, 1813	Eliau de Selomoh Hu y Lz DA FONSECA	Esther de Selomoh Mord L. MADURO y L. MADURO	200 "
Oct. 30, 1814	Jacob de Selomoh de Abm	Clara de Mord ABINUN DE LIMA [y C. PEIXOTTO ?]	
Jan. 18, 1815	Mosse de Mord Mosse y SASSO	Sarah de Jacob Abraham SASSO y SASSO	500 "
Aug. 28, 1816	Ishac de Selomoh y Lz DA FONSECA	Gracia de Jb Imanuel ABENATAR Jr. y LEVY	600 "
Before 1828	Samuel Jr. de Selomoh de Mord y L. MADURO	Judith de Abraham SASSO	
" 1834	Jeremia	Sarah	
June 24, 1835	Selomoh de Mord y NAMIAS DE CRASTO	Rachel de David COHEN Hz y PENSO	
Aug. 30, 1837	Samuel Jr. de Mord y NAMIAS DE CRASTO	Sarah de David NAMIAS DE CRASTO y LOPEZ DA FONSECA	
Dec. 5, 1838	Irmeyahu de Isaac	Leah de Rephael NAMIAS DE CRASTO y L. MADURO, wid. of Jeosuah Mord Henriquez	800 fls.; see above, p. 341.
About 1839	Isaac	Esther de Jacob JN LINDO [y L. MADURO ?]	
?	Selomoh de Mord y NAMIAS DE CRASTO, widower	Ribca de David COHEN Hz y PENSO	
March 28, 1849	Selomoh de Eliau y L. MADURO	Ribca de Eliau Ephraim CURIEL y PENSO	2,000 fls.
Before 1856	Jacob	Judith JESURUN LINDO	
Sept. 1, 1858	Salomoh de Samuel Jr. y SASSO	Esther de Jeosuah PIZA y SASSO, wid. of Henry Ms Belissario	
Between 1855 and 1873	Mordechay de Salomoh y Rachel COHEN Hz	Salome de Isaac ABINUN DE LIMA y COHEN Hz	
"	Jacob de Salomoh y Ribca COHEN Hz	Rachel de Isaac ABINUN DE LIMA y COHEN Hz	
"	Abraham de Samuel Jr. y SASSO	Anna de Jeudah SASSO y PIZA	

LEVY MADURO (cont.)

Marriage Date	Bridegroom	Bride	Dowry and/or Remarks
Between 1855 and 1873	Mordechay de Samuel Jr. y Sasso	Clara de Salomon Bravo	
" 8, 1873 "	Jacob de Samuel Jr. y Sasso	Esther de Jacob Fidanque	
Jan. 8, 1873	Moses de Samuel Jr. y Sasso	Sarah de Isaac Sasso	
March 29, 1874	David de Salomon	Betzi de Isaac Nunes Vaz	
	Jacob de Isaac	Esther de David de Castro y Jn Sasportas	
June 16, 1880	Mordechay de Salomoh y Curiel	Emma de David Jb Lz Penha y Henriquez	8,000 fls.
Dec. 15, 1880	Elias de Selomoh y Curiel, illus. 176, 191	Sarah de Elias Jn Henriquez y Dovale	25,000 "
Aug. 31, 1887	Moises de Selomoh y Curiel	Adela de Jeosuah Abm Naar y Pereira Brandao	6,500 "
Dec. 28, 1887	Ephraim de Selomoh y Curiel	Serafina de Abm Jb Jesurun y Jesurun	16,566 "
About 1888	Jeosuah de Salomoh y Piza	Blanche Brandon	
After 1888	Ditto, widower	Estella de Salomon B. Delvalle y Piza	
June 13, 1894	Samuel Ernesto de Moses Samuel y Sasso	Rosalinda de Moses Sasso y Castro	
March 25, 1908	Salomon de Mord y Lopez Penha	Bequita de Moses L. Maduro y Naar	
Dec. 4, 1912	David de Mordechay y Lz Penha	Clara de Moises Benj de Marchena y Marchena	50,000 "
May 20, 1915	Jeosuah de Moses y Naar	Rebecca Deborah de Elias L. Maduro y Jn Henriquez	
May 22, 1915	Mordechay Moses Montefiore de Elias y Jn Henriquez	Edith Rachel de Prospero Baiz y Pereira Brandao	Divorced
June 24, 1917	Salomon Abm de Ephraim y Jesurun	Rachel Louise de Joseph William Pereira Brandao v Delvalle	

Jan. 29, 1930	Milton Haïm de Samuel Ernesto y Sasso	Delia de Jacob Capriles y Lz Penha	6,000 fls.
Dec. 17, 1932	David de Samuel Ernesto y Sasso	Gladys de Manrique Capriles y Gs Casseres	6,250 "
Dec. 19, 1934	Stanley de Samuel Ernesto y Sasso	Esmée de Isaac Baiz y Cohen Hz	Divorced
Jan. 29, 1936	Jack de Jacob Fidanque y Fidanque	Ruth Senior de Benjamin Delvalle y Maduro Lopez	Divorced
Oct. 15, 1954	Muriel de Milton Hm L. Maduro y Capriles	Marvin James de Edward Isidore Gersch y Jaffe	
Aug. 29, 1964	Rene David de Jack y S. Delvalle	Debora de Jacob de Vries y Stern	

See allied families: Abenatar, Andrade, Ascoli, Pereira Brandao, Brandon, Calvo, Castro, Cayo, Alvares Correa, Henriquez Cotinho, Delvalle, Lopez Dias, Da Costa Gomez, Henriquez, Cohen Henriquez, Gabay Henriquez, Jesurun Henriquez, Lopez Henriquez, Moreno Henriquez, Jesurun, Henriquez Juliao, Machorro de Leon, Levy, Abinun de Lima, Jesurun Lindo, Marchena, Rodrigues Marques, Mendes, Henriquez Moron, Motta, Naar, Namias de Crasto, Nunes, Cohen Peixotto, Lopez Penha, Penso, Rodriguez Pereyra, Pinedo, Rodriguez, Salomon, Sasso, Senior, De Sola, Suares, Valencia.

Genealogy:

Moseh Levy = Rachel Maduro → Salomoh = Hanah de C. → Moses = Esther D. S. → Samuel =
Esther V. → Isaac = Esther L. M.↗ Esther V.F. ↗ Salomoh = Jochebed L.F. →
Sarah L.M. Samuel = Deborah L. M.

Eliau = Esther L. M. → Salomoh = Ribca C. → Mordechay = Emma L.P. → Salomon =
Bequita L. M. → Mordy, single.

MARACHE

Before 1708	Mosseh Marache, a.k.a. Meers	Raquel
" 1737	Moses	Esther Machorro
" 1756	Benjamin de Joseph	Esther de Samuel (?) Iftagh
Dec. 12, 1756	Jacob	Sarah de Aron Mendes Machado

Marriage Date	Bridegroom	Bride	Dowry and/or Remarks
	MARACHE (cont.)		
About 1760	. Moses	Sarah de Abraham Sasso y Campanal	
See allied families: Garcia, Levy Maduro, Aboab Osorio, Sasso, De Sola.			
	DE MARCHENA		
Before 1638	Abraham, a.k.a. Martienne	Sarah, a.k.a. Leonore de los Angeles	Pr. St., p. 155
Jan. 24, 1659	Isaac de Abraham y Sarah	Rebecca de David (?) Cary or Carilho	Mar. in A'dam
July 15, 1682	Abraham de Isaac y Carilho	Sarah de Mordechay de Crasto	Ditto, illus. 269
After 1691	Ditto, widower	Sarah Carilho	
About 1702	Aron	Ribca de Marchena	
" 1720	Isaac de Abraham y Crasto	Esther de Mord Namias de Crasto y Carilho	
Before 1736	Abraham de Isaac y Namias de Crasto	Rachel de Jacob de Molina y Gaon	
June 15, 1751	Isaac de Isaac y Namias de Crasto	Rachel de Moseh Penso y Namias de Crasto	
May 25, 1760	Isaac de Abraham y Molina	Esther de Moseh Penso y Namias de Crasto	
June 21, 1787	Isaac de Isaac Abm y Namias de Crasto, widower	Abigail de Moseh Penso y Namias de Crasto, wid. of Abraham Hz Moron	10,000 pesos
Oct. 14, 1795	Abm de Isaac Abm y Esther Penso	Esther de Jacob de Sola y Jn Henriquez	6,000 "
(Children: Isaac, Jacob, Moses Jr., Esther, Leah, Mordechay, Jeosuah, Benjamin, Raphael and Gabriel)			

Date	Groom	Bride	Amount / Notes
June 1, 1814	Moseh de Isaac Abm y Esther Penso	Abigail de David Isaac Henriquez	2,000 fls.
Dec. 8, 1824	Isaac de Abm de Isaac y de Sola	Esther de Abraham Pinedo y Marchena	6,500 "
Feb. 17, 1836	Mordechay de Abraham y de Sola	Jael de Ephraim Curiel y Penso (Children: Esther, Isaac, Elias, Rebecca, Lea, Ephraim and Abraham)	4,000 "
Sept. 7, 1847	Benjamin de Abm Isaac y de Sola	Clara de Abm L. Maduro y Athias Robles	Mar. in Sto. Domingo
May 23, 1860	Abraham de Mordechay y Curiel	Sarah de Eliau Curiel y Penso	3,000 fls.
Jan. 18, 1865	Isaac de Mordechay y Curiel	Clara de Haim Daniel Lz Penha y L. Maduro	5,000 "
About 1870	Elias de Mordechay y Curiel	Julia de Mordechay A. Correa y da Costa Gomez	
Aug. 5, 1874	Abraham de Isaac y Pinedo	Leah de Manuel A. Correa y Pinedo, illus. 259	Mar. in Rio Hacha
April 3, 1881	Jacob de Benjamin y L. Maduro	Olimpia de Gabriel de Marchena	Mar. in Sto. Domingo
June 21, 1882	Ephraim de Mordechay y Curiel	Abigail de Abm Ms Chumaceiro y Lz Henriquez	
Jan. 18, 1885	Moise de Benjamin y L. Maduro	Julia de Isaac de Marchena y Lz Penha	10,000 fls.
Nov. 29, 1893	Mordechay de Abraham y Curiel	Elvira de Isaac de Marchena y Lz Penha	10,000 " (?)
March 26, 1896	Abraham de Mordechay y Curiel, widower	Rachel de Eliezer Lz Penha y Hz Juliao	
June 16, 1898	Mordechay Morris de Elias y A. Correa	Clarita de Morris Jr. Pinedo y A. Correa	Mar. in Rio Hacha
Aug. 27, 1898	David Ernesto de Isaac y Lz Penha	Lucila de Moses Pinedo y A. Correa	
June 27, 1900	Rudolfo de Isaac y Lz Penha	Esther Silveria de Cheri Moises Leon y Marchena	1,500 fls.

DE MARCHENA (cont.)

Marriage Date	Bridegroom	Bride	Dowry and/or Remarks
March 11, 1908	Elias de Isaac y Lopez Penha	Angelina de David M. Jesurun y Cohen Hz	
June 25, 1908	Benjamin Ernesto de Isaac y Lz Penha	Abigail de David Haim Salas y Abinun de Lima	
Aug. 14, 1913	Virgilio de Elias y A. Correa	Rebecca de Cheri Moises Leon y Marchena	1,500 ,,
Oct. 3, 1914	Mario de Ephraim y Ms Chumaceiro	Selina de Isaac Hz Moron y Pinedo	
Aug. 3, 1918	Moises de Isaac Mord y Lz Penha	Sarah de David Haim Salas y Abinun de Lima	
Aug. 17, 1918	Ismael de Ephraim y Ms Chumaceiro	Abigail de Josias Ms Chumaceiro y Marchena	
July 8, 1922	Atilio de Ephraim y Ms Chumaceiro	Sarah de Abm Capriles y Ms Chumaceiro	
Jan. 17, 1946	Ernesto de David y Pinedo	Noemi de Isaac Senior y Marchena	
Aug. 8, 1946	Armando de Moises y Salas	Eunice de Albert Delvalle y Cohen Hz	
April 11, 1949	Hector de Moises y Salas	Elaine de Victor Jesurun y Valencia	

See allied families: Amon, Baiz, Capriles, Aboab Cardozo, Mendes Chumaceiro, Curiel, Delvalle, Gaon, Jesurun, Leon, Levy Maduro, Roiz Mendes, Naar, Namias de Crasto, Osorio, Pinedo, Sasso, Senior.

Genealogy:

Abraham = Sarah → Isaac = Rebecca C. → Abraham = Sarah de Cr. ↘ Isaac =

Esther N. → Abraham = Rachel M. → Isaac = Esther P. → Abraham = Sarah Ca.

Esther De S. → Mordechay = Jael C. → Isaac = Clara L.P. →

Moises = Sarah S. → Armando = Eunice D. → Nadya, born 1947.

↘ Hector = Elaine J. → Stanley, born 1950.

942

RODRIGUEZ MARQUEZ

May 27, 1722   Jacob   Esther de Salomoh Levy Maduro

See allied families: Athias, Levy Maduro, Cohen Peixotto.

VAZ MARTINEZ

1666	Jacob	Esther Lopez Alvin
About 1680 (?)	Ditto, widower	Esther Leon Guedes
Before 1746	Samuel de Jacob y Leon Guedes	Reyna Levy Suares
April 8, 1764	David Vaz Martin, b. London	Rachel Gabay Letob, b. Jamaica

See allied families: Jesurun, Naar.

Mashud, see Henriquez Moron.

MATTOS

Before 1743	David	Sarah Israel Monsanto	1,650 pesos
Feb. 10, 1745	Ditto, widower	Lebana Luna de Jacob Suares	1,400 ,,

See Rodriguez Miranda.

OROBIO DE MATOS

Before 1716   Abraham   Sarah

DE MEDINA

Before 1709   Salomoh   Esther de Benjamin Carvalho

See allied families: Dias Cotinho, Delvalle, Levy, Levy Maduro.

Meers, see Marache.

HENRIQUEZ MELHADO

Marriage Date	Bridegroom	Bride	Dowry and/or Remarks
Nov. 19, 1722	Jacob, b. Barbados	Leah VAEZ NUNEZ	
May 23, 1762	Abraham	Esther de Isaac SUARES	

See allied families: De Casseres, Pinheiro de Nogueira, Suares.

ABENATAR MELO, see Abenatar.

MENDEZ

Marriage Date	Bridegroom	Bride	Dowry and/or Remarks
Aug. 26, 1739	Guidon de Jeosuah	Rachel de Elias SALAS y ROBLES	Mar. in A'dam
May 20, 1753	Isaac, b. Bordeaux	Ribca de Salomon Aron L. MADURO y SALOM	Mar. in Curaçao
Oct. 16, 1763	Sabetay Israel, b. A'dam	Sarah MENDEZ CARDOZA, b. A'dam	Ditto
July 21, 1765	Guidon de Jeosuah y SALAS	Benvenida de Abm MONIS y MORON TELLES	Ditto

(This family, as all families listed in this appendix, is pure white. The statement that it had colored blood is absolutely untrue.)

See allied families: Moreno Henriquez, Levy, Namias de Crasto, Quiros, Salas.

FRANCO MENDES, see Lobo.

GABAY MENDES, see Cohen Peixotto.

LEVY MENDEZ, see Levy.

ROIZ MENDES

Marriage Date	Bridegroom	Bride	Dowry and/or Remarks
March 12, 1747	Abraham Michael, b. A'dam	Abigail de Abraham CAMPOS PEREIRA, b. Curaçao	

April 29, 1804	Abraham Haim de Abm y Campos Pereira	Jeudith de Jacob Is Hz Moron y Pessoa	2,350 pesos
Dec. 5, 1827	Abraham Jr. de Abm y Hz Moron	Ribca de Isaac Haim Salas y Souza Britto	2,266 fls.
About 1830 (?)	Moses de Abraham	Gracia Jesurun Sasportas	
Dec. 4, 1833	Jacob de Abraham y Hz Moron	Esther de Isaac Haim Salas y Souza Britto	600 ”
Jan. 16, 1839	Aron de Abraham y Hz Moron	Esther de Moises de Marchena y Henriquez	
March 15, 1862	Abraham	Sarah Roiz Mendes	Mar. in Barranquilla

See allied families: Aboab, Alvares Correa, Henriquez Juliao, Henriquez Moron, Osorio, Salas.

DE MERCADO

About 1685 (?)	David Rephael	Gracia de Casseres
June 29, 1777	Samuel, b. Jamaica	Sarah de Abraham Calvo [y Lz Penha ?]

See Delvalle, Piza.

Gomez de Mesquita, see Henriquez Farro.

Henriquez de Mesquita, see Henriquez Fereyra, Levy Maduro, Salom.

MEYER

May 12, 1847	Herman de Moses y Frederica Meyer	Sarah de Jeosuah Piza y Sasso
Feb. 11, 1874	Ludwig de Emmanuel Y Pauline Polly	Leonor de David Lobo y Sarah Cortissoz

Marriage Date	Bridegroom	Bride	Dowry and/or Remarks
		MEYERSTON	
Before 1820	Marcus (Meyer)	Rebecca de Abm David DE MEZA y ATHIAS ROBLES	
Aug. 21, 1839	Abraham de Marcus y DE MEZA	Abigail de Moises ABINUN DE LIMA y DE SOLA	
May 17, 1899	Abraham Arthur Rolando de Mauricio	Leah de Mordechay CAPRILES y SENIOR	
Feb. 8, 1900	Abraham Alfonso de Abraham y ABINUN DE LIMA	Rachel Rosalina de Menases CAPRILES y SENIOR	
See Capriles.			
		DE MEZA	
Before 1736	Abraham	Sarah PRETTO	
About 1793	Abm de David Abm	Esther de Jacob ATHIAS ROBLES y DA COSTA ANDRADE	Pr. St., p. 449
April 20, 1796	David de Salomon	Rachel de Isaac CARDOZO DA COSTA	1,025 pesos
March 1, 1826	Raphael de Abm y ATHIAS ROBLES	Gracia de Jacob DE CASTRO y JN SASPORTAS	
Sept. 23, 1829	Jacob Haim de Abm y ATHIAS ROBLES	Esther de Abm SALOM DELVALLE y DE MEZA	2,500 fls.
April 4, 1832	David Hu de Abm y ATHIAS ROBLES	Hanah de Abm S. DELVALLE y DE MEZA	
See allied families: Pereira Brandao, Delvalle, Pretto Henriquez, Mendes de Sola.			
		FROIS DE MEZA	
March 23, 1766	Abraham	Esther [de Rephael ?] GOMEZ	

946

See Mendes de Sola.

MIRANDA, see Vaz Farro, Touro.

RODRIGUEZ MIRANDA

Before 1733	Isaac de Abraham	Esther DE (MARTOS) [MATTOS]	
Nov. 23, 1755	Isaac	Sarah de Benjamin DE LA ROSA y Rz MIRANDA	4,500 pesos 12,000 fls.
June 12, 1763	Abraham	Hanah CAMPOS DE LEON	
Before 1773	Elias	Ribca LOPEZ PENHA	
Sept. 27, 1795	Abraham de Elias [y Lz PENHA ?]	Leah de Is Abm Is SENIOR [y L. MADURO ?]	
May 17, 1801	Elias de Isaac	Esther de Elias Rz MIRANDA	
Dec. 23, 1835	Isaac Jr. de Eliau y Lz PENHA	Hanah de Elias Jn HENRIQUEZ y Lz PENHA	

See allied families: Curiel, Jesurun, De Leon, Lopez Penha, De la Rosa.

MOCATTA, see Henriquez Moron, Naar, Pinto.

DE MOLINA

Before 1691	Abraham	Leah
About 1695	Jacob	Ribca GAON
June 2, 1734	Aron de Jacob y GAON	Clara de Benjamin DA MOTTA y BARUCH HENRIQUEZ
Oct. 27, 1735	David de Jacob y GAON	Rachel de Benj DA MOTTA y BARUCH HENRIQUEZ
Before 1746	Abraham de Jacob y GAON	Simha BARUCH LOUZADA

See De Marchena.

947

MONIS

Marriage Date	Bridegroom	Bride	Dowry and/or Remarks
Sept. 4, 1737	Abraham de Isaac	Rachel de Jeudah MORON TELLES	Mar. in A'dam
Before 1774	Isaac de Abraham	Esther CUNHA	

See allied families: Ailyon, Curiel, Mendes.

FROIS MONIS, see Gomes Casseres.

MONSANTO and ISRAEL MONSANTO
(apparently one and the same family)

Marriage Date	Bridegroom	Bride	Dowry and/or Remarks
Dec. 6, 1733	Isaac de Jacob Israel	Esther de Rephael JESURUN y SASPORTAS	
1736	Jacob de Isaac	Judith ABENDANA PEREIRA, widow	
Aug. 12, 1742	Abraham Israel	Ribca Ulloa	1,500 pesos
June 20, 1756	Jacob de Isaac Israel y JESURUN	Sarah [de Aron ?] VAZ FARRO [y MIRANDA ?]	
About 1763 (?)	Raphael de Isaac y JESURUN	Rachel JESURUN SASPORTAS	
Feb. 28, 1773	Moses de Isaac y JESURUN	Ribca de Moses TABOADA y Lz DA FONSECA	
April 20, 1777	Josias de Isaac [y JESURUN ?]	Esther LOPEZ REPHAEL	
Sept. 7, 1783	Isaac de Rephael Israel	Batsebah (a.k.a. Simha) de Jacob Israel MONSANTO y VAZ FARRO	200 "
March 2, 1806	Isaac Jr. de Josias y LOPEZ REPHAEL	Esther de Jacob Imanuel ABENATAR	1,400 "
March 5, 1809	Isaac de Moses Hu	Sarah de Jacob PINEDO y MARCHENA	2,400 "

See allied families: Abravanel, Henriquez Cotinho, Cohen Henriquez, Abinun de Lima, Mattos, Pardo, Rodriguez Pereira, Pinto, De Sola.

MENDES MONSANTO

Date	Husband	Wife	Dowry
May 22, 1749	Jacob, b. Lisbon	Esther de Moseh DE TOVAR	500 fls.
Aug. 17, 1777	Moses de Jacob y TOVAR	Clara de Abm Lz PENHA y Rz MIRANDA	
About 1804	Abraham de Moses y Lz PENHA	Esther, b. Cape Haiti, 1784; d. St. Thomas, 1856.	
Sept. 24, 1817	Elias	Judith DE SOLA	4, 126 pesos
Before 1818	Joseph de Moses y Lz PENHA	Esther PEREIRA	
Nov. 3, 1824	David de Moses y Lz PENHA	Rachel de Moise CARDOZE y CAPRILES	8,400 pesos
Oct. 8, 1850	Moises de Joseph y PEREIRA	Leah de Abm Jb JESURUN y HENRIQUEZ	72,997.37 fls.
Before 1855	Jacob	Judith	

See allied families: Cardoze, Henriquez Cotinho, Fidanque, Pardo.

MOLINA MONSANTO

Date	Husband	Wife
Before 1750	Raphael	Rachel de Moses ALVA y GOMES SILVA

See Morales.

RODRIGUEZ MONSANTO

Date	Husband	Wife	Dowry
Aug. 13, 1678	Isaac de Abraham	Jael de Isaac FEBOS	3,350 fls.

See Alvares Correa, Motta.

MORALES

Date	Husband	Wife
May 23, 1762	David	Sarah de Rephael MOLINA MONSANTO
Jan. 26, 1775	Ditto, widower	Abigail de Aron Hz MORON y PENSO, widow of Is Motta

Marriage Date	Bridegroom	Bride	Dowry and/or Remarks
	MORALES (cont.)		
Before 1783	Salomon	Esther Ries	
„ 1809	Abraham de David y Molina Monsanto	Sarah [de Isaac Victoria ?]	

See allied families: Henriquez, Da Costa Lemos, Robles.

Henriques Morao, see Henriquez Moron.

	MORENO		
1743	Abraham de Jacob [y Sanchez ?]	Jael de Gabriel A. Correa y Febos	

See Moreno Henriquez.

Henriquez Moreno, see De Sola.

	HENRIQUEZ MORON		
About 1662	Isaac de Aron	Ribca	Pr. St., p. 145
„ 1694	Abraham de Isaac [y Ribca ?]	Ribca [Mocatta ?]	
Before 1700	Jacob de Isaac [de Aron ?]	Sarah	
About 1705	Ditto, widower	Judith de Abm Barucha Carvalho, wid. of Moseh Frois	
Sept. 3, 1710	Aron de Isaac, b. Curaçao	Esther de Moseh da Costa, widow of Abm Da Fonseca	Mar. in A'dam
Sept. 23, 1718	Isaac de Abraham	Ribca da Fonseca y da Costa	Ditto
Jan. 13, 1719	Isaac de Abraham y Ribca	Esther Mocatta	Ditto
Before 1727	Jacob de Abraham y Ribca	Leah [de David ?] Namias de Crasto	3,500 pesos
1730	Aron de Abraham y Ribca	Esther de Abraham Penso y Pereira	

950

Rachel Semah Barrios

(Her daughter Ribca Hz Moron, who was born in Curaçao, married in Amsterdam in 1760.)

Date	Groom	Bride	Notes
1730 (?)	?	Rachel Semah Barrios	
Dec. 31, 1732	Isaac de Aron	Esther de Samuel Abarbanel Souza y Judith Machado	Mar. in A'dam
1742	Jacob de Abraham, widower	Esther de Jacob Jn Henriquez y Carilho	
Nov. 17, 1743	Ditto, widower	Batsebah de Jacob Jn Henriquez y Carilho	
Before 1743	Isaac de Jacob	Judith Lopez	
May 28, 1749	Jacob de Aron	Sarah de Abm David Levy	
Nov. 2, 1755	Abraham de Aron y Penso	Abigail de Moses Penso y Namias de Crasto	
March 21, 1762	Nachson de Jacob y Namias de Crasto	Sarah de Abm Belmonte y Naar	
About 1765	Abraham	Esther Roiz Mendez	
Before 1766	Isaac de Aron y Penso	Esther de Isaac Motta y Chaves	
Oct. 26, 1766	Abraham de Isaac	Esther de Abraham Pessoa	
May 19, 1768	Aron de Isaac de Aron	Rachel de Joseph Mashud, widow of Aron Bocaro	Mar. in A'dam
March 31, 1776	Jacob [de Isaac y Lopez ?], known as Jb Hz Moron de Lucena	Sarah de Abraham Pessoa Senior	
June 11, 1809	Isaac de Jacob y Pessoa	Clara de Samuel Is L. Maduro y L. Maduro	500 pesos
About 1842	Samuel de Isaac y L. Maduro	Sarah de Jacob Baiz y Oliveyra Isidro	
Before 1842	Abraham de Isaac y L. Maduro	Rebecca de Jacob Baiz y Oliveyra Isidro	
About 1859	Isaac	Rachel (of St. Thomas)	
Jan. 5, 1876	Ignacio (Isaac) de Abm y Baiz	Clara de Gabriel Pinedo y Delvalle	4,000 fls.

951

HENRIQUEZ MORON (cont.)

Marriage Date	Bridegroom	Bride	Dowry and/or Remarks
Oct. 27, 1886	Frederico de Abm, a.k.a. Antonio, y BAIZ	Abigail de Selomo CURIEL y DELVALLE HENRIQUEZ	
June 20, 1908	Prospero de Ignacio (Isaac) y PINEDO	Esther de Moses Lopes DE LEAO LAGUNA y OUDS	

See allied families: Capriles, Carilho, Orobio de Castro, Alvares Correa, Henriquez Cotinho, Dovale, Henriquez Fereyra, Nunez Ferro, Da Costa Gomez, Leao (Leon), De Marchena, Rois Mendes, Morales, Motta, Namias de Crasto, Pereira, Pinedo, Cohen Rodriguez, Salas, Suares.

LEVY MORTEIRA, see Pardo.

DA MOTTA

Marriage Date	Bridegroom	Bride	Dowry and/or Remarks
Before 1678	Abraham	Clara	
„ 1709	Benjamin [de Abraham ?]	Esther BARUCH HENRIQUEZ	
„ 1742	Isaac de Benj y BARUCH HENRIQUEZ	Deborah de Is CHAVEZ y LEVY	
„ 1742	Aron de Benj y BARUCH HENRIQUEZ	Rachel de Is Hz COTINHO y DOVALE	
„ 1748	Abraham de Benj y BARUCH HENRIQUEZ	Ribca NETTO	
June 30, 1748	Selomoh de Benj y BARUCH HENRIQUEZ	Rachel ALVARES CORREA	
July 7, 1748	David de Benj y BARUCH HENRIQUEZ	Sarah de Selomoh Sam. L. MADURO y CALVO	A house and a half interest in another in Otrabanda
July 7, 1748	Mordechay de Benj y BARUCH HENRIQUEZ	Hanah de Selomoh Sam. L. MADURO y CALVO	A house and a half interest in another in Otrabanda

Date	Groom	Bride	
About 1750 (?)	Moseh de Benj y BARUCH HENRIQUEZ	Sarah ROSETTA	
„ 1750	Salomon (Selomoh) de Benj y BARUCH HENRIQUEZ, widower	Ribca Hanah	
Before 1762	Salomon	Jael ROIZ MONSANTO	
Aug. 7, 1763	Isaac de Benj y BARUCH HENRIQUEZ, widower	Abigail de Aron Hz MORON y PENSO	
Oct. 16, 1768	Benjamin, b. St. Thomas	Sarah ANDRADE	
June 15, 1783	Benjamin de Mordechay y L. MADURO	Sarah de Semuel Hm de Salomoh L. MADURO [y KEYZER ?]	1,500 pesos
Dec. 18, 1793	Aron de Isaac y Hz MORON	Judith de Benjamin COHEN Hz y CASTRO	7,000 „

See allied families: Castello, De Castro, Henriquez Cotinho, Delvalle, Dovale, Garcia, Cohen Henriquez, Silva Leyba, Levy Maduro, Molina, Pereira, Ricardo.

NAAR

Date	Groom	Bride	
1620	Moise Naar, a.k.a. DE PINA	Rebecca NAAR [ABAS ?]	
About 1620	Manuel DE PINA, a.k.a. Elijah (?) NAAR	Leah SENIOR	
March 19, 1626	Francisco Ramirez Pina, a.k.a. Isaac Naar	Abigail de Baruch OSORIO	Mar. in A'dam
1640	Ditto, widower	Sarah de Manuel NAAR	Ditto
April 4, 1641	Benjamin	Reina de David CHILON	Ditto
July 17, 1648	Salomon, a.k.a. Manuel Ramirez Pina y SENIOR	Hester SALOM	Ditto
June 1, 1657	Moses de Manuel y SENIOR	Sarah de Jacob GABAY HENRIQUEZ	Ditto
Dec. 13, 1657	Dr. Isaac de Manuel y SENIOR	Rachel SENIOR	Ditto
Aug. 30, 1669	Moses	Sarah de Isaac PENSO	Ditto
March 25, 1675	Salomoh de Eliau	Ribca de Matatia ABOAB y NAAR	Ditto
March 27, 1675	Elias de Salomon	Abigail de Matatia ABOAB y NAAR	Ditto

NAAR (cont.)

Marriage Date	Bridegroom	Bride	Dowry and/or Remarks
About 1676	Jacob de Abm, a.k.a. Manuel de Pina [y SENIOR ?]	Ribca de Jeosuah HENRIQUEZ y BARZILAY	Mar. in Curaçao
May 28, 1688	Abraham de Isaac y SENIOR, wid. of Leah Naar	Gracia de Jacob MOCATTA	Mar. in A'dam
Before 1705	Abraham de Jacob y HENRIQUEZ	Leah de Moses Lz HENRIQUEZ y HENRIQUEZ	
About 1705 (?)	Jacob de Moses y GABAY HENRIQUEZ	Ribca de Jacob VAZ MARTINES y LEON GUEDES	
„ 1710 (?)	Jeosuah de Jacob y HENRIQUEZ	Sarah [de Moses ?] Lz HENRIQUEZ [y HENRIQUEZ ?]	
Dec. 29, 1712	Salomon	Rebecca NAAR	Mar. in A'dam
May 7, 1716	Isaac	Judith PRETTO y NAAR	Ditto
Jan. 17, 1731	Benjamin [LOPEZ y NAAR]	Rachel de Abm NAAR y Lz HENRIQUEZ	
	(Son of Dr. Daniel Lopez, according to the late Jossy L. Maduro [above, pp. 103-104])		
April 6, 1735	Jacob de Eliau	Gracia de Gabriel A. CORREA y FEBOS	Mar. in A'dam
Feb. 22, 1737	David de Isaac	Masaltob ALPRON	
Dec. 15, 1743	Jacob de Jeosuah y Sarah Lz HENRIQUEZ	Sarah de Gabriel LEVY y TOURO	Ditto
May 10, 1744	Jacob de Abraham y Lz HENRIQUEZ	Miriam de Jeosuah NAAR y Lz HENRIQUEZ	
Sept. 9, 1746	Moses de Jeosuah y Sarah Lz HENRIQUEZ	Esther de Jacob PINEDO y A. CORREA	
1748	Moses de Jacob y VAZ MARTINES	Sarah de David VAZ FARRO	

Date	Groom	Bride	Notes
About 1752	Jacob de Jeosuah y Lz Henriquez	Rachel de Jacob Pinedo y A. Correa	
Nov. 9, 1755	Moses de Jb y Vaz Martines, widower	Ribca de David Levy	
May 13, 1759	Abm de Jeosuah y Sarah Lz Henriquez	Leah de Benjamin Naar y Naar, wid. of Moses Benj Lz Henriquez	
May 18, 1760	Abraham de Benjamin y Naar	Leah de Moses Touro y Ulloa	
May 24, 1761	David de Jeosuah y Sarah Lz Henriquez	Sarah de Benjamin Naar y Naar	
July 2, 1769	Jacob de Moseh	Ribca de Mordechay Fundao [= Fundam]	Separated
April 17, 1774	Jeosuah de Jacob Abm y Naar	Leah de Moses Isaac L. Maduro y Lz Dias, wid. of Abraham Lz Dias	
Jan. 22, 1775	Jeosuah de Jacob Jeosuah y Levy	Ribca de Isaac Levy y Medina	2,670 pesos
Jan. 14, 1776	Jeosuah de Jacob Jeosuah y Levy, widower	Leah de Abraham David Jesurun y Lz Henriquez	
Before 1786	Abraham	Rebecca Rodriguez	Mar. in A'dam
April 28, 1793	Jeosuah de Abraham [y Naar ?], b. 1768 in Curaçao	Sol de Daniel Nunes Henriquez	Mar. in St. Eustatius
Oct. 26, 1803	Jacob de Jeosuah Jb y Jesurun	Abigail de Daniel David Gs Casseres y Jesurun	6,500 pesos
Dec. 5, 1814	Abm de Jeosuah Jb y Jesurun	Esther de Abm de Marchena [y de Sola ?]	2,500 pesos
March 8, 1823	Jeosuah de Jacob y Gs Casseres	Judith de David Jesurun y de Castro	7,150 ,,
June, 1849	Jacob de Jeosuah y Jesurun	Abigail de Jose Jb Henriquez y Jesurun	*47,928 fls.

(Children: Sarah, Rebecca, Esther, Jeosuah, Joseph and David)

* According to the lawyer Abraham Mendes Chumaceiro in his pamphlet, *Wie heeft beheerd? en Hoe is beheerd?* (above, p. 447)

955

Marriage Date	Bridegroom	Bride	Dowry and/or Remarks
		NAAR (cont.)	
March 27, 1850	Jacob de Abraham y MARCHENA	Jael de Isaac PENSO y SUARES	3,500 fls.
March 15, 1854	Jeosuah Jr. de Abm Hm y MARCHENA	Sarah de Elias Pa BRANDAO y COHEN Hz	2,500 "
About 1860	Raphael	Perla HOHEB	
May 21, 1879	Jeosuah de Jb Jeosuah y HENRIQUEZ	Rebecca de Isaac BAIZ y PEREIRA	4,000 "
March 16, 1892	Abraham de Jeosuah Jr. y Pa BRANDAO	Dagmar de Morris Osorio y COEN	

See allied families: Baiz, Belmonte, Aboab Cardozo, Gomes Casseres, Ezra, Henriquez, Cohen Henriquez, Jesurun Henriquez, Lopez Henriquez, Hoheb, Jesurun, Lopez, Levy Maduro, Athias de Neyra, Lopez Penha, Penso, Jesurun Pinto, Valencia.

Genealogy:
Jacob = Ribca H. → Jeosuah = Sarah L.H. → Jacob = Sarah L. → Jeosuah = Ribca L.

Abraham = Esther M. → Jeosuah Jr. = Sarah P.B. → Abraham = Dagmar O. Leah J.

NAFTALI, see Lopez Da Fonseca.

Marriage Date	Bridegroom	Bride	Dowry and/or Remarks
		NAMIAS DE CRASTO	
About 1600	Michiel DE CRASTO NEHEMIE	Philippa (a.k.a. Rachel ?) NUNES	Mar. in Holland
March 10, 1607	Rafael CARDOZO NEMIAS, a.k.a. DE CRASTO	Catharina MENDES	Mar. in A'dam
Dec. 24, 1643	Isaac de Abm NEHEMIAS, a.k.a. CARDOZO	Sultana GAMIS	Ditto
?	Imanuel NAHAMIAS	Rachel, d. A'dam in 1672	
?	Imanuel NAHAMIAS DE CRASTO	Sarah, d. A'dam in 1681	
Before 1656	Daniel de Imanuel NAHAMIAS DE CRASTO	Sarah	

956

Date	Groom	Bride	Notes
„ 1656	Eliau de Imanuel NAMIAS DE CRASTO	Sarah de David BRANDON, a.k.a. HOHEB	Mar. in A'dam
July 13, 1656	Simon NEHEMIAS	Sarah CARDOZA	
April 21, 1673	Imanuel NAHAMIAS DE CRASTO	Sarah TEIXEIRA	
Aug. 19, 1676	Imanuel de Eliau y BRANDON	Esther de Isaac HOHEB, a.k.a. BRANDON	8,000 fls.
Before 1688	Mordechay de Eliau y BRANDON	Rachel de David CARILHO	
Feb. 5, 1691	David de Eliau y BRANDON	Sarah de Jacob BRANDON, a.k.a. HOHEB	10,000 „
July 23, 1692	Jacob de Daniel	Sarah de Abraham ZUZARTE	
Before 1697	Jacob Namias de Crasto	Leah NAMIAS DE CRASTO, widow of Benjamin Henriquez	
„ 1709	Elias de Manuel Elias y HOHEB BRANDON	Sarah de Mord NAMIAS DE CRASTO y CARILHO	
May 2, 1709	Elias de Mordechay y CARILHO	Sarah de Manuel Elias NAMIAS DE CRASTO y HOHEB BRANDON	
Before 1718	David de Mordechay y CARILHO	Leah de Abraham DE MARCHENA y CARILHO	
April 3, 1719	Manuel Jr. de Mordechay y CARILHO	Rachel de Abraham NAMIAS DE CRASTO, widow of David Escapa Torres	
About 1732	Mordechay de Jacob	Sarah de Jacob SEMAH FERRO y A. CORREA	4,166:5:2 pesos; Pr. St., p. 295
Nov. 23, 1749	Ditto, widower	Rachel de Jacob SEMAH FERRO y A. CORREA, wid. of David Moseh Lz Henriquez	2,500 pesos
June 15, 1751	Jacob de Mord y SEMAH FERRO	Sarah de Moses PENSO y NAMIAS DE CRASTO	
Sept. 5, 1751	Elias de David y MARCHENA	Esther de Rephael A. CORREA y Rz MONSANTO	3,500 „
Sept. 3, 1752	Abm de [David y MARCHENA ?]	Rachel de David Is SENIOR y GAON	

957

NAMIAS DE CRASTO (cont.)

Marriage Date	Bridegroom	Bride	Dowry and/or Remarks
Before 1759	Jacob de Manuel	Ribca de Jacob HENRIQUEZ MORON	
Sept. 25, 1759	Isaac de David y MARCHENA	Sarah de Jacob HENRIQUEZ	
Dec. 7, 1760	Isaac de Mord y SEMAH FERRO	Leah de David Lz HENRIQUEZ y SEMAH FERRO	2,264 : 5 : 1 pesos
Feb. 9, 1766	Jeosuah de Mord y SEMAH FERRO	Esther de David Lz HENRIQUEZ y SEMAH FERRO	3,000 pesos
About 1770	Abraham de Mord y SEMAH FERRO	Gracia de David Lz HENRIQUEZ y SEMAH FERRO	
Before 1776	Isaac	Esther CUNHA	
Dec. 21, 1785	David de Mord y SEMAH FERRO	Leah de Isaac PINHEIRO DE NOGUEIRA y Hz MELHADO	2,000 "
Feb. 22, 1786	Raphael de Elias y A. CORREA	Hanah de Salomoh L. MADURO y L. MADURO	5,200
March 22, 1801	David de Isaac y Lz HENRIQUEZ	Sarah de Jeosuah NAMIAS DE CRASTO y Lz HENRIQUEZ	800 "
Sept. 20, 1812	David de Isaac Dd y HENRIQUEZ	Abigail de Jacob Lz DA FONSECA y FERNANDEZ	6,000 "
	(Children: Sarah, Abigail, Leah and Isaac)		
Sept. 3, 1817	Eliau de Rephael y L. MADURO	Gracia de Joseph COHEN PEIXOTTO y L. MADURO	2,250 "
March 31, 1824	Salomoh de Rephael y L. MADURO	Sarah de Jacob DE CASTRO y JN SASPORTAS	
Dec. 6, 1837	Eliau de Rephael y L. MADURO, wid.	Leah de Joseph COHEN PEIXOTTO y L. MADURO	
Aug. 23, 1843	Isaac de David y Lz FONSECA	Rachel de Jacob MORENO HENRIQUEZ [y PENSO ?]	Mar. in Coro

Aug. 25, 1852	Rephael de Selomoh y CASTRO	Ribca de Aron Abm Hz JULIAO y Hz JULIAO	
Nov. 10, 1858	Haim de Selomoh y CASTRO	Jeudith de Joseph Jacob SASSO y CARDOZE DA COSTA	
Nov. 6, 1861	Ditto, widower	Ribca de Joseph Jacob SASSO y CARDOZE DA COSTA	
April 9, 1862	David de Selomoh y CASTRO	Judith (Julia) de David Hz JULIAO y ROIS MENDES	
April 20, 1864	David de Selomoh y CASTRO, widower	Judith de Jacob JN PINTO y COHEN Hz, wid. of Gabriel E. Cohen Henriquez	4,000 fls.
Jan. 26, 1870	Haim de Selomoh y CASTRO, wid. of Ribca S.	Judith de Isaac Jb DE CASTRO y MOTTA	
Sept., 1873	Abraham de Selomoh y CASTRO	Rachel de Isaac Moses Hz JULIAO y BUENO VIVAS	Mar. in Coro
Dec. 18, 1878	Moises de Selomoh y CASTRO	Sarah de Rephael NAMIAS DE CRASTO y Hz JULIAO	
Jan. 14, 1880	Selomoh de Rephael y Hz JULIAO	Sarah de Benjamin CURIEL y NAMIAS DE CRASTO	
June 14, 1884	Aaron de Rephael y Hz JULIAO	Rachel de Benjamin CURIEL y NAMIAS DE CRASTO	
Dec. 8, 1906	Mauricio Mordechay de Abm y Hz JULIAO	Sarah de Jacob PINEDO y DA COSTA GOMEZ DE LA PENHA	
Oct. 21, 1931	Amilcar de Mauricio y PINEDO	Rebecca de Joseph CURIEL y SASSO	

See allied families: Amiel, Alvares Correa, Curiel, Henriquez Fereyra, Henriquez, Jesurun Henriquez, Lopez Henriquez, Jesurun, Henriquez Juliao, Levy Maduro, Marchena, Henriquez Moron, Penso, Ricardo, Senior.

Genealogy: Imanuel → Eliau = Sarah B. → Mordechay = Rachel C. → David = Leah M. → Eliau = Esther A. C. → Raphael = Hanah L. M. → Salomoh = Sarah d. C. → Abraham = Rachel H. J. → Mauricio M. = Sarah P. → Amilcar = Rebecca C. → Edith Esther = Maurice Amiel.

Marriage Date	Bridegroom	Bride	Dowry and/or Remarks
	NATHAN		
March 27, 1850	Haim Henry de Nathan NATHAN y MARKS	Sarah de Rephael LINDO y HOHEB	4,000 fls.
	NETTO, see Aboab, Da Motta.		
	NUNES NETTO		
Before 1761	Isaac	Ribca SARETTE	
Feb. 13, 1763	Joseph	Judith RODRIGUEZ	
See Dias Lorenso.			
	ATHIAS DE NEYRA		
About 1700	Joseph de Benjamin	Deborah de David LEVY MENDES y BRANDON, wid. of Abm Touro	
Before 1725	Jacob, a.k.a. Antony	Leah de Isaac de CHAVEZ y LEVY	
Dec. 15, 1743	Benjamin de Jacob y CHAVEZ	Rachel de Jeosuah NAAR [y Lz HENRIQUEZ ?]	
See allied families: Carvalho, De Castro, Mendes de Castro, Flores.			
	DA COSTA NOBLE		
Before 1761	Jacob	Rachel RODRIGUEZ PEREIRA	
	PINHEIRO DE NOGUEIRA		
April 26, 1752	Isaac, b. Lisbon	Judith de Jacob HENRIQUEZ MELHADO	
Dec. 22, 1788	Abm de Isaac y Hz MELHADO	Sarah de Jacob Lz DA FONSECA y FERNANDEZ	2,000 pesos

Oct. 29, 1845	Isaac de Abm y Lz da Fonseca	Sarah de Selomoh Salom Delvalle y Motta

See allied families: Casseres, Cohen, Levy (a.k.a. Levison), Namias de Crasto.

NONES

Before 1839	Samuel Benjamin	Hannah Carolina Isacson
Dec. 24, 1862	Alfred de Samuel Benjamin y Isacson	Esther de Joseph Pereira Brandon y Penso

See Pereira Brandao.

NUNES

March 28, 1687	Mosseh de Abraham	Deborah de Selomoh Levy Maduro y Crasto	200 fls.
Before 1722	Isaac	Rachel Aboab	

See allied families: Aboab Cardozo, Namias de Crasto, Cohen Peixotto, Nunes Redondo.

Fernandez Nunes, see Lopez Penha.

LEAÔ NUNES

April 24, 1774	Abraham	Esther de David Bueno Vivas
June 27, 1779	Ditto, widower	Sarah de Abraham Curiel y Fidanque

RODRIGUEZ NUNES

Before 1744	Daniel	Rachel Gomes Silva
Oct. 6, 1748	Isaac	Esther de Mosseh Haim Alva y Gomes Silva
Before 1758	Jacob	Miriam

See Rosetta.

Marriage Date	Bridegroom	Bride	Dowry and/or Remarks
		VAZ NUNES	
Before 1698	Abraham	Sarah	
„ 1741	Abraham	Sarah ABENDANA	
See allied families: Lopez Henriquez, Henriquez Melhado, Barzilay Robles.			
	OBADIA, see Sarfatti, Yohay.		
		OBEDIENTE	
Before 1781	Joseph Jr. de Joseph	Judith de Samuel RODRIGUEZ PIMENTEL	
See Henriquez.			
	OLIVEIRAS, see Da Costa Andrade.		
		JESURUN DE OLIVEYRA	
About 1765	Jacob	Judith de Aron ISRAEL ST. CRUS y MORENO Hz	
Jan. 31, 1798	Aron de Jacob y ST. CRUS, b. Paramaribo	Rachel de Eliau PENSO	
See allied families: Curiel, Penso, Santcroos.			
		VAZ DE OLIVEYRA	
Sept. 16, 1770	Isaac Henriquez de David	Violanta de Isaac BELMONTE y A. CORREA	
See allied families: Pereira Athias, Dias.			

OSORIO and ABOAB OSORIO

Jan. 4, 1767	Jacob de David	Gracia de Moses A. Correa y Semah Ferro, wid. of Isaac Semah Ferro	
May 25, 1794	David Jr. de Jacob y A. Correa	Judith de Moses Marache, widow of Is Abm Sasso	
Nov. 2, 1800	Moises de Jacob y A. Correa	Rachel de Jacob Is Hz Fereyra y Pereira, wid. of Moshe Haim de Emanuel Moseh A. Correa	500 pesos
	(Children: David, Jacob Haim, Gracia, Clara, Ribca and Judith)	
Before 1808	Moses Jr.	Sarah Roiz Mendes
„ 1838	Jacob Haim de Moises y Hz Fereyra	Rebecca Cardoze
Jan. 30, 1839	David de Moises y Hz Fereyra	Esther de Isaac Cardoze	2,000 fls.
About 1863	Emanuel Correa de Jb Hm y Cardoze	Clara Fidanque
June 10, 1863	Isaac Jr. de David y Cardoze	Esther Henriquez de Benjamin S. Delvalle y Castro	5,000 „
Between 1870-75	Moses Morris	Perla Coën
March 23, 1881	Isaac de David y Cardoze, wid.	Jael Julia de Elias Curiel y Oliveyra
Dec. 24, 1892	David de Isaac Jr. y Delvalle	Eveline de Murray A. Correa y Jesurun
Aug. 28, 1895	Moses de Isaac Jr. y Delvalle	Rebecca Emmeline de Mord Cardoze y Finsi
Oct. 13, 1917	Benjamin Delvalle de Isaac y Delvalle	Esther de David Isaac Osorio y A. Correa
March 11, 1925	Hubert de Moses Morris y Coen	Aura de Morris Elias de Marchena y Pinedo

See allied families: De Castro, Alvares Correa, Curiel, Fidanque, De Jongh, Abinun de Lima, Naar, Pereira.

Marriage Date	Bridegroom	Bride	Dowry and/or Remarks
	Ouds, see Leao Laguna.		
	Pacheco, see Pardo.		
	Palache, see Piza, Querido.		
		PARDO	
Sept. 12, 1619	David de Joseph	Rachel de Josias Sanchez	
1648	Josiau de David y Sanchez	Sarah de Saul Levy Morteira	
Nov. 10, 1668	Rachel de Josiau y L. Morteira	Isaac de Emmanuel Baruch	
March 15, 1679	David de Joseph de David	Esther de Imanuel Aben Atar	3,000 fls.
Before 1694	Saul de Josiau y L. Morteira	Esther	Pr. St., p. 198
" 1694	David de Josiau y L. Morteira	? ?	
	(Children: Abraham, Isaac, Josias, Saul, Joseph; Ribca = Samuel Abenatar of London)		
Dec. 6, 1733	Josias de Saul, b. New York	Esther de Jacob Israel Monsanto	
Before 1749	Abm de David Josiau David	Hanah Pacheco	Mar. in Surinam
May 1, 1749	Isaac, b. London	Abigail de David Vaz Farro y Carvalho, widow of Moses Vaz Farro	
Aug. 15, 1756	Saul	Rachel Fundam	
June 25, 1775	David de Isaac y Vaz Farro	Sarah Lopez de Paz, b. Bordeaux	
Aug. 11, 1776	Mordechay de Is y Vaz Farro	Rachel de Josiau Dovale y Ulloa	
Aug. 27, 1783	Aron de Isaac y Vaz Farro	Hanah de Jacob Abendana Belmonte	
Jan. 28, 1784	Saul Jr. de Isaac y Vaz Farro	Sarah Hanah de Hu David Israel Ricardo y Semah Aboab	
March 24, 1784	Moses de Isaac y Vaz Farro	Gracia de Nathan Pua	

964

May 2?, 1788	Josiau de Saul y Fundam	Sarah de Mord Jo Henriquez y Senior	3,000 pesos
Dec. 12, 1787	Saul Jr. de Is y Vaz Farro, wid.	Rachel de Hu David Israel Ricardo y Semah Aboab	
Sept. 18, 1799	Isaac de David y Lopez de Paz	Esther de Samuel Lopez Salzedo	
May 22, 1803	Isaac de Mordechay y Dovale	Leah de David de Mord Abinun de Lima y Calvo, widow of David Abm Senior	760 "
May 22, 1803	Josiau de Mordechay y Dovale	Sarah de David de Mord Abinun de Lima y Calvo	
	(Children: Mordechay, Rachel, Clara, David, Isaac, Abigail and Daniel)		
Aug. 30, 1812	Isaac Jr. de Aron y Abendana Belmonte	Esther de Moses Ms Monsanto y Lz Penha	2,300 "
	(Children: Aron, Moses and Hannah)		
Aug. 31, 1817	Selomoh de Aron y Abendana Belmonte	Ribca de Moses Ms Monsanto y Lz Penha	5,360:6 "
Jan. 13, 1836	David Jr. de Josiau y Abinun de Lima	Sarah de Moses Elias Penso y Suares	4,000 fls.
Oct. 13, 1841	Moise Jr. de Isaac y Ms Monsanto	Esther de Jacob de Aron Pardo	Mar. in St. Thomas
March 10, 1847	Isaac Cadet de Josias	Esther de Isaac Pardo y Ms Monsanto	Mar. in Coro
Aug. 10, 1887	Josiao de David Jr. y Penso	Leonie (Leah) de Mord A. Correa y Jesurun	8,000 fls.
See allied families:	Casseres, Idanha de Casseres, Castro, Vaz Farro, Fidanque, Henriquez, Jesurun, Pinedo, Seixas, Senior, Valencia.		

ANTUNES PAREDES

About 1685	Abraham	Rachel de David Levy Dovale Mendes y Brandon

965

Marriage Date	Bridegroom	Bride	Dowry and/or Remarks
	ANTUNES PAREDES (cont.)		
June 20, 1707	Aron de Salomon	Leah de Abm ANTUNES PAREDES y LEVY DOVALE MENDES	
See Machorro.			
	DE PAZ, see Levy.		
	ABOAB DE PAZ, see Benveniste.		
	GARCIA DE PAZ		
Before 1674	Jacob	Sarah Ribca	
„ 1752	Jacob	Sarah de Mord PENSO y DA COSTA CARDOZO	750 pesos
Jan. 24, 1762	Ditto, widower	Rachel de Daniel Israel RICARDO y ABAZ	
See allied families: Vaz da Costa, Campos de Leon, Penso.			
	LOPEZ DE PAZ, see Pardo.		
	PEIXOTTO, see Cohen Peixotto.		
	COHEN PEIXOTTO		
Oct. 8, 1623	Dio [Diego ?] PEIXOTTE, b. Portugal in 1598	Ester de Abraham DE LA FAYA	Mar. in A'dam
Before 1660	Mozes COHEN PEIXOTTO	Rachel COHEN PEIXOTTO, b. Brazil	PJCAA, Dotar, y. 5395
„ 1663	Joseph	Esther COHEN PEIXOTTO	Mar. in A'dam
„ 1670	Jeosuah	[Sarah ?], Haham Isaac Aboab's daughter	
„ 1688	David de Moshe	Rachel COHEN PEIXOTTO	Mar. in A'dam

Date	Groom	Bride	Notes
Feb. 16, 1688	Ditto, widower	Esther de Samuel Lz HENRIQUEZ	800 fls.; mar. in A'dam
Oct. 5, 1688	Josuah de Moshe y Rachel C.P., b. "Keyana" (Cayenne) in 1663	Esther de Jacob COHEN PEIXOTTO, b. Bordeaux	2,600 fls.; mar. in A'dam
June 21, 1690	Moses de Joseph	Abigail de Imanuel ABEN DENAN	Mar. in A'dam
Sept. 5, 1691	Moseh (a.k.a. Joseph) de Jacob, b. Bordeaux	Esther de Josuah COHEN PEIXOTTO y ABOAB, Haham Aboab's grand-daughter	Mar. in A'dam (PJCAA, Ket., vol. 4, no. 209)
Before 1696	Moseh de Abraham, b. Barbados	Esther PEIXOTTO	
July 6, 1696	Ditto, widower	Sarah de Benjamin ARARI, b. Barbados	3,500 fls.; mar. in A'dam
March 6, 1705	[David] Jeosua de Jacob PEIXOTTO, b. Bordeaux	Judica de Josuah COHEN PEIXOTTO	Mar. in A'dam
Oct. 20, 1706	Isaac de Josuah y ABOAB, Haham Aboab's grandson	Esther de Moseh Israel NUNES	Mar. in London
April 6, 1707	Abraham de Josuah y ABOAB, Haham Aboab's grandson	Rachel de Moseh Israel NUNES	Mar. in London

(According to Vaz Dias, this marriage was registered in Amsterdam on April 26, 1714.)

Date	Groom	Bride	Notes
Dec. 18, 1709	Josuah de Joseph	Siporah de Aron DE LA PENHA, a.k.a. DE LA FAYA	Mar. in A'dam
About 1711	Mozes	Rachel, widow of Isaac Rz MARQUES	
Nov. 17, 1712	Jacob de Diego Mendes PEIXOTTO, b. A'dam, 35	Leah ABENSUR y XIMENES, b. Hamburg	Mar. in Barbados
April 26, 1713	Aron de Jacob, b. Bordeaux	Sarah de Mozes COHEN PEIXOTTO	
March 17, 1719	Mozes de Josuah	Esther de Mozes (Joseph) PEIXOTTO	
Jan. 31, 1721	Jacob de Abm, b. Bordeaux	Ribca de Mozes COHEN PEIXOTTO	
May 7, 1722	Aron de Joseph (Josuah)	Bona CAMIS	
Before 1727	Aron	Sarah PEIXOTTO	
Feb. 3, 1729	Joseph de Mozes	Abigail GABAY MENDES	
May 31, 1730	Jacob de Joseph (Mozes)	Ribca de Abm COHEN DE LARA y Rachel ABENATAR	1,550 fls. plus; mar. in A'dam

COHEN PEIXOTTO (cont.)

Marriage Date	Bridegroom	Bride	Dowry and/or Remarks
Feb. 2, 1731	Josuah de Isaac y NUNES	Sarah de Abm PEIXOTTO y NUNES (Haham Aboab's great-grandchildren, both were born in London.)	
Feb. 5, 1740	Josuah de Moses (Joseph) Peixoto da Silva, b. Barbados	Esther COHEN PEIXOTTO, sister of Daniel Cohen Peixotto	Mar. in A'dam
About 1742	Daniel [de Josuah ?], descendant of Haham Aboab	Gracia de Abm CAMPOS PEREIRA	Most probably mar. in Curaçao
June 27, 1760	Josuah de Moses, widower	Leah de Jacob PEIXOTTO, descendant of Haham Aboab	Mar. in A'dam
March 3, 1762	Samuel	Sarah de Daniel MENDES DA COSTA	Mar. in London
May 29, 1767	Abraham de Moses	Sarah de Abm ISRAEL RICARDO	
Nov. 21, 1773	Jeosuah de Daniel y CAMPOS PEREIRA	Esther de Salomoh LEVY MADURO y CALVO	Mar. in Curaçao
Before 1776	Isaac	Rachel de David LEVY MADURO	Mar. in A'dam
July 20, 1783	Joseph de Daniel y CAMPOS PEREIRA	Rachel de Samuel Moseh L. MADURO y COHEN PEIXOTTO	950 pesos; mar. in Curaçao
March 15, 1804	Daniel de Jeosuah y L. MADURO	Ribca de Jacob Selomoh L. MADURO [y SASSO ?]	425 pesos
Dec. 24, 1809	Salomon de Jeosuah y L. MADURO	Rachel de David Is SUARES y L. MADURO	660　　"
March 20, 1811	Jeosuah de Isaac y L. MADURO	Esther de Mord BARUCH LATES	Mar. in A'dam

See allied families: Abinun de Lima, Levy Maduro, Jesurun Sasportas.

DE LA PENHA, see Da Costa Gomez, Peixotto.

LOPEZ PENHA

Marriage Date	Bridegroom	Bride	Dowry and/or Remarks
Before 1730	Jacob	Amada Rachel MENDEZ DA COSTA	Pr. St., pp. 424-26

968

Date	Groom	Bride	
„ 1745	Abraham	Rachel RODRIGUEZ MIRANDA	
Feb. 22, 1749	Jacob Lz P., a.k.a. Rz CAMPOS, b. Lisbon	Rachel (Kiña) de Joseph FIDANQUE y JN HENRIQUEZ	1,500 (?) pesos
April 18, 1753	Moseh de Jacob y Mz DA COSTA	Esther de Selomoh FERNANDEZ NUNES [y GARCIA ?]	
April 28, 1771	Daniel de Jacob y Mz DA COSTA	Rachel de Moseh Lz PENHA y FERNANDEZ NUNES	8,000 pesos
April 9, 1775	Abraham de Jacob	Rachel de David DA SILVA	Both born in A'dam
Aug. 17, 1777	Isaac de Abm y Rz MIRANDA	Ribca de Jacob Jeosuah NAAR y LEVY Ribca	
About 1778 (?)	Isaac de Jacob y Mz DA COSTA	Ribca	
July 2, 1780	Eliau Haim de Abm y Rz MIRANDA	Ribca de Benjamin VAZ FARRO y A. CORREA, wid. of Jacob P. Brandon	Pr. St., pp. 371-72
Aug. 21, 1811	Moseh de Daniel y Lz PENHA	Clara de David C. HENRIQUEZ y MOTTA	4,000 pesos
Sept. 22, 1811	Jacob de Daniel y Lz PENHA	Sarah de David C. HENRIQUEZ y MOTTA	14,000 „
Nov. 19, 1842	Haim Daniel de Moseh y COHEN HENRIQUEZ	Rachel de Abm. L. MADURO y ATHIAS ROBLES	
March 13, 1850	David de Jacob y COHEN Hz	Rebecca de Joseph HENRIQUEZ y JESURUN	3,300 „
May 9, 1855	Eliezer de Moseh y COHEN Hz	Jeudith de David Hz JULIAO y BUENO VIVAS	
Oct. 25, 1876	Haim Daniel de Moseh y COHEN HENRIQUEZ, wid.	Rachel de Abraham CURIEL y HOHEB	
Before 1879	Moses Benjamin de Haim Daniel	Adelaida DE MARCHENA	
Sept. 13, 1879	Julius de David Jacob y HENRIQUEZ	Esther de Jacob Jeosuah NAAR y HENRIQUEZ	8,000 fls.

(Children: Rebecca, Abigail, David, Julius Jr., Henry, Ida, Eduardo, Sarah, Nora and Wilfrid)

LOPEZ PENHA (cont.)

Marriage Date	Bridegroom	Bride	Dowry and/or Remarks
Sept. 7, 1904	David Haim de Eliezer y Hz JULIAO (Children: Romelia and Isaac)	Esther de Isaac Moses DE CASTRO y DE CASTRO	
Oct. 15, 1916	Julius Jr. de Julius y NAAR	Rebecca de Ephraim L. MADURO y JESURUN	15,000 fls.
March 1, 1933	Edward de Julius y NAAR	Jael de Mordechay L. MADURO y Lz PENHA	561,365.41 fls.
June 23, 1943	Isaac de Castro de David Haim y DE CASTRO	Isolina de Joseph CURIEL y SASSO	

See allied families: Baiz, Calvo, Capriles, Cardoze, Casseres, Mendes Chumaceiro, Curiel, Jesurun Henriquez, Jesurun, Levy Maduro, Marchena, Mendes Monsanto, Rodriguez Pereira, Jesurun Pinto, Senior, Valencia.

Genealogy: Jacob = Amada Rachel M. d. C. → Daniel = Rachel L. P. → Moseh = Clara C. H. → Eliezer = Jeudith H. J. → David Haim = Esther De C. → Isaac = Isolina C. → George Haim, born 1948.

PENSO

Marriage Date	Bridegroom	Bride	Dowry and/or Remarks
Before 1650	Diego Fernandez, a.k.a. PENSO	Simone, a.k.a. Abigail Pessoa de Jeronimo GOMES PESSOA	Mar. in Portugal
About 1687	Abraham P. y PESSOA	Sarah de Isaac PEREIRA y NAMIAS DE CRASTO	
Sept. 29, 1729	Mordechay de Abraham	Rachel DA COSTA CARDOZO	Mar. in A'dam
Before 1731	Moseh de Abraham y PEREIRA	Ribca de Mordechay NAMIAS DE CRASTO y CARILHO	
„ 1736	Isaac de Abraham y PEREIRA	Rachel de Elias PEREIRA y BUENO VIVAS	3,000 pesos

Date	Husband	Wife	Amount
Sept. 5, 1751	Moseh de Abm y Pereira, wid.	Abigail de Rephael A. Correa y Rz Monsanto, wid. of Mord A. Correa	2,570 pesos
Sept. 9, 1759	Mordechay de Moseh y Namias de Crasto	Sarah de Abm Isaac Senior y Penso	2,200 "
August, 1762	Ditto, widower	Abigail de Abm Isaac Senior y Penso	
April 12, 1767	Elias de Moseh y Namias de Crasto	Esther de Abm Isaac Senior y Penso	
Feb. 24, 1771	Rephael de Moseh y A. Correa	Esther de Is de Marchena y Penso	
Nov. 17, 1771	Abm de Mordechay y da Costa Cardozo	Rachel de Jacob Garcia de Paz y Penso	
Sept. 26, 1773	Elias de Moseh y Namias de Crasto, widower	Jael de Isaac Belmonte y A. Correa	
Aug. 7, 1774	Moseh de Moseh y A. Correa	Sarah de Manuel de Rephael A. Correa y Semah Ferro	
Aug. 8, 1790	Elias de Moseh y Namias de Crasto, wid. (Children: Mosseh, Isaac, Ribca, Rachel, Abigail, Esther and Jael)	Esther de Isaac Belmonte y A. Correa	949 : 4 pesos
Feb. 10, 1796	Moseh Haim de Moseh de Moseh y A. Correa	Leah de Rephael A. Correa y Jn Henriquez	5,000 "
Dec. 24, 1797	Moseh de Elias y Belmonte (Children: Elias, Jacob Haim, Benjamin, Joseph, Sarah, Isaac, Jael, Miriam and Esther)	Jael de Jacob Suares y Garcia	3,200 "
June 8, 1803	Manuel de Moseh de Moseh y A. Correa	Esther de Rephael A. Correa y Jn Henriquez	5,000 "
April 19, 1815	Isaac de Eliau y Belmonte	Sarah de Jacob Suares [y Garcia ?]	
Feb. 19, 1823	Moses de Moses Haim y A. Correa	Judith de Aron Jn de Oliveyra y Penso	3,500 "
Nov. 23, 1831	Eliau de Moseh [y Suares ?]	Sarah de Manuel Penso y A. Correa	13,333.33 fls.
March 20, 1833	Jacob Haim de Moseh [y Suares ?]	Miriam de Benjamin Suares y Penso	8,000 fls.
May 18, 1842	Benjamin de Moseh y Suares	Jael de Benjamin Suares y Penso	8,000 fls.

PENSO (cont.)

Marriage Date	Bridegroom	Bride	Dowry and/or Remarks
June 14, 1843	Ishac de Moseh y Suares	Ribca de Hu Moseh Jesurun y L. Maduro Peixotto	
May 10, 1860	Jacob de Abm y Garcia de Paz	Batsebah de Abigail Penso	
Jan. 20, 1869	Emanuel de Eliau y Penso	Sarah de Manuel A. Correa Jr. y Jn Sasportas	8,000 fls.
Dec. 22, 1869	Joseph de Moseh y Suares	Rachel de David Delvalle Hz y Penso	6,000 ,,
Jan. 4, 1871	Jacob de Eliau y Penso	Gracia de Manuel A. Correa Jr y Jn Sasportas	8,000 ,,
March 17, 1871	Moises Haim de Eliau y Penso	Hannah Esther de Salomo L. Maduro y Curiel	16,000 ,,
Dec. 5, 1888	Jesurun de Isaac Moseh y Jesurun	Sarah de Jacob Jeosuah Naar y Henriquez	8,000 ,,
March 25, 1896	Elias de Manuel y A. Correa	Abigail de Moises Delvalle Hz y Penso	8,000 ,,

See allied families: Pereira Brandao, Alvares Correa, Curiel, Delvalle Henriquez, Lopez Dias, Gerstl, Cohen Henriquez, Moreno Henriquez, Hoheb, Jesurun, Jeudah Leon, Marchena, Henriquez Moron, Naar, Namias de Crasto, Jesurun de Oliveyra, Pardo, Garcia de Paz, Pereira, Pinedo, Senior, Suares.

Genealogy:

Diego Fernandez P. = Abigail P. → Abraham = Sarah P. → Moseh = Ribca N. de C. ↘ Eliau =
Esther S.   Abigail A. C.
Jael B.   → Moseh = Jael S. → Elias = Sarah P. → Moseh Haim = Hannah Esther L. M. →
Esther B.
Salomo, d. 1956.

Alvares Penso see Ricardo

PEREIRA

Date	Groom	Bride	
About 1672	Isaac	Rachel [de Eliau ?] Namias de Crasto	
Before 1698	Eliau de Isaac y Namias de Crasto	Sarah de David Bueno Vivas	
" 1704	Jacob de Isaac y Namias de Crasto	Ribca de David Carilho	Pr. St., p. 236
July 15, 1727	Mordechay de Isaac y Namias de Crasto	Esther de Eliau y Bueno Vivas	3,000 pesos
Before 1737	Isaac de Jacob y Carilho	Hanah de Abraham Penso y Pereira	
" 1740	Jacob de Eliau	Esther de Jacob Jeudah Leon y Hz Moron	2,500 "
Nov. 17, 1743	David de Elias y Bueno Vivas	Esther de Jacob Pereira	3,700 " ; divorced
1749	Jacob de Eliau, widower	Ribca de Jacob Jeudah Leon	3,000 "
Before 1750	Elias de Jacob	Rachel Jesurun Henriquez	
Feb. 25, 1759	Elias Haim de Jacob	Sarah de Mordechay Pereira y Pereira	
Aug. 14, 1768	Jacob de Eliau, widower	Rebecca de Abm Hz Cotinho	
Sept. 25, 1768	Jacob de Mordechay y Pereira	Esther de Aron Motta y Hz Cotinho	
June 16, 1771	Joseph [Pereira] of Paris	Abigail de Mord Abinun de Lima y Halas	
Jan. 5, 1777	Isaac Haim de Jacob y Leon	Clara de Abraham Jeudah Leon y Penso	
About 1777	Isaac	Ribca Henriquez Moron	
Aug. 12, 1798	Jacob de Isaac Haim y Leon	Esther de Jacob Aboab Osorio Jr. [y A. Correa ?]	3,317:4 pesos
Sept. 3, 1820	Ditto, widower	Sarah de Isaac Sebastiaan Hz Cotinho	

(This marriage is not recorded in the MIA Ketuboth Registers since it took place during the Piza Affair, Chapter XV.)

See allied families: Abenatar, Baiz, Henriquez Fereyra, Da Costa Gomez, Jesurun Henriquez, Jeudah Leon, Levy, Penso, Piza.

Marriage Date	Bridegroom	Bride	Dowry and/or Remarks
		ABENDANA PEREIRA	
Before 1674	David	Sarah	Pr. St., pp. 220-21
Sept. 4, 1699	Joseph de David, b. Curaçao	Judith Lopes Telles	Mar. in A'dam
See Monsanto.			
		CAMPOS PEREIRA	
Before 1726	Abraham	Sarah Gomez	
See allied families: Roiz Mendez, Cohen Peixotto, Pessoa.			
		CORONEL PEREIRA	
Before 1792	Abraham	Simha Vieira	
		LOPEZ PEREIRA	
Before 1763	Jacob (in Curaçao in 1763)	Esther de Antonio Gomez Casseres y Frois Monis	Mar. in Bordeaux
Medina Pereira, see Da Costa Gomez.			
Nunes Pereira, see Tovar.			
		RODRIGUEZ PEREIRA (also without "Rodriguez")	
Before 1745	Isaac	Esther	
Aug. 1, 1762	Jacob Haim	Judith de Abm Israel Monsanto [y Ulloa ?]	

974

Date	Groom	Bride	Amount
Oct. 17, 1762	Abraham	Ribca de David Lz Henriquez y Lz da Fonseca	
March 26, 1809	Samuel de Jacob Haim y Monsanto	Hanah de Samuel Is L. Maduro y L. Maduro	500 pesos
Nov. 26, 1834	Jacob Haim de Samuel y L. Maduro	Sarah de Mord L. Maduro y Namias de Crasto	
Jan. 24, 1838	Samuel Jr. de Samuel y L. Maduro	Sarah de Moseh Daniel Lz Penha y Cohen Hz	
Feb. 7, 1849	Moseh de Samuel y L. Maduro	Jochebed de Eliau L. Maduro y L. Maduro	3,920 fls.
Jan. 31, 1872	Isaac Haim de Jacob Haim y L. Maduro	Julia Jael de Abm Jb Senior y Senior	15,000 ,,
Nov. 22, 1876	Samuel de Moses y L. Maduro	Hannah de Moses Lindo y Senior	
Aug. 21, 1881	Salomon de Jacob Haim y L. Maduro	Hannah de Jeudah Senior y Senior	
Feb. 8, 1905	Henry de Isaac Haim y Senior	Else de Gustave Julio Sturmthal y Senior	

See Curiel.

PEREZ, see Levy Maduro, Sasso.

PESSOA

Before 1742	Abraham	Rachel de David Bueno Vivas
,, 1751	Abraham Sr	Rachel de Campos Pereira

See Henriquez Moron, Penso.

PIMENTEL

Before 1790	Samuel	Sarah Souza

See Lopez Henriquez, Senior.

Marriage Date	Bridegroom	Bride	Dowry and/or Remarks
	HENRIQUEZ PIMENTEL		
Before 1764	David	Ribca MENDES DE SOLAS	
	RODRIGUEZ PIMENTEL		
Before 1734	Samuel	Sarah de Abraham LOPEZ	
1744	Abraham Sr	Esther LOPEZ HENRIQUEZ	
Before 1764	Abraham Jr.	Simha de Abm SASPORTAS y PIMENTEL	
See allied families: Obediente, Rodrigues Rivera, Ricardo, Sasportas.			
	PINEDO		
Before 1719	Jacob [de Gabriel ?]	Sarah de Manuel A. CORREA y FEBOS	Pr. St., pp. 354-57
Nov. 2, 1755	Gabriel de Jacob y A. CORREA	Clara de Aron Hz MORON y PENSO	
	(Children: Jacob, Aron, Manuel, Abraham, Rephael and Esther)		
Nov. 2, 1755	Manuel de Jacob y A. CORREA	Ribca de Aron Hz MORON y PENSO	
Jan. 8, 1783	Jacob de Gabriel y Hz MORON	Ribca de Isaac DE MARCHENA y PENSO	6,000 pesos
	(Children: Gabriel, Clara, Rachel, Sarah, Isaac and Esther)		
Nov. 10, 1784	Aron de Gabriel y Hz MORON	Leah de Isaac Haim Rz DA COSTA y A. CORREA	14,000 "
Feb. 4, 1795	Rephael de Gabriel y Hz Moron	Abigail de Moseh de Moseh PENSO y A. CORREA	8,000 "
June 4, 1800	Abraham de Gabriel y Hz MORON	Ribca de Is Abm DE MARCHENA y PENSO	6,500 "
Sept. 3, 1806	Gabriel de Iacob y MARCHENA	Judith de David Is HENRIQUEZ y CASTRO	6,400 "

Date	Groom	Bride	Amount
June 1, 1814	Gabriel de Aron y Rz da Costa	Abigail de Isaac Abm de Marchena y Penso	6,500 "
April 7, 1824	Moseh de Aron y Rz da Costa	Esther de Rephael Pinedo y Penso	3,400 "
Dec. 15, 1824	Moses de Rephael y Penso	Clara de Aron Pinedo y Rz da Costa	7,000 "
Nov. 19, 1828	Gabriel de Abraham y Marchena	Esther Juliette de Elias Delvalle y Pinedo	8,000 fls.
March 11, 1835	Rephael de Rephael y Penso	Ribca de Mordechay A. Correa y Pinedo	2,666.64 fls.
April 15, 1856	Isaac Jr. de Abm y Marchena, 47	Ribca de Gabriel Pinedo y Delvalle, 18	
March 23, 1859	Abraham de Gabriel y Delvalle	Deborah de Haim Josiau Cohen Hz y Jesurun	12,000 fls.
April 6, 1859	Mordechay (Murray) de Rephael y A. Correa	Clara de Imanuel A. Correa Jr. y Jn Sasportas	8,000 "
June 17, 1863	Eli de Gabriel y Delvalle	Roserfina Alvares Correa	Mar. in Rio Hacha
July 1, 1868	Moises de Rephael y A. Correa	Miriam de Imanuel A. Correa Jr. y Jn Sasportas	16,000 fls.
?	Morris Gabriel	Hanah de Imanuel A. Correa	
Sept. 13, 1871	Jacob Jr. de Gabriel y Delvalle	Jeudith de Daniel da Costa Gomez de la Penha y Hz Moron	
Sept. 6, 1876	David de Rephael y A. Correa, 18	Rachel de Isaac Josias Dovale Mendez y Abinun de Lima, 14	49,000 "
July 4, 1877	Emmanuel de Rephael y A. Correa	Emma de Moise Pardo Jr.	36,000 marks; mar. in Hamburg
Feb. 27, 1884	Rodolfo de Murray (Mord) y A. Correa	Rebecca de Murray A. Correa y Jesurun	
June 7, 1893	Alvares Correa de Murray (Mord) y A. Correa	Rosa Amalia de Elias Moreno Hz y P. Brandao	1,280 fls.
Nov. 29, 1899	Moises Michael de Moses y A. Correa	Rebecca de Moses Ephraim Curiel y Curiel	3,500 "

977

PINEDO (cont.)

Marriage Date	Bridegroom	Bride	Dowry and/or Remarks
Nov. 29, 1903	Emmanuel de Morris Jr. y A. CORREA	Roserfina de Elias DE MARCHENA y A. CORREA	
April 20, 1904	Enrique de Murray y A. CORREA	Abigail de Raymondo A. CORREA y ROIZ MENDEZ	Mar. in Coro
June 15, 1911	Rowland de David y DOVALE MENDEZ	Rosaura de Ephraim DE MARCHENA y Ms CHUMACEIRO	
April 9, 1913	Jacob de Isaac Jr. y PINEDO	Judith de Morris Gabriel PINEDO y A. CORREA	
Dec. 21, 1935	Victor de Moises Michael y CURIEL	Emma de David L. MADURO y MARCHENA	
March 14, 1937	Isidore de Alvares Correa y MORENO Hz	Nilda de Elias Penso DELVALLE y PENSO	
Nov. 18, 1939	Victor de Moises Michael y CURIEL, widower	Else de Jacob Naar COHEN Hz y A. CORREA	
Nov. 9, 1940	Michael Herbert de Mozes Michael y CURIEL	Enid de Salomon Mozes LANSBERG y HENRIQUEZ	

See allied families: Baiz, Pereira Brandao, Capriles, Cardoze, Alvares Correa, Delvalle, Lopez da Fonseca, Da Costa Gomez, Henriquez, Cohen Henriquez, Jesurun Henriquez, Jesurun, Marchena, Monsanto, Henriquez Moron, Naar, Namias de Crasto.

Genealogy: Jacob = Sarah A.C. → Gabriel = Clara H.M. → Rephael = Abigail P. → Rephael = Ribca A.C. → Moshe = Miriam A.C. → Moises Michael = Rebecca C. → Michael Herbert = Enid L. → Herbert Michael.

PINHEIRO, see Mendes da Gama.

PINTO

Marriage Date	Bridegroom	Bride	Dowry and/or Remarks
Jan. 23, 1671	David de Mordechay	Leah MOCATA	

Dec. 13, 1675	Ditto, widower	Rachel de Crasto, a.k.a. Maria Cardozo	Mar. in A'dam
May 7, 1677	Ditto, widower	Sarah Henriquez Alvares	Ditto
About 1715 (?)	Samuel de David y Hz Alvares	Sarah de Rephael Jesurun Alvares	
Nov. 13, 1746	Rephael de Samuel y Jn Alvares	Sarah de Moses Pereira Athias y Vaz de Oliveyra	

See Bueno, Jesurun.

JESURUN PINTO

(Though known as Pinto, this family belongs to the Jesurun family and is descended from Haham Rephael Jesurun.)

Jan. 6, 1734	Moseh de Rephael Jesurun y Sasportas	Leah de Samuel Pinto y Jn Alvares	2,400 pesos
Before 1763	Samuel de Moses Jesurun y Pinto, a.k.a. Jesurun Pinto	Judith de Isaac Monsanto y Jesurun	
Dec. 29, 1790	Isaac de Samuel y Monsanto	Rachel de David Naar y Naar	1,600 ”
About 1805 (?)	Abraham de Samuel y Monsanto	Sarah Gomez Fonseca	Pr. St., p. 429
Aug. 21, 1811	Jacob de Samuel y Monsanto	Rachel de David Haim Cohen Hz y Motta	2,000 pesos
Sept. 9, 1835	David de Jacob y Cohen Hz	Esther de Moseh Lz Penha y Cohen Hz	
Aug. 28, 1872	Jacob de David y Lz Penha	Abigail de Benjamin Henriquez y Hz Juliao	4,000 fls.

See allied families: Cortissoz, Henriquez, Cohen Henriquez, Jesurun, Namias de Crasto, De Sola, Wolff.

Torres Pinto, see Israel.

979

PIZA

Marriage Date	Bridegroom	Bride	Dowry and/or Remarks
Before 1702	Haim de Haim, b. Constantinople	Sarah Gabay	
June 1, 1702	Ditto, widower	Miriam de Jacob Aubi, b. Belgrade	300 fls.
June 16, 1723	Jeudah de Haim y Aubi	Luna de Samuel Sphorni	1,400 ”
March 5, 1727	Jacob de Haim y Aubi	Rose de Jeudah y Esther Granada	1,300 ”
Jan. 25, 1731	Joseph de Haim y Aubi	Buena de Abraham Baessa	
March 16, 1759	Samuel Haim de Jeudah y Sphorni	Esther Ventura	
April 6, 1759	Abraham de Joseph y Baessa	Abigail de Joseph Siprut y Gabay	
Feb. 11, 1763	Samuel Haim de Jeudah y Sphorni, wid.	Rebecca Nunes Bernal	
Sept. 21, 1763	Moses de Jeudah y Sphorni	Sarah de Joseph Palache	
April 13, 1764	Haim de Joseph y Baessa	Marianna de Isaac Mercado	
Feb. 23, 1770	Salomon de Joseph y Baessa	Buena de Joseph Baessa	
Jan. 6, 1775	Haim de Joseph y Baessa, wid.	Rachel del Sotto, wid. of David Keyzer	
April 27, 1775	Abraham de Jeudah y Sphorni	Sarah de Daniel Azulay y Deborah Musafia	
May 22, 1792	Esther de Moses Piza y Palache	Abm de Hu Ishac de Joseph Palache	
Aug. 9, 1793	Jeudah de Moses y Palache	Judith de Isaac Jesurun	
March 20, 1795	Luna de Moses Piza y Palache	Moses de Isaac Pereira	
Aug. 13, 1802	Joseph Jr. de Haim	Judith de Jacob Suzarte	
Oct. 12, 1804	Samuel de Moses y Palache	Judith de Isaac de Moses Pereyra	
Nov. 25, 1808	Jeudah de Moses y Palache, wid.	Simha de Jehiel Salomo Salem	
About 1810 (?)	Jeosuah de Moses y Palache	Benvenida de Isaac Zacutto	Above, pp. 305-326
Dec. 12, 1815	Ditto, widower	Esther de Isaac Zacutto	Mar. in Curaçao
Sept. 15, 1816	Ditto, widower	Hanah de Jacob Sasso y Sasso	Ditto, illus. 82-83
Jan. 1, 1822	Haim de Joseph	Ribca de Abraham Casseres	
Aug. 3, 1827	Nathan Rephael	Leah de Eliezer Abendana	

Aug. 5, 1827	Abraham Rephael	Esther de Jacob Nunes Vaz	
1835	Moses de Jeosuah y Benvenida Zacutto	Ribca de David Lz da Fonseca y Hz Cotinho	
June 8, 1837	Moses de Jeudah	Jochebed de Jacob Pinheiro	
1845	Jeudah de Jeosuah y Benvenida Zacutto	Leah de David Lz da Fonseca y Hz Cotinho	
1858	Jacob de Jeosuah y Sasso	Bendita Ascoli	
1862	Samuel de Jeosuah y Sasso	Rachel de Moses Piza y Lz da Fonseca	

See allied families: Mendes Belissario, Delvalle, Jesurun Lindo, Luria, Levy Maduro, Meyer, Sasso.

POLLY

| Before 1860 | Raphael de Salomon y Sarah Meyer | Rachel de Salomon Lobo | |
| June 20, 1860 | Ditto, widower | Rachel de Abm Haim Senior y Cohen Hz | 11,500 fls. |

See Jesurun, Meyer.

PORTO

| Aug. 14, 1783 | David de Samuel, wid. of Rachel Costa | Rachel de Moses Finzi, wid. of Salomon Saruco | |

VAN PRAAG

| Sept. 29, 1822 | Ishac de Jeudah | Batsebah Esther de Samuel Hoheb [y Cohen Hz ?] | |

PRADO, see Lopez Fonseca.

PRETTO, see Aboab, D'Almeida, Frances, De Meza, Naar, Sarate.

PUA, see Pardo.

Marriage Date	Bridegroom	Bride	Dowry and/or Remarks
		QUERIDO	
Before 1906 (?)	David de Isaac y Rachel Hond	Sarah Palache	
Aug. 16, 1911	Ditto, widower	Estella de Mord Fidanque Curiel y Rz Miranda	
		QUIROS	
Aug. 5, 1759	Moses, b. Portugal	Leah Mendes, b. Amsterdam	
		LOPEZ RAPHAEL	
Before 1766	Abraham	Rachel de Leon	
April 16, 1780	Joseph, b. London	Leah de David Ricardo	

See Cardozo, Monsanto.

VILLA REAL, see Serano.

Marriage Date	Bridegroom	Bride	Dowry and/or Remarks
		NUNES REDONDO (originally Nunes)	
March 26, 1687	Mosseh de Abraham Nunes	Deborah de Selomoh L. Maduro y Crasto	200 fls.
About 1726	Abraham de Mosseh Nunes Redondo y L. Maduro	Esther de David Machorro de Leon y L. Maduro	766:5:2 pesos
Aug. 20, 1736	Salomo de Mosseh y L. Maduro	Abigail de Daniel Aboab Cardozo, wid. of Jeremias L. Maduro	1,500 pesos; Pr. St., p. 328
Before 1759	Isaac [de Abm y M. de Leon ?]	Sarah Levy Barrios	

See allied families: Calvo, Aboab Cardozo, Lopez, Lopez Salzedo, Suares.

NUNES RIBEIRO

Date	Person	Spouse	Notes
Before 1780	Isaac	Leah Tovar	

RODRIGUES RIVERA

Date	Person	Spouse	Notes
1741	Jacob	Hanah de Samuel Rz Pimentel, wid. of Abm Saportas	

ISRAEL RICARDO

Date	Person	Spouse	Notes
Aug. 29, 1693	David, b. Livorno in 1652 to Diana Israel	Strellia Amadios	Mar. in A'dam
Jan. 15, 1694	Benjamin y Diana Israel	Reyna de la Faya	Ditto
July 5, 1697	Rephael y Diana Israel	Jael Jesurun Alcobasa	Ditto
Feb. 5, 1721	Joseph de David y Amadios	Hanah Bath Abraham Avinu [a proselyte], a.k.a. Hannah Abas, d. of Sarah Abas	Ditto
Oct. 13, 1723	Daniel de David y Amadios	Leah de Abraham Abas	
Nov. 6, 1732	Abm de Rephael y Jn Alcobasa	Sipporah Alvares Penso	
July 22, 1735	Samuel de Benjamin y de la Faya, b. New York in 1701	Rica Israel [Ricardo ?]	
June 20, 1756	David de Daniel y Abas, b. A'dam	Sarah Mendes Solas, b. St. Christopher	Mar. in Curaçao
Sept. 15, 1762	David Jr. de Joseph y Abas	Batsebah de Mordechay Isaac Semah Aboab y Hanah de Abm Senior	Mar. in A'dam
March 4, 1764	David de Daniel y Abas, wid.	Esther de Moses Motta y Rosetta, b. St. Thomas	Mar. in Curaçao
Oct. 28, 1770	Aron, b. Amsterdam	Leah de Samuel Israel Ricardo	
Before 1783	Samuel	Esther Rodriguez Pimentel	Ditto

983

ISRAEL RICARDO (cont.)

Marriage Date	Bridegroom	Bride	Dowry and/or Remarks
March 29, 1797	Ribca de Hu David de Joseph ISRAEL RICARDO y SEMAH ABOAB	Daniel Haim de Isaac Abm DA COSTA	Mar. in A'dam; parents of the poet Isaac Da Costa
Feb. 6, 1799	Joseph de David y SEMAH ABOAB	Ribca de Aron Haim ISRAEL SAGACHE y Esther GERMAN	Mar. in A'dam
March 24, 1802	Mordechay de David y SEMAH ABOAB	Esther de Moises Frois D'ANDRADE y DE SOLA	9,000 pesos
March 21, 1817	David de Aron y RICARDO	Rachel de Rephael NAMIAS DE CRASTO y L. MADURO	
Before 1846	Moises Frois de Mord y FROIS D'ANDRADE	Henriette TAVAREZ	
March 15, 1871	David de Moises Frois y TAVAREZ	Miriam de Salomon Joseph DE JONGH y DELVALLE	
July 16, 1913	Louis Joseph de David y DE JONGH	Hannah Haydée de Abm CAPRILES y Ms CHUMACEIRO	

See allied families: Aben Habib, Aelyon, Alascar, Capriles, Mendes Henriquez, Leon, Pardo, Garcia de Paz, Cohen Peixotto, Lopez Raphael, Jesurun Sasportas, De Sola.

Genealogy:

David = Strellia A. → Joseph = Hanah A. → David Jr. = Batsebah S.A. → Mordechay =
Esther F.D'A. → Moises = Henriette T. → David = Miriam D.J. → Louis Joseph =
Hannah Haydée C.

RIES, see Morales.

ROBLES

Marriage Date	Bridegroom	Bride	Dowry and/or Remarks
June 30, 1748	Abraham	Esther de Benjamin JESURUN y ISRAEL	
Before 1830	Jacob	Sarah de Abm David MORALES [y Victoria ?]	

984

See Athias Robles, Salas.

ATHIAS ROBLES, see Athias.

BARZILAY ROBLES

| Before 1749 | Joseph | Hanah de Jeudah SASSO y PEREZ | |
| „ 1753 | Jacob | Rachel VAZ NUNES | |

See Athias Robles.

RODRIGUEZ

Before 1746	Rephael	Rachel ABOAB	
April 17, 1791	Jacob de Abraham, b. Bayonne	Ribca de Abm FLORES y ATHIAS DE NEYRA	6,000 pesos
Dec. 10, 1797	David de Isaac	Branca de Abm CARDOZO DA COSTA y SUARES	500 „ ;
March 7, 1812	Ditto, widower	Ribca de Abm CARDOZO DA COSTA y SUARES	Pr. St., p. 433
March 3, 1824	Isaac de David y CARDOZO DA COSTA	Leah de Isaac L. MADURO PEIXOTTO y LOPES DIAS	

See allied families: Gomez, Cohen Henriquez, Levy Maduro, Naar, Nunes Netto.

COHEN RODRIGUEZ

| Before 1708 | Aron | Ribca de Jacob HENRIQUEZ MORON |

See Lopez.

DE LA ROSA

| Before 1737 | Benjamin | Ribca RODRIGUEZ MIRANDA |
| July 11, 1756 | Isaac de Benjamin y Rz MIRANDA, b. Barbados | Rachel de [Moses ?] ISRAEL KEYZER |

See Rodriguez Miranda.

Marriage Date	Bridegroom	Bride	Dowry and/or Remarks
		ROSETTA	
Before 1755	Elcana	Sarah de Daniel Rodriguez Nunes	
See Motta.	Sagache, see Ricardo.		
		SALAS	
Before 1724	Eliau de Isaac, b. Livorno	Prudencia Sadika de Leon	
June 21, 1724	Ditto, widower	Sarah Robles, b. Seville	Mar. in A'dam
May 19, 1728	Abraham de David, b. Livorno	Rachel de Haim Cohen y Hanah Motelbot	Ditto
May 21, 1730	Ditto, widower	Judith de Isaac Frois	
About 1752	Moses de Eliau y Robles	Rebecca de [Jeosuah ?] Mendes	Pr. St., p. 399
Feb. 28, 1779	Guideon de Moses y Mendes	Esther Cardozo da Costa, b. A'dam	
March 18, 1800	Isaac Haim de Moses y Mendes	Sarah de Gabriel Souza Britto y Abinun de Lima	1,300 pesos
	(Children: Clara, Esther, Moises and David)		
Sept. 16, 1835	Moises de Isaac Hm y Souza Britto	Abigail de Abm Roiz Mendes y Hz Moron	
Before 1839	Gabriel de Isaac Haim y Souza Britto	Rachel Gomes Casseres	
Oct. 29, 1862	Abraham de Moises y Roiz Mendes	Deborah Delia de Isaac de Valencia y Abinun de Lima	4,000 fls.
April 15, 1863	Isaac de Moises y Roiz Mendes	Leah Julia de Isaac Baiz y Pereira	See illus. 255
April 3, 1872	Gabriel de Moises y Roiz Mendes	Leah de Abm Hz Moron y Baiz	
May 23, 1875	Jacob de Moises y Roiz Mendes	Esther de Isaac Baiz y Pereira	4,000 "
July 26, 1882	David Haim de Moises y Roiz Mendes	Ribca de Haim Abinun de Lima y Cohen Hz	4,000 "

March 3, 1894	Isaac George de Abm y VALENCIA	Lunita de Haim ABINUN DE LIMA y COHEN Hz
Sept. 20, 1903	Jacob Arnold de Abm y VALENCIA	Eleonor de Abm Delvalle DE JONGH y OSORIO
Oct. 29, 1903	David Dario de Abm y VALENCIA	Rachel Noemi de Jacob SALAS y BAIZ
Before June, 1909	Moises Hm de David Hm y ABINUN DE LIMA	Ethel de Mord ATHIAS ROBLES y SASSO
Aug. 30, 1913	Haim de David Hm y ABINUN DE LIMA	Julieta de Alberto HENRIQUEZ y SENIOR
Aug. 24, 1918	Julio Abm de David Hm y ABINUN DE LIMA	Clara de Josias Ms CHUMACEIRO y MARCHENA
Feb. 15, 1947	Oscar de David Dario y SALAS	Louise de Emilio Lz HENRIQUEZ y SALAS
Feb. 7, 1951	Abm Edgardo de Arnold Jacob y DE JONGH	Margarita de Abm Oscar SEMAH DE VALENCIA y HENRIQUEZ
Aug. 8, 1956	Elias de David Haim y ABINUN DE LIMA	Noemi de Isaac SENIOR y MARCHENA, wid. of Ernesto de Marchena

See allied families: Gomes Casseres, Fontein, Van Gelder, Henriquez, Cohen Henriquez, Lopez Henriquez, Leezer, Abinun de Lima, Levy Maduro, Marchena, Mendez, Roiz Mendes, Senior, De Sola, Valencia.

Genealogy:

Isaac → Eliau = Prudencia Sadika D.L. / Sara R. ⌐ Moses = Ribca M. → Isaac Haim = Sarah S. B. →

Moises = Abigail R. M. → Abraham = Deborah Delia V. → Jacob Arnold = Eleonor D. J. →

Abram Edgardo = Margarita V. → Ralph Joel, born 1955.

CARILHO SALDAÑA

Before 1759	Abraham, b. A'dam	Esther ABOAB
Sept. 16, 1759	Ditto, widower	Ribca de Jacob COHEN Hz y ABOAB

See Cohen Henriquez.

SALEM, see Piza.

987

Marriage Date	Bridegroom	Bride	Dowry and/or Remarks
		SALOM	
Before 1709	Jacob	Sarah de Abraham HENRIQUEZ DE MESQUITA	
1748	Samuel de Isaac	Leah SALOM	2,500 pesos
See Levy Maduro, Naar.			
		SALOMON	
About 1890	Edward	Anna de Salomon Samuel L. MADURO y PIZA	
See Van Lier.			
		LOPEZ SALZEDO	
1765	Abm de Moses y Miriam DELVAILLE, b. France	Deborah de Isaac NUNES REDONDO y LEVY BARRIOS	
See allied families: D'Aguilar, Levy Maduro, Pardo.			
	SAMPSON, see Mendes Chumaceiro.		
		SANCHES	
Aug. 26, 1764	Isaac	Ribca GARCIA	
See Pardo.			
		ISRAEL SANTCROOS, also ST. CRUS	
Before 1732	Aron de Moses, b. Amsterdam	Judith ANDRADE	
Dec. 6, 1733	Ditto, widower	Esther de Daniel MORENO Hz y ULLOA	

988

June 3, 1795	Abraham Haim DE Jacob	Rachel de Jacob Hu Jn DE Oliveyra, b. Amsterdam	1,800 pesos; separated
Nov. 2, 1859	Haim Jeudah de David y Luna Piza	Simha de Aron Ms Chumaceiro y Lz Cardozo	2,100 fls.

See allied families: Souza Britto, Henriquez, Jesurun de Oliveyra.

DE SARATE

Before 1729	Joseph	Judith Pretto

See Nunes Netto.

Dias Sardo, see Levy Maduro.

SARFATTI

Aug. 13, 1943	Salomon de Moises y Romi	Rebecca de Salomon Obadia y Obadia

See Behar, Levaton (a.k.a. Levantou).

Saruco, see Porto.

SAPORTA, also SASPORTAS

About 1685	Abraham de Jacob, b. London	Esther Saportas	
March 24, 1700	Ditto, widower	Ribca de Joseph Medina Lobo	
Jan. 26, 1735	Abraham	Hanah de Samuel Rz Pimentel	1,400 pesos

See Jesurun, Rodriguez Pimentel.

JESURUN SAPORTAS or SASPORTAS
(originally Jesurun)

Oct. 28, 1708	Haham Rephael de Moseh Jesurun	Rachel de Abraham Sasportas y Esther	4,800 fls.

JESURUN SAPORTAS or SASPORTAS (cont.)

Marriage Date	Bridegroom	Bride	Dowry and/or Remarks
1746	Abraham de Rephael y Sasportas	Deborah Ulloa	950 pesos
July 2, 1748	Isaac de Rephael y Sasportas	Rachel de Jacob Lz da Fonseca y Benveniste	
Aug. 24, 1777	Jacob de Isaac y Lz da Fonseca	Sarah de Daniel Cohen Peixotto y Campos Pereira	
Oct. 8, 1780	Rephael de Isaac y Lz da Fonseca	Leah Hannah de Eliau Lz da Fonseca y Mendes de Sola	
Jan. 21, 1784	Ditto, widower	Sarah de Samuel Israel Ricardo	1,050 ,,
Dec. 29, 1813	Daniel de Jacob y Cohen Peixotto	Sarah de Abm Gs Casseres y Uziel Cardozo	

See allied families: De Castro, Alvares Correa, Curiel, Levy Maduro (Peixotto), Roiz Mendes, Monsanto.

SASSO

Marriage Date	Bridegroom	Bride	Dowry and/or Remarks
1730	Jeudah, b. London	Sarah Perez	
Before 1734 (?)	Abraham de Jeudah y Perez, b. London	Judith Israel Campanal	
	(Children: Joseph, David, Moseh, Salomon, Jeudah, Aron, Elias, Isaac [a.k.a. Joakim] Jacob, Rubin, Benjamin, Ribca, Esther, Sarah, Hanah and Samuel [C 1209])		
Nov. 1, 1744	Joseph de Jeudah y Perez, b. London	Rebecca de Benjamin Jesurun y Israel	
June 4, 1769	Moses de Abraham y Campanal	Judith de Joseph Sasso y Jesurun	
Jan. 16, 1780	Isaac de Abraham y Campanal	Judith de Moses Marache y Sasso	
July 25, 1782	Moses de Abraham y Campanal, wid.	Abigail de Joseph Vaz da Costa, wid. of Abraham Garcia	

Date	Groom	Bride	Amount
June 15, 1783	Elias Haim de Abraham y CAMPANAL	Ribca de Moses MARACHE y SASSO	600 pesos
Before 1783	Mordechay	Esther MENDES BALBORDA	
June 2, 1793	Jacob de Abraham y CAMPANAL	Judith de Moses SASSO y SASSO	444 "
Oct. 6, 1793	Rubin de Abraham y CAMPANAL	Ribca de Jacob GABAY Hz y Hz JULIAO	1,127:4 pesos
About 1795	Abraham	Leah	
" 1814	Isaac	Ribca de Jacob SASSO y SASSO	
" 1816	Abraham	Sarah de Jacob SASSO y SASSO	
Before 1833	Mordechay	Rebecca de Jb JESURUN LINDO y L. MADURO	
	(Children: David, Samuel, Moses, Abraham, Leah, Judith, Rachel, Esther, Abigail [and Jacob ?])		
About 1833	Isaac	Leah	
1834	Jeudah de Jacob y SASSO	Judith de Jeosuah PIZA y SASSO	
Nov. 30, 1836	Joseph de Jacob y SASSO	Sarah de Daniel CARDOZO DA COSTA y SASSO	
Before 1862	David de Mordechay y JN LINDO	Sarah	
	(Children: Isaac and Coleman)		
About 1868	Abraham de S.	Abigail	
Aug. 14, 1872	Samuel de Mordechay y JN LINDO	Clara Osorio de David DE CASTRO y ABOAB OSORIO	
Aug. 21, 1872	Moses de Mordechay y JN LINDO	Judith Osorio de David DE CASTRO y ABOAB OSORIO	
Dec. 11, 1878	Daniel de Joseph y CARDOZO DA COSTA	Miriam de Jacob L. MADURO y JN LINDO	
Before 1879	Mordechay de S.	Esther	
About 1884	Moses de David	Rosa de Ephraim ATHIAS ROBLES y L. MADURO	
Before 1887	Isaac Abraham de Mordechay	Julia NUNES HENRIQUEZ	

991

Marriage Date	Bridegroom	Bride	Dowry and/or Remarks
		SASSO (cont.)	
Sept. 3, 1890	Isaac de David y SASSO	Leah (Leonie) de Abm Ms CHUMACEIRO y Lz HENRIQUEZ	
Oct. 15, 1900	David de Moses y DE CASTRO	Esther Benilda de Mord L. MADURO y BRAVO	
About 1903	Moses de David, widower	Essie de Joseph ATHIAS ROBLES y CARDOZE	
Oct. 5, 1904	Mordechay Milton de Moses y CASTRO	Rachel Rosinda de Isaac DE MARCHENA y Lz PENHA	
Jan. 18, 1911	David Leslie de Is Abm y NUNES Hz	Sarah de Isaac David SASSO y Ms CHUMACEIRO	
About 1926	Abram de Coleman	Madeleine de Elias ATHIAS ROBLES y SASSO	

See allied families: Athias Robles, Cardozo da Costa, Curiel, Halman, Henriquez Juliao, Levy, Jesurun Lindo, Baruch Louzada, Levy Maduro, Marache, Namias de Crasto, Piza, Barzilay Robles.

Marriage Date	Bridegroom	Bride	Dowry and/or Remarks
		SEIXAS	
May 27, 1840	Abraham de Isaac y VALENCIA	Hanah de Isaac PARDO Jr. y Ms MONSANTO	4,000 fls.
		SENIOR	
Dec. 13, 1616	Philippe Henriquez, a.k.a. Jeudah SENIOR	Esther de Sebastiaan PIMENTEL y de Sarah LINDA	Mar. in A'dam
Sept. 22, 1656	Ribca de Jeudah SENIOR y PIMENTEL	Jacob FUNDAM	Ditto

Date	Groom	Bride	
Feb. 28, 1658	Mordechay de Jeudah SENIOR (a.k.a. HENRIQUEZ) y PIMENTEL (Children: Jeudah, Jacob, Esther, David, Ishac, Abraham; Rachel = Abm de Jb Fundam y Senior in 1686; Benjamin, Mosseh; Ribca = Ishac de Daniel Semah Aboab in 1699; and Salomon)	Sarah de Moses LOPEZ y Rachel MENDES DEL SOTTO	9,000 fls.; mar. in A'dam; Pr. St., pp. 302-304
Feb. 28, 1658	Jacob Henriquez de Jeudah y PIMENTEL	Esther de Moses LOPEZ y Rachel MENDES DEL SOTTO	Mar. in A'dam
Dec. 6, 1679	Jeudah de Jacob y LOPEZ	Esther de Mordechay SENIOR y LOPEZ	8,000 fls.
Jan. 29, 1681	Jeudah de Mordechay y LOPEZ	Esther de Jacob FUNDAM y SENIOR	4,500 "
Nov. 24, 1683	Ditto, widower	Sarah de Jacob FUNDAM y SENIOR	6,000 "
About 1689	David de Mordechay y LOPEZ	Sarah de Ishac de MARCHENA y CARILHO	Mar. in Curaçao
June 27, 1699	Benjamin de Mordechay y LOPEZ	Rachel de Jacob SENIOR y FUNDAM	
Before 1704	Salomon de Mordechay y LOPEZ	Esther [de Ishac DE MARCHENA y CARILHO ?]	Mar. in Curaçao
" 1710	Isaac Haim de David y MARCHENA	Rachel de Abm DE MARCHENA y CARILHO	
April 14, 1710	Abraham de Mordechay y LOPEZ	Batsebah de David ABOAB CARDOSO y Hanah DE CASSERES	Mar. in A'dam
About 1721	Mordechay Haim de David y MARCHENA	Sarah de Selomoh SENIOR	4,000 pesos
Before 1731	Jacob de David y MARCHENA	Leah de Mordechay HENRIQUEZ y NAAR	3,000 "
After 1731	Mordechay Haim de David y MARCHENA, widower	Leah de Abraham JESURUN y LEVY MENDES, wid. of Abraham Mendes da Gama	4,800 "
Dec. 6, 1733	Abm de Isaac Haim y MARCHENA	Leah de Abraham PENSO y PEREIRA	
Before 1738	Abraham de David y MARCHENA	Esther de Jacob Ephraim JN HENRIQUEZ y DA COSTA ANDRADE	4,000 "

Marriage Date	Bridegroom	Bride	Dowry and/or Remarks
	SENIOR (cont.)		
1746	Jacob de David y MARCHENA, wid.	Batsebah de Joseph FIDANQUE y JN HENRIQUEZ	2,000 pesos
Before 1748	David de Isaac Haim y MARCHENA	Ribca GAON	
June 6, 1751	Salomoh de Mord Haim y SENIOR	Rachel de Jacob SENIOR y HENRIQUEZ	
May 11, 1753	David de Mord Haim y SENIOR	Rachel de Isaac FUNDAM	Mar. in A'dam
Oct. 21, 1759	Abm de Mord Haim y JESURUN	Leah de Abraham SENIOR	
May 19, 1765	Isaac de Abraham y PENSO	Sarah de Salomoh Is L. MADURO y MEDINA	8,000 pesos
May 31, 1767	David de Jacob y FIDANQUE	Sarah de Jacob FIDANQUE y JN HENRIQUEZ	
June 19, 1768	Isaac Haim de Jacob y HENRIQUEZ	Ribca de Eliau Lz DA FONSECA y Ms DE SOLA	Separated
Feb. 21, 1779	Isaac de Abm y PENSO, widower	Esther de Isaac LEVY	3,900 pesos
Sept. 30, 1781	David de Jacob y FIDANQUE, wid.	Hanah de Jacob FIDANQUE y JN HENRIQUEZ	
May 16, 1787	Mord Haim de Abm Mord y SENIOR	Leah de Isaac Hm NAMIAS DE CRASTO y HENRIQUEZ	600 pesos
May 5, 1790	David Jr. de Abm Isaac Hm y PENSO	Sarah de Abm Jacob LOPEZ DIAS	4,400 "
June 29, 1796	David de Abm de Mord Hm y SENIOR	Leah de David de Mord ABINUN DE LIMA y CALVO	1,200 "
?	Abraham de Isaac	Abigail TABOADA	
Oct. 18, 1809	Jacob de Abm Mord Hm y SENIOR	Hanah de David Haim COHEN Hz y MOTTA	2,000 "

(Children: Leah, Abraham, Esther, David, Mordechay, Jeudah, Sarah and Salomon Haim)

Nov. 15, 1809	Selomoh de Abm Mord Hm y SENIOR	Abigail de Eliau PENSO y BELMONTE	2,600 "
May 22, 1814	Isaac Jr. de David Abm y LOPEZ DIAS	Leah de Mord Haim SENIOR y NAMIAS DE CRASTO	
May 19, 1817	Isaac de Abm Mord Hm y SENIOR	Esther de Jacob BELMONTE y A. CORREA	1,568 "
Aug. 8, 1819	Abraham de Mord Hm y NAMIAS DE CRASTO	Leah de David SENIOR	See appendix 27.
June 25, 1820	Abraham Jr. de David y ABINUN DE LIMA	Rachel de Jacob CALVO	
	(Only on June 7, 1822, was this marriage registered in the MIA. See Chapter XV and appendix 27.)		
June 12, 1822	Abraham Hm de David Jr. y LOPEZ DIAS	Abigail de Selomoh COHEN Hz y CASSERES	
	(Children: David, Salomon, Sally, Leah, Rachel, Priscilla, Esther, Ribca, Agatha, Ametyste and Sylvia)		
Oct. 19, 1825	Jacob Jr. de David y Lz DIAS	Rachel de Isaac PARDO [y ABINUN DE LIMA?]	
	(Children: Dr. Isaac, David Haim, Sarah, Abraham Haim, Leah, Mordechay and Clara)		
Dec. 7, 1836	Abraham de Jacob y COHEN Hz	Leah de Selomoh SENIOR y PENSO	
Nov. 30, 1842	Jeudah de Jacob y COHEN Hz	Jael de Selomoh SENIOR y PENSO	
1849 (?)	Jacob de Isaac y BELMONTE	Leah de Jacob DE CASTRO	
Sept. 17, 1851	Dr. Isaac de Jacob y PARDO	Ragel de Ovadia MENDES DA COSTA y FONSECA BRANDON	34,000 fls.
?	Mordechay Haim	Ribca de Abm SENIOR Jr. y CALVO	
March 17, 1852	Mordechay de Jacob y COHEN Hz	Eleonor de Mord COHEN Hz y DE SOLA	
Feb. 13, 1856	David de Abm de Mord y SENIOR	Sarah Sally de Haim Josiau COHEN Hz y JESURUN	12,000 "
June 16, 1858	David de Abm Haim y COHEN Hz	Ribca de Haim Josiau COHEN Hz y JESURUN	12,000 "

Marriage Date	Bridegroom	Bride	Dowry and/or Remarks
		SENIOR (cont.)	
Jan. 9, 1861	Isaac de Abraham M.	Raquel de Josiau Lz HENRIQUEZ y NAMIAS DE CRASTO	Mar. in Coro
Before 1864	Abraham de Isaac	Rebecca TAVARES	
Jan. 12, 1865	Salomoh de Abm Haim y COHEN Hz	Emma de Alexandre COHEN DEITELZWEIG y EPHRAIM	
Dec. 14, 1865	Jacob Haim	Esther HENRIQUEZ JULIAO	
Dec. 20, 1865	Abraham de Isaac y BELMONTE	Sarah de Jacob SENIOR y COHEN Hz	5,000 fls.
Nov. 13, 1868	Salomoh Jr. de Jeudah y SENIOR	Esther de Daniel JESURUN Jr. y Rz MIRANDA	13,000 "
June 20, 1877	Jacob de Isaac y BELMONTE, wid.	Sarah de Haim Daniel Lz PENHA y L. MADURO	
July 20, 1878	Jacob M.	Esther de Benjamin DE MARCHENA y L. MADURO, illus. 260	Divorced
May 8, 1880	Salomoh de Abm Hm y COHEN Hz, widower	Abigail de Benjamin DE CASSERES y SENIOR	5,000 fls.
July 3, 1882	Jacob de Isaac y MENDES DA COSTA	Clara de Abm Jacob JESURUN y JESURUN	5,000 "
April 14, 1886	Haim de Abraham Jb SENIOR y SENIOR	Esther de Benjamin DE MARCHENA y L. MADURO, divorcée of Jacob Senior	10,000 "
March 30, 1887	Josiau de Isaac, a.k.a. Lopez Senior, y Lz HENRIQUEZ	Carmen (Sarah) de Reymundo A. CORREA y ROIS MENDES	
Dec. 25, 1895	Edwin de Salomon y DEITELZWEIG	Rosaura de Benjamin HENRIQUEZ y COHEN Hz	2,000 fls.
Jan. 27, 1897	Edgar de Salomon y DEITELZWEIG	Selina de Jacob Eliau PENSO y A. CORREA	50,000 "
Aug. 28, 1897	Morry de Isaac Abm y Lz HENRIQUEZ	Emma de Reymundo A. CORREA y ROIS MENDES	

March 16, 1898	Jacobo de Isaac Abm y Lz HENRIQUEZ	Amelia de David JESURUN y COHEN Hz
1899	Benjamin F.	Esther Emma CORTISSOZ
April 11, 1900	Isaac Jr. de Jacob Is y Lz PENHA	Celina de Isaac Mord DE MARCHENA y Lz PENHA
Sept. 26, 1900	Alexander de Salomon y DEITELZWEIG	Emma de William DEITELZWEIG y KAUFMAN Mar. in Hamburg
July 4, 1903	Jacob de Abm Isaac y TAVARES	Anna Marianne de Moises Lz PENHA y MARCHENA
July 12, 1905	Morry de Isaac y Lz HENRIQUEZ, widower	Esther de Moises ABINUN DE LIMA y COHEN Hz
Nov. 29, 1905	Henry de David Jr. y COHEN Hz	Else de Manuel PENSO y A. CORREA
Feb. 12, 1925	Salomoh Alfred de Edwin y HENRIQUEZ	Edith Rachel de Prospero BAIZ y PEREIRA, divorcée of M. M. Montefiore L. Maduro 26,784.16 fls.
June 20, 1931	Otto de Isaac Jb y MARCHENA	Rosalina de David Hm SALAS y ABINUN DE LIMA
Nov. 22, 1933	Ruben Dario de Morry Is y A. CORREA	Beatrice Grace de Isaac James A. CORREA y PENSO 45,000 " ; divorced
June 19, 1941	Ruben Dario de Morry Is y A. CORREA, divorcé	Rachel Edith de Jacob Naar COHEN Hz y A. CORREA

See allied families: Capriles, Casseres, De Castro, Curiel, Lopez Dias, Dovale, Edwards, Henriquez, Jesurun Henriquez, Lopez Henriquez, Jesurun, Jeudah Leao, Abinun de Lima, Lindo, Lobo, Rodriguez Miranda, Naar, Namias, Penso, Rodriguez Pereira, Polly, Salas, Serphos, De Sola, Sturmthal, Valencia, Weil, Wolff.

GENEALOGY

1st Branch: Jeudah = Esther P. → Mordechay = Sarah L. → David = Sarah M. → Isaac Hm = Rachel M. → Abraham = Leah P. → David → Sarah L.D. → Abraham Hm = Abigail C.H. → Salomon = Emma D.

Abigail d. C. ↗ Edwin = Rosaura H. → Salomon Alfred = Edith B.

997

GENEALOGY (cont.)

Marriage Date	Bridegroom	Bride	Dowry and/or Remarks
2nd Branch:	Jeudah → Mordechay → David = Sarah M. → Mordechay Hm = Leah J. ↗		Sarah S. Abraham = Leah S.
	→ Isaac = Esther B. → Jacob = Leah d. C. Sarah L.P. ↗ Isaac Jr. = Celina M. → Otto = Rosalina		
	S. → Marguerita = Moses Serphos.		

SERANO

Marriage Date	Bridegroom	Bride	Dowry and/or Remarks
Before 1735	David	Hanah de Selomoh VILLA REAL	

SERPHOS

Marriage Date	Bridegroom	Bride	Dowry and/or Remarks
April 28, 1951	Moses de Isidor y ISRAELS	Marguerita de Otto SENIOR y SALAS	
Aug. 10, 1963	Mark Alexander de Isidor y ISRAELS	Yvonne de Max DE CASTRO y KYWI	

DA SILVA, see Lopez Penha.

FRANCO DA SILVA, see Curiel.

GOMES SILVA, see Alva.

LOPEZ SILVA, see Bueno Valensi.

SIMMONDS

Marriage Date	Bridegroom	Bride	Dowry and/or Remarks
Before 1853	Coleman	Esther de Moses Abm JESURUN y SENIOR	

SIMONSON, see Cardoze.

SIPRUT, see Piza.

SOBERHEIM, see Baiz.

DE SOLA

Date	Groom	Bride	Amount / Notes
Before 1733	Benjamin	Abigail HENRIQUEZ MORENO	
May 26, 1754	Isaac de Benjamin y Hz MORENO	Ribca de Jeudah NUNES DA COSTA	800 fls.
Jan. 31, 1759	Rachel de Benjamin y Hz MORENO	Aron de Isaac aCOHEN	
May 31, 1767	Jacob de Benjamin y Hz MORENO	Leah de Elias JN HENRIQUEZ y NAMIAS DE CRASTO	
Feb. 19, 1786	Benjamin de Isaac y NUNES DA COSTA	Esther de Jacob MARACHE y Ms MACHADO	2,500 pesos
March 16, 1794	Jeudah de Isaac y NUNES DA COSTA	Sarah de David RICARDO	2,000 „
March 12, 1797	Aron de Isaac	Rachel de Samuel JN PINTO y MONSANTO	1,500 „
Feb. 6, 1799	Jeosuah de Jacob y JN HENRIQUEZ	Esther de Moseh Hu MONSANTO y TABOADA	2,000 „
April 25, 1800	Elias de Jacob y JN HENRIQUEZ	Rachel RIBEIRO FURTADO	Mar. in A'dam
Jan. 15, 1802	Ditto, widower	Esther de Abm Moses MENDES DA COSTA	Ditto
March 19, 1809	Jeosuah de Jacob y JN HENRIQUEZ, wid.	Hanah de Haim ABINUN DE LIMA y DOVALE	5,000 pesos
Before 1824	Isaac Haim	Sipporah HOHEB	
June 7, 1826	Jacob de Jeosuah y MONSANTO	Leah de Selomoh COHEN Hz y CASSERES	
	(Children: Joshua, Haim Salomon, Esther, Sarah, Mozes, Hannah, Elias, David, Benjamin, Samuel and Daniel)		
Feb. 24, 1858	Moses de Jacob y COHEN Hz	Rachel Roselfina de Jacob Hm OSORIO y CARDOZE	
March 16, 1859	Jeosuah de Jacob y COHEN Hz	Abigail de Daniel COHEN Hz y MONSANTO	4,000 fls.
Feb. 1, 1860	Eliau de Jeosuah y MONSANTO	Sarah de Jacob SENIOR Jr. y PARDO	5,523.75 fls.

DE SOLA (cont.)

Marriage Date	Bridegroom	Bride	Dowry and/or Remarks
Jan. 23, 1861	Benjamin de Jeosuah y ABINUN DE LIMA	Hetty de Eliau ABINUN DE LIMA y COHEN Hz	3,250 fls.
Feb. 11, 1863	Benjamin Jr. de Jacob y COHEN Hz (Children: Jacob, Walter, Rachel, Theodore, Eleonor and Edgar)	Leah de Jacob SENIOR y PARDO	2,500 „
March 17, 1865	Haim Salomon de Jacob y COHEN Hz	Sarah de Eliau ABINUN DE LIMA y COHEN Hz	3,250 „
Feb. 5, 1868	Samuel de Jacob y COHEN Hz	Raquel Rosalvina de Moises JESURUN y SENIOR	4,000 „
About 1890	Herbert	Miriam de Salomoh L. MADURO y PIZA, widow of M. Ascoli	
March 31, 1897	Jacob Charles de Elias y SENIOR	Leah de Haim Salomon DE SOLA y ABINUN DE LIMA	
June 9, 1897	Frederic de Elias y SENIOR	Eleonor de Benjamin DE SOLA y SENIOR	
April 27, 1899 1899 (?)	Jacob Haim de Moses y OSORIO B. Edward	Sarah de Mord L. MADURO y BRAVO Beatrice M. DE SOLA	See illus. 262
March 16, 1900	Abraham de Jeosuah y COHEN Hz	Rose de Moses Marius A. CORREA y VALENCIA	
Aug. 13, 1902	Isaac de Haim Salomon y ABINUN DE LIMA	Leah de Benjamin DE SOLA y SENIOR	
Oct. 11, 1937	Samuel Maduro de Jb Hm y L. MADURO	Deborah Beatriz de Arnoldo Jb SALAS y DE JONGH	
July 25, 1964	Jaime Herman de Samuel y SALAS	Marie Madeleine de †Laurens LUCKMANN y L. MADURO	

(Marriage recorded in the Congregation Register as the bride's mother was Jewish)

See allied families: Frois d'Andrade, Castro, Ettedgui, Cohen Henriquez, Jesurun, Leon, Abinun de Lima, Lindo, Luria, Marchena, Mendes Monsanto.

GENEALOGY

Benjamin = Abigail H.M. → Jacob = Leah J.H. → Jeosuah = Esther M. ⟶ Jacob =
Hanah A.d.L.
Leah C.H. → Moses = Rachel Ros. O. → Jacob Hm = Sarah L.M. → Samuel = D. Beatriz
S. → Jaime = Marie Mad. L. → Michel, b. 1966.

MENDES DE SOLA

June 8, 1723	Samuel de David, illus. 67	Leah de Jeosuah de Ishac HENRIQUEZ	Mar. in A'dam
June 2, 1734	Isaac, b. Bayonne	Esther DE MEZA, b. London	
Nov. 9, 1749	Isaac de Samuel y HENRIQUEZ, b. Amsterdam	Abigail de Jacob Lz DA FONSECA y BENVENISTE	
Aug. 1, 1762	Aron	Hanah de Rephael GOMEZ	
Nov. 30, 1779	Samuel de Isaac y Lz DA FONSECA	Gracia de Abraham Ms COUTINHO y Ribca CURIEL	Mar. in A'dam
June 22, 1781	Jacob Hu de Isaac y Lz DA FONSECA	Hanah de Abraham aCOHEN	Ditto
Oct. 12, 1806	Rephael de Aron y GOMEZ	Esther de Isaac FROIS DE MEZA	
April 11, 1808	Jacob Hu de Isaac y Lz DA FONSECA, widower	Reyna de Matathia DE LA BELLA, wid. of Jacob Pinheiro	Ditto

See allied families: Bueno Vivas, Casseres, Henriquez Coelho, Henriquez Cotinho, Lopez Da Fonseca, Henriquez Juliao, Henriquez Pimentel, Ricardo.

DEL SOTTO, see Piza.

ABARBANEL SOUZA, see Henriquez Moron.

SPHORNI, see Piza.

SPINOZA, see Casseres, Cohen Henriquez.

Marriage Date	Bridegroom	Bride	Dowry and/or Remarks
SPRITZER			
Aug. 15, 1943	Eno de Wolf y Weiss	Ivy de Jacob Capriles y Lz Penha	
STURMTHAL			
Aug. 16, 1882	Gustav Julio y Ephraim	Elisa de Isaac Senior y Mendes da Costa	
SUARES			
About 1698	Daniel	Clara Vaez	
Before 1712	Isaac Hisquiau	Sarah da Costa de Andrade	
„ 1714	Jacob	Esther da Costa de Andrade	
Dec. 6, 1733	Jacob Hu Jr. de Abm, b. Barbados	Sarah de David Samuel Hoheb y Fidanque	
1746	Benjamin	Ribca Burgos	
Dec. 10, 1758	Jacob de David	Ribca de Abm Ns Redondo y Machorro de Leon	1,500 pesos
Before 1762	David Jr.	Rachel Henriquez Fereyra	
„ 1762	Isaac	Jael Henriquez Melhado	
March 3, 1765	Jacob de David, widower	Sarah de Jacob Henriquez Melhado	
May 31, 1767	Isaac de David	Rachel de Abm L. Maduro y Rz Marques	
Sept. 8, 1776	Jacob de Isaac	Miriam de Garson Garcia y Iftag Deborah	
Before 1778	David de Jacob y Nunes Redondo		
May 19, 1784	David de Isaac	Rachel de Salomoh Abm L. Maduro y L. Maduro	500 „
March 11, 1798	Jacob de Isaac de David	Ribca de Nachson Hz Moron y Belmonte	2,031 : 6 : 5 pesos

Aug. 24, 1844 | Benjamin de Jacob y GARCIA | Esther de Eliau PENSO

June 19, 1850 | Jacob de Benjamin y PENSO | Ragel de Joseph P. BRANDAO Jr. y PENSO | 1,000 fls.

Dec. 12, 1851 | Eliau de Benjamin y PENSO | Esther de Jacob MORENO Hz y PENSO | Mar. in Coro

See allied families: Cardozo Da Costa, Curiel, Levy Maduro, Mattos, Henriquez Melhado, Cohen Peixotto, Penso, Tovar.

LEVY SUARES

Before 1709 | Aron | Sarah VAZ MARTINES

See Vaz Martines.

SUZARTE or ZUZARTE, see Namias de Crasto, Piza.

TABOADA

June 30, 1748 | Moses, b. Bayonne | Hanah de Jacob LZ DA FONSECA y BENVENISTE

Nov. 9, 1749 | David de Jacob, b. Bordeaux | Rachel de Mordechay CALVO y D'ANDRADE

See allied families: Calvo, Monsanto, Senior.

TAVAREZ

1787 | David | Sipporah DE LEON | 2,844:4 pesos; separated

See Ricardo, Senior.

TEIXERA, see Namias de Crasto.

LOPES TELLES, see Abendana Pereira.

MORON TELLES, see Monis.

TORRES, see Semah Ferro, Gomez.

1003

Marriage Date	Bridegroom	Bride	Dowry and/or Remarks
		TOURO	
Oct. 4, 1663	Abraham T., a.k.a. Gaspar Fernandez Vega	Sarah DE MIRANDA	Mar. in A'dam
June 2, 1688	Isaac de Abraham y MIRANDA	Leah de Jacob ULLOA	Mar. in Curaçao
Nov. 2, 1697	Abraham de Jeudah	Deborah de David LEVY MENDES y BRANDON	5,000 fls.
1713	Moseh de Eliau	Hanah de Isaac HABILIO DA FONSECA	
Oct. 8, 1717	Jeudah de Isaac y ULLOA Samuel	Clara HALLAS	Mar. in A'dam
Before 1725		Leah	
After 1725	Ditto, widower	Sarah de Elisah ABOAB	
Before 1728	Jeudah de Abraham Israel	Leah de Gabriel LEVY y TOURO	
About 1730 (?)	Joseph Israel de Isaac y ULLOA	Esther de Abraham ULLOA Jr. y TOURO	
Before 1740	Moseh de Isaac y ULLOA	Deborah de Abraham ULLOA Jr. y TOURO	3,000 fls.
Dec. 15, 1743	Ditto, widower	Sarah ULLOA	3,750 pesos
About 1746 (?)	Jeosuah de Samuel [y ABOAB ?]	Jocheved de Moseh Lz DA FONSECA y NAFTALI	
Nov. 13, 1746	David de Isaac y ULLOA	Rachel de David BUENO VIVAS, wid. of Abm Hz Juliao	3,500 " ; divorced
Before 1753	Isaac de Samuel	Leah de Elisah ABOAB	
April 15, 1753	Isaac de Joseph Israel y ULLOA	Clara de Dr. Isaac CARDOZO y TOURO	

See allied families: Bueno Vivas, Cardozo, Lopez da Fonseca, Moreno Henriquez, Levy, Levy Maduro, Naar, Ulloa.

TOVAR

Before 1787	Abraham de Isaac	Esther NUNES PEREIRA	

| July 29, 1787 | Ditto, widower | Ribca de Jacob David SUARES |

See Mendes Monsanto, Nunes Ribeiro.

ULIEL, see Capriles.

ULHOA, also ULLOA

About 1668	Jacob	Esther ABOAB [CARDOZO ?]	
Before 1725	Abraham Hu Jr.	Sarah de Isaac TOURO y ULLOA	
„ 1730	Abraham de David Israel	Ribca de Jacob ULLOA	
„ 1753	Jacob	Gracia ALVARES CORREA	

See allied families: Andrade, Souza Britto, Bueno Vivas, Uziel Cardozo, Dias Cotinho, Dovale, Moreno Henriquez, Lopez de Leon, Monsanto, Jesurun Sasportas, Touro.

VAEZ, see Suares.

SEMAH DE VALENCIA, known as VALENCIA

Dec. 6, 1750	David	Sarah de Jacob JN HENRIQUEZ	Pr. St., pp. 445-46
May 1, 1774	Jacob de David y JN HENRIQUEZ	Sarah de Moses NAAR y PINEDO	
May 16, 1779	Benjamin	Esther de Abm ABOAB CARDOZO y Ns REDONDO	
Jan. 29, 1783	Ditto, widower	Ribca de Abm ABOAB CARDOZO y Ns REDONDO	500 pesos
Before 1791	Moises	Sarah de Isaac PARDO y VAZ FARRO, wid. of Salomon Vaz Farro	
Jan. 5, 1817	David de Jacob y NAAR	Deborah de Isaac Abm SENIOR	
About 1830	David Jr. de Benjamin y ABOAB CARDOZO	Rachel de Jacob JN LINDO [y L. MADURO ?]	
About 1845 (?)	Isaac de David y SENIOR	Judith Julia ABINUN DE LIMA y SALAS	
March 25, 1874	David de Isaac y ABINUN DE LIMA	Hannah Henny de Manuel A. CORREA y JN SASPORTAS	8,000 fls.

1005

SEMAH DE VALENCIA, known as VALENCIA (cont.)

Marriage Date	Bridegroom	Bride	Dowry and/or Remarks
Dec. 22, 1875	Julius Jacob de Is y ABINUN DE LIMA	Rachel Amalia de David Lz PENHA y HENRIQUEZ	House at No. 74 Pietermaai
	(Children: Charles and Rebecca who died in infancy; Julia, Clarita, David, Adelaida, Arnold, Horatio, Eduardo, Emma, Alberto, Abram Oscar, Gustavo and Ernesto)		
Aug. 23, 1919	Gustavo de Julius Jb y Lz PENHA	Hilda de Samuel B. P. BRANDAO y COHEN Hz	12,000 fls.
Dec. 28, 1921	David Penha de Julius Jb y Lz PENHA	Abigail Semiramis de Jacob SALAS y BAIZ	
?	Octavio de David y A. CORREA	Blanche de Isaac A. CORREA y PENSO	According to H.M.A. Correa, p. 39
July 21, 1926	Arnold de Julius Jb y Lz PENHA	Ida de Julius Lz PENHA y NAAR	12,000 fls.
Oct. 27, 1928	Abram Oscar de Julius Jb y Lz PENHA	Julia de Jacob HENRIQUEZ y HENRIQUEZ	12,500 ”
March 12, 1932	Horacio de Julius Jb y Lz PENHA	Deborah Dilia de Mord L. MADURO y Lz PENHA	
Jan. 7, 1957	Elsie de Arnold VALENCIA y Lz PENHA	Alexander Irvi de Salomon BRICHTA y FRANKEL	

See allied families: Alvares Correa, Lopez Henriquez, Jesurun, Abinun de Lima, Salas.

Genealogy: David = Sarah J.H. → Jacob = Sarah N. → David = Deborah S. → Isaac = Judith Julia
A.d.L. → Julius Jb = Rachel Amalia L.P. → Abram Oscar = Julia H. → Oscar Jr.

BUENO VALENSI

Marriage Date	Bridegroom	Bride	Dowry and/or Remarks
Jan. 25, 1730	David	Abigail de Abraham LOPEZ SILVA	Mar. in Curaçao

NUNES VAZ

Dec. 2, 1846 — Isaac de Pinhas, b. Jamaica — Ribca Roselvina de Joseph CAPRILES y RICARDO — 8,000 fls.

See Levy Maduro, Piza.

VENTURA, see Piza.

VIEYRA, see Levy Maduro, Coronel Pereira.

DE VRIES, see Alberga.

WEIL

June 11, 1862 — Sigismondo de Isaac y Jeannette ALEXANDER, b. Hamburg — Clara de Abraham Mordechay SENIOR y SENIOR — 2,000 „

WEINSTEIN

July 6, 1957 — Lester de Joseph y Mary ABRAMS — Myrna de Richard Abram COHEN Hz y L. MADURO

WOLFF

About 1835 — Raphael — Judith JESURUN PINTO

March 10, 1870 — Abraham de Raphael y Jn PINTO — Esther de Jacob SENIOR — Mar. in Barranquilla

See allied families: Cardoze, Cohen Henriquez, Moreno Henriquez, Abinun de Lima, Levy Maduro.

YOHAY

Aug. 13, 1943 — Alberto de Samuel YOHAY y YOHAY — Raquel de Salomon OBADIA y OBADIA

Jan. 9, 1965 — Samuel de Isaac y FRIEDLER — Frieda de Samuel FRUCHTER y FAERMAN

ZACUTTO, see Piza.

ZUZARTE, see Suzarte.

EXTRACTS FROM SEVERAL HEBREW MANUSCRIPTS
BY RABBIS OR CANTORS OF MIKVE ISRAEL

HAHAM JOSIAU PARDO

I. Notes on his ספר מזבח הזהב — "Book of the Golden Altar,"[1] a collection of 56 sermons written and delivered in Rotterdam between 1648 and 1651

ספר מזבח הזהב

וחוא חבור דרשות יקרות, אמרות טהורות, אשר דרש בילדותו בקהל ה על ענינים שונים:
עולת שבת בשבתו: החכם השלם יאשיה בכמור״ר דוד פארדו   ז״ל ברוטירדם

Volume 1

Sermon 1. "Since Jewish History does not record a case of 'a stubborn, rebellious son,' why does the Torah [Deut. 49: 18-21] mention it?" y. 5408 [1648].

Sermon 4. Sabbatical Portion *Balak* on the marriage of Ishac [son of Abraham] de Pinto, y. 5408 [1648].

Sermons 5 and 6. On the Simḥath Torah service of 5409 [1648] when Abraham Pereyra and Abraham Nunes were Bridegrooms of the Law. Sermon 6 was delivered in their honor the following Sabbath discourses on the reasons man was created last.

Sermon 8. He mentions his grandfather, "the Chief Rabbi" [Joseph Pardo], y. 5409.

Sermon 12. Sab. Portion *Terumah*. Pardo takes up "two important questions and handles them well: 1) How is it possible that God ordered Cherubim to be made in the Tabernacle; 2) Why

דרוש א״ ־ יחקור אם בן סורר ומורה לא היה ולא נהיה למה בא בתורה. בשנת הת״ח.

דרוש ד״ ־ בפ [רשת] בלק, בחתונת יצחק די פינטו, בשנת הת״ח.

דרוש ה״ ־ בשמחת תורה ... בשנת הת״ט. אברהם פירייירה ואברהם נוניס חתנים. דרוש ו״ בשבת בראשית לכבוד אברהם נוניס חתן בראשית ואברהם פירייירה חתן תורה. ויחקור למה נברא האדם באחרונה. שנת הת״ט.

דרוש ח״ ־ שמעתי אומרים בשם הרב הגדול זקני זצ״ל שנת חת״ט.

דרוש י״ב ־ בפ״ תרומה וחקרתי בו ב״ חקירות גדולות: הא״ למה ואיך צוה השי״ת לעשות כרובים במקדשו. הב״ למה האריך כ״כ במלאכת

---

[1] Ms. at the Ets Haim Library, in two volumes, 34 and 22 sermons, respectively.

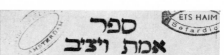

אותׁיׁרׁוׁתׁ אלה יקרו עדיהם וׁיׁדׁקו בׁרׁכׁ לׁפׁני הׁבׁחׁור הׁנׁחׁמׁד דׁוׁד חׁיׁים לׁופׁיׁם פׁינׁיׁא וׁגׁאׁל וׁנׁמׁי

**285. LICENSE TO SLAUGHTER CATTLE AND FOWL GIVEN BY
HAHAM DA FONSECA TO DAVID HAIM LOPEZ PENHA, 1782**

**286. HAHAM JOSIAU PARDO'S
"MIZBAḤ HAZAHAB," 1649**

ספר
אמת ויצׁיב

**287. DAVID ABOAB CHRONICLE, FIRST
PAGE (APPENDIX 19)**

288. THE NEWPORT, R. I., CONGREGATION'S APPEAL TO MIKVE ISRAEL, CURAÇAO,
FOR A CONTRIBUTION TO PAY OFF THEIR MORTGAGE, 1764 (APPENDIX 21)

Moses devoted four lengthy Sabbatical Portions to relate the work done for the Tabernacle" (y. 5409 [1649]).

Sermon 16. Sab. Portion *Emor.* Eulogy on the death of David Imanuel de Pinto [*alias* Rodrigo Alvares Pinto, Abraham de Pinto's brother]. Pardo "raises a mighty question: How can God take away perfect young souls and why? He gives four cogent reasons and explains why we should mourn the departed although they have gone to enjoy the happiness reserved to them in the next world" (y. 5409 [1649]).

Sermon 23. Sab. Portion *Vaethanan.* Pardo gives four reasons why Moses and not Aaron prayed to God to enter the Land of Israel, and why God did not accept the prayer — "Y. 5409, on the Sabbath after the happy marriage of Jacob de Pinto (May God protect him!) celebrated in the Holy Congregation."

Sermon 29. "Sabbatical Portion *Bereshith,* I [Pardo] being bridegroom of finishing the reading of the Law, and Moshe, son of the venerable Abraham de Pinto,[2] bridegroom of the beginning, year 5410 [1649]. May God give me children blessed by Him, Amen."

Volume 2

Sermon 5. Sab. Portion *Bemidbar.* This mentions the marriage of Pardo's brother Joseph[3] (y. not given).

Sermon 6. Sab. Portion *Naso.* On the

המשכן ד̄ פרשיות. וישיב יפה. הת״ט.

דרוש י״ו - בפרשת אמור שדרשתי להספד תשלומין הר̄ דוד עמנואל די פינטו נׄע. וחקרתי בו חקירה עצומה איך ולמה [ה̄] נושא אליו נפשות שלמים וכן רבים בקיצור ימים. וישיב ד̄ סיבות גדולות וגם יתן טוב טעם למה נצטער עליהם בהיות שנוסעים מרעה לרב טוב הצפון להם. שנת הת״ט.

דרוש כ״ג - בפרשת ואתחנן. ויתן ד̄ סיבות למה התפלל [משה] על הכנס לארץ ישראל ולא אהרן ע̄ה. ומה היתה כוונתו? ולמה לא נעתר לו השי״ת. הת״ט. לשורת החתן הר̄ יעקב די פינטו י[שמרהו] צ[ורו]... ואת זה אייחס לפיליסׄו שורה ק̄ שׄ שׄ שׄיליברה בק״ק מזיווג הר̄ יעקב די פינטו יצ״ו.

דרוש כ״ט - שדרשתי בשבת בראשית בהיותי חתן תורה ת[ודה] ל[אל] י[תברך] ומשה בן הנכבד אברהם די פינטו חתן בראשית. הת״י... ויתן לי זרע ברך ה״ אמן.

דרוש ו״ - שדרשתי בפרשת נשא

---

[2] Abraham de Pinto (a.k.a. Don Gyl Lopes Pinto) was the founder of the Yesiba de los Pintos in Rotterdam.

[3] He was hazzan of the Rotterdam synagogue and one of twelve students of the Yesiba de los Pintos; later, hazzan of London until his death in 1677. He wrote the *Shulhan Tahor* (Amsterdam, 1686) which had 14 editions.

birth of a son to Jacob de Pinto (y. not given).

Sermon 10. Simḥath Torah (5409 [5410-1649]), the treasurer of the synagogue Ishac de Pinto being bridegroom of the finishing of the reading of the Law, and Ishac Pereyra bridegroom of the beginning.

Sermon 18. Sab. Portion *Vayyeẓe* (5410 [1649]).

Sermon 19. Sab. Portion *Bereshith*, "Ishac de Pinto and Ishac Pereyra being Bride-grooms of the Law. A remarkable sermon on the great value of circum-cision" (y. 5410 [1649]).

Sermon 20. Sab. Portion *Lekh Lekha* (5410 [1649]).

Sermon 21. Sab. Portion *Vayyesheb* (5410 [1649]).

Sermon 22. "Sabbatical Portion *Vay-yiggash* where Joseph reveals himself to his brothers. He [Pardo] raises five important questions and answers them well during the attendance of the emissary[4] from Hebron" [5410-1649].

Sermon 23. Sab. Portion *Shemoth* (y. 5410 [1649]).

לשורת הבן הנולד ליעקב די פינטו.

דרוש י״ ~ שמחת תורה שנת (הת״ט) [הת״י]... והיו החתנים יצחק די פינטו ח[תן] ת[ורה] וגבאי הק״ק (ו)ה״ר יצחק פיריירה ח[תן] ב[ראשית].

דרוש י״ח בפרשת ויצא הת״י.

דרוש י״ט בשבת בראשית שנת הת״י בהיות יצחק פינטו ויצחק פיריירה חתנים. והוא דרוש נחמד על מצות המילה ומעלותיה עצמו מספר.

דרוש כ״ ~ לך לך הת״י.

דרוש כ״א וישב הת״י.

דרוש כ״ב שדרשתי בפ״ ויגש בהתודע יוסף אל אחיו. ויקשה ה קושיות גדולות וישיבם היטב. והיה שליח חברון בבית הכנסת.

דרוש כ״ג ~ שמות הת״י.

II. RITUAL SLAUGHTERING LICENSE ISSUED BY HAHAM PARDO IN 1666
INTRODUCTION

A certain Ishac Aboab (probably a son of Matatia Aboab) had learned the laws of *Sheḥita* from Haham David Pardo (father of Haham Josiau). He had received a license to kill animals in 1657, shortly before his teacher's death. Having lost his license, Aboab requested Haham Josiau for another. Although familiar with the case, Haham Josiau nevertheless made Aboab repeat the one-year course with him before issuing the following document.

ב[עזרת] ה[שם]

הן אל ישגיב בכחו ליריאיו וחושבי שמו, בהערות עליהם רוח ממרום שמי מעונו, רוח דעת ויראת ה״, לעשות את כל דברי התורה בקדושה ובטהרה כמשפט.

---

4 Unknown to Yaari.

הן אמת מודעת זאת בכל הארץ, ובפרט לשרידים אשר ה׳׳ קורא, כי אחד מן העניניס אשר
מאד ראוי לשים על לב, להיות ירא וחרד עליהם, לעשותם באימה ויראה, נודעת היא
השחיטה והבדיקה, כי רבו כמו רבו פרטיהם, ומה עצמו ראשיהם. ושבח אני את המֹתים, מתי
ישראל, אשר היושב בשבת תחכמוני עליהם לראש ומורה צדק, הוא לבדו השולח ידו לשחוט
ולבדוק, ועליו יסמכו כל בני שער עירם, ולא יערב לגשת זולתו, פן בחֹרם יצאו לקראתו.
אמנם זאת לפנים בישראל, על השחיטה ועל הבדיקה, לקים קֹול דבֹר ומנהיג הדור, אשר
על שכמו המשרה, ביד הבא אליו, למלא את ידו, לידע ולהודיע, כי ראוי הוא לסמוך עליו,
ולא יראה ולא ימצא פוצה פה ומערער נגדו.

הן לזאת עתה באתי, במגלת ספר כתוב עליו, כי בא הלֹום ברוב ענין, חמד בחורים, תמים
דעים, מאד נעלה, כמֹר יצחק אבוהב יץ (?) [ישמרהו צורו], אשר אומר כי הוא זה, יראת
ה׳׳ היא אוצרו, אושרו ועושרו. וידבר אלי לאמר: הלא נפשך יודעת מאד, כי הרשות נתונה
בידי, מאת הרב הקדוש אביך זצֹל, לשחוט ולבדוק, כי הוא זֹל לימדני והנחני במעגלי יושר
הדינין, וענתה השורה כתב ידו לפני לעד לעד משנת [ו]יֹתֹא ראשי עם⁵ לפֹק. אכן צר לי עד מאד,
כי מכתב יושר זה, מעשה ידיו זֹל להתפאר, נעלם מעיני, לא ידעתי איפה הוא, בקשתיהו ולא
מצאתיהו. על זאת מאנה הנחם נפשי עד אשר תטה לי חסד, וסמכת את ידך עלי, ובעשרת
הדברים תבא על החתום באמרי יושר, ואשימה עיני עליהם, כאשר תברכני נפשך.

כשמעי את דבריו ישרים ונכוחים ברכתיהו, גם ברוך יהיה. ועתה הנני בא לצרף מחשבתו
הטובה למעשה, כי ידעתיו חרד על דבר ה, עושה מעשהו באמונה. זאת ועוד אעידה לו עדות
נאמנה, כי שנה תמימה עמדי ובחברתי המתיק סוד יסוד דיני השחיטה והבדיקה. גם באימן
וחזקת היד מצאתיו זריז ונזֹכר, לבדוק בחוטין ובסדקין כמשפט, חכם ירא וסר מרע. ולכן כל
איש ישכיל בלב שלם, שקט ובוטח, יסמוך על שחיטתו ובדיקתו כעל שאר השוחטים ובודקים
מומחים אשר בעם ה׳׳ וצאן מרעיתו. אולם את זה ישמור לעשות, לקרות הדינין אחת בחדש
למען יהיו שנונים ושגורים בפיו כמשפט. ומובטח אני לא תצא תקלה מתחת ידו. וכל מן דין
סמוכו וקריבו לנא לקרבה אל המלאכה לעשות אותה ביתר שאת, הן חכמה הן יראה. נאם
הכותב וחותם חונה פה קֹק רוטֹרדם יֹאֹ בֹי חשק לחדש סיון שנת תבֹו לפֹק⁶ וסימנא טבא
ישחֹוט היטֹב בזֹה ואכֹול בגימטריא.

יאשיהו בכמהר דוד פרדו זלהֹה.

⁵ Deut. 33:21.
⁶ June 13, 1666.

HAHAM SAMUEL MENDES DE SOLA

LICENSE FOR RITUAL SLAUGHTERING
INTRODUCTION

In a general way various planters and sailors were obliged to learn the ritual laws of slaughtering poultry and animals for their personal consumption. The following license,[7] limited to the slaughter of poultry, was issued to Daniel da Costa Gomez on March 14, 1757, by Haham Samuel Mendes de Sola as rabbi of Mikvé Israel and Neve Salom. It was subject to revocation if Da Costa Gomez ate non-kosher (Gentile-made) cheeses as some Jews then did, whereupon poultry killed by him would be considered forbidden food. De Sola made him swear, on pain of excommunication, to abstain from such cheeses.

The same text, with very minor changes in one word or another, was employed by Haham Jacob Lopez da Fonseca when he granted licenses to kill poultry and animals to Moshe de Jacob Mendes Monsanto[8] in 1773 and to David Haim Lopez Penha[9] in 1782.

אותיותי אלה יתנו עדי ה״ וצדקו, כי בא לפני הבחור הנחמד דניאל דא קושטא גומיז ושאל
ממני רשות לשחוט כל מין עוף טהור אשר יאכל, ואחר שבדקתיו, חקרתיו וגם דרשתיו בכל
דיני שחיטה ומצאתיו בקי ומומחה בהם ובשמותיה״, ובהרגשת הסכין מצאתיו ג[ם] כ[ן] קולע
אל השערה ולא יחטיא, וגם שחט לפני ולפני טבחא דמתא נאמן קהלתינו [מקוה ישראל ונוה
שלום] כדין וכהלכה, נתתי לו הרשות אשר שאל ממני, וכל אשר בשם ישראל יכונה מותר
לו לאכל משחיטתו, בתנאי שיחזור ע[ל] כ[ל] דיני שחיטה לפחות פעם א״ בחדש. ויען כי
ראה ראיתי שבעוונותינו הרבים רבו כמו רבו הפריצים בבני עמנו, בני בליעל, הפורקים
מעליהם עול יראת שמים, באכלם מגבינות הגוים, גמרתי בלבי שלא ליתן סמכת שחיטה או
בדיקה לשום אדם, יהיה מי שיהיה, עד שיקבל עליו בפני, בגזרת חרם חמור, שלא יאכל
מגבינות הנ״ל. ובהיות שהבחור הנ״ל קבל עליו לפני את דברי האלה הזאת, בתנאי זה נתתי
לו הסכמתו זו. ואם ח[ו] יעבור על החרם הריני מבטל מעכשיו הסכמתי זו כאילו לא נתתיה,
ומכריז אני כל שחיטותיו לנבלה. ולמען תהיה זו לו (למנה) [לעדה] חתמתי שמי פה באי
קוראסאו, בק״ק מקוה ישראל, ביום ג״ י״ג יום לחדש אדר, שנת תקי״ז לפ״ק. כ[ה] ד[ברי]
העומד לשרת בקדש ורובץ תחת עבוד״ משאת בקה״ק ה״ה ק״ק מקוה ישראל וק״ק נוה
שלום ה״י.

הצעיר שמואל בלא״א [10] דוד חזקיהו מינדיש די סולה זלה״ה.

---

[7] Ms., Ets Haim Library, doc. no. 51. [9] Ms., in author's possession.
[8] *Ibid.*, no. 87. [10] בן לאדוני אבי

HAHAM JACOB LOPEZ DA FONSECA

Haham Da Fonseca, like his predecessors, designated Curaçao in the *Ketuboth* as follows: "In the island of Curaçao, in the city called Willem Stad, port situated in the sea of the West Indies."[11]

באי קוראסאו במתא דמתקרייא ווילים שטאד דיתבא על

כיף ימא דהודו מערבאה.

ASSESSOR DANIEL LOPEZ PENHA

There is a loose sheet in the Mikvé Israel Archives entitled: "Order of Sermons on the Important Days of the Academy אור תורה [held] in the Home of Dan[ie]l Lopez Penha in Curaçao." It is undated, but must have been written before 1780. *The Light of the Torah* Academy or Society appointed its own Bridegrooms of the Law. The following poem of unknown authorship was composed in honor of their Bridegroom of the Law Ishac ben Jahacob, probably Isaac de Jacob Lopez Penha. The poet may have been Daniel Lopez Penha, second administrator of this society, for Moses Lopez Penha tells us that his father wrote many poems in Hebrew.

יִזמר לשוני בגילה ושמחה

צִחק גם רננה להוד חתן תורה

חִדשות תהלות בפאר התורה

קִדושה נעימה בהוד ושיבה

בִאושר וכבוד בשלום ומנוחה

נִעימות לשון כל ירננו לאמר

יִברך אלהים חתן דת וישמר

עִטרת בראשו ברוב גיל וזמרה

קִדוש יעקב בהדר ותפארה

בִרכה ישים לו ובעתו יגמר

ASSESSOR MOSES LOPEZ PENHA

I. PRAYERS AND POEMS

For the celebration of the first centenary of the synagogue Moses Lopez Penha,[12] ex-merchant, composed several prayers and poems in Hebrew which he called קול רנה וישועה — The Voice of Rejoicing and Salvation.[13] They were sung during the evening and morning services of Passover, 1832. Although without poetical merit, some of these verses are presented to show that until the end of the 18th and early 19th centuries there were some people in Curaçao who were fond of the Hebrew language and poetry. Born in Curaçao, Penha studied under his father Daniel and Haham Da Fonseca.

SCHEDULE OF PRAYERS

סדר

שמחת בית הכנסת של ק״ק מקוה ישראל

בקורסא״ במלאת מאה שנים של חנוכתו

1. A short prayer: תודה לאל
2. A psalm of 18 verses on the order of the Psalms of David, punctuated and accented:

מזמור שיר לשמחת הבית:

חסדי ה נשירה לדור ודור נספר גדלתו

3. Ten verses sung to the tune of the Hallel of Hosha'na Rabbah:

יום זה ישמחו אמוני עם ועדת מקוה ישראל

כי בא מועד, הגיע עת, לזמר שיר במקדש אל

4. Twenty verses, each set of four sung to a different melody customarily sung in Amsterdam[14] and Curaçao in honor of Bridegrooms of the Law:

א

לחן לאל נורא

לאל עולם בקול רנה

גודלו אזכיר בעוז ואל:

לטוב העם אשר בנה

דביר זה מקוה ישראל:

---

[12] See above, pp. 339-40; *Precious Stones*, pp. 454-55.

[13] Ms., Ets Haim Library, no. 20 C 13.

[14] Penha indicated the other four melodies as follows:

לחן יאיר כיום ~ לחן ישלם שלם ~ לחן אזמר שיר ~ לחן אחלה נא

(*Tefilath Yesharim* [Amsterdam, 1779], p. 138).

5. The following verses to be sung in the evening service before removing the Scrolls of the Law from the Holy Ark:

ב	א
נגדילה שם האל בשירים נעימים:	קול מבשר יום זה השמיע ברינה
ובקול תודה ורון ביום המילואים	כי בא מועד ששון ועת לחנונה:
חינוך מאה שנים בנין בית תפילה:	על כן רנו שירו בחצרות אל
נגילה בליל זה בתוך עם סגולה:	תנו שבח ויקר למקוה ישראל:
הושיעה וגו''	ואומר החזן הושיעה את עמך

ד	ג
תשכון בהיכל זה קבל רנתנו	נוה יקרינו זה והיכל החביב
שועתנו רצה ושעה מנחתנו	זורח בליל זה כאש נוגה סביב
מהר הביאנו בנוה הדרך	לכבוד וגדולה לאדון השלום
לרנן ולזמר שם תהלתך	ולגוי עם סגלה זוהרת כיהלום
הושיעה וגו''	הושיעה וגו''

6. An adaptation of the *Yigdal* customarily sung at the end of the evening service during festivals:

לחן י[ום] ט[וב]

יגדל אלהים חי בטובתו, עדה נאמנה באהבתו:

יזרח ברוב חסדו וישועתו, בית מקוה ישראל בראשיתו:

7. Four verses on the order of those chanted in Amsterdam before the final blessing:

תקובל לפני אל תפילה ושבחה

כתודה ושלמים ומנחה מרקחה:

ופניו אחלה יברך את עם אל

וישכון עדי עד במקוה ישראל

8. Morning service, introduction to the *Kaddish:* רשות לקדיש

ב	א
לחן יאיר כיום	לחן לאל נורא
בשיר חדש זמרו נא	לאל מרום נורא עליון
יתנו הלל כרוב גודלו	בנועם פה אשירה לך
לאדון הכל פצחו רינה	קבל שיחי שוכן ציון
בקול ערב להללו	ביום שמחת בית היכלך

1015

ד	ג
לחן יצמח יציל	לחן ישלם שלם
קחו כנור לנצח	במלאת היום מאה שנים
לאדון עולם תוך היכלו	דביר היכל ובית מקדש
ובקול נעים לשבח	תנו תודה גם רננים
במקהלים זמרו לו	בתוך עדה בשיר חדש

ה

לחן גם כתמר

בקול תודה ובקול זמרה

שאו מנחה לגדולתו

ביום גילה ביום שירה

כי בא מועד שמחת ביתו

9. Two hazzanim to sing the [eight] verses customarily sung in Amsterdam on the anniversary of the Synagogue, starting with:

ישיר ישראל שיר נועם

10. Piyyut sung by the Congregation to the tune of *Todoth El:* לחן תודות אל

א

מלך רב נשגב עליון לך נשיר בקהל רב

שעה זמרת בני ציון וקול יערב

ב

ביום המילואים הזה נזמרך ברוב שמחה

נהללך בשיר יום זה וממנו רצה מנחה

ג

שמי מרום ובית זבול לא יכילון יקרך

ומה קיר זה והגבול היות מכון לשבתך

ד

פה תשכון שכינתך ותרצה יסודותיו

לפאר בית תפילתך וליסדו במכונותיו

ה

ולמנהיגי וראשי עם ונדיבי לב קהלנו

יגדיל שמם, ירבה הונם, מאד ישגו לעינינו

ו

תפלתנו ירצה יואל כקרבן ושיר נערב

ולקהל זה מקוה ישראל בטוב יהיו ושלום רב

ז

תנו הלל בקול תודה ביום ששון וביום שמחה

נדיבי לב בתוך עדה שאו ידכם בהרוחה

ח

נוחיל שוכן בהר ציון לפאר בית בית מקדשנו

ואז הבית יהיה עליון בעת ביאת משיחנו

11. Piyyut in six verses adapted to the text and melody of the Adon 'Olam:

לחן אדון עולם הידוע. לחזנים המשוררים שנים כאחד,

זה קורא וזה עונה:

אדון עולם אשר ברך, לעם בחר באור תורה

בעת אשא לחפצו קול, ואשיר לו ואחבירה

בידו אפקיד שיחי, לצור עוזי ביום שירה.

12. Pizmon to the tune of "A Los Campos":[15]

ב	א
כן נחנו ביום זה בתוך עם סגלה	כדוכן לויים אז בבית המקדש
גם באנו לזמר בנעימה יתרה	כאסף ואיתן בכלי שיר ומינים
לשמחת בית זה ולתת גדולה	לזמר בכל עוז בכל יום שיר חדש
למקוה ישראל בעוז ובתפארה	בתהלה בתודה מזמורים ורנים

ג

בשמחה רבה נרים קולינו

לאדון הכל כקרבן חובותינו

ברינון וזמר ושירי תהלה

כי יום יובל הוא וגילת קהלה

13. Pizmon to the tune of the Adon 'Olam as sung in New York:

לחן אדון עולם של נויורק

ב	א
מרום מקום מקדש מהרה יתחדש	אפתח שיר בשפתי גם לשוני תרון
נזמר שיר חדש בבית אחרון	אשיר אל אל שדי עת פותחים לו ארון

[15] An old Spanish ballad. The prayer book *Tefilath Yesharim*, pp. 140a-142b, cites the titles of six old ballads whose melodies were adapted to various liturgical songs of Simḥath Torah in Amsterdam: "Tres Colores en Una," "Pues Vos Me Paristes," "Porque No Me Hablas?" "En Campos Derma"(?), "La Mansanica," "Partistes, Amiga." For the adaptation of the melodies of these ballads to the liturgical songs of Salonika and for many more titles of these ballads, see Emmanuel, *Histoire des Israélites de Salonique*, pp. 199-200.

<table>
<tr><td style="text-align:center">ד</td><td style="text-align:center">ג</td></tr>
</table>

על ירושלים רחם אדון שמים	ישוב לפני לפנים יקר מפנינים
אז במצלתים יושר השיר ברון	ולוחות אבנים ואבני זכרון

ה

מקוה ישראל למפוזר כמו שה

את מאמר עשה [כ]משה בנסוע הארן

14. Last verses before the final blessing:

תקובל שמחתכם ותפילת אמונים

אלהים ישמורכם ותהיו דשנים

השגחתו יגן על עם סגלתו

ובהיכל זה לעד תשכן שכינתו[16]

בשנת... וַיְדַבֵּר מֹשֶׁה אֶת כֹּל דִּבְרֵי הַשִּׁירָה הַזֹּאת לפֹק.[17] המדלף סט [הצעיר משה דניאל לופס פנייה סופי טוב].

Then follows a special prayer in Hebrew prose, five pages long, probably undelivered because of its length.

II. PRAYERS OF CIRCUMSTANCE

While in Curaçao in 1963, I found in a drawer of a synagogue pew a small manuscript in Hebrew entitled: סדר התפלות. It is a collection of prayers of circumstance: In honor of King William II (1840-49); "for sicknesses;" for the sea traveller; for smallpox, and for a couple before the marriage ceremony (1846). Most probably Moses Lopez Penha was the author.

---

[16] These four verses were adapted to similar verses sung in Amsterdam at the end of the services honoring Bridegrooms of the Law (*Seder Hatefiloth Keminhag Kahal Kadosh Amsterdam* [Amsterdam, 1857], p. 161).

[17] [5]592 [1832].

UNKNOWN AUTHOR

When the Mikvé Israel Synagogue celebrated its 200th anniversary in 1932, the choir sang the following verses in Hebrew (transliterated into Latin characters), Spanish and Dutch. It is quite probable that they were composed in 18th century Amsterdam to be sung on happy occasions, and that Hazzan Duque adapted them to Curaçao, substituting Mikvé Israel for Talmud Torah. The Hebrew and Spanish texts follow.

לאל עולם

"LAEL NGOLAM"

A El Señor del Universo mundo
Creador y venerable siempre es,
Un canto elevo con fervor profundo
En este Recinto Augusto de paz.

לאל עולם סגולי רם
בקהל רב אשא זמרה
בסוד עדה אתן תודה
לשם קדשו ולתורה

Hoy es para nos día de contento
Que en medio pués de esa santa alegría
Se una nuestra voz en dulce concierto
Fiel intérprete de alma simpatía

חנון ! שמע שירת לבנו
ביום זה יום שמחתנו

De año en año Mikwe Israel
Florezca como arbol primaveral
Que sus frutos, dulces como la miel
Causen nuestra dehesa cardinal

מקוה ישראל תציץ כשושנה
תרבה שנה, שנה הדרה

1019

THE DAVID ABOAB CHRONICLE ON THE CONFLICT OF 1745-46

DAVID ABOAB'S "EMETH VE YAẒIB" — The Irrefutable Truth — is a bitter polemic born out of the harsh treatment he suffered at the hands of the parnassim and particularly of Haham De Sola (pages 187-89). As is usual in such circumstances, he is unsparingly biting and offensive toward his adversaries. He uses relatively good biblical Hebrew punctuated with numerous puns, and reveals a thorough rabbinical training which would have benefited the Curaçoan Jewry of that day immensely. He took his chronicle with him to Amsterdam for printing. The Amsterdam parnassim forbade its publication at the request of their Curaçao colleagues and requisitioned the manuscript.

A few excerpts from this interesting pamphlet of 24 pages follow. For the sake of brevity or out of respect for Haham De Sola, the parnassim of that era and the families Fidanque, Maduro and Redondo, certain expressions are deliberately omitted as the ellipses indicate. Insulting remarks and scandalous or exaggerated accounts have been purposely left out.

INTRODUCTION

ספר אמת ויציב

הוא ויכוח אמיתי, גנוז הוא אתי, מודיע אמֹת באמונֹה, קריֹאה נאמנה, צדק ילין בה, ובקרבה
ישים אוֹר בֹה . . . לא תשא פנים לשום אדם, נשיא ומלך בשר ודם, אם דל ואם עשיר . . .
לכן עתה באתי לגלות נבלתם, ולקרב חרפתם, כי יגֹלו בראש גֹלים.

Aboab laments the parnassim's suppression of the truth. He praises the Netherlands Government for protecting the Jews and describes Curaçao as being full of God-fearing Jews.

כי תהלות לאל יתברך היתה העיר הזאת קוראסֹאו עיר גדולה לאלהים ואנשים מיראת ה
מלאים . . . והיא היתה עיר ואם בכל איי האמרֹיקא.

HAHAM DE SOLA AND THE PARNASSIM

בשנת התקֹה . . . שבא שמֹץ . . . שֵׁמואל מֹנדיס צֹולא . . . בבא . . . זה לעיר הזאת אוי לעינים
שכך רואות, היה בדק על בדק, פרץ על פרץ . . . . מצא מין את מינו . . . . , איש חֹמֹס . . .
מֹרדכי חֹיים סֹניאור ושֹונא אֹור[1] . . . כשמו כן הוא . . . והאחרון שֹנֹרא בישא . . . שֹלמה גֹוניס

---

[1] A pun on the name Senior.

רִידוֹנדוֹ . . . כי אכלו וגזלו את מקוֹה ישראֹל . . . ידברו עתק על נוה הֿ נוֹה שלוֹם . . . תחת
שלֹש רזגה ארץ ותחת ארבֹה לא תוכל שאת הפרץ, תחת עֹבד כי ימלוך ונבל כי ישבע לחם.
תחת שׁנֹיה כי תבעל ושפחֹה כי תירש גבירתה . . .

Then, without reference to Penso, he names in disparaging terms the two rabbis
and the ten parnassim and councillors opposed to Penso and Penso's party. While
speaking of De Sola, he reveals the Haham's modest origin in Alentejo, Portugal.

THE QUESTION OF *Senif* OR ASSISTANT

יש כמו שלשים שנה שהיה משמש בעיר קוֹראֹסוֹ זקן אחד ללמדן ודרשן. ומשנעשה ישן נושן
ותלמודו שכח ובעוברו עליו חלוצי צבא נלקח ונלכד מהזקנה . . . שלחו קהל קוֹראֹסוֹ מהכא
להתם לעיר אמשטרדאם . . . לשאול מהם . . . איש אחד . . . ולסייע להההוא סבא . . . והם שלחו
לאיש הזה שמֹ . . . כדי להיות מסייע וסנֹיף לזקן הנ"ל . . . כמו שכתב הוא בעצמו באגרתו
השלוחה אל הזקן מאתו . . . אך בבואו לעיר הזאת . . . איני סנֹיף כי אם גביר גברא רבא
וכביר . . . אני למדן, אני פסקן . . . וילמוד להם מסכת ברכות . . . ויחדל מלבוא לב[ית]
הֿ[מדרש] כבראשונה כי אם פעם או שתים בשבוע . . . לקבל ת"ק מאות שקלי כסף בעבודה
מידי שנה בשנה.

HAHAM DE SOLA IS ASSAILED FOR PERMITTING THE SHEARING
OF THE BEARD DURING THE FIRST 33 DAYS OF THE 'OMER

והוא [די סולֹא] . . . היה הראשון לכל בית יוסף אשר בטל המנהג ההגון הזה שהיה פשוט
בעיר קוֹראֹסוֹ בין החסידים ואנשי מעשה. ענה ואמר למדו ממני, כזה ראה ועשה . . . בימי
העומר והספירה ליפות פניו . . .

THE PARDO-MADURO INCIDENT[2]

איש נמצא בעיר הזאת שמואל לוי מאדורו שמו איש . . . מאינן משפחות . . . ששלחו מהֿתם
להֹכֿא . . . קיים שטר חוב . . . ויהי אחרי כן נתחרט ממה שעשה . . . וימצא את הגביר הנעלה
כהר שמואל אידֹניא [די קאסיריס] נר"ו אשר סדר לו שטר מודעה . . . וסופר המודעה הזאת
היה הבחור הנחמד כה"ר יצחק פארדו נר"ו, מודע להגביר הנ"ל ושאר בשרו . . . ויהי
מימים . . . ותהום כל העיר . . . אז קמו כל בני המשפחה [של מאדורו] . . . להעמיד השטר
חוב על חזקתו . . . וגמרו לעות אדם בריבו הלא הוא כהֹר יצחק פארדו . . . ענה שמֹ . . .
ביום לג לעומר משנת התק"ה בתוך קהל ועדה . . . חלֹם בקרבך ישראל וירוק בפני הבחור
הנ"ל בגאוה וזדון, וישים אותו כעבד לפני אדון . . .

ALTERATION IN THE MOVEMENTS OF THE LULAB INITIATED
BY HAHAM DE SOLA [3]

שהיה [די סולא] משתרר עלינו במערצה להטיל אימה על הצבור שלא לשם שמים, מחרף
ומגדף . . . הקדושים אשר בארץ המה, בארץ האים, חלקם בחיים, הלא הם החכמים
השלמים, בני אלים ותמימים, כמוהר״ר יאשיהו פארדו וכמוהר״ר אליהו לופיס זלה״ה, ועוד
דבר סרה נגד חכמי ורבני הולנדא המהוללה . . . כולם כאחד היו נוהגים המנהג קדמון . . .
מזרח, צפון, מערב, דרום, מעלה ומטה ופשיטא ודאי דיש להם על מה שיסמוכו.

JOSEPH FIDANQUE AND THE HESSED VE EMETH BROTHERHOOD

ידוע תדע כי . . . יוסף פידנקי . . . עושה עושר ולא במשפט, כל ממונו משאו ומתנו כל שאין
רוח הבריות נוחה הימנו . . . ידו בכל ויד כל בו. ומפני זדונו . . . גרשו אותו מהסתפח בנחלת
ה . . . החברה הקדושה מרוחצי המתים . . . [4]

HAHAM DE SOLA INSULTS MEMBERS OF THIS BROTHERHOOD
AND DANIEL BELMONTE IN PARTICULAR

לגביר הנעלה המרומם על כל שבח ותהלה, בן של קדושים, ואחד מבני האיתנים, מהינון
הרים גבנונים, ההר חמד אלהים לשבתו, כה״ר דניאל בילמונטי בכ״ר יעקב בילמונטי נר״ו [5]
. . . בן יכבד אב . . . ובעבור שנתן [בילמונטי] טעם לדבריו . . . נגד שמץ . . . חרף וגדף בו
גם במשפחתו וכל הטף, בעבור השוחד שנתן לו [פידנקי] . . . הנקטף חבית של שרף הנוטף
מעצי הקטף.

CONSTRUCTION OF SYNAGOGUE NEVE SALOM AND THE
DISTURBANCES OF ELUL, 5506

איש חמס [סיניייור] ושנרא [רידונדו] לא שלו ולא שקטו מלהשים לפניהם [יחידי אוטרה באנדה]
מכשולות ופחים . . . אך לריק יגעו . . . ויבן את הבית ויכלהו הגביר הנעלה המרומם על כל
ברכה ותהלה . . . ה״ה כה״ר יצחק קאלבו נר״ו . . . ויעש לה חומה מחוץ ומבית . . .

THE TOBATH MARHE BROTHERHOOD AND DAVID ABOAB

חברה אחת יש בעיר קוראסו יהא [6] מאנשים חכמים ונבונים, גדולי הדור ובני האתנים, אנשים
חשובים ועריצים, בן של קדושים, עובדים את ה ביראה, גומלי חסד לבעלי תורה ולעוסקים
בה סמא דחיים, ותהילות ה יגידו באים העוברים ושבים לאמר הטיבה ה לטובים וזה שמה

---

[4] Fidanque was a founder of this brotherhood (*Precious Stones*, p. 63; see *ibid.*, pp. 288-91, for his biography and epitaph).

[5] For the Curaçao Belmontes' kinship to the Belmonte nobility of Amsterdam, see pp. 205-206, note 99.

[6] ישמרה השם אמן

אשר קראו לה טובֹת מראֹה, חן חן לה, כי טובת מראה היא במעשיה בקֹול שהיא תפארת
לעושיה ... ויהי היום יצאו בני החברה ... לרעות בגנים ולשמוח בשמחת של מצוה ...
לראות חנוכת בית אלהינו [נוה שלום] ... אחרי גמר התשבחות ... שִׁיר השִּׁירים ושֹׁפר תהֹלים
נדבו כל הקהל ... ועל כולם רבו ... חברת טובֹת מראֹה המהוללה אשר התנדבו יותר
ממאתים שקלי כסף בגילה ... אך ... שמֹץ ... לא רצה לגשת את בית ה ... בקרוא אותו
מושב לצים ...

לקרוא את ת[למיד] ח[כם] אחד [דוד אבוהב] מבנן של קדושים וצדיקים, הבא מאיי הים
ומארץ מרחקים. והאי צורבא מרבנן היה שקט בביתו ושאנן, לומד עם תלמידיו היקרים תורת
ה ... [לדרוש] בבית הכנסת החדש של נוֹה שלוֹם דברי תוכחות גידופים איומים וחירופים
נגד הבית ונגד אנשיה, כי היא בית פריצים והם אנשים רקים ולצים ... ומה אני[7] ... כי
אעלה להוכיח את עם ה ... שקבלו אותי[7] באהבה וחיבה ...

אחר תפלת מנחה בא לבית הכנסת ויחלוץ מנעליו ויעלה על התיבה, בענוה ויראה, ושאל
מחילה וסליחה ובפרט לזקן [ישורון] ולשמֹץ ... וכזה יתירו לו הנדוי ... מה יעשה טלה[8]
בין הזאבים, יחיד ורבים הלכה כרבים, וכן פעל ועשה ליום המחרת ויתירו את נדויו ...

וימסרו אותו בידי גוים ... וילילך מעיר קוראסֹו בתוך שמונה ימים, ויום השמיני היה ערב
ראש השנה ... שנת התק"ז ... שלשה המה [מתנגדיו] שמֹץ פיסול ואיש חֹמֹס ... וההוא
שונֹרא ... והרביעי בנימין לופיס [הנריקיס] שרי"ר.[9]

The Tobath Marhe nevertheless helps him financially.

Aboab then exposes Haham De Sola's domestic difficulties and the Haham's
previous suspension from the Yeshibah Ets Haim of Amsterdam. In conclusion he
upbraids De Sola for his incosistency over the *lulab*. Although De Sola had once
recognized the validity of the willow used in Curaçao, the following year he
entered the synagogue with the palm, myrtle and citron, but without the willow.
The polemic closes with this short prayer:

יה בגדול חסדך לטובים הטיבה
רחם על עבדך פס יד"א[10] בכתיבה.

---

[7] This passage again confirms David Aboab as the author of this pamphlet.
[8] The "Memorias Senior" do not picture Aboab as a docile person (see p. 188).
[9] שם רשעים ירקב
[10] דוד אבוהב

FAMILY HEADS AND MEMBERS OF THE COMMUNITY
1746 AND 1769

I N 1746 ALL MARRIED MEN, widows and widowers were required to sign a declaration promising to respect the laws of the *ketubah* or marriage contract — particularly the clause referring to the dowry a wife brought her husband. Practically everyone in the community signed it except the bachelors, aged maiden ladies, several planters and, of course, those temporarily away from the island. Twelve families opposed it (see p. 182).

In 1769 the parnassim tried to introduce the *Finta* or communal tax. This time also the entire community was called upon to support it. Almost everyone signed it with the exception of the Haham Da Fonseca, the teachers and ecclesiastical employees who were exempted from the payment of all taxes. Most of the wealthy members (whose names are also listed) were against it (see pages 255-56).

The lists are offered for two reasons. They give us an idea of the names of the families — some long since extinct. They also make it possible for us to estimate the number of Jews living in Curaçao in 1746 at some 1,450, and in 1769 at some 1,350 souls. Those who were relatively young in 1746 make their reappearance in the list of 1769. By the same token, various families living in 1746 disappeared by 1769.

Various additions have been made to these lists which are in a bundle of loose papers in the PJCAA. To the first one have been added the names of several married people and widows who failed to sign it for one reason or another; to the second, several members who then dwelled in Curaçao but did not sign.

1746	1769
A	A
Isaac Abarbanel	Isaac Abenatar*
David Abenatar	Semuel Aboab
Isaac Abenatar	Aron Ailyon*
Jacob Abenatar	Joseph Jochem Alexander*
Mosse Aboab	Isaac Andrade*
Samuel de Castro Almeyda	Jacob de Abraham Andrade
Ribca Alvares	Jacob de Mordechay Andrade*

* Refused to sign.

1746

Abraham Andrade
Isaac Hisquiau Andrade
Widow Mordechay Andrade
Abraham da Costa de Andrade
Benjamin da Costa de Andrade
Jacob da Costa de Andrade
Jacob Guadaloupe Andrade
Joseph Antunes [Paredes]
Branca Athias
Efraim Athias
Mosseh Pereira Athias

B

Abraham Belmonte
Daniel Belmonte
Ishac Belmonte
Jacob Belmonte
Widow Hana Benveniste
David Souza Britto
Abraham Bueno Vivas
Widow Isaac Bueno Vivas

C

Jacob de Mordechay Calvo
Ishac Calvo*
Widow Mordechay de Jacob Calvo
Sarah Israel Campanel
David Cardozo & Son
Abraham Aboab Cardozo
Jacob Gomes Casseres
Samuel Idanha de Casseres
Ephraim Castelo
Mosseh de Castro
Aron de Chavez Jr.
Esther de Chaves
Mosseh de Abraham de Chaves
Mosseh de Chavez
Abraham Alvares Correa
Manuel de Rephael Alvares Correa

1769

Abraham da Costa Andrade Jr.
Michael da Costa Andrade
Semuel da Costa Andrade*

B

Daniel Belmonte
Jacob de Abraham Belmonte
Jacob Rodriguez Brandam
Moseh Souza Britto
David Bueno Vivas
Joseph Bueno Vivas

C

Moseh Callo
Abraham Calvo
Dr. Joseph Capriles*
David Cardoze*
Daniel Aboab Cardozo
Gabriel Cardozo
Isaac Cardozo
Abraham Aboab Cardozo
Benjamin Aboab Cardozo
Aron de David Uziel Cardozo
Mosseh de Casseres
Jacob Gomes Casseres*
Jacob [David?] Gomes Casseres
Josiau Idanha de Casseres
Saul Idanha de Casseres
David [Haim] Castello*

* Refused to sign.

1746	1769
Mordechay Alvares Correa	Jacob de Moseh de Chaves
Mosseh Alvares Correa	Raphael Alvares Correa*
Widow Raphael Alvares Correa	Ishac Cardozo da Costa
Abraham Henriquez Cotiño	Isaac Haim Rodriguez da Costa**
Jacob Henriquez Cotiño	Mosseh Rodriguez da Costa
Widow Isaac Henriquez Cotinho	Abraham de Manuel Namias de Crasto
Mosseh Henriquez Cotiño	Abraham de Mordechay de Crasto
David Namias de Crasto*	David de Mordechay de Crasto
Mordechay de Crasto	Haim Isaac Namias de Crasto
Abraham Rodriguez Cunha	Ishac de Mordechay de Crasto
Jacob Curiel	Jeosuah de [Mordechay de] Crasto
Selomoh Curiel	Manuel Namias de Crasto
	Mordechay Namias de Crasto
	Ishac Curiel
	Moseh Curiel
	Selomoh de Jacob Curiel

D	D
Abraham Diaz	Abraham Lopez Dias*
Isaac Diaz	Abraham de Jacob Lopez Dias
Abraham de Isaac Lopez Dias*	David Lopez Dias
Isaac Lopez Dias*	Semuel Lopez Dias
Jacob de Isaac Lopez Dias*	David Haim Dovale
Moseh Lopez Dias	Josiau Dovale*

F	F
Abigail Vaz Farro	Selomoh Vaz Farro*
Benjamin Vaz Farro	Abraham Fidanque
Widow David Vaz Farro	Jacob Fidanque & Sons
Mosseh Vaz Farro	David Lopez Fonseca
Ishac Henriquez Fereira	David de Jacob Lopez Fonseca
Ishac de Jacob Henriquez Fereyra*	Eliau de Aron Lopez Fonseca
Jacob Semah Ferro	
Abraham Flores	
Widow Abraham Lopez da Fonseca	
Widow Aron Lopez Fonseca	
Widow Jacob Lopez Fonseca	
Mosseh Hisquiao Lopez da Fonseca	
Mordechay Fundam	

* Refused to sign.
** Not in the list although he initiated the project.

1746

G

Gerson Garsia
Widow Ribca Garsia
Rephael Gomez
Mother of Rephael Gomez
Isaac da Costa Gomez
Joseph da Costa Gomez
Abraham Gonzales
Jacob Dias Guadalupe

H

Widow Raquel Halas
Benjamin Rephael Henriquez
Jacob Henriquez
Jeosuah Henriquez Jr.
Widow Mordechay Hisquiau Henriquez
David de Jeudah Cohen Henriquez
David de Mosseh Cohen Henriquez
J[acob]. Cohen Henriquez
Jeudith, wid. Mosseh Cohen
  Henriquez
Abraham Jesurun Henriquez
Efraim Jesurun Henriquez
Eliau Israel Jesurun Henriquez
Jacob de Benjamin Jesurun Henriquez
Josseph Jesurun Henriquez
Benjamin Lopez Henriquez
Widow David H.º Lopez Henriquez
Widow Rachel de Selomoh L. Henriquez
Selomoh Lopez Henriquez
Benjamin Moreno Henriquez
Esther Moreno Henriquez
Father [= Jacob] of Mosseh Naar
  Henriquez
Mosseh Naar Henriquez
Semuel de David Hoheb

J

David Jesurun

1769

G

Moseh Gomez
Jacob da Costa Gomez*
Samuel de Gabriel da Costa Gomez*
Samuel de Joseph da Costa Gomez*
Moseh Gonsales
Barugh Guedella

H

David Hallas
David Henriquez
Moseh Henriquez
Benjamin Cohen Henriquez*
David & Jacob Cohen Henriquez*
Moseh de David Cohen Henriquez
Jacob Eliau Israel Jesurun Henriquez
Jacob de Joseph Jesurun Henriquez*
Jeosuah Jesurun Henriquez
Abraham Lopez Henriquez
Jacob de Benjamin Lopez Henriquez
Jacob de Selomoh Lopez Henriquez
Mosseh de Jacob de David L. Henriquez
Moseh de Selomoh Lopez Henriquez
Aron Moreno Henriquez
Aron Benjamin Moreno Henriquez
Isaac Moreno Henriquez
Jacob Moreno Henriquez
Jacob Pretto Henriquez
Semuel Hoheb*

J

Abraham de David Jesurun

* Refused to sign.

1027

1746

Ishac Jesurun
Mosseh de Benjamin Jesurun
[Haham] Rephael Jesurun
Widow Abraham Henriquez Juliaõ
Isaac Henriquez Juliaõ

K

Mosseh Keyser

L

Abraham de Jacob Jeudah Leao*
Jacob Jeudah Leao*
Semuel de Jacob Jeudah Leao*
Abraham Levy
David Levy
Eliau Levy
Ishac Levy
Manuel Levy
Mordechay Abinun de Lima
Branca Linda
Widow Abraham Lopez
Eliau Lopez
Manuel Lopez
Abraham Baruh Louzada
Isaac de Abraham Baruh Louzada

M

Aron Mendes Machado
Abraham Samuel de Moseh L. Maduro
Abraham de Selomoh Levy Maduro
Widow Aron Levy Maduro
Irmiau de Isaac Levy Maduro
Isaac de Semuel Levy Maduro
Isaac Levy Maduro
Jacob Levy Maduro
Jacob de Selomoh Levy Maduro
Mordechay Levy Maduro

* Refused to sign.

1769

Benjamin Jesurun
David Jacob Jesurun
Ishac Jesurun
Jacob David Jesurun
Mosseh Benjamin Jesurun

L

David Lopez Laguna*
Jacob de Eliao Jeudah Leao
Abraham a Levy*
Gabriel de Manuel Levy
David Abinun de Lima
Ishac [de Mordechay] Abinun de Lima
Mordechay Abinun de Lima
Eliau Lopez
Son-in-law of Eliau Lopez Jr.
Jacob Henriquez Moron de Losena
Abraham Barugh Louzada

M

Abraham de Isaac Levy Maduro
Ishac de Jacob Levy Maduro
Ishac de Moseh Levy Maduro
Ishac de Semuel Levy Maduro
Isaac de Semuel Hº Levy Maduro
For my brother Jacob de Moseh Levy
    Maduro
Jacob de Selomoh Levy Maduro
Mordechay de Selomoh Levy Maduro*
Moseh de Aron Levy Maduro

1746

Moseh de Isaac Levy Maduro
Moseh de Selomoh Levy Maduro
Moseh de Semuel Levy Maduro
Samuel de Isaac Levy Maduro
Semuel Levy Maduro
Semuel de Selomoh Levy Maduro
Selomoh de Isaac Levy Maduro
Selomoh de Samuel Levy Maduro
Widow Selomoh Levy Maduro
Selomoh de Moseh Levy Maduro
Abraham de Marchena
Widow Isaac de Marchena
Ester Rodriguez Marques
Reyna L. Suares, wid. Vaz Martinez
David de Mattos
Isaac Castro Mattos
Eliao Miranda
Ester Miranda
Mosseh Miranda
Ester, wid. Jacob Rz. Miranda
Widow Abraham Molina
Aharon de Molina
David de Molina
Abraham Monsanto
Isaac Israel Monsanto
Widow Abraham Molina Monsanto
Rephael Molina Monsanto
Aron Henriquez Moron*
Isaac de Jacob Henriquez Moron
Jacob Henriquez Moron
Abraham Motta
Aron Motta
Benjamin Motta
Isaac Motta

1796

By order of Moseh de Selomoh L. Maduro
Selomoh de Isaac Levy Maduro
Selomoh de Moseh Levy Maduro
Selomoh de Abraham Levy Maduro
Selomoh de Jacob Levy Maduro
Semuel de Isaac Levy Maduro
Semuel Levy Maduro Jr.
Ishac de Abraham de Marchena
Ishac de Medina
Abraham Henriquez Melhado
Sabbathay Israel Mendes
Abraham Michael Rodriguez Mendes
Elias Rodriguez Miranda*
Eliau Rodriguez Miranda
Ishac Rodriguez Miranda
David de Molina
    For my father Ishac de Molina
Jacob Mendes Monsanto
Rephael Molina Monsanto
Abraham de Ishac Henriquez Moron
Aron Motta*
Mordechay Motta
Mosseh Motta

N

Abraham Naar
Benjamin Naar
Father of H. de Jeosuah Naar
Jacob de Abraham Naar

N

David Naar
Eliau de Jacob Naar
Hezra Naar
Jacob de Abraham Naar

* Refused to sign.

1746

Jacob de Jeosuah Naar
Benjamin Neira's mother
Benjamin Athias de Neira
Daniel Vaz Nunes
Ishac Nunes

1769

Jeosuah de Jacob Naar
Mordechay Naar
Ishac Athias de Neyra*
Isaac Rodriguez Nunes
Abraham Haim Vaz Nunes
Mosseh Vaz Nunes

O

Joseph Obediente
Joseph Obediente Jr.
Jacob Aboab Ozorio*

P

Josiau Pardo
Daniel Cohen Peixotto
Isaque Penso
Mosseh Penso*
Jacob de la Peña
Abraham Lopez Peña
David de Eliau Pereira
Widow Eliau Pereira
Ishac de Jacob Pereyra*
Jacob Pereira
Jacob de Eliau Pereira
Mordechay Pereira
Abraham de Campos Pereira
Ester Rodriguez Pereira
Abraham Pessoa
Abraham Pimentel
Jacob Pinedo
Rephael de Samuel Pinto

P

Isaak Pardo*
Jacob Garcia de Paz
Manuel Hisquiao Penedo
Abraham [de Jacob] Lopes Penha
Ishac Lopes Penha
Moseh Lopes Penha
Abraham Penso
Mordechay de Moseh Penso
Eliau Haim Perreira
Ishac Pereira*
Abraham Rodriguez Perreyra
Jacob Haim Rodriguez Perreyra
Abraham Pessoa
Abraham Pimentel
David Henriquez Pimentel
Gabriel Pinedo*
Ishac Tores Pinto

R

Mosseh Ramos
Selomoh Rivero
Widow Jacob Robles
Raphael Rodrigues
Widow Aron Cohen Rodriguez

* Refused to sign.

1746

S

David Salom's mother
Aharon Mosseh Israel [St. Crus]
Mosseh Jesurun Saportas
Abraham Jesurun Sasportas
Abraham Sasso
Joseph Sasso
Abraham Senior
Abraham de Isaac Senior
David Senior
David de Isaac Senior
David Isaac Senior's mother
Jacob de David Senior
Mordechay Haim Senior
Salamaõ Senior
David Serrano
Semuel Gomez Silva
[Haham] Semuel Mendes de Solla
Abraham Hisquiau Suares
Benjamin Suares
David Suares
Widow Isaac Suares
Jacob Suares
Jacob Suares Jr.

T

Isaac de Semuel Touro
Joseph Israel Touro
Lea Touro
Mosseh Touro
Samuel Touro

1769

S

Moses Salas
David Salom
Abraham Salzedo
Abraham Jesurun Sasportas
Isaac Jesurun Sasportas
Jeudah de Abraham Sasso
Mosseh de Abraham Sasso
Abraham de Mordechay Senior
David Abraham de Isaac Haim Senior
For my son-in-law David Jacob Senior
Ishac de Abraham Senior
Ishac Haim de Jacob Senior
Ishac Haim Senior
Joseph Senior
Selomoh de Mordechay Senior
Ishac Dias da Silva
Jacob de Solla
Aron Mendes Solla
Binjamin Suares
David Suares
David de Jacob Hisquiao Suares
Ishac Suares
Ishac de David Suares
For my lord father Jacob Suares
Jacob Hisquiao Suares
Jacob de David Suares

T

David Taboada
Selomo Jeudah Leao Templo
Abraham Touro
David Touro
Ishac Touro
Jacob de Joseph Israel Touro
Jeosuah Touro

V

David Semah de Valença

1746

Married Men, Widows and Widowers who for one reason or another did not sign the declaration***

Ribca Silva, wid. Mosseh Alva
Judith Jesurun, wid. Samuel S. Barrios
Dr. Isaac Cardozo [Sr.]
Moses Aboab Cardozo
Benjamin de Semuel de Casseres
Semuel de Benjamin de Casseres
Sarah Gomes Casseres, wid. Abraham
    Gomes Casseres
Abraham Dias Coutinho
Joseph Fidanque
Judith Pretto, wid. Isaac Frances
Sarah da Costa Gomez, wid. Aron da
    Costa Gomez
Gabriel da Costa Gomez
Jacob Mordechay Henriquez
Mosseh Jeosuah Henriquez
Ribca Touro, wid. Gabriel aLevy
David Baruh Louzada
Isaac de Mosseh Levy Maduro
Lea Chaves, wid. Jacob A. de Neira
Sarah Pereira, wid. Abraham Penso
Sarah Lopez, wid. Samuel Rodriguez
    Pereira
Abraham Nunes Redondo
Selomoh Nunes Redondo
Sarah Vaz Martinez, wid. Aron L. Suares

Bachelors 20 years old and above in 1746

David Aboab
Semuel Aboab
David da Costa Andrade
Samuel da Costa Andrade
Jacob de Isaac Calvo
Samuel de Isaac Calvo
Aron de David Cardozo

1769

Men over 20 years of age, besides the Haham da Fonseca and Ecclesiastical Functionaries, who did not sign the declaration***

David Abenatar
Isaac Hisquiau Andrade
Benjamin da Costa de Andrade
David da Costa Andrade
Jacob da Costa Andrade
Ephraim Athias
Jacob de Mordechay Calvo
Mordechay de Isaac Calvo
Salomoh Haim Calvo
Dr. Isaac Cardozo [Jr.]
Jacob Aboab Cardozo
Josias de Casseres
Daniel Gomes Casseres
David Gomes Casseres
Daniel Lopez Castro
Daniel Mendes de Castro
Abraham de Chaves
Moses de Abraham de Chaves
Manuel de Mosseh Alvares Correa
Manuel de Rephael Alvares Correa
Abraham Dias Coutinho
Abraham Henriquez Coutinho
David Eliau Namias de Crasto
Jacob de Manuel de Crasto
Moses de Crasto
Abraham Curiel
Jeosuah de Jacob Curiel
Joseph Curiel
Jacob Lopez Dias
Isaac de Jacob Henriquez Fereira
Jacob Henriquez Fereira
Raphael Gomez
Abraham da Costa Gomez
David de Gabriel da Costa Gomez
Samuel Aben Habib
Benjamin Rephael Henriquez

*** These lists have been compiled from divers archives of the years 1746-1770. Most of these names also appear in my Catalogue of the Old Jewish Cemetery of Curaçao, *Precious Stones of the Jews of Curaçao*, pp. 495-548.

FAMILY HEADS – MEMBERS OF THE COMMUNITY, 1746 AND 1769

1746	1769
Aron de Moseh Cardozo	Jeosuah Henriquez
David Uziel Cardozo	Mordechay Henriquez
Mordechay Carvalho	Mordechay de Jacob Henriquez
Abraham Mendes de Castro	Daniel Cohen Henriquez
Abraham de Chaves	David de Moseh Cohen Henriquez
Jacob Alvares Correa	Jacob Cohen Henriquez
Manuel de Abm. Alvares [Correa]	Jeudah Cohen Henriquez
Isaac Henriquez Coutinho	Jacob Gabay Henriquez
Abraham Namias de Crasto	Jacob de David Lopez Henriquez
Elias de David de Crasto	Mordechay Lopez Henriquez
Elias de Manuel de Crasto	Mosseh de David Lopez Henriquez
Jacob de Mordechay de Crasto	Selomoh Lopez Henriquez
Mordechay de Crasto Jr.	Jacob de Moseh Naar Henriquez
Abraham de Selomoh Curiel	Moses Naar Henriquez
Semuel Curiel	David Hoheb
Jacob Dias	David Henriquez Juliao
David de Isaac Lopez Dias	Selomoh Israel Keyser
Abraham Dovale	Isaac de Elias Jeudah Leao
Josias Dovale	Abraham Jacob Jeudah Leon
Abraham de Jacob Hz. Fereira	Isaac Levy
Abraham Fidanque	Elias Lopez Jr.
Benjamin Fidanque	Aron Machoro
Elias Fidanque	Abraham de Selomoh Levy Maduro
Jacob Fidanque	Irmiau de Jacob Levy Maduro
David [de Abraham] Lopez da Fonseca	Jacob de Isaac Levy Maduro
Abraham Gomez	Moseh de Isaac Levy Maduro
David de Isaac Henriquez	Moseh de Jacob Levy Maduro
Jacob Menaseh Jesurun Henriquez	Selomoh de Samuel Levy Maduro
Abraham de David Jesurun	Jacob Marache
David Lopez Laguna	Abraham de Isaac de Marchena
Abraham de Eliau Jeudah Leao	Isaac Mendes
Isaac de Eliau Jeudah Leao	Jeosuah Guideon Mendes
Ishac de Jacob Jeudah Leao	Aron de Molina
Jacob de Eliau Jeudah Leao	David Morales
Michael de Jacob Jeudah Leao	Aron Henriquez Moron
Samuel de Eliau Jeudah Leao	Nagson Henriquez Moron
Jacob Hisquiau de Leon	Benjamin Moses Motta
Gabriel Levy	Isaac Haim Motta
Eliau Rephael de Abraham Lopez	Selomoh Motta
Gabriel Lopez	Abraham Naar Jr.
Aron Machoro	Jacob de Jeosuah Naar
Abraham de Isaac Levy Maduro	Moses Naar
Irmiau de Samuel Levy Maduro	Jacob David Ozorio

1746

Moseh de Aron Levy Maduro
Isaac de Medina
Abraham Michael Rodriguez Mendez
David Motta
Selomoh Motta
Benayahu Naar
David Naar
Josiau Naar
Mordechay Naar
Moseh de Jeosuah Naar
Isaac Athias de Neyra
Jacob Athias de Neyra
Moseh Nunes
Isaac Pardo
Elias de Jacob Pereira
Isaac de Elias Pereira
Joseph de Campos Pereira
Abraham Pinedo
Gabriel Pinedo
Manuel Hisquiau Pinedo
Isaac Nunes Redondo
Isaac de Selomoh Villa Real
David Salom
Samuel Salom
Jacob Israel St. Crus
Isaac Suares
Moses Taboada
David Touro
Daniel Ulloa
David Ulloa
Elias Ulloa
Isaac Ulloa

1769

Saul Pardo
Daniel Cohen Peixotto
Daniel Lopez Penha
Elias Penso
Jacob de Elias Pereira
Jacob de Mordechay Pereira
Manuel Pinedo
Samuel Jesurun Pinto
David Ricardo
Abraham de Isaac Senior
David Ulloa

THE NEWPORT PARNASSIM'S LETTER

(IN THE ORIGINAL SPANISH) TO THE MIKVE ISRAEL, CURAÇAO,
APPEALING FOR A CONTRIBUTION TO PAY OFF THE MORTGAGE ON
THEIR SYNAGOGUE *

Dignissimos Señores Miembros del K. K. Mikve Israel

Animados con la esperança q' nos promete La Pia protecion del Senr Frederick De Wit, Solicitamos por manos de dicho Caballero el Liberal auxilio dessa Virtuosa Congrega a fim [de] poder redemir el empeño, e Hypoteca q' nos fue preciso hacer de S[an]ta. Fabrica p^a acabar de pagar Los Obreros q' La construyeron. Por dos Años havemos con dificuldad consegido con q descargar los intereses de 8 p^r C^t desembolso, que añadido a Los annuales gastos q' requiere el suporte de la Esnoga, ha sido sumam^te arduo a esta pequeña Congrega en tan calamitosos tiempos. El periodo del tercer año de la Hypoteca estando a mano, y ... riendo Sernos impracticables, no tan solamente pagar el principal, pero [si] aun el Interes, hallamos forzoso el esclarecer a Nuestros Devotos Hermanos y relatarles N[ues]tra deplorable situacion, especialmente quando reflexemos en el eminente riesgo de con el tiempo perder nuestra estimable Fabrica!

El Señor De Wit, siendo testigo ocular de nuestro dilema, generosam^te nos anima ofreciendo protejer y Patrocinar una Subscripcion PARA RESGATE DE LA ESNOGA, y como effectivo Orador propone mostrar el camino a dicha Subscripcion; Offerta de inespressable commendacion; y peculiar a pensam^tos nobles: Lisonjeamonos q' Siendo en VM^des notorio Caracter el exercitar Misvot, Se muestren unanimes en concurrir a este desempeño y DIOS que assy Les dirija los animos sea servido remunerarles el desembolço con prorrogam^to de Vidas, Augm^tos de gracia, y prosperidades a esse numeroso K. K. por m[uch]os añ[o]s.

Newport K. K. Nephutsé Israel 7 de Tisry de 5525 [October 3, 1764].

Desse Pio K. K.
Muy ciertos Siervos
Q[ue]. S[u]s. M[ano]s. B[esa]n.

Naphtali Hart Jun[ior] Aaron Lopez Parnas
Jacob Hart Moses Seixas
Hazan Ishac de Ab[raha]m Touro Jacob Rod[rigue]z Rivera
Isaac Hart
Moses Lopez
Isaac Plizen

* MIA, loose papers. The English translation of this letter appears in Jacob R. Marcus, *American Jewry-Documents-Eighteenth Century* (Cincinnati, 1959), p. 88. See illus. 288 and p. 166.

1035

THE MOST COMPLETE LIST OF CURAÇOAN SLAVEHOLDERS
(July 1, 1764 - July 1, 1765)

DURING THE SECOND HALF of the 17th century Curaçoan slaveholders had to pay the Dutch West India Company a head tax of six reales per slave. This tax was increased to eight reales or one peso in 1698 when a total of 3,621 pesos was collected on 3,621 slaves. The directors of the Company had reason to deplore the progressive decrease in the number of slaves reported. Between 1720 and 1725 the slave tax brought in the respective amounts of 2,003; 1,931; 1,910; 1,791; 1,739, and 1,675 pesos, or a yearly average of 1,841.66⅔ pesos. There were 2,127 slaves registered in 1748. Between 1755 and 1764 this source of revenue averaged 2,057 pesos annually.

While the Company complained that "there was no country on earth where residents paid less taxes than in Curaçao" (WICA 71, p. 204), it nevertheless took the advice of their Curaçao governors not to employ strict enforcement measures. In 1764 it sought to remedy the situation by reducing the tax to one-half peso per slave provided that all declarations would be controlled by the Fiscal.

The list that follows is the first one prepared after this arrangement (OAC 907, no. 66, littera a). Doubtlessly it is the list most closely approximating the true number of slaves then owned. Despite the large total of 5,534, one gathers the impression that slave children of a certain age level were not included.

The Jewish slaveholders are indicated by an asterisk. The spelling of several Jewish names has been corrected.

Slaveholder	Slaves Owned	Slaveholder	Slaves Owned
Anna Kenningum & children	80	Anna Maria de Veer	1
*Abraham & Isaac de Marchena	80	*Abraham Rodrigues Mendes	1
Anthony Hebbelingh	2	Abraham Royer	2
*Abraham de Jacob Juda Leon	6	*Abraham de Pina Junior	4
*Aron Motta	4	*Aron de Molina	1
*Abraham Dias Cotiño	1	*Abraham de Mordechay Senior	2
*Abraham Curiel	3	*Abraham de Mordechay de Crasto	2
*Aron Henriquez Moron	20		
*Abraham Henriquez Moron	8	*Abraham de Benjamin L. Henriquez	1
*Abraham de Jacob Lopez Dias	2		

Slaveholder	Slaves Owned	Slaveholder	Slaves Owned
*Abraham de David Jesurun	4	Barend Hendrik Joosten	2
Adriaan Adriaansz	5	Benjamin de Maffe	
*Aron Mendes Sollas	3	[da Motta?]	19
Adriaan Webb	2		
*Abraham de Isaac Senior	6	Total:	77
Adriaan Pietersz van Steen	1	[Jewish-owned:	22][1]
*Abraham Lopes Penha	1		
*Abraham Henriquez Cotiño	4	Cornelis Berch	100
*Abraham de Salomon		Cornelis Stuylingh	46
Levy Maduro	2	Coenraad Visser	20
Abraham Bruyningh	8	Cornelis Raaven	6
*Abraham Rodriguez Pimentel	1	Cornelis Anthony Roelands	32
Albertus Delfftvos	4	Christiaan Hermes	3
Adriaan van Groot Davelaer	18	Casper Lodewijk van Uytrecht	150
*Abraham de Isaac Levy		Coleta Born	2
Maduro	4	Cornelis Pletsz	1
*Abraham L. Dias	2	Cornelia Kock	2
*Abraham Calvo	4	Cornelis Coeyens	4
*Abraham Henriquez Melhado	3	Catharina Nieuwkerk	1
Abraham Vermeulen	2	Christiaan Weeshuysen	2
Anthony Baret	1	Catharina Gijsels	1
Archibald Campbell	2	Christiaan Teltingh	3
Adriaan Graval	1	Christoffel Theodorus Saesbach	1
Abraham Evertsz	8	*Cohen Henriquez Junior	2
Anna Geysels	1	Christiaan Boom	3
		Claas Schotborgh Jansz	4
Total:	307	Cornelis Star Ligtenvoort	10
[Jewish-owned:	169]	Catharina Seenenbergh	1
		Claas Schotborgh Claaszoon	1
Borchard Specht	10	Coenraad Otto Royer	2
Barend Wassum	4	Casper Hendrik Zeep	1
Bartholomeus Holtman	6	Christoffel Adriaan van Ruysein	1
Barent Veeris	2	Christiaan Samuel Severeyn	8
Baptista La Pompe	1		
*Benjamin Raphael Henriquez	15	Total:	407
Balthasar Jansz	1	[Jewish-owned:	2]
*Benjamin Vaz Faro	5		
Bernardus van Starckenborgh	10	Children of Jurriaan Brugman	2
*Benjamin de M. Jesurun	2	Daniel Bir	1

[1] If de Maffe really is *da Motta*, then the "B" total for Jews is 41.

Slaveholder	Slaves Owned	Slaveholder	Slaves Owned
David Luydens	2	*David Ulloa	3
David Hansz	9		
Dirk Reyken	3	Total:	146
Daniel Boom	5	[Jewish-owned:	62]
Diederik M. Verplaats	20		
Dirk Willems	4	Ebbe Daal	10
Daniel Ellis	12	*Elias Lopes	1
*David de Gabriel da Costa		*Elias Haim Parera	2
Gomez	3	Evert Evertsz	15
*David Lopez Laguna and		*Elias Rodrigues Miranda	3
Samuel de Joseph da		Eva van Houten	2
Costa Gomez	8	Ernst Houtschild	4
*David Haim Castillo	1	Eva Constantia Zeeman	2
*David de Molina	2	Estiene Lougie	2
*David Ricardo	3		
*Daniel Lopez Castro	2	Total:	41
*David Morales	4	[Jewish-owned:	6]
*David da Costa Andrade	6		
*David Jesurun	6	Francoys Bollenslee	2
Dirk de Windt	5	Frans Grotenstam van Uytrecht	15
*David Bueno Vivas	6	Frans Grotenstam	36
*Daniel Aboab Cardozo	1	*Francisco Lopes Henriquez	40
Dirk van der Meer Eylbrecht	5	Fredrik A. Hersfeld	2
Dorothea Willemina Horst	4	Frans Royer	1
*David de Isaac Senior	2	Ferdinand Henricus	1
*David Taboada	1	Fredrik de Witt	3
*David de Jacob Lopes			
de Fonseca	1	Total:	100
David Muschard	2	[Jewish-owned:	40]
Children of Jeremias			
D. Bernard	2	Gs. Jacobus Ribbius	21
David Godfried Lugters	2	Gerrit Semerel	15
*David Abenatar	2	Gerard Striddels	6
Dirk Wijn	2	Gerrit Specht	44
*David Gomes Casseres	4	*Gabriel Pinedo	3
*David Suares Junior	2	Geysbert van Heumen	6
Domingo Cotiño[2]	2	Glaudy Vernie (or Vemie)	2
Dirk A. Kool	2	Gerrit Harmesen	2
*Daniel Mendes de Castro	5	Gillis Popp	8

[2] If Jewish, then the Jewish "D" total would be 64.

Slaveholder	Slaves Owned	Slave-holder	Slaves Owned
Gaspar Servester	1	Jan Veeris	30
		*Isaac Mendes	40
Total:	108	Jan Gerard Ellis	20
[Jewish-owned:	3]	Jannetje Martha Ellis	3
		*Josias de Casseres	1
Hendrik Siedrechts	8	Jan van der Linde	12
Hendrik de Neys	1	*Isaac Haim Rodrigues da Costa	25
Hendrik Cornelis Vos	18	Jan Hendriksz	70
Hendrik David Horst	12	Jacobus Vos	7
Hendrik Barent Resthuysen	8	Jacob Wouters	6
Harmen Theysen	8	Jurriaan Brugman	40
Hermanus Olderop	8	Josephus Hermanus Steegman	4
Hendrik Cassingh	3	Jan Deveylder	2
Harmen Kool	1	Jan Hendrik Brugman	20
Hendrik Hamer	13	Jan Hendrik Rudelof	3
Hendrik Boekhout	1	*Jacob Monsanto	3
		*Jacob Haim Rodrigues Parera	2
Total:	81	*Isaac Pardo	12
[Jewish-owned:	—]	*Isaac Suares	4
		*[Dr.] Joseph Caprillis	10
Jean Rodier	50	*Jacob de David Suares	1
Jacobus Otto van Brandt	64	*Joseph Jesurun Henriquez	6
Jan Nicolaas van Starckenborch	6	*Jacob de Joseph Jesurun	
Jonas Samuel de Barry	5	Henriquez	2
Jacob Weyts	8	*Jacob Levy Maduro	6
Jan de Veer	5	*Isaac de Jacob Levy Maduro	4
Jan G. Baumgard	1	*Jacob Fidanque	6
Jan Mattheus Graaff	4	*Jacob Gabay Henriquez	2
Jan Vos	12	*Jeosuah Henriquez Junior	6
Johannes Theysen	2	*Isaac de Elias Juda Leon	2
Jan & Jannetje Lixraeven & Co.	44	*Isaac de Jacob Juda Leon	2
Jan Hendrik Pletsz	12	*[Dr.] Isaac Cardozo	1
Johan Willem Heynel	1	*Jacob de Elias Jesurun	
Johannes Peeters	3	Henriquez	2
Jan Evertsz	20	Jan Nicolaas Kock	8
Johannes de Veer Abrahamszoon	2	*[Haham] Jacob Lopes de Fonseca	3
Johannes Schonewolt	1	*Josias Dovale	6
Jan Pieterse Six	5	*Isaac Parera	8
Johannes Ellis	60	*Jacob de Mordechay Andrade	3
Jacobus Lesire	6	*Jacob de Abraham Andrade	4
*Jacob de David Jesurun	25	Jan Hendrik Specht	42

Slaveholder	Slaves Owned	Slaveholder	Slaves Owned
*Isaac Motta	10	Isaac Paul van Schaegen	5
Isaac Daal	3	Johan Jacob Reymers	2
*Jacob Aboab Cardozo	4	Jean Baptista Groc	1
*Jacob Garcia de Pas	2	*Isaac Jesurun	1
*Isaac Touro	1	*Joseph Obediente	4
*Jacob de Josuah Naar	4	Jan Blauwart	2
*Jacob de Abraham Naar	3	Jan Beekman	2
*Joseph Curiel	4	Jacobus Spencer	6
*Isaac Curiel	2	Jan Ellis Nathanaelzoon	
*Josias Idanha de Casseres	4	& children	14
*Isaac de Mordechay de Crasto	2	Johannes van den Kerkhoven	1
*Isaac Hisquiau Andrade	1	Juan Pedro Martijn	2
Johan George Muller	5	Jan Willemsz Th. zoon	12
Johan Casper Huick	2	Jacobus Semerel	1
*Isaac de Jacob Hz. Fereyra	6	Johan Ekhard Sandrock	2
Johannes van Vilkens	1	*Isaac de Abraham Senior	3
Jan Schoon	4	Jan Fredrik Eilingen	2
*Jacob Hisquiau Suares	10	*Jeosua Naar	12
Jacoba de Witt	1	*Jacob de David Senior	2
Jan Ringelingh	2	*Jacob Pinedo	2
Juriaan Boom	2	Johannes Evertsz	6
Jacob de Peeters	6	Jan Copius	4
Johannes Jansz Baltharszoon	8	*Isaac Mendez Sollas	2
*Isaac Rodrigues Miranda	3	Jan Hendrik Bronswinkel	12
Jean Marie de Saint Chijn	2	Johan Ellis Herozoon	4
Jacob Charje	24	*Judah Cohen Henriquez	2
Jacob Radelieff	2	Jan Scholten	6
Jacob Bennebroek Berch	16	Jan Hendrik Spillenaar	2
Jan Christoffel Duringh	4	Jan Baptista Labadie	1
Jacob Josias (a Jew?)	2	*Isaac de Salomon Levy Maduro	3
*Jacob Lopez Dias	1	Jan Hartogsveld Junior	1
Jan Rudolph Faesch	4	Jacobus Croes	2
Johannes de Pool	12	Jacob Crane	2
Jan Lucas Fielen	5	Jurriaan de Pool	90
*Isaac Haim Namias de Crasto	2	*Jeosuah Henriquez	40
Jochem Wisman (a Jew?)	4	Isaac Lamont	8
Juan Anthony Marion	2	Johannes Stuylingh	30
*Jacob Cohen Henriquez	2	Johannes Vrolijk	2
Jurriaan Crisson	2	Jan Gomes Tesselaar	6
Jannetje Crisson	1	Jan Hansz	4
Jan Droogcop	4	Jan Adam Krell	6

Slaveholder	Slaves Owned	Slaveholder	Slaves Owned
Jan Fredrik Groen	4	*Manuel Pinedo	2
		*Moses Lopez Penha	1
Total:	1,256	*Moses Naar Henriquez	3
[Jewish-owned:	320[3]]	Michiel Joubert	6
		Mourens E. Franken	4
Lourents de Mey	60	Maria Pichot	3
Lourents de Mey Scholten	40	Maria Nieuwkerk	1
Lourents Laan	8	Maria Niemant	5
Ludolph Johan Iden	4	Margaritha Houtvat	2
Louis Adolph Winkler	2	*Moses de Benjamin Jesurun	2
Lodewijk Wielix	10	Marten Daniel Daal	7
Lourents Luydens	5	*Moses Henriquez	6
Lodewijk de Mendoza	1	Michiel van der Meulen	6
		*Mordechay de Salomon	
Total:	130	L. Maduro	4
[Jewish-owned:	—]		
		Total:	199
Mijndert Carel Six	3	[Jewish-owned:	92]
Michiel Römer	2		
*Manuel de Raphael Alvares		Nathanael Ellis	160
Correa	32	Nathanael Ellis Junior	3
*Moses de David Lopes		Nicolaas Hendrikse Pietersz	2
Henriquez	12	Nicolaas Verkuyl Winkler	8
Marten de Pool	5	Nicolaas Henricus	10
Maria Lupke	50	Nicolaas Schotborch	5
*Mordechay Henriquez	4	Nicolaas Ten Toorn	1
*Mordechay de Moses Penso	1	Nicolaas Bart	5
Matthias Pabest	6	Nicolaas Gomes	4
*Manuel de Moses Alvares		Nicolaas Klinkert	3
Correa	12	Nicolaas Evertsz	4
*Mordechay de Jacob		Nicolaas Willemsz	12
Henriquez	1	Nicolaas Dam	2
Martinus Oostenrijk	2	Nicolaas Daniel Crisson	1
*Mordechay Motta	2	Nicolaas Hellingh	1
*Mordechay de Crasto	8	Nicolaas Hendrik	
*Moses de Isaac Levy Maduro	2	Weerenbergh	2
Maria S. L. de Beaufort	3		
Maria de Veer	1	Total:	223
Matthias Gruys	1	[Jewish-owned:	—]

[3] This figure includes Jacob Josias' two slaves.

Slaveholder	Slaves Owned	Slaveholder	Slaves Owned
Pieter Pletsz	4	Costa Gomez	4
Pieter Huysman	2	*Samuel de David Hoheb	5
Pieter Jansz	5	*Samuel & Manuel Juda Leon	8
Philip Dirksz	2	*Saul & Josias Idanha de	
Pierre Cholyn	2	Casseres	2
Pieter Diedenhoven	170	*Saul Idanha de Casseres	2
Pieter Daal	24	*Salomon de Jacob Curiel	2
Pierre Brugman	30	*Salomon de Salomon	
Pieter Reyke	18	Levy Maduro	2
Pieter van Eyken	3	*Salomon de Jacob de Salomon	
Pieter Kier & Co.	4	Levy Maduro	2
Pieter Kier	7	*Salomon Lopes Henriquez	5
Paulis van Voorts Kup	3	*Selomon Keyser	1
Pieter Keegel	1	Simon van der Veen	1
Pieter van der Knieren	4	*Samuel Habib	1
Pieter Royer	3	*Salomon de Mordechay Senior	2
Philip Theysen	7	*Saul Pardo	7
Paulis Poppe	2	*Samuel de Isaac Levy Maduro	4
Pierre La Barbe	1	*Sara da Costa Gomez	6
Paulis Hill	1	Sigismundus Weiber	2
Pieter de Lange	2	Samuel Exon	2
Pieter Krull	1	Sigismundus Druschke van	
Pieter Quant	4	Starckenborg	3
Pieter Monsel	2		
Pieter Prins	1	Total:	61
Pieter Fredrik Kleeff	2	[Jewish-owned:	53]
Pieter Jansz	1		
		Theunis D. Kock	12
Total:	306	Theunis Jansz de Ronde	2
[Jewish-owned:	—]	Thomas Pietersz Beek	16
		Thomas Lodewijk Richard	3
Roeloff Meyboom	10	Theunis Pietersz	5
*Raphael Alvares Correa	3		
*Raphael Molina Monsanto	2	Total:	38
Richard Raeven	4	[Jewish-owned:	—]
*Rachel Bueno Vivas	3		
		Widow Fredrik Willem	
Total:	22	Hermes	120
[Jewish-owned:	8]	Willem Lesiere	2
		Widow Wigboldus Rasvelt	70
*Samuel de Gabriel da		Widow Matthias Schotborgh	60

Slaveholder	Slaves Owned	Slaveholder	Slaves Owned
Widow Jan Gerard Pax	20	Widow Steeven Rasmijn	8
Wigboldus Reyninck	54	Willebord Horst	5
Widow Jan Martin	200	Widow Casper S. Hansz	10
Widow Dirk van Uytrecht	100	Widow Jacob de Hoyer	2
Wid. Dirk van Uytrecht & Co.	140	Widow Hendrik Pletsz	3
Widow Daniel Lesire & children	100	Widow Nicolaas Ten Toorn	5
		Widow Cornelis Jansz	2
Widow Elias Luydens	5	Widow Martinus Niepage	6
Willem van Gorcum	20	Widow Cornelis Paradijs	1
Widow Gerard Schonenboom	61	*Widow Isaak Levy	3
Willem Lackrum	16	Widow Jacob Stoel	20
Widow Nicolaas Pieterse	10	Widow Jan Plaat	6
Widow Samuel Daal	20	Widow Jan Theunis Vos	6
Wid. Willem van Uytrecht	24	Widow Johannes Clemens	6
Wid. Rudolphus Bughij	80	Widow Gerrit Burgh	4
Willem Web	2	Wid. Johannes Stuylingh Samuelzoon	4
Wid. Cornelis Verplaats & Andries Verplaats	20	Widow David Sterling	6
Wid. Pieter Redoch	50	Widow Van der Burgh	2
*Widow Moses de Abm. de Chaves	4	Widow Hendrik Ladigh	2
		Willem Huyblingh	4
Widow Anthony G. Meyer	7	*Widow Moses Naar	2
Widow Samuel Francisco Stuylingh	6	*Wid. Benjamin de E. Jn. Henriquez	1
Widow Pieter van Keulen	5	Widow van Gorcum	4
*Widow Moses Penso	10	Widow Willem Kock	70
*Widow Salomon de Is. Levy Maduro	4	Widow Lourents Pletsz	8
		Widow Roeloff Linquist	2
Widow Jan Luess	7	Widow Abraham Visser	6
Widow Jeronimo Bulthe	2	*Widow Abraham Flores	3
*Widow Benjamin de Casseres	8	*Wid. Moses Cohen Henriquez	1
*Widow Abraham de Chaves	3	*Wid. Benjamin Athias de Neyra	4
*Widow Isaac Penso	7		
Widow Samuel Striddels	70	Widow Philip Webb	16
*Wid. Benjamin da Costa Andrade	1	Widow Jeronimo Durell	4
		Widow Pieter Bernje	3
Widow Theunis L. Vos	1	Widow Andries Blom	3
Widow August H. Leesten	7	Widow Dirk van der Meer	6
*Widow David Cohen Henriquez	2	Widow T. Neeve	1
Widow Adolph Crats	4	Widow Jurriaan du Pont	1
*Widow David Baruh Lousada	2	*Widow Joseph Israel Touro	2

Slaveholder	Slaves Owned	Slaveholder	Slaves Owned
Willem Martingh	2	Willem de Windt	14
Widow Jan Swart	1	Widow Jan van der Biest	6
*Widow Jacob Pinedo	2	Widow Geysbert Vos	3
Widow Jan Gerner	2	Widow Geysbert Vos Jansz	4
Widow Davelaar	6	*Wid. Moses de (Crasto)	
Widow Jan van Schaegen	2	[Castro]	3
Widow Jacob Sterling	2	Widow Nicolaas Guyot	1
Widow Hendrik Simon Landt	5	Widow Willem Lackrum	4
Widow Geysbert Somer	2	Wid. Willem Visser Claaszoon	2
Widow Jan Coster Pietersz	4	Widow Henricus Ds. Hobbens	6
Widow Frans Burger	3	Widow Jan Gulinkhuysen	2
Widow Bs. Glauman	8	Wa. Petronella Beek	2
Widow Jan Daal	5	Willem van Uytrecht	5
Widow Jan Duyking	7	Widow Willem Jansz	
Widow Jan Paul Schotborgh	2	Vermeulen	2
Widow Pothoven	2	Widow Bastiaan Pabest	2
Willem Stuylingh	5	Willem Hoevertsz	2
Widow Gerrit Martijn	1	Willem Klinkert	3
Widow Hero Ellis	41	Willem Kraneveld	1
Widow Valentijn Minnehoven	3	Widow Marten Copius	10
Willem Crisson	6	Widow Willem Webb Kok	2
Widow Hendrik A. Kool	2	Widow Carel Dörffel	10
Widow Cornelis Verplaats	6	Widow Claas Reyninck	83
Widow Coenraad Wendrick	2	Widow Pistolphie	13
Widow Fredrik Evertsz	4	Widow Adriaan Vermeulen	6
Widow Maak	6	Widow L. van Keulen	3
Widow Johannes Ch. Marquant	4	Widow Jacob Vos	1
Widow Albert Urdaal	16	Widow Caspt. de Wind	2
Willem Blom	6	*Widow Elias Judah Leon	1
Widow Gebel	2	*Widow Jacob Curiel	6
Widow Cornelis Dorcas	14	Widow Isaac Lamont	73
Widow Jan A. Kool	4	Widow Thomas de Mey	6
Widow Jan Bell	4		
Widow Christiaan Stridbeck	1	Total:	2,032
Widow Dirk Rasmijn	1	[Jewish-owned:	69]
Wid. Frans Hendrik Ricauw	5		

Slaveholder	Slaves Owned	Slaveholder	Slaves Owned
Totals by Letters		L	130
		M	199
A	307	N	223
B	77	P	306
C	407	R	22
D	146	S	61
E	41	T	38
F	100	W	2,032
G	108		
H	81	Grand Total:	5,534
J	1,256	[Jewish-owned:	867[4]]

[4] This figure includes the 19 slaves of Benjamin de Maffe, two of Domingo Cotiño and two of Jacob Josias.

BOOKS, RELIGIOUS OBJECTS, PICTURES AND WEARING APPAREL LISTED IN THE ESTATE INVENTORIES OF CURAÇOAN JEWS

THE INVENTORIES of decedents' estates — especially of the personal effects — afford one a deep insight into the life of the 18th and 19th century Jews of Curaçao.

BOOKS. Almost everyone left prayer books on his death — some richly bound in "carete" — probably tortoise shell — fitted with hinges and locks of silver. Mordechay de Jeudah Senior left the record number of 1,000 books in 1756 (OAC 873, no. 13); Dr. Benjamin de Sola, nine cases of books in 1817. Several people left books in Ladino — Jacob Dias Guadalupe, the record number of 33 books in "Spanish Hebrew" in addition to 28 in Hebrew.[1]

RELIGIOUS OBJECTS. God-fearing as they were, the Curaçoan Jews left a quantity of religious articles. These objects consisted of the *Taleth* (sometimes of silk since 1741),[2] the *Tefillin*, the *Zizit*, Sabbath and Ḥanukkah lamps, and so on. Usually of copper, these lamps were worth four pesos each in 1744 (OAC 854, no. 44). There also were silver Sabbath and Ḥanukkah lamps. In 1761 Sarah, the widow of Abraham Gomes Casseres, left four Sabbath lamps — one of silver — and a silver Ḥanukkah lamp too (OAC 880, March 29, 1761).

Many left *Keminhas* or amulets of silver and sometimes of gold provided with silver or gold chains. Among those who left gold amulets were Benjamin de Elias Jesurun Henriquez in 1765; Esther, widow of Abraham Flores, in 1770; and Mordechay Penso in 1790.[3]

Sometimes one encounters an *Homer* to keep count of the 49 days between the second day of Passover and Shabu'oth.[4] On his death in 1754 Jacob Dias Guadalupe left an indicator for the New Moon (Rosh Ḥodesh) in Hebrew (OAC 872, no. 1).

Since several sailors and planters were licensed to slaughter chickens, and even cattle, for their private use, the inventories of their estates list butcher knives and whetstones. In 1759 Jacob Jeudah Leao left the record number of six butcher knives (OAC 875, no. 339).

Many wealthy households, as earlier observed, kept a Sepher Torah, sometimes with the pertinent ornaments.

[1] OAC 872, no. 1, y. 1754.
[2] OAC 847, no. 88.
[3] OAC 897, no. 123; OAC 907, no. 187; OAC 983, no. 112.
[4] OAC 932, no. 521, y. 1781.

PICTURES. The tombstones of the Old Cemetery are mute witness to the Curaçoan Jews' feeling for art.[5] Nevertheless, it is surprising to encounter such a large assortment of pictures or paintings in the inventories up to 1855. Some Jews probably sold the pictures which they imported from Holland or Italy. In 1747 Isaac Mendes left 344 small, gilt-framed pictures, 23 large ones, ten others, and twenty covered with glass (OAC 862, no. 46). The surgeon Jacob Israel St. Crus left "a quantity" of paintings in 1759. In 1797 Samuel Josias de Casseres had 33 paintings, fourteen of which were large (OAC 997, no. 166). David de Salomon de Meza left 41 pictures in 1804 (OAC 1014, no. 32); Abraham Lopez Penha, 26 in 1816 (OAC 1047, no. 29); Abraham Salom Delvalle, 16 in 1819 (OAC 1056, no. 43); Abraham Henriquez, "two large family portraits, 16 pictures, ten others in stained glass, and a smaller one" in 1838 (CEOE 776, no. 56); Esther, widow of Abraham Haim de Meza, left eleven paintings in 1854 (MIA, loose papers). Even Haham Da Fonseca left two paintings in 1815 (MIA, *ibid.*).

Among these paintings were family portraits handed down from father to son, and representations of the Ten Commandments or the story of Mordechay and Esther.[6] The 34 pictures left by Isaac da Costa Gomez in 1811 included a reproduction of the Portuguese synagogue of Amsterdam (OAC 1034, no. 108). Most wealthy families left pictures or paintings. Like the Sabbath and Hanukkah lamps, these too have disappeared.

WEARING APPAREL, ACCESSORIES. In Curaçao, as in Holland, one or another Jewish man sported a wig. (There is a record of one in Curaçao in 1741.) The rabbis of both lands tolerated this and did not denounce it as being in imitation of a woman's article of clothing (Deut. 22:5). The cane or walking stick was very fashionable then. Several Jews owned canes with golden knobs, e.g., Jacob de Mordechay Calvo in 1772, and Haham Da Fonseca in 1815. Very often Curaçoans left thimbles of silver and gold.[7] Jacob de Mordechay de Calvo left a silver sword, a silver "Fontel doos" (?), a pair of boots inlaid with emeralds, and a gilt bedpan.[8] In 1811 Isaac da Costa Gomez left silver sandals encrusted with gold. Two years later Johebed, widow of Salomo L. Maduro, left a "paraplui" — better said, a parasol since it seldom rains in Curaçao. From the end of the 18th century the snuffbox was a popular accessory. Many were wrought in silver, some in gold.[9]

These inventories on the one hand and the magnificent tombstones on the other prove once again the religious ardor of the Jews of that age and their capacity to enjoy the wealth that God gave them.

---

[5] *Precious Stones*, pp. 123-29.
[6] Y. 1765, 1783, 1797, 1854.
[7] OAC 907, no. 187, y. 1770.
[8] OAC 944, nos. 207-209, y. 1772.
[9] OAC 1054, no. 87, inventory of David L. Maduro, d. 1819.

ST. EUSTATIUS

A. LETTER SENT BY THE JEWS ON FEBRUARY 16, 1781, TO ADMIRAL RODNEY

Petition of the Jews at St. Eustatius to Admiral Rodney
and General Vaughan.

To their Excellencies, the Commanding Officers in Chief of his Britannic Majesty's Army and Navy in the West Indies.

May it please your Excellencies,
To permit us, in the name and on the behalf of ourselves and others of the people of the Hebrew nation, residents in the island of Saint Eustatius, humbly to approach your excellencies, and with heartfelt anguish, to lay our grievances before you, and say: that it was with the utmost concern and astonishment, we have already, not only received your excellencies afflicting order and sentence, to give up the keys of our stores with an inventory thereof, and of our household plate and furniture, and to hold ourselves in readiness to depart this island, ignorant of our destination, and leaving our beloved wives and helpless children behind us, and our property and effects liable to seizure and confiscation; but also find, that these orders are for the major part carried into execution, a number of our brethren having, on Tuesday the thirteenth instant, been sent on board a ship, and have not since been heard of. Such unexpected orders as these from British commanders, whose principal characteristic is "mercy and humanity," have not only been productive of the most horrid and melancholy scenes of distress and confusion, that ever British eyes beheld under the fatal consequences of a rigid war, but numbers of families are now helpless, disconsolate, and in an absolute state of indigence and despair.

Unconscious of deserving so severe a treatment, we flatter ourselves that your excellencies will be pleased to hear this our humble petition, and not involve in one complicated scene of distress and misery, our helpless women and innocent babes; confidently relying upon, and earnestly hoping that, through your excellencies justice and humanity, we shall not supplicate in vain.

It is the peculiar happiness of those who live under British constitution, to be indulged with their own sentiments in matters of religion, when these principles of religion are not incompatible with, or subversive of the constitution in church or state; and it is the peculiar happiness of the Hebrew nation to say, that their religion teaches peace and obedience to the government under which they live; and when civil dissentions have threatened to subvert the constitution, the Hebrew nation have ever preserved a peaceful demeanour, with true loyalty to the King, and a firm and steady attachment to the laws and constitution.

For what reason, or from what motive we are to be banished from this island, we are at a loss to account. — If any among us have committed a crime for which they are punishable, we humbly beg those crimes may be pointed out, and that such persons may be purged from among us. — But if nothing can be alledged against us but the religion of our forefathers, we hope that will not be considered a crime; or that a religion, which preaches peace and recommends obedience to government, should point out its sectaries as objects of your excellencies rigour, and merit exclusion from a British island, by the express orders of British commanders. A moment's reflection must discountenance the idea, and leave us in perfect confidence of your excellencies favourable answer.

Permit us then to assure your excellencies, that we ever have, and still are willing, to give every conscientious testimony of obedience to government; and those of us in particular, who claim to be natural-born subjects of Great Britain, most humbly intreat your excellencies to order us before you, or before such person or persons as your excellencies shall please to appoint, there to prove our loyalty and fidelity, and to repeat and take our oaths of allegiance.

May the God of all mercies incline your hearts to listen to the prayers and supplications of your petitioners, and in this confidence, we humbly submit ourselves to your excellencies determination, hoping that you will pardon us for the intrusion of this address; and that through your excellencies lenity and humanity, your excellencies will be pleased to grant us such favourable terms, as you in your judgment and wisdom shall think most advantageous to his majesty's interest, and the honour and glory of his successful arms.

And your petitioners, as in duty bound, will ever pray, &c. Saint Eustatius, Feb. 16, 1781.[1]

---

[1] *Annual Register*, vol. 24 (London, 1782), y. 1781, pp. 308-10.

B. MARRIAGES, 1786-1796 [2]

Abbreviations: Adam = Amsterdam; b = born in; bgw = bridegroom's witness or witnesses; brw = bride's witness or witnesses; Cur = Curaçao; NY = New York; RI = Rhode Island; StE = St. Eustatius; StC = St. Christopher, St. Kitts; wid. = widow or widower of; the symbol "=" denotes married.

Dec. 17, 1786, Levy ABRAHAMS, b London = Kitty ABRAHAMS, b Herford Shire [Hereford], England; bgw Samuel Hoheb Az., brw Jacob Robles [the hazzan].

Jan. 21, 1787, David de Jacob NUNES TAVAREZ, b Bayonne = Zipporah DE LEON, b St. Kitts, bgw Samuel Hoheb Az., brw David Abendanone.

Jan. 28, 1787, Mozes GOMES DA FONSECA, b Bayonne = Sara de David RODRIGUES DA COSTA, b Adam, bgw Isaac Gomes Silva, brw her father David.

Jan. 27, 1788, Samuel Mozes FRANK, b Nimeguen [Nijmegen], 34, wid. Breina Hart = Lowe de Naphtalie and Shiepra HART, b RI, 24, bgw Izaack Hart, brw bride's parents. In the presence of the honorable councilmen of the island, Jacobus de Windt and A. Salomons, and Government Secretary Herman Brouwer.

Jan. 27, 1788, Salomon de David NUNES MERCADO, b Surinam, 22 = Sarah de David HENRIQUEZ PIMENTEL, b Cur, nearly $17\frac{1}{2}$, brw the bride's father and mother Rebecca Mendes Sol(e)[a]s. The bride did not know how to sign her name. The bridegroom presented the consent of his separated parents David Nunes Mercado and Rachel Turgeman, which was signed in Paramaribo, Surinam, and there legalized by the Government Secretary.

March 20, 1791, Benjamin LINDO, b London, 30 = Grace DE LEON, b StC, 23. In the presence of Governor P. A. Godin and the Councilmen Lucas Godet and Jan Schimmel Henriquez.

April 3, 1791, Salomon SALOMONS, b StE, nearly 27 = Hannah de Abraham HOHEB, b StE, nearly 19, bgw Judah Benjamin Loco [Lobo?] and his mother Rachel Gompas, wid. Salomon Levy; brw the bride's mother Rebecca Benjamin, wid. Abraham Hoheb, and Samuel Hoheb [most probably the bride's brother].

May 22, 1791, Benjamin Mozes HÜNIG, a.k.a. Simon Aaron Cappé, b Kúttenplaan [Kuttenberg?] in Bohemia, 36, wid. Rebecca Israels = Mariam LEVY, b NY, 24, bgw Salomon Salomons, brw Rachel Gompas, wid. Salomon Levy, as stand-in for the bride's mother Rebecca Tores, recent widow of David Juda Hart.

[2] OA Sint Eustatius, Sint Martin en Saba, no. 24.

June 15, 1791, Isaac HENRIQUEZ DE MESQUITA, b Adam, 32 = Rachel DE LA PENHA, b Adam, 27, wid. Abraham Nunes Cardoso; bgw Joseph Vieyra, brw Elias Pinna.

Aug. 28, 1791, Daniel LEVY, b NY, 28 = Judith ABARBANEL, b Cur, about $40\frac{1}{2}$, wid. Jacob de Porto. In the presence of the Island Councilmen Hendrik Pandt and Pieter Cavilje Cz.

April 29, 1792, David PARERA, b Maarsen-Utrecht, 34 = Mary Ann de Abraham ABENDANONE, b StC, nearly 17, P.J.N. [= of the Portuguese Jewish Nation]; bgw David H. Abendanone, brw bride's father and mother Rebecca Abendanone.

Oct. 21, 1792, Elias de PINNA, b Adam, about 36 = Gratia de David ABENDANONE, b StC, about 19, bgw Benjamin Lindo and his wife Graice (sic) de Leon, brw bride's father and mother Rachel de Leon.

April 28, 1793, Josua de Abraham NAAR, b Cur, 25 = Sol de Daniel NUNES HENRIQUES, b Surinam, 22, bgw Samuel Hoheb, brw Government Secretary Herman Brouwer under proxy given by the bride's father D. N. Henriques.

Sept. 21, 1794, Mozes WOLFF, b Berstof, Germany, 38 = Rebecca ROBLES, b StE, 19, bgw and brw Catharina Levy, wid. Jacob Robles, and Leon Jacob and his wife Lea Levy. In the presence of the Island Councilmen Daniel Roda and Pieter Petersen.

Nov. 27, 1796, Samuel Mozes FRANK, b Nimeguen [Nijmegen], about 46,[3] wid. Love Hart = Mehettibel [daughter of Naphtalie?] HART, b RI, about 26, bgw F. C. Ten. Zijthoff, brw. the bride's mother Sypora Hart. In the presence of Captain-Commander Burans [Burgher?] D. Roda, Ordinary Councilman L. J. Holm and [Government] Secretary H. Brouwer.

[3] The bridegroom gave his age as 34 in 1788 and 46 in 1796. It seems that he married his deceased wife's sister as was then customary.

C. DEATHS, 1793-1813 [4]

Abbreviations or symbols: rep. = reported; † before a name = Gentile

March 10, 1793, Miriam FRANK, daughter of Samuel Mozes Frank, b. StE,..., rep. by Naphtali Hart.

April 6, 1793, Abraham PENHA, 70, rep. by †J. Heyliger.

April 23, 1793, Meriam SALOMONS, daughter of Salomon Salomons and Hannah Hoheb, b StE, 15 mos., rep. by Daniel Nunes Henriques.

Oct. 13, 1793, Sarah de SARAH, b Jamaica, 95, rep. by Abraham Jacobs.

Dec. 12, 1793, Isaac M. FRANK, son of Samuel Mozes Frank, b StE, 11 months, rep. by N. Hart.

May 8, 1794, Branca JACOBS, wife of Abraham Mozes LEVY, b Maents [Mayence] on the Rhine, 82, rep. by Joseph Gomes de Mesquita.

Oct. 13, 1794, Salomon SALOMONS, b StE, 30, rep. by Judah Levy.

Dec. 26, 1794, Abraham ABENDANONE, b StC, 47, businessman, rep. by Elias de Pinna.

June 9, 1795, Daniel NUNES HENRIQUES, b Surinam, about 64, clerk to the Government Secretary and translator from Spanish and Portuguese into Dutch; rep. by Gomes Silva.

June 20, 1795, Moses Cappel FRANK, b Nimeguen [Nijmegen], about 48, rep. by Gomes Silva.

March 8, 1796, Love FRANK [b RI], 33 yrs., 5 mos. and 25 days, daughter of Naphtaly and S[ipporah]. Hart, wife of Samuel Mos: (Hart) [Frank]. Her newborn daughter died with her.

Nov. 18, 1797, Nathan SAMUELS. No details given.

July 7, 1801, Ester de SARAH, wife of Salomon JACOBS, b Jamaica, 56 yrs. and 9 mos.

Oct. 12, 1801, Salomon JACOBS, b Hamburg, 62.

Aug. 7, 1802, David DE LEON, son of David and Edith De Leon, b StE, about 4 years.

May 11, 1803, Judith Abraham LEVY, wid. Nathan Samuels and lately wife of Josiah Moses HOLLANDER, b Adam, 54.

Oct. 26, 1813, Hannah ROBLES, 55. [4]

No record of these seventeen deaths is to be found in the cemetery. [5] Twelve of them figure among the St. Eustatius Jewish residents of 1790, below, p. 1066.

---

[4] OA Sint Eustatius, Sint Martin en Saba, no. 246.

[5] See below, D. Epitaphs, 1742-1843.

D. EPITAPHS, 1742-1843

The Portuguese and English texts of 17 of the 21 epitaphs reproduced below were copied for the late J. M. L. Maduro who graciously passed them on to the author. Samuel S. Strouse photographed some of them for the American Jewish Archives (illus. 290-292). Florence (Mrs. Robert) Abraham took various notes and made copies of one and another tombal inscription in Portuguese and English for the American Jewish Archives. The Reverend J. Willingham copied seventeen inscriptions, eleven of them wholly or partly in Hebrew (ms., AJA).

A comparison of the texts with the photographs shows the copy in Portuguese and English done for Maduro to be most accurate.

The dominant language of these epitaphs, as in the Old Cemetery of Curaçao,[6] is Portuguese (nos. 1, 2, 6, 8, 10, 12, 13, 14, 16, 17); English and Hebrew also are employed.

The residents of St. Eustatius are to be commended for the respect they have always shown toward this historic cemetery despite the absence of Jews on the island. It would be a good thing if these precious stones, as well as the remaining synagogue walls, were placed under government protection.

Here follow the texts of the epitaphs in chronological order.

1

ויشא אברהם את עיניו וירא את המקום[7]

s̲ᴬ

DO BEM AVENTURADO

E, VIRTUOZO ABRAHAM

HISQUIAŨ DE LA MOTTA

F̲ᵒ EM 6 YIAR A̲ᵒ 5502

QUE CORRESPONDE

A 10 MAYO A̲ᵒ 1742

ת" נ" צ" ב" ה"[8]

---

[6] *Precious Stones*, pp. 112-13.

[7] Abraham lifted up his eyes, and saw the place (Genesis 22:4).

[8] May his soul be bound up in the bond of life.

2

ויקרבו ימי דוד למות[9]

SEPULTURA

DO

ANJO DAVID FILHO DE

IMANUEL & JEUDITH DE

LEAO FALLECEO EM 4

TAMUZ A$^{\underline{o}}$ 5520 QUE

CORRESPONDE 18 DE JUNIO

1760 DE IDADE DE 2 ANNOS

8 MEZES & 26 DIAS

HERE LYETH INTERED THE BODY OF DAVID HAIM HEZECIAH

THE SON OF EMANUEL &/ JUDITH DE LION WHO DEPARTED

THIS LIFE THE 4TE OF/ TAMUZ A$^{\underline{o}}$ 5520 HEBREWS STILE

WHICH CORRESPONDS THE 18TH OF JUNE 1760 AGED 2

YEARS 8 MONTHS 26 DAYS

The English lines border two sides and the head of this marble tombstone which has two allegorical representations (illus. 290).

3

ויהי יוסף בן ששים שנים

בלכתו לחיי עולמים

יום א' ט"ו לאייר שנת התקכ"א

אהביו ורעיו בגדו בראותם

יוסף סוף ימיו קנה שם מאבותם:

ת נ צ ב ה:

PROSECUTED ALL HIS DAYS

ENVEY'D TO THE GRAVE

IN SPITE OF FALSE FRIENDS

IS PRAISED BY THE BRAVE

JOSEPH BUZAGLO DE PAZ

AGED 60 YEARS MAY 15, 1761

[9] Now the days of David drew nigh that he should die (I Kings 2:1).

289. SYNAGOGUE RUINS, ST. EUSTATIUS

290. GRAVESTONE OF DAVID DE LEAO, 1760,
ST. EUSTATIUS

5

וישכב דוד עם אבותיו

פנ

דורש ומבקש היה לחסד ואמת

ובמתים היה גמל חסד ואמת

דבר פיו היה ישר ואמת

כל מעשיו היה עושה בכושר

(בה)[בה"] הי[ת]ה דבק[ה] נפשו ביושר

היה מתגבר כארי וקל כנשר

במצותיו היה מתגבר ונערץ

גופו שוכן (ב)[עם] קדושים אשר המה בארץ

ונשמתו בגן עדן מאירה מפז ומחרץ

הה כהרר דוד בן (המענקי) [המעולה?] המנוח?]

ל(נ)[ו]י פרענגר

מאמשטרדם נפטר ביום ה נ ניסן

ונקבר למחרתו ביום ו עשק ד ניסן

תקל

ת נ צ ב ה"

Our translation

AND DAVID SLEPT WITH HIS FATHERS (I KINGS 2:10).
HERE LIES ONE WHO SEARCHED FOR [OPPORTUNITIES]
TO DO CHARITY AND PURSUED TRUTH. TO THE DEAD HE
DISPENSED TRUE CHARITY. HE SPOKE RIGHTEOUSNESS
AND TRUTH, TRANSACTED HIS AFFAIRS HONESTLY, AND HIS
SOUL WAS DEVOTED TO GOD IN RIGHTEOUSNESS. HE WAS
AS STRONG AS THE LION AND AS SWIFT AS THE EAGLE TO
DO GOD'S BIDDING AND THEREFORE ADMIRED. HIS BODY
NOW RESTS IN THE EARTH AMONG THE SAINTED ONES.
IN PARADISE HIS SOUL OUTSHINES THE BRILLIANCE OF

11 Copied by the Rev. J. Willingham (ms., AJA).

SHE DIED AT THE AGE OF 68 YEARS/ ON THE 5TH OF ADAR
I/ IN THE YEAR 5543 WHICH IS FEBRUARY 7/ 1783 IN THE
CHRISTIAN[16] ERA/ MAY HER SOUL BE BOUND UP IN THE
BOND OF LIFE

The doctor-midwife Hannah Benjamin De Leon placed her house at the disposition of the worshipers during the rebuilding of the synagogue destroyed by the hurricane of 1772.

10

SEPULTURA

DO BEMAVENTURADO

IACOB CANTER FAL.O

26 SEBAT 5545

CORRESPONDI A 6 DE

FEB.RO 1785 DA IDADE

DE 44 ANNOS

S B A G D G

11

מצבת
קבורת הבחור הנחמד חיים די
ליאון נל״ע ביום א׳ ערב יום
הכיפורים שנת תקמז לפ״ק היה
תם וישר וירא אלהים סר מרע [17]
ומכבד את אביו ואת אמו על
כן היה נאהב מכל יודעיו
ויהי ימי חייו תשע עשרה שנה
תִנְצֹבֹה

---

[16] The expression, "era of the Christians," seldom appears on the tombstones (see epitaph 4).
[17] Compare Job 1:1.

HERE LYE THE REMAINS OF THE
WORTHY YOUTH HAIM DE LEON
WHO DEPARTED THIS LIFE ON
SUNDAY BEING THE EVE OF THE
GRAND DAY OF ATONEMENT IN
THE YEAR 5547 OF THE CREATION
WHICH ANSWERS TO THE 1 DAY
OF OCTOBER ANNO 1787[18] HE WAS
FOR HIS VIRTUES HIS FEAR OF
GOD OBEDIENCE TO HIS PARENTS
& FAIR DEALINGS WITH ALL
MANKIND BELOVED BY EVERY
ONE WHO HAD THE PLEASURE
OF HIS ACQUAINTANCE HE WAS
SNATCH'D FROM THIS TROUBLESOM
WORLD TO ENJOY ETERNAL BLISS
AT THE AGE OF NINETEEN

Our translation of the Hebrew text

TOMBSTONE/ OF THE PRECIOUS BACHELOR HAIM DE/ LEON
HE WENT TO HIS WORLD ON SUNDAY YOM KIPPUR EVE/
IN THE YEAR [5]547 HE WAS/ PERFECT AND UPRIGHT
FEARING GOD AND ESCHEWING EVIL [JOB 1:1]/ HE
RESPECTED HIS FATHER AND MOTHER/ AND SO WAS LOVED
BY ALL HIS ACQUAINTANCES/ AND THE DAYS OF HIS LIFE
WERE NINETEEN YEARS/ MAY HIS SOUL BE BOUND UP IN
THE BOND OF LIFE

The English text of the epitaph was published by Samuel S. Strouse in the *Jewish Digest*, vol. 7, in August, 1962, p. 21, in an article entitled: "The Genesis and the Exodus, Life and Death of the Jews of St. Eustatius" (pp. 21-25). Strouse incorrectly gave the date of death as October 7 instead of October 1 which is the date appearing in his photograph of the monument and the date furnished to me by Maduro. In passing, one and another comment Strouse makes about the Jews of St. Eustatius, about Jewish participation in the Dutch West India Company, and about the Jews of Dutch Brazil are not quite accurate. This epitaph also was copied by the Rev. J. Willingham (ms., AJA).

[18] The year should be 1786 to correspond to Sunday, 9 Tishri, 5547.

12

ואברהם שב למקומו [19]

S<u>A</u>

DO BEM^{DO} AB^M DE SEM^L

HOHEB F<u>O</u> 16 TISRY

A<u>O</u> 5548

תנצבה

Abraham, probably the son of Samuel Hoheb (no. 14), died on September 28, 1787.

13

SEPULTURA

DO

ANJINHO RACHEL

F^A DE IS. H^M DE D^D

H<u>O</u> YSR^L PEREIRA

FALECEO EM

6 HESVAN 5548

QUE CORRESPONDE

A 18 OUT<u>O</u> 1787

DA IDADE DE 3 A^{OS}

2 M^S E 9 DIAS

S. A. G. D. G.

Little Rachel died at the age of three years, two months and nine days. Her father Isaac Haim de David Hisquiao Ysrael Pereira was treasurer of the community in 1790.

14

S<u>A</u>

DO BEM^{DO} SEM^L HOHEB

F<u>O</u> 17 SEBAT A<u>O</u> 5548

Samuel died on January 26, 1788. Most probably he was the husband of Jael (no. 8), the father of Abraham (no. 9), and the very same prominent Jewish leader who was victimized by Admiral Rodney.

[19] And Abraham returned unto his place (Genesis 18:33).

15

ויעמד [העם מרחק]
ויהי קול השופר

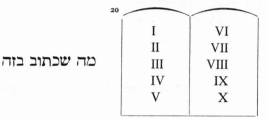

מה שכתוב בזה   קיים זה

ומשה עלה אל האלהים

מצבת

קבורת איש הלך תמים ופעל צדק הה החכם

המשכיל ונבון מורה ורב (?) דרך (?) החסיד וענין הישיש הנכבד

הגביר הנעלה פינחס משה בר יהודה[21] נע אב היה

לאביונים ולב אלמנה הרנין המליט עני מְשַׁוֵּעַ

ויתום ולא עוזר לו מנתא (?) היה בקהילתו זכה

לגמילות חסדים ולהכנסת אורחים קבע עתים

בתורה נשא ונתן באמונה ציפה לישועה והקרן

קיימת לו לעולם הבא נלע בן סב שנים ושבע

חדשים בכב לחדש תמוז שנת התקמט ליצירה

ת נ צ ב ה[22]

HERE LIETH THE REMAINS OF
MR. SALOM[N] LEVY[21] WHO WAS A
BRIGHT EXAMPLE TO VIRTUE A
LOVING HUSBAND FATHER TO
HIS RELATIONS & ORPHANS
BENEVOLENT TO ALL MANKIND

[20] In the top center is a basrelief of a man above the two Tablets of the Law.

[21] Note the difference in name in the English and Hebrew texts.

[22] To the Reverend J. Willingham we are especially grateful for the Hebrew text, although the Hebrew copy is not always accurate (ms., AJA). The English text was copied also by Florence (Mrs. Robert) Abraham for the American Jewish Archives file on St. Eustatius.

HE DEPARTED THIS LIFE
BELOVED AND LAMENTED BY
ALL WHO KNEW HIM
16 OF JULY 1789 AGED 62
YEARS & 7 MO[TS]

Our translation

AND THE PEOPLE STOOD AFAR OFF (EXODUS 20:21), AND THE VOICE OF THE HORN [WAXED LOUDER AND LOUDER] (*ibid.*, 19:19). HE LIVED UP TO WHAT IS HERE [THE TORAH] WRITTEN (BABA KAMA, 17A). AND MOSES WENT UP UNTO GOD (EXODUS 19:3). TOMBSTONE OF THE MAN WHO WALKED UPRIGHTLY AND WORKED RIGHTEOUSNESS (PSALMS 15:2), THE WISE, INTELLIGENT, EXPERIENCED TEACHER AND RABBI (?) GUIDE (?), THE PIOUS AND MODEST, THE RESPECTED AND VENERABLE, THE DISTINGUISHED GENTLEMAN PINHAS MOSES, SON OF THE DECEASED JUDAH.[21] HE WAS A FATHER TO THE DESTITUTE. HE CAUSED THE WIDOW'S HEART TO SING FOR JOY (JOB 29:13). HE DELIVERED THE POOR THAT CRIED AND THE FATHERLESS, AND HIM THAT HAD NONE TO HELP HIM (JOB 29:12). HE WAS BELOVED (?) BY HIS CONGREGATION FOR HIS KINDNESS AND HOSPITALITY. HE DEVOTED HOURS TO TORAH STUDY, TRANSACTED HIS AFFAIRS HONESTLY, AND SOUGHT SALVATION AND REWARD IN THE LIFE TO COME. HE DEPARTED TO HIS WORLD AT 62 YEARS AND 7 MONTHS ON TAMUZ 22, YEAR 5549 OF THE CREATION. MAY HIS SOUL BE BOUND UP IN THE BOND OF LIFE.

16

SEPULTURA

DA

BEM AVENTURADA

RACHEL QUE FOY

MULHER DE YACOB

GARCIA DA IDADE

DE CIRCA 58 ANOS

FALECEO EM 29

SIVAN 5551 QUE

CORRESPONDE A

PRIMEIRO DE JULIO

1791

S. A. G. D. G.

17

ויעקב הלך לדרכו ויפגעו בו מלאכי אלהים [23]

SEPULTURA

DO

BEM AVENTURADO

AMASQUIL VENABON

AGUEBIR ANEHELA

NEHIM ZEMIROTH

BEJISRAEL YAHACOB

HISQUIAO ROBLES

FALECEÕ DA IDADE

DE 40 ANNOS SERVINDO

O CARGO DE

HAZAN N'ESTA ILHA

ST. EUSTATIUS

EM 2 TEBET ANNO 5551 [24]

[23] And Jacob went on his way, and the angels of God met him (Genesis 32:2).

[24] Both Maduro and Willingham give the year as 5551. It should be 5552 according to a letter of the parnassim of St. Eustatius to Curaçao announcing the death of their Hazzan Robles. The deceased was the husband of Catharina Levy and the father of Rebecca who married Mozes Wolff in 1793.

ST. EUSTATIUS

QUE CORRESPONDE
28 DEZEMBRO 1791
תנצבה

18

MORDECA [25]
Y. WELCOM
E

19

SIMON [25]
ABENDANON(I)[E]

20

HERE LIES
INTERRED THE REMAINS OF
MOSES WAAG
BORN THE 11 MAY 1758
AND DEPARTED THIS LIFE
O(F)[N] THE 25 FEBR. 1825
SACRED TO HIS[26] MEMORY
HIS BELOVED AND AFFECTIONATE
WIFE HAS PLACED THIS STONE

21

SACRED
TO THE MEMORY OF
JUDITH JACOBS
WHO DEPARTED THIS LIFE
ON THE 22ND OF DEC. 1843
AGED 63 YEARS
THIS MONUMENT IS ERECTED
BY HER DISCONSOLATE SISTER
SARAH WAAG
THE SUMMONS CAME AND TO HER GOD SHE WENT
T'ENJOY THE BLESSINGS OF A LIFE WELL SPENT

[25] Epitaphs 18 and 19 bear no date. Welcome and Abendanone probably died in the second half of the 18th century.
[26] The Rev. J. Willingham's copy reads, "whose."

E. JEWISH RESIDENTS IN 1790

At the demand of the States General of Holland, Prince Willem V sent Willem August Sirtama thoe Grovestins and Willem Cornelis Boey to the Dutch West Indies in 1789 to compile a report on conditions in these islands. These commissioners also visited St. Eustatius. On their orders community treasurer Isaac de David Parera furnished an abstract of the yearly expenses of the community (page 527) and a list of the Jewish residents on the island. This list is reproduced below with all the misspellings encountered in the original copy.

LIST OF THE HEBREW NATION, AS COULD BE RECOLLECTED

					[Total]
David Abendanone	Parnas President	wife	7	children	[9[
Isaac Parera Davids	Treasurer	do.			[2]
Benjamin Willcome	Present assistant	do.	2	„	[4]
Abraham Abendanone	Adjunto	do.	6	„	[8]
Jacob Robles	Reader	do.	3	„	[5]
Judah Haim De Leon	Treasurer of the sick	do.			[2]
Nathan Levy	Sexton	do.			[2]
Emanuel de Leon	widower		2	„	[3]
Isaac Abrams	do.				[1]
David Henriquez Pimentel		wife	1	„	[3]
Naphtali Hart		do.	6	„	[8]
Salomon Jacobs		do.	6	„	[8]
Lyon Jacobs		do.	2	„	[4]
Jacob Garsia		do.			[2]
Judah Benjamin		do.	7	„	[9]
David Mendes		do.			[2]
Nathan Samuels		do.			[2]
Abram Mozes Levy		do.	1	„	[3]
Daniel Nunes Henriquez		do.	1	„	[3]
David Nunes Tavares		do.	2	„	[4]
Jacob Phillips		do.	2	„	[4]
Mozes Gomes Fonseca		do.	2	„	[4]
Samuel Mozes Franks		do.	4	„	[6]
Levy Abrams		do.	1	„	[3]
Haim Abendanone		do.			[2]
Isaac Henriquez da Meskitta		do.			[2]
Moses Waag		do.			[2]

Abigael Wellcome		widow	[1]
Sarah de Sarah		do.	[1]
Rebekah Garsia		do.	[1]
Rachel Mendes Balborda		do.	[1]
Esther Mellado		do.	[1]
Rachel Levy		do.	[1]
Leah Henriquez		do. 4 children	[5]
Esther Sasso		do. 2 „	[3]
Rebekah Hoheb		do. 4 „	[5]
Rebekah Benjamin		do. 1 „	[2]
Miriam De Leon	Husband absent	1 „	[2]
Dinah De Leon	do.		[1]
Miriam Levy	liveth with Rachel Levy unmaried		[1]
Hannah De Leon	do. „ Judah H. de Leon do.		[2]
Jacob Jesurun Oliveyra	wife absent		[1]
Elias Gomes	do.		[1]

Bachelors & Youngsters

Moses van David Parera	[1]	Isaac Gomes Silva	[1]
Michael da Costa Andrada	[1]	Levi & Moses Furtado	[2]
Elias de Pina	[1]	Jacob of Isaac Cohen	[1]
Joseph Vieyra	[1]	Barnet Levy	[1]
Philip van Praag	[1]	Moses Levy	[1]
Simha[27] Coppee	[1]	Judah Levy	[1]
Israel Zappurt	[1]	Isaac & Moses Martines	[2]
Lazarus Marcus	[1]	Jacob Benjamin	[1]
Ralph Benjamin	[1]	Isaac Wellcome, absent	
Solomon Solomons	[1]	Aron Josephs	[1]
Solomon Abrams	[1]	Abm. Messiah	[1]
Samuel of Ancona	[1]	Jacob Moses Franks	[1]

Strangers

Zipporah Abendanone		Hannah de Leon	[1]
& daughter	[2]	David Levy	[1]
Abraham Capadosa	[1]	Jesiah de Chavos	[1]
Joseph Bellinfante	[1]	Abm. Naar	[1]
Jacob Chaves	[1]		
		[Total:	170]

St. Eustachius 13th January 1790
(signed) I:. Parera Davids[28]
Treas.

[27] *Simha* for Sephardis is a girl's name; for Ashkenazis, a boy's name.
[28] WICA 257, document Lᵃ P 6, courtesy of the late J. M. L. Maduro. This list shows that two-fifths of the membership was of Ahskenazic origin if we include the Harts and Benjamins who had already married into Sephardic families for two generations.

F. RESOLUTION TAKEN [IN SEBAT, 5498 (1738)] WITH REGARD
TO A SEPHER TORAH GIVEN TO ISHACK DE LA PENHA
FOR DELIVERY TO ST. EUSTATIUS [29]

Termo de se haver entregado a Ishack de la Penha Hum Sepher torah, para Remetelo a s: Eústaçius:

Em Sebat, Foy Suplicado aoss^res do Mahamad, por Ishack de la Penha de parte dos Jehidim que se achaõ em S: Eustaçius, lhes quisesem Conseder hum Sepher torah, para uzo daquela Congrega, o qual lhe foy otorgado pelos ss^res do Mahamad, & Se lhe entregou ad? Penha hum Sepher torah de Gevil Com Capa de Seda Vermella, Com flores negras, que Se obrigou ditto Penha aremeter a ditto S: Eustacius.

[*firmado*]

David Mendes da Costa
Manuel de Jacob Curiel
Moseh de Abraham Pereyra
Isaac de Pinto
Ishac de Josseph de Meza

TRANSLATION

In Sebat [5498 — between January 22 and February 20, 1738], the gentlemen of the Mahamad were requested by Ishack de la Penha, in behalf of the Jews of St. Eustatius, to give him a Sepher Torah for the use of that congregation. This was granted by the gentlemen of the Mahamad, and a Sepher Torah of fine parchment with its black-flowered, red silk cape was presented to said Penha, who promised to deliver it to St. Eustatius.

[*Signed by*]   (The five parnassim above)

[29] PJCAA, Livro de Termos das Entregas..., 5489-5516, p. 151.

APPENDIX 25

ST. MARTIN

RESOLUTION ADOPTED THE 21ST OF HESVAN, 5544 (NOVEMBER 16, 1783), FOR OBTAINING THE SOVEREIGN'S APPROVAL OF ST. MARTIN'S REQUEST FOR COMMUNITY AND BYLAWS[1]

[21 Hesvan, 5544] Havendo recebido húa carta dos Parnassim do K. K. de St. Martin com aviso que dezejaõ formar húa quehila & Ascamoth cuyos Suplicaõ de fazer aprovar, & octrogar (sic) do Soberano; Sobre oqual se resolveo commeter a nosso Secret⁰ Lobo para ther húa intervista com o Avogado da Compª do Weste, & Consultar Sobre este cazo, & do resoltado nos fará raporte para emtaõ resolver o que convier.

TRANSLATION

[We, the gentlemen of the Mahamad,] Having received a letter from the Parnassim of the Holy Congregation of St. Martin stating that they wish to form a community and bylaws, for which purpose they request us to obtain the Sovereign's approval and authorization;

[Now, on this 21st day of Hesvan, 5544 (November 16, 1783), hereby] resolve to delegate our Secretary Lobo to arrange for a meeting with the attorney for the [Dutch] West [India] Company in order to discuss the matter, and subsequently to report the results to us for further deliberation.

1 PJCAA, Rezoluçoems dossʳᵉˢ do MM, 5539-5545, p. 264.

ARUBA

T HE FOLLOWING TWO EPITAPHS were copied by the author on his first visit to Aruba in 1940.

JAEL DE JACOB MORENO

ESTOS RESTOS MORTALES CUBRE ESTA FRIA

. . . .

ANGUSTIADA FAMILIA EN EL

9 DE NOVIEMBRE DE 1857 PARA

EL MUNDO DE LA REALIDAD. ALLI DISFRU

TARA PAZ DE SUS VIRTUDES, LA TRANQUI-

LIDAD DE SU CONCIENCIA Y EL SOCIEGO

DE SU ETERNA SALVACION

SUS DEUDOS DESOLADOS, CONSA

GRAN SUS LAGRIMAS Y ESTE MONU

MENTO A SU MEMORIA.

Lingstuil Curaçao

Like most of the monuments executed by Lingstuil, this too is difficult to decipher. Jael was the daughter of Eliau Penso and the sister of Isaac Penso, also of Aruba.

DAVID CAPRILES JR.

NACIO EN CURACAO 22 ENERO 1799

FALECIO EN ARUBA 22 NOVIEMBRE 1883

SU MOTE FUE LA HONRADEZ, ACATANDO

SIEMPRE LA VIRTUD, Y A SUS SEMEJANTES

UN AFECTO GENEROSO

Q. D. E. P.

David was the son of Isaac Capriles and Sarah de Haim David Dovale, and grandson of Dr. Joseph Capriles.

No tombstone could be found for David's father Isaac (d. Aruba, Dec. 13, 1837) in the Old Jewish Cemetery of Curaçao; he probably lies buried in one of the six old nameless adult graves of this small cemetery. David's mother, who died in 1850, reposes in the Old Jewish Cemetery of Curaçao (C 1335).

293. ABRAHAM DAVID CAPRILES, 1862-1936, MAJOR COMMANDANT OF
THE CURAÇOAN MILITIA, PAGE 487

294. SOL ABRAHAM H. SENIOR, 1839-
1908, BANKER AND CAPTAIN OF THE
CURAÇOAN MILITIA

295. ELIAS MANUEL PENSO, MEMBER OF
COLONIAL COUNCIL, 1912-26, AND
CAPTAIN OF THE MILITIA

296. ISHAC H. CAPRILES, AIDE-DE-CAMP
TO THREE GOVERNORS, 1918-23

297. IVAN LANSBERG, AIDE-DE-CAMP TO
GOVERNOR P. KASTEEL, 1942-48

DOCUMENT WITH RELATION TO THE PIZA AFFAIR

T HE SEPARATISTS, as Chapter XV disclosed, were obliged to conduct their religious marriage ceremony without the consent of the community.[1] After the reconciliation the Mahamad sought to legalize those unions. By synagogue announcement of Adar 8, 5582 (March 1, 1822), all Separatists who had married during the dispute were urged to register their religious marriage contracts in the Ketuboth Register of the community. Simultaneously the men were to receive the qualifying title of *Guevir* — the title used for a married man when called to the reading of the Torah but denied to one whose marriage was not recognized by the Mahamad.

Here follows the text of a "legalized" marriage contract as recorded in the Mikvé Israel Ketuboth Register, vol. VII, 2d numeration, no. 4.

לזכרון

אתיותנו אלו יתנו עדות נאמנה [איך] בכח ההכרזה כמאמר מעלת שרי המעמד ביום
שמונה לחדש אדר שנת ֗חמשת אלפים וחמש מאות וש(נ)ת[י]ם ושמונים לבריאת עולם הסכימו
מעלתם הנ"ל ליזהר ולהודיע לכל בני הקהילה הזאת לקר(ו)[א]ת(ן)[ם] בכ(י)נוי של **גביר**
לכל אחד מאותם שיוכלו להביא ראי(א)[ה] שנשאו כ(א)[ה]ונן וכשורה כדת משה וישראל **תוך**
הזמן אשר היה ענין הקטטה שהקהל היו נפרדים (ל)[ב]שתי הסעיפים לראות אם **היו**
נשואין כדת וכתובת(ק)[ם] כראוי בעדים נאמנים כתקנת חז"ל כדי לסמוך עלי(ו)[הם] ולהעתיקה
בספר כתובות הקהל להעמיד הדת על ת(י)לה. וכען אתא (ל)קדמנא הגביר אברהם בן
מ(ו)רדכי חיים שניאור בשטר כתובתו, לאשתו מרת לאה בת הגביר דוד שניאור מ"בג'ע,
העשוי (בזמן הפרישות הנז[ל'] [2] בפני עדים נאמנים. ואנחנו בי דינא חתמנו למטה בריר(ה)[א]
לנא להעתיק בספר כתובת אנתי(א)[ה] כראוי. וכדו לא אשכחנא טעות(ה)[א] **בסדר כתובתו**
הנזכרת לע(י)ל ועל כן העתיקוה(ו)[י] ואישר[נ]ו[ה](ו)[י] וקיימנוהי כדחז(ה)[י]. וזה נוסח כתובתו.
באחד בשבת, שבעה עשר יום לחדש מנחם, שנת חמשת אלפים חמש מאות תשע(ה) ושבעים
לבריאת (ה)עולם, למנין שאנו מונים פה באי קוראסאו, במתא דמתקרייא וויליים שטאט, **דיתבא**
על כיף ימא דהודו מערבאה, בא הבחור הנחמד אנחמד[3] [אברהם] בן הגביר הנעלה **מרדכי**

---

[1] See p. 310 above.

[2] So in the original text.

[3] So repeated in the original text with the name Abraham omitted.

חיים שניאור יצ״ו, ואמר לה, לבתולה הצנועה מרת לאה, בת הגביר הנעלה דוד שניאור נ״ע,
הוי לי לאנתו כדת משה וישראל. ואנא בס״ד אפלח ואוקיר ואזון ואפרנס ואכסה יתיכי
כהלכת גוברין יהודאין דפלחין ומוקרין וזנין ומפרנסין ומכסין ית נשיהון בקושטא ויהיבנא ליכי
מוהר בתוליכי כסף זוזי מאתן דחזו ליכי מדאוריתא ומזונויכי וכסותיכי וספוקיכי ומיעל לותיכי
כאורח כל ארעא. וצביאת מרת לאה בתולתא כלה דא והות להבחור אברהם חתן הנ״ל
לאנתו.⁴ וכך אמר לנו החתן הנ״ל אחריות וחומר שטר כתובתא דא קב(י)לית עלי ועל ירתאי
בתראי להתפרעא מכל שפר ארג [נכסין] וקנינין (ונכסין) דאית לי תחות כל שמיא דקנאי
ודעתיד אנא למקני, נכסין דאית להון אחריות, ואגבן דלית להון אחריות, כלהון יהון אחראין
וערבאין למפרע מנהון שטר כתובתא דא דקב(י)לית עלי ועל ירתאי (ברתאי) [בתראי] וחומר
כל שטר[י] כתובות דנהיגי בבנ[ו]ת ישראל העשוין כתיקון ח״ז״ל מן יומא דנן ולעלם דלא
כאסמכתא ודלא כטופסי דשטרי. וקנינן מהחתן הנ״ל למרת הכלה הנ״ל על כל מה דכתיב
לע[י]ל, במנא דכשר למקני ביה. והכל שריר ובריר וקיים.

Esta firmado ó Noivo   Abm. d Mordy. Senior
Firmado como testigos   Mordy Levy Maduro,
                              Abm. Jn. Henriquez

Esta firmado Com traducto da Idioma Rabinica a Lussitana. Esplicado por
mim em Portuguez   Jeosua de Sola.   Passa Adiante.

ובכן בעדות נאמנה יצדקו כל הנזכר לע[י]ל וה(ו)[י]א העתקה נאמנת כהוגן מכתובתו אשר
הראונו החתן עצמו. ולפי שהיו כהוגן וכדין גמרנו שלהבא יקרא(ו) בכ(י)נוי הגביר אברהם די
מרדכי חיים שניאור והחזרנו לו כתובתו. ואנ[ו]חנ[א] בי דינא חתימו דא עם סעדותי מעלת
הפרנסים (ה)[ד]קהל קדוש מקוה ישראל בקוראסאו, ארבעה עשר יום לחדש סיון שנת
ת̃ ק̃ פ̃ ב̃ לפרט קטן.

דניאל לופיס פיניא ס̃ט   Mordy Ricardo
דוד נאמיאס די קראסתו   Is. Capriles

A LASTING MEMORIAL OF THE MATTER

These letters of ours will give faithful testimony, by virtue of announcement
by synagogue crier made in accordance with the order of the exalted
members of the Mahamad on the 8th of the month of Adar, 5582 years
since Creation, to the decision of the excellencies abovementioned, warning
and advising all members of the Community who can prove that they had
married in due form and in compliance with the Law of Moses and Israel

---

⁴ There is no *tosefeth* or 50% augmentation of the dowry since there was an antenuptial contract.

during the period of the dispute when the Community was divided into two parties, to come forth to receive the qualifying title "Guevir" (married man); and

Whereas, the Mahamad, in order to determine whether or not each candidate was married according to Law and if the Ketubah was properly written and signed by competent witnesses in conformity with the ordinance promulgated by our sages of blessed memory, took as a basis the Ketubah, and registered it in the Ketuboth Register of the Community, and thus set the Law on its pedestal;

Before us has appeared the married man Abraham, son of Mordechay Haim Senior, with his Ketubah in favor of his wife Mrs. Leah, daughter of David Senior — may he rest in Paradise — made during the separation above referred to, in the presence of two competent witnesses; and

Whereas, we, the members of the Tribunal below undersigned, declare this as his authentic signature,

Now, therefore, the "Guevir" mentioned, asks and urges that we duly register in the Ketuboth Register his wife's Ketubah; and since we have not found anything unfavorable in the text thereof, we have registered, legalized and duly confirmed it, and hereby give the contents of this Ketubah.

A translation of this Ketubah is not deemed necessary, but these are its salient features. It was made on Sunday, the 17th of Menaḥem, 5579 (August 8, 1819), on the day of the civil marriage (CGA, MR, 1819), and was signed by the bridegroom Abraham de Mordechay Haim Senior and by the witnesses Mordechay Levy Maduro and Abraham Jesurun Henriquez. The officiant's name does not appear. This Ketubah was orally translated from Hebrew into Portuguese by Jeosua de Sola. The Beth Din's legalization of the document then follows.

Thus, we faithfully attest that the foregoing is a true and correct copy of the Ketubah which the bridegroom himself showed us; and whereas, it was executed in due form and in accordance with law, we have decided in the future to call him "Guevir Abraham de Mordechay Haim Senior," and we returned his Ketubah.

We, the members of the Tribunal, hereby affix our signatures in the presence of the attesting witnesses, their excellencies the Parnassim of this Holy Congregation Mikvé-Israel in Curaçao, the 14th of Sivan of the year [5]582 (June 3, 1822).

The Beth Din
By: Daniel Lopez Penha — May my end be good!
David Namias de Crasto

The Parnassim
By: Mordechay Ricardo
Isaac Capriles

It is noteworthy that Abraham David Senior who was married civilly on the 25th of June, 1820, to Rachel de Jacob Calvo (CGA, MR, 1820), did not celebrate the religious ceremony until the 18th of Sivan, 5582, or June 7, 1822 (Ket. Reg., *ibid*., no. 5). Four other couples who married during this period did not register their religious marriage documents with the community. One is therefore led to believe with Moses L. Penha, a contemporary of that time, that the reconciliation was in form only.

JEWS IN THE NATIONAL GUARD

THE JEWS served in the National Guard since the early days of the colony, and formed a separate company. In 1821 it was reorganized into five companies: Caucasians, Jews, mestizos, mulattoes and Negroes, and sailors of whatever color or creed.

The provision concerning the Jews reads: "All men of the Mosaic Religion shall form a company in order to render service more easily, and they also shall be ready to substitute for absentees of another company whenever those men are ordered to serve regularly on the Sabbath or other festivals when the Jews cannot bear arms."*

* OAC 237, June 21, 1821. The Dutch text reads: "Dat alle manschappen van den Mozaischen Godsdienst eene Compagnie zullen uitmaken, ten einde alsoo hunnen dienst gemakkelijker te maken en daardoor ook voor te komen het uitvallen van die manschappen uit andere Compagnie, wanneer dezelfve tot gewonen dienst mogten worden gecommandeerd het zij op Sabbath of andere feestdagen waarop Joden geene wapenen mogen dragen."

PETITION OF DR. DANIEL LEVY MADURO PEIXOTTO TO THE GOVERNOR OF CURAÇAO FOR A PERMIT TO PRACTICE MEDICINE IN CURAÇAO

> To His Excellency, Knight in the Order of the Dutch Lion, Rear Admiral in the service of His Majesty, the King of the Netherlands, Governor of Curaçao and its island dependencies, Commander-in-Chief of the Land and Sea Forces there, &. &. &.

The undersigned, Daniel L. M. Peixotto, approximately twenty-two years old, residing here, respectfully shows:

That the petitioner, in accordance with the annexed documents, was born in Amsterdam, capital of the Kingdom of the Netherlands, of a father born in this Colony and a Dutch mother.

That in early childhood he left Amsterdam with his father for this Colony where he lived six years. Afterwards the petitioner went with his father to North America to continue on to Holland, this route having been taken because of the [impending] war. Shortly thereafter war broke out between the United States and Great Britain, making it impossible for petitioner's father to carry out his plan [of going to Holland]. Meanwhile he deemed it advisable to let the petitioner study medicine. That the petitioner in effect completed his studies and received a proper diploma of Medical Doctor, which petitioner has the honor of producing herewith.

That five weeks ago, on the advice of his parents and of his own desire, petitioner came to this colony (where he has many relatives) with the intention of practicing medicine.

That the petitioner, in accordance with the ordinances of this island, particularly His Excellency's Regulation of February 13 of this year, respectfully addresses himself to His Excellency to approve his application and admit him to the practice of his profession as Doctor of Medicine.

> So doing, &c.
> D. L. M. Peixotto MD

Curaçao, May 14, 1821.

To this request the governor wrote: "The petition of the applicant has been taken under advisement, Curaçao, May 15, 1821" (OAC 294, no. 47).

At the same time, the Messrs. I. L. Penha and I. Pardo declared that shortly after Daniel's birth in 1799, they were in Amsterdam and visited the home of the petitioner's father, Moises L. Maduro Peixotto, and that the applicant's statements were correct. Governor Cantz'laar was not satisfied with this declaration and found fault with it. Finally he granted the license provided that Peixotto would take out Curaçao citizenship (OAC 237, no. 482, May 16, 1821).

The excuse offered by Dr. Peixotto to justify his father's remaining in New York does not coincide with the historical facts. His father left for New York in 1807 and established himself there immediately (above, page 425). Although Great Britain had been impressing United States' seamen on and off, the United States did not declare war against Great Britain until June 18, 1812.

COMMUNITY ASSESSMENT — DISTRIBUTION OF SYNAGOGUE SEATS
1862   1863

IN NOVEMBER, 1862, the Mahamad, with the approval of the Council of Elders, assessed the members with the *finta* or communal tax payable for the years 1863-64.[1] The minimal annual tax was three florins; the maximal, 210. In March, 1863, the parnassim assigned to each adult Jewish man on the island a synagogue seat free of charge as usual. To save space, both lists have been combined although there is a certain variation in the names.

These lists give us an idea of

1. The economic situation of every member between 1862-64;
2. The number of adult Jews then living in Curaçao;
3. The number of old families like the Dovales, Fidanques, Henriquez Juliaos, De Leons [Leaos], Pereiras, Pintos, and others that were still in existence and have since disappeared;
4. The fact that the Jews of 1863 still bore their Jewish names with pride.

Only five Ashkenazic families appear in these lists: Jadowmsky, Kristeller (an employee of the community), Edwards, Lansberg and Myerston. The last three married Portuguese Jewish girls born in Curaçao. The De Jongh family was of Sephardic origin. The Wolffs had been in the Caribbean for generations and were allied to the Portuguese Jewish families.

ASSESSMENT AND SEATING ARRANGEMENT
SEATS TO THE RIGHT, OPPOSITE THE PARNASSIM'S BENCH

Seat No.	Name	Tax in fls.	Seat No.	Name	Tax in fls.
1	David Cohen Henriquez	36[2]	19	Elias M. Penso	18
5	Jacob Wolff		22	Haim Benjamin Penso	
8	Elias Cardoze da Costa		23	Elias Penso Suares	9
14	Moses de Aron Hz. Juliao		24	Daniel B. Jesurun	18
18	Jacob Joseph Sasso		25	Jacob Suares	105[3]

[1] This refers to Chapter XVII, The Community Before the Schism of 1864.
[2] Reduced to 30 fls.
[3] Reduced to 90 fls.

Seat No.	Name	Tax in fls.	Seat No.	Name	Tax in fls.
26	David Penso		72	Daniel Joseph Sasso	
28	Jeosuah da Costa Gomez	18	73	Isaac Moses Salas	
29	Jacob H. Penso	18	74	David Isaac Abinun de Lima	
30	Jacob Henriquez	36			
33	David M. C. Henriquez		75	Abraham C. Henriquez	75
34	Benjamin Penso	15	76	Elias Namias de Crasto	3
35	Mordechay Henriquez Cadet	15	77	Haim Elias Curiel	
36	Mordechay de Marchena	3	78	Rafael Sº Namias de Crasto	3
37	Daniel da C. Gomez de la Penha	3	79	Jacob G. Pinedo	
			80	Isaac P. N. Vaz	
38	Isaac Pinedo Jr.	210[4]	81	Abraham Daniel Jesurun	24
39	Selomoh A. Capriles		82	Elias Daniel Jesurun	24
40	David Josias Dovale	6	83	Jacob Maduro Lopez	
41	Benjamin de Is. de Crasto[5]		84	David J. L. Henriquez	
44	Guideon Salas		85	Samuel L. Maduro Jr.	120
46	Jeosuah Jesurun	6	86	Jeosuah Naar Jr.	3
47	David Pardo Jr.	6	87	Isaac Namias de Crasto	18
48	Jacob de M. Salas		88	Benjamin de Marchena	12
49	Abraham Jadowmsky		89	Abraham Hz. Juliao	6
50	Manuel E. Penso	12	90	Selomo H. Pereira	
51	Gabriel Hz. Juliao		91	Isaac A. Curiel	
52	Benjamin Mord. A. Correa		92	Isaac Hz. Juliao	6
53	Jacob Ephraim Curiel		93	Josias Ic. Dovale	18
54	David Selomoh de Jongh		94	Mordechay Hm. Pereira	3
55	Jacob Isaac de Castro	3	95	Samuel da Costa Gomez Jr.	30
56	Daniel Jesurun Jr.	120	96	Mehir Myerston	
57	Benjamin Jesurun Jr.	150	98	Daniel Jacob de Sola	
58	Abraham de B. Jesurun	24	99	Abraham Cardozo da Costa	
61	Henry Nathan	30	100	Benjamin Gomes Casseres	
62	Jacob J. Naar	90	101	Moises Pereira	18
63	Mordechay Senior	24	102	Jacob Rois Mendes	105[6]
64	Manuel Penso Curiel		103	David Haim Lopez Penha	
65	S. E. L. Maduro	90	104	Raymond Alvares Correa	
66	S. M. Lansberg	36	105	Abraham Alfonso Myerston	24
70	Samuel de Casseres	18	106	Raph. de Is. Abinun de Lima	
71	Abraham de Meza Myerston		107	Josias D. Pardo	
			108	Isaac Abinun de Lima Jr.	3

[4] Reduced to 150 fls.
[5] Most probably Castro in place of Crasto.

[6] Reduced to 75 fls.

Seat No.	Name	Tax in fls.	Seat No.	Name	Tax in fls.
109	Jacob H. Pereira	3	118	Jacob Leaõ Nunes	
110	Joseph Penso	12	119	David Namias de Crasto	3
111	David M. de (Crasto)		120	Isaac H. Pereira	6
	[Castro]	12	121	Jacob Hz. Juliao	3
112	Edward Ricardo		122	Jacob Pinedo	3
114	Jacob E. Penso	12	123	Dob Kristeller	3
115	Elias My. de Marchena		126-138	Reserved for Soldiers	
116	Moises Salas	12	142	Elias B. Jesurun	3
117	Samuel Curiel				

ASSESSMENT AND SEATING ARRANGEMENT
SEATS TO THE LEFT, OPPOSITE THE PARNASSIM'S BENCH

No.	Name	Tax	No.	Name	Tax
1	A. M. Chumaceiro	18	34	Jacob Mord. A. Correa	
3	Rephael Pinedo	12	35	Mordechay Capriles	12
4	Moses Ic Ns de Crasto		36	Mordechay F. Curiel	15
5	M. Daniel Henriquez	6	37	Isaac Rz. Miranda Jr.	66
6	Isaac Gabriel Cardoze		38	Elias Rz. Miranda	
7	Elias Abinun de Lima	24	39	Ephraim Curiel	12
8	Aron A. Capriles		40	Elias Mosé Curiel	9
10	Gabriel Cardoze	3	41	Isaac de (Crasto)	
12	Moises Capriles			[Castro] Jr.	12
15	Manuel Alvares Correa	12	42	Jeudah Abinun de Lima	9
16	David Jesurun Penso	3	43	Manuel R. Pinedo	
17	Jacob David Pinto		44	Daniel Cohen Henriquez	30
18	Levy de Jongh		46	David Delvalle Henriquez	6
19	Moises Benj. Lopez Penha		47	Samuel da Costa Gomez	3
20	Isaac de Marchena	3	48	David Abinun de Lima	30
21	Benjamin de Sola Jr.	24	49	Jacob Delvalle Henriquez	6
22	Abraham Capriles	24	50	Mordechay Pinedo	
23	Mordechay (Murry) R. Pinedo	15	51	Benjamin Joseph Henriquez	12
24	Joseph Capriles Jr.	3	52	Jacob M. A. Correa	
27	Mordy M. D. C. Henriquez		53	Jacob Capriles	
28	Selomoh Elias Curiel	12	54	Jacob David de (Crasto)	
29	Abraham Delvalle Henriquez	15		[Castro]	12
30	Benjamin A. Correa	48	55	Haim de My A. Correa	
31	Abraham Ns de Crasto	3	56	Manuel Penso	75
32	Selomoh Abinun de Lima	24	57	Jacob de Sola	6
33	Mordy de Is. Hz. Juliao		58	Benjamin de Sola	15
			59	Mordechay Henriquez	42

Seat No.	Name	Tax in fls.	Seat No.	Name	Tax in fls.
60	Jacob A. Jesurun	210	91	Jacob H. Senior	9
61	Morris Curiel	42	93	Moises E. Curiel	3
62	Elias Jesurun Henriquez	120	94	Anjel J. Jesurun	
63	Jeosuah de Sola	98	95	David Jesurun Jr.	
64	Daniel Hm. Lopez Penha	3	96	Isaac Capriles	15
65	Benjamin de Casseres Jr.	24	97	Manuel Mordy A. Correa	
66	Sol C. Henriquez	42	99	Raphael Delvalle Henriquez	
67	Herman C. Henriquez	36	100	David Fidanque	
69	Mordy de M. A. Correa Jr.	18	101	David Valencia Jr.	150
70	Manuel A. Correa Jr.	66	102	David Osorio	3
71	D. A. Jesurun	24	103	Moises Delvalle Henriquez	12
72	Moises Wolff	6	104	Selomoh Ns de Crasto	
73	Jacob A. Curiel	6	105	Selomoh Delvalle Henriquez	6
74	A. M. Chumaceiro Az.	15	106	Benjamin Delvalle Henriquez	
75	D. M. Jesurun	12			
76	D. A. Senior	30	107	Abraham Jb Senior	24
77	Jacob Mosé Curiel		108	Jeosuah Rephael Henriquez	6?
78	A. J. Jesurun	120	109	Selomoh D. C. Henriquez	30
79	Benjamin Pereira Brandao	57	110	Jacob My L. Maduro	
80	Moises Frois Ricardo[7]		111	Moses Jb Jesurun	48
81	Abraham Mordy Senior	3	112	Haim Abinun de Lima	
82	Isaac J. Senior	105	113	Haim Namias de Crasto	
83	Samuel de Sola		114	Raphael Jeosuah Henriquez	36
84	Salomon de Leon	6			
85	Selomoh Senior	18	115	Elias Curiel	
86	Isaac Osorio	6	116	Moises Sasso	9
87	A. M. C. Henriquez	12	117	David Ricardo	
88	Mosé de Marchena	75[8]	119	[Joseph] Haim M. Chumaceiro[9]	12
89	David R. Capriles	18			
90	Josias P. Fidanque		120	Aron da Costa Gomez	6

IN ADDITION, THE FOLLOWING VACANT SEATS WERE ASSIGNED TO PEOPLE CURRENTLY ON THE ISLAND:

To the Right

32	Elias Joseph Pereira Brandao	31	Moses Lindo	
45	Abraham Mordechay de Marchena	59	[Dr] Salomon de Leon	36[10]

[7] His seat was changed to seat no. 27 then vacant (to the right).

[8] Reduced to 57 flrs.

[9] Then only 18, he later became the preacher and cantor of the community.

[10] His assessment was annulled as illegal, for he was in Curaçao less than a year. He was the father of the American Socialist Daniel de Leon.

To the Left

5	Name missing	25	Abraham Wolff
6	Abraham Isaac Senior	41	Abraham I. de Marchena

The resolution on the seating arrangements was made in Curaçao on March 9, 1863, and signed by Sol Cohen Henriquez as president and Moises Jesurun as secretary (MIA, Juntas de Mahamad, pages 38-40).

It is significant that the women had no reserved seats. They sat in the gallery, usually in the seats formerly occupied by their deceased mothers and relatives. But they were nevertheless taxed. The maiden ladies, of whom Curaçao has always had a large number, generally carried their father's given name as their middle name. The assessment for the widows, matrons and maiden ladies follows.

Name	Tax in fls.	Name	Tax in fls.
Widow Jeosuah J. Henriquez	75	Widow Benjamin Jesurun	3
„ Benjamin Suares	12	„ Jacob Lopez Penha	3
„ Haim J. C. Henriquez	210	„ Mordy A. Correa	12
„ Abraham J. Henriquez	36[11]	„ S! C. Henriquez	9
„ Raphael Wolff	12	„ Isaac Henriquez Moron	3
„ M. A. Jesurun	30	„ M[iriam] Ezra	30
„ Selomoh Senior	3	„ Sarah B. de Casseres	3
„ Jacob Senior Jr.	30	„ Rachel Calvo Senior	3
„ Myerston	3	„ Selomoh Pardo	6
„ Joseph Fidanque	3	„ Aron Henriquez Juliao	3
„ Josias Abinun de Lima	3	„ Abraham Pinedo	12
„ Selomoh de Jongh	3	„ Jos[iau]. L. Henriquez	6
„ Mordy Cohen Henriquez	3	„ Clara M^y A. Correa	3

Matrons

Leah de Moises Mendes Monsanto	120
(Her husband was abroad.)	
Jael de Jacob Naar	6

Maiden Ladies

Leah Abraham Haim Senior	9	Sarah A. Jesurun	6
Prescilla Senior	9	Leah de Casseres	6
Ribca Senior	9	Leah de Jacob Senior	6
Agata Senior	9	Rachel M. Jesurun	3
Amestiste Senior[12]	9	Jeudith M. Jesurun	3

[11] Reduced to 18 flrs.

[12] The first five were the maiden daughters of Abraham Haim Senior.

Name	Tax in fls.	Name	Tax in fls.
Rebecca D. Dovale	9	Abigail M. Jesurun	3
Esther D. Dovale	9	Gracia M. Jesurun	3
Hanah D. Dovale	9	Esther M. Jesurun[13]	3
Esther Jos. Pª Brandao	24	Esther Capriles	3

Many members were not taxed in November, 1862, either because of their modest position or because they were exempt for having less than a year's residence in Curaçao. On the other hand, the following individuals taxed in November, 1862, did not figure in the seating arrangement probably because they had meanwhile left the island or were officiants.

Name	Tax in fls.	Name	Tax in fls.
Abraham Moses Jesurun	36	Jacob Isaac L. Maduro	6
Aron N. de Crasto	3	Joseph Pª Brandao Jr.	9
A. Da Costa Gomez de la Penha	3	Joseph Jacob Henriquez	75
David Senior Jr.	66	Joseph Gomez Casseres	120
David Cardoze	12	Jeos. de Jeos. R. Henriquez Jr.	18
David Pardo Cadet	30	Jeudah Senior	120
David H. Dovale	30	Moises H. C. Henriquez	150[14]
Efraim Edwards	48	Mosé Sasso	9
Eliezer Lopez Penha	3	Moses Jesurun	12
Abraham Abinun de Lima	18	Mosé Jᵇ de Castro	3
Hm. Jʰ Israel Santcroos	9	Manuel N. Curiel	18

This assessment was signed by the president Dr. Isaac J. Senior and by the temporary secretary J. A. Curiel on November 6, 1862 (MIA, *ibid.*).

This tax-seating list shows that 212 adult men had been assigned seats in the synagogue, and that 202 members (men and women) had been assessed a total of 5,241 florins. Twenty-one families noted in these lists have since disappeared or have no descendants in Curaçao. The Osorios, Sassos and Fidanques have been living in Panama.

[13] The last five Jesuruns were the maiden daughters of Moises Jesurun.
[14] Reduced to 120 florins.

USAGES AND CUSTOMS

THE OLDER GENERATION of the community is in the process of disappearing and with it all the old usages and customs. Some of these customs have quite an ancient origin. We have therefore compiled them to keep a record for the history of the community.

Toward this goal we have pored over (1) the prayer book *Tefilath Yesharim* (Amsterdam, 1779) with marginal notes by Daniel Lopez Penha; (2) the Mikvé Israel Archives, (3) the "Memorias Senior" and (4) the "Memorias Curiel." We have also made use of some information given to us by David Lopez Penha, sexton of the community for fifty-three years. Over the years some of these Sephardic customs went out of use. Now that the Curaçoan Jews have given up the Sephardic ritual of their fathers for Liberal Judaism and the inconsistent Reconstructionist ritual (above, pages 507-508), there are almost none.

DAILY PRAYERS

There was the custom of the cantor's repeating *Hashem elohekhem emeth* — the Lord your God is true — after reading the *Shemah* although these three words are not printed in the ritual.[1]

The *Hashcaboth de Legados* were recited on Monday, Thursday and the New Moon before the reading of the Torah. On other days these prayers were said after the *Kaddish Tithkabbal*. However, the *hashcaboth* during the first eleven months of mourning were recited after the *Kaddish Tithkabbal* and before returning the Torah to the Ark.

It was customary to go to the altar and contribute in behalf of the parnassim and the families in mourning.

The service ended with the prayer *Zadik Ata Hashem* — Righteous art Thou, O Lord — and a *hashcabah* for one deceased seven days, thirty days or eleven months.

In the evening after the pupils of the *medras* had read the *Perashah* and the *Haftarah, kaddish* was recited and the afternoon prayer (*Minḥah*) began.

Morning and evening services were conducted daily as late as 1888.

Friday evening the *hashcaboth* were recited before sunset between *Minḥah* and *'Arbith,* and offerings were made for the health of the parnassim and mourning families.

[1] See Emmanuel, *Guedolé Saloniki Ledorotam,* no. 160, p. 106, about this custom.

The custom was to say *Boré peri haguefen* — who creates the fruit of the vine — and not *hagafen*.[2]

Before saying grace after meals, the entire family would sing the following verses, now chanted only twice yearly in the *sukkah* of the synagogue:

BENDIGAMOS[3]

-1-

Bendigamos á el Altísimo,
Al Señor que nos creó,
Démosle agradecimiento,
Por los bienes que nos dió.

-2-

Alabado sea su santo nombre,
Porque siempre nos apiadó,
Odu Ladonai ki tob,
Ki legnolam jasdó.

-3-

Bendigamos á el Altísimo,
Por el pan primeramente,
Y después por los manjares,[4]
Que comimos juntamente.

-4-

Pues comimos y bebimos alegremente,
Su merced nunca nos faltó,
Load al Señor que es bueno,
Que para siempre su merced.

-5-

Bendita sea la casa esta
Que nunca manque en ella fiesta,
Tarde, mañana y siesta,
A nos y á los hijos de Israel.[5]

Before the reading of the Torah, a *hashcabah* was said for persons deceased during the week and for those dead thirty days or eleven months. Then followed the *hashcaboth de legados*. Today the *hashcabah* text has been modified to conform to Reconstructionist ideology. This literally is a breaking of faith with those testators who made their bequest confident that the traditional text would be maintained forever (page 505).

Every time the Ark is opened on Saturdays and festivals the rabbi or his substitute intones the following prayer in Portuguese for the Queen, the Royal Dutch Family and for the Governor and Magistrates of Curaçao:

A Sua Majestade Juliana, Rainha dos Paises Baixos e a seu Real Consorte. As sereníssimas Princesas suas filhas. Aos descendentes da Casa Real de Orange Nassao; aos ilustres membros que concorrem no Governo destas terras e ao nobre venerável Excelentíssimo Senhor Governador desta ilha e a todos Magistrados en ela.[6]

---

[2] Subject of debate during the Piza affair (see above, p. 306).

[3] See Kayserling, *Revue des Etudes Juives*, XXII:124, and Remedios, p. 180, regarding these verses.

[4] The old text was *conduchos*.

[5] These verses recall several of this type formerly sung in Salonika.

[6] At the remonstrance of the author the original text of this prayer has been maintained by the United Congregation.

A person called to the Torah is designated as *Habaḥur* if he is a bachelor; as *Hagebir* if married, and as *Hayyashish* if he is sixty or over. If these people served or are serving as *parnas*, they are designated, respectively, as *Habaḥur Hanehmad* (the precious young man), *Hagebir Hane'ela* (the distinguished gentleman) and *Hayyashish Hanikhbad* (the honorable elder). The rabbi is entitled in accordance with his learning and hierarchic level: *Morenu Harab do Kahal Kadosh* for Chief Rabbi; *Haham Hashalem* for associate rabbi, and *Haham Hane'ela* for a learned hazzan rabbi-substitute; *Hamaskil ve Nabon Ne'im Zemiroth Israel* for the first cantor; and *Ribbi* for a teacher in the *medras*.[7]

Before distributing the honors the hazzan would say: *Bekhavod leḥalek hamiẓ-voth* — the honors will be distributed with reverence. These were apportioned as follows: the first to a member of the Cohen (priestly) Family, the second to a Levite provided that a Cohen preceded him, the third to a very honorable man, the sixth to a respected person, and the seventh to an elder. In the absence of a Cohen in the synagogue, a respected man was called up first. A Levite was never called second in the absence of a Cohen, or third. On the other hand, a lad was called to read the *Haftarah*. The custom of reading the *Haftarah* for the deceased was never practiced. Today only four people are called to the Torah, and the Cohen and Levy are no longer privileged.

A newly-married man or the father of a boy born during the week was called up third on the first Saturday of his marriage or birth of his son, while the father of a girl was called sixth.

The rabbi or his substitute was called up third on the Sabbaths of *Beshallah* (Song of Moses) and *Vaethhanan* (Ten Commandments); seventh on the Sabbath of *Itro* (T. C.), and fifth on the first day of Shabu'oth (T. C.) and on the seventh day of Passover (S. M.).

While the father went up to the Torah his sons, and sometimes his daughters, remained standing until he descended from the pulpit.

On the Sabbath of a Bar Miẓvah, circumcision, marriage or installation of parnassim, as well as on Simḥath Torah, a *surah* of from twelve to fourteen persons was called to the Torah.

Everyone called up to the Torah was required to offer in behalf of the deceased, for the health of a friend in mourning, and lastly for the health of the president and parnassim. The donations were made in *patacas* and its units, especially in *soldos*. Up to recent years the *franco*, worth a half florin, was the general monetary unit offered. Today the amounts given are no longer announced (see page 507).

Rosh Ḥodesh was announced on *Shabbath Yehi Raẓon* in the following manner: *Mahar umahorató manan e pois manan, primeira feira, segunda, terça, cuarta, quinta, sexta-feira, Shabbath Kodesh es Rosh Hodesh*.

Saturday afternoon, after the reading of the Torah and just before the 'Amidah, the *hashcaboth* were recited. If the first seven days of mourning ended on Saturday night, the *Ẓiduk Hadin* prayer for the deceased was said after 'Arbith.

---

[7] See our *Precious Stones*, pp. 84-85, about these titles.

ROSH HODESH

A special prayer for rain was recited on the first of every month during the reading of the 'Amidah at the paragraph beginning with *Shemah Kolenu* — Hear our voice.

On the occasion of a circumcision, the "pizmon" *Berukhim Atem* — Blessed be Ye — was chanted before Psalm 117 of the *Hallel*.

The Mahamad would inform the members of the community of the decisions taken during the previous month and announce certain important communal events. This was called *Hakhraza*.

ROSH HASHANAH AND YOM KIPPUR

On Rosh Hashanah people greet one another with: *escrito*, and on Yom Kippur, *escrito y sellado*, that is, May you be inscribed and sealed in the Book of Life. Until about 1930 Rosh Hashanah was still observed two days.

The conservative members did not permit any reform relating to the rites of Yom Kippur. However, Hazzan Duque introduced the organ and Hazzan Jessurun Cardozo eliminated certain portions of the liturgy as well as the 'Arbith prayer in order to enable the public to observe the blessing of the moon.

The honors on Yom Kippur are distributed in this fashion: Before nightfall the treasurer kindles a special candlestick. The oldest member of the Council of Elders opens the doors of the Ark during the *Kal Nidre* and the president of the community does so at *Ne'ilah*. On Yom Kippur Eve before the chanting of the *Kal Nidre* (whose melody was similar to that chanted by the Sephardim of Turkey and the Balkans), ten Scrolls of the Law were brought forth from the Ark to be carried by the parnassim. Haham Chumaceiro reduced them to three ever since Yom Kippur, 1863. The scrolls and the *tebah* are covered with a white silk velvet cloth on Yom Kippur and formerly on Hosha'na Rabbah also. The Bridegroom of the Law accompanied the hazzan to the *tebah* during the morning prayers.

A *Mi Sheberakh* prayer was recited for the people imprisoned by the Inquisition: *A todos nossos irmaõs presos por la Inquisição*.

The rabbi or his substitute did not descend from the *tebah* on Yom Kippur Eve. The assistant hazzan accompanied the Scrolls of the Law to the altar.

During the morning service the body of parnassim was called up individually to the Torah.

Before *Ne'ilah* a *hashcabah* is recited for all those who bequeathed forty *patacas* or more to the synagogue. Although this list is very long, the parnassim of the United Congregation, at my written disapproval, did not and I hope they will never dare to abridge it, above, pages 282, 511. In this manner the community pays well-merited homage to previous generations.

The *Ne'ilah* prayer used to be recited by the *Morenu Harab* who was accompanied to the *tebah* by two parnassim.

HOSHA'NA RABBAH

Seven Scrolls of the Law were removed from the Ark and placed on the *tebah*. Seven circuits, without the scrolls but with the *lulab*, were made. At the end of each circuit the *shofar* was sounded. People wished one another *escrito y sellado en libro de vidas*. This beautiful service has been abolished.

SHEMINI 'AZERETH

Before starting the prayer for rain in the *Musaf* service, the honor of opening the doors to the Holy Ark was assigned to the oldest plantation owner.

SIMHATH TORAH

Until about a century ago it was a great honor to be named *Hatan Torah* — Bridegroom of the Law, or *Hatan Bereshith* — Bridegroom of the beginning. The *hatanim* were accompanied to the altar by two respected members of the community. The *Hatan Torah* and his companion took places on the north side of the altar while the *Hatan Bereshith* and his companion seated themselves on the south side. On *Shabbath Bereshith* the *hatanim* changed places. Ten Scrolls of the Law were taken out on *Simhath Torah* with each bearer accompanied by a person holding a lighted candle in hand. In honor of the *hatanim*, fourteen people designated by the *hatanim* were called to the Torah. The cantor chanted several verses composed by the brothers David and Abraham de Imanuel da Silva, by Aaron David Hamis Vas, Moshe Jeudah Piza and Isaac de Jacob Hizquiau Lopez. The sexton L. Penha was not sure about the custom of making circuits with the Scrolls of the Law. After *Sukkot* a feast was held for the slaves.

A special service was celebrated in honor of the *hatanim* during *Shabbath Bereshith*. Also on this day fourteen persons designated by the *hatanim* were called up to the Torah. Since the merged Congregation adopted the triennial cycle of Torah reading, these joyful services almost disappeard.

HANUKKAH

The sexton distributed a candle to every member to kindle the Hanukkah lights in the home. The Hanukkah lamp was properly set on the south side of the synagogue; today, before the altar. The hazzan would not descend from the *tebah* the nights of Hanukkah. His assistant lit the Hanukkah lights.

PURIM

On the Sabbath preceding Purim the *Mi Kamokha* of Rabbi Jeudah Halevi was chanted, and the second Parnas of Talmud Torah was installed. After the recital of the *hashcaboth* and the prayer for sailors and sea travelers, the *Kupoth Hashekel* — four silver bowls — were passed out to the public for a collection. (The proceeds of one bowl was destined for the poor of Jerusalem.) The public then made offerings to the hazzanim and servants of the synagogue. Afterwards the Book of Esther was read. Before starting the hazzan would say: *Bekhavod likro Hamegillah* — the Book of Esther will be read with reverence. During the reading he was accompanied by one of the parnassim.

In the home the celebrants chanted fitting verses in Spanish, such as Moses L. Penha's "El Triumfo de Esther" (1847), which follows. (He also composed two other Purim songs: "La Gloria Israelita" [1842] and "Heroismo de Mordoqueo" [March, 1849].)

EL TRIUMFO DE ESTHER [8]

-1-

Celebremos amigos este dia - Viva!
Purim con placer la alegría - Viva!
Salvos, libres de Aman atroz.
Cantemos juntos en alta voz - Viva, viva, viva...

-2-

La bella Esther cual sol brillante - Viva!
Gran Sultana por su Rey amante - Viva!
Gracia le pidió por su nación,
Y se la concedió con afección - Viva, viva, viva...

-3-

Acusa al vil cual condenado - Muera!
Senténciale Asuero guindado - Muera!
Sublima al fiel hebreo,
A mayor pompa que el reo - Viva, viva, viva...

-4-

Protegidos por la divina mano - Viva!
Vengados del infernal tirano - Viva!
Castigado su vil altivez,
Repetiremos a cada vez - Viva, viva, viva...

-5-

Reunidos pues hoy festejamos - Viva!
Con banquetes, bailes celebramos - Viva!
Al gran Mardoqueo grata memoria,
Y á la inmortal Esther la gloria - Viva, viva, viva.

Early in the 19th century, at the request of the parnassim, the governor authorized the Jews to use fireworks and parade in the streets in costume and mask. Skits were presented. These festivities sometimes lasted as many as eight days.

Up to a hundred years ago Purim was celebrated with much enthusiasm in Curaçao and possibly was the gayest of all the festivals.[9] People still greet one another with: *Purim Alegre* — Happy Purim.

[8] According to a manuscript in our possession.
[9] *WIG*, 1927-29, p. 516.

PESAḤ

Two days before Passover the sexton distributed a candle to each member *para escombrar el Hamez* — to search after leaven. On Passover Eve everyone received *ḥaroseth*.

The *Hallel* was chanted during the 'Arbith service. Each person conducted the *Seder* in his home. Hazzan Duque changed this practice by having the *Haggadah* read in the synagogue courtyard. Today a large *Seder* is held at a club in the city. The text of the *Haggadah* is Reconstructionist, and the dietary laws are not observed.

On the first day of Pesaḥ, after the reading of the *hashcaboth*, the president opens the Holy Ark. The cantor chants the 67th Psalm and the choir sings the *Tehilath*, thus to commemorate the anniversary of the synagogue. In the 18th century the boys of the *medras* would sing *Los Cantares* — Song of Songs.

'OMER

This is the period of counting the days between Passover and Pentecost. On Saturdays during this period, after the first *Kaddish Tithkabbal* prior to the recitation of the *hashcaboth*, the hazzan would say to the public: *A os Senhores que não contaraõ o Homer que contem sem bençaõ* — Those gentlemen who have not counted the 'Omer should do so without the preliminary blessing.

Until two generations ago no one moved to another house during the first thirty-three days of the 'Omer. Sexton Lopez Penha was not familiar with any special service for Lag la 'Omer — the 33rd day of the 'Omer. This was a very popular service among Sephardim of the Middle East. On the last day of the 'Omer the hazzan would add the words: *Sheem shib'ah shabu'oth temimoth* — which are seven full weeks.

SHABU'OTH

On Shabu'oth Eve, after supper, the faithful returned to the synagogue to read with their rabbi the *Tikun*, a special ritual. Until 1864, the anniversary of the synagogue of 1703 was celebrated on this holiday. Also, the first Parnas of Talmud Torah was installed.

TISH'AH BE-AB

On *Shabbath Ḥazon*, the Sabbath preceding Tish'ah be-Ab, the Parnas of Hebra (burials) was installed. The *haftarah* of this Sabbath was recited in Hebrew and in Spanish as well. On Tish'ah be-Ab the pulpit and at least one Scroll of the Law were draped in black. The dirges were chanted by the rabbi, cantors and certain pious members previously chosen by the rabbi. The *haftarah* was recited in Hebrew and Spanish. At the end of the service, as the hazzan was about to leave the synagogue, he said to the public: *Morir debemos* — We must all die one day. They responded: *Ya lo sabemos* — That we know.

In the past the observants would close their stores on this day while their less observant brothers conducted business *a media puerta* — with the door half open.

SELIḤOTH

Seliḥoth (penitential) prayers were recited during Elul in the morning service by a special hazzan. Usually he was a very pious, venerable man who was called *Hazzan de Seliḥoth*.

SERVICES ON SPECIAL OCCASIONS

CIRCUMCISION

A special service was conducted in the home of the newborn son on the night preceding the circumcision which took place in the synagogue the following morning. The community still has the special chair formerly employed for this ceremony (illus. 57). When the infant was returned to his mother's room, he was accompanied by several boys bearing lighted candles.

YONATI

This service to name a newborn girl took place in the home usually forty days after birth. The first verse of the *Yonati* prayer (Song of Solomon 2:14) was chanted in Spanish.

HAGOMEL

As soon as she is able to leave the house after a wholesome confinement, the mother presents herself with the child before the Ark on any week day to recite the *Hagomel*. This is the blessing on escape from danger. The rabbi accompanies her.

BAR MIẒVAH

The celebrant used to read from the Torah the *Perashah* coinciding with the Sabbath of his celebration. Haham Chumaceiro introduced the reading from a second scroll of Deuteronomy X:12-22.

WEDDING

The *Ketubah* or marriage contract was written entirely in Hebrew after the text used by the Sephardim of Amsterdam. Since women formerly were not protected by Dutch Law, the *ketubah* was a very important document in her behalf. This document contained the dowry, at times with a brief inventory of the goods she brought. It was signed by the bridegroom, the rabbi, the president and the treasurer of the community. Today it is signed by the young couple, the rabbi and the parnassim who, in keeping with old tradition, retain a copy in the synagogue archives.

1091

The bridegroom had to include as *tosefeth* (a supplement), in behalf of his wife, fifty percent of the dowry she brought to the marriage. If he died before his wife, then she had the right to receive payment of her original dowry plus the supplement. Only after this payment was the decedent's estate divided among his heirs, even if they were his own children.

If the wife predeceased her husband without leaving any issue of the marriage, her heirs were entitled to half the original dowry, but not the fifty percent addition. If she left children, the husband inherited her entire dowry. However, it was subject to parnassim control if the children were minors (see page 386n).

The wedding ring for the bride is inspected by the rabbi and the parnassim to make certain that it has the required value.

Marriages took place in the synagogue in the morning on any day of the month whether the moon was growing or waning. Since 1887 marriages usually are performed in the evening.

MISCELLANEOUS PRAYERS

TEVILAH

The women took their ritual bath at nightfall except on Friday and the eve of Jewish festivals when they bathed in the afternoon.

BIRKATH COHANIM

The Priestly Blessing was said only during the holy days, festivals and *Shabbath Bereshith*. It was abolished after the schism of 1864 (page 383) for want of members of the Cohen Family.

TIKUN

The *Tikun* is the prayer the rabbi recites at the dedication of a new home. Members of the family nail a *Mezuzah* on each doorpost of the house.

LEVAYAH

This prayer was recited in the synagogue before one set out on a trip. Friends and other travelers made donations to the synagogue for his safe return.

RESGATE DE ALMA

This prayer was said for the ransom of the soul of someone gravely ill. Afterwards the name Hisquiau or Rephael was added to a man's name, and Hannah to a woman's.

LAST MOMENTS

If the dying person was conscious, he recited the special confession in the presence of the rabbi. Otherwise the rabbi said the prayers for him. During these agonizing moments, seven candles were lit. Immediately upon death, two were left. See *Precious Stones of the Jews of Curaçao*, pp. 75-96, for full details on burial and mourning services.

FORMULAS USED ON SPECIAL OCCASIONS

The prayers used in the offerings contained the following formulas in Portuguese intermingled with several Spanish and Hebrew words.

For the deceased:	Tantos soldos Shemen Lamaor por el descanso de (name of the deceased) . . . .
For the health of the survivors:	Para que Deus lhes conceda vidas largas.
For a speedy recovery:	Para que Deus lhe conceda Refua Shelema e para que continue em saude perfeita.
For an anniversary:	Que Deus lhe deixe contar muitos anos de bom.
On escape from danger:	Hagomel- Que sua saida seja para bem.
For rain:	Para que Deus nos conceda chuva de benção.
Traveling:	Para que Deus lhe leve ao porto de seu desejo e lhe livre de todos maus encontros.
Safe arrival:	Que sua chegada seja para bem.
For the receipt of good news:	Que Deus lhe mantenha com bem e mande boas noticias de él.
No specification:	Por sua intenção.
For the health of the parnassim and members of the community:	Pela saude dos senhores Parnassim, Yehidim deste Kahal Kadosh, para que Deus lhes aumente e prospere.
For the health of the president of the community:	Pela saude do Rosh Hakahal.
For the health of the Chief Rabbi:	Pela saude do Morenu Harab.
On the installation of the parnassim:	Pela saude dos Senhores Parnassim salientes e entrantes.
For the health of the Ḥatanim:	Pela saude dos senhores Hatanim, que sempre se entreguem ao cargo de Misvoth.

For the newlyweds:	Pela saude dos senhores noivos, para que Deus lhes haga felizes.
On the birth of a son:	Pela saude de Bangal a Berit, sua esposa e recem-nascido, pais e mães, parentes que vejam grandes gustos.
For a *Bar Miẓvah*:	Pela graça de haver chegado a este estado, pais e mães, parentes que vejam grandes gustos.
On Rosh Hashanah and Yom Kippur:	Para que Deus nos escreva em livros de vida.
On the three festivals:	Para que Deus lhe (*or*, nos) conceda festas alegres.
The Rabbi, Hazzan and Sexton solicit their own health:	Pela mi propria saude e que Deus me conceda muitos anos no serviço desta Santa Casa.[10]

These, in general contour, are the most important rites and customs which the Curaçoan Jew zealously transmitted from generation to generation. With very few exceptions they have been abandoned.

[10] See Emmanuel, "El Portugues en la Sinagoga 'Mikvé Israel' de Curaçao," *Oẓar Yehudé Sefarad*, I (Jerusalem, 1959), pp. XXV-XXXI.

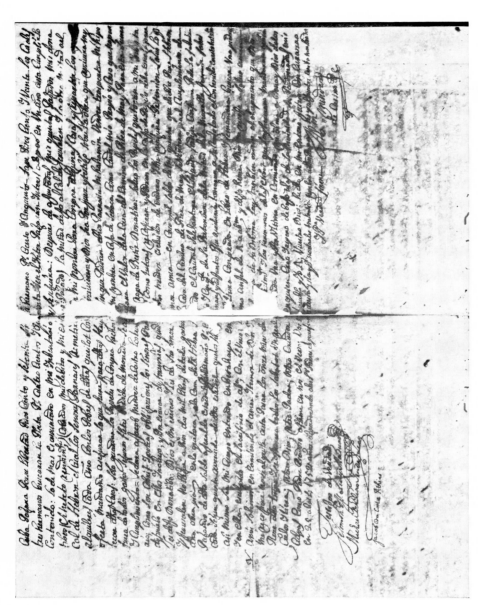

298. WILL OF ABRAHAM MENDES DE CASTRO (LAST PAGE) WITH SIGNATURES OF
TESTAMENTARY WITNESSES SELOMOH DE ISAAC LEVY MADURO, MICHAEL DE ELIAO
JEUDAH LEAO, JACOB DA COSTA ATHIAS, 1752

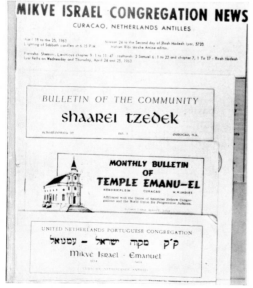

INTRODUCCION.

Desde que el Pueblo de Ifrael fueron captivados a *Babilona*, mefclaron fu *Lengua fanta* con la *lengua Chaldea*; por lo qual muchos de fus hijos los nafcidos ally, aprendieron defde la Cuna aquella lengua, perdiendo la Noticia y la perfeccion de la lengua Hebrayca; por lo que ordenó *Ezrá* para que el pueblo entiendieffe lo que leian en los Libros de la Ley, que fe traduxeffe en lengua Chaldayca; de modo que havian dos Lectores, uno que dizia el verço por el *Sepher Torá*, y otro lo paraphrazeava en Chaldaico.

Bien es verdad, que al tiempo prezente, tambien la Lengua Chaldayca, no es comunmente Conocida, no obftante nos quedó de obligacion, meldar cada qual *la Paraffa de la femana* una vez en Chaldaico defpues de haverla dicho dos vezes en Hebrayco: pero es Jufto que para mayor Inteligencia de la *Biblia*, tenga cada qual la traducion en la *lengua Materna*, por lo que fe ha Imprimido muchas vezes la *Biblia Efpañola* con mucha exactitud, por fer la Traducion della la mas propia a la Letra, no anteponiendo una Palabra por otra, ni tan poco efcufando palabras; pues la Palabra de Dios, es perfecta, por lo que es mucho mejor feguir tal qual en la traducion, como eftá en el original.

Con todo effo de haver varias ediciones, no fervia de Provecho Imediato, a los que meditando en la Biblia Hebrayca, y dudando el fentido de alguna Palabra, no podian luego, hallar la repuefta de fu duda, y aun que pudian tomar dos Biblias al tiempo de la Meditacion, cauzaria efto no poco de travajo, para bufcar el Texto en que dudavan.

Eftas razones (y puede fer) que aun otras muchas, le movieron al Muy Zelozo y Magnanimo Sr. *Abraham Mendes de Caftro, morador de Curaçao* a poner en execucion, efta prezente obra de la *Biblia Hebraica y Efpañola en dos Colunas*, empeçando y finiendo cada una de las Colunas Igualmente, fin difcrepcion de una palabra; y para mayor facilidad, eftán en ambas las Colunas *los Numeros de los Capitulos y verfos*, por lo que nos perfuadimos ferá efta obra acepta con el aplauzo general;

299. INTRODUCTION, ABRAHAM M. DE CASTRO BIBLE, 1762

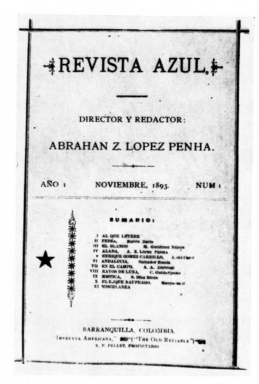

300. REVISTA AZUL OF ABRAHAM Z. LOPEZ PENHA, FIRST ISSUE, 1893, PAGE 454

301. CONGREGATIONAL BULLETINS, CURAÇAO

302. CURAÇOAN PAPERS OWNED OR EDITED BY CURAÇOAN JEWS

PERSONALIA

ABRAHAM MENDES DE CASTRO
1689-1762

EIGHTEENTH CENTURY JEWRY of Curaçao counted among her men of good will a certain Abraham Mendes de Castro. He was born in 1689, most probably in Spain. His father was also called Abraham, sure proof that both were Marranos, as his mother Esther most probably was. Castro arrived at Curaçao from Bordeaux about 1707. That year he is encountered in Curaçao purchasing slaves from the Dutch West India Company (WICA 202, p. 225). He was joined a little later by his brother Isaac and his nephews Jacob and Daniel, also from Bordeaux. Isaac died in 1733 and his bachelor son Jacob in 1754.

Castro dealt in lumber. Like most businessmen of the day, he owned a boat, the *Arke Noach*, jointly with Abraham and Joseph Sasso.

Many of his coreligionists in Curaçao contributed funds to various benevolent societies in Amsterdam, among them the Misheneth Zekenim of which Castro was a member. He also belonged to three benevolent societies in Curaçao. In 1751 he donated to the Mikvé Israel three mahogany beams for the Holy Ark which is still in use.

Castro had a special fondness for the Holy Land and the diffusion of the Bible. On April 30, 1760, he sent 900 pesos to Moses de Chaves, his representative in Amsterdam, to have Proops print a two-column Hebrew-Spanish Bible in two volumes. Chaves meanwhile died and certain difficulties arose. Castro then requestes Chaves' son Aron to have Ribbi Jeudah Piza and a certain Manuel Calo take charge of reviewing, binding and distributing the book. Half the profits from its sale was destined for the community of Jerusalem and the other half to the Hebron community, this in addition to the 3,000-4,000 pesos he had intended to bequeath to these holy cities. Castro also requested the Amsterdam parnassim to meet with Proops in order to "come to an understanding and settle the differences between the parties." His letter closed with a prayer to God to "remove us from the Captivity of over 2,000 years, installing Ruler and King in Jerusalem" (OAC 879, Dec. 4, 1760).

Castro never saw his Bible; he died on October 10, 1762. The first volume appeared, in folio, later in the year. In the preface Proops, while crediting Castro with the idea of the publication, stated that he had printed the Bible at his own expense since Castro's remittance was insufficient. At least he mentioned Castro as author of the project. Not so the poet Abraham Yehisquiya Bassan who had words of praise only for Proops. Of course there was no question of profits going to the two holy cities. With great difficulty Castro's nephew Daniel obtained a few copies of the Bible in 1772 in return for the 900 pesos his uncle had remitted (OAC 944, no. 29).

This handsome Bible is a reprint of the Ferrara de Usque edition. It has a feature seldom encountered in other Bibles: The introduction carries verses formerly sung before and after the reading of each important book. These were peculiarly Sephardic and were sung in Salonika until a short while ago. See illus. 299.

A prudent man, Castro drew up his will in 1752. It is one of the most original encountered in the old archives of Curaçao. It is a testimony to his deep faith in God, his love for the Holy Land and his humanity toward the sick poor of his community and his slaves. He charged his executors to conduct the memorial services for him in keeping with Spanish-Portuguese Jewish custom, and made a magnificent plea to his nephews to revere God, and observe His Divine Law. Written in Spanish and translated into Dutch, both copies of the will are preserved in the old archives of Curaçao at The Hague. Our English translation follows.

> Realizing that life is not in the hands of man but is governed by the only living God Almighty in whom I believe and adore, whose Divine Mosaic Law I, His slave, follow and venerate with all my heart and soul and His greatness and mercy profess, I Ab^m Mendez de Castro, son of Ab^m Mendez de Castro and Mrs. Ester Mendez de Castro, of Jewish origin, in full possession of my senses, declare this to be my last will and testament, irrevocable by virtue of divine and human laws.
>
> I leave all that I possess and what He has granted to me and is [therefore] His, to my heir, the Almighty God of Ysrael, disowning all sorts of blood relations on earth; and so with His permission and Divine help I make these bequests and testament in His Holy Name as I submit to His Divine will, amen.
>
> I appoint as executors and guardians the Parnassim and adjuntos of this island.
>
> I bequeath to the Hebra [Guemiluth Hasadim] of this island the house purchased from Marcos Basarne located between [that of] the Widow Jacob Fos [Vos] and [of] Mr. Jan Amaño opposite the worthy Haham's house. It shall be rented to tenants approved by the Messrs. Parnassim who shall pay the rent regularly and deliver same to the parnas of the Hebra to help maintain the sick poor under its care. The Hebra shall not distribute said rents to any other charity or mortgage or sell said house. For carrying out this objective, God will approve the work and grant complete health and prosperity to the Congregation for many years.
>
> The house purchased from Yshak Pereira and that from the wife of Elias Dubernar and the one located on Pi[e]ter de May (Maai) Road where the wood is, I bequeath to Daniel and Jacob Mendez de Castro (equally) for them and their legitimate heirs through marriage. The deeds to said houses shall remain in the Chest of Documents at the Synagogue. Neither the said

Mendez nor their heirs shall be able to mortgage, transfer or sell said houses to anyone. In the event of the death of the abovenamed [nephews], God forbid, one-third of the rent or value of said houses shall go to the Hebra [Guemiluth Hasadim] of this island, another third to the Congregation of Jerusalem and the remaining third to the Congregation of Hebron, without prejudice. The said [legatees] shall take care of repairs and painting out of the rents received so that the houses are saleable when there are no living heirs. Of course, while they are still alive, there would be no reason to break this, my last will and testament.

I give and bequeath to Daniel and Jacob Mendez de Castro a parcel of land on Pi[e]ter de May (Maai) Road purchased from Mordhay Pereira, opposite the house formerly of Selomoh Senior and that of the Widow Craneveld to the left on the way to Pi[e]ter de May (Maai).

The canuco [cunuco] shall not be sold while Serafiña lives; afterwards, the earnings therefrom shall become part of my residuary estate, the deed to same having been registered in my name by Johannis Evertsz in the Government Secretariat.

I order the following gifts and escaboth [bequests for memorial prayers] to be made: For memorial prayers for my father, Abm Mendez de Castro, who died on the 10th of Kislev, forty pesos; for my mother, Mrs. Ester Mendez de Castro, who died on the 15th of Kislev, forty pesos; for my brother Yshak Mendez de Castro, forty pesos; one hundred pesos for my memorial services that God may receive me. To the Esiva [Yeshiva] of the elderly [Misheneth Zekenim] of Amsterdam, eighty pesos which shall be remitted by bill of exchange to the parnassim then presiding; to the three esibot [Yeshivot of Curaçao] of which I am a member, namely, the Honen Dalyn [Dalim], Pene Sabat and the Esiba of Semuel de Casseres, twenty-five pesos each; to the daughter of Benjamin de Rosa, to the daughter of Aron Machado and to the daughter of Ysaque [Mendez?] de Castro, twenty-five pesos each; fifty pesos to be distributed monthly among the poor of the Sedaca, I repeat, fifty pesos.

I also order that all work started by my negroes shall be finished and supplied with what I would have adjusted. Any lumber then remaining, white or mahogany, shall be sold at public auction for the benefit of my estate. Each of my negroes and negresses shall take his chest without opposition. Certificates of manumission shall be given to those hereinbelow named: Serafiña, children, grandchildren and her entire family; Esperanza, children, grandchildren and her entire family. Sesilia, Bastiaan and Inguito are discharged and shall be given a certificate of manumission. Acara owes forty pesos for his freedom while Agustin owes fifty (50) pesos. Caba must pay one hundred seventy pesos for his freedom; Sire, his brother, one hundred fifty pesos, and Sape, one hundred twenty pesos; said three brothers to look for the money [namely], four hundred forty pesos on which they shall meanwhile pay interest at 8 pc. per year until fully paid off. The rest [of the slaves] are mentioned in my inventory.

After the settlement of my accounts and payment of my debts, funeral expenses and legacies, I leave half of the remainder of my estate to the Community of Jerusalem and the other half to the Community of Hebron, to be remitted by the Messrs. Parnassim, in my name, for the purpose of buying several houses and annually distributing the rent realized therefrom among the poor of said communities, as the monies are received. And may God be judge and witness over the work that will receive my gift. [The Parnassim of Curaçao] shall send over whomever they wish to said communities to make certain that neither the Hahamim nor the Parnassim of those communities [i.e., Jerusalem and Hebron] sell, transfer or mortgage said houses, their mission being only to keep the deeds to such investment, in my name, in the Poor Chest. And should there not be enough after costs, insurance, postage or loss of money, then there shall be added the value of the house on Pi[e]ter de May (Maai) Road to make up the deficit.

To Jacob Mendez de Castro I make a gift of the household furniture and wearing apparel, excepting the papers concerning my estate. As these constitute deeds, mortgages and obligations, the Messrs. Parnassim, as my executors, shall collect them and place them in the Record Chest of the Synagogue for their use exclusively. In order to avoid disputes, [I declare that] the said Mendez are excluded as heirs and shall have no claim whatsoever except to the legacies made to them. God is my heir and may He impart to them love and reverence for Him.

In the event that the balance of my account set aside for Hebron and Jerusalem does not reach 2,000 pesos net (free of all costs), the house of Pi[e]ter de May (Maai) Road shall be sold to make up the deficit for such charity. If there is any money left over in my estate, then to the house bequeathed to the Hebra shall be erected another story as required, payment of one hundred fifty pesos to be made from said remainder to Gerard Striddels and Jan Amaño for their claim to half the party wall built according to the bill received from said Striddels.

The Messrs. Parnassim and adjuntos in charge of the administration of my estate and execution of my last will and testament shall also see that my body is buried in the betahayn [Beth Hahaim] in the prepaid grave recorded in the Cemetery Register, and they shall send away for a tombstone on which shall be engraved Ab[raha]m's Sacrifice, with the verse: "And the angel of the Lord called unto him out of heaven, and said: 'Abraham, Abraham.' And he said: 'Here am I.'" May God gather me unto Him, amen.

To my nephews I recommend the love and reverence of God and the observance of His Holy Law. I also order that the apartment from whence God will call me unto Him should not be rented until eleven months after my death, and that the members of the esibot [yeshivot] to which I belong shall send someone to pray during that period, and every Saturday one real shall be offered for each [yeshiva].

Finally, I commend my soul to Adonay, God of Heaven and Earth, our God, our Father, our Creator in whom I believe and hope under the wings of His Divinity to be forgiven for all my sins, as promised us by the Merciful Father in the verse: "You the People, and I Adonay, your God."

Done in my full senses in Curazao, the 25th [of] April, year 1752. Though grateful to the Fathers of the Orphans of this island and [but] wishing to spare them trouble, I designate the said Parnassim and adjuntos abovenamed [as administrators of my estate],

And verily sign Ab.ᵐ Mendez de Castro
True Witnesses:
Selomoh de Is. Levij Maduro:
Michael de Eliao Jeudah Leao
Jacob Da Costa Athias*, illus. 298

A few days after his death, the parnassim took an inventory of Castro's estate. Among other assets it listed thirteen books, a Sabbath lamp, a *hanukkiah*, five houses, two parcels of real estate, four slaves with two children (others had been freed earlier), and accounts receivable of 630 pesos (OAC 887, no. 97). In accordance with this instructions the parnassim sold the houses left for the Holy Land cities Jerusalem and Hebron, and remitted the moneys to the Amsterdam parnassim for transmission to the beneficiaries (page 154).

HIS TOMBSTONE

Castro left a beautiful house for the sick poor of the community, and several bequests to his nephew Daniel. Nevertheless, neither the parnassim nor Daniel carried out his wish to head the gravestone with the verse from Abraham's Sacrifice (Genesis 22:11). We have therefore added it to his epitaph as follows:

[ויקרא אליו מלאך ה" מן השמים
ויאמר אברהם אברהם ויאמר הנני]

S.ᴬ

DE EL AIASIS BE

ANIHBAD AB.ᴹ MENDES

DE CASTRO QUE

FALESIO EN 23 DE

TISRY A.ᵒ 5523 QUE

CORESPONDE A 10 DE

OCTUBRO A.ᵒ 176(3)[2]

ת" נ" צ" ב" ה

* OAC 834, no. 267; OAC 884, no. 196; OAC 887, no. 25.

The venerable Castro's epitaph — listed as C 968 in my Catalogue of the Old Jewish Cemetery of Curaçao — is one of 2,536 epitaphs in manuscript copied by me between 1937 and 1938 from the tombstones and saved from total obliteration by the gases emitted from the adjacent petroleum refinery (illus. 8, 9, 74).

JOSSY M. L. MADURO

1891-1964

I had intended to write short biographic sketches of Curaçao's most illustrious Jews of the past 120 years. The material had been prepared. But after the merger of the communities (Chapter XXV), it seemed pointless to bring these Sephardic notables to life. Then Jossy M. L. Maduro died suddenly. Suddenly it became imperative to perpetuate this man for the great pride and interest he took in the history of his community.

He was born in Curaçao on October 12, 1891, to Moses L. Maduro (1863-1911), a direct descendant of the first Moshe Levy Maduro to reach Curaçao in 1672, for whom he was named. Until about a generation ago the Jews of Curaçao perpetuated the names of their grandfathers and great-grandfathers, and rightly so. A Jew of Curaçao called Jeosuah, Josias or Manuel is descended, either on his mother's or father's side, from the following forebears: the first, from Jeosuah Henriquez; the second, from Haham Pardo, and the third from Manuel Alvares Correa. The first was in Curaçao before 1656 and the others came in 1674. Jossy Maduro also believed in this lineage. His father Moses married Adela, the daughter of Jeosuah Naar Jr. and Sarah Pereira Brandao in 1887, and had five children: Salomo, b. 1890; Jossy; Benjamin, b. 1897; Rebecca, b. 1889 and m. 1908 to her cousin Salomon de Mordechay Levy Maduro; and Sarah, b. 1907 and m. 1928 to Frank Pereira Brandao. Although the son of Salomon Elias Levy Maduro (1814-1883), founder of Maduro & Sons, Jossy's father went into business for himself. He ran the Palais Royal and also had several business interests in Coro.

Jossy's maternal grandfather Jeosuah Naar Jr., whose biblical name Jossy proudly bore and so highly proclaimed, was a descendant of the pioneer Jeosuah Henriquez above-mentioned and of Jacob Naar who arrived in Curaçao about 1676 (*Precious Stones*, pp. 174-75). Jacob Naar married Jeosuah Henriquez' daughter and, as customary, named his second son Jeosuah. This name has been carried down, especially in the Naar and Henriquez families, from generation to generation, until now. Jossy's grandfather, Jeosuah Naar Jr., for many years was hazzan of the Reform community founded in 1864 (page 389).

Like all the boys of the community, Jossy also attended the Reverend Joseph H. M. Chumaceiro's Hebrew School. Spirited and independent, he would not submit to a certain discipline, even in the island's elementary school, and was expelled. Nevertheless, his father (a member of the well-known Curaçao Historical Society founded in 1896, member of the Algemeen Nederlandsch Verbond and other cultural societies) gave him the best education that Curaçao

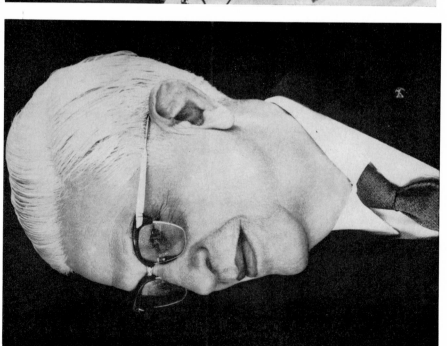

304. PRINCE BERNHARD OF THE NETHERLANDS
DECORATING JOSSY M. L. MADURO WITH THE
OFFICER'S CROSS OF ORANGE-NASSAU, 1951

303. JOSSY M. L. MADURO, 1891-1964

305. BENJAMIN M. L. MADURO, 1897-1966, ENGLISH CONSUL FOR MANY YEARS

306. SALOMON ELIAS L. MADURO, 1881-1951, ASSOCIATE OF S.E.L. MADURO & SONS

307. CHARLES ELIAS L. MADURO, 1883-1947, SONG WRITER AND ASSOCIATE OF S.E.L. MADURO & SONS

308. MONTEFIORE M. ELIAS L. MADURO, 1884-1956, ASSOCIATE OF S.E.L. MADURO & SONS

then afforded. Jossy thus learned to speak, read and write perfect Dutch, Spanish and English. He also spoke French and understood Portuguese.

Jossy was only twenty on his father's death in 1911. He continued with the business. Once his economic position was assured, he married his cousin Rebecca Debora on May 15, 1915. The daughter of Elias S. L. Maduro and Sarah de Eliau Jesurun Henriquez, she inherited her philanthropic father's kindness and docility and her mother's intelligence and prudence. It was a happy marriage. They had a son and a daughter. George was born in Curaçao in 1916 and died in the concentration camp at Dachau in 1945 (page 501). Sibyl married Jacob C. Michiel Alvares Correa in 1946 and had three sons: George Maduro, Michel Roland and José Manuel.

As grandson of the founder of Maduro & Sons, Jossy joined the renowned firm (of which he was proxy in 1916) and stayed on until 1945 when he resigned probably because of his son's death. In 1921 he was proxy of Maduro's Bank, of which he was a founder and stockholder pro forma (page 474).

At the same time he took an active part in the life of the island. He served in the National Guard as third, second, and finally as first lieutenant; consul of Guatemala in 1911; consul-general of the same country from 1913 to 1916, and consul from 1928 to 1962; consul of Sweden from 1917 to 1939; member of the Colonial Council in 1931, and of various government commissions, including one which examined students of the upper classes, and so forth. In 1938 he was the Curaçao delegate of the Netherlands Participation Committee to the New York World's Fair, 1939-41.

In 1913 he started to interest himself in historical studies and entered into correspondence with the Société Académique d'Histoire Internationale from which he received a gold medal that year. He also became interested in the Cuban Red Cross and in 1913 was decorated Honorary and Meritorious Knight of the Cuban Red Cross, 4th class. In 1923 he received a medal of honor from the Department of Public Instruction of the Venezuelan Government, and in 1930 was decorated Officer of Public Instruction of France.

Following the steps of his father and forebears, he served as parnas of the Mikvé Israel community from 1917 to 1918, and died while a member of the Council of Elders.

In 1928 he left for Holland with his family for the education of his children. That year a colonial exposition of books was held in Holland, and he was called to participate in the organizing commission. He was amazed to see how poorly Curaçao was represented in books. While in Holland he consulted the old archives of Curaçao preserved in the Royal Dutch Archives at The Hague, and many rare books on Curaçao.

Meanwhile the Mikvé Israel community of Curaçao was preparing to celebrate the bicentennial of its synagogue. Jossy was entrusted by the parnassim to write a documented history of the community. For the purpose he enlisted the aid of the historian Jacob S. Da Silva Rosa, then librarian of the Ets Haim.

In 1934 he wrote a serious study, in Dutch, on the history of the Jews of Curaçao: "De Portugueesche Joden in Curaçao." It appeared in *Gedenkboek-*

Nederland-Curaçao 1634-1934 (pp. 69-79), which was published to celebrate Curaçao's 300 years under Dutch rule.

His particular hobby was to reconstruct the genealogies of the Jewish families of Curaçao. In fact, he was a member of the Heraldisch-Genealogisch-Historisch Genootschap De Nederlandse Leeuw at The Hague. The author often consulted him on genealogical questions. In 1951 he turned out, also in Dutch, a very well-done, detailed genealogy of the Levy Maduro family from 1612 to 1948. It appeared in Dr. Ds. A. J. C. Krafft's *Historie en Oude Families van de Neder-landse Antillen* (The Hague, 1951), pp. 99-118. Shortly afterward he wrote a genealogical note on Jacob Rodrigues Rivera for the Publication of the American Jewish Historical Society (*PAJHS* 42:303-4).

Unfortunately he never published his history of Curaçao, probably because of the deep grief over his son George's death, and his love of perfection. Although he had consulted the old archives of Curaçao at The Hague, Amsterdam and Curaçao for many years, he still believed himself inadequately documented. Because he insisted on perfection, he would become indignant over breezily or hastily written articles about the Jews of Curaçao that appeared from time to time. When my "De Nederlandsche Graftschriften op 'Beth-Haim'" appeared in 1943, he made certain remarks to me, particularly on genealogy, and asked how I had the courage to write about the Jews of Curaçao without having seen the archives [of Holland]. This struck home. I decided to go to Holland with my wife, who passed away on April 26, 1969, to consult not only the old archives of Curaçao and of the Dutch West India Company, but also the precious archives of the Portuguese Jewish Community of Amsterdam, until that time accessible to none.

In the fifteen months before his passing, Jossy Maduro cooperated with me fully. A few hours before he was stricken, he went, at my request, to the archives of the Mikvé Israel to check certain facts for me. These never came. Toward the end of 1963 he had a presentiment of death and in one of his letters to me wrote: "I want to see your book published before I die." Alas, he died without realizing that wish.

He was interested not only in the history of the Jews of Curaçao, but also in the history of the island. Numerous were the notes and clarifications which he sent professors, writers and journalists to correct or amplify certain data. Several of those notes were printed anonymously.

For a while he was curator of the Museum of Curaçao. That is why the museum's carillon player played different musical pieces at the funeral.

Like his relations he was modest. Although richly endowed with earthly goods, he was not haughty and did not lead a life of luxury. He was a true gentleman, the aristocrat of the Jews of Curaçao.

As earlier stated (page 484), in 1952 he founded Madurodam in memory of his son George, for which purpose he contributed 100,000 florins. This Lilliputian city has among its tiny reproductions of Holland's most important buildings, the respective synagogues of Amsterdam and Curaçao. It is a tourist attraction that yields some 100,000 florins annually for the beneficiary, the sanatorium

309. UNVEILING OF MONUMENT ERECTED TO ELIAS
S. L. MADURO, JULIANA SQUARE, 1912

IN MEMORIAM

GEORGE J.L.MADURO

JURIDISCH CANDIDAAT
VAN DE RIJKSUNIVERSITEIT TE LEIDEN
RESERVE-TWEEDE-LUITENANT
VAN HET WAPEN DER CAVALERIE

GEBOREN OP CURAÇAO 15 JULI 1916
ALS ACHTERKLEINZOON VAN DE STICHTER
VAN DE FIRMA S.E.L.MADURO & SONS
EN VOORBESTEMD TOT EEN LEIDENDE
FUNCTIE IN DEZE ONDERNEMING
OVERLEDEN IN HET CONCENTRATIEKAMP
TE DACHAU OP 9 FEBRUARI 1945

HEM WERD POSTHUUM HET RIDDERKRUIS DER
4E KLASSE DER MILITAIRE WILLEMSORDE
VERLEEND VOOR HET VOLGENDE WAPENFEIT:

"HEEFT ZICH IN DEN STRIJD DOOR HET BEDRIJVEN
VAN UITSTEKENDE DADEN VAN MOED, BELEID EN TROUW
ONDERSCHEIDEN, DOOR OP 10 MEI 1940 ALS COMMANDANT
VAN EEN PELOTON JONGE SOLDATEN MET VEEL BELEID
EN OP EIGEN INITIATIEF DE VERMEESTERING TE
ONTWERPEN EN VOOR TE BEREIDEN VAN DE ACHTER
DE VLIET BIJ RIJSWIJK (DORREPAAL) MET ZIJN PELOTON BEZETTE
VILLA "LEEUWENBURG" (DORREPAAL) MET ZWARE
MOED AAN HET HOOFD VAN TWEE GROEPEN DE ONDER
VIJANDELIJK MITRAILLEURVUUR LIGGEND BRUG OVER DE
VLIET OVERSCHREDEN, DEN AANVAL OP HET VERSTERKTE
STEUNPUNT (VILLA "LEEUWENBURG") PERSOONLIJK
GELEID EN BIJ DEN STORMAANVAL ALS EERSTE
BINNENGEDRONGEN, HET VERZET ALDAAR GEBROKEN
EN DE BEZETTING KRIJGSGEVANGEN GEMAAKT
(K.B.VAN 10 MEI 1946 N° 6)

"MET TROTS ZAL IK ZIJN DADEN BLIJVEN GEDENKEN"
(BRIEF VAN H.M.KONINGIN WILHELMINA AAN ZIJN OUDERS)

311. GEORGE L. MADURO MEMORIAL
PLAQUE AT S.E.L. MADURO & SONS,
CURAÇAO

310. MONUMENT ERECTED TO ELIAS S. L. MADURO, PHILANTHROPIST,
JULIANA SQUARE, 1911

at Laren, Holland, a tidy sum indeed. In consideration of its founder, the Dutch flag at Madurodam was lowered at half-mast the day of his death.

In addition to the above-mentioned decorations conferred upon him, he was also decorated in the following orders: Officer in the Order of the Liberator (Simon Bolivar) of Venezuela, 4th class, in 1911, and Commander 3rd class in 1922; Knight 1st class of the Order of Wasa of Sweden in 1924; Knight in the Order of the North Star of Sweden in 1937; Commander of the Honorary and Meritorious Order of the Cuban Red Cross, 3rd class, in 1938; Commander of the Meritorious Order of Bernardo O'Higgins of Chile in 1948; Officer in the Order of Orange-Nassau in 1951; Knight in the Order of the French Legion of Honor in 1952, and finally Commander in the Order of Quetzal of Guatemala in 1958.

Jossy Maduro, a man so deeply esteemed and appreciated by kings and princes, by presidents and cabinet ministers, by his countrymen and coreligionists, departed this life on May 27, 1964. His funeral was heavily attended. The governor and vice governor of Curaçao, the consular corps, the Masonic lodges, the press and a multitude of several hundred mourners turned out to pay their last respects. All the local newspapers of Curaçao and several of Holland carried the obituary and eulogies.

The father of genealogy of the Jews of Curaçao has disappeared. He was a sincere and conscientious historian, a man who did honor not only to the Levy Maduro family and to Curaçoan Jewry, but also to the island of Curaçao. Que Sua Bendita Alma Goze Da Eterna Gloria, Amen!

GLOSSARY

The words explained are Hebrew unless indicated by these abbreviations or spelled out in full: A = Aramaic; D = Dutch; L = Ladino; P = Portuguese; S = Spanish. The often erratic spellings of the words as they appeared in the texts are retained and their correct transliterations are given.

AB, Abb. Fifth Jewish month starting between July 6 and August 7.

AB, FAST OF. Occurring on the ninth day of the month of Ab. *See* Tish'ah be-Ab.

ABODATH AKODES, Abodat Hakodes, *see* Habodat Akodes.

ABI YETOMIM, Aby Yetomim. "Father of the Fatherless," Psalms 68:6. Brotherhood founded in Amsterdam in the 17th century.

ABI (or ABY) YETOMIM VE DAYYAN ALMANOTH. "Father of the fatherless, and judge of the widows," Psalms 68:6. Brotherhood founded in Curaçao in 1733.

ADAR. The twelfth Jewish month starting between February 10 and March first.

ADAR RISON (Adar Rishon). Adar I. The twelfth month in the Jewish leap year starting between January 30 and February 11.

ADAR SENI, Adar Seny (Adar Sheni). Adar II. The thirteenth month in the Jewish leap year starting between March 1 and March 13.

ADJUNTO (pl., Adjuntos) [S, P]. Member of the council or governing body of the community or fraternal organization.

ADON 'OLAM. Lord of the Universe. Opening words of a synagogue hymn.

AGOMEL, *see* Hagomel.

AMIDA, 'Amidah. Standing. The main prayer of each service said standing and in silence.

ANSHE HESED, Anse Hesed. Men of Charity. A pallbearers society founded in Curaçao in 1754.

APHTARA, *see* Haftara.

APODERADOS DA NAÇAO [P]. Empowered by the Nation. Delegates of the Jewish community to the Government.

APPROBACION [S, P]. Imprimatur or license given by the Rabbis of the Portuguese Jewish Community of Amsterdam for the printing or publication of a book.

'ARBIT, Arbith. Evening prayers.

ASCAMA, *see* Hascama.

ASCAVA, *see* Hashcaba.

ASHKENAZI (pl. Ashkenazim). Jew residing in or descended from those who live in the countries of Central and Northern Europe, as contrasted with Sephardi or Sepharadi.

ASPACA, *see* Haspaca.

ASURA, Surah, *see* Shurah.

AZ YASHIR MOSHE. Then sang Moses. Opening words of the Song of Moses (Exodus 15:1).

BAHAL ASURA (Ba'al Hashurah). Lord of the row. Privilege given to a father of a newborn child or of a Bar Miẓvah, to a bridegroom or Bridegroom of the Law, to the newly-elected Parnassim, or others, to call up to the reading of the Torah, on the Sabbath of his respective festive occasion, as many as 14 or 20 friends and relatives in place of the usual seven.

BAHALE BERIT. Lords of the Covenant, i.e., fathers of newborn sons to be circumcised.

BALAK. Name of a king of the Moabites. The Sabbath portion of the Torah, Numbers 22:2-25:9.

BANADEIRA [P]. Bather. A woman in charge of the ritual bath.

BANCA [S, P]. Seat or bench reserved in the synagogue for the president or vice president of the community.

BANCA DE PARNASSIM [S-P, H]. The bench reserved for the president and officers of the community.

BANCA DE PARNAZES, see Banca de Parnassim.

BARAJA, Beraja, see Beraha.

BAR MISVA, Bar Mitsvah, Bar Mitzvah (Bar Miẓvah) [A-H]. The son of Commandment. A boy who reaches the age of religious duty on his 13th birthday when he takes part in the synagogue services, usually on the first Sabbath after that event.

BEDEHA (Bedika). The inspection of a slaughtered animal, especially the lungs, to pass upon its fitness for consumption.

BEMAVENTURADO [P]. The blessed one. Said of a deceased person in his epitaph.

BEMIDBAR. In the wilderness. The Sabbath portion of the Torah, Numbers 1:1-4:20.

BERAHA (Berakhah). Blessing, euphemism for Kelalah, curse or small excommunication.

BERESHITH. In the beginning. First word of the Book of Genesis. The Sabbath portion of the Torah, Genesis 1:1-6:8.

BERIKH SHEME [A]. Opening words of a prayer recited at the opening of the Altar (Zohar, Vayyakel, p. 206a).

BESIMANTOB. With good sign, or with good augury; the equivalent of the Ashkenazic Mazaltov.

BETAHAYN, Beth a Haim, Beth-Haim (Beth Hahaim). House of life; the cemetery.

BETH DIN. House of judgment; the religious court.

BICUR HOLIM, Bikur Ḥolim. Visit to the sick. Society to aid the infirm.

BIRCATH COHANIM, Birkath Cohanim. The priestly blessing.

BODEK. Examiner and inspector of ritually slaughtered meat, especially the lungs.

BOTICA [S, P]. Pharmacy.

BRIDEGROOMS OF THE LAW or ḤATANE HA-TORAH. There are two: Ḥatan Torah (Bridegroom of the Law) and Ḥatan Bereshith (Bridegroom of the Beginning). Chosen from the wealthy or respected members of the congregation, the first is given the honor of closing the annual reading of the Pentateuchal cycle in the synagogue, and the second of commencing it. This ceremony takes place on the festival of Simḥath Torah.

CAMARA DE ORFAOS [P]. The Orphans Chamber or Orphans Fund founded by the Portuguese Jewish Community of Curaçao in 1810 for the administration of orphans' affairs. It was dissolved in 1876.

CASER, Casser (Casher). Clean, ritually permissible as applied to food.

CLASSIS [Latin]. The ministers and ruling elders in Amsterdam making up the governing body of the Dutch Reformed Church.

COENOEKJE [Hollandized Spanish-American]. Small "cunucu." See cunucu.

COHANIM (s., Cohen). The Cohen Family. Priests; descendants of Aaron.

CONTRABANDISTA [S, P]. Smuggler, contrabandist.

COPIADOR DE CARTAS [S, P]. Letter file.

CUENTAS DE TESORERO [S]. Treasurer's Accounts.

CUNUCU [Spanish-American, corruption of conoco]. A patch of ground for planting corn.

DAYYAN (pl., dayyanim). Judge of a religious court.

DIN (pl., dinim). Law, judgment.

DIN TORAH. Legal opinion according to Jewish Law.

DOTAR, see Santa Companhia de Dotar Orphas.

ELUL. The sixth Jewish month starting between August 5 and September 6.

EMOR. Speak unto. The Sabbath portion of the Torah, Leviticus 21:1-24:23.

ERUB, Irub, Iruv. The law concerning the transportation of objects from one place to another on the Sabbath, and the setting up of an "enclosure" permitting such transportation within that enclosed area.

ESCAMA, see Hascama.

ES HAIM, Eshaim, Ets Haim, Ez Haim. Tree of life. To set or remove the twin silver bells crowning the scrolls of the Law. Name of an early brotherhood of Curaçao.

FAMILIEGELD [D]. Income tax.

FEAST OF TABERNACLES. The festival of Sukkot occurring between Tishri 15-21, usually the end of September and early October.

FINTA [S, P]. Jewish community tax.

FISCAL [D]. Chief of police, public prosecutor.

GABAY. Treasurer.

GAT [D]. Hole, opening, gap (in a wall).

GEMARA [A]. The part of the Talmud containing the commentaries and amplifications of the Mishnah.

GEMILUT HASADIM, Gemiluth Hassadim, Guemiluth Hasadim. Deeds of Mercy. A sick benefit burial society.

GET [A]. A divorce granted by a Jewish religious tribunal.

GOURDES [French]. The silver monetary unit of Haiti worth about 20c; originally it was equal to five francs.

GUEVIR (pl., Guevirim). Lord; a wealthy man. A married man.

HABDALAH. Separation. Benediction at the conclusion of the Sabbath or festival.

HABODAT AKODES. Service of saintliness. A pall-bearers society of Curaçao founded in 1783 and still existing in 1844.

HADAYYAN HAMEZUYAN. The distinguished judge.

HAFTARA, Haftarah. Conclusion. That portion of the Prophets read immediately after the reading of the Torah in the morning services of the Sabbath, feast and fast days; also, in the afternoon services on fast days.

HAGBAA. The raising of the Torah before the congregation.

HAGGADAH. Narration. The telling of the story of the redemption from bondage in Egypt, in the home on the first two nights of Passover.

HAGOMEL. He who bestows. A prayer of deliverance recited before the Holy Ark or the Torah.

HAHAM (Hakham; pl., Hakhamim). Sage. Title given to a rabbi of a Sephardic community.

HAHAM HAMEROMAM. The exalted rabbi.

HAHAM HANE'ELA. The outstanding rabbi.

HAHAM HASHALEM. The omniscient sage.

H: H: = Haham Hashalem. See definition immediately above.

HAHAM MAYOR [H-S]. Chief Rabbi.

HAHAM MOR [H-P]. Chief Rabbi.

HALLEL. Praise. Psalms 113-118 sung on the New Moon, Hanukkah and festivals.

HAMASKIL VE NABON, Hamaskil ve Navon. The intelligent and wise.

HAMOHEL HAMUBHAC. The expert circumciser.

HANUKKAH. Dedication. The eight-day festival of lights starting the 25th day of Kislev, i.e. between November 25 and December 27.

HANUKKIAH [L]. Hanukkah lamp.

HARAB HAMUBHAC. The brilliant rabbi.

HARBIT, see 'Arbit.

HAROSETH, Harosset. A mixture of apples, oranges, nuts, raisins, wine and cinnamon used in the services the first and second nights of Passover.

HASCABA, Hascabah, see Hashcaba.

HASCAMA, Hascamah, Haskama (pl. Hascamoth). Decision: agreement; an article of the bylaws of a congregation or brotherhood.

HASHCABA, Hashcabah (pl., Hashcaboth). Lying down. Memorial prayer for the soul of a deceased person. Bequest for memorial prayers.

HASHCABA DE LEGADOS [H, S-P]. Memorial prayers for the soul of a deceased person who left a legacy for the purpose.

HASPACA, Haspacah, Haspaka, Aspaca (pl., Haspacoth). Maintenance. Periodic stipendium or allowance given to a rabbinical student, an orphan, widow and the like.

HATAN, Hathan (pl. Hatanim). Bridegroom.

HATAN BERESHIT, Hatan Bereshith, Hatan Beresit. See Bridegroom of the Law.

HATAN TORAH, Hatan Torra, Hathan Thora. See Bridegroom of the Law.

HAZAN, Hazzan (pl., Hazzanim). Cantor; synagogue reader.

HAZAN DE SELIHOTH [H, S-P, H]. Cantor leading the penitential prayers.

HAZAROTH. Songs by Solomon ben Gabirol sung on Shabu'oth.

H: C: = English for K[ahal]. K[adosh]. Holy Congregation.

HEBRA, Hebrah (pl., Hebroth) [A]. Company, society, fraternity. The society for tending the sick and burying the dead.

HEBRAH KADDISHAH [A]. The Holy Brotherhood — burial society.

HECHAL, HEJAL (Ekhal). Palace. The Holy Ark or cabinet where the holy scrolls of the Law are kept.

HEREM. Excommunication.

HERMANDADES, IRMANDADES (s., Hermandad, irmandade) [S, P]. Brotherhoods, fraternal organizations.

HESED VE EMETH. Kindness and truth. Name of

the brotherhood to wash the dead founded in Curaçao in 1726.

HESHVAN, Hesvan. The eighth Jewish month starting between October 3 and November 3.

HOMER, *see* 'Omer.

HOSANA RABBA, Osahana Raba (Hosha'na Rabbah) [H-A]. The great hosanna. The 7th day of the Feast of Tabernacles.

HYAR, *see* Iyar.

IAR, Iiar, *see* Iyar.

IESIBA, Iesibot, *see* Yeshibah.

IMPOSTA DA NAÇAO [P]. Tax of the Nation. Sales tax imposed by the Jewish community.

INSINUATIE [D]. Summons and complaint.

IRMANDADES, *see* Hermandades.

IYAR (Iyyar). Second Jewish month starting between April 9 and May 11.

JAR, Jiar, *see* Iyar.

JESIBA, Jesibot, *see* Yeshibah.

JODE KWARTIER, Joden Quartier, Joode Quartier [D]. Jewish Quarter where the Jews of Curaçao lived in the early days of their settlement.

JOHANNES [Modern Latin]. A Portuguese gold coin (falsified or altered since 1793) whose official weight and value were placed at 22 carats, and 11 pesos 2 reales, respectively.

KAAPVAARTKAS [D]. Privateering Fund.

KADIS, Kadish, Kaddish [A]. Originally a glorification of God, for many centuries it has been a mourner's prayer also.

KAHAL, Kehila, Kehillah (pl., Kehilot). Congregation.

KAHAL KADOS, Kahal Kadosh. Holy Congregation.

KAL NIDRE [A]. All vows. Opening words of the prayer intoned on the eve of the Day of Atonement.

KASHER, Kasser, Kosher, *see* Casher.

KASHRUTH. The state of being *Casher*.

KAT [D]. Battery.

KEMINHAS, *see* Quemihot.

KETUBA, Ketubah (pl., Ketuboth). Marriage contract.

KIDDUSH. Sanctification. Ceremony and prayer proclaiming the holiness of the Sabbath or festival, performed with glass of wine in hand and finished by sipping of the wine.

KINOTH (s., Kinah). Dirges. Usually read on the Fast of Ab.

KIPUR, Kippur, Yom Kippur. The Day of Atonement occurring on the tenth day of Tishri.

KISLEF, Kisleff, Kisleu, Kislev. The ninth Jewish month starting between November 1 and December 3.

K: K: = Kahal Kados, Kahal Kadosh. Holy Congregation.

K: K: do T: T: = Kahal Kados do Talmud Torah [H-P]. Holy Congregation of Talmud Torah (the Portuguese Jewish Community Amsterdam).

K: K: T: S: = Kahal Kados do Terra Santa [H-P]. Holy Congregation of the Holy Land.

KLIP [D]. Rock, crag.

LADINO [S]. Judaeo-Spanish. Dialect spoken by the Jews of the Balkans and Middle East or by their descendants in which Old Spanish predominates the blend of Portuguese, French, Hebrew, Italian and Turkish. (It is written in Hebrew characters.)

LEES-BIBLIOTHEEK [D]. (Public) lending library.

LEGADO [S, P]. Bequest, synonymous with Hashcabah. An amount of money left to the Synagogue by Curaçoan Jews for perpetual memorial prayers for the dead.

LEGAJO [S]. File, bundle of letters.

LEKH LEKHA. Get thee out. The Sabbath portion of the Torah, Genesis 12:1-17:27.

LEVANTADOR (pl., Levantadores) [S, P]. By the Sephardim, the person who raises up the Scroll of the Law before the reading of the Torah.

LIVRO DE CIRCUNCISIONES [S]. Circumcision Register.

LULAB, Lulav. A cluster of palm, willow and myrtle carried with a citron in the morning services during the seven days of the Feast of Tabernacles, excepting the Sabbath.

MAFTIR. One who concludes, especially the reading of the Torah.

MAHAMAD. Standing committee. The executives of the congregation; also, Board Room.

MASA, Massa, *see* Matza.

MATZA (Maza) [pl., Matzoth, Mazzoth]. Unleavened bread eaten during Passover.

MAYOR COMANDANTE [S]. Commander-in-Chief of the Civil Guard.

MEDRAS (Midrash). Institute for learning; religious school.

MEDRASIM, Medrassim (Midrashim). Plural of Medras.

MEZUZAH. Doorpost. A container having a tiny parchment inscribed with the first two parts of the Shemah prayer (Deut. 6:4-9; 11:13-21).

MIKVE ISRAEL, Mikveh Israel. Hope of Israel. Name of the old congregation of Curaçao before the merger of 1963.

MINJAN, Minyan. Number. The quorum of ten Jewish males above the age of thirteen required to conduct collective religious services.

MINUTAS DE ANCIANOS [S]. Minutes of the Council of Elders.

MISHEBERAH, Mi Sheberakh. May He who blessed. Opening words of a prayer invoking a blessing on the entire congregation or on certain individuals named therein.

MISHNA, Mishnah. Teaching. The oldest collection of Jewish legislative writings — apart from the Pentateuch — that forms the basis of the Talmud.

MISVA, Misvah, Mitsvah, Mitzvah (Miẓvah; pl., Miẓvoth). A commandment, good deed. The corpse of a Jew or its burial. An honor involving participation in the synagogue service.

MODA'AH. Confession of faith.

MOHEL. A Jew qualified to perform circumcisions.

MORENU HARAB. Our Chief Rabbi.

MORENU VE RABENU. Our teacher and rabbi.

MUSAF. Additional. The additional service to the regular morning service on the Sabbath, holy days and festivals.

NASO. Take the sum of. The Sabbath portion of the Torah, Numbers 4:21-7:89.

NEDABAH. Donation. A synagogue appeal for funds in favor of an individual or institution.

NEHILA, Ne'ilah. Closing. The concluding prayer on the Day of Atonement.

NISAN, Nissan. The first Jewish month starting between March 10 and April 11.

'OMER. Sheaf. The seven weeks between Passover and Pentecost, counted day by day.

OSAHANA RABA, see Hosha'na Rabbah.

OTRABANDA [S, P]. The "other side." The City of Willemstad, Curaçao — divided into two parts by the Santa Anna Bay — is joined together by the Queen Emma Bridge. The area east of this pontoon bridge is called Punda (point, center) and that to the west, Otrabanda.

PAPIAMENTO [Curaçoan]. A dialect spoken by the natives of Curaçao, it is a blend of African, Dutch, English, Spanish, Portuguese and French, with Portuguese predominating.

PARASA, Parasah, see Perashah.

PARNAS, Parnaz (pl., Parnassim). Provider. Warden or trustee of the community; administrator or president of a society, brotherhood or yeshibah.

PARNAS DE FABRICA [H-S]. Administrator and inspector of the community buildings.

PARNAS DE HEBRA [H-S-A]. Burial and cemetery administrator.

PARNAS DE TALMUD TORAH [H-S-H]. Administrator and inspector of the community schools

PARNASSIM DE BANCA [H-S]. Officiating president and officers of the community.

PARNAZES DE BANCA, see Parnassim de Banca.

PATACA (pl., Patacas) [P]. See peso.

PATINTJE (pl., Patintjes) [Danish (?) with Dutch suffix]. An 18th century coin of St. Thomas then worth almost two pesos.

PENNING [D]. A very small 18th century coin that was worth one-sixteenth part of the stuiver.

PERASHAH (pl., Perashiot) [A]. The equivalent of the Ashkenazic Sidra. The weekly liturgical reading from the Pentateuch.

PESAḤ. Passover. Festival starting the 15th of Nisan. See Nisan.

PESO, PEZO (pl., Pesos, Pezos) [S, P]. Ancient Spanish and Portuguese silver money used in the Americas; originally worth eight reales or 2.50 florins.

PIYUT, Piyyut (pl., Piyyutim). Religious poem, hymn.

PIZMON (pl., Pizmonim). Song. A religious poem sung in the home or synagogue.

PLACAAT, Plakaat [D]. Government publication or edict.

Punda [S, D]. Point. Formerly, the city; now the largest business center of Willemstad, Curaçao.

Purim. Feast of Esther occurring the 14th and 15th Adar. *See* Adar.

Quemihot (s., Quemeha). [A]. Charms or amulets.

Rabino [S]. Rabbi.

Reales (s., real) [S, P]. Ancient Spanish and Portuguese silver money varying between 15 and 31 Dutch cents in value. Eight reales were equivalent to a peso or a pataca. *See* Peso.

Rebbi, Rebi, Ribbi, Ribi, Ribby, Rubi, Ruby [A]. My master. A teacher of religion. Sometimes this title was given to highly respected cantors of the Curaçao community.

Reglamentos (s., Reglamento) [S, P]. Regulations; bylaws.

Responsa [Latin]. Collection of answers and decisions handed down by eminent rabbis on questions put to them.

Ribbi, Ribi, Ribby, *see* Rebbi.

Rimonim, Rimmonim. Pomegranates. The twin silver bells crowning the Scrolls of the Law.

Ros, Rosh. Head. Chief or president of a brotherhood or dean of a college for Jewish learning.

Rosasana, Ros-Ashaná, Rosassana, Rosassanah, Roshashana (Rosh Hashanah). Head of the year. The Jewish New Year occurring on the first and second of Tishri. *See* Tishri.

Ros Hodes, Rosh Ḥodesh. The head of the month. The first day of the Jewish month.

Rubisim, Rubissim (s., Rubi), *see* Rebbi.

Sabath, Shabbath. The Sabbath.

Sabath Agadol (Shabbat Hagadol). The great Sabbath, the Sabbath before Passover.

Saliah, Shaliaḥ (pl., Sheliḥim). Messenger. Usually a lettered, respected person sent by a Jewish community, particularly of the Holy Land, to collect funds for a charity.

Samas, Shamas, Shamash (Shammash). Servant. The beadle and sexton of a synagogue.

Santa Companhia de Dotar Orfas [P]. Holy Brotherhood to Dower Orphaned Maidens. Founded in Amsterdam in 1615 to provide dowries for poor or orphaned girls.

Santa Irmandade [P]. Holy Brotherhood.

Sebat, Sebath, Shebat (Shevat). The eleventh Jewish month starting between December 30 and January 31.

Sebuoth, Shavuoth, Shebuot, Shevuot (Shabu'oth). Weeks. The Feast of Weeks occurring on the sixth and seventh of Sivan. *See* Sivan.

Sedaca, Sedacca, Sedaka (Ẓedakah). Righteousness, charity. The general funds of a Portuguese-Jewish community.

Seder. Order. The order of service conducted in the home on the first two evenings of Passover.

Sefer, Sefre, *see* Sepher.

Sehita, Shehitta (Sheḥita). Slaughtering. Slaughter of poultry or cattle in accordance with Jewish ritual prescription.

Selihoth. Forgiveness. Penitential prayers for forgiveness.

Sephardi, Sepharadi (pl., Sephardim. Sepharadim). A Jew originally of Spain or Portugal, or his descendants, as contrasted with Ashkenazi.

Sepher, also Sepher Torah. The book par excellence, the Book of the Law, the Pentateuch written on parchment; the Holy Scroll of the Law.

Shabat Bereshit, Shabbat Bereshith. The Sabbath when Genesis 1 : 1-6 : 8 is read.

Shabbat Naḥamu. Sabbath of Comfort. Also known as Shabbat Vaethḥanán. The Sabbath after the Fast of the Ninth of Ab when, among others, the Ten Commandments (Deut. 3 : 23-7 : 11) and the comfort of Prophet Isaiah (Isaiah 40 : 1-26) are read.

Shema, Shemah. Hear. The sublime prayer of a Jew proclaiming the unity of God (Deut. 6 : 4).

Shemini 'Aẓereth. A separate festival although it is the eighth day of Sukkot.

Shemoth. Names. The Sabbath portion of the Torah, Exodus 1 : 1-6 : 1.

Shofar. Ram's horn. Sounded on Rosh Hashanah and at the end of the Day of Atonement.

Shohet (pl., Shoḥatim). Ritual slaughterer.

Shomer [= Mashgiaḥ]. Guard. One who watches over the preparation of food according to Jewish ritual.

SIMHA TORRA (Simḥath Torah). The Rejoicing of the Law. The ninth day of the Feast of Tabernacles (or the second day of Shemini 'Aẓereth) when the yearly cycle of the reading of the Torah is ended and started again.

SIVAN. The third Jewish month starting between May 8 and June 9.

SOGET, Sohet, see Shoḥet.

SOHET-BODEC (Shoḥet-bodek). Ritual slaughterer and examiner of the carcass slaughtered, especially the lungs.

SOLDO (pl., Soldos) [P]. A coin worth five centimes.

STIVER, see Stuiver.

STOCKFISHOUT, Stockvishout [D]. Logwood.

STUIVER [D]. Penny.

SUCOT, Suçoth (Sukkot). Booths. The Feast of Tabernacles, Tishri 15-21.

SUKKAH. Booth. A structure whose roof is covered with branches and the interior walls are decorated with fruits and vegetables symbolic of the festival period during Tishri 15-21.

SURAH (Shurah). Row. The number of people called to the Torah over and above the usual seven.

TALETH [A]. A prayer shawl with fringe at each of its four corners used by male Jews during certain religious services.

TALMID HAHAM (pl., Talmidé Hahamim). Pupil of the sage. A student of theology; a Sephardic Rabbi without an official community post as contrasted with the Haham, the Chief Rabbi of a community.

TALMUD. The rabbinical collection of Jewish Law and so forth.

TALMUD TORAH, Talmut Tora. School. Torah instruction. Name of the Sephardic congregation of Amsterdam.

TAMUS, Tamuz (Tammuz). The fourth Jewish month starting between June 7 and July 9.

TAREF. The adjective of Terefah. See Trefa.

TEBA, Theba (Tebah). Box. The platform or reading desk in the synagogue used mainly by the Haham and Reader.

TEBET, Tebeth. The tenth Jewish month starting between December 1 and January 2.

TEFILLIN. Phylacteries.

TEHILATH. Praise. The first word of verse 21 of Psalm 145.

TERMO [P]. Limit. Decision or resolution made by an executive body.

TERRA SANTA [P]. The Holy Land; soil from Israel.

TERUMAH. Contribution; offering. The Sabbath portion of the Torah, Exodus 25-27:19.

TESHUBA, Tesuba. Penitence.

TEVILA, Tevilah. Immersion. Ritual bath.

TIKUN, Ticum (Ticun). Improvement. Service for dedicating a home. Also, a prayer conducted in the synagogue the first night of the Feast of Weeks.

TISABEAB, Tishnabeab (Tish'ah be-Ab). The Ninth of Ab. The fast commemorating the twofold destruction of the Temple of Jerusalem and the expulsion of the Jews from Spain.

TISHRY, Tisri, Tisry (Tishri). The seventh Jewish month starting between September 3 and October 5.

TORAH. The Pentateuch, the Five Books of Moses.

TREFA, Treffa (Terefah). Torn. Food and meat not ritually fit for consumption, as contrasted with kasher.

TSITSIT, Tsitsith, see Ẓiẓit.

T:T: = Talmud Torah. See Talmud Torah.

VAETHHANAN. And I besought. The Sabbath portion of the Torah, Deut. 3:23-7:11.

VAYYESHEV. And dwelt. The Sabbath portion of the Torah, Genesis 37:1-40:23.

VAYYEẒE (Vayetse). And went out. The Sabbath portion of the Torah, Genesis 28:10-32:3.

VEADAR. See Adar Sheni.

VESALOM (Veshalom). And peace. A greeting.

YESHIBAH, Yeshivah, Yesiba, Yesibah, Jesiba (pl., Yeshiboth). Session. House of study, school; college for Jewish learning.

YIAR, see Iyar.

YOM KIPUR, Yom Kippur. Day of Atonement.

ZEMIROTH. Songs. Psalms or hymns recited in the morning service.

ẒIẒIT. The fringe on the four corners of the prayer shawl; also, the short undergarment with fringe on its four corners, known by the Ashkenazim as Arbah Kanfoth.

BIBLIOGRAPHY

Numerous books have been consulted for the *History of the Jews of the Netherlands Antilles*, principally those dealing with the Portuguese Jews of Europe and America. But archival material forms the backbone of this work. Most of the archives listed in my *Precious Stones of the Jews of Curaçao* published in 1957 apply to this history too. As it is now out of print, a summary of those archives follows. Combined with them are the records investigated on four subsequent trips I made to Curaçao and one to Holland to complete my research.

ARCHIVES CONSULTED IN CURAÇAO

CONGREGATION MIKVE ISRAEL OF CURAÇAO
(now UNITED CONGREGATION MIKVE ISRAEL-EMANUEL)

Nine boxes of records from 1724 to 1845, containing:

Accounts of several 18th century Community Parnassim (incomplete).

Documents on the Andrade case.

Documents on the Piza affair.

Minute Books of 19th century Parnassim (incomplete).

Records of the Hesed ve Emeth Brotherhood, 1726-1878.

Several Documents of the Neve Salom Synagogue.

> The foregoing records are in poor condition. Formerly at the home of a past parnas, they now are kept in the Office of the Secretary of the United Congregation.

Account Books from 1836.

Birth Registers since 1799 (incomplete).

Correspondence from 1852.

Death Registers from 1857.

Hascamoth of 1755-1756 (appendix 1).

Hashcaboth Registers from 1674.

Ketuboth Books from vol. 6, Sivan 16, 5542 (May 29, 1782).

Manuscript of 1840, in Portuguese and Hebrew, of occasional prayers recited in the synagogue (probably written by Moses Lopez Penha). This I discovered in 1963 in a drawer of a synagogue pew.

Minute books from 1854 (in excellent condition).

Pulpit Announcements, 1858-1891.

Register signed by employees and others acknowledging receipt of salary or allowances, from 1863.

1111

THE FOLLOWING DOCUMENTS CITED IN THE VARIOUS ARCHIVES CONSULTED
ARE MISSING:

Account Books before 1836.

Account Books (six) lost in 1863 by Abraham Mendes Chumaceiro, bookkeeper for the Community.

Account Books and Minute Books of the Orphans Fund from 1810, still mentioned in the Community minutes of 1862.

A major part of the records on the communal rift over Hazzan Piza, 1818-1822.

Correspondence exchanged with the Island Governors before 1856.

Decisions of the Mahamad, Treasurer and Beth Din mentioned in the Memorias Curiel and Memorias Senior.

Old Birth Registers.

Old Records and Old Death Registers of the Parnas de Hebra.

Privileges granted to the Community by the Dutch West India Company or the States General of Holland from 1651 to 1740. (See above, p. 335).

Records inventoried by Community Secretary J. Capriles Jr. in 1878.

Records of Synagogue Neve Salom of Otrabanda.

Records of the numerous yeshiboth and hermandades (excepting the Hesed ve Emeth which turned up in Curaçao in 1957 after *Precious Stones of the Jews of Curaçao* had been published).

Records of the Representatives of the High Commission on Israelitic Affairs in Holland.

The first five Ketuboth Books which disappeared between 1868 and February 13, 1881.

The original Hascamoth, in their entirety, from 1672-1749.

These missing documents are conservatively estimated at seventy volumes. Some were lost in one way or another. But the rest probably were deliberately destroyed or secreted by some peace-loving member wishing to blot out all trace of the frequent stormy differences between the Parnassim and members, or among the members themselves. Did he bury them near the synagogue or in the cemetery? In 1936 an iron box with Community records was discovered when Community houses along Kerkstraat were demolished in order to widen the street leading to the Synagogue. I saw that box empty.

On his departure in 1897 Hazzan Joseph M. Corcos took many old documents, certainly with the intention of returning them to the Community. The few which I looked over at the American Jewish Historical Society, New York City, are virtually in fragments.

DUTCH JEWISH REFORM COMMUNITY OF CURAÇAO

Cash Books from 1864.

Correspondence from 1864.

Marriage Register from 1864.

Minute Books from 1864.

Unbound Documents from 1864.

PRIVATELY OWNED DOCUMENTS

The Jossy M. L. Maduro Notes on Curaçoan Jews as Captains and Shipowners culled from the OAC and WIC archives and given to me for consultation.

BIBLIOGRAPHY

The Jossy M. L. Maduro Notes on the Jews of St. Eustatius, including the Maduro-ordered copy of 17 epitaphs of the Jewish Cemetery of St. Eustatius given to me for consultation.

The Memorias Curiel and Memorias Senior: Chronicles in Portuguese owned by the late S. A. L. Maduro, Curaçao.

These two chronicles indisputably are the most precious documents on the island related to the Jews of Curaçao. But I do not believe that they ever formed a part of the community archives.

MEMORIAS CURIEL (49 pp., in good condition)

Written by a son of Ephraim de Selomoh Curiel (C 2379), it covers the period mainly from 1716-1739. The list of Parnassim and Bridegrooms of the Law started in the Memorias Senior is repeated and added to by Curiel, and continued after him by a member of the Maduro family.

MFMORIAS SENIOR (230 pp., two pages in poor state)

Written by Jacob de David Senior (*PAJHS* 44:217) it is a sort of index of the important decisions handed down by the Community Treasurer, the Mahamad, and Beth Din. It starts from the death of Haham Lopez in 1713 and goes up to Sivan 18, 5523 (1763). Toward the end several events occurring between 1811 and 1815 are recorded in another hand. It lists Community Treasurers from 1671-72, Parnassim from 1671/73 (appendix 12), Bridegrooms of the Law since 1675; Hahamim, Rubissim, Hazzanim, and other officiants of the Community; Parnassim of Talmud Torah, Representatives of the Jewish Nation (i.e., the Community) to the Government (appendix 13), the Women in charge of the ritual bath, and so forth. A son of the chronicler completed these lists.

The original Lopez Penha Family Chronicle owned by Otto Senior, Curaçao.

The Lopez Penha Family Chronicle (principally genealogy) owned by Mrs. Julius Lopez Penha Jr., Curaçao.

The Lopez Penha Family Documents given to the author by the late Sexton David H. Lopez Penha.

CURAÇAO GOVERNMENT ARCHIVES

Applications for Marriage Licenses.

Land Registry Office Records from 1807 to the present day: surveys, contracts of purchase and sale of real estate and boats; deeds, mortgages, and other documents from May, 1869.

Maritime Records of Curaçao, in Charge of R. F. W. Boskaljon, Government Archivist:
Crew lists from 1844.
Harborage and Security Charges, 1854-1864.

Marriage Registers from 1817.

Notarial Records from January, 1846: transfers of real estate, deeds, mortgages, antenuptial agreements, wills, partnership agreements, and so forth.

Old Slaveowners Lists.

Old Tax Lists.

Unpublished Colonial Reports (Koloniaal Verslag), 1821-1833.

ARCHIVES CONSULTED IN HOLLAND

MUNICIPAL ARCHIVES OF AMSTERDAM

Index Cards on 17th century matter prepared by Dr. Simon Hart, Archivist.

Index Cards (several hundred) on 18th century matter made by various archivists of the Municipal Archives.

Several documents of the period from 1650-1730.

Several Notarial Records of the 17th century, in Portuguese.

The Classis of Amsterdam

Correspondence between the Classis of Amsterdam and the Protestant Church of Curaçao from the second half of the 17th century to the end of the 18th century.

The A. M. Vaz Dias Card Index relating to civil registrations of intention to marry.

The A. M. Vaz Dias Notes on many Notarial documents of the 17th and 18th centuries.

ARCHIVES OF THE PORTUGUESE JEWISH COMMUNITY OF AMSTERDAM

Mrs. Emmanuel and I were the first to consult these priceless archives dating from 1614. In addition to the vast number of bound records, we also pored over bundles and bundles of loose papers, both at the Secretary's Office of the Portuguese Jewish Community of Amsterdam and the Municipal Archives of that city. Since then Dr. (Miss) Wilhelmina Christina Pieterse has prepared an excellent catalog of these voluminous archives: *Inventaris van de Archiven der Portugees-Israelitische Gemeente te Amsterdam* (Amsterdam, 1964), 85 pages. Outside of some thirty old registers including the Ketuboth Books from 1673 and records of modern times since 1871 at the Office of the Secretary of the Portuguese Jewish Community of Amsterdam, all the documents are kept at the Municipal Archives of Amsterdam. History forever will be indebted to A. le Cosquino de Bussy,* archivist of the Municipal Archives. He realized their immense value and had the presence of mind and courage to transfer these records to a secret hiding place during the Nazi occupation.

ETS HAIM LIBRARY (Portuguese Jewish Community, Amsterdam)

Several manuscripts and rare books related to Curaçao and other islands of the West Indies.

TOMBAL INSCRIPTIONS (Portuguese Jewish Cemetery at Ouderkerk).

ROYAL LIBRARY AT THE HAGUE (KONINKLIJKE BIBLIOTHEEK)

The J. H. J. Hamelberg Collection of notes in manuscript.**

STATE ARCHIVES AT THE HAGUE (RIJKSARCHIEF)

Curaçao Archives, 1708-1845.

The old archives of Curaçao, designated as OAC (= Oud Archief van Curaçao, i.e., Old Archives

---

* See the W. J. van Hoboken introduction to Dr. W. Chr. Pieterse's Catalog above mentioned.
** For a list of this collection see Dr. A. J. C. Krafft, *Historie en Oude Families van de Nederlandse Antillen* (The Hague, 1954), p. 427.

of Curaçao), run into 1,701 numbers, exclusive of the records entitled "Curaçao en Onder-hoorigen Eilanden 1828-1845" (Curaçao and its Island Dependencies, here designated as CEOE). The latter group comprises 1,285 numbers. I have pored over many of these often bulky,   volu-minous tomes.

Dutch West India Company Archives here designated as WICA.

Letters or instructions of the Company to Curaçao from 1675.

"Letters and Papers of Curaçao to the Chamber of Amsterdam," 1680-1791.

I have consulted a good portion of this correspondence to and from Curaçao.

Decisions of the "Gentlemen X" (Second Council of the Dutch West India Company) related to Curaçao, from 1675.

Dutch West Indian Miscellany.

Index Cards (several hundred) on 18th and 19th century OAC documents and 18th century WICA records, in charge of Dr. (Mrs.) M. A. P. Meilink-Roelofsz.***

ARCHIVES CONSULTED IN THE UNITED STATES OF AMERICA

AMERICAN JEWISH ARCHIVES, CINCINNATI, OHIO

A collection of 25 epitaphs from the Jewish Cemetery of St. Eustatius.

Birth Registers of the Mikvé Israel Community, Curaçao, for some of the years between 5461 and 5574 (1701-1814), copied by Selomoh Cohen Peixotto.

Documents originally from England, the Antilles and elsewhere related to Curaçao that were brought to my attention by Dr. Jacob R. Marcus.

NATIONAL ARCHIVES, WASHINGTON, D.C.

Despatches from United States Consuls at Curaçao to the Secretary of State and others, 1793-1906.

Despatches from United States Consuls at St. Eustatius to the Secretary of State and others, 1793-1838.

These despatches, condensed into 14 large rolls of microfilm containing several miles of ex-posures, were graciously ordered by Dr. Jacob R. Marcus, at my request, for the American Jewish Archives where they now are.

PRINTED MATTER

Books, too numerous to list, bearing on Curaçao in general, and on the history of the Portuguese Jews of Europe and America, as cited in the footnotes of this work.

Corcos, Joseph M., *A Synopsis of the History of the Jews of Curaçao*. Curaçao, 1897, 48 pp.

Emmanuel, I. S., "Jewish Education in Curaçao (1692-1802)," *PAJHS* 44:215-36.

— "De Nederlandsche Grafschriften op 'Beth-Haim' op Curaçao," *Geschiedkundige Opstellen*. Curaçao, 1943, pp. 55-78.

*** See Dr. (Mrs.) M. A. P. Meilink-Roelofsz, "A Survey of Archives in the Netherlands pertaining to the history of the Netherlands Antilles," *West Indische Gids* (The Hague, 1954), pp. 1-38.

— "New Light on Early American Jewry," *American Jewish Archives*, VII. Cincinnati, 1955, pp. 3-64, particularly pp. 20-21, 64, which touch on the Jews of Curaçao (published on the occasion of the American Jewish Tercentenary).

— "Het Oude Joodsche Kerkhof op Curaçao," *Lux*. Curaçao, January-February, 1944, pp. 143-149.

— *Precious Stones of the Jews of Curaçao*. Assen, 1957, 584 pp., out of print.

— ולצפת הקדושה' ל'ארץ ובקוראסאו באמשטרדם הספרדים קהילות של סיועין *Sefunoth*, VI. Jerusalem, 1962, pp. 400-424; on Curaçao, pp. 409-411.

Maduro, Jossy M. L., "Portugeesche Joden in Curaçao," *Gedenkboek Nederland-Curaçao, 1634-1943*. Amsterdam, 1934, pp. 68-78.

Old newspapers and magazines of Curaçao.

Rare pamphlets printed in Curaçao.

Studies and reports involving Jews of Curaçao, directly or indirectly, that have appeared in publications cited in the footnotes of this work and particularly in:

Archives Israélites. Paris (19th century).

The Occident. Philadelphia (19th century).

Publications of the American Jewish Historical Society.

West Indische Gids. Amsterdam.

INDEX

Since very often the same name appears in different spelling (i.e. Cardoso, Cardozo; De Leao, De Leon; Mendes, Mendez; Morao, Moron; De Sola, De Solas, De Solla, De Sollas, etc.) or incomplete (i.e. Aboab in place of Aboab Cardozo; Da Costa, in place of Da Costa Andrade, Namias ,in place of Namias de Crasto, etc), to save space we selected the most appropriate one.

The page numbers in boldface type refer to the marriages of that family, as recorded in appendix 17, pages 843-1007.

Four-digit numbers in italics represent years.

INDEX

Guarico, Ven., 830
Guayanilla, Puerto Rico, 835
GUEDALIA, Abraham(?), 156
GUEDALIA, David, 170
GUEDELHA, Baruch, 777, 898, 1027
GUEDELLA, Semah, 158
GUER, Samuel, 768
GUERMAN, Isaac Baruch, 226, 778
Guide, The, Kingston, 242
GUITERMAN, Vida Lindo, 32
GUTIERES, Abraham de Aron Mattos, 225
GUTIERES, Aron de Mattos, 836
GUTIEREZ, Salomon, 233n
GUTTIERES, Jacob, 108, 764
GUTTIERES, Joseph, 743

HABIB; see Aben Habib
HABILHO, Raquel de Isaac, 130
HABILHO, Sipora de Isaac, 130
HABILLO, Isaac Hisquiau, 518, 765
HAGUEL, Mosseh, 156
HAIM SABETHAY, 181n
Haiti, 301, 468n, 828, 830
HALAS (Hallas), David, 263, 899, 1027
HALAS, Mordechay Raphael, 759, 899
HALAZ, Isaaq, 108, 764, 770, 898
HALMAN, 899
Hamburg, 41, 51n, 399n, 490, 913, 922, 967,
  977, 997, 1007, 1052
HAMELBERG, Johannes Hermanus Jacobus,
  48, 105, 138, 287n, 413n, 443, 447-48,
  667n, 747, 1114
HAMER, Hendrik, 1039
HANSE, Abraham, 152n
HANSZ, Casper S., 644, 1043
HANSZ, David, 1038
Hanukkah Lamps, 94, 1046-47, illus. 55
Harborage charges, 1113
Haroseth, distribution, 236, 613
HART, David Juda, 1050
HART, Isaac, of Newport, 1035
HART, Izaack, 1050
HART, Jacob, 1035
HART, Lowe (Braina), 1050-51
HART, Naftali, 219, 1035, 1050-52, 1066
HART, Nathan, 723
HART, Shiepra (Sypora), 1050-51
HART, Simon, 9, 41n, 47n, 1114
HART, W. F. de, 675
HARTOG, Johan, 376n, 458n
HARTZ, Dr. Philip H., 436
Hascamoth of Mikvé Israel, 1651-88, 52, 56-68,
  541-46;1696-1750, 91-92, 547-79; 1750-53,
  231-33; 1752-60, 250, 586-606; 1756-68,
  610-12; 1786, 275, 606-7; 1810, 290,
  580-609; 1825-33, 336-37, 613, 615;
  1849-75, 615-17; of Neve Salom, 151-52
HASETH, C. de, 670
HASETH, C. G. de, 637, 643

HASETH, Ch. J. de, 662
HASETH, Clasina de, 429, 638
HASETH, P. F. de, 655
HASETH, P. L. de, 638
Hashcabah; see Legado, memorial prayer
HASSON, Abraham ben, 163
HASSON, David, 164
HASSON, David Polokhron, 754, 756
Hatereth Bahurim u-Malbish Harumim brother-
  hood, 126, illus. 34
Havana, 215, 221, 225-26, 334n, 827-28
HAYON, Nehemiah, 116
HAYUNGA, Rudolph, 299, 325
HAZAN, Jacob Lebeth, 161
HAZAN, Selomoh, 163
Hazard games prohibited, 91, 232, 592
Hazzanim, 245, 250, 263-64, 341-42; conflict
  with, 275-77, 306-26, 343-44; election of,
  594-95; innovation in the prayers forbidden
  to, 250
Head-covering, 359, 506
Hebrew Educational Society, 406
Hebrew Union College, 514; library of, 9, 32,
  516n
Hebron, 125-26, 131, 154-65, 191, 251, 256,
  522, 753-56, 1010, 1095, 1097-99
Heerenstraat built mainly by Jews, 101-2, 143,
  illus. 60
HEINE, Heinrich, 334
HELFRICH, O. L., gov., 487
HELLER, Bernard, 392
HELMUND, Gotlob W., 676, 679
HEMPEL, Marten, 687
HENDRICKS, Jan, 212, 671, 1039
HENDRIK, Prince Willem Frederik, 338
HENDRIKSZOON, Jan Schotborgh, 361n
HENDRIKZ, J. A. K., 703
HENRICUS, Nicolaas, 646, 1041
Henriques & Francisco Henriquez, 108, 227n,
  766, 769, 771
HENRIQUES; see Henriquez
HENRIQUEZ, 899-902
HENRIQUEZ (Cohen), 902-907
HENRIQUEZ (Delvalle), 881-883
HENRIQUEZ (Jesurun), 907-909
HENRIQUEZ (Lopez), 909-911
HENRIQUEZ (Moreno), 911-912
HENRIQUEZ, Abigail Delvalle, 128n
HENRIQUEZ, Abraham, 630, 640, 676
HENRIQUEZ, Abraham, of St. Croix, 836
HENRIQUEZ, Abraham Daniel Moreno, illus.
  230
HENRIQUEZ, Abraham Delvalle, 531, 636,
  648, 651, 805, 1080
HENRIQUEZ, Abraham Haim Cohen, 372,
  374-76, 378-79, 456, 804, 1079, illus. 108
HENRIQUEZ, Abraham Isaac, 79, 338, 622,
  629-30, 641, 645, 654, 677, 799-802, 1047
HENRIQUEZ, Abraham Israel, 69
HENRIQUEZ, Abraham J., wid., 1082

1135

Jewish, attachment to Curaçao and Holland, 411-15; contribution to the general development of Curaçao, 465-88; of music in Cur., 482; emigration to the Mainland, and elsewhere in the Americas, 347-48, 822-40; philanthropy, 364, 483-85; population in *1702, 1713, 1725, 1728, 1737, 1745, 1749-50, 1785, 1818, 1833-35, 1865, 1894*, 93, 109, 115, 137, 144, 180, 193n, 206, 234, 277, 279, 302, 346-47, 368, 448; in Aruba, 531-32; in St. Eustatius, 524, 527; Sephardic survival in danger, 516

Jewish South, New Orleans, 408

Jews, and Christians in Curaçao, 114-15; in consular service, 366-67; contribute for the fortifications, 100, 113, 228-29; to governor Lauffer's administration, 285-86; control the shipping, 83, 133; in the Island's Council, 337; loyal to the House of Orange, 283-84; marine insurance underwriters, 82, 143, 213-14, 217-19; in the National Guard, 148-49, 285-87,